THE
COUNTERFEIT
COUNTESS

The Jewish Woman Who Rescued
Thousands of Poles During the Holocaust

ELIZABETH B. WHITE
AND JOANNA SLIWA

SIMON & SCHUSTER

New York   London   Toronto   Sydney   New Delhi

1230 Avenue of the Americas
New York, NY 10020

First Simon & Schuster hardcover edition January 2024

SIMON & SCHUSTER and colophon are registered trademarks of Simon & Schuster, Inc.

Simon & Schuster: Celebrating 100 Years of Publishing in 2024

For information about special discounts for bulk purchases,
please contact Simon & Schuster Special Sales
at 1-866-506-1949 or business@simonandschuster.com.

The Simon & Schuster Speakers Bureau can bring authors to your live event.
For more information or to book an event, contact the Simon & Schuster Speakers Bureau
at 1-866-248-3049 or visit our website at www.simonspeakers.com.

Interior design by Ruth Lee-Mui
Maps by Paul J. Pugliese

Manufactured in the United States of America

1   3   5   7   9   10   8   6   4   2

Library of Congress Cataloging-in-Publication Data is available.

ISBN 978-1-9821-8912-9
ISBN 978-1-9821-8914-3 (ebook)

CONTENTS

USAGE NOTES

Place Names

The names of the places where Janina lived in Eastern Galicia (today's Western Ukraine) changed in the course of the twentieth century, sometimes more than once. Just between 1939 and 1941, the name of today's Lviv changed from Lwów to Lvov to Lemberg. This book uses the place names that Janina knew and used. For places that have different names today, the current name is provided in parentheses the first time the place is mentioned.

Usage of "Poles"

Prewar Poland was a multiethnic state. The majority consisted of ethnic Poles who were Polish-speaking, predominantly Roman Catholic, and did not belong to another ethnic group. Like Janina, many members of Poland's ethnic minorities considered themselves loyal Poles, and during World War II many would risk and even sacrifice their lives for their nation. Polish citizens generally identified themselves and one another by their ethnicity. In this book, when the term "Pole" is not modified, it refers to a person of Polish ethnicity.

THE
COUNTERFEIT
COUNTESS

Baltic Sea

U.S.S.R.

GERMANY

GERMANY

GERMANY

Treblinka
•Warsaw

Radom•
Lublin•
Sobibor
Majdanek
Zamość

GENERAL GOVERNMENT

VOLHYNIA

Belżec

•Kraków
•Dębica
•Lwów
•Żurawno
Przemyśl

Auschwitz-Birkenau

PROTECTORATE OF BOHEMIA AND MORAVIA

GALICIA
(added in August 1941)

U.S.S.R.

SLOVAKIA

KINGDOM OF HUNGARY

ROMANIA

Poland, During World War II

—— Borders of Poland on September 1, 1939

- - - - Line of Partition of Poland Between Germany and U.S.S.R. before June 22, 1941

0   100 miles

0   100 kilometers

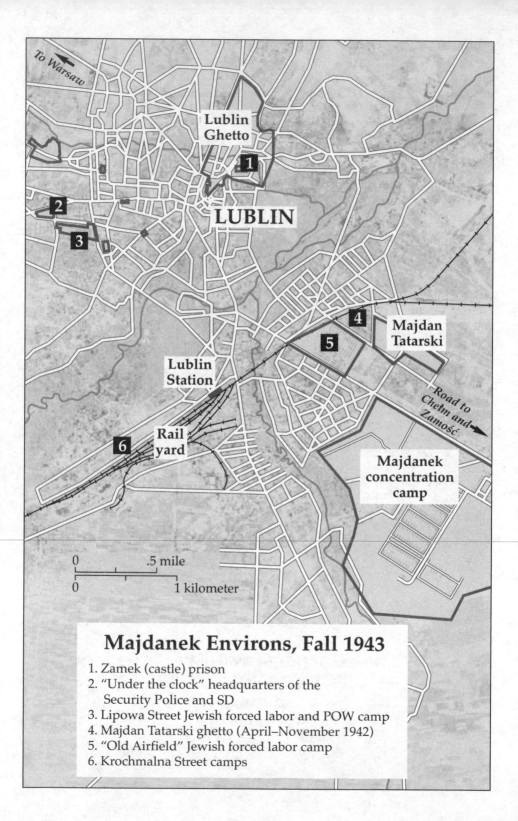

To Warsaw

Lublin
Ghetto

1

LUBLIN

2

3

4

5

Majdan
Tatarski

Lublin
Station

Road to
Chełm and
Zamość

6

Rail
yard

Majdanek
concentration
camp

0   .5 mile

0   1 kilometer

Majdanek Environs, Fall 1943

1. Zamek (castle) prison
2. "Under the clock" headquarters of the
   Security Police and SD
3. Lipowa Street Jewish forced labor and POW camp
4. Majdan Tatarski ghetto (April–November 1942)
5. "Old Airfield" Jewish forced labor camp
6. Krochmalna Street camps

Lublin City Center

1. Zamek (castle) prison
2. Border of the Lublin Ghetto
3. RGO office from fall 1942
4. Old Town
5. Janina's residence from December 1941
6. Lipowa Street Jewish forced labor
   and POW camp
7. RGO office until the fall of 1942
8. Office of the city administration
9. Adolf-Hitler-Platz, formerly Litewski Square
10. Location of Janina's apartment in July 1944
11. Office of the Governor of Lublin District

0   .25 mile

0   .5 kilometer

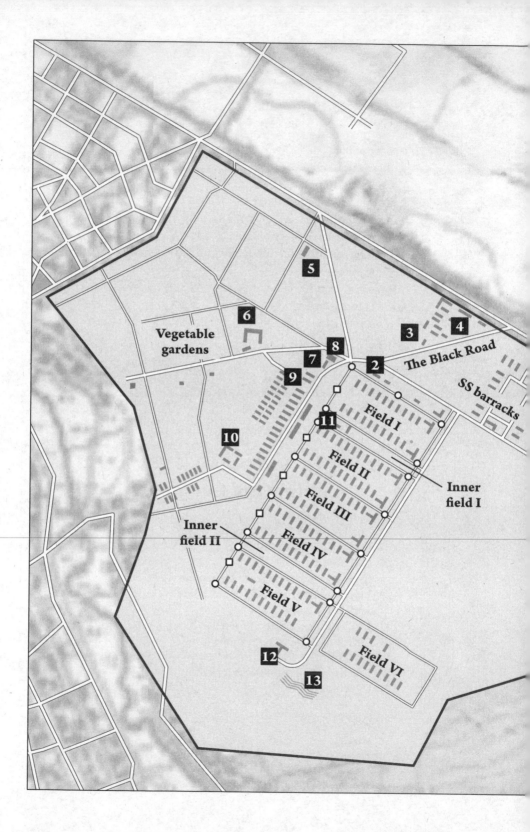

5

6

Vegetable
gardens

8

3

4

7

2

The Black Road

9

SS barracks

Field I

11

Inner
field I

10

Field II

Field III

Inner
field II

Field IV

Field V

12

Field VI

13

Majdanek Concentration Camp

1. Commandant's office
2. Post office
3. Physician's office
4. Construction material depot
5. Commandant's residence
6. Burning pits
7. "Rose Garden" selection area
8. Bathing and disinfection facility and gas chambers
9. Food warehouses
10. Kennels
11. Old crematorium
12. New crematorium
13. Ditches for mass executions

O Watchtowers   ◇ Guard Booths

Commandant's headquarters

1

Camp farm

0   .5 mile

0   .5 kilometer

PROLOGUE

August 9, 1943
Lublin, Poland

Once again, the commandant of Majdanek concentration camp found Countess Suchodolska in his office, making yet another absurd demand.

SS-*Obersturmbannführer* Hermann Florstedt had served at several concentration camps in Germany, but Majdanek, he had found, bore little resemblance to them. Located in Lublin in German-occupied Poland, the camp was primitive and chaotic compared to the concentration camps in the Reich. Florstedt's assignment as the camp's commandant in 1942 had been a promotion, but also punishment for suspected corruption at Buchenwald. He had arrived at Majdanek to find a massive construction site with unpaved roads, no running water, contaminated wells, and open latrines that gave off an overpowering stench. Towering billows of smoke regularly belched from the camp's crematorium chimney, raining down the ashes of men, women, and children murdered in the gas chambers. Currently 23,000 prisoners were languishing in unimaginable filth. Infectious diseases were so rampant that even the SS guards sickened and died.

Majdanek did have one compensation in Florstedt's view: it was the repository of the personal belongings of many of the hundreds of thousands of Jews being murdered by the SS in German-occupied central Poland. SS warehouses in Lublin held mountains of clothes, shoes, furs, and leather goods, and boxes full of currency, jewelry, watches, wedding bands, and gold teeth. It was Florstedt's responsibility to ensure that Majdanek prisoners processed these goods so that the SS could fully profit from them. But who would notice if Florstedt and his most trusted men took some of the riches as recompense for their service in plundering and murdering Germany's racial enemies?

One of the vexations of Florstedt's work, however, was the meddling of Polish aid organizations that sought to provide food and medicines for Majdanek's Polish prisoners. The Polish Main Welfare Council and the Polish Red Cross were far more assertive than any similar organizations in the Reich. They had actually obtained permission to make weekly deliveries of bread and food products for the prisoners' kitchens, to supply the prisoners with packages of food and necessities, and to provide medicines for the camp infirmaries. And yet Countess Janina Suchodolska of the Polish Main Welfare Council continually pressed for more: to make more frequent deliveries of more food and more medicines. She even proposed delivering prepared soup for the prisoners. Such things would be out of the question in any other concentration camp. But when told no, the Countess simply made the rounds of higher SS and Nazi authorities until she finally persuaded one that her requests were somehow in German interests.

To make matters worse, the Countess used her visits to Majdanek to spy on the conditions there. Efforts to deter her had proved fruitless. The petite brunette aristocrat remained utterly unflappable in the face of shouts and threats from the SS. Recently, she had even alerted health officials to a typhus epidemic among the prisoners, forcing Florstedt to arrange some semblance of treatment for them.

Now she was pestering Florstedt about the thousands of Polish peasants in the camp. The SS had dumped them there in July after evicting them from their farms to make room for German settlers. Since the SS quickly culled the able-bodied adults for forced labor in the Reich, the peasants still in the camp were mostly children or elderly. After just a few weeks in the camp, these prisoners were already dying of dehydration, starvation, and diseases at a rate that was extreme even for Majdanek. Somehow, the Countess had persuaded German authorities to release the 3,600 Polish peasants still on

Majdanek's rolls, but only on condition that her organization provided all the necessary paperwork and found places for them to live. In just a couple of days, Countess Suchodolska and her coworkers managed to do both.

The Countess had arrived at the camp gate in the morning to receive the civilians. There she was informed, with no further explanation, that nearly half of them were no longer "available" for release. The remaining civilians had been assembled in the third of Majdanek's five prisoner compounds, about a kilometer from the gate where the Countess awaited them. The distance had proved too far for many to walk: the Countess had watched with increasing alarm as prisoners, trying in vain to hold each other up, stumbled, fell, and lay helpless in the dust. And so here she was in Florstedt's office, insisting that he allow trucks and ambulances to enter the camp and pick up the prisoners. Allowing Polish civilian transport inside a concentration camp was in complete violation of SS security regulations! But Florstedt knew there was no point in refusing—the Countess would just go over his head.

Within two hours, trucks, buses, and ambulances arrived, recruited by the Countess from businesses and organizations throughout the city.

In the end, 2,106 peasants were released from Majdanek in August 1943. More than 25 percent of them wound up in Lublin's two main hospitals, and nearly 200 died within days, over half of them children under age twelve. But some 1,900 survived, thanks to the efforts of Countess Suchodolska and her many colleagues.

Her efforts to help the prisoners of Majdanek did not end there. The Countess relentlessly pressed Nazi authorities for more concessions, and gradually they agreed to permit increased deliveries of food, medicines, and supplies. They even allowed her to bring in decorated Christmas trees so that the prisoners could celebrate the holiday. By February 1944, the Polish Main Welfare Council was supplying soup and bread five times a week for 4,000 Polish prisoners in Majdanek, in addition to other deliveries of food and medicine. The Countess herself usually brought the soup into the camp, under the close supervision of SS guards.

Throughout all her dealings with Nazi and SS officials, no one ever suspected that the indomitable Countess, so self-assured and aristocratic in her
demeanor, was not a countess at all, nor was her name really Suchodolska.
She was Janina Spinner Mehlberg, a brilliant mathematician, an officer in
the underground Polish Home Army, and a Jew.

INTRODUCTION

In December 1989, historian Elizabeth "Barry" White received an unexpected package from a stranger. It contained a carbon copy on onionskin paper of an untitled, typewritten manuscript. The donor of the package, American History professor Arthur Funk of the University of Florida, explained that the manuscript was the memoir of Janina Mehlberg, a Polish Jew who survived the Holocaust by posing as the gentile Countess Janina Suchodolska in the city of Lublin. The memoir recounted how she had persuaded the SS to allow her to deliver food for thousands of prisoners in Majdanek (My-DAH-neck) concentration camp and how she used those deliveries to smuggle messages and supplies to resistance fighters imprisoned there.

Funk told Barry that, after the war, Janina (Yah-NEE-nah) Mehlberg immigrated to the United States. She died in 1969 in Chicago, where she was a professor of mathematics at Illinois Institute of Technology. After her death, her husband, the philosopher Henry Mehlberg, tried unsuccessfully to get her memoir published. Shortly before his death in 1979, he entrusted the memoir to Funk in the hope that the historian could publish it. Funk tried, but had been unable to interest any publisher in the memoir. He gave the manuscript copy to Barry because she had just delivered a paper on Majdanek at the American Historical Association convention, and so he hoped that she would find a way to make Janina Mehlberg's story known.

There was a Countess Janina Suchodolska in German-occupied Lublin during World War II, Barry knew. Postwar studies of the camp note that, as an official of the Polish Main Welfare Council, a relief organization, she personally made regular deliveries of food for prisoners at Majdanek and, as a member of the underground Polish Home Army, had worked to organize the resistance within the camp through smuggled correspondence. Many accounts of Majdanek by former prisoners mention the Countess, the brave and kind "lady with the sad smile" who brought them food, news of the war, decorated Christmas trees and Easter eggs, and Holy Communion wafers. Prisoners recalled how she never flinched when the SS screamed threats in her face, and they marveled at her success in winning astonishing concessions from Nazi officials, which they attributed to her knowledge of the German mentality. Some former prisoners credited her with providing not only the physical sustenance but also the hope that enabled them to survive. None of the studies or accounts, however, mentions that the Countess was using an alias, much less that she was a Jew.

Knowing the special circle of hell that was Majdanek, Barry read the manuscript with increasing astonishment—and skepticism. Lublin was the headquarters of the largest mass murder operation of the Holocaust, *Aktion Reinhard*. In connection with the operation, at least 63,000 Jews were murdered in Majdanek's gas chambers and shooting pits.[1] Thousands of non-Jewish Poles were imprisoned and died there as well. Yet, according to the memoir, a petite Jewish woman negotiated with top Nazi officials in Lublin, met frequently with SS officials at Majdanek, befriended Majdanek's SS guards, and regularly visited the camp's prisoner compounds. She continually and successfully pressed German authorities to permit her organization to provide ever greater quantities and types of relief for Majdanek's prisoners. It seemed from her account that she never accepted "no" as a final answer and always considered "yes" an invitation to ask for more. Even more incredibly, she used the deliveries as cover to smuggle correspondence and supplies to her fellow resistance members imprisoned in the camp, including tools to aid them in escaping. In addition to her work at Majdanek, she rescued Poles seized for forced labor in Germany and children taken from their families. The Gestapo threatened her, surveilled her, and sent spies to entrap her; on more than one occasion, she narrowly escaped arrest, torture, and death.

The gripping story told in the memoir seemed to Barry almost too fantastic to be true. On the other hand, the author had unusually detailed knowledge about Majdanek, its staff, and its prisoners that someone not personally involved with the camp was unlikely to possess. If the memoir was true, then it revealed a historically significant story that deserved to be made known. But if the memoir was true, why did Janina Mehlberg not come forward after the war to reveal her identity and take credit for her accomplishments? She only wrote the memoir in the 1960s, long after she had left Poland and become well established in the United States. If the memoir was untrue, why would Janina and Henry Mehlberg go to such lengths to perpetrate a hoax? Barry decided that she could not make any use of the memoir without first corroborating that Janina Mehlberg was Countess Suchodolska.

At that time, however, Barry had no way to verify the memoir. In 1989, the Internet was not yet generally available. Researching Janina Mehlberg's life then required poring over dusty files and peering at microfilm in Polish archives. Barry was then a new mother and working for the U.S. Department of Justice on investigations and prosecutions of Nazi criminals in the United States. She lacked the time and resources to conduct research in Poland, particularly as she did not know Polish. Since Funk also planned to give copies of the memoir to several archives, including the United States Holocaust Memorial Museum (USHMM), Barry hoped that some more qualified scholar would do the work necessary to verify the memoir and bring its story to light.

Years passed, then decades, with no indication that any scholar had examined the memoir. Funk died in 2007. The thought that she might be the only historian who knew about the memoir haunted Barry. What if its claims were true? Did she have a responsibility to ensure that they were verified and made known?

In 2017, working as a historian at the USHMM, Barry embarked on an effort to verify Mehlberg's claims and discovered a 1975 book review by a former Polish resistance member named in her memoir. Praising the contributions to the resistance at Majdanek of "Janina Suchodolska Mehlberg," he mentioned that her memoir had yet to find a publisher.[2]

While this discovery persuaded Barry that Janina Mehlberg likely was Countess Suchodolska, she concluded that further proof of the memoir's claims was needed in order to publish it. Determined to recruit a historian with the necessary qualifications to corroborate the memoir and tell Janina Mehlberg's story, she sent the manuscript to Joanna Sliwa, who is an expert on the Holocaust in Poland. After reading the memoir, Joanna offered to partner with Barry to research Janina Mehlberg's life and tell her story to the world.

Through records, interviews, photographs, and contacts in nine countries on three continents, we have not only succeeded in verifying the details of her memoir but also have uncovered far more about Janina Mehlberg's remarkable accomplishments as Countess Suchodolska than the memoir recounts. The incident in the prologue to this book, for example, is not mentioned in the memoir but is based on the wartime documents of the Polish Main Welfare Council. The SS official she persuaded to order the release of the civilians in Majdanek was the manager of *Aktion* Reinhard, a man with the blood of more than 1.5 million Jews on his hands. In addition to her relief work at Majdanek, she provided food, shelter, and medical care for tens of thousands of Polish civilians evicted from their homes or abducted from their villages, establishing soup kitchens, hospitals, rest and aid stations, and orphanages for children separated from their families. She negotiated the release of thousands of Poles from transit and labor camps as well as from Majdanek.

We also discovered that, in the course of her life, Janina Mehlberg underwent several reinventions, altering her name and occupation—and becoming increasingly younger. As Pepi Spinner, born 1905, she obtained a doctorate in philosophy and logic at age twenty-two from the prestigious Jan Kazimierz University in Lwów, Poland. As Józefa Mehlberg, she worked as a math teacher and lecturer in Lwów from 1935 until 1941, when she and Henry fled to Lublin and obtained false identities. As Countess Janina Suchodolska, she became the secretary and eventually the deputy of the top official in Lublin District of the Polish Main Welfare Council. At the same time, as "Stefania," she served in the anticommunist Polish Home Army, the largest armed resistance group in German-occupied Poland. When Soviet forces drove the Germans out of Lublin in 1944 and installed a communist government, she became Dr. Janina Suchodolska, social worker, born in 1909. She served in postwar Poland as the deputy director of a welfare agency, tending to the neediest in her war-ravaged country. In 1950, she defected in West Berlin and immigrated to Canada as Josephine Janina Spinner Bednarski Mehlberg. Finally, in 1961, she became a U.S. citizen as Dr. Josephine Janina Spinner Mehlberg, born in 1915.

Although "Janina" was not her name until 1941, Janina Mehlberg retained it as part of her name for the rest of her life, and it is the name she used in her memoir. In a preface to the memoir that her husband, Henry, wrote after her death, he identified her as Janina Spinner Mehlberg. For these reasons, we decided to refer to her as Janina throughout this book.

When we set out to verify Janina's memoir, we planned that, if we succeeded, we would try to publish it along with text that would explain its historical references and the context of the events it recounts. This approach would preserve Janina's voice and perspective while helping readers to understand her story. The memoir starts at the beginning of World War II and ends in 1944, when Soviet forces captured and occupied Lublin. It is not a strictly chronological account, however, but a series of vignettes reflecting some aspects of her activities and experiences. It is written with the assumption that readers will be familiar with the people, places, and events to which it refers. On its own, the memoir cannot convey to most of today's readers a full appreciation of how remarkable Janina's story is. For example, today few people outside Poland have heard of Majdanek concentration camp. Yet in 1944, it became internationally notorious when its liberation by the Red Army provided the first physical evidence that the Nazi regime systematically gassed Jews. The camp was even featured in a film shown at the postwar trial of the major German war criminals in Nuremberg. Before the name Auschwitz became a synonym for the Holocaust, Majdanek was the international symbol of Nazi criminality.

After finding so much more about Janina's life and remarkable accomplishments than the memoir reveals, we decided to write a biography of Janina instead. By drawing heavily from Janina's memoir, we tell her story largely from her perspective, incorporating her thoughts and observations as she recounted them. The dialogue in this book is either drawn directly from the memoir or is based on conversations that the memoir describes. In the epilogue, we discuss how we corroborated Janina's memoir, her motives for writing it, and what it reveals about her character and the lessons she drew from her experiences. We end with Janina's voice by quoting the final passages of her memoir.

This book recounts the story of Janina's life within the context of the events that shaped her actions, integrating her experiences into the larger story of the terror and suffering that the Germans visited upon Poles both Jewish and non-Jewish during World War II. German-occupied Poland was ground zero of the Nazi "final solution" policy, the place where the majority of the Germans' Jewish victims died in ghettos, camps, killing centers, and shooting pits. Janina became Countess Suchodolska in order to escape their fate. Yet even as a supposedly "Aryan" Pole, Janina remained under threat from German policies of racist persecution and mass murder. Nazi ideology portrayed the Jews as the most dangerous of the Germans' "subhuman" enemies, but ethnic Poles ranked only slightly higher on the Nazi racist scale of human worth. Poland's German occupiers unleashed a campaign of systematic carnage that in less than six years claimed the lives of three million Jewish Poles and nearly two million non-Jewish Poles. The Germans also seized more than two million non-Jewish Poles to perform forced labor in the Reich, separating them from their families, and abducted tens of thousands of Polish children to transform them into Germans. The Polish Jewish jurist Raphael Lemkin[3] coined the word "genocide" in 1944 to describe the Germans' efforts to exterminate both Jewish and non-Jewish Poles.

Janina's story illustrates how Poles sought to resist the German occupation and to help one another survive. She was rescued by a non-Jewish family friend, Count Andrzej Skrzyński, who brought Janina and Henry to Lublin and provided them with identity papers as Count and Countess Suchodolski (Suchodolski is the form used for a man and, in English, for a couple). Jews living on false papers during the Holocaust in Poland tended to lie low and avoid going out in public as much as possible, lest they be recognized by a former acquaintance, betrayed by the trace of a Yiddish accent, or forced to show papers that would not stand up to scrutiny. But Janina could not bear to remain passive as so many of her compatriots suffered and died around her. With Skrzyński's backing, she enlisted in the Polish Home Army, the armed forces of the Polish Underground State. Of all the countries occupied by Nazi Germany, Poland had by far the most extensive underground resistance organization, and women played vital roles in it. In addition to serving as a courier and a spy, Janina helped to organize and worked with networks of mostly women who smuggled messages and supplies to imprisoned members of the resistance.

For decades after World War II, there was almost no scholarly or public interest in the experiences of Jewish women during the Holocaust or in the women who fought Nazi Germany through resistance and intelligence work. Funk told Barry that, in his effort to get Janina's memoir published, he sent it to an eminent Holocaust historian in the United States. While the historian found the memoir's story interesting, he concluded that the experiences of one woman Holocaust survivor did not make a compelling case for publication. At that time, the field of Holocaust studies was in its infancy, and historians were mostly focused on the actions and motivations of the perpetrators. That focus has since broadened, and Jewish women's responses to the Nazi genocide have become an important area of study. This century has also seen burgeoning public interest in stories about women who fought Nazi Germany and sought to rescue its victims. In telling Janina's story, we recount the feats of some of the other Polish heroines who risked their lives for their country and whose activities intersected with Janina's.

It was also through Count Skrzyński that Janina obtained a position with the Polish Main Welfare Council, known by its Polish initials, RGO. The Germans did not permit the RGO to tend to all Polish citizens, only to those whom the Germans considered racially Polish. In the district of Lublin, the RGO cared for hundreds of thousands of Poles expelled from their homes and communities, robbed of their property and livelihoods, subsisting on starvation rations, or consigned to prisons or concentration camps. It was able to provide so many with shelter, food, medicines, and clothing largely thanks to the generosity of the people of Lublin, most of whom were themselves suffering from privation and malnutrition as the intended consequence of German policies. Their contributions also made it possible for Janina to feed thousands of prisoners at Majdanek by delivering tons of bread and hundreds of gallons of soup on a nearly daily basis. At no other concentration camp did such a program exist.

World War II and the Holocaust have given rise to numerous inspiring stories about daring and selfless heroes who fought Nazism and rescued its victims. Some of the best known stories occurred in Poland. German industrialist Oskar Schindler has been deservedly celebrated in the book by Thomas Keneally and in Steven Spielberg's film *Schindler's List* for risking his life and exhausting his fortune to save the lives of some 1,200 of his Jewish workers. Warsaw zookeepers Jan and Antonina Żabiński, who hid nearly three hundred Jews and Polish resistance fighters on zoo grounds, are the heroes of the book by Diane Ackerman and film directed by Niki Caro *The Zookeeper's Wife*. There are even more books and dramatic treatments of the life of Irena Sendler, a Polish social worker who smuggled hundreds of Jewish children out of the Warsaw Ghetto and placed them in private homes and religious institutions. Books and films have recounted the astounding courage and feats of resistance of such Polish Jews as the Bielski brothers of the book by Nechama Tec and film directed by Edward Zwick *Defiance* and, more recently, the "ghetto girls" of Judy Batalion's *The Light of Days*.

Janina's story is unique. She was a Jew who rescued non-Jews in the midst of the largest murder operation of the Holocaust. She witnessed the beginning of *Aktion* Reinhard with the bloody deportation to the Bełżec killing center of nearly 30,000 Lublin Jews, and she was one of the first Poles to learn of its apocalyptic end with the mass shooting at Majdanek and two other camps of 42,000 Jews. As often as five days a week, she descended into the den of death at Majdanek, knowing that she would be gruesomely tortured and murdered if the SS discovered either her smuggling activities or her true identity. Over and over, she met with mass murderers to persuade them to help her rescue their victims, and she did so with astounding success: based on wartime records, we have documented that she negotiated the release from German captivity of at least 9,707 Poles, 4,431 of them from Majdanek. The deliveries of food and medicines that she organized likely saved thousands more prisoners from dying of starvation or disease. It is impossible to determine how many Polish lives would have been lost but for Janina's efforts, but the number surely has five figures.

Janina's memoir is both an account of her life during World War II and a meditation on human nature that seeks to draw some meaning from what she observed and experienced. She witnessed both the worst and the best of human capabilities. She saw that people who engaged in murderous cruelty could still commit acts of surprising kindness and even self-sacrifice, and that people who routinely risked their lives to save others could be self-serving or hateful. She recognized that some of her compatriots—including possibly some of those who worked with her, were aided by her, and lit candles and said prayers for her safety—would have denied her identity as a Pole if they had known she was also a Jew. But one of Janina's qualities that shines through in her account is her deep compassion for human frailties, and so her realistic assessment of human nature did not diminish her commitment to saving every life she could.

Janina was extraordinarily intelligent, keenly analytical, and remarkably quick-witted and innovative. Her specialty as a mathematician was probability, which served her well when her survival and success depended upon accurately calculating the tremendous risks she took every day. Ultimately, however, her actions were not guided by risk assessments, but by a simple mathematical principle: the value of one life is less than the value of multiple lives, and her life, if she survived without seeking to save others, would have no value.

Throughout her life, Janina refused to be defined or restricted by stereotypes: she was a woman in the almost entirely male field of mathematics; a patriot in a country that discriminated against her based on both her gender and Jewish identity; a Jew who risked her life to save non-Jewish Nazi victims during the Holocaust; and an anticommunist who served a communist government in order to provide aid to those in need. She saw herself simply as one human, bound to all other humans regardless of their misogyny, racism, or ideology, and she valued her own life only as it served other lives. Her story deserves to be told. The world needs her story.

ONE

BEFORE

When, near the end of her life, Dr. Josephine Janina Mehlberg put to paper the experiences and reflections she felt were worth preserving, she made no mention of her first thirty-four years. Nor did she record her work directing aid for millions of the homeless, destitute, and orphaned in post–World War II Poland, or even write a word about her later life as a math professor in the United States. Instead, the memories and lessons that prompted, even compelled her to write were from the period when World War II shattered her comfortable life as a Polish Jewish intellectual and she seemed destined for murder at the hands of Poland's Nazi occupiers. That was when she made a fateful choice: she would spend her remaining days not in fear and false hope of a meaningless survival, but in bold action to save as many others as she could before meeting a meaningful death. That was when she transformed into Countess Janina Suchodolska, a woman unknown to the many whose lives she saved, a woman haunted to the end of her days by the many she failed to rescue.

Janina was born Pepi Spinner on May 1, 1905, entering a life of rare privilege for a Polish Jewish girl.[1] Her father, Pinkas, was a wealthy estate owner, and she enjoyed a childhood of comfortable elegance.[2] The Spinners were well assimilated in local society and experienced little overt antisemitism. They mixed socially with the Polish nobles who owned the neighboring

1

estates and whose children were Janina's playmates. Like their aristocratic friends, Janina and her older sisters, Chaja and Bluma, were taught at home by nannies and tutors who imparted to them the manners, skills, and knowledge expected of girls in Polish genteel society.

Janina's birthplace, the town of Żurawno (today Zhuravno), was in Eastern Galicia, a region that has had multiple rulers over the past millennium. Today it is part of Ukraine, but for centuries it was a Polish realm. In the late eighteenth century, Austria, Prussia, and Russia successively carved up the once mighty Commonwealth of Poland and Lithuania until they had swallowed it all. Austria helped itself to Galicia.[3]

All three powers tried to force their Polish subjects to assimilate. The Poles, however, refused to give up their identity, culture, and national aspirations, even after their uprisings were brutally suppressed. In 1867, as Austria struggled to hold its multinational empire together, it transformed into the constitutional monarchy of Austria-Hungary and granted some autonomy to other ethnic groups. Eastern Galicia, especially its capital, Lwów, became a center of Polish nationalism and culture.

Janina was fluent in German, the language of Austria, studied English and Russian, and could chat in Ukrainian with the peasants who worked her father's fields. She likely knew some Yiddish as well. Mostly, however, she spoke Polish and French with her Polish friends and aristocratic neighbors, and she absorbed their nationalist sentiments and veneration for Polish culture. This background of multilingual privilege provided her essential skills that she would draw on when, as an adult, her survival and freedom would depend upon her ability to be a convincing imposter.

When Janina was nine, World War I broke out and her happy childhood soon ended with loss and tragedy. Eastern Galicia was ravaged as a major battleground in the fight between the Russian Empire and the Central Powers of Austria-Hungary and Germany. In the first months of the war in 1914, Russian forces swept across Eastern Galicia and promptly confiscated all estates owned by Jews. The armies of the Central Powers drove the Russians out in 1915, but not before the retreating forces abducted hundreds of landowners and leading businessmen.[4] Among them was Janina's father. In 1918, her family received word that he had died.

and mathematicians who viewed philosophy as a branch of science that was essential for understanding and advancing scientific and mathematical reasoning. Their intellectual meeting ground was the field of logic. Twardowski accepted women and Jews as his doctoral students and preferred graduate students with expertise in fields other than philosophy. By pursuing a doctorate in philosophy under Twardowski, Janina could advance her work in mathematics while also participating in the exciting explorations and discourse of his seminar. She applied to study under him, and he welcomed her as his student.[7]

Janina obtained a doctorate in philosophy in February 1928.[8] In her dissertation, titled "Mathematical Reasoning and Traditional Logic," she demonstrated that the principles of traditional logic alone are insufficient for mathematical reasoning, which must also draw on other sources of thought, particularly imagination and intuition. In the dark days to come, Janina would apply logic, imaginative innovation, and intuitive insight into human character to the task of resisting her nation's enemies and saving its citizens' lives.

Janina received an exciting opportunity to gain recognition for her work when the Polish Philosophical Society in Lwów invited her to present a lecture in May 1928. It was a bitter disappointment when a health crisis forced her to cancel. By the fall, she had recovered sufficiently to travel to Paris for a year of study at the Sorbonne. Then she returned to Lwów, where she found employment as a math teacher.

Sometime after her return, Janina crossed paths again with another Twardowski student, Henry (then Henryk) Mehlberg.[9] Just seven months older than Janina, he had obtained a master's degree in French in 1924 and a doctorate in philosophy in 1926 from Jan Kazimierz University, then spent two years studying in Austria, Germany, and at the Sorbonne. After he returned to Lwów in 1928, the only employment he could obtain was teaching French at a private preparatory school in the city of Lublin. He found the pay miserable and the city a boring backwater compared to Lwów.[10] With Twardowski's help, he obtained another position teaching languages in the city of Stanisławów (today Ivano-Frankivsk, Ukraine).[11]

When Henry reconnected with Janina, he found that the serious

The war rekindled the hope and determination of the Poles to win back their sovereignty, especially after the entry of the United States. The Fourteen Points program of President Woodrow Wilson called for an independent Polish state comprising all the lands where Poles were in the majority. Eastern Galicia, however, had a Ukrainian majority. As the Central Powers prepared to surrender in the fall of 1918, Eastern Galicia again became a battleground. Polish and Ukrainian forces fought each other as well as Bolshevik Russia's Red Army. In the grip of ultranationalist and ideological frenzy, soldiers on all sides slaughtered Jews. Well over 100,000 Jews were murdered in these post–World War I conflicts, and estimates range as high as 300,000, leading some historians to characterize the pogroms of that period as a prelude to the Holocaust.[5]

When the carnage finally ceased in 1921, Poland's eastern border enclosed large areas where Ukrainians, Belarusians, or Lithuanians were in the majority, including Eastern Galicia. Janina settled in Lwów with her mother, Tauba, and became a star student at her private girls' prep school, displaying a keen and curious intellect and a remarkable talent for mathematics. She was also ambitious and aspired to a career that would make full use of her intellectual gifts.

Lwów's Jan Kazimierz University accepted Janina to study under two of Europe's leading mathematicians: Stefan Banach and Hugo Steinhaus. Banach was then pioneering the field of functional analysis, but it was Steinhaus's work on probability theory and mathematical reasoning that particularly intrigued Janina. She obtained the equivalent of a master's degree in Exact Sciences, which qualified her to teach mathematics at the secondary level. But she aimed higher, to obtain a doctorate and teach at a university. Mathematics was not a welcoming field for women anywhere then, including Poland. Only five women obtained doctorates in mathematics in Poland before World War II, and only one of them in Lwów. Steinhaus, in particular, took a dim view of women in the highest level of his field.[6]

Janina was not one to let misogyny stand in the way of her goals. Jan Kazimierz University was also famous as the birthplace of the intellectual movement known as the Lwów-Warsaw School. Led by the charismatic philosopher Kazimierz Twardowski, it was a circle of mostly philosophers and mathematicians who viewed philosophy as a branch of science that was essential for understanding and advancing scientific and mathematical reasoning. Their intellectual meeting ground was the field of logic. Twardowski accepted women and Jews as his doctoral students and preferred graduate students with expertise in fields other than philosophy. By pursuing a doctorate in philosophy under Twardowski, Janina could advance her work in mathematics while also participating in the exciting explorations and discourse of his seminar. She applied to study under him, and he welcomed her as his student.[7]

Janina obtained a doctorate in philosophy in February 1928.[8] In her dissertation, titled "Mathematical Reasoning and Traditional Logic," she demonstrated that the principles of traditional logic alone are insufficient for mathematical reasoning, which must also draw on other sources of thought, particularly imagination and intuition. In the dark days to come, Janina would apply logic, imaginative innovation, and intuitive insight into human character to the task of resisting her nation's enemies and saving its citizens' lives.

Janina received an exciting opportunity to gain recognition for her work when the Polish Philosophical Society in Lwów invited her to present a lecture in May 1928. It was a bitter disappointment when a health crisis forced her to cancel. By the fall, she had recovered sufficiently to travel to Paris for a year of study at the Sorbonne. Then she returned to Lwów, where she found employment as a math teacher.

Sometime after her return, Janina crossed paths again with another Twardowski student, Henry (then Henryk) Mehlberg.[9] Just seven months older than Janina, he had obtained a master's degree in French in 1924 and a doctorate in philosophy in 1926 from Jan Kazimierz University, then spent two years studying in Austria, Germany, and at the Sorbonne. After he returned to Lwów in 1928, the only employment he could obtain was teaching French at a private preparatory school in the city of Lublin. He found the pay miserable and the city a boring backwater compared to Lwów.[10] With Twardowski's help, he obtained another position teaching languages in the city of Stanisławów (today Ivano-Frankivsk, Ukraine).[11]

When Henry reconnected with Janina, he found that the serious twenty-year-old he had known in his last year of graduate school had grown into a charming, lively, and stylish woman in her prime. She was now going by "Józefa" as her first name, which sounded more Polish and sophisticated than "Pepi." Henry thought her very pretty: petite and slim, with blue-green eyes and luxurious dark hair that framed a lovely face. He admired her combination of femininity with fierce intelligence. Henry tended to be intense and to dominate intellectual discussions, which sometimes caused his male colleagues to grumble. Janina, on the other hand, had no problem interrupting him or holding her own in their discourse, and she managed to do so with such gentle good humor that Henry did not take offense when they disagreed and could even be swayed by her opinion. Like him, Janina was well versed in many subjects outside her field, particularly European literature and history, and they engaged in wide ranging conversations. Henry, enchanted, concluded that he had met his intellectual match. Janina appreciated the man capable of reaching such a conclusion.

In 1933, some calamity befell Janina that left her suffering deeply in body and spirit. Its precise nature is unclear, although it may have been connected with her mother's death that year. Henry supported Janina throughout the difficult time and their love for each other grew. The two married on August 6 in Henry's hometown, Kopyczyńce, before settling in Stanisławów. Henry hoped that in new surroundings and under his care Janina would recover. Her spirits did revive enough by the summer of 1934 for her to submit an article on mathematical pedagogy for a volume Twardowski was editing, but her physical health did not improve. In May 1935, with Twardowski's help, Henry was able to obtain treatment for Janina in a hospital in Lwów. After a two-week stay, her health and strength began to rebound.[12]

Janina and Henry had additional reason to rejoice in the summer of 1935: he had obtained a teaching position in Lwów and they were able to move back to their beloved city. Once again, they had Twardowski to thank. The professor had encouraged and critiqued Henry's writings on the philosophy of science and made sure that others in the Lwów-Warsaw School were aware of them. In 1934, the president of the Polish Philosophical Society in Lwów—former Twardowski student and renowned scholar Roman Ingarden—invited Henry to speak to the society about his theories.[13] The next year, he published (in French) his first essay on the causal theory of time. Even those who questioned his theory recognized the brilliance of his reasoning. The Lwów circle of the Lwów-Warsaw School wanted Henry among them and helped him find work in the city. Janina, too, obtained a position, teaching math at a girls' high school.[14]

After they moved to Lwów, Janina and Henry sat for studio photographs. Janina appears pale and thin in her photo, perhaps from the effects of her long illness, but exhibits her individual sense of style. She did not wear her hair in the short waves that were universally fashionable then, for she had never bobbed the long, thick locks that fell to her knees in gentle curls when she let it down. Instead, she wore her hair that day in a long chignon tied slightly to one side. For his photo, Henry struck the pose of a serious scholar, his blue eyes cast down in deep thought, his blond, wavy hair combed back from a high forehead and a hairline that was beginning to recede.[15]

The Mehlbergs settled into a comfortable life in Lwów. In addition to their teacher salaries, Janina received a yearly stipend from her father's estate, while Henry received some income as a titular partner in his father's distillery business in Kopyczyńce.[16] They rented a four-room apartment in a fashionable neighborhood near the university and furnished it to suit Janina's elegant taste.

But the atmosphere in the city had changed since their student days. The hopes and ideals that Poles had shared when they were fighting for their sovereignty faded and fragmented as they faced the challenges of self-government. Integrating three regions that for more than a century had operated with different legal, social, political, and economic systems and that had been ravaged by seven years of warfare proved difficult, divisive, and painfully slow. In the late 1920s, just as the economic situation finally began to improve, the Great Depression brought devastation.

Even more worrying was the political polarization that made the country increasingly difficult to govern. Poland had begun its independence as a parliamentary democracy that guaranteed the rights of the ethnic minorities who made up more than 30 percent of its population. But there were competing visions of who truly "belonged" to the Polish nation. The right-wing National Democrats believed that ethnic Poles should enjoy advantages that members of other Christian ethnic groups should only be able to acquire by assimilating, while Jewish Poles should be forced to leave the country altogether. Opposing this view was the hero of Poland's independence, Józef Piłsudski, a socialist who maintained that all residents of the Polish state should be full citizens. Fed up with the instability of Poland's multiparty system, Piłsudski overthrew the government in 1926, replacing it with a nonpartisan authoritarian regime.[17]

The economic misery of the Great Depression stoked ethnic hostilities and popular unrest. The Organization of Ukrainian Nationalists (OUN) embarked on a terror campaign against the Polish "occupiers," while the National Democrats and their fascist offshoot encouraged boycotts of Jewish businesses and even fomented pogroms. Much of the violence occurred in Eastern Galicia. In Janina's birthplace, Żurawno, perpetrators of a pogrom in April 1937 demolished Jewish shops and homes and beat Jewish residents.[18] At the beginning of January 1938, Jewish students at Jan Kazimierz University were forced to sit in the back of classrooms on what were called "ghetto benches"; many were beaten up, some were even murdered.[19]

The Polish regime responded to the growing unrest by becoming even more authoritarian, especially after Piłsudski's death in 1935. It also sought to co-opt the National Democrats' followers by adopting their rhetoric. It renounced the minority treaty that protected the rights of ethnic groups, exacted collective punishment on Ukrainians for OUN attacks, and called for the emigration of Poland's three million Jews.[20] Coupled with the bitter legacy of post–World War I ethnic violence, Poland's official repression of minorities fueled ethnic hatreds that were ripe for exploitation by its enemies.

Poland's most dangerous potential enemies were also its two largest neighbors: Germany to the west and the Soviet Union to the east. Both countries aspired to regain the swaths of territory they had lost to Poland in the aftermath of World War I. Despite Poland's best efforts to steer a neutral path between the two, its relations with them grew increasingly tense, especially after Adolf Hitler and his Nazi Party took power in Germany in 1933.

Hitler launched a campaign of territorial expansion in March 1938, when Germany annexed Austria. He then proceeded to wipe Czechoslovakia off the map by attaching the Czech lands to the Reich and establishing a self-governing satellite state in Slovakia. By April 1939, there was little doubt that Hitler had chosen Poland to be Nazi Germany's next victim. But Britain and France promised to come to Poland's aid if Germany attacked, and in the summer of 1939 they sought an alliance with the Soviet Union aimed at checking German aggression. Polish leaders thought that even Hitler would not be fool enough to risk a two-front war with Germany's three major European adversaries from World War I.

Then, on August 24, the world received stunning news: Nazi Germany and the Soviet Union, sworn ideological enemies, had signed a nonaggression pact, agreeing not to attack each other for ten years. Within two days, German troops were moving toward the Polish border.[21]

And yet, in 1939, Janina and Henry had reasons to be pleased with their status and optimistic about the future. Lwów's intellectual circles had welcomed them with open arms. Both were recognized members of the Lwów-Warsaw School, which had become one of Europe's leading philosophical circles. Janina was elected to the Polish Mathematical Society and published a critique in *The Journal of Symbolic Logic*.[22] Henry began work to obtain the habilitation, the postdoctoral certification that would qualify him to teach in a university. His published work was attracting notice and respect from philosophers both in Poland and abroad. He was regularly lecturing at the Philosophical Society and Jan Kazimierz University and was giving talks on the radio about Twardowski's philosophy. On at least one occasion, Janina joined him on air, to debate the question "Is Truth Relative?"[23]

Henry and Janina had a wide circle of friends, both Jewish and non-Jewish, who admired the couple's brilliance and enjoyed their warmth and kindness. Janina, generous and empathetic, was especially adept at forging friendships with people from many different backgrounds and walks of life.

Nothing about their lives prepared Janina and Henry for what was to come.

TWO

THE BEGINNING OF THE END

Shortly after dawn on September 1, 1939, the residents of Lwów heard the drone of German warplanes overhead, then felt the shattering blasts of bombs falling on their beautiful city. In shock and disbelief, Janina and Henry, like most others in the city, did not follow official instructions to retreat to the basement of their building, for they were confident that Poland's mighty air defenses would soon put a stop to the unpleasantness.

Two days later, however, with German bombers still dropping their payloads and Lwów's buildings crumbling, a rising sense of panic drove residents to their basements. Still, they took comfort from exciting news: France and Great Britain had declared war on Germany. Surely, Poles thought, Germany would soon be forced to withdraw its troops and concede defeat.

Then, a week into the war, the refugees began to arrive from the west, first in a trickle but soon in an unending river that filled the main roads as far as the eye could see. The trains had ceased running and only the wealthy had cars, so the refugees traveled mainly on foot, bicycles, or in conveyances drawn by horses or cattle. They arrived panicked and traumatized by the German blitzkrieg, having seen their homes and communities obliterated and hundreds of their fellow travelers killed on the way by bombs, shells, and strafing warplanes. With them came unsettling rumors: Polish forces were being routed; the government was fleeing the country.

9

Janina and Henry huddled in the stuffy basement of their building with the other residents. For long days and nights, they endured excruciating boredom broken by moments of terror as they listened to whistling bombs and screaming artillery shells and held their breath when their building shuddered from the impact of nearby explosions. Still, people clung hopefully to the assurances of Poland's leaders that the Polish Army was far superior to the German Wehrmacht and that the retreats of Polish forces were merely strategic.[1]

On September 17, as German forces were poised to take Lwów, news came that Soviet forces had crossed into Poland. For a fleeting moment, some Lwów residents grasped the hope that the Soviet Union had abandoned its nonaggression pact with Nazi Germany and was coming to Poland's rescue. In fact, the Soviets came to fulfill their part of the bargain with Nazi Germany. In a secret codicil to their pact, the Nazi and Soviet governments had agreed to divide Poland between them.

Janina and Henry had retreated to their basement as proud citizens of Poland. When the bombing and shelling finally ceased on September 22, they emerged as subjects of the Union of Soviet Socialist Republics. Per their secret agreement with the Germans, the Soviets occupied and annexed Poland's provinces east of the Bug River, including Eastern Galicia. The rest of Poland fell to Nazi Germany, which annexed Poland's western and northern provinces to the Third Reich. The remaining area, about one quarter the size of prewar Poland, became a German possession. Dubbed the General Government (*Generalgouvernement*), it was essentially a colony, ruthlessly ruled by a German administration for the benefit of its overlord. Just two decades after proudly declaring its sovereignty, the Polish nation again found itself without a state and occupied by enemies intent on eradicating not only its independence but also its identity.

On the heels of the Red Army, a wave of violence swept through Eastern Galicia. The occupying soldiers looted and raped at will. Incited by the Soviets to take up "scythes and axes" and destroy "Polish fascism," some Ukrainians complied with gusto. They looted estates and businesses and attacked their owners, sometimes murdering them. Most of the victims were ethnic Poles, followed by Jews. Believing that the land they seized would be theirs,

Ukrainian peasants welcomed the Red Army with bread and salt. The Soviets might preach about a workers' paradise without ethnic, religious, or social distinctions, but they understood the value of manipulating ethnic hostilities.[2]

In Lwów, renamed Lvov, Janina and Henry faced the prospect of homelessness. The Red Army confiscated thousands of homes and apartments of the city's mostly Polish and Jewish residents, or forced families to live in one room and serve the soldiers billeted in the rest of their abode.[3] Soon after the city was occupied, two Red Army officers arrived at Janina and Henry's door to determine how to dispose of their apartment's four rooms. Henry was not at home.

Greeting the officers in Russian, Janina graciously showed them around, hoping she could persuade them to let her and Henry remain in one of the rooms. The officers stared agape at the walls covered with shelves of books.

"Why do you own all these books?" one officer asked Janina.

"My husband and I are professors and needed to acquire them for our work," she replied.

The other officer, pointing to a book on the desk, noted that the author's name matched that on the apartment door.

"Are you related to the author?" he asked.

"He is my husband."

"So, your husband is not only a professor but a writer, and you teach as well."

Janina confirmed his conclusion. To her astonishment, the two officers then took their leave.

Under the Soviet regime, it turned out, teachers had a special status and could be allotted two rooms each.[4] Thus, Janina and Henry could remain in their apartment as before. The tenants in the apartment below, however, had to house four officers and their families.

But to keep their apartment, the Mehlbergs had to be approved for teaching positions. The Soviets strictly surveilled the personnel and curriculum at all schools to ensure the ideological purity of instruction. Ukrainian, Russian, and Yiddish replaced the Polish and Hebrew languages in primary and secondary schools. At Lwów's university, renamed Ivan Franko University after a nineteenth-century Ukrainian writer, the language of instruction was changed to Ukrainian, and many Polish and Jewish professors were dismissed. The philosophy department was expected to teach Marxist materialism, not the unorthodox views of the Lwów-Warsaw School.[5]

As the daughter of an estate owner, Janina qualified as a class enemy, while the Mehlbergs' activities in the Lwów-Warsaw School could have disqualified them from teaching. When they registered with authorities, Janina claimed that her father had been a simple bookkeeper on a Polish estate. She and Henry presented themselves as high school teachers, she of math and he of foreign languages. Neither field was ideologically suspect, and since Janina could teach in Ukrainian and Henry did not need it to teach French, they were approved to continue their work.

On October 22, Janina and Henry had to vote to "choose" what had already been decided for them: that Eastern Galicia would unite with the Ukrainian Soviet Socialist Republic. Every resident of Eastern Galicia was required to submit a ballot. Those who failed to come to a polling station were sought out and transported there, or the ballot box was brought to them. As she approached the ballot box, Janina, like all voters, had to show how she had filled her ballot.

The unsurprising election result was announced: 90.83 percent of Galicians voted for union with Ukraine.[6]

Hunger and want descended on Lwów. The Soviets confiscated most private enterprises and closed the banks, seizing all but a paltry sum in depositors' accounts. Even that amount became worthless when the ruble replaced Polish currency. The only legal way to acquire income was through wages, but there was massive unemployment thanks to the dislocations caused by the confiscations. There was an acute food shortage as well, and by the start of the unusually harsh winter of 1939–1940, no coal could be obtained for heating. Even the black market had little to offer, and its prices quickly spiraled beyond what workers' wages could afford. The search for food became an all-consuming quest. So little was available that the state-run stores simply listed the few goods they had for sale on their windows. People stood in line for hours, often overnight, in the dwindling hope that something would still be available when they finally reached the head of the queue.

The Mehlbergs had taken in a colleague of Henry's, and the two men shared in the search for food for their household. Bundled in all their warm clothing, they would set out in the dark hours before dawn, carrying knapsacks to hold whatever they could find. One early morning, they saw a store that was open, and in its windows were jars of liquid concentrate of ersatz tea. Excited at the prospect of surprising Janina with what had become a rare delicacy, the men bought two jars. The rest of their foray proved similarly successful, for they succeeded in buying a half pound of horsemeat after standing only six hours in line.

The two men returned to the apartment and, with conspiratorial grins, proposed to Janina that they warm up with a nice cup of hot tea. Then, in response to her look of puzzled surprise, they triumphantly opened their knapsacks to pull out the two jars, only to find that both had frozen and shattered while the men waited to buy the horsemeat. Trying to console them, Janina served up cups of ersatz lemon powder in hot water. In such trying times, ingenuity and imagination were necessary coping strategies.

People's constant food anxiety actually played into the hands of Soviet authorities. As a teacher, Janina had a front-row view of how the Soviets used food to indoctrinate children and students in Marxist ideology and turn them into active supporters of the Communist Party. Children received a hot meal daily at school and were organized into communist youth groups that met in beautiful confiscated homes and supplied sumptuous treats. Given the austerity they endured at home, children needed little encouragement to attend the meetings. At the universities as well, cafeterias supplied students and teachers with hot food. Numerous unions, committees, and professional associations were organized, and at each of their many meetings there were food counters with bread and sausages for sale. Janina noted that hungry stomachs tended to develop a strong appetite for political discussion.

But the Soviets relied much more on the stick than the carrot to ensure conformity and obedience to Marxist totalitarianism. Thousands of agents of the Soviet secret police, then known as the NKVD, descended upon Eastern Galicia to identify and determine the fate of all suspected enemies of the state. In February 1940, they carried out the first of four massive deportations of people categorized as threats to Soviet rule based upon their professions, class, or ethnicity. The victims included Polish landowners, civil

servants, and police, landowning Ukrainian peasants, Jewish business owners, and the Polish and Jewish refugees from German-occupied Poland who
refused to accept Soviet citizenship. Packed tightly into boxcars, the victims
traveled with little food or water for days or sometimes weeks until they
arrived at labor colonies in the tundra of Siberia or the steppe of Kazakh-
stan. According to the wartime Polish government in exile, 1.25 million
Polish citizens were deported by the Soviets between February 1940 and
June 1941, 400,000 of them from Eastern Galicia.[7]

Although forced to perform backbreaking labor, the deportees at least
had a chance of surviving. In April 1940, the NKVD murdered 21,892 Polish Army officers, policemen, and members of Poland's intelligentsia in the
Katyn Forest in western Russia and at four other sites.[8]

Certain that spies and traitors were everywhere plotting to overthrow
Soviet rule, the NKVD and its informants relentlessly hunted for suspects.
In Lwów, thousands disappeared into the four NKVD prisons to be tortured
until they confessed and named others. The lucky prisoners were sentenced
to eight years in a Siberian gulag; the rest received a bullet in the back of the
neck.[9]

Like so many citizens of Lwów, Janina and Henry lived in constant
dread that the NKVD would set its sights on them, perhaps as members of
a suspect group or because of an allegation wrenched from an acquaintance
desperate to escape torture. They listened nightly for the knock on the door
signaling that their time had come.

Nevertheless, whether under German or Soviet occupation, Polish pa-
triots like Janina and Henry maintained faith that their nation's subjugation
was only temporary. After all, this was not the first time that Poland had
been wiped off the map. The Poles found strength in the words of Poland's
national anthem:

> Poland is not yet lost
> As long as we're alive.

Poland would rise again, Janina and Henry were sure. This was not
the end.

THREE

TERROR COMES TO LWÓW

Shrieking in terror, young women were fleeing through the streets of Lwów. Those caught pleaded for their lives as their pursuers stripped and flogged them. Other rioters were dragging men out onto the streets and bludgeoning them. Hundreds were dying in the bloody frenzy. The victims were Jews, and their murderers were their neighbors. It was June 30, 1941, and German forces had just taken the city.

Since Nazi Germany's attack on the Soviet Union eight days earlier, Ukrainian nationalists had been preparing to vent their rage at their Soviet oppressors. The gruesome discovery of some 1,500 corpses of NKVD prisoners in Lwów's prisons added to their fury. Unable to get their hands on actual Soviet officials, Ukrainian militia groups settled upon Jews as scapegoats, even though many of the murdered prisoners were Jews. The slaughter continued for two days until German military officials finally stepped in and restored order on July 2. By that time, more than a thousand and possibly as many as 4,000 Jews had been murdered.[1]

Then a *Kommando* (detachment) arrived in the city from one of the SS *Einsatzgruppen*. These were the notorious task forces of the German Security Police and SD that enforced security behind the German front lines during military operations. The Security Police, consisting of the Gestapo and the Criminal Police, was a state agency, while the SD

(*Sicherheitsdienst*; Security Service) was the intelligence service of the SS (*Schutzstaffel*; Protection Squads), the armed security force of the Nazi Party, but the two were joined under one office at the start of World War II. One of the tasks of the *Einsatzgruppen* in the seized Soviet territories was to eliminate "Judeo-Bolshevism," the Nazi term for communism, through mass murder of communists, members of the intelligentsia, and above all, Jews.[2]

Janina and Henry did not witness the first Ukrainian rampages, as their neighborhood near the university was not predominantly Jewish. But two nights after the *Einsatzkommando* arrived in the city, its officials burst into the nearby homes of some two dozen prominent university professors, most of them Poles. The Germans arrested not only the professors but also family members and servants. By the end of the next day, nearly all were dead, shot in mass graves in the hills above the city.[3] Among the victims were three mathematicians whom Janina knew and respected.

Murders of Jews continued as well, although under the direction of the SS, the Ukrainian militia conducted them in a more orderly and targeted fashion. Between July 2 and 5, the militia rounded up thousands of male Jews and took them to an open-air sports arena, where they were brutally beaten and tortured. Most of the Jews were then marched to the woods outside the city, where, with the help of the Ukrainians, the SS shot them. The *Einsatzkommando* did not make an exact count of the victims but reported that they numbered between 2,500 and 3,000.[4]

The Wehrmacht, the German armed forces, established a military administration in Lwów, which the Germans renamed Lemberg. The city commandant placed ethnic Ukrainians in positions of power. Although Nazi ideology considered all Slavs, including Ukrainians, to be racially inferior, the Germans were as adept as the Soviets at exploiting ethnic divisions. The Wehrmacht had organized units of the OUN that marched into Eastern Galicia with German troops. With German encouragement, Ukrainian nationalists called on their ethnic brethren to seize villages and towns and take revenge against their enemies, especially Jews and Poles. Contrary to OUN expectations, however, Germany's Nazi leaders had no intention of granting sovereignty to the Ukrainians. After an OUN faction declared Ukrainian statehood in Lwów, its leaders soon found themselves guests of the SS in Sachsenhausen concentration camp.[5]

One of the military administration's first acts was to order all Jews between ages fourteen and sixty to register and wear armbands with the Star of David. For the SS and Ukrainian militia, the markings simplified the task of finding victims to murder.[6] Janina could only watch in sorrow as her friends in mixed marriages were forced by the armband requirement to choose between terrible options. Some non-Jewish partners divorced their Jewish spouses and took the children, in hopes of saving them. Some non-Jewish mothers even tried to claim that their children were illegitimate, since bastardy was better than having a Jewish father. Janina also had friends who had been practicing Christians all their life yet were classified as Jews by the Germans. They might have been able to hide their parentage from the Ukrainians, but not from the Germans. A professor of Polish literature well known to Janina and Henry was a devout Catholic whose Jewish parents were converted Christians and had baptized him at birth. After learning that he was required to wear the armband, he slit his wrists in his bathtub.

Janina and Henry donned the armband and experienced the full force of Nazi persecution. One of the first decrees banned Jewish ownership of radios. When Janina went to turn in hers at the designated place, she found a long line of other Jews lugging radios in the July heat. A few hours after she joined it, two armed Ukrainian militiamen guarding a small group of young men passed by. Suddenly, Janina was startled by a heartrending wail from an older Jewish woman standing near her in the line.

"That's my son! They are taking my son!"

Dropping her radio, the woman ran toward the men. One of the Ukrainians roughly shoved her away, but she continued to follow them, wailing for her son. The other militiaman grabbed her head in his hands and smashed it on the curb until she was dead. Then he kicked her body and rejoined the group. Janina could do nothing but keep her place in the line as it slowly shuffled past the bloody corpse. Such scenes had become common in the city.

On July 25, the Ukrainian militia embarked on a new, two-day pogrom. They targeted wealthy Jews, dragging them into the street, beating them, and then taking them off to be shot.[7] This time, they came to Janina and

Henry's neighborhood. Janina became aware of the danger when, drawn to her window by a commotion in the street below, she saw that a group of Ukrainian militia had dragged out the Jewish landlord of a neighboring building. The landlord was kneeling before one of the militiamen, whom Janina recognized as the building's janitor. As the landlord pleaded for his life, she heard the janitor snarl:

"No! Under the Bolsheviks you said I stole from you. Now it's my turn to send you to hell. I'm not going to lift a finger to save a rat like you!"

Janina was shocked. Often when the janitor was working outside the building, she would stop to chat, always remembering to ask about his children, who were clearly his pride and joy. When she learned one day that one of the children was seriously ill, she arranged medical treatment for the child. She could not fathom how the loving father and friendly neighbor she knew, who had shown no animosity toward her as a Jew, could so heartlessly consign another human being to a cruel death.

The next day, a truck pulled up in front of Janina and Henry's building and disgorged Ukrainian militia. Janina saw them enter the building and, assuming that they were looking for Jewish men, insisted that Henry hide while she pretended to be a visitor. When the knock came, Janina answered the door—and saw that the janitor was among the men. Somehow swallowing her fear, she stated that she was a houseguest of the Mehlbergs, who were not at home. Then the janitor spoke up.

"That's right, I remember seeing the Mehlbergs leave earlier."

The group moved on in search of other victims.

Janina closed the door and leaned against it, trying to process what had just happened. The man she knew to be responsible for the murder of at least one Jew had just saved the lives of two others, at considerable risk to his own. The two acts appeared incompatible, yet both were performed by the same person. Over the next three years, she would observe further instances of the human capacity to perform logically irreconcilable acts, and her observations would influence her calculations of risk as she daily put her own life on the line to save others.

By the time the pogrom ended on July 27, the Ukrainian militia had murdered some 1,000 victims in Lwów. The city commandant reacted the

next day by imposing a two million ruble fine upon the city's Jews as punishment for "provoking" the Ukrainians.[8]

Things got even worse for Lwów's Jews on August 1, when Eastern Galicia became *Distrikt Galizien*, the fifth *Distrikt* or province of the General
Government, the area of Nazi-occupied Poland that Germany did not annex
in 1939. It was run by Nazi civilian administrators who ruthlessly exploited
its resources and people and enriched themselves in the process. Some of
the most corrupt and brutal veterans of Nazi rule in the General Government obtained leading positions in Galicia District, earning it the derisive
nickname "Scandalicia" (*Skandalizien*). In fact, the district's first governor
so far overstepped even Nazi standards for graft that he was recalled, tried,
and executed in 1942.[9]

The new civilian administrators barred Jews from employment, schools,
and public spaces. All Jews between ages fourteen and sixty became liable
for forced labor. Civilian officials inspected Jewish residences, registered the
furnishings, confiscated what was valuable, and evicted the inhabitants.[10]
There was such a barrage of constantly changing regulations and decrees
from different offices that Janina was never sure whether what she had done
permissibly the day before had become prohibited overnight.

Lwów's new administration immediately levied an additional fine
against the Jewish community. Janina and Henry did not have the cash to
pay their part of the fine and so, like thousands of other Jews in the city, she
went to St. Mary's Square in the city's Old Town to sell her two most valuable items, a ring and a custom fountain pen ornamented in 22-karat gold.
The square was one of the most beautiful in the city, but now it seemed
like something out of a fever dream. It was packed with people shoving and
shouting in the stifling heat. Mixing among the desperate men and women
seeking to sell their belongings were German soldiers, officers, and SS men
with greedy grins. Some seemed to specialize in specific items, for Janina
saw one hold up a hand with wedding rings to his fingertips, while another
drew back the sleeve from his raised arm to show bracelets.

Janina recognized a friend in the crowd, the wife of a professor, who was
trying to sell a bracelet, and the two women stood together. A German came
over to inspect their items, asked Janina the price for hers, and then offered

to buy them for half the amount she named. Civilians clustered around to watch. One of them spoke to Janina in German:

"Don't sell it to him. The pen alone is worth three times that much."

The German snorted in disgust and walked away. Whereupon an SS man simply snatched the pen from Janina's hand and sauntered off into the crowd. The civilian who had advised her not to sell tossed her a few złoty and quickly followed the SS man. That, Janina learned, was how business was done in St. Mary's Square.

Hunger became a constant companion for Janina and Henry. Their official rations provided less than 8 percent of the calories needed to survive, and they were only allowed to buy the few permitted foodstuffs—if they were even available—at a single market between the hours of 12:00 and 4:00 p.m. There they ran the risk that Germans or Ukrainians would attack and rob them or abduct them to perform grueling labor, from which many never returned.

Adding to the misery of daily life, typhus arrived in September with Ukrainian soldiers returning from German POW camps. Malnourished Jews living in crowded quarters proved especially vulnerable to the disease, which soon ran rampant in the city. This added to the Germans' determination to "solve the Jewish question" in Galicia. There were more than half a million Jews in the district, more than 100,000 of them within the city of Lwów. Nazi officials decided to cut the Jews off completely from the rest of the population by enclosing them in ghettos. Not all of them, though—first there would be a culling.[11]

Janina began to notice trucks full of Jews speeding toward Piaskowa Góra (Sandy Hill) in the city's heights in early October. And at night she would hear long bursts of gunfire coming from those heights. One day, she ran into a friend from her school days, a Pole, whose haggard appearance alarmed her. The distraught woman explained that she had fled from her home on Piaskowa Góra because it was just twenty yards from an execution site. Sleep continued to elude her, however, because the sounds of the gunshots and screams she had heard for so many nights never ceased echoing in her head.

The raids on Jews intensified, always for the announced intention of taking them for work. Sometimes that proved to be true, but the gunfire in the hills indicated that for many it was not. For Janina, like the other Jews of Lwów, every day involved a desperate calculation of the probability that venturing to the market, visiting a friend, or even staying at home would end either in abduction to perform agonizing labor or in death. There was no safe place for a Jew in Lwów.

People tried different strategies to avoid being taken. One day, Janina paid a visit to a young couple she knew from the university and was surprised to be greeted at the door by a gray-haired woman. After a double take, Janina recognized her friend. She had dyed her hair because she had to go stand in line to buy food at the market and feared that, as a healthy young woman, she would be taken for labor. Her strategy proved successful for several shopping forays, until the day she went out and never returned. The SS were seizing elderly women that day—and not to take them for labor.

Like the other Jews not yet taken, Janina kept a constant vigil for the trucks that carried SS men and Ukrainian auxiliaries. As she was watching out her apartment window early one morning, she saw a truck pull up and Ukrainian policemen enter the apartment building across the street, shouting that they had come to take the residents to work. A young, partially disabled Jewish clerk lived there with his pretty wife. The Ukrainians passed him over as unfit for work but seized his wife instead. The clerk reassured himself that his wife must have been taken for work, because the Ukrainians logically would have seized him if they were looking for victims to murder. At five the same evening, Janina watched as the clerk began standing outside the entrance to his building, waiting for his wife's return. At eight he was still there, leaning heavily on his cane. The next morning, he was still there, no longer waiting expectantly but crumpled in the doorway, sobbing. No one could get him to leave the entryway, so his neighbors finally notified his parents, who came and took him.

And then one night around 3:00 a.m., terror pounded on Janina and Henry's door. They tried to dress quickly as the pounding became louder. Shaking with fear, Janina opened the door. Ukrainian policemen barged past her and seized Henry.

"We're taking him for work," they announced.

Janina pleaded with them in Ukrainian, "He's a teacher, he's not much good for physical labor."

But they stomped out with Henry in tow, only partially dressed. Janina followed them, filled with despair and wanting only to share Henry's fate. But when she tried to follow them into the police station, one of the policemen pushed her away.

"What's your hurry," he sneered, "don't you know where they're taking him?"

This confirmation of her worst fear suddenly filled Janina with a reckless stubbornness. She stared into the policeman's eyes and did not move. Enraged, he screamed, "Get the hell out of here!" and cracked her in the face with his rifle butt.

A Wehrmacht officer entering the building witnessed the assault. He steadied Janina and advised her to leave, but she refused to budge. This seemed to impress him. Promising to find out what was happening to Henry if she left the station, he finally persuaded her to go stand in a doorway across the street. After half an hour, he returned.

"I took your husband out of the transport and am sending him to the Wehrmacht bakery for work. Now you can go home."

But, reeling and nauseous from the blow to her head, Janina continued to wait, not daring to trust the officer's assurances. Soon, she saw a truck depart with the other Jewish men collected at the station, and it headed toward Piaskowa Góra. Just then, she saw Henry emerge from the station's entry, escorted by two German soldiers. They turned and headed in the other direction, toward the Wehrmacht bakery. Another soldier came and told her that Henry would return at six that evening.

Still she stood in the doorway as the hours dragged by. At six, she cried out in relief as she spotted Henry walking toward her. And, amazingly, he was carrying a loaf of wheat bread, something they had not tasted in months. Back at their apartment, Janina tended to Henry's chest and arms, raw and blistered from his shirtless labor hauling hot loaves from the ovens. Yet, as they feasted on the loaf of bread, they were almost giddy with gratitude. The irony of their feelings was not lost on Janina, who remarked, "If a man has been beating you brutally for years, then suddenly stops and offers you a sip of water, he may seem to you the Lord of Mercy at that moment."

FOUR

TRANSFORMATION

Two small suitcases packed with only the bare necessities stood at the door, ready for Janina and Henry to grab them on their way out. It was December 7, 1941, and they knew they had to get out of Lwów. The city's nearly 120,000 Jews had received orders on November 8 to move into a ghetto by December 15. Reports of what was already happening there were horrifying, and not just because of the massive overcrowding and raging epidemics. To enter the ghetto, the Jews had to funnel through two gates under railroad bridges. As they filed in on foot, carrying the few possessions they were allowed to bring, German and Ukrainian police searched, robbed, and beat them. Men and women who seemed particularly poor or weak were seized and taken to the Security Police prison. Now it seemed that the prison must be full, for the police had blocked off the roads between it and the sand pits in the city's heights and dozens of trucks were speeding back and forth daily, traveling up with covered loads and returning empty. Gunfire constantly echoed from above.[1]

Even if they survived the gauntlet into the ghetto, Janina and Henry understood what awaited them there. News had reached Galicia's Jews that thousands of Jews were dying of starvation and diseases in the ghettos already established in German-occupied Poland. In Warsaw alone, the death rate was between 4,000 and 5,500 per month.[2] Janina and Henry lacked the kind of physical labor skills and connections that might get them a work card and, with it, the possibility of better rations, perhaps even an entire half of a room to live in, and most important, protection from mass shootings. For it was illogical to expect that the Germans would stop murdering Jews once they were all sealed into the ghetto, where finding victims would no longer require any effort. Janina and Henry were nothing if not logical. Going into the ghetto, they concluded, meant going to their deaths.

They had decided to join Henry's family in Kopyczyńce, where there was no ghetto yet, and Henry's father was sending a horse-drawn carriage to collect them. When it arrived, they opened their door and stopped short in surprise: an unexpected visitor stood there, about to knock. It was Count Andrzej Skrzyński (AHN-jay SKSHIN-skee), an old friend of Janina's family. He had taken the first civilian train allowed to cross into Galicia to seek out Janina and make her a proposition: she and Henry should travel back with him to Lublin. Skrzyński promised he could get them false papers, living quarters, and jobs.

Janina and Henry weighed the odds and concluded that the Count's proposal offered the best chance for long-term survival. But only if they could get to Lublin. Galician Jews could not travel outside the district without official permits, for which Janina and Henry did not qualify. That meant they must travel without wearing the Star of David armband or carrying papers that identified them as Jews, both offenses for which they would be shot if caught. Count Skrzyński was confident, however, that if they stuck with him during the journey, he could get them to Lublin.

On the morning of December 8, Janina and Henry gazed out the window and bid a silent farewell to their beloved city as their train departed the Lwów station. Janina remembered that the day was the Catholic holiday of the Feast of the Immaculate Conception, and she fondly recalled the processions, festivities, and fireworks of past years in the city. Lublin is about 130 miles northwest from Lwów, but when the railroads were built, Lwów was in Austria-Hungary while Lublin was part of the Russian Empire. The rail route between the two cities was circuitous and required several changes for which there were no set schedules, since civilian trains were regularly shunted aside for Wehrmacht transports that were speeding soldiers and supplies to the Eastern Front. The journey would take days.

The day was dark and frigid, and the passenger cars were unheated and unlit. Janina and her traveling companions jostled on the hard wooden benches for hour after long hour. The train would occasionally stop, and a German official would board with a flashlight to conduct a random check. Each time, Janina observed a young man who shrank back into the shadows, trying to hide a face pale with fear. She guessed that he, too, was a Jew.

After twenty-four hours, they had traveled little more than fifty miles to Przemyśl, where they had to change trains. Informed that they had to wait ten hours, Skrzyński and Henry went in search of food while Janina stayed in the cold, dark station with the two suitcases. After a while, she noticed bobbing lights slowly moving her way. Panic seized her. German police were examining all passengers and demanding to see their papers.

Janina was standing in a corner of the station and had no way to escape. How could she explain her lack of papers? Paralyzed with fear and despair, she could not think. Her luck, she concluded, had run out. A wave of relief washed over her that Henry and the Count would not be caught with her, followed by a wave of sorrow for their coming grief. As two policemen turned their lights on her and approached, she resolved to meet her fate with dignity.

"What do you have in these valises?" demanded one policeman.

Without replying, she bent to undo the latches, but her fingers fumbled with cold and nerves as she waited for the next demand: her papers. The other policeman shone his flashlight on her face, then said, "She doesn't look like a smuggler. Let's leave her alone." And they moved on to the next passenger. Janina slowly straightened and stood in a shivering daze for she knew not how long before Henry and the Count returned.

After a further day of travel, they arrived at Dębica—still 130 miles away from their destination—and faced another long wait for the next train. They were desperately tired, but German bombs had destroyed most of the city in 1939 and there were no hotels. Count Skrzyński found a railway worker who took them to a building with a number of bare cots. All but one were occupied by Polish travelers. The men insisted that Janina take the available cot with the Count's overcoat as a blanket, and they sought space to sleep on the floor.

They were startled from their sleep by harsh shouts of *"Raus, Alle!"* In the darkness, Janina could hear people groaning and a baby's wail. They all filed out, wondering whether they were about to be arrested, only to discover that the order came from a drunk German soldier seeking a place to sleep it off and unwilling to share space with "Polack swine." There was nothing to do but return to the station.

After three days and three nights, they arrived at Lublin. Hoping to slip out of the station quickly without encountering any police checks, the men went to retrieve the luggage while Janina sought a cab. She found one easily, then waited with increasing anxiety, straining for a sight of Henry and the Count, while the cab driver complained about losing other fares. Finally, nearly an hour later, she saw Count Skrzyński approach. He was alone.

"You and I are going home now," he said, taking her arm. "Henry was detained by some German police for something, and he'll come after us."

Janina broke away from him and ran back into the station. There she saw Henry being berated by a German official who was shouting that taking any baggage out of Galicia was strictly prohibited. Henry looked pale. At any moment, the official would demand to see his papers. Janina sprang into action.

"What do you want of my husband?" she demanded in German as she stepped in front of Henry and fixed the official with a haughty look.

Startled by her peremptory tone and apparent lack of fear, the official lost his swagger and replied in a lower voice, "He has broken a strict regulation on baggage."

"He could do no such thing," Janina retorted, "because when we left Lwów there was no such regulation!"

The official backed down and said lamely, "Anyway, he has to pay a fine."

If they agreed to the fine, Janina realized, they would have to show papers so it could be recorded.

"We are not going to pay any fine," she declared firmly, "because there was no regulation about this, and if you will put through a call to Lwów, you will hear it for yourself."

Now flustered and fuming, the official ordered them to get out, "and don't let me catch you another time!"

Careful not to give away their relief, Janina and Henry sauntered out of the station with their two bags. "Never has a harshly bellowed order sounded so sweet," Janina thought.

Decades later, she would reflect on the lesson she learned in this encounter and that she would use again and again to save lives in the years that followed it:

> What do you do with your fear and trembling in a confrontation with a swaggering bully? You confine it to the small prison of the heart, letting none seep into the muscles of the eyes, hands, or legs; you quake within and show calm authority without—you pull off a hoax. You must not toady to them, you must not let them sniff blood. Composure and coolness toward them implied the backing of power, and in the face of power they might very well shrink.

Three days earlier, Pepi Mehlberg had departed Lwów for Lublin. Countess Janina Suchodolska arrived there in her place.

FIVE

THE DYSTOPIAN UTOPIA

After the misery of their three-day journey, Janina and Henry were yearning for a bite to eat, a place to lay their heads, and a chance to thaw their frozen marrow. Their horse-drawn cab took them to 22 Narutowicza Street, where Count Skrzyński had arranged for them to stay. It was an elegant neoclassical building, with shops on the street level and four stories of residential space above lined with wrought iron balconies.[1] Passing under two grime-streaked caryatids that supported the arch over the entry drive, they rang the bell at an imposing set of carved wooden doors. A porter answered and led them through to the rear courtyard and the building's entry. As they followed him up an unlit staircase, Janina noted that the temperature inside seemed no warmer than outside.

The porter led them to a landing where an elderly lady was waiting and welcomed them warmly in French. The landlady was not at home, she explained, but she could take the Mehlbergs to the room that would serve in part as their living quarters. She led them to a vast, hall-like drawing room, with high ceilings and five huge French windows that opened to balconies. Janina thought it the perfect setting for a chamber music recital, with elegantly dressed ladies and gentlemen seated in gilded chairs. Now it was sparsely furnished and crisscrossed with lines of laundry. As Henry stowed their luggage in the corner that was to be theirs, Janina reached up to the lines to take down some linens, only to discover that they were frozen stiff. As she had feared, the room was freezing cold.

Just then, the landlady fluttered in, apologizing in French that she had not been present to greet their arrival. "But I never miss Vespers," she explained. She was Countess Władysława Strus, about seventy-three years old, petite, fine-boned, surprisingly agile, and with a face that radiated kindness. In addition to her Lublin home, her family had once owned large estates in Beresteczko and Hrubieszów, but the Germans had confiscated them. The lady who had first greeted Janina and Henry was Countess Władysława's sister, Madame Maria Czernecka, age seventy. She had been expelled from her husband's grand estate after the Germans arrested him. Since she had received no notice of his fate, she clung to the false hope that he was alive in the concentration camp that the Germans had established for Polish prisoners in Oświęcim in annexed Poland. The Germans called the camp Auschwitz.

Countess Władysława shared one room in her building with her sister and rented the others to tenants. When Count Skrzyński told her he was seeking living quarters for his wife's distant cousins, she readily offered part of her drawing room. Now the sisters clucked about the "nice young couple," endeavoring to make them feel welcome. Seeing the frozen linen in Janina's hands, Countess Władysława assured her that she needn't worry about the room's temperature.

"I had an iron stove brought in the minute I knew you were going to rent it, and I am going immediately to get some nice black coal, so we shall soon be as cozy as toast!"

Clutching her worn fur coat against her thin frame, the Countess bustled out of the room. The sight of a small stove in a corner did not reassure Janina. Her heart sank further when the Countess returned with "the nice black coal"—five lumps in a small dustpan. Clearly, the lady had no idea how much coal it would take to heat such a large room. Janina thought the scene could almost be a French comedy, were it not so cruelly real. The Countess proceeded to light the stove, getting coal dust on her hands and face. "Whatever would her butler in Beresteczko think if he saw her now?" Janina thought.

The stove was actually the sisters' cookstove. The Countess took charge of preparing the daily meal, a broth thickened with a bit of flour. She tended to it over the sickly flame with the same care as the roasts and stews that her servants had cooked for hours at Beresteczko, which raised rueful but affectionate smiles in Janina and Henry. If Janina suggested raising the flame, the Countess scolded her. "Janka, my dear," she said, using a diminutive form of Janina, "don't you know that the very best in any food is brought out by careful, watched over, very slow cooking?"

On Sundays, the Countess made pancakes of water and flour fried with bits of bacon and served with a tiny bit of jam. For weeks before her Saint's Day, however, the sisters would forgo the pancakes to save the flour, preparing to hold a real party for their friends. When the day arrived, they opened the dining table to seat twenty-four and covered it with a beautiful embroidered tablecloth, fine china, and flowers. From the pound of flour she had saved up, the Countess made shortbread cookies. Served on the lovely plates, with flowers between each place and ersatz tea in the delicate cups, they created a festive feeling in the guests. The Countess presided over the table like the lady of the manor she had once been. Her guests, including Janina and Henry, wore their Sunday best and spoke French in animated conversations. It brought back to Janina happy scenes from her childhood.

In addition to the little rent the Countess collected, the sisters lived off the wages of Madame Maria, who worked as a domestic for the Rylskis, members of the lower aristocracy. She went to and from work in dirty, worn bedroom slippers, saving her only pair of shoes for church. She performed numerous chores, including washing floors and carrying heavy baskets of coal, but she was given nothing to eat during her entire workday, because Madame Rylska complained that food was just too expensive. When Janina expressed outrage at this treatment, Madame Maria scoffed, "These are no hardships, my child. Hardship is what my poor husband must suffer in Auschwitz—if indeed he is still alive. What one does as a free man or woman, that should not be called hardship, unless we want to blaspheme against God's mercy!"

Whatever the temperature in their room, Janina and Henry always felt warmed by the tender kindness of the sisters. In time, they were able to re turn it by looking out for them and helping to support them.

Janina and Henry were now living in a part of Poland scarred and trau- matized by more than two years of Nazi racist persecution. For Hitler, the conquest of Poland in 1939 was just one step toward fulfilling the mission that he believed Providence had assigned him: winning the *Lebensraum* des- tined for the German *Volk*. This vast "living space" would stretch from Ger- many to the eastern border of the European continent and would be settled by people of "German blood" from all over Europe. There they would pro- duce the food, goods, and sons needed to ensure victory in the never-ending war for racial dominance. The fact that this future *Lebensraum* was already inhabited by tens of millions of Slavs as well as millions of Jews presented no moral or practical impediment, since Hitler considered both groups to be "subhuman." A minority of the Slavs would be retained to provide brute labor for their German masters; the rest, along with all the Jews, would in one way or another be made to disappear.[2]

German-occupied Poland became the laboratory where the measures for realizing the Nazi racist utopia were developed and tested. In September 1939, Hitler ordered that the western Polish provinces annexed to the Reich be made entirely German as quickly as possible by deporting their Jewish and Polish inhabitants eastward and replacing them with ethnic Germans imported from the territories occupied by the Soviet Union. All non-Jewish Poles were to be corralled in the occupied area east of the annexed territo- ries, with the exception of one corner on the Soviet border. That area would become a "reservation" where all the Jews under Germany's control, both those in the Reich and in occupied Poland, would be forced to live. An enor- mous, unbreachable wall was to be erected along the reservation's western border to ensure that no Jews could return. This was to be a temporary ar- rangement, however, for eventually all of German-occupied Poland would be made entirely German.[3]

Hitler handed responsibility for realizing his vision to Heinrich Himm- ler, *Reichsführer* of the SS and Chief of the German Police.[4] He had at his disposal all the types of forces needed to impose the Nazi racist "new order" upon occupied Poland. His SS "race experts" would sort those genetically qualified to join the German racial community from those whose "blood" doomed them to servitude, ethnic cleansing, or mass murder. His concentration camps would permanently remove from society anyone seen as a potential threat to German rule, while his police forces along with his military formations, the Waffen SS, would sniff out, round up, and murder those considered too dangerous or unfit to be worthy of life.

To prevent the Poles from mounting any effective resistance to German rule, Hitler ordered the elimination of their leaders and educated classes. Following Germany's invasion of Poland, Himmler sent in his special task forces, the *Einsatzgruppen*, to track down 61,000 members of Poland's intelligentsia whose names had been collected by the SD before the war. The units summarily executed thousands of civilians, especially targeting Polish politicians, intellectuals, aristocrats, and even priests, teachers, doctors, and lawyers. By the end of 1939, these forces had shot some 40,000 Poles and 7,000 Polish Jews and sent tens of thousands more Polish civilians to the concentration camps in the Reich.[5] By the end of the war, the Germans would murder 25 percent of Poland's intelligentsia, including 15 percent of its schoolteachers and 18 percent of its Catholic priests. The losses were much higher for the professions in which Jews played a substantial role: Poland lost 45 percent of its doctors and dentists and 56 percent of its lawyers.[6]

Himmler wasted no time in launching the ethnic cleansing program to rid the Reich of Poles and Jews, an estimated six to eight million people. On October 30, 1939, he ordered that the first million be dumped into the General Government in the following four months. According to Himmler's plan, once all the Poles were deposited in the General Government, his race experts would screen them so that the few deemed "racially valuable" could be sent to the Reich to be assimilated. Annual screenings would follow of all Polish children between the ages of six and ten, and those selected would be sent off for assimilation as well. Once all their natural leaders had been murdered, the remaining "subhuman" Poles would lose their national and ethnic identities and become a reservoir of cheap, unskilled laborers.[7] Himmler proposed that the children of this underclass be schooled at most through the fourth grade, since Polish children would only need to be taught "simple counting up to 500 at most, writing one's name and   that it is divine law to obey the Germans. . . . I do not think that reading is necessary."[8]

As for the Jews, Himmler's race experts were developing proposals for getting rid of them all by shipping them somewhere outside of Europe. The French colony of Madagascar was the leading candidate, but others were also under consideration, such as Siberia above the Arctic Circle. Whichever remote, undeveloped, inhospitable destination was chosen, the expectation was that the four million people confined there under SS supervision would not long survive.[9]

For all his ambitions for the General Government, however, the reality was that Himmler was not in control there. Hitler assigned the task of ruling the General Government to Hans Frank, his personal lawyer and a committed Nazi since 1923. Frank's assignment was to govern the Polish territory just as Germany had once ruled over its African colonies: by seizing or exploiting everything of value, using the forced labor of its indigenous inhabitants, and eradicating all those who resisted. He answered only to Hitler and ruled by decree according to the *Führer's* wishes.[10]

In the late fall of 1939, freight trains began arriving at stations in the General Government and disgorging thousands of men, women, and children forcibly deported from their homes in the annexed territories. Without warning, they had been rounded up at night by SS and police forces and forced to leave behind nearly all their possessions for the ethnic Germans who were to take over their homes, farms, and businesses. Just between December 1 and 17, 1939, the SS and police shipped 87,838 Poles and Jews to the General Government without giving prior notice to its officials. Frank protested vociferously that the resulting chaos was undermining his ability to exploit the region for Germany's benefit. In March, Himmler finally had to halt the deportations and agree that all future operations would be conducted in consultation with Frank and his officials.[11] This was just the opening round in a power struggle between the *Reichsführer* and the governor general that would continue for five years.

There was little disagreement between the two ideologically, however, especially when it came to rabid hatred of Poles and Jews. Frank yearned for the day when his realm would be *Judenfrei*—free of Jews—and populated by Germans, with a Polish minority as the servant class. The self-styled top legal mind of the Nazi Party, he abolished the Polish legal code but did not replace it with German law, since even its limited restraints on state power were more than he would brook in his realm. His non-German subjects could have no recourse against German excesses because nothing his officials did could qualify as an excess.[12]

Directly beneath Frank and answerable to him were the governors of the districts—Warsaw, Kraków, Radom, Lublin, and, from 1941, Galicia. Beneath the governors were the heads of the *Kreise*, local districts or counties. The applicants for these and other positions in Frank's administration tended to be minor civil servants, small businessmen, and Nazi Party officials seeking advancement that was unobtainable for them in the Reich because of their personal limitations, past failures, or criminal activities. They all had wide latitude to rule their individual fiefdoms as they pleased, provided they showed initiative in realizing Hitler's dreams of a racist new order. Competence and relevant experience were not requirements for positions in the General Government, only, as Frank explained, readiness to act as "warriors totally dedicated to the liquidation of the Poles."[13]

With no legal restraints upon its officials, theft and corruption became the hallmarks of the General Government administration. As the German head of the city of Lublin put it, "We have decided to behave, as officials, exactly the other way round than at home, that is, like bastards." Officials confiscated estates, factories, and businesses—especially those owned by Jews—and gave charge of them to relatives, cronies, or Germans who offered the right price. These "trustees" then brazenly embezzled the assets entrusted to them. Since it was official policy to eradicate every vestige of Polish culture, officials systematically plundered palaces, churches, and museums, destroyed national monuments and memorials, and closed libraries, looting or burning their works. In Kraków, the General Government's capital, Frank ensconced himself in the Wawel Royal Castle and confiscated a string of other palaces for his personal use, decorating them with all the finest trappings he could steal. His subordinates eagerly copied his example. German officials could enrich themselves by taking what they wanted or by demanding payment for not taking it. Bribery became the oil of the administrative machinery. For the right inducement, almost anything could be done; without it, almost nothing.[14]

Count Skrzyński, who served in the Polish resistance, helped Janina and Henry acquire identity documents that enabled them to pass as Poles. Henry became Count Piotr Suchodolski and Janina Countess Janina Stanisława Bednarska Suchodolska.[15] To obtain the documents, they first had to acquire birth certificates based upon the records of the churches where they were supposedly baptized, as well as a record of their wedding from a marriage registry. With these, they could register as residents of Lublin and obtain the all-important *Kennkarte*, the identity document that the Germans required all residents of the General Government to carry. But the Germans were well aware that many *Kennkarten* were forgeries or based on forgeries and so regularly changed the regulations, requiring extra stamps or adopting a new format for which the old *Kennkarten* had to be exchanged. With every change, Janina's and Henry's documents came under fresh scrutiny and, as the Gestapo expanded its investigations, increased risk of exposure.[16]

Shedding their Jewish identities only enabled Janina and Henry to exchange one form of persecution for another, somewhat less deadly, form. In the General Government, as well as in the Reich, a system of strict apartheid was imposed not only upon the Jews but also upon the "Poles," a term that for the Germans applied exclusively to persons of Polish ethnicity. Fraternization between Poles and Germans was strictly forbidden. Poles were barred from parks, gardens, museums, public swimming pools, and certain neighborhoods, as well as from all the better shops, restaurants, cafés, and most theaters and cinemas. They could only shop at certain hours, could only use designated areas of bus and train stations, and had to sit in the rear of public transport. University and secondary school education were banned for Poles. The Germans confiscated so many school buildings and shot or incarcerated so many teachers that Polish children lucky enough to attend elementary school could only do so for a few hours a week in unheated classrooms with seventy or more pupils.[17]

Food policy was one of the Germans' favorite tools for persecuting racial enemies. The General Government's economy was primarily agrarian, but much of the food it produced was sent to the Reich. In the fall of 1941, the official rations for Poles only supplied between 20 percent and 30 percent of the calories an adult needs to survive.[18] Instead of receiving rations directly, Polish Jews had to subsist on the tiny quantities of food their Jewish community was permitted to buy. In January 1941, the amount of flour authorized for the Lublin *Judenrat* (the Jewish council assigned to fulfill German demands and to provide for Lublin's Jewish residents) came to less than one pound per person—for the entire month.[19] Carbohydrates— mainly potatoes, beans, and bread—accounted for nearly all the calories in Poles' rations. The goal of Nazi policy was to weaken and decimate the Polish population so that it could not resist German rule or long-term Nazi plans to make most of the Poles and all of the Jews disappear from their native land.[20]

On top of starvation rations, General Government officials imposed a labor requirement upon Poles between the ages of fourteen and sixty and a forced labor requirement upon Jews twelve and older. Like the Jews, Poles could be seized at any time to perform heavy labor at construction or road-building sites or in labor camps. Unlike the Jews, they could be sent off to the Reich to work, a fate that had befallen more than half a million by the time Janina arrived in Lublin. At first, some Poles volunteered, believing German promises that they would experience better conditions and be better able to support their families back home. By now, however, Poles knew the truth: in Germany, they were given the worst jobs with the worst pay, could not change jobs, and had no recourse against employers who beat or raped them. Even before German Jews were ordered to don the yellow star, Polish laborers in the Reich had to wear a special badge marking them as Poles. When employers reported their Polish workers as lazy or disruptive, the Gestapo incarcerated them in "labor education camps" or even in concentration camps.[21]

Through Count Skrzyński, Henry obtained employment with Społem, the largest agricultural cooperative in Lublin District. He worked as an agricultural expert with a specialty in egg production. It was a job that allowed him to keep a low profile throughout the war.

Given Henry's long work hours, the task of obtaining groceries and supplies fell to Janina. The few stores that catered to Poles in Lublin could not be counted on to supply even the meager amount and types of food permitted under the ration system, and since these were insufficient for long-term survival, there was no choice but to seek provisions on the black market. Finding illicit vendors with the goods one needed and then bargaining to obtain them with cash or through barter was difficult and risky. As the war dragged on and shortages increased, people spent more and more of their time in the search for food and essential items. A popular Polish joke at that time summed up the situation:

> Two friends who had not seen each other for a long time met in the
> street:
>> "What are you doing?"
>> "I am working in the city hall."
>> "And your wife, how is she?"
>> "She is working in a paper store."
>> "And your daughter?"
>> "She is working in a plant."
>> "How the hell do you live?"
>> "Thank God, my son is unemployed."[22]

When she first wandered the streets of Lublin, Janina thought the city rather lovely, despite Henry's complaints about his earlier stay there. But everywhere she went, she found its beauty marred by the German occupiers. Litewski Square, lined with palaces of the local nobility and the Church of Saints Peter and Paul, had been renamed Adolf-Hitler-Platz. In its center, a huge map displayed the advance of Nazi control over Europe, and a loudspeaker, which the Poles dubbed "the Bellower," blared news of German victories and spewed antisemitic propaganda. The elegant shops and cafés of the broad boulevard Krakowskie Przedmieście bore signs barring entry to Poles. Walls were plastered with posters depicting Jews as dirty and lice-ridden and accusing them of everything from selling poisonous liquors to spreading typhus. Most appalling to Janina was the sight of the gaunt and sickly faces of the Polish children she encountered outside the crowded tenement buildings where their families were forced to live after the Germans took their homes.

Passing through the Gothic Kraków Gate, Janina entered the cobblestone streets of Lublin's Old Town. Its half-timbered houses with painted frescoes were crumbling yet still exuded charm. Heading toward the eighteenth-century Grodzka Gate, however, she found that the street was blocked and police were inspecting all who entered. A sign warned of the danger of typhus and identified the area beyond as the ghetto.[23]

The section of Lublin between Grodzka Gate and Zamek, the castle that loomed over the city, was the historic Jewish quarter, which dated back to at least the fifteenth century. Lublin's population of over 42,000 Jews had spread well beyond the quarter by 1939. In spring 1941, Lublin District Governor Ernst Zörner ordered that all Lublin city's Jewish residents be confined in a ghetto in one section of the Jewish quarter. In October 1941, Governor General Frank decreed that all Jews caught outside their assigned ghetto were to be arrested and shot, as well as any Poles discovered to have aided them. Entrance to the Lublin Ghetto was prohibited for all non-Jews except General Government officials on December 9, 1941, just before Janina and Henry arrived in the city.

By the start of 1942, more than 35,000 Jews were living in the ghetto, packed into synagogues, schools, warehouses, tenement buildings, and ancient wooden houses. With rare exceptions, there was no electricity or running water. It was no secret that starvation and typhus were rampant— as one SS official described it, the residents were "dropping like flies."[24] Hearing about conditions in the ghetto, Janina could not help but think with despair of her friends and colleagues who now suffered under similar conditions in Lwów.

Janina observed how German policies aimed to set Poland's different ethnic communities against one another. The Germans published antisemitic propaganda in the Polish language in order to inflame the Poles' prejudices against Jews. Lublin had a significant Ukrainian population and, as in Galicia, the Germans privileged it over Poles and Jews. Ukrainians received better rations, could educate their children through university, were allowed to frequent some establishments barred to Poles, and could even convert some Catholic churches to Greek Catholic or Orthodox. Poles with German ancestors could do even better by registering as *Volksdeutsche*, ethnic Germans. If accepted, they enjoyed the same rations and many of the same privileges as Reich Germans in the General Government. Some ethnic Germans welcomed the chance to join the supposedly superior Germans and support their new fatherland, including by looting and slaughtering Jews. But there were many Poles of German ancestry who had always considered themselves loyal Poles and resisted the temptation to obtain the privileges that Germans enjoyed, even though doing so branded them as suspected enemies.[25]

Not all Poles suffered equally under German policies, Janina discovered. The social order had turned topsy-turvy, with professors lucky to work as waiters and aristocratic ladies as maids. But some Poles fared considerably better, while a few even improved their standard of living, at least for a while. This was chiefly thanks to the black market. Like many other residents of the city, Janina's search for food took her into the countryside around Lublin to visit savvy farmers who had saved or hidden enough of their produce from German requisitioners to offer some for sale for cash or goods. She was surprised by the quantity and variety of luxury items she saw in the simple peasant households where she sought food. In one, there was a concert piano that no one could play; in others she saw record players that sat silent, given the lack of electricity. One day she visited a farmer who proudly showed her five radios and five sewing machines that he was saving as dowries for his daughters. Some of the peasant women she dealt with wore makeup and gave off the scent of expensive perfumes. Many of these goods came from Jews who had been forced to trade their most prized possessions in order to stave off starvation.

Madame Maria's employer, Madame Rylska, provided an example of how some people in the city managed to profit from Nazi persecution. Beneath her beauty and charm, Janina discerned, lay a rare talent for making money. Officially, Madame Rylska operated an elegant pastry shop and café, as well as a store selling baby carriages. Her main source of income, however, was smuggling, at which her son Olek proved particularly adept. One of their specialties was shoes, for which only Germans and *Volksdeutsche* received rations, but they also traded in the diamonds and gold that they acquired from Jews, their principal clients.

Janina understood that black marketeering and bribery were essential survival strategies in German-occupied Poland, and that they depended upon turning a profit and taking advantage of others' needs. Staying true to one's values could be a luxury few were willing to afford when Nazi policies set the price for doing so as survival for oneself or one's family. She observed this in one of Countess Władysława's tenants, a half-German young man who refused to register as *Volksdeutsch*. Janina admired how he shivered in his thin coat and ate boiled unpeeled potatoes like his other housemates. But then he married, a baby soon followed who turned sickly, and finally he traded in his Polish nationality for food and medicine to save his child.

It was not her place, Janina decided, to judge the choices others made to survive Nazi oppression. Had not she and Henry abandoned their families and friends for a chance to escape the Nazis' murderous plans? That knowledge would burden them both for the rest of their days.

SIX

ANNIHILATION

Of all the failed Nazis who found a second chance in occupied Poland, none was a greater fanatic or had a larger cloud over his head than Odilo Globocnik. An Austrian, he had served as the first Nazi head of Vienna after the *Anschluss* (annexation) in 1938. The appointment was an award for his service to the illegal Nazi movement in Austria, during which he had earned several prison sentences for treason and a reputation as a terrorist and assassin. But after just eight months in the Vienna post, he was dismissed for incompetence and threatened with arrest for allegedly enriching himself through bribery and embezzlement, especially of Jewish assets.

Luckily for Globocnik, he had made an important friend in Berlin: Heinrich Himmler. The pedantic *Reichsführer* SS, who had been plying Globocnik with his favorite works on racist theory, saw his pupil as a fanatically committed man of action who would stop at nothing to impose Nazi rule. That was a skill set Himmler knew he could use, and Poland's conquest offered the perfect opportunity to apply it. In November 1939, Himmler appointed Globocnik SS and Police Leader in Lublin District, with command over all the Waffen SS and police forces stationed there. The position effectively put Globocnik beyond the reach of the investigators who were pursuing him for his misdeeds in Vienna. It also ensured that he would be forever beholden to Himmler.[1]

As the SS and Police Leader in a General Government district, it was Globocnik's responsibility to terrorize the non-German population into unquestioning obedience to their German masters. His standard duties included incarcerating or murdering members of the Polish intelligentsia and applying disproportionate violence in response to any signs of resistance.[2]

In addition to his regular duties, however, Globocnik pursued several special assignments from his mentor and protector. Lublin was slated to serve two important purposes in Himmler's plan to achieve his racist utopia. First, it was to be the location of the reservation to which all the Jews under Germany's control, as well Roma (then called Gypsies) and other "undesirables," would be confined. But Himmler also believed that Lublin District had untapped human potential in the descendants of the Germans who had migrated into the region centuries before. Once identified and re-Germanized, this progeny would form the vanguard for Germanizing all of the General Government after Germany won the war. Creating the reservation and Germanizing the General Government became Globocnik's two most cherished goals.[3]

For the reservation, Globocnik chose a swampy region near the Bug River, where he planned to put 2.5 million Jews and Roma to work digging a giant antitank trench along the General Government's eastern border. Governor General Frank adamantly opposed the reservation plan, however. The General Government was already overburdened by the hundreds of thousands of Poles and Jews being expelled from the annexed territories, he complained. Globocnik suggested a simple solution to the problem of the expellees: if the Polish and Jewish communities of the General Government could not care for them, then they should be left to starve. This modest proposal did not meet with Frank's approval. In March 1940, he persuaded Hitler to call off the reservation plan.

Globocnik arrived in Lublin before most of the district's civilian administrators and immediately claimed complete control over the district's Jews, including their labor and assets. To make good on his power grab, he formed an auxiliary police force, called the *Selbstschutz* (self-defense), made up of ethnic German Poles who served as his private army. He deployed it to loot Jewish homes and businesses, rob Jews on the streets, and seize and abuse Jewish forced laborers. He also established camps where the *Selbst-schutz* forced Jews to perform heavy labor on a variety of military and civilian projects in Lublin District. By the fall of 1940, 50,000 to 70,000 Jews were being forced to work in seventy-six camps in Lublin District. Thousands died from the primitive conditions or from being beaten or shot by their *Selbstschutz* guards.[4]

Jews were not the only victims of the *Selbstschutz*. Globocnik also deployed his private army in reprisal actions against Polish communities and in roundups of Poles for forced labor, during which his mercenaries robbed, raped, and murdered at will. Fed up with its excesses, civilian officials succeeded in forcing Globocnik to disband the *Selbstschutz* in fall 1940 and to give up all but one of his forced labor camps.

Janina discovered Globocnik's remaining camp, at 7 Lipowa Street, soon after she arrived in Lublin. Its prisoners included 2,500 Polish Jewish POWs.[5] Janina would sometimes watch as the SS guards escorted the camp's prisoners to labor sites in the city. The sight of the Jewish POWs in their Polish uniforms, marching in disciplined formation, their heads held high, filled her with pride. But her heart was also heavy with the knowledge that some non-Jewish Poles believed the national uniform was defiled when worn by a Jew.

While his reservation plans came to naught, Globocnik made good progress on the project he dubbed "Search for German Blood." When Himmler visited Lublin in October 1940, Globocnik enthralled him with proposals for Germanizing both the city of Lublin and the agriculturally rich Zamość region in southeastern Lublin District. The city would become a center of German culture and industry. In the Zamość region, the SS would expel the non-German peasants to establish idyllic villages populated by settlers chosen for their "German blood." Leading regimented lives governed by the SS, these happy settlers would produce the food and the offspring that Germany would need to wage its future wars. These plans had to remain on paper for the present, but Himmler ordered Globocnik to have them ready when the time was finally ripe to put them into action.[6]

That time already seemed to be approaching in the spring of 1941 as Germany prepared to attack the Soviet Union. German generals were certain that the Wehrmacht would defeat the Red Army in a matter of weeks. After the Soviet Union's inevitable collapse, it would finally be possible to realize Hitler's vision for the German *Lebensraum* in Eastern Europe. Following a meeting with Hitler in March, Frank triumphantly announced exciting news to his subordinates: "Where 12 million Poles live today will one day live four to five million Germans. The General Government must become as German a land as the Rhineland."[7]

At Hitler's direction, Wehrmacht leaders planned the Soviet campaign as a *Vernichtungskrieg,* a "war of annihilation" to be ruthlessly waged against the "Judeo-Bolshevik" enemy without regard to the rules of warfare. Military and civilian planners drew up occupation policies for the territories to be seized that would cause "umpteen million" civilians to die of starvation in just the first year. Himmler took charge of long-range planning for imposing the new racial order in the German *Lebensraum*. His *Generalplan Ost* (General Plan East) envisioned eliminating 30 to 45 million indigenous inhabitants by forcing them to starve or to migrate beyond the Urals. These victims would account for up to 85 percent of the Poles, 75 percent of the Belarusians, and 64 percent of the Ukrainians. The ten million Germanic settlers who would take their place would be led and controlled by the SS.[8]

Just four weeks into the Soviet campaign, victory against the Soviet Union already seemed at hand. Eager to put his plans in motion, Himmler met with Globocnik in Lublin on July 20, 1941, to give him several important assignments. The first was to begin the Germanization of the General Government by expelling non-Germans from the Zamość region and settling ethnic German colonists in their place. The second was to develop SS and police bases that would take the lead in pacifying and colonizing the territories farther east.

The third assignment Himmler gave Globocnik was to transform the city of Lublin into a military and industrial base that would provide the manpower, equipment, and supplies to support SS dominion in the "German East." The city would become a garrison for 60,000 SS and police forces and the site of a wide variety of SS-owned industries. To make way for the troops and industries, Globocnik planned to expel the city's Polish residents.

Lublin's transformation could not be achieved without an adequate labor supply, but for as long as the war lasted, Poles would be needed for labor in the Reich. Himmler fixed on two other sources for workers. One, at least for the time being, was Jews. Much to Globocnik's satisfaction, Himmler authorized him not only to expand the Lipowa Street Jewish forced labor camp but also to build a new one at a former airfield on the edge of the city. The other labor source would be Soviet prisoners of war. Himmler ordered construction of two huge concentration camps for Red Army prisoners, one in Lublin and the other in Birkenau, adjacent to Auschwitz. By March 1942, the planned capacity of the Lublin concentration camp expanded from 50,000 to 250,000.[9]

Eager as he was to attack his Germanization assignment, Globocnik first had a major logistical problem to solve: what to do with all the non-Germans living in the areas designated for German colonists. As usual, he hit upon a ruthlessly simple solution. If the two million Jews living in the General Government were killed, the Poles in the Germanized areas could be deposited in the ghettos. The conditions there would then simplify the task of getting rid of the Poles once they were no longer needed.[10]

That left the question of how to kill the Jews. This was a problem other Nazi and SS officials were wrestling with as well. Enthusiasm for sending the Jews to live elsewhere had waned as the war continued. On July 31, 1941, Hitler's deputy, Hermann Göring, formally authorized Reinhard Heydrich, the head of the Security Police and SD, to develop a plan for the "comprehensive solution" to the "Jewish question" in Europe, something Heydrich had long been working on. His *Einsatzgruppen* immediately proceeded to murder entire Jewish communities in territories seized from the Soviet Union. This approach had distinct drawbacks for the General Government, however. Shooting two million men, women, and children in an area the size of Belgium would inevitably attract international notice, might spark resistance, and would require manpower and resources needed for the war. And so Globocnik, ever the man of action, sought a way to annihilate the General Government's Jews that would be cheap, efficient, and easy to keep relatively secret.

Since the start of the war, Nazi Germany had developed a new mass killing technology for its "euthanasia" program to murder Germans with mental or physical disabilities. Institutionalized patients were sent to six special "sanatoriums," where they were asphyxiated with carbon monoxide in special gas chambers designed to look like showers. These facilities dispatched more than 70,000 victims before Hitler, in response to some grumbling among the Germans, ostensibly ended the program in August 1941 (although patients with disabilities would continue to be routinely murdered in sanatoriums and asylums until two months after Germany's defeat). The next month, Globocnik brought members of the technical staff that had developed the euthanasia gassing facilities to Lublin to advise him how to murder the Jews in the General Government with carbon monoxide.[11]

Globocnik met with Himmler on October 13, 1941, to present a plan for murdering the General Government's Jews. In isolated villages along the major rail lines, he would erect special compounds to which the SS would bring Jews in large transports and, within a few hours, asphyxiate them hundreds at a time with carbon monoxide in sealed chambers. These compounds would be cheap to build, as only the gassing barracks required any special materials; the only other buildings would be wooden warehouses for the goods looted from the victims and barracks for the small force needed to murder the victims. The carbon monoxide would be piped into the gassing barracks from the engine of a tank or large truck. Tall wooden fences around the compounds would hide the activities within from any outsiders who dared to come near.

To perform the hands-on labor of rounding up and murdering Jews, Globocnik planned to use a new private army he was recruiting from the Soviet POW camps. Designated by the location of their training base, the "Trawniki men" would become notorious for their brutality.[12]

Other SS officials developed variations of the euthanasia technology in the fall of 1941. Heydrich's technical experts produced gas vans, mobile transport into which carbon monoxide was pumped from cylinders or engine exhaust, killing the passengers while carrying them to their gravesite. At Auschwitz, SS officials successfully tested on Soviet POWs a different, readily available poison: hydrogen cyanide. Sold as Zyklon B, it was already in heavy use at concentration camps as a delousing agent.[13]

By the time Janina moved to Lublin in mid-December 1941, work was progressing on the first of Globocnik's killing centers, at Bełżec near the district's eastern border. At that same moment, Nazi Germany's Jewish policy was undergoing a momentous change, one that would expand the scope of Globocnik's murder operation beyond the borders of the General Government. After Hitler declared war on the United States on December 11, he announced to top Nazi Party officials that the time had come to fulfill the promise he had made in January 1939. In a speech broadcast around the world, he had then "prophesied" that if the "international Jewish financiers" of the world succeeded "once more" in fomenting a world war, "the result will be not the Bolshevizing of the earth, and thus the victory of Jewry, but the annihilation of the Jewish race in Europe!" He had meant the threat as a warning to Britain, France, and the United States not to interfere with Germany's conquest of Eastern Europe. Now that the war was truly global, however, he was determined to fulfill his prophesy.[14]

Reinhard Heydrich received the go-ahead for his "comprehensive" plan. On January 30, 1942, he assembled top German officials at a villa in Wannsee outside Berlin to assign them their tasks for achieving the "final solution of the Jewish question": the murder of all the Jews in Europe. To avoid unpleasant repercussions, the SS and police would ship the victims living outside Eastern Europe to occupied Polish and Soviet territories, where they would be dispatched with poison gas or bullets.[15]

Between March and late July 1942, Globocnik established three killing centers—Bełżec, Sobibor, and Treblinka—that daily murdered tens of thousands of Jews from all over Europe. In June, Globocnik named his mass murder program Aktion (Operation) Reinhard, in honor of Reinhard Heydrich, who had just died of wounds from an assassination attempt. In the twenty months of the operation, more than 1.5 million Jews and an unknown number of Roma were murdered in the three killing centers, and another 200,000 Jews were shot. Aktion Reinhard was the deadliest mass murder operation of the Holocaust—Auschwitz, with its 960,000 Jewish victims over nearly three years, ran a distant second.[16]

Aktion Reinhard's purpose was not just to murder Jews but to exploit them in every possible sense, right down to their hair and gold teeth.

Globocnik temporarily spared some *Aktion* Reinhard victims so he could force them to work in the SS enterprises he was developing in and around Lublin city. These enterprises were funded with the proceeds from looted Jewish valuables; operated with looted Jewish tools, materials, and machinery; and transformed Jewish personal possessions into goods for use by Germans. The huge prisoner of war camp complex being built on the outskirts of the city was to become a major site for these enterprises and for Jewish forced laborers. Its official name was *Kriegsgefangenlager* (Prisoner of War Camp) Lublin but, based on the camp's location in the Majdan Tatarski suburb, the locals dubbed it Majdanek.

Janina's first inkling that a new Nazi plan for Lublin's Jews was in the works came from Madame Maria, who relished imparting the gossip she heard at work. The café of her employers, the Rylskis, was near the Lipowa Street workshops, where their prewar Jewish tailor was forced to work. He would surreptitiously visit them on his return to the ghetto in the evening to alter clothes for them. He accepted food, which he took home to his daughter, but refused their money, explaining that when the time came, he hoped they would give him another form of payment. Then in February 1942, he came to them in anguish. The Germans had begun dividing the ghetto into two parts with barbed wire and now announced that the Jews had to apply for new identity cards. Jews who had jobs like his that the SS deemed important were to receive different cards from those who, like his daughter, did not. Rumors were flying that he and the other "privileged" workers would soon be moved into the smaller part of the ghetto.[17] The tailor felt sure that the Jews left in the larger ghetto section would be subjected to some new form of suffering and he feared that his daughter would not survive it. He begged the Rylskis to save her.

As March approached and the division of the ghetto neared completion, the tailor's visits became more frequent and his pleas more urgent. He even brought money to pay the Rylskis to save his daughter. But no amount of money could compensate for the risk he was asking them to take. The Germans had begun to execute Poles, sometimes including their family members, for trying to help Jews hide.

Much to everyone's astonishment, twenty-two-year-old Olek Rylski decided to save the tailor's daughter, whom he had never seen, and to do so by staging a sham wedding. He bribed a Polish family living next to the ghetto to take the girl in when she fled there one night. The next day, he moved her to a residence in another part of the city and secured an identity card for her from a Polish girl of the same age and physical description. The following morning, dressed in his best and accompanied by Father Santi, an Italian priest who had agreed to the scheme, he called upon his "bride," who looked lovely dressed in silk and tulle. They made an elaborate show of processing toward the town hall to register their marriage. Afterward, she moved into another place he had arranged for her and managed to survive the war passing as a Pole.

This story fascinated Janina. She had met Olek Rylski and taken him for an enthusiastic black marketeer who was utterly indifferent to the suffering from which he reaped his profits. He seemed, in fact, the type of Pole around whom Janina and Henry had to be most on their guard to avoid any suspicion of their Jewish identity. And yet he had risked his own life as well as the lives of his family to save a Jewish girl he did not know. Here was another example of people's ability to act against interest in ways that seemed out of character and irreconcilable with their previous actions. There were hidden variables at work in human nature, she concluded, that could defy logical inference.

The tailor returned once more to the Rylskis, brimming with happiness and gratitude for the safety of his child. They never saw him again.

Late on March 16, 1942, German police and Globocnik's Trawniki men surrounded Lublin's ghetto and then stormed in. Lublin residents outside the ghetto heard shouts in German, shrieks and cries, and intermittent bursts of gunfire. They glimpsed Jewish bodies lying in the ghetto streets in pools of blood. Poles living near a sand mine outside the city witnessed the shooting of the children from the ghetto orphanage. At night, people living along the route from the ghetto to the municipal slaughterhouse observed hundreds of Jewish men, women, and children shuffling by, clutching bags or suitcases containing the few items they were permitted to take with them. From the area behind the slaughterhouse, where there was a railroad siding, more gunfire could be heard. The Underground reported that the Jews, including the corpses of those shot, were packed into freight cars that some-times sat on the siding for days before heading eastward.

Day after day, but especially at night, the shouts, shrieks, shots, and shuf-fling reverberated in Lublin. By April 14, some 28,000 residents of Lublin's ghetto had been murdered. More than a thousand were shot; the rest were gassed at the Bełżec killing center. The remaining 7,000 Jews were moved into a new ghetto in Majdan Tatarski. Three thousand were then selected and sent to Majdanek; all were shot. On April 20, 1942, Hitler's birthday, the liquidation of the Lublin Ghetto was complete.[18]

Lublin's ghetto was the target of *Aktion* Reinhard's inaugural operation. Its second target was the ghetto in Lwów.

The fate of the deported Jews was a hot topic of whispered discussions in Lublin. The Germans said that the Jews had been sent to perform labor "in the East," but people noted that many of the deportees were too old or young to work, while only able-bodied workers had been allowed to re-main. Railway workers reported that the Jews were being taken to a small SS camp next to the village of Bełżec. Poles living in the vicinity described what they could witness from a distance: thousands of Jews were disappearing daily into the facility, which had only three small wooden barracks; no Jews were ever seen leaving; no food was being delivered, but carts piled with personal belongings regularly departed the camp for the rail station ware-house; a strong odor was emanating from the facility. By mid-April, word was spreading around the district: the Germans were murdering the Jews at the camp at Bełżec. Opinion was divided as to how, with the three chief guesses being electrocution, gas, or suffocation with a vacuum pump.[19]

The shocking realization that the Germans were murdering the Jews caused Poles to ask: "Will we be next?" They had good reason to wonder. After the prediction of a swift victory in the war failed to come true, Nazi leaders doubled down on their ruthless exploitation of the Polish popula-tion in 1942. They cut Poles' rations, increased the agricultural levies, and plundered Polish homes, farms, and businesses so that Germans on the home front would not have to experience shortages. Brutal raids became the order of the day. German forces swooped into villages, neighborhoods, and marketplaces to seize victims, or dragged them out of churches and off of trains and streetcars. The victims might be put to heavy labor on some local road building or construction project, sent to the Reich or to one of the hundreds of forced labor camps in the General Government, or they might be held as hostages, to be shot in reprisal for the next real or perceived act of resistance.[20] People were afraid to sleep in their beds and fled their homes at the merest hint of a raid. As one Pole wrote in his diary in March 1942, Poles were living with "the constant sensation of death, violence and injustice. The population is being terrorized. . . . The number of victims continually multiplies."[21]

Janina felt caught in a vise between horror and fear. The sounds of the Lublin Ghetto liquidation kept ringing in her ears, tormenting her with thoughts of her many loved ones in the Lwów Ghetto who were experiencing the same unspeakable fate. She was constantly conscious of the danger that she and Henry would be murdered as well. If Henry were seized in a raid, a physical examination would immediately expose him as a Jew, since he was circumcised, and they would both be murdered. But first would come the torture to discover who had helped them. Gruesome stories abounded in Lublin of the methods and implements that the Gestapo employed at Security Police headquarters. Janina worried that suspicion would fall on Count Skrzyński, or perhaps even Countess Władysława, if she and Henry were exposed as Jews. The constant tension she felt made it nearly impossible to sleep, and even breathing sometimes seemed to take effort.

One night, she started out of a fitful sleep to see circles of light dancing on the ceiling. Instantly she realized: flashlights! She ran to the window and carefully peeked out from a side of the curtain. German soldiers were going into the houses and apartment buildings along the street. Just two buildings away, she saw them bang on the door, rush in, and begin to drag men out to a waiting truck. In a panic, Janina ran to her landlady's room and woke the two sisters.

"Auntie Władzia, quickly, they're coming for Henry! Give me the key to the cellar so he can hide," Janina begged.

"I'll do no such thing, my child," Władzia exclaimed. "You're so upset that you can't think straight right now. If they take him from here, it's for labor or a concentration camp. But if they find him hiding in the basement, they will shoot him on the spot.

"Besides," she added more softly, "they are not going to take him. We have our special prayers for such occasions. Just go back to your room and wait and see."

Returning to their room in despair, Janina found Henry already dressed. She darted to the window. The truck was now right across the street. She watched as the Germans, brandishing bayonets, forced some men into it. The doors slammed. And then the truck drove off, taking the Germans as well.

Janina went back to the elderly ladies' room and found them both on their knees, praying fervently. Countess Władysława's face gleamed with tears and a strange peace. Janina told them the Germans had left, and after a few more minutes, they arose.

"Didn't I tell you that God hears our prayers?" Władzia asked. "Such prayers, anyway!"

Janina was not going to argue the point. She understood that the sisters' faith was what had enabled them to persevere through so many hardships. But Janina recognized that there would be other raids, and neither luck nor divine intervention could be counted on to spare Henry from being taken. No matter how she calculated the probabilities, the odds always pointed to the same result. Sooner or later, she and Henry would meet their fate: annihilation.

SEVEN

"BETTER TO DIE A SOLDIER"

Once Janina accepted that she would not survive the war, fear's grip on her began to loosen. The problem she needed to solve, she realized, was not how to survive, but how to live what remained of her life. The answer appeared obvious. She would devote herself to thwarting however she could the Nazi plans to destroy Poland and its people. For that struggle, she enjoyed one peculiar advantage: her false identity as a Polish countess. European class consciousness, even among the Nazis, bestowed an automatic deference on the nobility that she could exploit—as long as she could carry off the role of someone who took her privilege for granted.

So Janina went to Count Skrzyński and persuaded him to sponsor her membership in the Polish Home Army. It seemed best not to reveal her true identity. The Home Army, or AK (*Armia Krajowa*) as it was called, was the armed force of the Polish Underground State, the clandestine resistance organization that was active throughout occupied Poland and answered to the Polish government in exile in London. Recognized by the Allies, the government in exile was an uneasy alliance of prewar Polish political parties ranging from the right-wing, antisemitic National Democrats to the Polish Socialist Party. The members of the AK and the Polish Underground within Poland reflected the same range of attitudes toward Jews as did the parties in the government in exile. Jewish Poles did serve in the AK, but those who served openly as Jews were the rare exception, and some local AK commanders refused to admit Jews in their ranks. Skrzyński and Janina recognized that she was more likely to win the trust and acceptance of AK leaders as a Polish Christian aristocrat than as a Polish Jew.[1]

With Skrzyński vouching for her, Janina passed the vetting process to join the ranks of the AK. In a training cell consisting of a few other new recruits, all unknown to one another and using pseudonyms, she learned such skills as coding and how to spot and evade surveillance, as well as what to do and say if arrested. On the day of her induction, Janina took the oath of loyalty. Holding a crucifix, she swore:

> Before Almighty God and the Holy Virgin Mary, Queen of Poland, I take in my hands this Holy Cross, the sign of Suffering and Salvation, and swear loyalty to Poland, the Republic of Poland, to unyieldingly guard her honor and to fight for her liberation from slavery with all my strength—and unto death.[2]

Taking the oath and joining the fight against her nation's oppressor liberated Janina. "No more passive endurance of suffering and helpless fear," she thought. "Better work, risk, danger—better to die a soldier than a victim!"

The ultimate aim of the AK and the Underground State was to prepare a national uprising against the occupier. This was to occur when Nazi Germany was on the brink of defeat. The AK planned at that point to attack the German forces remaining in the country, drive them out, and then proclaim and defend sovereignty over Poland's prewar boundaries.[3] Collecting intelligence was an essential aspect of preparing for the uprising, and the AK relied heavily on women to spy on and transmit information about German plans and operations. Women tended to attract less scrutiny from the Germans than men, and they were less likely to be seized in raids, which made it easier for them to move about, observe German military movements and installations, and overhear conversations. Polish women who knew German and obtained clerical jobs in General Government offices were able to report on the contents of documents they handled and provide blank forms that the AK could use to forge orders or passes.[4]

The Lublin AK assigned Janina the code name "Stefania." One of her earliest assignments was as a courier, carrying information, orders, money, and other items between AK cells and commands. This was one of the most common tasks assigned to women not only in the AK but also in other clandestine resistance organizations. Janina often made her courier runs at night. Dressed in dark clothes and rubber-soled shoes, she slipped between buildings and kept to the shadows of alleyways. Periodically, she would stop to determine the direction of the gunfire that regularly echoed through the city, signaling that the police were either firing on another curfew-breaker, conducting a raid, or drunkenly proclaiming their mastery over the "Polack swine."

Sometimes, when Janina could not make a delivery immediately, she would entrust the packet to Countess Władysława. "Auntie Wladzia" would take it without question, her eyes shining with pride, and she insisted that Janina not know where she had put it, so that suspicion would not fall on Janina if it were discovered. She also urged Janina not to hand her anything in her sister's presence or to confide in her sister. The warning was not needed, for Janina knew that Madame Maria, cheerful and gregarious, tended to babble about whatever she had heard or seen, oblivious to the potential consequences.

Another focus of AK activities was sending news and instructions to the Poles via clandestine publications and radio broadcasts. Count Skrzyński played a role in these efforts, and Janina joined him. Their assignment was to listen to foreign radio broadcasts, especially the BBC, take down their contents, translate them if in another language, and encode them. Like the Jews in the General Government, the Poles were ordered to turn in their radio sets, while members of ethnic groups permitted to have radios had to obtain a special license to use them.[5] Janina and Skrzyński's listening station was in the home of Mrs. Santi, mother of the Italian priest who had feigned to marry Olek Rylski and the Jewish tailor's daughter. As an Italian citizen, Mrs. Santi could own a radio, but Janina and Skrzyński did not use it for their clandestine work. Instead, they listened on the receiver of a Wehrmacht major who was billeted in Mrs. Santi's home and was often away in the evening. As they tuned and listened to his radio, Mrs. Santi would turn up the volume on hers while her daughter watched for anyone approaching the home. The daughter's warnings gave Janina and Skrzyński just enough time to slip out of the major's room. Anyone who entered the premises would find them with Mrs. Santi in her living room, attending to the German broadcast. The major's room also served as a meeting place for the members of the AK cell to which Janina and Skrzyński belonged.

In May 1942, Count Skrzyński accepted the position of the lead official in Lublin District of the Polish Main Welfare Council. Known by its initials, RGO (*Rada Główna Opiekuńcza*), it provided welfare services and relief to ethnic Poles and was the only Polish civil society organization permitted to exist and operate in the General Government. Skrzyński's was an almost impossibly challenging job in which he would be of immeasurable service to the people of Poland. It was also a job that would ultimately repay him with indignity and slander.

There had been an RGO in German-occupied Poland during World War I, and its founder, Count Adam Ronikier, proposed to reactivate it after the General Government was established. Since General Government officials took no interest in the welfare of the "alien" people they ruled, they welcomed the opportunity to offload responsibility for providing the neediest victims of German policies the bare essentials to support life. They were not about to allow a single Polish organization to provide services to all former Polish citizens, however. Instead, relief officials limited the RGO to aiding Poles and set up separate organizations to provide for Polish Jews and Ukrainians. To fund its operations, the RGO received a small portion of a special welfare tax imposed upon the Poles and could also seek donations, including from Polish diaspora organizations abroad, especially in the United States. These donations largely ceased after Germany declared war on the United States in December 1941. From then on, the RGO relied primarily upon donations in money and in kind from the malnourished and impoverished population of the General Government.[6]

The RGO's work was closely supervised by the General Government's Department of Population Matters and Welfare, known by its initials, BuF (*Bevölkerungswesen und Fürsorge*). Although part of the civil administration, it was established and led by some of the top race experts in the SS and was dedicated to realizing Himmler's vision of a racist new order in the General

Government. The section that directly oversaw the RGO also handled all "Jewish questions."[7]

Based in Kraków, the RGO organized a Polish care committee in each *Kreis* or county of the General Government's five districts. Each county committee organized branches within its *Kreis*. In Lublin District, the Polish Care Committee for the county of Lublin consisted of two committees, one for the county and one for the city of Lublin, that operated jointly, answering to the same board of directors and sharing offices and some personnel. Most of the people who organized and provided the care services were unpaid volunteers. Skrzyński's job was to oversee and coordinate the work of the committees and branches throughout Lublin District, report on their activities and needs to RGO headquarters, and conduct all communications on their behalf with district officials. His official title was Advisor to the Governor, meaning the German governor of Lublin District.

Skrzyński's immediate superior in the RGO was also his predecessor as advisor, Prince Henryk Woroniecki, who had moved to Kraków to serve as vice director of the RGO's central office. Woroniecki wanted to expand the RGO's operations in Lublin District and to develop it into an effective advocate for the Polish people. Before moving to Kraków, he had forced the head of the Lublin Polish Care Committee to resign because, in Woroniecki's view, he devoted far too little energy to the committee and far too much to his private business. Skrzyński would give no cause for such concerns.[8]

The title of advisor came with little support. Skrzyński used the office space of the Lublin Polish Care Committee and largely relied upon its staff. He needed an assistant to monitor the RGO's expenditures and distributions, submit the required reports to German authorities, and manage the various initiatives he was undertaking. It had to be someone with a good head for numbers, fluent German, and the tact and standing to interact effectively with both the RGO's overseers and its clients. He knew someone who not only met those requirements but whose noble title would be seen as an additional qualification by the many aristocrats who held leading positions in the RGO. But before she could take the job, Countess Suchodolska had to be vetted by the Lublin District BuF office, which among other things required proof of Aryan ancestry going back at least two generations. Somehow,

Janina passed muster. She was appointed Secretary to the Advisor, a position that combined the duties of personal assistant and office manager.[9]

Her new duties revealed to Janina the full measure of the misery that the Germans had visited upon the Polish population of Lublin District. Their needs were staggeringly great. The RGO was providing support and relief for tens of thousands of people in the district, many of them children. It ran soup kitchens, temporary shelters, and orphanages; provided support for the families of Polish POWs and forced laborers sent to the Reich; and supplied food, clothing, shelter, and medical care for the Poles expelled into the district from the annexed territories. The challenges Janina faced in her job could seem overwhelming, but the work was unquestionably meaningful. She embraced it with all her energy and determination.

The RGO had no institutional relationship either with the AK, the Home Army, or with the Underground State, and some RGO officials opposed any cooperation with them, justifiably fearing that they would be arrested and the RGO disbanded should the Germans discover that it was aiding resistance activities. Nevertheless, Skrzyński and Janina were far from the first or only members of the AK to obtain positions in the RGO. In fact, the AK actively sought to embed members in the care committees and may have played a role in obtaining Skrzyński and Janina's appointments. Having an RGO identity card was extremely useful to AK members because it entitled them to rations, exempted them from being seized for forced labor, and, most important, permitted them to travel about the counties and the district to provide RGO services. One perk of Janina's job was a special permit that allowed her to own and use a bicycle. Under the cover of their official duties, AK members working for the RGO acted as couriers, spies, and distributors of clandestine press.[10]

Janina came to play a key role in the AK's penetration of the RGO. It was her job to prepare and submit the identity cards of RGO employees for German approval, and she took advantage of this task to create cards for agents of the Underground. She was one of the few members of the AK who knew the identities of comrades working for the RGO.

Janina's position in the RGO exposed her to scrutiny from the Germans. The Security Police were deeply suspicious of the RGO, aware that its employees' duties and ability to travel could serve as cover for espionage and sabotage activities. The hostility was only deepened by RGO officials' many appeals to German civilian authorities to oppose reprisal actions by the SS and police and to secure the release of hostages and of Poles seized for forced labor. The Gestapo regularly surveilled and searched RGO employees and not infrequently arrested them. In fact, eleven RGO employees in Lublin District were arrested in the year before Janina took up her duties. Under the German occupation, 385 RGO employees would be executed for resistance activities, at least forty of them in Lublin District.[11]

Through the services it provided and its interventions with German authorities, the RGO mitigated the suffering of millions of Poles and rescued untold thousands who faced death from starvation, disease, exposure, or execution. Nevertheless, there were some Poles who viewed the RGO as collaborating with the Germans. General Government officials encouraged that perception, claiming that the RGO was evidence that they were working with and on behalf of the Poles. RGO officials were ordered to attend German-sponsored events and issue German-dictated announcements to the Polish population. Although the Polish government in exile granted Polish social organizations permission to cooperate with the German occupiers in work that aided Poles, there were some in the Underground who thought that RGO officials, especially RGO president Count Ronikier, went too far in accommodating the Germans. When Ronikier refused to participate in the fourth anniversary celebration of the General Government's founding in November 1943, however, he was arrested, and the RGO was threatened with disbandment. RGO officials had to tread a thin line between service to Poland and collaboration with its enemy.[12]

One initiative Skrzyński immediately sought to pursue as RGO advisor in Lublin was to provision the prisoners in the prison camp being built at Majdanek. Despite its official designation as a prisoner of war camp, it was in all but name a concentration camp, part of the system of camps in which the SS starved and worked to death political and racial enemies from all the countries under German control. Himmler did supply thousands of Soviet POWs in the fall of 1941 to build both Majdanek and Birkenau, the latter part of Auschwitz concentration camp. The POWs arrived at the two camps in what the SS termed a "catastrophic state," however, and proved incapable of labor.[13] The Wehrmacht captured 3.3 million Red Army soldiers by the end of 1941 and corralled them in open enclosures, providing almost no food or medical care, and transferring tens of thousands to the SS to be murdered. By February 1942, 2.2 million died. At Majdanek, almost 95 percent of the 2,000 Soviet POWs who arrived in October 1941 were dead three months later.[14]

In early 1942, Majdanek's prisoners included Polish peasants arrested for failing to meet the agricultural quota, Polish civilians seized as hostages, local Jews rounded up for forced labor, and prisoners of various nationalities transferred from concentration camps in the Reich. As the camp was established on land with no infrastructure, the SS had to hire local civilians with specialized construction skills. These workers returned to the city nightly with gruesome tales of what they had witnessed in the camp, of whippings and shootings and pits that had to be continually expanded to hold the ever-growing number of corpses.[15]

After his dreams of exploiting hundreds of thousands of Soviet POWs were dashed, Himmler fixed on a new purpose for Majdanek and Birkenau: they were to play vital roles in the "final solution." Majdanek was to serve principally as a site for Jews temporarily spared from the gas chambers of *Aktion* Reinhard's killing centers to work in SS enterprises, while Birkenau would perform the functions of both a Jewish forced labor camp and a killing center.

Lublin's residents first learned of Majdanek's new role in April 1942, when long trains of freight cars began arriving at the Lublin station from Slovakia. The wails and cries from inside the cars, begging for water or a breath of fresh air, identified the cargo as men, women, and children. Hundreds of men would descend from the trains, wearing the star on their clothing that marked them as Jews. Surrounded by shouting SS men and snarling guard dogs, they would be marched under curses and blows to Majdanek.[16]

By midsummer 1942, there were more than 10,000 male Jewish prisoners in Majdanek as well as over 500 Polish men. People in the Lublin area could see some of the prisoners on a daily basis as they were marched to worksites around the city. They were a frightening sight: filthy, skeletal figures in striped or painted rags, stumbling along in wooden clogs. As they returned at night, they would carry the corpses of the prisoners who had died or been killed at the worksite.[17]

In the fall of 1942, transports arriving in Lublin sometimes discharged all their passengers: Jewish men, women, and children. They disappeared into Majdanek. The next day, the clouds of smoke billowing from the chimney of the camp's crematorium and its nearby burn pits spread a noxious odor through Lublin. It became an open secret in the city that Jews were being murdered en masse at Majdanek.[18]

Skrzyński and Janina believed they might get permission to feed Majdanek prisoners because the RGO was able to provide food for Poles incarcerated in prisons in some parts of the General Government. The indomitable Countess Karolina Lanckorońska had almost single-handedly created the prison aid program. The daughter of a high-ranking Polish nobleman who served in the Austro-Hungarian Imperial Court, she had divided her childhood between a family palace in Vienna and another in Eastern Galicia. Her father's magnificent art collection inspired her to obtain a PhD in art history, and she became head of the art history department at Jan Kazimierz University in Lwów. When the Soviets occupied the city, she joined the Polish Underground, but then had to flee to the General Government, barely one step ahead of the NKVD. As a Red Cross nurse in Kraków, she learned that Poles were starving to death in General Government prisons. Outraged, she visited Count Ronikier to insist that the RGO provide food to the prisons and that she be put in charge of the effort. She met all three of the key qualifications for the position, she asserted: 1) she was a woman, so less likely to attract German suspicion; 2) she had no husband or children whose lives the Germans could threaten; 3) her German was flawless. The Countess was not a person one easily said no to. Ronikier accepted her proposal.[19]

Countess Lanckorońska discovered that in order to feed Polish prisoners, she had to obtain approval from the local German authorities in charge of each prison. And so, by train, bus, cart, sledge, and on foot, she traveled from prison to prison to negotiate permission for food deliveries. Civilian officials were generally amenable, but the Security Police viewed both her and her proposal with suspicion. In fact, the suspicion was justified, since the Countess regularly reported to her commanding officer in the AK all the information she was gathering about the number of prisoners and conditions in the prisons.

The Countess proved an effective negotiator. By autumn 1941, a growing number of prisons were receiving deliveries of food products or prepared meals from the local RGO care committees. She also negotiated permission for the Jewish social welfare organization to deliver food to Jewish prisoners. In addition, using her AK connections, she established local networks that smuggled food and clothes into the prisons. It was Lanckorońska who established the precedent for providing overt and clandestine aid to prisoners through the RGO that Janina was to follow in Lublin.

After Galicia became a General Government district in 1941, Countess Lanckorońska returned there to set up feeding operations in the district prisons and to oversee RGO activities in Stanisławów. There she incurred the wrath of the city's Gestapo chief, Hans Krüger. The Countess could be a formidable figure: tall, self-assured, decided in her opinions, unshakable in her values, and unafraid to speak her mind. Krüger considered her a traitor because, although her mother had been Prussian, she assured him that she was a Polish patriot. He was particularly infuriated by her persistent demands to learn the whereabouts of 250 members of Stanisławów's Polish intelligentsia whom he had ordered arrested. To silence her, Krüger had Lanckorońska arrested as well. Before consigning her to the execution squad, he boasted to her about his role in murdering not only the Stanisławów intelligentsia but also the university professors of Lwów.

Krüger did not get to execute Countess Lanckorońska, however. Through her relatives, she had contacts with the royal family of Italy, Nazi Germany's ally, and they intervened directly with Himmler on her behalf. Himmler ordered that she be transferred to Lwów and her case investigated there. In the Lwów prison, the Countess wrote a report detailing all that Krüger had revealed to her about the mass murder of Poland's intelligentsia. This placed Himmler in a dilemma: executing the Countess was politically inadvisable; releasing her was out of the question. So he consigned her to Ravensbrück, the women's concentration camp located fifty miles north of Berlin, where he expected the conditions would soon finish her off. Once again, Countess Lanckorońska defied expectations of her demise. She survived Ravensbrück—where she taught the prisoners art history—and outlived the *Reichsführer* SS by fifty-seven years.

In Lublin District, the RGO obtained permission to supply food products for the inmates of several prisons, the largest of which was in the Lublin castle. Lublin's Polish Care Committee also sought permission to supply food for prisoners at Majdanek in early 1942 but were met with refusal from the camp's commandant. Skrzyński intended to get a different answer.[20]

His first attempt failed. Karl Otto Koch was one of the "old-school" commandants, having served in the camp system almost from its beginning. In 1937, he became the first commandant of Buchenwald, then the largest concentration camp in Germany. Through embezzlement and extortion, he and his wife, Ilse—dubbed by the prisoners the "Beast of Buchenwald"—led a life so extravagantly lavish that the local SS and Police Leader arrested him for corruption. Himmler had Koch released and sent him and some of his staff members to Majdanek, where they would have a chance to redeem themselves.[21] Koch detested all concentration camp prisoners as dangerous enemies and viewed the "subhuman" Poles and Jews imprisoned at Majdanek with murderous contempt. No Polish civilian organization would be allowed to bring food to any camp he controlled.

The RGO tried paying civilian workers employed at Majdanek to smuggle food in for the prisoners. The cost proved prohibitive and the risk too great, for workers caught smuggling were beaten and imprisoned in the camp. By the time Janina began working for the RGO, it had abandoned this effort.

Janina did learn of one clandestine network that was successfully smuggling small amounts of food and medicines to the prisoners' infirmary in Majdanek. It had been established by the fearless thirty-five-year-old Saturnina Malm, who had been a volunteer social worker before the war. In January 1942, Malm began seeking to help a friend get messages to her husband, a physician imprisoned in the camp. Malm spent days scouting Majdanek's environs, getting as close as she could until the SS threatened to shoot her. Finally, she noticed that the camp's SS staff were bringing their laundry to a small house in a village near the camp. The laundress agreed to help Malm, and they recruited an SS guard to get a message to the prisoner physician, who was secretly treating the guard for a venereal disease. Malm succeeded in establishing regular contact with members of the Polish Underground imprisoned in the camp who worked in the infirmary. To provide the medicines and medical supplies they requested, she persuaded a Lublin physician to be the "finance minister" for her network. He collected funds from other Lublin physicians to buy the medicines, and Malm enlisted the aid of certain pharmacists to source and provide them.[22]

Through Malm's network, prisoners were able to inform the Underground about conditions in the camp. Prisoner physician Dr. Jan Nowak reported that Koch's approach to containing a typhus epidemic was to have 2,000 infected prisoners shot. In July 1942, word got out that eighty Soviet POWs had managed to escape one night, after which Koch ordered the slaughter of the forty remaining POWs.[23]

Koch could not prevent news of the escape from reaching Berlin. He claimed that the murdered POWs had been part of a massive, violent breakout that had overwhelmed the undisciplined guards. Himmler did not credit Koch's excuses. During a visit to Lublin shortly afterward, he fired Koch and had him placed under investigation for criminal negligence.

Janina could not stop thinking about Majdanek and the suffering of its prisoners, the vast majority of whom, she knew, were Jews. Everything she could learn about the camp, both through her own observations and Underground reports, filled her with horror. Finding ways to help not only the Poles but also all the victims imprisoned there, became her personal mission. She and Skrzyński hoped that they could persuade the new commandant to accept their proposal to deliver food to the camp. But, after a brief interlude under Ravensbrück commandant Max Koegel, Majdanek's command passed to Koch's protégé, Hermann Florstedt, who had served as deputy commandant at Buchenwald. According to SS gossip, Florstedt had also served Ilse Koch as one of her lovers. When Skrzyński and Janina tried to meet with him about feeding Majdanek prisoners, Florstedt's response was as emphatically negative as his mentor's.[24]

Janina had a mission, however, and refused to accept no as a final answer. She and Skrzyński were determined to continue pressing their request until somehow, eventually, they got to yes.

EIGHT

FROZEN CARGO

In the predawn hours of November 27, 1942, residents of the village of Skierbieszów in Lublin's Zamość County lurched out of sleep into a nightmare. SS and police forces were storming into their homes.

"You are being resettled," they were told. "Gather only what you can carry and report immediately in front of the church. SCHNELL!"

Less than two hours later, the Poles of Skierbieszów were carried off on open carts into the bitterly cold night and away from the homesteads where their families had lived for generations. Few would ever see those homes again.[1]

Other villages were hit that same day, and more and more in the days that followed. Janina learned of the resettlements as soon as they began from an Underground contact in Zamość. Shortly afterward, she began receiving panicked messages from the Zamość Polish Care Committee that many members of its branches had been seized in the raids. She and Skrzyński tried desperately to find out which villages had been resettled, where the expellees had been taken, and what was planned for them so that the RGO could intervene on their behalf. Janina had an additional task from the AK: find out which villages were slated for future resettlement so that the Underground could warn the residents and help them flee.

Janina reached out to both her official and her clandestine contacts within the district and local civilian administrations, but none could provide any information. The rivalry between Frank and Himmler extended to their underlings in the General Government, where the SS and police operated as a law unto themselves. SS and Police Leader Globocnik, in particular, had nothing but disdain for the governor of Lublin District, Ernst Zörner, and was not about to brook any interference in his pet project. On Globocnik's orders, civilian officials were excluded from all aspects of the resettlement operation.

In the weeks before the operation began, there had been a growing dread among the Poles of the Zamość region that the Germans would soon unleash a new terror upon them. Just a month earlier, the last ghettos in the county had been liquidated in brutal and bloody operations. Aware that they were being sent to their death, many of the Jews had sought to hide or flee. So for weeks after the roundups in the ghettos, massive manhunts ferreted out hundreds of Jews and slaughtered them, often in public view. The perpetrators were not just the Germans and the Trawniki men but also Polish policemen, firefighters, and even ordinary citizens. Some Poles watched aghast to see their brethren murder their Jewish neighbors; some even tried to save Jews. Few failed to grasp that the Germans might subject them to the same fate.[2] The commander of the AK warned his superiors in London that the moment all the ghettos had been cleared, "the Germans will begin to liquidate the Poles in the same fashion."[3] When the expulsions in Zamość began, many Poles assumed that the moment had arrived.

There was in fact a connection between the liquidation of the ghettos and the start of the resettlement operation. In July 1942, with Nazi leaders again confident of imminent victory over the Soviet Union, Himmler visited Globocnik in Lublin to accelerate the process of achieving the racist utopia. By the end of the year, he ordered, all the Jews in the General Government should be annihilated, except for a small minority who would be forced to work under SS supervision in closed labor camps or at Majdanek or Auschwitz. Once the ghettos were empty, Globocnik should begin Germanizing Lublin city and the Zamość region by expelling their Polish inhabitants and settling ethnic Germans in their place.[4]

Globocnik was overjoyed. "[N]ow all our most secret wishes will be fulfilled," he crowed to an SS colleague. He began the resettlement of Lublin at the start of October 1942, expelling the Polish residents of entire sections of the city as well as nearby villages. Many of the expellees turned to the Lublin Polish Care Committee for help, but even before the expulsions began it lacked the resources to provide for all those who already qualified for its aid. To make matters worse, some of its own workers were falling victim to the expulsions, including two who were placed in the new women's camp at Majdanek.

Then, on November 11, the Germans evicted Skrzyński, Janina, and the Lublin Polish Care Committee from their shared office space, which was located in the designated German district of the city. The RGO was allocated a formerly Jewish-owned building on Lubartowska Street, on the border of the former ghetto, but it required extensive renovations before Janina and her colleagues could work there. She and Skrzyński were still frantically scrambling to find shelter and supplies for the Lublin expellees when they learned of the expulsions in Zamość.[5]

Globocnik aimed to expel more than 33,000 Poles from the Zamość region and settle ethnic Germans onto their lands before the start of the spring planting season. His forces temporarily imprisoned the Polish victims in a former Soviet POW camp in the city of Zamość (renamed Himmlerstadt), where race experts conducted selections. The few children and adults deemed to be of German stock were to be drilled into good Germans. The remaining children between the ages of six months and fourteen years along with adults too elderly or disabled to work were slated to be dumped in vacant ghettos. Globocnik planned to send about 20 to 25 percent of the remaining youths and adults to Auschwitz, the rest to forced labor in the Reich or in the East.[6]

Globocnik's plans went awry from the start. As word of the expulsions spread, Poles fled into the region's forests. Globocnik's forces often arrived at a village slated for resettlement only to find it almost entirely deserted. The SS resettlement commission called in the officials of the RGO's Zamość care committee and forced them to issue a proclamation to the Poles in the region. It called on them to keep calm and remain in their villages, assuring them that only some Poles would be resettled and that no harm would come to them. But, the proclamation warned, the Germans would punish all those who fled. The SS also threatened to punish any attempt by the RGO to provide relief to the expellees.

The proclamation had no effect. By early December 1942, the RGO estimated that thousands of Poles had fled into the forests, while as many as 5,000 had been seized and placed in the Zamość camp. Rumors had come to the RGO about the selections in the camp and that families were being separated. Janina and Skrzyński assumed that the able-bodied adults would be sent for forced labor, but they tried in vain to learn what fate was planned for the rest.

The answer came in mid-December 1942. The RGO received notice that hundreds of families of Zamość expellees were to be resettled in vacant ghettos in Warsaw and Radom Districts. The local care committees urgently requested resources and advice from the RGO in Kraków, because the homes in those ghettos had been so thoroughly vandalized and looted that they were uninhabitable.

Before the month was out, transports from Zamość deposited more than 2,000 expellees in one county alone. They did not consist of families, however. Half of them were unaccompanied children, while most of the rest were elderly or disabled adults.

Globocnik's forces did not try to seize all the Poles in the resettled villages, mainly only those who owned land. Those left behind became virtual serfs, forbidden to leave their villages and forced to labor for the ethnic German settlers who took over the emptied homes and farms. The German masters whipped their workers, robbed their food stores, and demanded the clothes off their backs and the shoes off their feet.

By the end of December 1942, Globocnik's forces had snared almost 10,000 Poles, less than 30 percent of his goal.[7] About twice as many had fled, and those hiding in the forests were suffering terribly from lack of food and shelter in the midwinter conditions of deep snow and temperatures below 0°. Skrzyński and Janina could find no way to get aid into the region. The Count's protests to German authorities were ignored, his requests to send food and supplies to the Zamość camp went unanswered. The local care committees were no longer operating, as those members who had not been seized had fled. All Janina could do was to prepare the supplies and personnel so that the RGO could send them as soon as it received authorization to help the Poles in Zamość.

Increasingly, Poles in Zamość resolved not just to evade the Germans' resettlement plans but to fight back. Families fleeing into the forests took with them whatever they could of their produce and livestock and destroyed the rest, even burning their homes. In the forests, peasants formed or joined armed bands, some associated with the AK, that attacked the villages where ethnic Germans had been settled. In reprisal, SS and police forces burned villages that had not been resettled and slaughtered their Polish residents.

In Lublin and in Kraków, the RGO was ceaselessly protesting the resettlement action to General Government authorities. Shocked by the increase and ferocity of attacks by armed resistance groups, civilian officials grew more sympathetic to the RGO's pleas and began to suggest that the expulsions be halted. Globocnik ignored them. To him, the answer to resistance should always be ever more disproportionate violence.

The state of the expellees transported to Warsaw and Radom Districts evidenced the horrifying conditions in the transit camp at Zamość. When they were being expelled from their homes, Polish families were given so little time to collect their things—often just ten minutes—that some could not dress all their children in coats and shoes. In the camp, the adults and children selected as worthless for German purposes were separated from their families and penned in a compound surrounded by barbed wire. In the uninsulated wooden barracks, some without floors, barefoot and thinly clad children were consigned to the care of adults who were often unable to care for themselves. Exposure, severe malnutrition, lack of hygiene, and diseases quickly took their toll. By early January, dozens of children were dying daily.[8]

Conditions in the Zamość camp were little better for the youths and adults selected for forced labor. When hundreds of Zamość expellees arrived at Auschwitz in mid-December 1942, SS officials there complained that most were too starved and weak to perform labor. Per standard concentration camp practice, the SS had to "liquidate" those who could not work so that they would not burden the camp's resources. This complaint caused

SS resettlement officials to consider whether it would be better to ship all the expelled Polish children to Auschwitz to be murdered instead of sending them to the ghettos. Doing so would ensure that the children did not survive and pass on their "undesirable blood."[9]

Even worse than what they suffered in the Zamość camp was the agony the elderly and children expellees endured during transport to vacant ghettos. As they had when deporting the Jews, the Germans sealed the Zamość expellees into train cars and provided them with little or no food or water for their journey. The cattle and freight cars packed with expellees were often shunted aside to allow higher priority transports to pass, so it generally took days for the trains to reach their destination. When they arrived, members of the local population were there to greet them, organized by the RGO care committees. The Poles unloaded the expellees, provided hot meals for the ambulatory, rushed the weak or unconscious to local hospitals, and carried to the morgue the corpses of those who died in transit. It was not always possible to identify the dead, particularly the children. Such was the case with a six-month-old barefoot girl in a pink sweater and striped cap who died on a transport to Siedlce, about 130 miles from Zamość.[10]

The surviving expellees were entirely dependent upon the RGO care committees for shelter and the means to live. The RGO assisted some to go to relatives, recruited families to take in children, and arranged shelter for the rest. Care committee workers spent countless hours helping expellees register with authorities, access medical care, and apply for ration cards. Much of the food, clothing, and basic necessities that the care committees provided to the expellees was donated by Polish populations that were already suffering from severe shortages of all three.

Meanwhile, the able-bodied youths and adults shipped off to the Reich to perform brute labor lost all contact with their family members. Anguished letters poured into Janina's office from expellees pleading for news of their children and parents. Janina was desperate to help them, but helpless to do so.[11]

Finally, on February 9, 1943, the RGO received permission to care for the Poles in the Zamość camp.[12] Janina immediately dispatched to the camp the supplies and personnel she had readied for this moment. Among the workers were ten women members of the Underground experienced in running nurseries and kindergartens. Janina had recruited them and supplied them with RGO identity cards so that they could enter the camp. Their task was to register the hundreds of children and persuade their parents to transfer them to the RGO's custody. The workers promised that the RGO would send the children to relatives or provide shelter for them.

Janina had already arranged for a children's home to be established on Lublin's outskirts to house the children rescued from the Zamość camp. Many mothers, understanding the danger their children faced, readily consigned custody of them to the RGO, but some refused, desperately wanting to believe German assurances that they would be able to keep their children with them. Janina's women workers asked for guidance in dealing with these reluctant mothers.

Just at that time, Janina received a report from Underground contacts in Warsaw District about a Zamość transport found sitting silently on a railroad siding. When the doors were pried open, the frozen corpses of five hundred children were found inside. The Germans quickly resealed the wagon and directed its cargo to Sobibor to be incinerated in the killing center's burning pits.[13]

Utterly horrified, Janina was in no doubt about her next step. She responded to her workers in Zamość: ignore the mothers who refuse to consign custody of their children. By whatever means necessary, she directed, "take the children."

NINE

THE POLISH QUESTION

On the frigid morning of February 26, 1943, Janina set out with Prince Woroniecki and Count Skrzyński for a momentous appointment. Their mood was tense but optimistic as their car headed out of the city on the road leading to Zamość. About one kilometer out, Janina saw on her left, behind barbed wire, the giant warehouses of Globocnik's forced labor camp for Jews that was commonly called the Old Airfield camp because of its location. After another kilometer, she saw on her right the barbed wire that marked the boundary of Majdanek. Behind it in the distance, she could glimpse barbed wire fences and watchtowers surrounding an area that stretched nearly to the horizon. Within it, dark barracks hunkered in the dirty snow and a chimney spewed smoke that wafted over the road, its odor making Janina feel slightly nauseous.

Then the car pulled in at a gate guarded by armed SS men. Janina and her companions showed their papers and stated their business: an appointment with the commandant. They had come to present a plan for feeding Majdanek's prisoners. And this time, Janina knew, Florstedt could not refuse.

It was the turning tide of the war that led to German authorities' change of heart regarding RGO aid for Majdanek prisoners. Nazi Germany had been at the pinnacle of its power in early fall 1942, but since then British and

American forces had landed in North Africa, the Red Army had crushed German forces at Stalingrad, and Allied bombs were turning German cities into rubble. Germany needed more workers to replace the men it was shipping to the crumbling fronts, and it needed more food imports to prevent shortages from sapping morale at home. Nazi leaders looked to the General Government for both.

This led Governor General Frank to suggest a reconsideration of German policy toward the Poles in December 1942. As he sagely observed to his subordinates, "one cannot simultaneously annihilate the Poles and count on Polish labor power." The General Government would accomplish all that it was called upon to do for the German war effort, he asserted, but first the fundamental question needed to be answered: "Should . . . we starve the Poles to death, or feed them?"[1]

Heinrich Himmler was mulling a similar question with regard to the 110,000 prisoners in his concentration camps. Germany needed workers, and he had a captive workforce. He dreamed of turning his camps into major industrial sites where prisoners would produce matériel for arms industries that would pay the SS for the forced labor. The principal impediment to this plan was that the whole point of the concentration camps was to destroy the prisoners, not develop them into productive workers. He would be able to offer German industry far more laborers if only 80,000 prisoners hadn't died in the last half of 1942, nearly 90 percent from starvation, exhaustion, disease, or injury. This number only included registered camp prisoners, not the Jews who were murdered on arrival at Auschwitz and Majdanek. If Himmler was going to extract maximum profit from his concentration camps, then he needed not only to acquire more prisoners but also to find ways to keep them alive and able to work—preferably ways that did not require additional expenditures by the SS.[2]

So in late October 1942, Himmler decreed that families and private persons could send monthly packages of food and clothing to individual concentration camp prisoners. This was soon followed by directives to the concentration camp commandants and doctors to lower the mortality rate among their prisoners. Instead of annihilating prisoners through labor, the camps were now to be reservoirs of forced laborers that served the economic interests of the SS.[3]

This change in policy did not enable Janina and Skrzyński to get permission to feed Majdanek's prisoners, however. Even though Majdanek was part of the concentration camp system, it still carried the official designation of a prisoner of war camp. Moreover, it was primarily a camp for Jews, who accounted for nearly 90 percent of the camp's prisoners at the end of 1942. In fact, Globocnik considered it one of "his" *Aktion* Reinhard camps and demanded that its commandants cater to his demands. Although thousands of Polish hostages and peasants were also imprisoned in Majdanek during 1942 as collective punishment for resistance to German rule, they were considered temporary detainees who were supposed to be released after a few weeks, provided they survived that long.[4] Since Majdanek was not a concentration camp with Polish political prisoners, Florstedt could reject RGO claims that it had standing to feed Majdanek prisoners.

But in February 1943, Majdanek's prisoner population became more diverse. In his quest for prisoner laborers, Himmler directed that able-bodied Polish inmates in General Government prisons be transferred to his concentration camps, particularly Majdanek and Auschwitz. He also ordered mass roundups of unemployed able-bodied Poles and anyone suspected of participating in the resistance, all to be placed in Majdanek, Auschwitz, or the camps in the Reich. Majdanek and Auschwitz were also to take in men, women, and children seized in anti-partisan operations in territories captured from the Soviet Union. Himmler even directed that a special camp for Soviet children be established within Majdanek's women's compound. Except for the few selected for Germanization, these children would be trained to labor for the rest of their lives in the workshops of the concentration camp system.[5]

Following Himmler's directives, in early 1943 the Security Police shipped to Majdanek several thousand Poles gathered from General Government prisons or seized in raids. By early February, Poles outnumbered the Jews among the camp's inmates. Reflecting its new status as a camp for Polish political prisoners, Majdanek was designated a concentration camp on February 16, 1943. Its official name was Waffen SS *Konzentrationslager* Lublin.[6]

At the same time, the RGO was taking advantage of Frank's increased interest in preserving the lives of his Polish subjects, at least until the end of the war. With the civilian administration's support, on February 9, 1943, the RGO finally obtained blanket permission from the Security Police and SD in the General Government to deliver food, clothes, and necessities for Polish inmates in all the prisons. Since Majdanek's Polish political prisoners were under the jurisdiction of the Gestapo, which was part of the Security Police, Skrzyński and Janina realized that the RGO now had a basis for claiming the right to feed those prisoners. There was no time to lose, for they had learned that Polish prisoners were dying in Majdanek after just a few weeks of captivity there. It was even rumored that Polish prisoners no longer able to work were being murdered in the camp's gas chambers along with Jews.[7]

To obtain authorization to feed Majdanek prisoners, Skrzyński and Janina had to navigate the bureaucratic maze of the General Government's administration. Skrzyński generally brought Janina with him when he met with General Government officials so that she could take notes, provide information that supported his requests, and communicate the instructions received at the meetings to the care committees. There may have been a psychological advantage to bringing her as well. German officials generally displayed their contempt for their Polish visitors by refusing to extend them common courtesies, such as standing to receive them or inviting them to sit. Yet class consciousness was so ingrained even in SS officers that they tended to rise instinctively when presented to a German-speaking noblewoman. This then confronted the official with a dilemma. Sitting while the lady stood might feel uncomfortable, which left the options of either standing throughout the meeting—perhaps facing away to display disdain—or inviting the lady to sit, in which case the men present would sit as well. Once this point of order was resolved, the meetings generally followed a pattern: Skrzyński would state the reason for his intervention; the official would then harangue them about the lazy, uncivilized Poles and their failure to appreciate the justness and magnanimity of German rule; finally, they would get down to business.

When Skrzyński and Janina renewed their quest to feed Majdanek prisoners, their first visit was to the BuF department for Lublin District, the civilian agency whose permission was needed for any RGO initiative. In 1942, the Lublin BuF had been reluctant even to allow the RGO to raise public donations. Now that Frank was pushing a somewhat conciliatory policy toward the Poles, however, the BuF was obliged to be more open to Skrzyński's requests. When Skrzyński and Janina presented their proposal to organize a relief operation for Majdanek prisoners together with the Polish Red Cross, the BuF consented.[8]

Skrzyński and Janina's next stop was at the Gestapo office in Lublin. It was housed in a corner building with a distinctive curved façade and a clock high above the entry that had become the symbol of terror to Lublin's residents. It was well known that "under the clock" dark and airless basement cells were stuffed with bloody, mangled prisoners awaiting their next turn at interrogation by the Gestapo's torture specialists. Janina and Skrzyński's visit was brief, for the official they met immediately cut them off. If the RGO wanted to feed Majdanek's prisoners, it would have to get permission from the chief of the Security Police and SD for all of Lublin District, SS-*Hauptsturmführer* (Captain) Hellmut Müller. For that meeting, Skrzyński brought in more firepower: Prince Woroniecki, the RGO's vice director in Kraków.

Skzyński's strategy worked: Woroniecki won Müller's permission for the RGO and the Polish Red Cross to provide food, medicines, and supplies for the Polish prisoners under Security Police jurisdiction at Majdanek. When Florstedt received Müller's notice to this effect, he had no choice but to make some concessions to the RGO delegation.

In any event, now that he was under strict instructions to reduce prisoner mortality, Florstedt saw the value in accepting the RGO proposals. He agreed that the RGO and the Polish Red Cross in Lublin could organize the delivery to Polish prisoners of packages containing food and necessities sent by the prisoners' relatives. Each package, weighing no more than 2 kilograms (4.4 pounds), had to be properly addressed to a specific prisoner at the camp, and relatives could pay the RGO's Lublin Polish Care Committee or the Polish Red Cross to prepare the packages in their name. In addition, he authorized the Lublin Polish Care Committee to make a weekly delivery to Majdanek consisting of one kilogram of bread for each Polish prisoner as well as beans, potatoes, and vegetables to be added to the prisoners' soup. The care committee could also deliver blankets and straw for the Polish prisoners' mattresses, while both the RGO and the Polish Red Cross could supply medicines requested by the camp doctor. Woroniecki won another concession that was nearly as important to the Polish prisoners and their families as the food and package deliveries: the right for Polish prisoners to send one letter or two postcards a month.

On the return from Majdanek, Janina shared her two companions' joy over the concessions Woroniecki had won, but she was anxious to get to work. Although the Lublin Polish Care Committee and the Polish Red Cross in Lublin would be supplying the packages and food, the Germans specified that Skrzyński's office had overall responsibility for the delivery of aid to Majdanek. Skrzyński immediately entrusted the details of the operation to Janina. As soon as she got back to her office, she had to send notice to all the RGO care committees about soliciting packages for Majdanek prisoners and publish an appeal for donations in money and kind. She also planned to solicit donations personally from Lublin businesses and organizations and to enlist the help of her Underground contacts. Now that she could finally pursue the mission she had set herself, she would make sure that it did not fail for lack of resources.

As Janina expected, her colleagues at the Lublin Polish Care Committee and the Polish Red Cross sprang into action the moment they received the go-ahead to supply aid to Majdanek. The Red Cross was in charge of receiving and delivering packages from prisoners' relatives, including those that relatives paid the Lublin Polish Care Committee to prepare. By mid-March 1943, the two organizations were providing an average of 1,700 packages to Majdanek per week.

In addition, the Lublin Polish Care Committee had to obtain the blankets and straw for the prisoners' beds, collect the ingredients to be added to the prisoners' soup, and bake more than six tons of bread for delivery every week—one kilogram for each of the 6,000 Polish prisoners who according to Majdanek authorities were being held in the camp. Obtaining and preparing the food was the responsibility of Antonina Łopatyńska, the head of the Lublin Care Committee's Nutrition and Care Department. Although she did not speak German, she had a special knack for extracting allocations of strictly rationed goods from German officials, cowing the clerks by sternly lecturing them through an interpreter on international law pertaining to the treatment of populations in occupied territories.[9]

For Janina, the permission to feed the prisoners at Majdanek was a rare cause for hope in the midst of the massive suffering that, despite their ceaseless and exhausting efforts, she and her RGO colleagues could do so little to alleviate. If only they could arrange for enough packages to be sent to Majdanek, then, combined with the bread and soup ingredients the Lublin Polish Care Committee was providing, it would be possible to substantially increase the Polish prisoners' chances for survival. What is more, Janina knew that each of Majdanek's compounds housed not only Poles but also prisoners from other national and ethnic groups, including Jews. Since the kitchen in each compound fed all the prisoners from the same cauldrons, the products that the RGO provided for those kitchens would enrich the soup that was fed to all of the camp's prisoners. Although the RGO was barred from providing aid to non-Polish prisoners, Janina envisioned eventually supplying sufficient quantities of products to stave off starvation for all of Majdanek's prisoners, not just the Poles.

Problems ensued immediately, however. Both Janina's office and the Polish Red Cross were inundated with pleas from people desperate to learn whether their loved one was a prisoner in Majdanek. Some had received notice months earlier that the person they sought was consigned to Majdanek, but they had learned nothing more since; some had only heard rumors that their relative had been sent there. But Florstedt and Müller refused to provide a list of Polish prisoners in Majdanek or even to identify the prisoners who had died.

Moreover, it quickly became evident that few of the thousands of packages being sent to confirmed prisoners at Majdanek were actually reaching them intact. Each package was accompanied by a preprinted postcard that the recipient was supposed to return to acknowledge receipt. But prisoners' families were complaining to Janina that they were not receiving the cards, or that the signatures on the cards they did receive were forged. She learned that the camp SS inspected every package and seized many of the contents before sending them on to the "kapos"—concentration camp prisoner functionaries—in the prisoner compounds, who looted them as well. When a package actually got through to a prisoner, it generally contained nothing but moldy bread.

Problems also arose with the director of the Lublin Polish Care Committee, Tadeusz Dąbrowski, and the head of the Polish Red Cross in Lublin, Ludwik Christians. Because the care committee did not have its own transport, it relied upon the Polish Red Cross to deliver not only the packages but also all the other goods it provided for Majdanek prisoners. In the first three weeks of March 1943, the care committee sent to Majdanek via the Polish Red Cross nearly twenty tons of bread in three shipments. There had been no deliveries of the products that were to enrich the prisoners' soup, however. The estimate for the monthly cost of those products came to a staggering sum, and food prices were continually rising. Dąbrowski decided it would be best to delay delivering the products for soup until the care committee had one or two months' supply on hand. Christians had an additional concern about providing the products to Majdanek: they would be consumed by all the camp's prisoners, not just the Poles. That, of course, was exactly Janina's intention. As a prewar politician, Christians had represented the radical wing of the antisemitic National Democrats. He firmly believed that the mission of the Polish Red Cross should be to aid ethnic Poles, and only ethnic Poles.

Skrzyński brought in Woroniecki to settle the matter. In late March, the Prince met separately with Christians and Dąbrowski to hear them out, and he rejected the arguments of each. Regardless of who consumed the products provided by the care committee, he lectured, providing the products for the Polish prisoners was "our great and absolute duty." There was no time to lose, for the Germans might revoke permission for the Majdanek food deliveries at any moment. Lest there be any doubt about his instructions, the Prince put them in writing: "Begin the feeding action immediately."

It appeared that Janina's mission to feed all the prisoners at Majdanek might succeed after all.

TEN

MAJDANEK

If Hermann Florstedt entertained any hope that his assignment as Majdanek's commandant bode well for his career, his first day at the camp in
November 1942 must have quickly dispelled it. The rumors of rampant corruption at Buchenwald when he served there as Koch's deputy had cast a
pall over his reputation, so his posting to Majdanek was less a vote of confidence than a last chance at redemption. His instructions were clear: clean
up the mess Koch had left behind, establish order and discipline, and develop Majdanek into a center of industrial enterprises where prisoners produced goods for the SS. His first tour of the camp made it equally clear that
his chances for success were exceedingly slim.

Florstedt had served at Sachsenhausen as well as Buchenwald, but Majdanek bore little resemblance to those two concentration camps in the heart
of the "Old Reich."[1] It was, instead, a primitive outpost of German rule in a
hostile territory. When he arrived there, Florstedt found a vast, chaotic construction site on an expanse of open land that was four times larger than Buchenwald.[2] There were no paved roads or pathways, and the autumn rains
had turned the sandy soil into mud so deep it sucked even the boots off the
feet of the SS men. At one point, the SS drew up blueprints for the camp to
hold 150,000 prisoners and the factories they would work in, but—as with
many of Himmler's ambitious plans—the continuing war forced the project

to be curtailed. Until Germany's victory, when there would be no lack of construction materials and transport, Majdanek was slated to have a capacity of 25,000 prisoners and an industrial area with sixty-four workshops and warehouses. Theoretically, it already had sufficient barracks to house 25,000 prisoners in November 1942, though many lacked windows, doors, and furniture. But only six buildings had been erected in the industrial area, and the barracks for the guards and the camp administration were still under construction.[3]

What had been constructed appeared improvised and shoddy. The "protective custody camp"—the SS term for the area of a concentration camp where prisoners were detained—covered more than seventy-five acres and consisted of five rectangular compounds called "fields" and two narrower "inter-fields," all adjacent and surrounded by a double barbed wire fence and watchtowers. Unlike the sturdy prisoner barracks at Buchenwald, which had quarters for dining and sleeping as well as lavatories, the barracks at Majdanek were uninsulated wooden buildings with no internal divisions and no running water. In some compounds, the barracks were actually horse stables with barn doors, dirt floors, and only an opening under the eaves to let in light. The tar paper that covered the barrack roofs quickly curled and flaked into the swirling wind.

Alongside the barracks were the latrines: cement troughs in the ground crossed lengthwise by boards on which the prisoners perched to relieve themselves in the open. Afterward, they could not clean themselves, since the compounds had no running water or bathing facilities, and the SS rarely allowed the prisoners to fetch buckets of well water for washing. In any event, health authorities had condemned the water in the camp's three wells as contaminated with E. coli and ammonia. There were bathing and disinfection barracks just outside the protective custody camp, but they were largely reserved for newly arriving prisoners.

Because of the food shortages in the General Government, the prisoners' diet at Majdanek made the sparse meals at Buchenwald seem sumptuous. Starving prisoners drinking contaminated water, unable to bathe, and continually plagued by lice and fleas created the perfect conditions for epidemics of dysentery, scabies, tuberculosis, typhoid, and the dreaded typhus that sickened and killed even the SS guards. The three barracks in Field I that served as the "hospital" were overflowing with sick and injured patients who could expect little treatment other than a brief reprieve from hard labor. Once prisoners appeared incapable of returning to work, however, they were left to die or were murdered. There were over 8,000 prisoners in Majdanek when Florstedt arrived, but more than three times that many had been registered at the camp in the previous eight months. In November 1942 alone, 2,999 died. Smoke poured constantly from the chimney of the crematorium located between Fields I and II. The two oil-fired ovens, which could burn at most one hundred bodies in twelve hours, could barely keep pace with demand. The stench in the camp compounds from open latrines, thousands of unwashed bodies, and burning corpses was so overpowering that Florstedt determined to visit the protective custody camp as rarely as possible. When he did, it was always in his car and with a lit cigar clenched firmly in his teeth.

Thousands more victims were dying at Majdanek than the official death statistics indicated. Between March and September 1942, Majdanek's role in *Aktion* Reinhard had been to work to death the Jewish men temporarily spared from the gas chambers of the killing centers in order to labor in SS enterprises. By October 1942, however, Majdanek had two operational gas chambers and began serving as a small-scale killing center as well. Jewish men, women, and children arrived by the hundreds from the last ghettos and labor camps that Globocnik's forces were clearing in Lublin District, including Majdan Tatarski and Zamość. The pace of arrivals picked up when gassing operations ceased at Bełżec in November. Newly arrived Jews rated unfit for work and all the children and elderly were immediately gassed or, when their number exceeded the camp's gassing capacity, shot in the Krępiec woods, where the victims' corpses were burned. *Aktion* Reinhard's year-end report on the number of Jews it had "resettled" in 1942 tallied the victims of four sites: Bełżec, Sobibor, Treblinka, and Majdanek. Of the operation's 1,274,166 victims, Majdanek accounted for 24,733.[4]

Keeping operations at Majdanek completely secret was nearly impossible, Florstedt found. There were no walls around the camp, just barbed wire fencing. Buildings on a hill at the edge of Lublin looked down into the camp, and houses in a neighboring village were close enough to have a view of Field V. There was no fence at all around much of the camp's southern perimeter, including where it abutted the part of the village of Dziesiąta that the SS had not razed and added to Majdanek. By day, the only thing separating the remaining villagers from the prisoners laboring in the camp's vegetable gardens was the line of sentries who guarded the area. At night, the villagers went onto the camp's grounds to fetch water from their only well.

Florstedt did not even have trained SS Death's Head guards to enforce security and discipline. Some of the officers and NCOs were experienced concentration camp hands, but the rest of the SS men were either older reservists or, increasingly, ethnic Germans from Croatia, Hungary, or Romania recruited to serve as cannon fodder for the Waffen SS. The recruits sent to Majdanek had been rated too weak or inept to serve at the front without first being whipped into shape at a concentration camp. They tended to be semiliterate and to speak in dialects Florstedt could barely understand.[5] The SS could not even cobble together enough of these cohorts to meet Majdanek's requirements, and so a battalion of Lithuanian auxiliary police served at the camp as well, few of whom spoke any German. They did share the Germans' contempt for Poles and Jews, however, and were notorious among the prisoners for being trigger-happy. In addition, to assist in the mass murder process at Majdanek, Globocnik assigned some of the Trawniki men who provided the manpower for *Aktion* Reinhard. These brutish guards, mostly Ukrainians, ignored regulations and went drinking and whoring in Lublin after curfew, then sullenly endured the lashes they received as punishment.[6] Florstedt found that resentment and discontent were rife among Majdanek's guard forces.

Florstedt's security challenges multiplied in early 1943 with the arrival of thousands of Polish political prisoners. Among these men and women were trained members of the Underground, and their co-conspirators on the outside, including Janina, immediately sought to contact and assist them. Some resistance members in Lublin secured jobs as civilian construction specialists in the camp so that they could scout for colleagues, smuggle food and medicines to them, and relay messages. Two Underground cells of women hid packages at night in several sites in the camp's vegetable gardens and then retrieved the messages that prisoners left there. One cell, based in Dziesiąta, also provided lodging for prisoners' family members and bribed the sentries to look the other way while the visitors spoke to prisoners laboring in the camp fields.[7] No matter how much Florstedt threatened to punish guards who had dealings with prisoners or civilians, there were some who could not resist the temptation to augment their meager wages and boring diet when offered the right amount of money or bacon.[8]

Although Florstedt granted the RGO permission to provide packages and food for the prisoners, he suspected it was planning to use the deliveries to support and expand the resistance within the camp. That was, in fact, Janina's assignment. As information came in to her about the location of Underground members in the camp, she saw to it that they were sent packages from "family members" in the resistance. Through the AK, she worked with several groups of women to obtain the ingredients and assemble the packages, among them the network that Saturnina Malm had established to provide medicine and food to the camp infirmary. Another group was headed by the baker Antonina Grygowa, a woman of modest means renowned in Lublin for her generosity to anyone in need. Together with her two daughters, she ran a bakery that produced bread for the Lublin Care Committee's soup kitchens during the day. At night, they baked more bread to add to the packages they provided for prisoners at both Majdanek and Zamek, the prison in Lublin's castle.

A problem soon arose with the bread in the RGO packages: it was turning moldy before the prisoners received it. The cause, Janina determined, was that in an effort to increase the prisoners' caloric intake, the Lublin Polish Care Committee was sending slices of bread with fat spread upon them. She conferred with Łopatyńska and Grygowa to come up with a solution. Sending the fat in a separate container was not an option, because it would be stolen before the prisoner received the package. After some experimentation, Grygowa devised a recipe for rolls baked with extra shortening that did not mold quickly. Since fats were strictly rationed, Łopatyńska had to work her magic with German officials to get the extra shortening for the bakers.

Once the delivery of food products for the prisoners' soup finally began in April 1943, Janina could visit Majdanek to collect receipts for the food and supplies from the RGO and to discuss future deliveries. She often rode there on the horse-drawn Red Cross truck with its driver, Ludwik Jurek, who was also an AK member. At Majdanek, she could get no farther than the commandant's headquarters, next to the main road and largely out of view of the protective custody camp. Somehow, she vowed to herself, she would eventually win access to places within the camp where she could directly observe and maybe even interact with the prisoners. In the meantime, she made sure on all her visits to chat up the SS guards at the checkpoint and the clerks in the headquarters. For many of those she interacted with, the kindly attentions from the distinguished lady with perfect German provided a welcome break from their tedious routine.

On a visit to Majdanek in early May 1943, Janina saw a sight that filled her with horror: a giant plume of thick, black smoke rising from an area west of the protective custody camp. She knew that the last inhabitants of the Warsaw Ghetto, despite heroic resistance, were being sent by the thousands to Majdanek. The smell of burnt hair and roasting flesh emanating from the plume left her in no doubt as to its source.

Relatives of Polish prisoners in Majdanek pleaded for the RGO's help in getting their loved ones released. In May, through interventions with the Security Police, Skrzyński was actually managing to win the freedom of dozens of Poles seized in street raids or held as hostages. Upon their release, these prisoners were taken to the office of the care committee and RGO in Lublin to be fed and given medical treatment, clothes, and money for the journey home.

Janina made a point of debriefing the released prisoners about their experiences and observations at Majdanek. What she heard exceeded her darkest imaginings. They told her that the prisoners' daily diet consisted of a bitter swill called coffee, soup made from rotten vegetables and weeds, and one eighth of a loaf of bread, with a tiny bit of marmalade and horsemeat sausage twice a week. Since they had no dishes assigned to them, they ate the soup sitting on the ground out of unwashed bowls that were used by several prisoners during the same meal, and the marmalade was delivered into their filthy hands. They talked of how prisoners driven mad with hunger would snarl and fight like animals over a bit of stale bread. They spoke of bodies covered with lice, scabies sores, mud, and feces from chronic dysentery, and of going for a month or more without bathing or even a change of clothes. And they described heavy artillery wagons with chest-high wheels, filled with skeletal corpses that daily traveled from the prisoner compounds to the crematorium, pulled and pushed along the deeply rutted camp road by twenty starving prisoners under constant whipping from kapos and SS men.

Janina also learned about the Jews newly arriving at Majdanek. Men, women, and children waited on bare ground sometimes for days without food or water in the "rose garden," the prisoners' term for a barbed wire enclosure next to the bathing facility. After finally undergoing a brief examination by camp officials, some were directed to the building with showers and disinfection tubs, while the rest, mostly children and people over forty, were forced to strip and then rushed to the gas chambers to be murdered. Usually, the SS conducted the gassings at night, while tractor engines were running to drown out the victims' screams. But now so many Jews were arriving that the SS were gassing them during the daytime as well. Every night, the protective custody camp was filled with the wails of Jews mourning the loss of their children, parents, wives, and husbands.

Prisoners released from the women's camp in Field V informed Janina that 2,000 Belarusian women and children seized in anti-partisan raids had been placed in the camp since March. The older children were held separate from their mothers in barracks surrounded by barbed wire. Since their arrival, typhus had broken out and was now raging in the compound.[9] The prisoners spoke with awe of a Polish physician, Dr. Stefania Perzanowska, who had persuaded the SS to let her set up an infirmary barrack and was providing medical treatment for prisoners. Since there were few other medical professionals among the women prisoners, she had established a nurse training program for volunteers. But she had little more than a stethoscope and some thermometers to work with and almost nothing in the way of medications, disinfectant, gauze, or bandages. There were so many typhus patients in the women's compound, Janina learned, that it had become impossible to quarantine them.[10] From former male prisoners, Janina heard that typhus was now spreading in the other prisoner compounds as well.

This information inspired Janina with an idea. So far, she had been unable to get a meeting with Majdanek's chief doctor, even though Florstedt had authorized the RGO to consult with the camp physician about supplying medicines for the Polish prisoners. Now she decided to use the new typhus epidemic in the camp to get the doctor's attention. In mid-May, she obtained a meeting with the German medical superintendent of Lublin District. Appealing to him for help was a risky gambit, but she calculated that he might agree, if not out of human decency, then out of self-interest.

As usual, she was left to wait until well after the appointed time before being ushered in to see the superintendent. He was standing when she entered, looking out a window, and he did not address her. She decided to dispense with the usual introduction.

"There is a typhus epidemic in Majdanek," she announced. "Our committee seeks permission to provide inoculations."

The doctor reacted predictably, spewing invectives against meddling Polish organizations that demanded rights, helped traitors, and coddled criminals. She waited until his harangue ended.

"I came to you because you are a physician, though now it seems I might as well have gone to the SS. But I came to you because you supposedly once swore an oath to relieve sickness and suffering, and I thought a doctor would surely help."

He turned from the window to face the petite woman who had just addressed him with such calm effrontery. Then he invited her to sit down.

"I'll think about it," he said in a different tone, "but how would you get it there?"

"We could send it to you," she replied, "and you could deliver it to the Majdanek authorities."

He began to pace his office while she explained what she had learned, that there were hundreds of typhus patients in the infirmaries and many more, including children, who were sharing bunks with prisoners who were not yet infected.

He interrupted her. "I'll go to the camp and see for myself what can be done. But," he threatened, "if any of you start spreading horror stories, you know what will happen to you!"

He then went to the telephone, first to call the district doctor, who hadn't heard anything about the situation. Then he called the head of the BuF department, who denied the whole thing. Nevertheless, the superintendent arranged a group tour of the camp hospital for the next day and invited Janina to accompany him. Janina readily accepted this opportunity to go inside the protective custody camp.

By the time of the inspection, Janina had received word that the infirmary barracks were being cleaned and aired and prisoners moved. Janina met the superintendent's group at the commandant's headquarters and then was transported with them to the men's "hospital" in Field I. As their car turned onto the road that ran by the prisoner compounds, Janina glimpsed to her right a building complex under a large wood awning that partially shielded what it covered from view. Based on drawings of the camp smuggled out by resistance members, she realized that the gas chambers were located somewhere under the covering.

At the first entry, they turned past a wooden guard booth and through a gate between two barbed wire fences. She was startled by the sight of flower beds riotous with colorful May blooms. On each side of the compound, a row of ten long wooden barracks stretched back some three hundred yards. She could see little of the rest of the protective custody camp, other than the chimney rising from the next compound on her right. It was impossible not to see and smell the smoke wafting from it or from an area some two hundred yards away, but no one remarked upon it.

The infirmary barracks that they visited seemed very basic but not overcrowded, and they could see that the patients were receiving treatment from prisoners who were well-qualified physicians. The SS orderlies acknowledged that there was some typhus but maintained it was well under control. The physician prisoners, looking ashamed and fearful, kept silent. In the course of the tour, however, one let slip that while the quarantine barrack had two hundred beds, four hundred prisoners had been diagnosed with typhus just the day before.

The medical superintendent recognized that typhus was becoming epidemic at Majdanek again and that it might spread to Lublin and to German soldiers. He told Janina that he would speak with the commandant and instructed her to come to his office the next day. She arrived promptly the next morning and, after a weary wait, received welcome news: she had an appointment to see a Dr. Blancke in Majdanek that very day.

SS *Haupsturmführer* Dr. Max Blancke had been exceedingly busy at Majdanek ever since his arrival from Natzweiler concentration camp in April 1943. Much of his time was immediately taken up with eyeballing the prisoners in each compound in order to determine which ones were incapable of work and unlikely to recover. Those he selected were placed in a *Gammelblock*, a barrack surrounded by barbed wire where prisoners were left without food or water, lying in their excrement on the dirt floor until they died or were finally taken out to be murdered. Because of the typhus in the women's camp, he had developed a method of selecting prisoners without getting too near them: he had them walk by him with bare legs and feet and sentenced to death those showing edema and sores. In addition, since the transports of Jews began arriving from Warsaw in late April, he had been working long hours day and night in the "rose garden" choosing victims for the gas chambers. Even though Blancke sent thousands to their deaths, Majdanek's population of registered prisoners had grown from 11,000 when he arrived to almost 25,000 by mid-May, more than two thirds of them Jews. He had no time or desire to meet with a woman from some Polish charity, but he could not ignore the medical superintendent's order.

When Janina arrived at Majdanek, two SS men escorted her to a white, two-story house located halfway between the road and the protective custody camp and left her to wait under guard. Eventually, a rather young, attractive man arrived and motioned her to enter an office.

"What do you want to see me about?" Blancke barked impatiently.

"As if he doesn't know," Janina thought, but she patiently explained the purpose of the RGO, Florstedt's agreement that it could provide medicines to the camp, and the medical superintendent's instruction that she meet with the camp doctor. Blancke continued to feign ignorance. When she mentioned the typhus epidemic, however, he exploded.

"There is NO typhus epidemic in this camp!" he thundered. "And as for your other concerns, I am not in the least interested in the welfare of Poles!"

Blancke's fury alarmed Janina, and she wondered whether he could have her arrested. Stilling her nerves, she said, "I have come to offer, on behalf of my organization, a shipment of serum against typhus for all the inmates of Majdanek. We have been delivering food parcels for the prisoners, authorized by Gestapo headquarters." She placed a tiny stress on the words "authorized" and "Gestapo." "We also take some care of prisoners when they are released, and having heard that there were typhus cases at Majdanek, we thought we would like to protect the camp's inmates."

"Doesn't your committee have any better causes than to help these scoundrels?" Blancke demanded. "What's the matter with you charity ladies? Don't you think that if serum were necessary, I, the chief physician here, would see to it that we got it? Anyway, the typhus cases are all quarantined, and the other inmates have no contact with them!"

Janina lowered her eyes and kept silent. Blancke's bullying was not going to deter her. If he refused the serum, she would just go back to the superintendent.

That thought apparently occurred to Blancke as well. After a pause, he said in a milder tone, "Of course, if your committee happens to have the serum, it wouldn't be bad to give it to the prisoners, preventatively, just as prophylaxis, you understand."

"That seems a good idea," she responded.

"Even with the greatest care in quarantining," he went on, "lice can travel from barrack to barrack, so maybe it's as well to inoculate them all and be done with it."

Blancke authorized Janina to send 4,000 vials of serum to Majdanek. She realized this was not enough even for all the Poles in the camp, but she considered this just the first step in the campaign she intended to wage to provide medicines to Majdanek. She persuaded Blancke to meet with the Lublin Polish Care Committee's physician, Dr. Tadeusz Krzyszkowski, to discuss the prisoners' medical needs. The result of their conference was a list of medicines that the Lublin Polish Care Committee and the Polish Red Cross scrambled to fill.

But every step forward toward saving Majdanek's prisoners met with reverses. By the end of May, the Polish Red Cross estimated that only

20 percent of the packages it was delivering were getting to the address-ees. Camp authorities now maintained that there were only 3,000 Polish prisoners in the camp, far fewer than the actual number. Consequently, the quantity of bread and food products that the Lublin Care Committee was authorized to supply was too little to make a difference in the diet even of the Poles, much less of the many thousands of other prisoners. Camp officials had started making difficulties even about these deliveries. And Florstedt reneged on his promise in February to allow Polish prisoners to write to their families. Mail had to be censored, and Florstedt had no desire to deploy staff to the task.

To break through the intransigence of Majdanek officials, Skrzyński appealed to Security Police Chief Müller, who instructed Florstedt to meet with the Count. When he arrived at the commandant's office on May 25, however, Skrzyński found not Florstedt but the chief of Majdanek's administration department, Heinrich Worster. The commandant had much more important matters to attend to, Worster explained. Nevertheless, he assured Skrzyński that the RGO could continue supplying bread and food products and could also provide certain medicines, especially vaccines. The food deliveries were to occur each Saturday before noon. In addition, the RGO could supply mattress straw twice a month, and Worster requested immediate delivery of as many blankets as possible. Worster even promised that Polish prisoners would be permitted to send a postcard to a relative and to receive correspondence in return. When Skrzyński pressed him about informing families when their loved ones died in Majdanek, however, Worster refused. He also insisted that the RGO could only supply food for 3,000 prisoners.

Following Skrzyński's conferences with Müller and Worster, Polish prisoners were assigned to work in the camp post office and the rate of package delivery began to improve. Camp authorities also distributed preprinted postcards to the Polish prisoners, along with strict instructions for filling them out. Even this limited ability to communicate with their families improved the prisoners' chances for survival, because it enabled the families to write back and send packages. For the prisoners, the emotional sustenance provided by the correspondence was as precious as the physical sustenance in the packages.[11]

Blancke's acceptance of typhus serum from the RGO was only for appearance's sake, for vaccinating less than 20 percent of Majdanek's prisoners could not possibly stop the disease from spreading among the unvaccinated. The camp's SS leaders were more intent on covering up the epidemic than controlling it. At the beginning of 1943, the Inspectorate of Concentration Camps had placed the camp under a two-month quarantine, during which even the SS were not permitted to leave, a situation that was ripe for mutiny. No one wanted a repeat of that experience. Not long after the medical superintendent's inspection, however, Florstedt received notice that a commission was coming from Berlin to check out a report that typhus was again becoming rampant in the camp. He made it clear to his subordinates that the commission was not to find evidence of the disease in the camp infirmaries.

When Dr. Perzanowska received the order not to report any cases of typhus, there were hundreds of typhus patients isolated in two barracks of the women's camp in Field V. She had no idea what she was supposed to do with them. Then Erich Muhsfeldt, the chief of the crematorium, paid her a visit. His job involved not just disposing of prisoners' corpses but also murdering prisoners selected for death who were not gassed. During his drunken binges he would sometimes barge into the women's infirmary, fire his pistol wildly, and accuse Perzanowska of committing sabotage by shielding malingerers. On this day, accompanied by a medical orderly, he watched as Perzanowska treated patients. Seeing a Jewish woman with the telltale rash, he asked Perzanowska whether the patient had typhus. When she nodded in the affirmative, he and the orderly took the woman into a storeroom and shut the door. After a few minutes, Muhsfeldt emerged and told Perzanowska to look inside. The patient lay dead. Muhsfeldt then screamed at her, "No more typhus in the women's hospital! Understood?"

Perzanowska and her staff spent all that night altering the records of the patients in the two isolation barracks, assigning them a variety of diagnoses. A few days later, Dr. Blancke rushed the group of medical inspectors from Berlin through the women's wards. As Dr. Perzanowska stated the fictitious diagnoses, the inspectors did not bother to look at the patients, who bore the visible signs of their true affliction. At the end, the commission leader addressed her:

"No typhus in the camp?"

"No typhus at all, sir," she replied.[12]

Haunted by the stories she was hearing from the released prisoners, Janina became obsessed with finding more ways to help Majdanek prisoners not just to survive, but to want to survive. "We must do more!" she said again and again to her colleagues and to herself, even crying out the words in her sleep. She conceived a plan for delivering prepared soup to the camp, but her colleagues in the Lublin Polish Care Committee and the Polish Red Cross scoffed at the idea. The Germans would never allow it, they insisted, and even if they did, the logistical challenges of preparing and delivering vats of soup for thousands of prisoners were insurmountable.

With more packages passing through SS inspection at Majdanek, Janina's Underground network began smuggling small messages in the parcels they were preparing, hiding them in a bread roll or at the bottom of a marmalade container. Janina wanted to let her comrades in the camp know that they were not forgotten, that there were many people on the outside who were taking great risks to help them, and so they must not give up hope. Many of them had been completely cut off from the world since long before their arrival in Majdanek and had undergone excruciating torture by the Gestapo. Some, she knew, had finally broken, and now they were suffering in a hell of shame in the camp, scorned by the other prisoners. Janina wanted to reach them as well, to let them know that their comrades on the outside saw them as martyrs, not traitors, deserving of honor, not shame. She arranged to send them messages of appreciation in parcels or passed news of a German defeat or partisan attack to them via comrades who were civilian workers in the camp.

For Janina, the sight and smell of the smoke over Majdanek felt like a constant reproach for her failure to help those who had been reduced to ashes. She had to devise more ways to help those still living. As long as they suffered, she could find no peace.

ELEVEN

JANINA'S LISTS

On July 6, 1943, Majdanek prisoners toiling in the sweltering heat near the main road noticed a billowing cloud of dust advancing from the direction of Zamość. It was not like the dust storms that had been swirling through the camp during the summer drought, coating everyone and everything with a fine, gray grit. This cloud kept over the road, steadily extending from over the horizon. Soon, the prisoners saw its cause: hundreds of exhausted, sweaty, grimy peasants lugging bags of belongings. Most seemed to be women, children, or elderly.[1]

These were the victims of Globocnik's latest operation to pacify and Germanize southern and southeastern Lublin District. It combined an anti-partisan campaign code-named "Wehrwolf" (a combination of the *Wehr* of the Wehrmacht with the word for werewolf, *Werwolf*) with a resumption of the resettlement program that had been suspended in March for the planting season. In late June, German army units along with Waffen SS and police forces set up a dragnet around villages in Zamość and two neighboring counties and proceeded to arrest all the Polish men between the ages of fifteen and forty-five, shooting any who put up resistance. While planes spotted from above, troops methodically combed the fields to find those who sought to flee. A few days later, Globocnik's forces returned to seize the men's families. In retaliation for partisan attacks and resistance to their methods, the Germans destroyed some villages entirely with bombs and fire and murdered all the inhabitants, including children, by shooting them or burning them alive.

Globocnik had the seized civilians placed in three transit camps in the region. After all the men underwent interrogation for ties to the Underground, the SS resettlement commission intended to conduct the usual sorting of the useful from the useless. Globocnik's plan for the latter was to house them in a former POW camp where they would be forced to perform light labor for however long they lived.[2]

Although Globocnik sealed the area and cut off telecommunications, word quickly reached Skrzyński and Janina of the attacks and the filling transit camps. Skrzyński immediately sought to travel to the region to investigate conditions and organize the care committees' response, but the SS and police forces refused to honor his travel authorization from civilian officials. On July 1, Skrzyński persuaded Security Police Chief Müller to issue him a police pass to travel in the affected counties. He spent most of the rest of the month there, regularly reporting to district civilian authorities and the RGO in Kraków about German atrocities and the disastrous effects of the resettlement operation.[3]

Janina was highly skeptical of the German resettlement authorities' promise that, unlike the winter resettlement operation, this time they would not separate Polish children from their families. A plea for help she received from a grandmother in Zamość confirmed her suspicion. The woman's four granddaughters were being held in a transit camp despite the fact that the Germans had shot their father and their mother's whereabouts were unknown.

Janina resolved to learn all she could about the children in the transit camps and to track them as they were placed on outgoing transports so that they could eventually be returned to their families. Reactivating her committee of child care workers from the previous resettlement operation, she dispatched them to the rail stations by the transit camps, where the RGO was allowed to provide some food and necessities to the expellees as they boarded the deportation trains. Janina assigned her workers, mostly members of the

Underground, to report back the number of children on the transports, the date and place when each transport departed, and whatever information about the transports' destination they were able to wheedle out of officials and railway workers. The women particularly looked for unaccompanied children and occasionally succeeded in slipping a few out of the transports.[4]

By early July, the transit camps were so overcrowded that the SS resettlement commission decided to send some of the expellees to Majdanek. In two days, nearly 6,000 Poles arrived at the camp, many of them forced to walk the fifty miles from Zamość. The escort guards shot those who fell behind as encouragement for the others to keep going. By the end of July, the commission had sent some 9,000 Polish expellees to Majdanek.[5]

The camp, already at its theoretical capacity, was completely unprepared for this influx of prisoners. Barracks intended for 250 prisoners held 1,500 or more, with multiple people to each bed and others sleeping cheek by jowl on the floor. All, including the children, had to stay outdoors during the day under the broiling sun and stand for excruciating hours during the roll calls before dawn and at dusk. They relieved themselves in the open latrines and had no way to wash their bodies or clothes, or their infants' diapers. Their suffering became immeasurably worse when Florstedt cut off the water to the protective custody camp and ordered the execution of anyone caught using water to drink or wash. Although Majdanek had finally been connected to Lublin's sewer system, the severe summer drought had caused the municipal waterworks to fail. The only liquid the prisoners received was the "coffee" given out in the morning and the disgusting soup that was passed around in unwashed bowls and, like everything else in the camp, was gritty with dust. The sight of prisoners hauling sloshing buckets of well water for the camp's flower beds only added to their torment.

Conditions at Majdanek were especially devastating for the children. Starvation and dehydration swiftly hollowed out their already malnourished bodies. They sickened from measles and mumps as well as the typhus that inevitably swept through the expellees. And they daily witnessed traumatizing scenes of vicious beatings and of naked corpses piled in wheelbarrows, arms and legs twitching like macabre puppets on the bumpy journey to the crematorium. More and more children died as each day passed.[6]

With Skrzyński away investigating conditions in the region of the Wehrwolf operation, Janina took charge of all interventions with German authorities concerning Majdanek. Camp officials did not regard the Zamość
expellees as concentration camp prisoners and so did not include them in
the tally of Poles the RGO was authorized to provide for. Janina did manage
to negotiate some increase in food, but it was not enough to make any significant difference in the prisoners' nutrition. Any joy she felt at being allowed
to provide 250 liters of milk for the children evaporated when she learned
that most of it was siphoned off by the SS and kapos. Her only real achievement was to arrange the transfer to Lublin's children's hospital of 153 desperately ill Polish children in Majdanek. Their extreme emaciation shocked
Janina and made her even more desperate to rescue those still in the camp.[7]

Meanwhile, on July 3, Janina learned that transport trains were depositing
whole families of starving expellees in the transit camp near the Lublin city
train station at 6 and 31 Krochmalna Street. Immediately after arriving, they
were being taken to be deloused at a facility outside the camp. Poles living
nearby had spontaneously set up a soup kitchen and were bribing the guards
to allow them to feed the expellees as they passed by. Seeing an opportunity
to rescue more children, Janina and a few of her AK colleagues joined the
feeding effort. As they served food to throngs of expellees awaiting delousing, the women offered to take children to be cared for, and they succeeded
in whisking some away. Once trains began departing from Krochmalna to the
Reich carrying entire families, however, fewer parents were willing to give
up their children. Janina decided that the risk involved in taking the children
now outweighed the potential reward.

Janina made the neighborhood soup kitchen an official RGO operation, and her call for the local population to donate food for the expellees
met with instant success. Since she could not get permission to distribute
food inside the Krochmalna camp, she had carts set up outside its gates for
receiving and distributing the donations. The commotion this caused in-
duced the Krochmalna commandant, the ethnic German Zdzisław Musielski, to relent. He gave Janina three passes for Lublin Polish Care Committee
workers to distribute prepared soup, food items that expellees could take
with them on their journey to the Reich, and milk and rolls for the camp

infirmary. The Polish Red Cross also provided bread, preserves, and milk. Janina often used one of the passes herself so that, while distributing food to the expellees, she could question them. She then passed on any useful information she gleaned to the Underground.[8]

Meanwhile, armed with Skrzyński's reports, the RGO's leaders in Kraków were petitioning for the resettlement operation to stop and its victims to be released. When RGO president Count Ronikier went to see Frank on July 23, he was astonished by the gracious reception he received. The governor general professed that he, too, opposed resettlement and pacification operations, and he promised to stop them. What's more, Frank granted the RGO significant new funding for its work and announced that the General Government would soon institute new policies to improve conditions for the Poles. The change would include an increase in rations for Poles who showed themselves to be loyal and productive subjects. Henceforth, Frank declared magnanimously, "no working person will have to starve *anymore*" in the General Government (emphasis added). It soon turned out that, thanks to *Aktion* Wehrwolf, the power dynamics in the General Government were shifting in a direction that would provide the RGO far more leeway for rescuing Polish victims of Nazi persecution.[9]

Earlier in the year, Frank's proposals for a somewhat kinder and gentler policy toward the Poles had found no support from Himmler or Hitler. Before *Aktion* Wehrwolf began, Frank pleaded with Hitler to put off the Germanization of the General Government until after the war and to stop the slaughter of women, children, and the elderly in reprisal actions. He complained that these tactics were only causing chaos in the countryside and threatening the harvest while driving the Poles into the arms of the Bolsheviks. Himmler insisted, however, that Globocnik would somehow manage to Germanize and pacify the region without harming the General Government's economy or security. As a sop to Frank, Himmler promised that once *Aktion* Wehrwolf achieved its goals, he would transfer Globocnik out of the General Government. Hitler backed Himmler, who authorized Globocnik to proceed with his campaign. Within days of its start, Frank's worst predictions began to come true.

By the time of his meeting with Count Ronikier, however, Frank had acquired an influential ally in his efforts to rein in the power of the SS and police in the General Government: the new governor of Lublin District. Globocnik's close relationship with Himmler had empowered him to ignore most of former governor Zörner's orders and decrees. But Governor Richard Wendler was Himmler's brother-in-law and even dearer to the *Reichsführer* SS than Globocnik. Wendler reacted with fury to the effects of Globocnik's operation, which Skrzyński was documenting in his letters of protest to the governor. The partisans were growing stronger by the day and were attacking the new ethnic German settlements so frequently that the settlers were abandoning their farms and refusing to return. Since the Polish peasants were either being seized by Globocnik's forces or were fleeing them, there was no one left to tend the fields, so the prospects for the harvest appeared dim. Even the SS general in charge of anti-partisan warfare conceded that Globocnik's tactics had failed. In a July 27 letter to "Dear Heinrich," Wendler informed Himmler that Globocnik had created a "spectacular fiasco" in Lublin District. The governor urged his brother-in-law to "install Globocnik in his new assignment as soon as possible and get him out of here."[10]

Himmler agreed to send a new SS and Police Leader to replace Globocnik in Lublin District by mid-August. In the meantime, on July 31, Globocnik had to concede that Wendler's civilian authorities would take control of prisoners in the transit camps who were not suspected of participating in the resistance. The District Labor Office would take custody of those selected for labor, while the RGO would take over the expellees rated as unfit for work.[11]

Globocnik did not immediately leave Lublin, however, in part because he still had some tasks connected with *Aktion* Reinhard. There was also some question about his next post. Himmler wanted to promote Globocnik to a Higher SS and Police Leader, but the number of positions was declining with the Germans' retreat on the Eastern Front. After Italy surrendered to the Allies in September 1943 and Germany occupied the northern half of the country, a new position opened up in Globocnik's hometown, Trieste. There, Globocnik proceeded with his usual gusto to slaughter civilians and ship Jews to their death.[12]

Globocnik's dismissal had immediate consequences for Janina's work. On August 2, she accompanied Skrzyński to meet with Wendler regarding a list of demands that the Count had submitted two days earlier. The governor acceded to nearly all of them. He assured them that there would be no more resettlement raids and that collective punishment in reprisal for partisan attacks would cease. While Wendler did not have the authority to close the transit camps, he had arranged permission for the RGO to take charge of the camp inmates who were ill, as well as all orphans and unaccompanied minors. The released expellees were forbidden to return to their villages, but the RGO could settle them elsewhere in the district. The SS and Police Leader would authorize RGO personnel to enter the five transit camps, including the one in Majdanek, and would instruct the commandant of each camp to provide information about all the Polish expellees who had been interned there. The governor further promised that local officials would cooperate with the RGO and issue passes to its workers so that they could perform their duties. Finally, the governor declared that, other than the people seized in pacification actions to be sent to the Reich, not one more person would be forcibly deported out of his district. He invited Skrzyński to contact him directly regarding any major issues he encountered and to continue keeping him fully informed about events in the region.[13]

Stunned by the sudden reversal in resettlement policy, Skrzyński and Janina left Wendler's office determined to make good on his concessions before the policy could change again. Their first step was to see Security Police Chief Müller, who arranged for them to meet that same afternoon with Globocnik's chief of staff about access to the transit camps. Janina recognized the significance of this appointment. Despite Wendler's promises and assurances, it was not he, but the SS and police who controlled the fate of the expellees. If she and Skrzyński could win the support of the SS and Police Leader's chief of staff, then their ability to aid the expellees would be assured. What Janina did not know was that she was about to confer with a mass murderer of her people.

SS *Sturmbannführer* (Major) Hermann Höfle was, like his boss, an Austrian, and had also done prison time before the *Anschluss* for illegal Nazi activities. After joining Globocnik's staff in 1940, he became the SS and Police

Leader's advisor for Jewish Affairs (*Judenreferent*) and, in 1942, the manager of *Aktion* Reinhard. His main responsibility was to handle the logistics of moving the operation's victims from their homes or from ghettos to the killing centers and forced labor camps. He established transit ghettos where Jews from Poland and beyond were concentrated and selected for labor or death. He coordinated the ghetto clearance operations with local police and civilian authorities and deployed units of Trawniki men to carry them out. Not content to manage operations from his desk in Lublin, he supervised many of the operations in person. His elevation to Globocnik's chief of staff was recognition for his managerial skills in organizing the murder of over 1.5 million Jews in just seventeen months. At the time Skrzyński and Janina visited him, Höfle was preparing to clear the Białystok Ghetto of its last 30,000 inhabitants.[14]

The meeting went well. Höfle promised that the RGO could obtain lists with the names of detainees in the transit camps who could be released to the Polish care committees. He also invited Skrzyński to contact him personally on any matters involving police orders. The memorandum on their meeting does not note whether Höfle stood to greet Countess Suchodolska.[15]

The next day, just after Skrzyński set out on another tour of the Zamość region, a summons arrived for him from Höfle. Janina showed up in Skrzyński's stead at the appointed time the next morning. She explained Skrzyński's absence and suggested that Höfle meet the next day with Count Stanisław Łoś, who was in charge of resettling the expellees after their release. But Höfle was seeking immediate action, and he recognized that Janina was, like himself, the person who acted behind the scenes in her organization to get its work done. Since Globocnik had accepted Wendler's demand that civilian authorities take control of the expellees, the SS and police now wanted to close the transit camps as quickly as possible. Höfle informed Janina that the RGO was to take custody of all the women and children and all the men rated unfit for work who were still in the camps. He instructed her to contact the commandants of the transit camps "immediately" to determine the number of detainees to be released.[16]

Janina rushed back to her office and sent instructions to RGO officials in the Zamość region to contact the commandants of the three transit camps there. Then she set out for Majdanek. She was confident that Musielski would provide the numbers for Krochmalna but suspected that Florstedt would raise difficulties. Since Janina had authorization from Höfle, Florstedt was obliged at least to meet with her. She explained to the commandant that she was to obtain the number of women, children, and disabled expellees in Majdanek who were to be released, and she told him of Governor Wendler's promise that the RGO would be allowed to send workers into the transit camps to provide care for the expellees. Florstedt dismissed both demands as irrelevant for him. The expellees in Majdanek were not listed in the camp's registry because they were under the jurisdiction of the SS resettlement commission. If Janina wanted to have them released, she would have to get their names elsewhere and provide them to Florstedt along with an official order transferring each one to the RGO's custody. As for the governor's promise, Majdanek might be serving as a transit camp for expellees, but it was still a concentration camp, he informed her, and the only way he would allow RGO workers to enter it would be as prisoners.[17]

Janina was annoyed but not discouraged. Florstedt could make things difficult, but he could not prevent the release of the expellees in Majdanek, and she intended to make that happen as quickly as possible. She would just have to get their names from the resettlement commission, and with Höfle's backing, she knew she would succeed.

The next morning, August 5, the BuF held a conference at its office that was attended by Höfle, Janina, and Łoś and Dąbrowski of the Lublin Polish Care Committee. They all agreed on a plan to settle the expellees released from the transit camps in Lublin and Puławy counties. Janina made a plea for the immediate release of the expellees in Majdanek and presented information about their rising mortality rate in the camp. The resettlement commission would provide her the information and authorizations she needed, Höfle assured her.

After the conference ended but before Janina left the BuF, an official of the resettlement commission strutted into the office. To Janina's surprise, he flatly rejected her request for information about the expellees to be released from Majdanek. With a dismissive glance at the BuF chief, he asserted that no matter what assurances the RGO had received from civilian officials, he had the final say on the fate of the expellees. There would be no releases from Majdanek until the commission had finished examining the children, since it was certain that some had German blood and so should be united with their racial brethren in the Reich.

Janina felt almost amused by this puffed-up SS sergeant who thought he could thwart her mission. She informed him that it was SS and Police Leader Globocnik (said with slight emphasis) who ordered the release of expellees from Majdanek, and his chief of staff had just this hour assured her of full compliance from the resettlement commission. At her suggestion, the BuF chief offered to put the commission official through to Höfle so that he could explain why he was refusing to comply.

The official's tone changed. There were 3,600 Polish expellees eligible for release in Majdanek, he told Janina, but he lacked the personnel to prepare all the necessary paperwork for freeing them in the near future. Janina quickly assured him that the RGO would happily relieve him of the paperwork burden. They then agreed that the RGO would receive the names immediately and the expellees would be released in stages starting on August 9.

Janina also pressed for permission to establish an aid station in Lublin where the released expellees would receive food and vaccinations against contagious diseases before journeying to their new residences. This the resettlement official refused, insisting that those freed proceed immediately to their place of resettlement before the residents of Lublin could observe their condition and make contact with them. In the end, though, Janina won on this point as well, for a short time later the resettlement official visited her office in a more conciliatory mood. He approved the aid station and agreed that Janina could bring a Red Cross doctor and a few orderlies to Majdanek to deal with expellees who required immediate hospitalization. The resettlement official assured Janina that one car would be sufficient transport for that purpose.

A massive mobilization effort ensued to prepare for the release of the expellees in Majdanek. The Lublin Polish Care Committee established a rest station in a church on Betonowa Street near the train station where it and the Polish Red Cross would feed hundreds of people a day, provide them parcels for their journey, and administer medical care and vaccines.

The care committee also recruited escorts to take the expellees to the communities where they were to settle and obtained the tickets and passes for the journeys. The local care committee branches prepared to house, feed, and clothe the new arrivals, register them with authorities, and help them obtain work and ration cards. Individuals, organizations, and businesses volunteered help and donated money, food, clothing, diapers, and medicines. Janina was easily able to recruit typists in the city to help the care committee's clerks prepare release certificates for 3,600 people and the lists of those to be released on specific dates.

On August 9, 1943, Janina and a Polish Red Cross physician arrived at the Majdanek guardhouse at the gate to the "Black Road" that led to the protective custody camp. This was the point where she was to receive custody of the eight hundred expellees on the list she had submitted the day before. But when the SS resettlement commission official handed her back the list at the guardhouse, her heart sank: half the names were crossed off. The only reason he would give for the change was that those persons were "no longer available."

Then Janina waited, staring at the point where the Black Road dipped down to the right and disappeared around the corner between Field I and the bathing facility with the gas chambers. She had been informed that the expellees to be released that day would depart on foot from Field III. The August sun was blazing and her eyes stung from the dusty air. Finally, they began to appear on the road, thin, gray figures progressing slowly up the slope toward her. Some were walking, some were staggering, many were struggling to carry children or to hold up sick or elderly relatives. More and more fell or simply gave up and were now lying on the dust-covered stones of the recently paved road. Looking closely at the stones, it was possible to find some that bore Hebrew letters. Previously, they had marked the gravestones of Lublin's Jewish cemeteries.

When the people who reached the transfer point saw the SS resettlement official, they were afraid to speak to Janina and hesitated to follow her instructions because they did not trust that they were really being freed. Eventually, some told Janina in anguish of relatives who were supposed to accompany them but were too weak to walk out of Field III or had collapsed soon after leaving it.

The moment that Janina and all Lublin had anticipated with such hope had turned into a disaster. Janina realized that many of the expellees who managed to get to the transfer point would not be able to walk two kilometers farther to the rest station on Betonowa Street. The one ambulance the Red Cross had sent could not possibly ferry all the people who clearly required hospitalization. And what was to be done about all the people who could not reach the transfer point? Of one thing she was certain: they could not be left in the camp, not even for one more day. She pleaded with the SS resettlement official to allow transport into the protective custody camp to bring out the expellees from Field III. Such permission could only come from Majdanek's commandant, he informed her.

Janina dashed to camp headquarters and marched straight into the commandant's office, demanding to speak with Florstedt. When he appeared, she matter-of-factly informed him that she needed to use his telephone to call for transport that would bring the expellees unable to walk from Field III to the rest station. She would then need passes for herself, the Red Cross physician, and the transport drivers to go to Field III to collect the expellees. Enraged by the Countess's brazenness, Florstedt was on the verge of ordering her out of his office, but then he reconsidered. He realized that, if he refused the Countess, she would eventually get her way by appealing to Höfle. The commandant was counting on Globocnik to recommend him for promotion and had no desire to incur the wrath of his chief of staff.[18] Florstedt instructed his staff to put through Janina's telephone calls and to issue her passes for six people to enter the protective custody camp.

Janina called the Red Cross, the volunteer fire department, the Społem agricultural cooperative, the Kucharski soap factory, Sochacki Company, and estate owner Count Smorczewski. Within two hours, horse-drawn trucks, ambulances, and wagons were pulling up to the gate of Field III. Janina and the Red Cross physician were waiting there and entered the compound to find a scene of ghastly chaos. Based on the physician's hasty triage, Janina instructed the drivers which expellees to take to the rest station or hospital. Janina willed herself to focus entirely on the task at hand lest she be overwhelmed by the sight, sound, and smell of the starving, sick, and dying all around her. Only that night, after everything was done, did the images flood into her mind that would haunt her for years to come. Especially of the children, skin-covered skeletons who stared blankly out of sunken eyes, too weak even to cry.

Janina received custody of just 399 people that day. So that the other transfers would proceed more smoothly, she persuaded the SS resettlement official not to be present, promising to provide him a full report. On each of the following four days, the transfer of custody began with Janina receiving the list of people to be released, on which hundreds of names were crossed off.[19] Polish transports then proceeded to Field III to collect those too feeble to walk. Once the transfer was completed, Janina handed back the list and made her report.

In all, Janina received custody of 2,106 expellees out of the 3,600 whose release she had requested. The Red Cross physician sent 394 of them immediately to Lublin's hospitals. At the rest station, Red Cross personnel vaccinated expellees in the hope of protecting them from typhus and preventing them from spreading it, but little could be done about the lice that visibly crawled on their skin and in their hair. Some of the released expellees, desperate to stay with their families, hid their symptoms. Within a few days of their release, another 140 were sent to Lublin hospitals from nearby villages. Of the 534 expellees released from Majdanek who were treated in Lublin hospitals, 183 died, most from typhus, including 101 children aged twelve or younger. An unknown number of the released expellees died in their new communities, as did some of their neighbors, felled by the spreading typhus epidemic.

Janina took little comfort in the fact that her efforts had served to free more than 2,000 people from Majdanek, most of them women and children. What had happened to the nearly 1,500 whose names had been crossed off her lists? Janina again appealed to Höfle, who asked the resettlement commission for an accounting. It was just a clerical error, the commission replied. It presented a tally purporting to show that all the rest of the 8,566 expellees it had sent to Majdanek had been selected for labor, except for 186 who had died in the camp. Janina immediately recognized that the commission's tally left 54 people unaccounted for. She suspected that they had died after the commission gave her the names of the expellees to be released.[20]

While she was seeking the releases from Majdanek, Janina also hounded the Lublin Labor Office about the expellees in the Krochmalna Street transit camp, which the Labor Office controlled. Thousands of expellees continued to arrive at Krochmalna as the transit camps in the Zamość region shut down. Janina informed the Labor Office of Governor Wendler's personal promise that no more expellees would be sent to the Reich against their will. Therefore, she insisted, the Labor Office was obliged to provide the RGO a list of all the Polish expellees who were in the camp and to grant the Lublin Polish Care Committee's workers unfettered access to them to help them find homes and jobs. When the Labor Office balked at fulfilling these obligations, Janina appealed to the offices of the governor and the SS and Police Leader. Soon afterward, the Krochmalna Street transit camp released three hundred sick expellees to the Lublin Care Committee and issued it ten passes for its workers to speak with the remaining expellees in the camp.

Even though it could no longer send the expellees to the Reich against their will, the Labor Office could still assign the able-bodied to work involuntarily at labor sites within the General Government where they faced abuse, deprivation, and unsafe conditions. Only a valid labor card could exempt a Pole from such assignment, and so Janina sought to get as many labor cards as possible for Krochmalna's able-bodied detainees. She and her colleagues with access to the camp questioned detainees about their professions and past work experience and compiled lists that Janina sent to large employers such as Społem, the forestry department, the school superintendent, and the various chambers for agriculture, artisans, and medicine. The employers then sent representatives to the camp to claim specific detainees as their workers.

In the second half of August, there were so many expellees in Krochmalna that it was taking the Lublin Polish Care Committee up to six hours a day to distribute food to them all. Generally, the new arrivals had already been selected for labor, but the epidemics spreading in the crowded conditions quickly caused hundreds to be rated as unfit. By the end of the month, Janina had obtained the release into RGO care of 1,022 Poles from Krochmalna. Hundreds were admitted to Lublin's overflowing hospitals. In the infectious disease wards, two adults or three children had to be assigned to each bed.[21]

In all, Janina managed to secure the release into RGO care of 3,128 expellees taken captive by the Germans during the resettlement operation in the summer of 1943. That number represented less than 10 percent of the 36,389 people the SS resettlement commission reported seizing. The commission sent 29,214 to forced labor, mostly in the Reich. Altogether, between November 1942 and August 1943, the Germans seized or drove 100,000 Poles from three hundred villages in the Zamość region and replaced them with 14,000 settlers deemed to have German blood.[22]

Even after confirming that the transports from the transit camps were carrying children together with their relatives, Janina continued to gather information about the children being sent out of the district. She was able to get copies of transport lists from a woman working in the district labor office. Janina also directed women working for RGO branches at border stations to keep watch for the transports and report back about which ones left the General Government and in what direction. Her fears for the children were confirmed when she began to receive letters from frantic parents reporting that their children had been taken from them once they had crossed over into the Reich. After the war, Janina would provide Polish investigators a list of children between the ages of two and fourteen who had been taken in the resettlement operation and sent to the Reich on twenty-nine transports between July 7 and August 25, 1943. Janina believed that many of the children wound up in the special camps where abducted children were drilled into little Germans and beaten if they cried for their families or spoke in their native language. The total number of children on the list came to 4,454.[23]

TWELVE

RESCUE

By the end of August 1943, Lublin's main cemetery contained row upon row of freshly dug graves, each containing the body of a Zamość expellee whose release from Majdanek or Krochmalna had come too late. So many children died that the city ran out of coffins for them, and so some had been buried in bags.[1]

The plight of the deportees released from Majdanek made a deep impression upon the people of Lublin and strengthened the resolve of many to resist the German occupiers. The AK networks that Janina worked with to aid Majdanek prisoners were expanding as a consequence. They were now under the direction of Irena Antoszewska of the Central Underground Care (*Centralna Opieka Podziemia*), known as OPUS, the organization within the AK that aided imprisoned members and sought to organize resistance cells in the prisons and camps. The manager of a restaurant, Antoszewska served Germans in the front of the premises while her AK colleagues assembled packages in the back. She obtained the food for the packages by soliciting donations from estate owners in the countryside and collecting products that AK units looted from German supplies. Janina gave her a pass as an official supplier of the RGO so that she could justify to German inspectors why she was transporting large quantities of food from the countryside into the city.[2]

The OPUS relief network included Saturnina Malm, who was producing packages for Majdanek prisoners at night in her tenement building with the help of family and colleagues. They had to mail the packages, because Ludwik Christians, as head of the Lublin Polish Red Cross, forbade his organization to accept them for delivery. He feared that Majdanek officials would bar the Red Cross from delivering any packages if they discovered that some came from people who were not relatives of prisoners.[3] To avoid suspicion, each member of Malm's group carried the packages out in intervals, using the building's three exits, and delivered them to workers at the post office who could be trusted not to reveal the packages' true origin. Malm was also corresponding regularly with prisoners in Majdanek via AK colleagues working as electricians in the camp. They used a small house near the Old Airfield forced labor camp for Jews as a letter drop.

The risks Malm was taking were enormous, yet in late August 1943 she took on perhaps her greatest risk of all. As she was carrying correspondence to the letter drop, she came upon a large group of Jewish women under SS guard who were being force-marched from the Old Airfield camp's railroad siding to Majdanek. They were among the 11,000 Jews sent to Majdanek in August and September from the Białystok ghetto. Malm quickly walked away from the road to avoid the SS, then felt a sudden tug at her elbow. Turning, she saw a terrified fourteen-year-old girl with a pleading look in her eyes who had somehow slipped away from the group unseen. In a split-second decision, Malm took the girl in hand and ducked out of sight with her. Malm's husband, Mikołaj, helped her get the girl to their building, where they hid her in an attic. Regarding the tremendous danger his wife had placed them in, Mikołaj Malm said simply, "What will be, will be . . ."

The girl was Sara Roth, the only survivor of her family. She might have passed as a non-Jewish Pole, but she spoke little Polish and her Yiddish accent marked her as a Jew as soon as she opened her mouth. Malm gave her books in Polish to study in the attic during the day and then took her out behind the building in the evening to give her air and teach her how to pronounce the words she was reading. Sara was a quick study and before long could speak and write Polish fluently. With the help of an orphanage director, Malm was able to get Sara documents with the identity of a deceased Polish girl. Sara survived the rest of the war as Jadwiga Naremska.[4]

Janina's work for the RGO had come to feel like bailing water on a sinking ship. The Lublin Polish Care Committee lacked sufficient resources to support all the expellees released from Majdanek and Krochmalna whom it had settled in Lublin County. Meanwhile, Krochmalna continued to fill with thousands of Poles seized in anti-partisan operations, and the Labor Office was now insisting on immediately releasing all those rated unfit for labor to the care committee before it had a chance to find them places to live. The rest station on Betonowa Street was so crowded that people were having to stand throughout the night. Skrzyński and Janina had been trying for over a year to get approval for the care committee to set up a night shelter in Lublin, but they could get no response from city officials. In addition, Lublin's hospitals were so overcrowded that they were releasing the care committee's charges before they had fully recuperated, and the only place the committee had to put them was in a school. There were no beds in the building, so the patients slept on the floor. But now the school year was about to begin, and the city administration had ordered the committee to vacate the premises.[5]

Janina's efforts to aid Majdanek prisoners were also foundering. While Polish prisoners were receiving more packages, they were no longer allowed to write to their families except for returning the card acknowledging receipt of a package. The camp's authorities were also curtailing the RGO's delivery of bread and products for soup. And yet, the SS and police were stepping up their raids in Lublin County, seizing Poles off the streets and out of public transit and sending them to Majdanek. Hostage taking was also on the rise. The Order Police, the uniformed branch of the German police, ran a special camp for hostages in part of Majdanek's Field IV, and its population swelled to nearly a thousand by early September. They were primarily Poles seized as collective punishment for communities that failed to meet the agricultural quota or in order to deter assistance to partisans. By regulation, hostages were supposed to be men between the ages of seventeen and forty. Only one man in a family was to be held as a hostage, and hostages were to be released after four weeks. In reality, whole families were sometimes detained as hostages, and the length of detention at Majdanek was more likely to be four months than four weeks. Although the hostages were not forced to work in the camp, starvation and disease still took their toll, and the majority of hostages died before release or shortly afterward.[6]

Still, Janina drew hope from the new power dynamic in Lublin District and resolved to take advantage of it while it lasted. Unlike Globocnik, the new SS and Police Leader, Jakob Sporrenberg, seemed inclined to cooperate with civilian authorities and to respect Governor Wendler's decrees. Given the governor's role in freeing the Zamość expellees, Janina decided to seek his aid in securing other releases and in forcing civilian officials to address the pressing needs of the Lublin Polish Care Committee. Skrzyński was now spending most of his time in the eastern and southern counties of Lublin District, so Janina was handling the work that was based in Lublin County, including most communications with German authorities there.[7] She lacked the status to approach the governor's office directly, however. So she called in Prince Woroniecki from Kraków.

Woroniecki contacted Wendler, who ordered the chief of his administration, Ernst Schlüter, to ascertain the RGO's concerns and determine what could be done to address them. When Woroniecki and Janina met with Schlüter on September 2, the Prince turned the meeting over to her. Impressed by the Countess's presentation regarding Polish civilians at Majdanek, Schlüter immediately contacted the camp administration about releasing all hostages detained there against the regulations, as well as all persons seized in raids who were not suspected of illegal acts. That same day, Majdanek released three hundred hostages. Then, in a triumph for Janina, Schlüter asked her to return the following week to discuss the situation of the expellees who were being settled in Lublin County. As they walked out of the meeting, Woroniecki congratulated Janina on its outcome. She now had a direct line to the governor's office, and she intended to make the most of it.

At the start of her meeting with Schlüter on September 8, Janina informed him that, despite his instructions to Majdanek authorities, many hundreds of Poles were still being held there as hostages or as victims of raids. Her statement had its intended effect, for Schlüter immediately called

Majdanek, this time with even better results: 1,400 Poles were released from the camp that day and 400 the next. At Janina's request, Schlüter also instructed Majdanek officials to return the belongings of the expellees who had been released and to give the belongings of those who had died to the Lublin Polish Care Committee.

Then Janina presented facts and figures about the needs of the expellees, about the hundreds who had died and the hundreds who were still overwhelming Lublin's hospitals. She informed Schlüter that the Labor Office was dumping the Poles at Krochmalna rated unfit for work onto the Lublin Polish Care Committee without any provision for housing or feeding them. In light of this situation, she requested his support in persuading civilian authorities to allocate space and furnishings to the care committee so that it could establish a shelter and a convalescent hospital. As in all her dealings with German officials, Janina framed her requests as matters that the Germans would care about—for example, as prophylactic health measures rather than humanitarian assistance to Poles—and emphasized how it was in the Germans' own interests to grant them.

Schlüter found Countess Suchodolska to be most persuasive and sympathetic. He promised that he would order the Building Office to allocate space for a night shelter and that he would look into the possibility of establishing a convalescent home. Then he made another phone call, this one to the chief of the Labor Office, whom he ordered to come to an arrangement with the Countess that would ensure proper care for the Poles in Krochmalna who were unfit for work.

Finally, Janina brought up the difficulties she was encountering in getting the special IDs and train passes that the care committees' personnel required to perform their work. Schlüter invited Janina to submit a list of the care committee personnel who needed the IDs and passes and promised that he would personally issue them. Janina made sure that many of the people on that list were her colleagues in the Underground.

Immediately after the meeting, the chief of the Labor Office contacted Janina, and within two days they had worked out an agreement regarding Poles in Krochmalna who were rated unfit for labor. They would remain in the camp until the Lublin Polish Care Committee arranged shelter for them, during which time the care committee would have complete access to them at any time and could take them out of the camp temporarily for medical treatment and appointments with officials. Until their release, they would be fed by the camp with support from the care committee. Having learned her lesson during the release of the expellees from Majdanek, Janina also negotiated for transportation for the deportees once they were released from Krochmalna.[8]

Janina's appeal to Schlüter for space to establish a convalescent home also succeeded. On September 15, the district administration allocated to the Lublin Polish Care Committee part of a building that it could use to house expellees released from the hospital but still too weak to travel to their new homes. The Polish Red Cross provided the personnel and administered the facility under the supervision of care committee medical officers.[9]

As the settlement of the released expellees from the Zamość region progressed, a new emergency confronted Skrzyński and Janina. Polish refugees were fleeing into Lublin District from the multiethnic former Polish territory of Volhynia (Wołyń), which was just to the east of the district and outside the General Government's borders. The region had become a battle zone. In response to increasing attacks from Polish, Ukrainian, and Soviet-backed partisans, the Germans were conducting pacification operations with their usual brutality. Simultaneously, inspired by the changing tide of the war on the Eastern Front, Ukrainian nationalists were conducting their own ethnic cleansing campaign against the Poles so that Ukraine could claim sovereignty over the region at the war's end. Units of the Ukrainian Insurgent Army (UPA) were destroying Polish villages and massacring their residents by the thousands in order to drive all other Poles out of the region. Polish partisans were attacking Ukrainian villages in retaliation.[10]

The Security Police were rounding up the refugees and placing them in transit camps along with Poles seized in pacification operations. Once the usual selection of the able-bodied for work in the Reich was completed, the question remained of what to do with those not fit for labor. The Security Police decreed that they should return to Volhynia, but the RGO denounced that policy as tantamount to sentencing the refugees to death. The Security

Police then proposed to place them in concentration camps. After urgent lobbying efforts by the RGO, the General Government administration in Kraków finally settled the matter. None of the Volhynian refugees would be sent to work in the Reich against their will, and only those suspected of ties with the resistance would remain under Security Police jurisdiction. All the rest were to be cared for by the RGO, which would be responsible for settling them within the General Government.[11]

Janina soon learned that, German promises to the contrary, Poles from Volhynia were still being sent to the Reich against their will. In Volhynia, the Germans encouraged frantic Polish civilians who had seen their homes burned and their loved ones slaughtered to sign up for transports that would take them to safety in the General Government, where they would be cared for by the RGO. Instead, healthy young adults who signed up for the transports discovered that they had been registered as volunteers for labor in the Reich. In addition, the Germans continued to conduct raids to seize laborers in Volhynia, and as a result many transports carried people who had not volunteered to go the General Government.[12] Determined to prevent as many as she could from becoming forced laborers in Germany, Janina devised a multifaceted rescue operation.

The RGO's vastly expanded responsibilities in Lublin District required it to recruit more personnel. Thanks to Janina, many of the new hires were members of the Underground. She assigned some of them to provide food and emergency supplies to the refugees when their transports crossed into Lublin District from Volhynia. When Janina received official notice of an incoming rail transport, she alerted the local care committee to set up a care station at the crossing point. The care station workers handed packages of food, clothes, and diapers to the refugees, many of whom had fled with just the clothes on their backs. The committees also set up field kitchens to serve soup to the refugees and guards during longer stopovers. While providing these services, Janina's Underground employees interviewed the refugees to determine whether any were being transported against their will. The same was done by the care committee members working in the temporary transit camps. The information was passed to Janina.

Sometimes Janina could use her official contacts to rescue Volhynians seized for labor. At others, she had to resort to clandestine means. Her Underground employees used various strategies to help individual refugees slip away from a transport or transit camp. These included bribing guards, smuggling people out on the carts that carried vats of soup, or supplying workmen's clothes so they could blend in with other workers as they left the camp. Far more daring and dangerous was the strategy used to rescue groups of involuntary refugees. Railway workers in the Underground would attach an empty car to the rear of a transport train and direct the passengers to be rescued to transfer to it. Then, at that station or the next, the car was uncoupled. When the train left, the car remained, and members of the Underground helped the passengers escape, often to join AK units in the area.[13]

Her Volhynian rescue operation soon put Janina in grave peril. As a result of her official interventions, the Germans realized that she was receiving specific information about Poles from Volhynia who had been designated for forced labor in the Reich. They also did not fail to notice that some of those persons were disappearing en route. Janina received a threatening letter from Governor Wendler. His officials had informed him that care committees under Janina's supervision were obstructing the orderly evacuation of people from the Eastern territory and persuading volunteers not to go on to Germany but to escape from the transports. He was therefore making her personally responsible for every act of sabotage and escape. He ordered her to send a copy of his letter immediately to all the Polish care committees in Lublin District along with her own instructions to confine their assistance to Volhynian refugees strictly to distributing food and clothes. Any other activity, the letter threatened, would be considered sabotage and subject every member of the committee to arrest.

Wendler's threats frightened Janina. Continuing her rescue efforts would endanger not only herself and her workers but potentially also the RGO's entire program of aiding the refugees. Abandoning her efforts and allowing Poles to be abducted to the Reich was not an option, however. She decided to comply with the letter of Wendler's orders but not with their spirit. She sent Wendler's letter to the care committees along with her own directive to refrain from any activity other than the provision of food and clothes. The dispatch of both the letter and the instructions was logged in her records and the copies were placed in the files of her office and of the committees. She made one exception, however. She did not send the letter and directive to the care committee of the city of Lublin, because she knew its leaders were meek enough to obey them. Then, she sent couriers to all the other care committees in Lublin District with instructions to ignore the letters and carry on as before. Henceforth, however, she decided that only members of the Underground would perform illegal activities so as not to endanger ordinary committee workers. And so, the escapes continued and the fugitives, supplied with false identity cards, disappeared.

The destination of many of the Volhynian transports was the Kroch-malna Street transit camp. The Lublin Polish Care Committee had responsibility for registering the refugees in the camp and provided physicians to ascertain the health status of all the detainees. The director of the care committee's aid to Krochmalna, Józefa Olbrycht, was also Janina's partner in the Volhynian rescue operation. Olbrycht instructed the AK members working under her in the camp to suggest to healthy detainees that they report certain symptoms to the physicians hired by the care committee. Consequently, a surprisingly large proportion of the young adults in the camp were being diagnosed with illnesses that precluded their assignment to forced labor.[14]

Officials of the BuF resented that Janina had circumvented their authority to get the support of Wendler's office for RGO initiatives. Her activities with the Volhynian refugees only deepened their anger and distrust. This was especially true of the director of the BuF office of Lublin city. Irmgard Villnow despised Poles in general and Countess Suchodolska in particular, whom she viewed as meddling in matters that came under Villnow's jurisdiction. One evening in October 1943, Villnow raided the offices of Janina and the Lublin Care Committee on Lubartowska Street. Somehow, she knew to go directly to Olbrycht's desk, where she found a list of Volhynian refugees who had been interviewed in the temporary transit camps. She absconded with the list and the correspondence log of the care committee for Lublin city.

The next morning, the head of the district BuF office ordered Janina, Christians, and Stanisław Kalinowski, counselor to the city care committee, to appear in his office at noon sharp. Seeing Villnow there, Janina knew she was in trouble, for she had learned of Villnow's raid on the care committee offices from the building's porter, fellow AK member Józef Wendrucha.

"Why are you sabotaging the orders of the German authorities and why have you not circularized our letter to all the care committees in the district?" Villnow demanded.

"But I *did* send that letter," Janina protested. "You need only check all the logs for proof that I did!"

Then Villnow, confident that she was about to destroy Janina, triumphantly produced the log of the Lublin city care committee as evidence that Janina had not sent it the letter. Next, Villnow presented the list she had taken from Olbrycht's desk and demonstrated that it contained names of people who had crossed into Lublin District from Volhynia but had not been registered at Krochmalna. She accused Janina of arranging for the unregistered persons to escape and insisted that she must have had the help of the Lublin Polish Care Committee and the Polish Red Cross.

The district BuF chief, Fritsche, began to shout at the three of them that they had committed treason and would be turned over to the Gestapo for prosecution. He continued with a tirade about German casualties and charged that "It is people like you three who are responsible for the bombardment of German cities!"

The two men were even more frightened than Janina. She had told them nothing about the Volhynian rescue operation, even though Christians also worked for the Underground. They both turned on her, demanding to know whether there was in fact an "Operation Volhynia" and insisting that if there were, then only she could be held responsible for it. "My colleagues, collaborating to get a confession from me!" Janina thought in dismay. But she managed to appear outwardly calm while she frantically searched for a plausible explanation.

"Yes," she responded evenly, "I direct the operation to assist Volhynians, but I do so in complete accordance with German regulations. The list that Frau Villnow found in our office is from September, before the Lublin Polish Care Committee was required to register the refugees, and some of those on the list undoubtedly departed before the registration was conducted.

Furthermore, not all the refugees who receive RGO care at the border are sent to Krochmalna. Obviously, the Lublin Care Committee could not register refugees who were no longer at the camp, much less those who never passed through it."

Then, with a touch of indignation and a slightly raised voice, Janina repeated that there was ample proof that she had circulated the German letter to every county care committee in the district.[15]

"Why not to the Lublin city committee?" her colleagues demanded.

"Frau Villnow has insisted that since she is the supervisor of the city care committee, I am not to give it orders. I therefore assumed that she would send the letter and an accompanying directive to the city committee. I followed the order I received exactly by sending the governor's letter to the county committees along with my own directive that the governor's orders be obeyed. If I was supposed to send it to the city committee as well, then the most I can be accused of is negligence, but no more so than Frau Villnow."

Fritsche, who had picked up the telephone receiver to call the Gestapo, put it back in its cradle. He ordered everyone but Janina to leave his office, as he had instructions for her that did not concern them. Once the others left, he continued in a mild tone.

"Well, we all forget things sometimes. Why not send out your recommendations when you get back to your office?"

"I certainly shall," Janina replied, "but Frau Villnow must do so, too, so that mine will follow hers."

Janina then expressed with apparent sincerity her appreciation for all the Germans were doing to save Poles in Volhynia from being murdered by Bolshevik and Ukrainian bandits. She regretted that the Poles sometimes misunderstood their German rescuers' intentions.

Upon leaving Fritsche's office, Janina found her two colleagues waiting for her, looking pale and shaken. Both attorneys, they congratulated her for conducting her defense "like the best lawyer."

"I had to," Janina replied dryly, "when my two would-be counselors, one the president of the Bar Association, were ready to sell me to the enemy!" She thought of the many other occasions she had experienced during the war when a woman had kept her head while the men around her lost theirs.

That evening, Wendrucha called on her at home. He asked her to go into the courtyard behind her building, where she found some young men who had escaped from a transport from Cumań (Tsuman) in Volhynia. There were about 450 persons on the transport, they explained, mostly young, strong single men and women. They had been told that they were being brought to the General Government to be given over to the RGO, but after they arrived at the Lublin station, they learned that they were about to be sent to Germany.

Janina was determined to help them but, considering Wendler's letter and her narrow escape that morning, decided to go through official channels. Realizing her odds of success would be stronger if no one were missing from the transport, she asked the young men to return to it.

"I give you my word as a Polish woman," she assured them, "that you will be freed along with all the others."

They accepted her word and returned.

After a sleepless night of worry that she would not be able to keep her word, Janina went to see the Labor Office official responsible for Krochmalna. Despite the Nazi Party badge he always proudly displayed on his lapel, Herr Geissler had often proved to be accommodating. Upon entering his office, Janina immediately demanded to know why an entire transport of people who had not volunteered for work in Germany was about to depart for the Reich. Forgetting to maintain her usual composed demeanor, she complained in a raised voice, "These people were told they were to be handed over to our committee. I talked to them at the station and have promised to take them under our care. If you won't release them, I'll go to Kraków and intervene with your top authority. After all, the decree against forced labor for Volhynians came from the governor general himself!"

She counted on Geissler's failure to recognize that technically she did not have authority to intervene for the persons in the transport, because they came from outside the General Government. She had ceased to be surprised at how little many German officials knew about the regulations they were supposed to enforce, probably because they had no background in government administration. Geissler, for example, had been a pharmacist in Germany before becoming an important official in Poland.

Angered by Janina's tone, Geissler ordered her to return to her office. An hour later, she received a call from her assistant, Janina Wójcikowa, who was working at Krochmalna. She reported that all the freight cars had been emptied and the whole Cumań transport was there in the camp. Then Geissler called Janina and ordered her to remain in her office to receive a visit from pertinent officials who would explain the situation to her. Uneasy about these "pertinent officials" and their "explanation," Janina decided she should have someone she trusted nearby and so called Wójcikowa back to the office. Hours passed, and when it was time for the office to close, Geissler called again, telling her to stay there. Wendrucha decided to remain at his post so that he could see who came for Janina.

Wójcikowa paced the floor nervously, worried that the longer the delay, the less likely Janina's visitors were coming merely to make explanations. Back and forth to the window she paced; then, while looking out it, she suddenly gasped.

"A car with two Gestapo officers—just at our building—just getting out of the car. My God, did you *have* to interfere?"

"I'm sorry," Janina replied quietly, "I *had* to, after those men went back to the transport because I promised to free them all."

So they waited for the steps in the hall. They seemed to take so long coming. Wendrucha slipped out and down the back stairs, then returned in a flash with the news that the officers had gone into the next building and had merely parked the car outside theirs!

Night fell and still they waited. They turned out all the lights except in Janina's office, and Wójcikowa sat in the dark room next to it, leaving the door open so she could see who came and hear what was said. Finally, two cars stopped outside the building and three men emerged, one of them Geissler. When they reached Janina's office, they found her busily writing a memo and referring to a file.

"Working late?" Geissler asked.

"Didn't you ask me to wait for you?" she replied with a shrug. "No use wasting time, there's plenty of work here." She knew better than to show anxiety to German officials.

"You're coming with us to the camp now," Geissler said.

"Fine," Janina answered. As they left, she directed a furtive glance toward the next room.

Geissler took Janina in his car while the two men traveled in the other. They arrived at Krochmalna, where Commandant Musielski was waiting to receive them. Geissler told him of Janina's claim that the people in the Cumań transport had not volunteered for labor in the Reich, which Musielski denied. Apparently, the people had been frightened into agreeing that they had volunteered. Janina asked that she be allowed to talk with them. Since Musielski knew Polish, Geissler agreed.

So the announcement went over the megaphone that all from Cumań should come to the yard because the RGO was there. Once they had assembled, Janina addressed them.

"I know that you were taken by force, and I promise you, on the honor of the RGO, that nothing will happen to you if you tell the truth. Did you, or did you not apply to work for the Germans?"

Her urgent question was answered by silence. She repeated it, and after another short silence, a few people came forward and anxiously stated, "They said that in the General Government they would hand us over to the RGO. That's why we went to register with them."

Janina turned to Geissler. "So that's the way it was, you see."

Taking Janina to the camp office, Geissler declared he would hand over all the families to RGO care, but only the sick ones among the single youths.

Stubbornly, Janina asserted, "If you don't give them all to me, I'll go to Kraków about it. Every single one."

He yielded, but only if she would take them immediately. She suspected he thought that would be impossible, but she agreed, certain that she could get Społem's transport manager, Piotr Kosiba, to send trucks, as he had when the expellees were released from Majdanek.

As she exited the camp to arrange the transportation, Janina encountered Wójcikowa, who was wiping tears from her eyes. She had followed

Janina in a cab and burst out crying with relief when she saw that the two cars were going to Krochmalna, not to the Gestapo.

Społem promised to send sufficient trucks by 1:00 a.m. Janina returned to the Volhynians and told them to be ready to leave with the committee that night. "I told you, we keep our promises!" They wept with relief, and she trembled at the thought of how close she had come to breaking her promise. The RGO later settled the group in a village fourteen miles from Lublin.

Despite her success in freeing the transport, Janina was thoroughly upset with herself. She realized that, in her worry and exhaustion, her intuition had failed her, causing her to misread Geissler. Her tone and behavior with him had escalated the situation into a confrontation that might easily have led to her arrest. It was good that she had learned how to prevent fear from paralyzing her, but she had also been trained that intelligence agents must sharply observe the enemy's moves, discern their promise and their threat, and tailor their own actions in response. She must never make assumptions about the future based on past success, for no two situations were alike and every action involved a unique set of risks. She must calculate those risks as precisely as possible to determine the probability of success and then weigh whether what was to be gained was worth the price of failure. Especially now, when she was on the verge of achieving her mission to feed all of Majdanek's prisoners.

THIRTEEN

SOUP WITH A SIDE OF HOPE

In mid-September 1943, Hermann Florstedt thought he had actually pulled it off. In the ten months since he became Majdanek's commandant, he had overseen the completion of most of the planned construction projects. The camp had new workshops and warehouses that employed prisoners in a variety of jobs, including producing furniture and uniforms for the SS and repairing hundreds of thousands of shoes reaped from *Aktion* Reinhard. A new crematorium with five coke-burning ovens was rising behind the protective custody camp. At last, the prisoner compounds had been connected to the municipal sewer system, and the prisoner barracks were gradually acquiring lavatories with running water. Globocnik had given him a glowing recommendation, asserting that Florstedt had been "extraordinarily valuable" to him and praising his success in remedying the "intolerable conditions" at Majdanek.[1]

Florstedt's crowning moment had come on September 7, when he attended a conference with top SS officials in Berlin. There he learned that all of Globocnik's forced labor camps for Jews were about to become subcamps of Majdanek. Florstedt was to command at least eleven camps in the General Government with well over 50,000 prisoners, the vast majority of them Jews. Along with this change would come his promotion to SS-*Standartenführer* (Colonel).[2]

But it was not to be. One of the "intolerable conditions" Florstedt had failed to remedy was the high mortality rate among Majdanek's registered prisoners, who did not include Jews sent there to be killed on arrival. An SS study presented to Himmler in September revealed that Majdanek was the only concentration camp where the mortality rate rose in August, to 7.67 percent for men and 4.41 percent for women. A male prisoner was ten times more likely to die at Majdanek than at Dachau. Auschwitz had the second highest mortality rate: 3.61 percent for its registered women prisoners.[3]

Even more worrisome to Florstedt was the revived SS investigation of Koch, his mentor at Buchenwald and Majdanek's first commandant. The SS investigators were now looking into corruption at both camps. Before they visited Majdanek in mid-1943, Florstedt had the prisoners murdered who worked in the *Effektenkammer*, the warehouses where all the belongings of incoming Jews and prisoners were sorted and searched for valuables. Florstedt's minions overlooked one of the prisoners, however, who was in the infirmary and survived to testify. The investigators learned that Koch and members of his staff routinely filched jewelry, money, and luxury items from the *Effektenkammer* and that the practice had continued under Florstedt. During the transports to Majdanek of thousands of Jews in spring 1943, the investigators heard, Florstedt held regular scavenger hunts in the "rose garden" following selections. Turning over the dirt with spades, he and his top henchmen found jewelry, gems, and gold currency buried there by the waiting Jews to hide them from the SS. Stealing the loot from the victims was not a crime, but pocketing it was.[4]

Koch and his wife, Ilse, were arrested on August 24, 1943. One month later, Florstedt was recalled to Germany for questioning, then officially arrested on October 20. Koch was tried, sentenced to death, and executed on April 15, 1945. Florstedt was still in prison in March 1945, but his fate after that remains a mystery.[5]

In Florstedt's absence, the routine for delivering packages and food products for Majdanek prisoners changed. The camp SS finally agreed that it would be more efficient if, instead of leaving everything at the camp headquarters, Jurek, the Red Cross driver, took the packages directly to the post office, which was next to the protective custody camp, and delivered the bread and the products for soup to the food warehouses, which were across from the entry to Field I. Unbeknownst to Christians, Jurek was now picking up the packages being prepared by OPUS, the AK prisoner aid organization, and delivering them with the packages from the Red Cross and the Lublin Polish Care Committee. The increasing number of packages from all three sources required a change to twice-weekly deliveries, on Tuesdays and Fridays, in addition to the delivery of RGO bread and soup products on Saturdays. During his deliveries, Jurek communicated covertly with the prisoners working in the post office and at the warehouses. He also smuggled messages with such regularity that the prisoners nicknamed him "the postman."[6]

When Janina accompanied Jurek on the Saturday deliveries, she could only get as far as the gate to the protective custody camp, where she turned in the record of the delivery and received the receipt. While she waited for Jurek to return, she would try to converse with the SS men who pulled duty there and so get to know which ones were friendly or at least willing to accept "gifts." Some would have nothing to do with her, but two of the regulars, the Polish ethnic Germans Alfred Bajerke and Alfred Hoffmann, proved quite approachable. She had also developed a good rapport with another Polish ethnic German who worked in the camp headquarters, SS Sergeant Wilhelm Karl Petrak.[7]

Janina was now able to witness some of the cruelty and suffering at Majdanek that she had heard about from released prisoners. From her post at the camp gate, she observed prisoner work squads going to and from labor outside Majdanek. They marched in rows under the guard of armed SS men and dog handlers and to the shouts and blows of kapos. The Jewish prisoners mostly wore the striped concentration camp uniform, but many of the non-Jews wore ill-fitting civilian clothes painted with the letters "KL" (for *Konzentrationslager*) in red. Seeing their gaunt and wounded frames, Janina wondered how they could possibly perform hard manual labor for eleven hours a day or more, six days a week.

One day, she watched a returning labor squad as it filed through the gate. They were required to stand at military attention as they waited to pass through, but one elderly prisoner was visibly drooping. Suddenly, an SS guard emerged from the sentry box and, in full view of Janina, kicked the prisoner and hit him so hard in the face with a truncheon that blood went flying. Taking evident pleasure in Janina's horrified expression, the guard sneered at her, "They don't know what discipline is. That's why we finish them off in less than twenty days!" Then he returned to the sentry box and took a swig from a bottle.

The guard may have hoped to frighten Janina, but, four years into the war, she had seen too much violence to be so easily shaken. It only strengthened her resolve to fight back by saving as many lives as she could.

When she learned of Florstedt's absence, Janina saw a potential opening for overcoming his officials' obstruction of the RGO's assistance to Majdanek prisoners. She persuaded Petrak to help her bring the matter of prisoner correspondence to the attention of the acting commandant, Martin Melzer, who was the commander of Majdanek's SS Death's Head Guard Battalion. Her approach succeeded: Melzer authorized her to make regular deliveries of postcards for distribution to the prisoners.

Janina personally brought 6,000 postcards to Majdanek, rejoicing that the Polish prisoners would finally be in contact with their families. Then she had her first run-in with the commander of the protective custody camp, SS Lieutenant Anton Thumann. His very name struck fear in the hearts of the SS guards as well as the prisoners, for he was a foul-tempered drunk who took sadistic pleasure in torturing prisoners with his whip, truncheon, and vicious dog, Boris. Thumann's motto was that prisoners who survived longer than three months at Majdanek were thieves and vermin that deserved to be exterminated. Florstedt had given him free rein in running the protective custody camp, and he did not see why that should cease under an interim commandant who had never run a concentration camp. When Janina tried to deliver the postcards, Thumann refused to accept them.[8]

Thumann probably assumed that the matter was closed, but he was about to learn that no issue with Countess Suchodolska was finally resolved until it was resolved to her satisfaction. She appealed to Melzer, and in the end, Thumann was obliged to take the cards from her. Accepting them was not the same as agreeing to distribute them, however. OPUS soon received a smuggled message reporting that the prisoners were still not allowed to write to their families.

Another smuggled message at the end of September 1943 reported that typhus was on the rise again in the camp, and tuberculosis was spreading as well. Although many more packages were reaching the prisoners, much of their contents continued to be plundered by the SS and kapos. Starvation was amplifying the toll of the epidemics, and mortality in the infirmaries had risen 50 percent.[9]

This was crushing news. It seemed to Janina that she had accomplished almost nothing in the seven months that she had been overseeing the aid program at Majdanek. It was time to escalate matters, she resolved. She would appeal to Lublin District authorities about Majdanek officials' failure to uphold the agreements regarding prisoners' correspondence and the delivery of packages, food, and medicines to the camp. This time, she planned to press for even more than what had previously been agreed. She had not given up on her plan for providing prepared soup to Majdanek prisoners. The epidemics at Majdanek, she realized, provided her a basis to argue that providing nourishing soup for at least the sick prisoners was in the Germans' interest. She consulted Łopatyńska, head of the Lublin Polish Care Committee's Nutrition and Care Department, who conceived a plan for how the care committee could prepare the soup in its kitchens in addition to all the other food it was serving to the needy. Figuring out how to deliver it would be up to Janina.[10]

So Janina paid another visit to the district medical superintendent. He did not question her report of epidemics at Majdanek and saw the sense in her proposal to provide not only typhus serum to the camp but also a special diet for sick prisoners. At his direction, she went to see Blancke.

Janina's meeting with Majdanek's chief physician followed the usual pattern. Blancke called Janina a nuisance, reminded her that Majdanek was a concentration camp, not a sanatorium, and then accepted her offer of typhus serum. When she proposed providing soup for the sick prisoners, though, he scoffed. For that she would need the commandant's permission, which Blancke clearly doubted she would get. To her surprise, however, Blancke authorized her to speak with a prisoner physician, Dr. Nowak, regarding the camp infirmaries' needs for medicines and supplies.

The news that Janina was going to speak with a prisoner named Dr. Nowak caused some excitement among her OPUS colleagues, because Malm had been corresponding for more than a year with a Dr. Jan Nowak, a member of the Underground imprisoned at Majdanek. Jan Nowak is a common Polish name, however, and there was at least one other Dr. Nowak at Majdanek. In the hope of determining whether the doctor she spoke with was Malm's correspondent, Janina tore a two-złoty note in half and had one of the pieces smuggled to him.

On the day of her appointment to speak with Dr. Nowak, Janina received strict instructions at camp headquarters: no physical contact with prisoners was permitted, and she must confine the conversation strictly to the purpose of her visit. Then she was driven to the guard booth just outside Field V, where the men's infirmary had recently moved. She immediately noticed a pathetically thin but bright-eyed Jewish boy about ten or twelve years old standing by the compound gate. His green armband identified him as one of the "runners," usually Jewish boys put to work as couriers in the men's fields. Between their courier runs they had to stand all day in every kind of weather in a small area between the barbed wire fences next to the gate. After Janina showed her pass to the SS guard, he ordered the boy to fetch Dr. Nowak.

Janina chatted pleasantly with the guard while she waited. In time, the boy reappeared with a prisoner who gave his name, Nowak, and his prisoner number. Janina nodded to him, smiling warmly, then looked at the boy with a raised eyebrow. "Izio," he whispered, which in Polish may be a diminutive for Izaak, Izrael, or Izydor. As Janina turned back to Nowak, she felt something brush her coat and then saw Izio scamper back to his post. As she and the doctor spoke, she casually reached inside her coat pocket and felt a torn bill, the other half of the two-złoty note.

In addition to enlisting the aid of the district medical superintendent, Janina sent an appeal to the new Security Police chief, Karl Pütz. She informed him that Majdanek officials were failing to comply with the directives of his predecessor, Müller, authorizing the RGO to feed Majdanek's Polish prisoners and permitting the prisoners to write to their families.[11] Not long after she submitted her appeal, Janina received a summons from Majdanek's interim commandant to meet with him at the camp on October 15.

Janina assumed that Melzer had heard from Pütz, but she did not know what instructions the latter had given. Her repeated interventions about conditions at Majdanek had made it clear that she was somehow receiving information that the Germans considered to be top secret. Every time she went to Majdanek, Janina was keenly aware that the SS might not allow her to leave because of suspicion that she was connected to the Underground or, even worse, that she was not who she claimed to be. So before setting out for Majdanek on October 15, she gave her keys as usual to Wójcikowa along with instructions on what to do should she not return. She also generally took an RGO employee with her to Majdanek who could report back if she were arrested. On this day, she took the office interpreter, who in fact was a priest from Poznań who had taken refuge in Lublin after being released from Dachau. Sensitive to what Father Juliusz Winiewski had suffered there, Janina had him wait for her in a cab outside the Majdanek headquarters gate.

Relatively speaking, the meeting began almost cordially. Melzer directed Janina to sit and present her business. Starting with the issue she thought most likely to meet with success, she informed Melzer that his order authorizing the prisoners to send postcards to their families was being ignored. Melzer called Thumann and the SS official in charge of the post office into the meeting. In no uncertain terms, the commandant ordered that the postcards Janina had brought be distributed immediately to the Polish prisoners along with an announcement that they were permitted to write to their families twice a month. He instructed Janina to bring a new set of cards to the camp in three weeks.

Janina moved on to her next issue: the packages being delivered by the Red Cross were not arriving to the addressees intact. The postal director protested that this was not his fault. His office was fulfilling its duty by forwarding all parcels to the compounds in which the addressees were held. This answer did not satisfy Melzer, who ordered the postal director to ensure that packages reached their addressees. Finally, Janina presented her offer to provide prepared soup for the patients in the prisoner infirmaries, framing it not as a new request but as conforming to the spirit of what had already been granted. Melzer's manner immediately turned brusque.

"This is a concentration camp," he lectured her, "and the only camp that permits outsiders to feed the prisoners. To grant further privileges here would be an injustice to the prisoners in the other camps, and justice, order, and discipline are the principles that guide *all* actions by the SS. The inmates here constitute an element hostile to German authority, rebels and bandits who would be sentenced to death by any court! Yet here, they are being held in protective custody, which you must surely recognize is better than prison. And whenever prisoners are found to be innocent, they are immediately released. You do know this, do you not?"

"No," Janina replied, "I am unfamiliar with the details of concentration camp administration. I only know that the inmates here are not free and that, since this concentration camp is in the General Government, my institution is obligated to provide for the Polish prisoners, just as it does for the inmates of prisons. I am simply proposing to feed the sick with an additional item, which hardly seems like an excessive privilege, and surely it is in the interests of SS authorities. After all, the district medical superintendent has endorsed the proposal."

Melzer ordered her to go wait in the reception area. After a long while, she saw Blancke enter the commandant's office. Then there was another long wait, during which she became increasingly gloomier about her prospects for success. The guard on duty even remarked that the commandant might have forgotten about her. Finally, she was called back in.

Melzer's first question revived Janina's hope: "How do you propose to deliver the soup?"

"The Lublin Polish Care Committee can make the soup in its twenty-four kitchens and transport it here on trucks," she replied. "If the trucks take the soup directly to the compounds with infirmaries, then the camp routine will not be disturbed."

Melzer handed Janina a document that he instructed her to read and sign. It was a formal agreement setting out the conditions for the RGO to deliver soup twice a week for 830 sick Polish prisoners, as well as other food products recommended by the Lublin Care Committee's physician. The agreement specified that Janina bore sole responsibility for the deliveries, which were to be made by her in person or by one other whom she could designate. She was to provide a list of the contents of each delivery to the guard at the camp gate, the commandant's office, and to Blancke or his staff.

Janina signed, trying not to look triumphant. "When shall the soup deliveries occur?"

Blancke answered, "On Tuesdays and Thursdays, starting next week."

"May I consult an infirmary physician about the kinds of soup to bring and other products and medicines that the patients need?"

Blancke nodded.

After Janina signed the agreement, Melzer interrogated her about her background, residence, activities, her husband and his job at Społem, and her affiliations. Then he released her with a warning: "One can always gain entrance here, but the exits may not be quite so obvious."

Elated, Janina returned to the cab and found the driver and Father Winiewski in astonished relief. After so many hours, they assumed that Janina had been arrested. Yet they had waited, the priest praying the Rosary. The cab driver knew Janina well and always picked her up when he saw her if he didn't have a fare. He would not take her money, saying, "An oldster like me, I don't need it anymore. But when I stand before St. Peter, I can tell him I always helped you on your errands of mercy, and he will like that." Now he swore that he would go to confession that evening and say thanks that the Countess had been spared.

Janina's colleagues could scarcely believe the news. She notified Woroniecki, who promised to wire her money from Kraków. Then she and Łopatyńska set to work on their plan. They would be delivering 1,250 liters of soup a week, plus special bread and other products approved by Blancke. Łopatyńska found sufficient volunteers among her kitchen staff to prepare the soup at night, but they needed extra kettles or vats to transport it. Janina thought of milk cans, which could hold 25 liters, and she called around to estates near the city hoping she could collect a total of fifty. They all arrived the next day. Since Jurek delivered packages to Majdanek on Tuesdays, Janina had to find other transport for the soup. As usual, Kosiba of Społem readily offered to provide the necessary trucks and drivers.

The next day, Saturday, Janina rode with Jurek to Majdanek to make the weekly delivery of bread and food products from the Lublin Polish Care Committee. In the headquarters office, Petrak issued her a pass to speak with Dr. Nowak after checking with Blancke. There was a heavy frost, and a bitingly cold wind raked Majdanek's plain. As an RGO official, Janina was permitted to have a fur coat, but she preferred to shiver rather than wear it around Majdanek's freezing prisoners. She rode with Jurek and an SS guard to Field V, where she found Izio on the porch of the guard booth. Before he ran to fetch Dr. Nowak, he whispered to her, "Today's guard isn't a beast. He even let me into his booth to warm up a while and gave me some tea, but he always looks around first to make sure no one sees."

That day's guard, a Tyrolean, welcomed Janina into the booth and proved especially talkative. Then Dr. Nowak arrived at the gate, and she exchanged a wordless greeting with him as he flatly stated his name and prisoner number. Janina was writing in her notebook the food and medicines needed in the infirmary when, suddenly, they heard the Tyrolean hiss, "Thumann's coming!"

Before they could turn, Thumann was upon them in a rage. "I will lock you in!" he bellowed to the guard and set to beating Dr. Nowak on the head with his truncheon.

"And you!" he screamed in Janina's face. "Do you think that this is a sanatorium? You will bring nothing here, and I'll see to it at headquarters!"

He turned on his heel and stomped off. Dr. Nowak, bloodied, disappeared. Izio looked ashen, and the guard muttered, "What a beast." When Janina returned to Jurek, who had observed the confrontation, he crossed himself and thanked the Holy Virgin for protecting the Countess this time.

On October 19 at 11:00 a.m., Janina set out from Lubartowska Street atop one of the Społem trucks laden with cans of soup and baskets of bread, while colleagues smiled and waved from the windows.[12] They arrived at Majdanek precisely at the appointed time. The guard at the gate to the protective custody camp had received no notice about the delivery, so they had to wait as he sent word to camp headquarters. After nearly an hour, a medical orderly entered the guardhouse with a woman in a striped prisoner uniform. The woman announced her name: "Perzanowska."

Janina started and felt tears come to her eyes. This was Dr. Stefania Perzanowska! Janina had heard so much from released women prisoners about Perzanowska's inspiring leadership and how she had single-handedly created an infirmary in the women's camp where prisoners received expert and tender care. And now Janina was meeting her, a true heroine. Perzanowska's appearance alarmed Janina, however. It was not just that the doctor was painfully thin but that she seemed drained of any color, listless and apathetic. But when Janina smiled warmly at her and gave her own name, a light seemed to kindle in the doctor's eyes.

Blancke had informed Perzanowska the day before that she was to take receipt of a special delivery for the women's infirmary the next day. He warned her not to engage in any conversation beyond the minimum necessary to conduct the transaction. That morning, wanting to make a good impression when she received whatever was in the delivery, Perzanowska had put on the least filthy of her uniforms and kerchiefs and resolved to try to smile, if she could only remember how. It was almost a year since she had been arrested in Radom for Underground activities. After fifteen brutal interrogation sessions, the Gestapo gave up trying to extract information from her and dumped her in Majdanek in January 1943. Since then, the camp's daily routine of unbearable suffering and unrelenting violence had steadily ground her down and drained her spirit. She tried to appear confident and caring to the desperately ill and dying women she could do so little to help, but in fact she felt almost devoid of human feeling, enclosed in a hard, cold shell of indifference.

As she approached the guardhouse, Perzanowska saw the trucks laden with cans and baskets and realized with a shock that this was the delivery she was to receive. Then she entered and saw a slender, handsome brunette with thick dark braids piled on her head like a crown. "Suchodolska of the RGO" Perzanowska heard the woman say. Somehow, her voice, her smile, her look of deep concern, and the warmth of her empathy penetrated Perzanowska's shell and made her feel human again.

The doctor stared in wonder at the woman as she read out the list of the food in the delivery and explained that the same delivery would be made twice a week and could include additional food and medicines as approved by the camp doctor. Here was someone, Perzanowska marveled, from that other world— "outside the wire"—that had come to seem a universe away. What efforts had been made, what risks taken to bring this largesse to the doomed? Perzanowska turned to the medical orderly and asked, "May I express the thanks of the prisoners to Madame?"

The SS duty officer, having become bored as Janina read the list, was attending to other things. The medical orderly indicated to the women that they should step outside. They did so, then Perzanowska, fighting back tears, struggled to find the words to thank Janina. "You don't know what it means to me to speak with you, a free woman. Everyone in Field I will be so grateful when I tell them what you have done, and so envious when they hear that I met with you!"

Janina looked at the orderly. "Will you allow me to shake hands with the prisoner?" She showed him her palms. "You see I have nothing in my hands, I will not give her anything, just shake her hand." The orderly looked around, saw no guard was watching, and said gruffly, "Shake hands, if you must, but make it fast!" Janina, tears on her cheeks and trembling, took Perzanowska's hand, squeezed it, and said, "Tell the others in the compound that this handshake is for all of them, from all of us who are still free!"

Suddenly, SS guards spilled out of the guardhouse and sentry box screaming at Janina to finish and leave. Perzanowska watched in awe as Janina did not even flinch but calmly informed them in proper German that she was authorized to speak with the doctor about the needs of the infirmary, to learn the number of patients needing special diets, and to write down what was needed. Furthermore, as there were different kinds of soups and breads in the delivery, she needed to show the doctor where they were placed in the truck. So Janina and Perzanowska climbed onto one of the trucks, and as Janina announced which can had what kind of soup and explained what was in the baskets, she asked Perzanowska under her breath in Polish whether she wished to send a message to anyone. Perzanowska, feeling the guards' eyes on her, gave a slight nod. Then Janina, notebook in hand, told the orderly that she had to take down the information of the persons who received the delivery. The oblivious orderly stated his name, while Perzanowska muttered an address in Lublin and a brief message to be sent there.

Finally, some SS men got in the trucks and drove them off to the protective custody camp. The officer of the day informed Janina that she was to pick up the cans outside the gate at 1:00 p.m. the next day. Then Janina watched as Perzanowska walked slowly back down the road to hell. It was a vision that would haunt her for days.

But Perzanowska was actually smiling. "There were brave people on the outside who were taking risks to help the helpless victims of Majdanek!" she thought with amazement. And she diagnosed the cause of the sensation that had just come upon her: hope.

When Janina returned with the next delivery, she met Perzanowska and a prisoner named Bargielski from Field V, whose prisoner number, 15, marked him as one of the "old-timers" in the camp. They were accompanied by an SS officer and a woman in the uniform of an SS *Aufseherin*, the term for a woman guard in the concentration camp system. She smiled graciously at Janina and held out her hand, apologizing that her gloves—which were immaculate—were too tight to remove. After Janina reported the contents of the delivery, the woman exclaimed:

"The soup is sure to be delicious, Polish women being such good cooks. I'm glad the patients will be so well nourished. Why, even the staff don't get such nutritious soup!"

Before she replied to this outlandish statement from the obviously well-fed *Aufseherin*, Janina saw Perzanowska brush her fingers to her lips. Janina said nothing.

The woman was Else Ehrich, commander of the women's concentration camp at Majdanek, known for her military bearing and the methodical way she daily beat prisoners bloody with a riding crop she tucked in her boot. During the roll calls in the women's camp, she sought out prisoners who appeared unable to work and sent them to be murdered in the gas chambers or crematorium. She also participated in the selections of newly arrived Jewish families, seizing children from their mothers and slinging them by their feet into the trucks that took them to be gassed. Once, when Perzanowska asked for milk for the Belarusian infants in the camp, Ehrich slapped her hard across the face and screamed, "This is not a sanatorium, this is an extermination camp!"[13]

Once that day's delivery was complete, Janina went to the headquarters office to turn in the list of contents. When she took off her coat, a note fell out of the pocket. Quickly snatching and concealing it, she felt her heart lurch. Had the *Aufseherin* slipped it in to compromise her? When she returned to her office, she found it was a note from Bargielski. "Ovomaltine and calcium preparations badly needed for the TB cases. Can't ask camp doctors because very sick are immediately sent to the crematorium. Please bring in next delivery—very urgent!" She had no idea how Bargielski had managed to get the note in her pocket under the eyes of the SS.

Janina consulted her OPUS colleagues about getting the products to Bargielski. They decided to fix false bottoms to some of the milk cans. The next day, a tinsmith sent by the AK completed the job. Then Janina had to figure out how to let Bargielski know where to find the goods. Even if Bargielski were the one sent to receive the delivery, she dared not try to tell him, because the duty officer on Tuesdays was often Hoffmann, who knew Polish.

On Tuesday, Janina made her first smuggling foray to Majdanek. Hoffmann was on duty and invited her into the guardhouse. "That committee of yours must care a lot about these prisoners," he said. "The Polish Red Cross sends some kid here, but your committee sends you in person." Janina was impressed that he knew the difference between the RGO and the Polish Red Cross, because most people attributed the RGO's activities to the latter.

Looking a little embarrassed, Hoffmann continued. "There's a poor devil of a woman working in the laundry, very sick, needs a bit of milk. I could pay for it, but I can't leave to get it. Would you be able to get some for her?"

Hoffmann's request could be a trap, Janina recognized, but her intuition told her otherwise. Weighing the probabilities, she decided that the chance to win his goodwill was worth the risk, particularly considering the contraband she was attempting to deliver that day. She gave the SS man a sympathetic look and replied, "If it means so much to you, of course I'll bring some milk for her. One of my colleagues used to own an estate and is still able to get milk there without a ration coupon."

Then Perzanowska and Bargielski arrived. As Hoffmann looked on, Janina pointed to one of the trucks and addressed Perzanowska: "There are the cans for your field, and I must say you women are much better dishwashers than the men—you scour the bottoms of the cans properly." "As to you," turning to Bargielski, "please be careful not to leave soup in the can, and pay better attention to cleaning the bottoms!" The prisoner, looking repentant, responded, "Considering what the committee is doing for us, we promise to see that everything is thoroughly cleaned."

Janina's relief that Bargielski evidently understood her message was countered by fear that Hoffmann had grasped it as well. Would the promise of milk buy his silence? She spent all night imagining she heard footsteps approaching that would soon be followed by a knock on the door and a journey to the Zamek prison. But she survived the night and the next day rushed to check the cans after they were retrieved. The smuggled products were missing, and in the bottom of one can she found a note: "All is in order. God bless your committee. Please continue. We know that the Countess can do everything. We can, too."

The SS had become accustomed to her deliveries, Hoffmann would soon be in her debt, and she had a way to smuggle messages and contraband into the camp. Time for her next step, Janina decided: to get past the camp gate and obtain access to the prisoner compounds. She called on Petrak in the headquarters office and requested a pass.

"You have permission to bring in the food," he said, "you don't need anything *more*. It depends on the man on guard, but if you have trouble with him, we'll do something. I hear that the prisoners are better off and your committee is working very well."

She left puzzled. Did Petrak mean that her permission to deliver the food did not specify where she was to leave it? She decided to test that.

On the next delivery day, with Ovomaltine, calcium, and tiny packages of butter tucked in the bottoms of the cans, Janina found Hoffmann on guard. "Wouldn't it be less complicated," she asked him innocently, "if we just drove up to the gates of the fields and deposited the cans there? After you check everything, of course." Then she handed him the milk for his girlfriend in the laundry.

Hoffmann thanked her but said she would have to get a pass from headquarters to go to the compounds. "Would you put in a call to Sergeant Petrak for me, then?" she asked. Her mention of Petrak seemed to make an impression on Hoffmann, and he called the headquarters office to arrange for Janina to see the sergeant. Petrak, evidently satisfied that Hoffmann would raise no objections, issued Janina a pass to the protective custody camp.

Janina returned to Hoffmann, who made a cursory inspection of the trucks, assigned an SS man to ride with her, and waved her on. And so, Janina passed through the gate with the trucks and their contraband. The risk she was taking was enormous, she knew, but it was outweighed by the greater opportunities she now had to help Majdanek's prisoners.

At Field I, neither the guard at the gate nor the *Aufseherin* on duty questioned the change in procedure for the delivery. Perzanowska looked at Janina with surprise and awe. The doctor had grown bolder in her interactions with Janina, and the two were developing their own language, based on gestures, facial expressions, quickly whispered Polish words, and the inflection of their official exchanges in German. After the contents of the truck had been unloaded, Janina instructed Perzanowska and the *Aufseherin* that the empty cans be placed outside the compound gate for retrieval the next day. "And," Janina said, turning to Perzanowska, "don't forget to scrub the bottoms." Looking steadily at Janina, Perzanowska nodded with a hint of a smile. Janina was certain the doctor understood her meaning.

The next stop was at Field III, which had a typhus infirmary. Since the compound was under quarantine, Janina could not interact with any of its prisoners. Then she proceeded to Field V, where the delivery went smoothly. Bright-eyed Izio beamed at Janina from his space between the wires. She smiled back, thinking of the plans she was already making for him. The Tyrolean had guard duty again in the booth and seemed pleased to have a chance for another chat with the Countess. He even told her how and where she should stand so that the guard in the tower could not observe her interactions with the prisoners.

On her next delivery, Janina brought along her assistant, young, vivacious, and astute Hanka Huskowska. As Janina anticipated, the SS men and male kapos were so eager to get Hanka's attention that they failed to keep theirs trained on Janina's activities.[14] She even managed to say a few encouraging words to Izio. That night, she knew, Izio was going to receive a precious gift. Janina had learned that his mother was working in the women's infirmary and had succeeded in getting a message from her to Izio, which was hidden in one of the soup cans in that day's delivery.

Riding back to the office, Janina felt almost happy. So much had changed in just a few weeks. Prisoners were now writing to their families, and consequently the number of packages continued to increase. They were arriving to the addressees intact as well, because a prisoner committee had been assigned to distribute the packages in each of the compounds that housed Poles. The typhus serum had been delivered and administered. Already, messages smuggled out of the camp were reporting that conditions had improved.[15]

It was not nearly enough, of course, but now she was confident that she could do much more. Since the SS weren't checking the actual quantities of the deliveries, she would steadily increase them. She would deliver other items to sustain and support the prisoners as well. Among the messages she was inserting in the soup cans were reports about the Germans' accelerating retreat in the East and the steady advance of British and American forces up the boot of Italy. Together with the increased food and medicines they were receiving, the knowledge that the Germans were losing the war and that the people of Lublin were going to such lengths to help them would provide the prisoners the strength and the hope that they needed to survive. And not just the Polish prisoners. Somehow, she would get enough food into the camp to feed all the prisoners at Majdanek, including Izio, his mother, and the thousands of other Jews in the camp. Her determination to achieve this goal had never lagged, but now she had logical reasons to hope for success.

It was Tuesday, November 2, 1943.

FOURTEEN

HARVEST OF DEATH

When Janina returned to her office, she found Father Santi waiting to report some troubling news. The SS at the Lipowa Street forced labor camp for Polish Jewish POWs had ordered the noncommissioned officers to change from their uniforms to civilian clothes, which some were refusing to do. Since the Germans' demand seemed to Janina to violate international law, she reported the news to her AK commander, a Polish Army colonel with the code name Łodzia.

During the night, Janina heard sporadic gunfire but did not consider it to be out of the ordinary. The next morning, however, she received an alarming report: all of the more than 2,000 prisoners of the Lipowa Street camp had been marched out under heavy SS escort in the direction of the train station and Majdanek, and some had been shot along the way. Janina checked with her contacts at the station: no prisoners had arrived there, and no transport trains were scheduled. It seemed most likely, then, that the prisoners had been marched to the Old Airfield Jewish forced labor camp just outside the city or a little farther on to Majdanek. Colonel Łodzia ordered Janina to investigate.

At the office, Janina found her assistant Hanka waiting for her in distress. Her family lived on an estate close to Majdanek, and since dawn that morning they had been hearing regular salvos of gunfire reverberating from the camp.[1]

Janina decided to go with the truck driver who was picking up the soup cans at Majdanek that day. As they passed the Old Airfield camp, she looked for activity there. She would normally see Jewish prisoners about the grounds, but today the camp appeared to be deserted. When they drew nearer to Majdanek, they found the road was closed, and armed sentries ordered them to turn back.

Janina had the driver pull over before they passed the Old Airfield camp. In the cold rain, she made her way to a house near the road and asked the woman who answered her knock whether she had observed anything unusual at the camp. The woman told Janina of being wakened before dawn that morning by a commotion on the road. Peering out her window, she had watched as thousands of figures passed by in the twilight while Germans shouted orders and dogs barked. They were heading in the direction of Majdanek.

Clearly, Janina thought, the prisoners from both the Lipowa Street and the Old Airfield forced labor camps had been taken to Majdanek. She knew the camp to be already near capacity and wondered how it could take in thousands more prisoners. Hanka's report of gunfire that morning suggested a horrifying answer: the SS were shooting some prisoners to make room for the rest.

Back at her office, Janina called Melzer's adjutant at Majdanek. He informed her curtly that Majdanek had a new commandant and he was far too busy to pay attention to her business. Janina explained that, since the Lublin Polish Care Committee had not been able to retrieve its soup cans that day, she wanted to confirm that the next day's delivery could occur as scheduled. No, it would not be possible to enter the camp on Thursday, either, the adjutant replied. Then he added with a chuckle, "There'll be too much food for the prisoners tomorrow, anyway."

Janina called back to Majdanek and asked to be put through to the office that granted entry passes. As she anticipated, Petrak answered the phone, but he did not identify himself. When would the RGO be able to make its next delivery? she asked. Call back tomorrow about making the delivery on Friday, he advised her.

Janina had orders from her commanding officer to find out what was happening, and she was determined to obey them. On Thursday, she visited Hanka and they borrowed her family's horse and buggy, saying they had business in Zamość. Finding the road blocked on either side of Majdanek, they took back roads through the fields and got to the border of the Majdanek farm. As they observed the camp, they saw black smoke begin to rise in the vicinity of the new crematorium. It was not coming out of the crematorium's tall chimney, however.

Back in Lublin, panicked rumors were circulating. The sound of gunfire coming from Majdanek had lasted all day on Wednesday. Some people who lived on a rise above the camp reported that from their rooftops they could see hundreds of armed SS and clouds of gun smoke behind the protective custody camp and catch glimpses of groups of naked people exiting the rear of Field V in the direction of the gunfire. And for two days, civilian workers had been barred from the camp. Thinking of the black smoke she had just witnessed rising behind the protective custody camp and remembering the adjutant's comment about "too much food," Janina shared the general fear that the SS had murdered all the prisoners at Majdanek. When she called about making the soup delivery on Friday, however, Petrak told her that the trucks would be allowed to enter.

Janina reported this news to Colonel Łodzia. It might be a trap, he pointed out, but they agreed it was worth the risk in order to confirm that Majdanek's prisoners still lived. There would be no contraband in the delivery, however.

On Friday, Hanka insisted on accompanying Janina to Majdanek. Before the camp came into view, they saw plumes of thick, black smoke rising from it. At the guardhouse, the friendly Tyrolean SS guard was assigned to be their escort. He climbed up on their truck looking glum and uncharacteristically said nothing as they drove to the protective custody camp.

They found Dr. Perzanowska waiting at Field I. Her face was ghastly pale and terror stared from her red-rimmed eyes.

"I'm surprised they let you in," the doctor whispered. "We are going through torture. Yesterday, and the day before. If they'd just finish us up, like the Jews, if they would only make it quick!"

Janina tried to suppress the nauseating horror that was rising in her.

Perzanowska was clearly in shock, she concluded, and so maybe the doctor's words did not really mean what Janina feared they did. She tried to show Perzanowska what was in the truck, hoping to rouse her, but the doctor paid no interest. "It's the end, anyway, for all of us," she said, as if in a trance.

"Do you need any medicines for your patients?" Janina urged.

"We need nothing anymore. We won't need anything." After a pause, the doctor looked at Janina. "I am glad that you could come today, that we could still see each other." Then she turned and walked back into the compound.

At Field III, Janina usually saw Jewish as well as Polish prisoners waiting behind the gate to take in the cans and baskets, but today she noticed that there were only Poles. The same was true at Field V, and the prisoners who unloaded the truck all looked despondent. Even the SS and kapos in the compound seemed sullen, despite Hanka's presence. Izio was not at his usual post.

"Where are the others?" she asked Bargielski.

"Gone," he answered.

"And Izio?"

"They are all gone." Then he added, "The days and the nights are horrible."

After the truck had been unloaded, Bargielski addressed her in a formal tone. "I would like to take leave of you, and may God protect all of us." Then he walked away.

Hanka pulled Janina toward her and whispered, "I can't stand it any longer! They all seem to know something terrible that's going to happen to them."

As they rode back to the guardhouse, the Tyrolean suddenly spoke quietly, "All the Jews are dead." He paused, then added, "What are they doing? Don't they know what human beings are?" Before dismounting the truck at the guardhouse, he looked at Janina and said, "May God protect you, lady."

Despondent, Janina and Hanka rode back to Lubartowska Street in silence. The truck was laden with the empty soup cans from Tuesday's delivery, and Janina had them checked. In the bottom of one, they found a long letter. It reported that over thirty-six hours, Majdanek's Jewish prisoners as well as the prisoners of the Lipowa Street and Old Airfield camps had been murdered. The authors of the letter felt certain that, because Germany was losing the war, the SS planned to exterminate all the prisoners so that no witness to their atrocities would survive. Although the letter's authors doubted they would see Janina again, they had to write down what had happened to keep from going mad. If she did receive the letter, they warned, she should not come to the camp again.[2]

The massacre had begun before dawn on November 3, the authors wrote. They heard the sound of gunfire, then music began to play from truck-mounted loudspeakers that had been brought into the camp. Waltzes, marches, and tangos blared, and in between each number came the sound of shots and screams. At morning roll call, the Jewish prisoners were ordered to gather, then they were steadily herded to Field V. An SS man told the authors that the Jews were being "finished off" and described what was happening. The Jews had to undress in a barracks at the back of Field V. In groups of ten, they were forced to run naked through an opening in the barbed wire and between a gauntlet of SS men that led to three 100-meter-long ditches lying in zigzags near the crematorium. For several days preceding the massacre, three hundred Jews had been forced to dig those ditches, supposedly for protection in air attacks. Now, each group of ten Jews, some made up of women and children, had to enter one of the ditches and lie on the ground or on the bleeding, twitching bodies of those who had gone before. Members of police and Waffen SS units assigned to the operation then shot the victims with machine pistols. It was rumored that some members of the camp SS participated in the shooting as well, none more enthusiastically than Thumann. Throughout the day following the massacre, Thumann directed a hunt in all the prisoner compounds to find Jews who had hidden and drag them to the ditches to be murdered.

The slaughter of an estimated 18,000 Jews at Majdanek on November 3, 1943, was just one scene in the bloody final act of *Aktion* Reinhard. To Himmler, 1943 had seen an alarming increase in violent resistance from Jews in Poland who were no longer in any doubt as to the fate the Germans planned for them. It had taken the SS nearly a month to put down the Warsaw ghetto uprising in the spring, at a cost of more than one hundred SS casualties. On August 2, prisoners at the Treblinka killing center set fire to it, and one hundred of them succeeded in escaping. The SS also met violent resistance from Jews in the Białystok and Vilna (Lithuanian: Vilnius) ghettos. The last straw for Himmler occurred on October 14, when more than three hundred Jews broke out of the Sobibor killing center, killing eleven of the SS staff and two Trawniki guards in the process.[3] *Aktion* Reinhard had practically completed its task of "resettling" the Jews of the General Government to mass graves and burn pits, and those who had been temporarily spared for labor now presented an unacceptable risk. So Himmler ordered the liquidation of the operation's camps and prisoners.

SS and Police Leader Sporrenberg received the assignment. He assembled a force of 2,000 to 3,000 men from the SS and police that murdered at least 42,000 Jews on November 3 and 4, 1943. It was the largest German mass shooting operation of the Holocaust. Sporrenberg gave it a celebratory code name: *Aktion Erntefest*, Operation Harvest Festival.

FIFTEEN

CHRISTMAS AT MAJDANEK

On Tuesday, November 9, 1943, Janina returned to Majdanek, to the place where, just a week earlier, she had entertained such hopes for a Jewish boy whose ashes now rose in the noxious black smoke that was smothering Lublin. She willed herself not to think about that. This was not the time for fear and anguish. She was no longer Pepi Spinner Mehlberg, whose own ashes ought to be mixed with those of her family and friends in Bełżec or in the bags of fertilizer that Majdanek sold to local farmers. She was Countess Janina Suchodolska now, and she had a mission. Now, more than ever, she would see it through.

As she visited the compounds, Janina could see that the prisoners' panic of Friday had dissipated. Some AK members among the prisoners had replaced the Jews who had worked in the camp's offices. From the records they could access, the prisoners concluded that the slaughter of the Jews was not the prelude to evacuating Majdanek and murdering its remaining prisoners. In fact, it was said that the new commandant took some interest in improving conditions for the prisoners. There had been a noticeable decrease in arbitrary beatings, and bedridden prisoners were no longer required to report for the morning and evening roll call.[1]

The prisoners' equanimity disturbed Janina. No longer fearing they were about to be slaughtered, they seemed almost sanguine about the

147

murder of their fellow prisoners and impervious to the smoke and the stench of thousands of rotting corpses that engulfed the camp. It would take weeks to dispose of all the bodies, and every time Janina saw the smoke as she approached Majdanek, her inner Countess had to reassert herself over the Pepi who yearned to howl her grief.

She had a mission to accomplish, and the rumors about the new commandant inspired her with an idea for expanding her deliveries—and her access—to Majdanek's prisoners. She immediately sought a meeting with the commandant, which Petrak arranged without any trouble.

When SS *Sturmbannführer* Martin Weiss first learned of his appointment to be commandant of Majdanek, he was told that he would be taking over an extensive system of camps that provided laborers for the growing SS industrial complex in the General Government. He arrived in Lublin just in time to witness the collapse of the SS industries on November 3 as most of their laborers were murdered. Weiss had been chosen for the Majdanek post based on his experience and accomplishments. A Nazi "Old Fighter," he had served in the concentration camp system since its birth in 1933 and rose to the position of commandant at Neuengamme in 1940. In 1942, he took command of the original SS concentration camp, Dachau, and in one year managed to decrease its monthly prisoner mortality rate to the lowest of all the concentration camps, 0.23 percent. Even though he lost more than 85 percent of his anticipated workforce in *Aktion Erntefest*, Weiss was still expected to preserve the labor capacity of the remaining prisoners.[2]

Janina found Weiss to be, if not cordial, at least somewhat interested in what she had to say. She started by introducing the functions of the RGO within the General Government and especially its duty to provide for Polish prisoners. In fulfillment of that duty, her organization was delivering soup and bread to the Majdanek infirmaries for the sick prisoners, as well as bread and food products for the rest of the prisoners. Currently, she informed him, the deliveries for the sick prisoners occurred on different days from the deliveries for the others, and her organization was also having to retrieve the soup cans between food delivery days. She explained that it would be much more efficient and less expensive for her organization if it could bake and deliver the bread for all the prisoners on the same days that it delivered soup. In fact, she concluded magnanimously, her organization now had the capacity to prepare the soup three times a week and would be willing to provide it if a more efficient delivery schedule could be worked out.

Weiss appeared to accept Janina's representation of the RGO feeding program at Majdanek as simply the way things were done in the General Government. He questioned her proposal, however. Majdanek was a concentration camp, a precisely organized and tightly run maximum security facility, he lectured her. Its purpose was to isolate dangerous criminals and enemies, not to accommodate the wishes of some social welfare organization. The current delivery schedule was dictated by the necessity of minimizing disruptions to the camp regime. The meal times for the infirmaries were different than for the rest of the prisoner compounds. Moreover, if the bread were delivered on the same days as the soup, then prisoners would have to be diverted from their weekday labor assignments in order to fetch it from the food warehouses.

Janina acknowledged Weiss's concerns but insisted that if the Lublin Polish Care Committee simply delivered the bread directly to the compounds, as it did the soup, then the baskets could be taken in at the convenience of the SS and there would be no need to divert prisoners from their labor. She said this as though it were normal for a civilian organization to be accessing the prisoner compounds. As long as Weiss accepted this, then her proposal for delivering the bread would seem perfectly logical.

Weiss agreed to Janina's entire proposal. The Lublin Care Committee could supply soup and food for the sick prisoners three times a week and make its weekly delivery of bread for the other prisoners directly to the compounds on one of the soup delivery days.[3] As she returned to her office, Janina allowed herself a moment to gloat. The baskets for the bread loaves and the heavy two-ply paper bags for bread rolls provided more opportunities for smuggling contraband in addition to the false bottoms of the soup cans. With access to each of the prisoner compounds, she could not only increase communications between prisoners and the outside world but also between prisoners in the different fields, making it easier to organize the resistance within the camp. Based on her reading of Weiss at the meeting, she felt confident that she could win more concessions from him. Commandant

Weiss did not yet realize, Janina thought, that when she asked for a finger, she meant to get the whole hand.

Now that Janina was authorized to expand the feeding program at Majdanek, she had to find more funds and products. She put out a public call for donations and contacted businesses, unions, social organizations, landowners, and farming cooperatives. Once again, the people of Lublin impressed her with their generosity. The nuns of the Ursuline convent provided hundreds of liters of cream soup per week for tubercular prisoners or other patients with special dietary needs. Teams of upper-class women volunteered to peel and chop vegetables and scrub the giant kettles that Łopatyńska had built into the Lublin Polish Care Committee's kitchens. Kosiba agreed to provide two more Społem trucks for each of the delivery days. Wagons and trucks arrived daily at the care committee's storerooms to drop off large quantities of food. Janina simply signed the receipts and did not ask after the origin of the goods or the legitimacy of the donors.

Społem's warehouses stored the food for the Germans in Lublin as well as the rationed products for Poles. Janina was in regular contact with its general manager, who sometimes complained to her about the challenges of his job, particularly the continual problem of loss and breakage. If he mentioned that 3,000 kilograms of sugar had just gone missing from a particular warehouse, Janina would notify the Lublin Polish Care Committee to send a rental truck to that warehouse to pick up the "missing" sugar.

No one in the camp SS raised any objections when Janina began delivering baskets of bread to each of the prisoner compounds in Majdanek, even when she made the bread deliveries on every day that she brought soup for the infirmaries. Nor did the SS show any interest in the quantities she was delivering or ask why deliveries often included additional items, such as apples and onions. She steadily increased the quantity of soup and rolls, so that there would be enough to feed all the Poles in the compounds with infirmaries. Because she could now speak with a physician in Fields I and V up to three times a week, she was fielding more requests for medicines, which she supplied either openly, with Blancke's approval, or clandestinely in the bottom of soup cans or in the bags of rolls, which also concealed hundreds of individual portions of butter.

In addition to medications, the prisoner physicians asked Janina to pro-
cure a new X-ray machine to replace their broken one, as well as a pneumothorax device for treating TB patients. X-ray machines were expensive and
not made in Poland, but Janina assigned the task of locating one to an RGO
physician. After just a few days, he reported that some doctors in Lublin were
willing to supply one. Since it would be impossible to smuggle the machine
into Majdanek and to hide its use, Janina decided to seek Blancke's approval
for it to be provided to the camp. She did not mention the pneumothorax
device, however, because the prisoner physicians were anxious not to draw
Blancke's attention to the growing number of prisoners with TB, lest he isolate them in a barrack and leave them to die without treatment. Blancke accepted the offer of the X-ray machine.

Janina had not consulted with the Polish Red Cross leadership about
the change in the RGO feeding program at Majdanek, although Jurek was
assisting in the soup delivery. When Christians learned of the new deliveries,
he demanded a meeting with Skrzyński and Lublin Polish Care Committee
chairman Dąbrowski to discuss the situation. Since Christians was in both
open and clandestine contact with the prisoner physicians at Majdanek, he
was receiving some of the same requests for medications as Janina, so he
had legitimate concerns about duplication of efforts. He also had his usual
concerns about the RGO using resources meant for Poles to feed the prisoners of other nationalities being held at Majdanek.[4]

At their November 16 meeting, Skrzyński sought to placate Christians
without actually agreeing to any changes in the RGO's assistance to Majdanek prisoners. The Count acknowledged the overall responsibility of the
Polish Red Cross for medical and hygienic assistance to Majdanek's infirmaries. The RGO stood ready to support the Red Cross in its efforts, he
assured Christians. For example, the RGO had just obtained permission for
a new X-ray machine from the camp physician and was sourcing one that
the Red Cross could deliver to the camp. The Lublin Polish Care Committee would still provide food products for weekly delivery to Majdanek by
the Red Cross, but it would also continue its own deliveries to the camp
of soup, bread, and other types of food, as well as medicines. Since the
food was being apportioned appropriately in each prisoner compound by

152   THE COUNTERFEIT COUNTESS

a committee of its Polish prisoners, Christians need not worry that non-Polish prisoners would receive it. Skrzyński promised that his office would henceforth consult with the Polish Red Cross beforehand about interventions with German authorities regarding aid to Majdanek and would notify it promptly regarding the outcome of RGO interventions.[5]

In order to deconflict the provision of medical assistance to Majdanek, the Polish Red Cross and the RGO asked Weiss to allow a committee of prisoner physicians to meet regularly with representatives of both organizations regarding the supply needs of the camp infirmaries. Weiss not only consented but also authorized the committee to meet with the organizations' representatives in the office of the Polish Red Cross in Lublin. Before each meeting, the Red Cross arranged for relatives of the committee members to be present on its premises that day. It then persuaded the committee's SS escorts to allow contact between the physicians and their family members by offering the escorts a lavish feast and entertainment.[6]

Janina was always under SS guard when she visited the protective custody camp, but now her visits had become such an accepted part of the camp's routine that she felt it was safer to observe her surroundings more openly and even move around. One day while she watched a truck being unloaded at Field IV, she saw a teenaged prisoner speaking to another youth in Polish. As he was telling a story with obvious relish, she moved closer to hear what he was saying.

"He went out that morning with his gang to break stones on the road. A bunch of Jews, the gang was. And awfully slow. So he took the hammers from the two slowest ones, made them lie down, and started banging on their heads with their hammers as they should have been doing to the stones! Nearly finished them off too, but the SS stopped him so there wouldn't be corpses in the work area. And then," he concluded, "you should have seen them work—like beavers!"

Janina glared at the boy, her first instinct to judge him a born psychopath. Then she considered once again the terrible choices that the German occupiers forced Poles to make in order to survive, choices that hardened many and drained them of their empathy. How much worse it was here in Majdanek, where survival for more than a few weeks required luck, cunning, and ruthless devotion to self-interest. Her glare turned to a look of pity. What child would not become warped under such circumstances?

The same was true for many of the SS men, she realized, for most of the guards she was getting to know were ethnic Germans who had not volunteered to serve at a concentration camp. Still, under the constant indoctrination, harassment, and threat of punishment from their superiors, they had acclimated to their role as brutal persecutors of the prisoners. They were not devoid of humanity, however, as Hoffmann and the Tyrolean guard had proved. Even some of the experienced camp SS whose routine brutality toward the prisoners she had observed would sometimes help her by looking away when she passed a package to a prisoner or by warning her when Thumann was expected to make his rounds. Human connection could sometimes evoke kindness even from the habitually cruel. That knowledge guided how she pursued her mission at Majdanek and factored into her calculation of the risks she undertook.

Via the false bottoms of the soup cans and the baskets and bread bags, a regular correspondence developed between Underground members in the camp and those on the outside. Prisoners sent out the names of others who were not members of the Underground but were not receiving packages. Janina forwarded those messages to the AK's OPUS aid organization, which then "adopted" those prisoners and sent them packages as well.[7]

Janina tried to ensure that only AK members employed by the Lublin Polish Care Committee were involved in secreting the messages and contraband she was smuggling into Majdanek and retrieving what the prisoners sent out. Her assistant Hanka was not in the AK, for she had sworn to her mother not to join any resistance organization after her father was taken hostage and killed. Hanka quickly figured out that the Majdanek deliveries were being used for smuggling, however, and she begged Janina to allow her to participate in the operation. Hanka had proved so valuable to Janina that she agreed, and she designated Hanka to be her replacement on days when Janina could not accompany the deliveries.

In November 1943, the Lublin Polish Care Committee provided 20,000 kilograms (44,000 lbs.) of bread, 15,700 liters (over 4,000 gallons) of soup, and various other foods to Majdanek. The quantities seemed enormous, and yet Janina knew all too well that they were not enough. This fact was driven home to her one snowy day as she was riding into the camp with a soup delivery. The trucks always wobbled on the stones of the "Black Road," but today hers was skidding as well. As it entered a curve, she realized that it was falling over, so she leapt from the seat and tumbled in the snow. She got gingerly to her feet, feeling pain in her side but finding that nothing seemed broken. Then she saw with horror that the contraband items she had been carrying in a small bag had scattered in the snow. Prisoners working nearby ran to the overturned truck, and when the first one neared her, she pointed at the items, signaling for help. He quickly organized retrieval of the items as the SS guard struggled with the horses, which were being choked by their harness. After righting the wagon and replacing the empty cans, the prisoners fell upon the spilled soup, scooping up the vegetables and drinking the soup-soaked snow. When Janina passed the same spot as she exited the camp, she saw that the ground was bare and there was no trace of the soup. She was moved that the prisoners all helped her before they started on the soup, but the incident impressed her with the urgent need to do still more for them.

So she visited Weiss to request another finger and came away with much of the hand. The commandant agreed that Polish prisoners could receive an unlimited number of packages and that family members could send prisoners clothing as well. He increased the frequency with which families could write to prisoners to three times a month. He even agreed that the camp would respond to inquiries about specific prisoners from their families and from the RGO if they provided precise data about the prisoners. Still Janina pushed for more: to provide soup for all the Polish prisoners in Majdanek, not just those in the infirmaries. That was not up to him, Weiss told her, she would need to get the consent of the chief of the Security Police and SD of Lublin District. Which Janina did. Consequently, in December 1943, the Lublin Care Committee began providing all of Majdanek's Polish prisoners soup, rolls, compote, and other food products three days a week.[8]

Shortly before Christmas, Janina finally obtained the pneumothorax device that Majdanek's prisoner physicians had requested. Her next challenge was to figure out how to deliver it, for it was far too large to fit in a bread basket or the bottom of a soup can. It would have to be incorporated into a truck in some way that would elude SS inspection. Her AK colleagues constructed a wooden case for it that fit under the floor of the driver's seat of one of the delivery trucks. This left the problem of how, once the truck got to Field V, the device could be unloaded without the SS seeing it. Through their secret communications with Janina, Bargielski and Dr. Nowak proposed a plan.

Now that the Lublin Polish Care Committee was providing meals for all the Polish prisoners, it had to send two trucks for every prisoner compound. The day before she planned to deliver the pneumothorax device, Janina informed camp authorities that one of the care committee's soup kitchens needed repairs and so she would send just one truck to Field V the next day. When she brought the delivery, Janina was riding on that truck. Hiding her nervousness, she bantered as usual with the duty officer while the SS inspected it. It passed, and she rode on to Field V, where Bargielski and Nowak awaited her. Feigning surprise that there was only one truck, Bargielski announced that there was no point in diverting prisoners from their labor to unload it when it could just go directly to the kitchen. This was part of the plan, for the truck driver knew he was to drive into the compound, had been trained to remove the device from the truck, and had willingly agreed to undertake the risk. But suddenly, Bargielski told the truck driver to get down so that he could drive the truck instead. Then he jumped on and drove off.

Janina cast a glance at the guard in the tower and held her breath. He had swung his machine gun around and was watching Bargielski driving the truck. Apparently concluding that Bargielski would not dare to do such a thing without orders, the guard did not fire.

Janina fretted. Would Bargielski know how to remove the case from the truck? Would he damage the device or mix up the parts so that Dr. Nowak would not be able to reassemble it with the coded instructions he had received? Would he be caught? And she questioned the wisdom of the enterprise, whether saving some tubercular prisoners was worth endangering the whole operation at Majdanek. Had she calculated the risks correctly?

Bargielski returned with the truck. Janina rode on it back to Lubartowska

Street, where the driver retrieved the case and handed it to her. Inside it was a package with a card that read "With thanks and Christmas wishes from the prisoners of Field V." Janina cried out in wonder when she opened it. The package contained a beautiful Nativity scene made with pieces of cardboard, matches, bits of bread, strips of colored paper from packages, and snips of cotton from the hospital. It contained the manger, the infant Christ and Mary, a tiny Christmas tree, and where the scene usually depicts shepherds or the Magi, three prisoners made of cotton wool, dressed in concentration camp uniforms. There were even tiny bulbs to light the whole scene. Janina wondered at the ingenuity, labor, and love that had gone into making this fantastic gift in utter secrecy inside a concentration camp. In the midst of their suffering, its creators still felt the need and found the strength to give something back to those who cared about them. Janina kept the gift for some years among her most prized possessions as evidence of the perseverance of humanity and creativity even in conditions designed to crush the human spirit.

Before receiving the gift, Janina had already been thinking about doing something special for Majdanek prisoners for Christmas. She consulted with her colleagues at the Lublin Polish Care Committee, suggesting that the committee might send in some delicacies in the double-bottomed cans.

"What about trees?" one asked in jest. "Surely you plan to smuggle in some of those."

Janina thought it over. "I'll ask the commandant," she replied.

Weiss had become quite accustomed to Janina's visits. She could never tell whether he regarded her as a nuisance that he had to put up with or as the ally she claimed to be in the effort to keep his prisoners alive. As usual, he listened impassively to her latest pitch. Christmas Eve would fall on a Friday, which was not a delivery day for the care committee. She proposed that the committee send in an extra delivery on that day of packaged and prepared food that the prisoners could have to celebrate Christmas the next day. Weiss consented. Then she brought up the question of the trees.

"Christmas trees," Weiss said. Janina thought she detected a slight tone of surprise—perhaps even amusement?—in his response.

"Yes. We happen to have enough from a generous donor to provide one tree for each of the prisoners' barracks."

"There could be no question of lighting them," Weiss admonished.

"Of course," Janina replied. And Weiss consented.

When the RGO brought the next soup delivery, Perzanowska noticed that Countess Suchodolska seemed genuinely cheerful. She always greeted the doctor with a warm smile, but today it lacked its usual hint of sadness. In the snatches of conversation they held while conducting their official business, the Countess said, "I've been to the commandant. He's allowing me to come to you on Christmas Eve. I will come at noon."[9]

Janina was sure the people of Lublin would provide the Christmas treats she planned to deliver to Majdanek, but she was overwhelmed by their actual response. All the candy and pastry shops offered sweets, farmers donated foods, stationery stores agreed to supply tree trimmings, and Spolem found an unusual amount of breakage in eggs and jam jars. As the items poured in, willing hands came forward to cook special hams, bacon, and sausages, and to bake babkas, macaroons, cookies, poppy seed cakes, and strudels. Together, employees and volunteers of both the Lublin Polish Care Committee and the Polish Red Cross worked day and night to assemble the delicacies in packages for 5,500 prisoners. Instead of the usual soup, the Christmas Eve delivery would bring borscht with meat pierogi, dried mushroom stew, cabbage rolls with rice, and the traditional Polish Christmas dessert, egg noodles with poppy seeds and sugar. Children in the care committee's shelters made decorations that were hung on the large trees for the barracks, while additional, smaller trees were added to the delivery for the prisoners to decorate themselves. Finally, the delivery would include wafers for the Polish Christian tradition of breaking wafers with loved ones on Christmas Eve, as well as Holy Communion wafers that priests imprisoned in the camp would distribute in secret nighttime ceremonies.[10]

At noon on Christmas Eve, Dr. Perzanowska stood at the guard booth outside Field I and thought she must be dreaming. One huge platform truck after another passed by, loaded with cans and barrels and piled high with evergreen trees. When the trucks for Field I arrived, she inhaled the trees' scent deeply. It was the smell of freedom, she thought, and tears began to roll down her cheeks. Then Countess Suchodolska approached, obviously very moved as well. She persuaded the guard to allow her to break a wafer with Perzanowska. While they shared the wafer, gazing into each other's tear-stained faces, Perzanowska felt that they had consecrated an unbreakable bond between the prisoners and their compatriots in freedom. Never again would she feel abandoned in the concentration camp, for she knew that there were many outside it who held her in their hearts.

Janina also got the guard's permission to shake hands with the prisoners who were unloading the truck. As she did, she expressed to each the Christmas greetings of the RGO and Lublin Polish Care Committee. Hanka, who had accompanied Janina to Majdanek, shared a wafer with one of the other prisoners. There were more tears, and even laughter as the women unloading the trucks wrapped their arms around the fragrant trees.

Suddenly, Janina heard several prisoners gasp and the guard snap to attention. A car had pulled up to the guard booth, and out of it stepped Weiss. Janina had heard that the commandant hardly ever visited the protective custody camp, and never for more than a few minutes. She had not seen him on any of the previous soup deliveries. But now he approached the unloaded barrels and ordered a prisoner to open one. It contained the noodles. Janina's joy evaporated and her heart became a heavy lump. Besides the packages and trees, she did not have permission to deliver anything other than the usual soup and bread. She racked her brain for an explanation.

"What do you have here?" Weiss demanded, pointing at the noodles.

"We had to change the menu. The soup we usually bring spoils in a day, and since we're not allowed to come on Christmas, we substituted noodles."

"Do the other prisoners get the same thing?" he inquired.

"Yes, Herr *Kommandant*, except for the hospital patients. For them, Dr. Blancke ordered a special diet," Janina lied. Blancke took no interest in the diet of sick prisoners, but she hoped that mentioning his name would help make her explanation sound plausible. Her stratagem apparently worked, for Weiss lost interest and returned to his car, which headed back toward camp headquarters.

At each prisoner compound she visited, Janina persuaded the guard to allow her and Hanka to break a wafer with a prisoner and to shake hands with the prisoners unloading the trucks. Not a few of the male prisoners cried, and she even saw the Tyrolean SS man wipe away a tear. One of the older, experienced SS officers was heard to mutter, "Man, at home in Germany, this would never happen."[11]

From Majdanek that day, Janina went to the Krochmalna Street transit camp, bringing a similar feast of borscht and noodles as well as articles of clothing. There, she participated in a celebration together with the district medical superintendent and an official from the labor office. As Janina distributed the wafers to the detainees, occasionally sharing one, they pressed upon her their tearful gratitude. Then they all joined in singing Christmas carols.

Janina also obtained permission to deliver extra parcels and food to Majdanek on New Year's Eve, although they were not as sumptuous as the Christmas Eve delivery. In the days following the holidays, she received a smuggled letter from a committee of Polish prisoners in each compound describing how they had celebrated Christmas Eve by decorating their trees, dining together, breaking the wafers, singing carols, and even putting on skits. The holiday committee from Field I sent their description of the celebration in verse. Janina was pleased to learn that many Polish prisoners had shared the bounty from their packages with non-Poles, especially in the women's camp and the camp infirmaries.

That Christmas at Majdanek became an indelible memory for the Polish prisoners who experienced it and survived the war. Even decades later, it would remain for many of them one of the most meaningful experiences of their lives. The indifference and selfishness that had possessed them in their struggle to survive dissipated, at least for a time, as they came together to feast, sing, and pray. Gazing at the huge Christmas tree in each barrack, sparkling with its handmade decorations, prisoners felt a deep, spiritual connection to their Polish culture and traditions, and to the compatriots who had provided them with this symbol of hope and token of love. That night, the sound of Polish voices carried from compound to compound at Majdanek. They were singing "God Save Poland."

SIXTEEN

CAT AND MOUSE

On a sub-0° day in early January 1944, a ghastly parade coursed slowly along the streets from Lublin's freight station to Majdanek. Hundreds of skeletons dressed in flimsy striped uniforms lurched through the snow in their wooden clogs, struggling to hold themselves upright in the unrelenting wind. Every few yards, a body fell, so the parade left a two-kilometer string of corpses in its wake. Three months earlier, these skeletons had been mostly young, healthy men from nearly every country that Germany occupied. Then, they had been forced to labor in the tunnels of the Buchenwald subcamp Dora, where the Germans planned to manufacture a new class of strategic missiles. Now, injuries, starvation, and disease had rendered these men worthless to the SS, which had packed them into unheated boxcars and sent them on the long journey to Majdanek without food or water. At the freight station, prisoners incapable of walking and the corpses of those who died en route were stacked on top of one another in trucks that delivered them to the camp.

This was just one of the transports that brought some 8,000 desperately ill and disabled prisoners to Majdanek in the first three months of 1944. Since the SS industries in Lublin were shut down following Operation Harvest Festival, Majdanek had lost its purpose as a reservoir of labor for the SS. In December 1943, it was designated a "convalescent camp," in reality, a place where prisoners deemed useless were sent from other camps to die. Their maladies included end-stage TB, intestinal infections, kidney failure, shattered bones, and blindness brought on by the conditions of their forced labor. The men of this transport from Dora, many of them French, were placed in barracks in Field IV and left there without any medical treatment to subsist on the meager camp diet. After three weeks, those still alive were moved to the lice- and flea-infested barracks of the men's infirmary. After three months, of the 250 young Frenchmen in the transport, only eight still survived.[1]

Soon after the Dora transport arrived, Janina received a coded message from Henryk Szcześniewski, an AK member imprisoned in Field III. The compound had received 1,500 prisoners from the sick transports who were desperately ill with dysentery, and one third of them had already died. He urged Janina to get medication to the compound as quickly as possible.

Janina immediately sent Lublin Polish Care Committee employees out to scour the city and nearby towns for antidysentery drugs, and by the next morning they had accumulated 1,000 doses. However, since there was no longer an infirmary in Field III, she could not obtain official authorization to deliver it there. Anxious to get the medicine to the compounds before that afternoon's soup delivery, she called Petrak and claimed that, because of a shortage of trucks, she needed to deliver the soup in two transports. He agreed to issue her two passes to the protective custody camp that day. Janina's AK colleagues in the care committee storehouse quickly loaded two trucks, secreting the drugs in the false bottoms of the soup cans, and she took them to Field III. Szcześniewski organized the administration of the drugs.[2]

Some days later, Szcześniewski sent word that five hundred of the patients were still alive and appeared to be recovering. Janina did not know whether to be pleased or appalled. She was determined to get more drugs to the sick prisoners in Fields III and IV, but smuggling was too risky given the types and quantities of medicines that were needed. So she paid a visit to Blancke.

She found Majdanek's chief physician packing up his office. He was being transferred to the new Plaszow concentration camp in Kraków. In the course of their many interactions over the previous months, Blancke's rudeness toward Janina had moderated to grudging respect. But as she presented her proposal to deliver medication to Fields III and IV, he cut her off.

"You have done enough. Too much, in fact. And you should be grateful that you are still at liberty."

"How much does he know?" Janina wondered, and that old intruder, fear, crept into her heart. She had realized going in that her explanation for how she knew about the sick prisoners in Fields III and IV was not very plausible. Had she fatally miscalculated in making this proposal?

"I am a physician, not a policeman," Blancke continued. "Leave well enough alone and stop making requests. I am not going to say anything to the commandant about your request but, personally, I believe that from now on you should be barred from the camp."

Then, with a look of special intensity, he concluded, "I think you understand what I mean. You have done more than enough!"

Janina's fear slipped away. She felt almost touched. Here was an SS officer who had sent thousands of Jewish and Polish prisoners to their deaths. Yet, although he evidently knew that she was conducting clandestine operations at Majdanek, he had essentially spared her life by not reporting her. Even a monstrous criminal could retain vestiges of humanity.

By 1944, the giant map in Adolf-Hitler-Platz in Lublin had been removed and the "Bellower" had ceased broadcasting. Instead of celebrating their latest military victories, the Germans were pasting up posters in the city announcing all the people who had just been sentenced to death for resisting German rule or shot as hostages in reprisal for partisan attacks. Governor General Frank had changed his policy toward his "foreign" subjects yet again. Furious that, despite his magnanimity, Polish partisan attacks were escalating, he abandoned his objections to reprisal actions and in October 1943 ordered the death penalty for every Pole who disobeyed any German order or in any way hampered the German "rebuilding effort" in the General Government. As usual, Frank's policy had the opposite of its intended effect. If a Pole could be murdered by the Germans just for living in the wrong place or failing to follow an impossible rule, what did the

Poles have to lose by actively resisting them? One Underground member calculated his odds of survival as follows: there were 30,000,000 Poles, and 3,000 were being seized every day; the likelihood that he would be seized on any given day was thus one in 10,000. Consequently, there was no point in worrying.[3]

Thousands of Poles made the same calculation and flocked to join the many, disparate armed organizations operating in the General Government. Attacks were occurring every day, in every district, and executions and reprisals increased accordingly. In January 1944, Janina received a report from Majdanek prisoners that new trenches had been dug next to the crematorium and loudspeakers placed on its roof. Soon afterward, buses began traveling up the new road that ran along the back of the prisoner compounds directly to the crematorium. The SS withdrew the prisoners working in the area whenever the buses arrived, but a few were able to hide in places in Field V from which they could observe. Prisoners, their hands bound with wire, were pulled from the buses in groups of two to five. The SS forced the men, women, and sometimes children to run through the snow into a trench and shot them with automatic rifles. Most of the victims were from the Zamek prison in Lublin, others had been seized in pacification operations. The buses continued arriving with regularity, usually multiple buses on the same day, bringing hundreds to their death. At the same time, a steady stream of prisoners was flowing into and out of the hostage camp in Field IV. When a hostage heard the SS call his name, he rejoiced at the prospect of being released, but his joy turned to terror when, after leaving the compound, he was marched not to the right, toward freedom, but to the left, to the slaughterhouse of the crematorium.[4]

In 1943, the typical punishment for a civilian caught smuggling items into Majdanek was incarceration in the camp for several weeks, which some did not survive.[5] Now, smuggling was a capital offense. Still, Janina was not about to pass up the opportunity her expanded deliveries to Majdanek offered for organizing the camp resistance. Every week, she was bringing 21,000 kilograms of bread, 5,400 liters of soup, and 6,600 rolls, along with other products, in three deliveries. The number of cans, bags, and baskets on each delivery was so large that the SS could not spare the time to inspect them all closely. Janina calculated that the odds of the SS discovering the false bottoms of the cans or the particular bag or basket that contained messages or contraband were low enough to justify the risk to herself and to the feeding program.

Prisoners serving in the AK organized cells in each of Majdanek's compounds and appointed at least one member to the prisoner committee that received the RGO deliveries. Every time she went to the camp, Janina was able to communicate with an AK comrade in each of the compounds. In Field V, her contact was Dr. Henryk Wieliczański. Before the war, he had been Izaak Halperin. Neither he nor Janina ever learned that the other was a Jew.[6]

Between Janina's verbal communications and the correspondence she was smuggling, the Majdanek AK cells were in regular contact with one another and able to establish an overall command for the camp based in Field V. It sent out weekly reports about the conditions in the camp and the personnel, strength, and plans of the SS. Dr. Romuald Sztaba reported information about V-1 missile production that he collected by interviewing the prisoners in the Dora transports. Janina also provided the AK intelligence information that she gleaned from her chats with SS guards and officials at the camp.[7]

The Gestapo at Majdanek knew that there were organized resistance operations in the camp and was constantly seeking to sniff them out. Through torture, threats, and inducements, it turned some Poles into spies and infiltrated them into the compounds. Janina received warnings from prisoners and from her AK commander to be on her guard. She was hardly blind to the risk she was undertaking, which was far greater than they realized, and she never entered the camp without a touch of paranoia. Was that prisoner working at the food warehouse just a little too eager to help her? She had a nagging suspicion of her AK contact in Field IV, Nowakowski. That compound had been the hardest to organize, because Poles were in the minority there, and most of them had been arrested for criminal rather than political offenses. One day, in light of rumors of a denunciation in the camp, Janina included no contraband in the delivery. At Field IV, an SS officer awaited the delivery and proceeded to inspect every can, bag, and basket. After he found nothing, he seemed to throw a glance at Nowakowski. Perhaps Janina imagined it, but she could never be sure.[8]

One day, Hanka confessed her fear that her aunt was going to betray Janina. The woman believed that Countess Suchodolska's activities at Majdanek were a cover for resistance work, and she accused her niece of breaking her promise not to join the Underground. Hanka argued heatedly with her, denying that the Countess was involved in any illegal activity. She was proud to work with the Countess and to be in her confidence, Hanka told her aunt, and in any case she would willingly risk her life for the Countess because hers was more valuable to Poland. Her aunt was garrulous and liked to boast of knowing secrets and so might bring suspicion on Janina, Hanka warned. Janina thought it best to pass Hanka's warning to Colonel Łodzia. Soon afterward, the aunt received a letter warning that if her loose talk led to anyone's arrest, she would be tried by a secret tribunal of the Underground.

As Janina was working in her office early one morning, a visitor entered and asked to speak with Count Skrzyński. The Count was not due to arrive for some time, Janina told the visitor, who appeared to be an estate owner. He said that he would wait. He did not sit, however, but paced about the room. Janina noticed that he was casting oblique glances at the reports and RGO identity cards lying on her desk. Then he asked her about the map and chart on the wall on which she kept track of the RGO's activities throughout the district. But as she explained them, he kept his eyes on her rather than what she was showing. She began to grow uneasy.

Wójcikowa, Janina's assistant, entered the office. "What shall I do about the gentleman's dog? It's becoming quite restless," she said.

A dog. Only Germans went around with dogs. But the visitor explained that he had brought the dog to the city to take it to the veterinarian. Since it was getting late, he asked to have a telephone call put through. Janina wrote down the number he gave her and immediately recognized it.

Looking the visitor in the eye, she said, "This is the number of the Security Police main office."

The man then identified himself as an officer of the SD and demanded to inspect the building.

Before they left her office, the SD official suggested that Janina bring her coat, since the building was cold and she was coughing. Seeing Janina go out with her coat over her shoulders, Wójcikowa immediately assumed that Countess Suchodolska was being arrested. Wendrucha, the building porter, had warned Wójcikowa when she arrived for work that "some Gestapo fellow is in the Countess's office." Janina calmly explained that the SD official had come to inspect the building, and she asked Mrs. Olbrycht, who ran the aid program at Krochmalna, to show him the storeroom. After finding nothing of interest, the official entered the office of the Lublin Polish Care Committee's secretary, Father Behnke, a young priest who dressed in lay clothing, as the RGO was forbidden to employ clergy.[9] The official demanded to know Behnke's name, birth date, address, and work duties, and then asked, "Have you been in the army?" This put Behnke in a quandary, because admitting he had not served would raise the question of why.

"No," Behnke answered nervously.

"Why not?"

"I was too young," he stammered, but the official quickly calculated that Behnke had been just the right age for the draft in 1939.

Janina stepped in to rescue the young man. "He didn't pass the physical. Category C, maybe even O. He doesn't want to talk about it with young girls around the office."

The official looked suspiciously at Janina. "How come you know so much about military classifications?"

The priest tried to help her out with "Oh, the Countess knows everything, even army ratings!"

But wary, the official said to Janina, "You must have had dealings with the army. Or was your husband perhaps an officer?"

"No," Janina responded. With sudden inspiration, she added sadly, "He is in another one of those excusable classes."

The SD official interrogated a few more employees and finally left. Janina concluded that the point of his visit had been to intimidate her and her colleagues. There could be no doubt now that they had come under the suspicion of German security officials. Janina's AK commander ordered her to obtain an extra identity card in case she had to flee. Tucking up her hair so that it looked short, she had a new photo taken and affixed to an identity card with the name Jadwiga Wojarowsan.

Despite the SD official's visit, Janina took on even more risks in her work at Majdanek. At Perzanowska's request, she began smuggling books into the camp, separating them into sections that she hid in the bread baskets. She brought in works by celebrated Polish writers as well as medical texts for Perzanowska. And to keep prisoners abreast of the progress of the war, she ensured that they received the Underground's daily radio digest, the *Biuletyn Informacyjny*. Sometimes the AK instructed her to make contact with a particular prisoner in one of the compounds. She would whisper the prisoner's name to the AK representative there, who then arranged for the prisoner to be present for the next delivery. With a nod of the head, Janina's comrade would indicate the prisoner, to whom Janina would pass a message or small parcel. Occasionally, Janina even arranged for family members of prisoners to see their loved one by bringing them on a delivery run and passing them off as RGO workers.[10]

As more and more sick transports arrived, Majdanek's weekly death tally shot up into the hundreds. The infirmary in Field V was overwhelmed with 3,600 patients, 1,000 of them Poles. There were thousands of Poles among the sick transport prisoners in Fields III and IV as well. Janina was supplying soup for them, and adding more fats and nutrients than the Germans allowed. At Perzanowska's request, she sent sauerkraut to Field I to combat scurvy in more than seven hundred sick prisoners sent from Ravensbrück.[11] In Field III, the Polish prisoners gave their soup to non-Polish prisoners in the sick transports, thanks to Janina's AK contact, Stanisław Zelent, who headed the food distribution committee for the compound. Zelent also requested packages for specific non-Poles in the compound. This was not happening in Fields IV and V, however, where so many of the Poles were themselves at death's door and desperately needed all the food they could get.[12]

Standing outside Field V with Hanka during one delivery, Janina observed a cart being pushed and pulled by prisoners as it passed in the direction of the crematorium. With a shock, she realized it was full of corpses.

But sitting on top was a living skeleton, his ribs and collarbone clearly visible through waxy yellow skin. Dark, burning eyes sunk deep in their sockets stared in horror and despair. Janina nearly cried out, but Hanka grabbed her hand and squeezed it. They must not draw the attention of the SS to what they had seen and understood.

This experience deepened Janina's obsession with finding ways to do more for the prisoners. She began pleading with Weiss to permit soup delivery five days a week. "It would really be the same overall amount," she lied, "but it's very hard on us to cook and deliver such quantities at a time." After obtaining approval from the Security Police, Weiss assented to the added deliveries.

Beginning in February 1944, Janina and/or Hanka delivered food to Majdanek every Tuesday through Saturday. Officially, the weekly quantity of the deliveries came to 7,250 liters of soup, 9,000 butter rolls, 4,000 kilograms of cabbage, plus bread, milk, butter, compote, cacao, and smoked meat, adding 935 calories to the daily diet of Polish prisoners. Janina calculated the caloric value of the actual deliveries to be 1,200 calories per day per Polish prisoner. Between the RGO deliveries and the packages they were receiving, Polish prisoners were faring far better than ever at Majdanek and were visibly healthier and stronger than the other prisoners.[13]

The feeding program at Majdanek was a relatively minor aspect of Janina's and the RGO's activities in Lublin District. In February 1944, the RGO was supporting 120,842 adults and 51,721 children in the district. It estimated that another 100,000 people qualified for its care. The Lublin Polish Care Committee was providing food for 3,000 prisoners at Zamek as well as the detainees passing through the Krochmalna Street transit camp. Refugees were arriving at Krochmalna not only from Volhynia but also from neighboring counties in Lublin District to which ethnic fighting had spread. Others in the camp had been seized in pacification operations or roundups for labor. There were so many sick and injured in the transit camp that Janina finally persuaded the Labor Office to establish a hospital there and even to provide beds, blankets, and straw mattresses. She also obtained the release of 787 Volhynian refugees between February 1 and mid-March, for whom the RGO provided shelter and support. During the same period,

832 victims of pacification operations were able to return to their homes from Krochmalna, thanks to the efforts of Skrzyński and Janina.[14]

Janina and the Lublin Polish Care Committee were able to meet the demands of five deliveries a week to Majdanek in part because the Polish government in exile was supporting the feeding program with substantial funds. This attracted the envy of Christians, who complained to the government in exile that the RGO was using its funds to feed not just Polish prisoners but also the prisoners of other nationalities at Majdanek. The Polish Red Cross should take over the program, he insisted, because it could be trusted not to misuse the funds.

The government in exile sent a representative to question Janina about Christians's claim. Exasperated, she freely admitted that her goal was to feed everyone in the camp, regardless of nationality. The only proof of eligibility she required was need and suffering. There were no limits to what she would willingly do to help the prisoners, but she had no heart for turf battles. If the Polish Red Cross were deemed more capable of running the feeding program at Majdanek, she would raise no objection, but she would no longer have any part in it. The government in exile put the question of who should run the feeding program to the AK command in the camp. It polled the prisoners and sent their response in a coded message: they wanted the RGO to continue feeding them.

RGO headquarters sent Janina a letter of commendation for her tireless service to aid Majdanek prisoners, but she found the whole affair disheartening. She collaborated closely with Polish Red Cross workers in providing both licit and illicit assistance to Majdanek, and Christians himself had taken great risks in the same effort. He sent reports to the Underground about Majdanek and even collected clandestine photos of the camp. Yet he seemed intent on destroying the collaboration between his organization and the RGO, apparently just so he could take sole credit for the Majdanek relief program.

Janina was equally discouraged by rivalries among the people she was trying to aid. The Polish political prisoners in Majdanek in 1944 represented nearly every resistance organization in Poland, and they organized corresponding cells within the camp. The organizations arranged for their members to receive packages, and most contributed to the RGO food deliveries as well. But the animosities between the various organizations were shared by their comrades within the camp. Janina found the evidence of their discord in soup cans that were returned from Majdanek still full of soured soup, because the prisoners could not agree how to distribute it.[15]

In late February, Janina frequently had the sense that she was being watched. Since the visit of the SD official, Wójcikowa had taken to accompanying Janina to and from work. As they started out for the office one morning, Janina noticed that a young man whom she had recently seen several times outside her building was walking some distance behind them. She ducked into a shop, pretending that she was looking for some article. When she and Wójcikowa exited, Janina saw the man across the street. When they passed the Kraków Gate, she felt that he was close behind them. Wójcikowa stopped to read a new poster on the wall listing the victims of the latest mass execution, all of them from her and Janina's neighborhood.

"How terrible!" Wójcikowa lamented.

"Can't be helped," Janina replied. "If they are guilty, what else is there to do but shoot them?"

Wójcikowa looked at her aghast. After they got to the office, Janina explained the reason for her remark.

"Oh!" Wójcikowa exclaimed. "I've seen that young man outside your building before and just assumed that he lived there."

Janina stopped seeing friends or anyone else she could avoid, fearing that the Gestapo would suspect them as her accomplices if she were arrested. The janitor of her building told her that a man had quizzed him about her comings and goings. She took to carrying the counterfeit identity card that she had received from the AK at all times, secreted on her body.

One morning in early March, Janina heard footsteps behind her as she turned into the carriageway beneath the Lublin Polish Care Committee's building. In the courtyard, Społem trucks were being loaded with bread. The drivers lifted their caps to her, as always, but the finger of one man as he did so seemed to point across the way. As she climbed the creaky steps to her office, she heard other steps below and realized that something was about to happen.

Janina rushed into her office, calling for Olbrycht and Hanka. She gave the counterfeit identity card to Olbrycht and asked her to warn Henry not to come home if Janina were arrested. As she finished, Wendrucha burst in.

"A suspicious-looking fellow just walked up, went out on a rear balcony, and is watching over the back entrance!"

Then things happened fast. Wendrucha and Olbrycht hustled Janina into a storeroom, and Wendrucha ran off. After a few minutes, he returned and pushed her into the next room, where the bread was stored. He directed her to crawl into a sack, then threw some loaves in after her. Suddenly, Janina was airborne as Wendrucha and two drivers tossed her into a truck. The engine started and Wendrucha called, "Go to the people's kitchen and get the soup."

The truck traveled some distance before stopping with a lurch. Janina heard a ripping sound and later learned that the driver was changing the license plates. The truck set out again, with Janina jostling uncomfortably among the sacks in the back. When it finally stopped and she was unpacked, she found herself before the home of the driver. He rushed back with the truck while Janina, feeling stiff and warped, was put to bed and made to drink hot tea. Less than an hour later, the driver returned in a cab to inform her that there had been no attempt to arrest her and it was safe to return to the office.

Upon her return, Hanka and Olbrycht greeted her with tears of relief and recounted what had transpired during Janina's "abduction." Just after Wendrucha and Olbrycht had put Janina in the storeroom, a gentleman and lady entered the office and asked to see the general manager of the RGO. Wendrucha showed them to the office of Stanisław Sikora, the manager of the Lublin Polish Care Committee. The lady asked Sikora that she be sneaked into Majdanek on one of the food delivery trucks, explaining that she had a sister there, and it was rumored she would soon be transported to another camp. If the RGO could not take the lady to see her sister, would it at least take a letter to the unfortunate woman with photos of her poor children? The gentleman said he would make the effort worthwhile and offered Sikora a considerable sum.

Sikora was a stickler for the rules and regulations and unaware of Janina's smuggling activities at Majdanek, so the couple's request and attempt to bribe him struck him as outrageous. "Are you out of your minds to ask us to destroy all our work for one favor?" he demanded, and then dismissed them.

The couple next sought out Janina's office, where they found only Hanka. The lady pleaded her case with great feeling, but Hanka, rather more politely than Sikora, informed her that what she requested was impossible.

"If only the Countess Suchodolska were here, I'm sure she would do it for us. She has the heart of a real Polish woman!" the lady lamented.

But Hanka asked them not to interrupt her work further. The man left, but the lady stayed on to kiss Hanka's hands, sobbing and imploring her to take the things into the camp. As Hanka got up to leave the room, the lady asked, "Won't you at least tell me when the Countess is coming? Has she been here this morning?" Hanka replied coolly that she had just come in and did not know the whereabouts of the Countess. Finally, the lady left.

Hanka had grasped the situation at once. She was sure that the couple had been sent by the Gestapo to trap Janina into doing something for which she would be arrested when she arrived at Majdanek. It seemed the Gestapo were still seeking confirmation of their suspicions before making such a high-profile arrest.

Despite the danger, Janina resolved to go with the food delivery to Majdanek that day. Not to appear might look suspicious. She ordered all contraband removed from the trucks and gave detailed instructions about the many matters that others would have to handle if she were arrested. She also destroyed the counterfeit identity card. Her disappearance now would implicate too many others, she realized.

Janina and Hanka, riding on the lead delivery truck, arrived at the gate to Majdanek's protective custody camp just as a sleek sedan was departing. Hanka tugged Janina's sleeve and threw a glance at the passing car. Inside it, Janina saw an elegantly dressed couple. She looked back at Hanka, who nodded and said quietly, "The same people."

Now on friendly terms with all the SS who manned the guardhouse, Janina asked the duty officer about the couple who had just left.

"Them?" he replied. "Just some folks who had an appointment with Thumann."

Janina continued chatting with him and learned that, until about an hour earlier, extra SS had been put on guard at the gate. She realized that, if the couple had won her consent to their request, the SS would have conducted a thorough inspection of the trucks that day and arrested her when they discovered her illicit cargo.

Janina had escaped the trap, but it caught Wendrucha instead. A few mornings later, Janina found Wendrucha's wife waiting for her at the office. A torrent of words poured out of the distraught woman. "They" had taken Wendrucha. Two of them had knocked on the door at midnight and, when she answered, pointed their guns at her and barged inside. They ordered Wendrucha to dress while they searched the home, ransacking drawers, looking behind pictures, rousting the children and turning over their beds. Finally, they pushed Wendrucha into a car and drove off.

The woman's news shook Janina to her core. Wendrucha, one of her closest accomplices in the AK, was likely at that moment being tortured by the Gestapo. She immediately sent an official inquiry to German authorities seeking information about the RGO employee who had been taken into Security Police custody the night before.

The next day there was still no response to Janina's inquiry, but the Polish custodian of the Zamek prison appeared unexpectedly to deliver a coded message from Wendrucha. "I know nothing. They beat me, asking about some woman. But I know nothing of her. I only want my three children to be cared for. I believe the Countess will provide for them. I believe that one has to choose those who can be most useful. I, a soldier, was fated to die in battle. Good-bye to all. No time to mention names. Please remember the orphans."

The risk he was taking so frightened the custodian that he was practically in a state of collapse and had to be revived. Fortunately, Janina had appropriate medication on hand, because it was not uncommon for people to come to the RGO office in extreme distress.

A few days later, Janina received another coded message from Wendrucha.

His torturers were accusing him of purposely taking the couple to the wrong office in order to buy time so that he could help Janina escape.

Finally, a response arrived to Janina's official inquiry. Wendrucha was dead. The cause of death: heart attack. Janina pulled every string she could to retrieve Wendrucha's body, which she viewed together with Father Santi. All the fingers on both of Wendrucha's hands were horribly broken.

Grief and guilt weighed heavy in Janina's heart. If she had not taken some prisoners' relatives into the camp to see their loved ones, the Gestapo would not have set that trap for her. And if she had heard the lady's pleas for help, she might have given in. She had let sentimentality overrule logic, and this was the consequence. Wendrucha had saved her life and lost his own as a result. All Janina could do was to give a job to Wendrucha's wife and provide financial assistance for his three children for some years after the war.[16]

SEVENTEEN

THE PLOT

Three weeks before Easter 1944, Janina arranged to meet with Majdanek's commandant to propose a holiday celebration for the prisoners. As usual, she brought an RGO employee with her, this time another priest in lay clothing, Father Michalski. When they arrived at the camp headquarters, the commandant's aide told them that Weiss was on his way and allowed them to wait in his office with the door open, just across from the aide's desk. As Janina made a show of unbundling herself from her coat and scarf, she glanced at a memo lying on Weiss's desk. The heading read "Re: Camp Evacuation."

"So this is it," she thought. With the Red Army advancing across Eastern Galicia, there had been speculation for weeks that the SS would abandon Majdanek. Now the order had come. At least, according to what little she was able to read, the plan appeared to be to transport the prisoners to other camps, not to shoot them.

Weiss appeared and approved Janina's proposal to provide traditional holiday treats for Majdanek's prisoners on the day before Easter.[1] "Just some eggs and sweets," she assured him, which, compared to bringing in decorated trees at Christmas, seemed practically business as usual. By this point, Weiss had decided that it generally wasn't worth his time to argue with the Countess, since she would just keep returning with the same request or would take it to the chief of the Security Police. She had a way of making her proposals sound so logical that it almost seemed irrational to refuse them.

As soon as her meeting ended, Janina rushed back to her office to send word of the evacuation to the Underground and to the AK command in Majdanek. The news of their impending evacuation dashed the hopes of Majdanek prisoners that they would soon be liberated by the advancing Soviet forces. But some speculated that the transports might offer the opportunity for escape. The AK cells in every prisoner compound sent a request to District Command that armed units attack and liberate at least one of the transport trains before it crossed out of the General Government into the Reich.

The AK District Command agreed in principle to the prisoners' demand and sent a request for approval and support troops to the AK high command. In the meantime, it ordered Janina, in collaboration with prisoners working in the camp administration, to collect precise information about the times and routes of the transport trains, which prisoners would be on each train, and the strength, arms, and disposition of the SS escort.[2] Janina wondered whether it was really possible to attack a train carrying more than 1,000 prisoners—some doubtless sick or injured—and liberate them without many being killed. But she was not going to question orders, despite the enormous personal risk involved. She understood how desperately her comrades in the camp yearned to be free. If the cost of achieving that at least for some of them was her own life, it was a bargain she was willing to make.

Once the news of Majdanek's evacuation became public, Janina met with Weiss to discuss the future of the RGO feeding program for the camp. As the prisoners were sent off, she pointed out, she would need to know how many Poles remained so that the food deliveries could be adjusted accordingly. She also asked permission to distribute food packages to the departing prisoners and to augment the rations they would receive for the journey. Weiss agreed that a day or two before each transport, Janina would receive information about the number of Poles it included. For each of them, the Lublin Polish Care Committee could supply one kilogram of bread, 0.5 kilogram of rolls, and 20 decagrams (7 ounces) each of bacon, sugar, and honey.[3]

A plan was beginning to take shape. AK members working in the camp registry were to obtain the evacuation transport lists and, through bribes and "clerical errors," ensure that one of the transports would contain a large contingent of their comrades. That transport would be the target for liberation. When Janina received word of the impending transport from Majdanek headquarters, she would notify her colleague Maria, who operated a secret radio transmitter in the Lublin Polish Care Committee's soup kitchen at the city train station. It would be Maria's job to discover the timetable and route of the train through her contacts at the station. Colonel Łodzia would then arrange for armed units to be deployed for the attack along with trucks to disperse the prisoners out of the attack area. Some of the resistance members on the transport would have to know the plan in advance so that they could spring into action and direct the other prisoners when the attack began. Janina would have to supply them with weapons that they could secrete on their bodies as well as precise instructions and hand-drawn maps showing where transport waited for them once they escaped the train.[4]

There were so many moving parts to this plan, so many ways it could go wrong or be discovered by the Germans, particularly given that Janina was already under Security Police suspicion and surveillance. For once, Janina tried not to calculate the probabilities and just kept focused on the task at hand. But the constant work and vigilance were wearing her down. She now weighed only eighty-six pounds.

All hope for liberating a transport seemed lost when, on the night of March 28, Majdanek was placed under total lockdown following the escape of nine prisoners. While working in the camp's vegetable gardens, the prisoners managed to pry open a sewer grate unseen and then slithered a few hundred yards through human waste to freedom. The lockdown was to last until the camp was evacuated, during which time no civilian workers would be allowed to enter, none of the SS could leave, and the prisoners were all confined to their compounds. The AK cells had no way to communicate with the outside world or even with one another.[5]

Not ready to give up on the plan to free her comrades, Janina decided to take a gamble. The next day, she arrived at Majdanek with trucks hauling the regular delivery of hundreds of gallons of soup and several tons of bread.

When the duty officer refused her entry, she adamantly refused to leave and insisted that he contact Weiss. It was out of the question, she declared, that in a time of such desperate food shortages, the commandant would allow all this food to go to waste. A call was put through to headquarters, and Janina got her pass to the protective custody camp.[6]

The deliveries restored communication with the AK command in Majdanek, which sent Janina a message via an empty soup can reporting what it had learned about the upcoming transports. There would be two on April 2, one to Bergen-Belsen and one to Natzweiler, with some AK members on the latter. Two more transports, both to the Gross-Rosen concentration camp in eastern Germany, would likely depart on April 4 and 5, taking most of the remaining Polish male prisoners. The AK members working in the prisoner registry were arranging for the majority of the AK members designated for Gross-Rosen to go on the second transport. The AK command urged that this transport be liberated.[7]

Janina immediately sent this information to Maria and to "Elżbieta," the head of "Sahara," the AK intelligence operation responsible for Majdanek. The AK District Command needed to know the route of the train as soon as possible in order to plan the attack, while Elżbieta had to provide Janina with the weapons and supplies for the prisoners who would lead the escape from the train in time for Janina to deliver them. She worried that the decision to allow the RGO deliveries would soon be reversed.

When Janina arrived at Majdanek with the food delivery on Friday, March 31, she was handed a notice that 730 Polish prisoners would be transported from the camp on Sunday, April 2. The extra rations supplied by the RGO for the departing prisoners should be delivered with the Saturday food delivery. Janina was pleased. The notice confirmed both that the AK command's information was accurate and that she would be allowed to make at least one more delivery. As she approached Field III, however, she found Thumann waiting for her. That was always a bad sign. Janina steeled herself for whatever was to come.

"Move on!" he ordered. "This compound is for transport prisoners. They don't need your food."

"But the transport isn't leaving for two days," Janina pointed out.

"How do you know that?" he demanded. There was a look of triumph in his eyes, and he stepped forward as if to seize Janina. He thought he finally had proof that Countess Suchodolska was a spy.

"Headquarters notified me this morning. I'm to bring packages and extra rations for all the transport prisoners tomorrow," Janina replied pleasantly.

Thumann stopped and scowled. "You'll bring nothing to this compound."

"But Commandant Weiss specifically authorized the packages for departing prisoners. Let's just check with him, shall we?"

Weiss overruled Thumann, who now had further reason for his enmity toward the Countess.[8]

Maria reported that the transports to Gross-Rosen would travel south from Lublin, through a forested area, before turning west. Via Elżbieta, Janina received packets of razor blades and flasks of liquor, some of it spiked with drugs. These were for the prisoners who would lead the breakout from the Gross-Rosen transport. Majdanek's guards were notorious for drunkenness, so the prisoners expected that they could easily ply the transport guards with the drugged liquor. Then the prisoners were to attack the intoxicated guards with the razors once the assault from outside units began. Having learned from Thumann that the prisoners selected for transports were being gathered in Field III, Janina had the items secreted in the soup cans to be delivered to that compound on Saturday, April 1.

As usual, Janina's first stop on her April 1 delivery was at Field I. She always looked forward to her largely wordless conversations with Perzanowska there, but today the doctor and the other prisoners receiving the delivery were unusually subdued, and some were crying. A tragedy was unfolding in the compound. Outside one of the barracks, Janina could see that a large group of Belarusian children had been gathered by the SS women overseers. The children were dressed in pretty outfits, the boys with caps and the girls with ribbons in their hair. From inside the barracks, Janina could hear women sobbing and crying out to the children, reminding them of their names and the names of their fathers and villages. Then trucks pulled up to the barrack. As the SS women began lifting the hysterically weeping children into them, the wailing and banging of their mothers locked inside the barrack grew to a deafening din. Janina felt so shattered by the women's anguish that she could barely keep from crying herself. Later, she obtained evidence that the children had been taken to Łódź for Germanization, and she would testify about their abduction after the war.[9]

At Field III, Janina arrived with the usual delivery plus a truck loaded with packages for the prisoners due to depart the next day.[10] She watched with trepidation as the truck with the soup cans and their contraband drove to the kitchen barrack. A prisoner on his way to unload the truck with the packages gave Janina a grin and a salute. As she returned the salute, Janina heard the crack of a whip and saw the prisoner flinch, then flee. Startled, Janina turned and saw Thumann mounted on a horse, his whip in hand. He rode right up to Janina and bent down over her.

"I am very sorry that you are not to be a prisoner here," Thumann snarled, "but someday soon you'll find yourself in a concentration camp, and you won't be any better off than they! The prisoners and kapos might pity you, but if it's my camp, I'll hang you from the nearest pole!"

He bent down farther, his nose nearly touching Janina's, and stared her down with a glare of such intense malice that Janina felt transfixed with fear. She did not show it, however, but kept her gaze evenly on his, willing every muscle to remain still. Time seemed suspended. Then Thumann sneered, straightened, and rode off into the compound.

Hanka began sobbing. She had been sure that Thumann was going to shoot Janina if she answered him. As Hanka urged that they leave Majdanek immediately, she saw Janina suddenly go rigid, as if she were frozen to the ground. Hanka thought the Countess was having a breakdown, but it was terror that had overcome her. She was watching Thumann ride up to the truck from which Zelent was probably at that moment unloading the contraband. Just before he reached it, Thumann veered his horse around and came cantering back toward her.

"What's in that damn truck of yours?" he bellowed.

Janina's nerves immediately snapped back into place. Looking up at Thumann with feigned composure, she replied, "Didn't you see, sir? Soup and bread, plus milk for the sick, as usual."

"You're lying," he shouted, "What else is there?"

Janina straightened up to her full five-foot, one-inch height and answered him again as he bent over her. "Nothing else. If you don't believe me, why don't you have it checked?"

She realized that her tone might spark a new explosion of fury from the SS officer, but hoped that it would at least distract him from the truck. With a grunt of disgust, he yanked the horse's reins and rode off. And the truck returned, relieved of its perilous load. Janina proceeded to complete that day's delivery in her usual, outwardly calm manner, while the prisoners who had witnessed her altercation with Thumann stared in awed relief. A few crossed themselves as they sent up a prayer of thanks for the Countess's escape.

Back at her office, Janina found another report on the upcoming transports in one of the empty soup cans. The second Gross-Rosen transport, scheduled for April 5, would carry eight hundred Polish prisoners, including some of the AK command and many of its members. Every freight car would be assigned a group of resistance fighters, including one who was in on the escape plot.[11] Janina forwarded this information to Elżbieta and Łodzia. On April 3, the final go-ahead for the operation arrived. With the message was a map showing the location in the forest near Kraśnik where armed units would be waiting to attack the train as it passed. Janina was ordered to watch for the departure of the prisoners from Majdanek and then go in person to the railway station to deliver a message confirming that the transport had begun and describing the strength of the SS escort. A liaison would take the message to Colonel Łodzia, who would then get the armed units into place. Maria would radio the time when the train actually departed.

That same day, Majdanek notified Janina that she should bring packages and extra rations on April 4 for all the Polish prisoners being sent to Gross-Rosen on April 4 and 5. When she arrived with the delivery—including maps and instructions for the escape operation—Janina was assigned the Tyrolean guard as her SS escort. He seemed even more jovial than usual, and she could smell alcohol on his breath. "I must bid you farewell, today, Madame," he said in a sentimental tone. "I am leaving with the transport and from there will go home on leave." Then he added with a grin, "With any luck, the war will be over before I report to duty again."

He handed Janina a pack of cigarettes that he hoped she could pass to Zelent, who always received the RGO deliveries to Field III and had developed a sort of friendship with the guard. Janina wished him well, and meant it sincerely. She felt some compassion and even admiration for this SS man who dared to be kind when kindness was punished as treason.

At Field III, the escort guards for that day's transport were already gathering. Some were obviously drunk. The relaxed atmosphere surprised Janina, until she learned that Thumann was not at Majdanek. She was riding on a platform truck with packages for the departing prisoners, and she stayed on it when it drove into the compound. The SS allowed each of the departing prisoners to collect his package from the truck and paid no attention as they spoke to Janina, many to express their thanks for the efforts of the RGO and the Polish Red Cross to help them survive. This allowed Janina to speak relatively freely with her AK contacts who would be on the second transport and knew of the proposal to liberate them, among them Dr. Nowak. She confirmed to them that the operation had been approved and indicated where on the truck they could find maps and instructions. They were all in good spirits, believing that they would soon be free. Their hope strengthened Janina's resolve.[12]

When she saw Zelent, Janina gave him the Tyrolean guard's gift, as well as a letter she had been carrying from Zelent's wife. Although she had stopped doing personal favors for prisoners' relatives, she made an exception for Zelent, whose courage, leadership, and ingenuity in building the camp resistance she deeply admired. She knew he was on the list for the second Gross-Rosen transport, but he informed her that he had managed to have his name removed. He would stay on at Majdanek, which would retain a small number of prisoners for some time longer. Janina questioned his decision, for he had three children, the youngest born after his arrest. "What would you do in my place?" he asked. Janina had to admit that he was right to stay. The Underground needed a contact in Majdanek for as long as it operated, and Zelent was the obvious candidate.[13]

Dr. Ryszard Hanusz approached Janina and furtively handed her his Bible. The brilliant physician had saved many prisoners' lives with a new procedure he developed for treating typhus. But he had been imprisoned in Majdanek since 1941 and in Sachsenhausen before that, and the years of concentration camp life had taken a psychic toll.[14] Tearfully, he begged Janina to find a way to get the Bible to him at Gross-Rosen, for he was absolutely convinced that without it, he would die. Seeing the doctor's desperation, Janina accepted the Bible and assured him that it would be restored to him. She did not admit that she had no idea how to accomplish that.

While she was at Majdanek that day, Janina learned that the camp post office had ceased delivering packages to the compounds after some of its workers shipped out on the first transports. As it happened, Petrak had just been put in charge of the post office, having been transferred away from headquarters after he made critical comments regarding the slaughter of the Jews on November 3. Janina quickly struck a deal with him: she could use her platform trucks to carry packages from the post office to Field III, where the contents of packages for prisoners who had already departed would be distributed. She was able to bring the first batch of packages that same day.[15]

Janina found another report from Majdanek prisoners that evening, and this one had disturbing news. Prisoners in the carpentry workshop were making wooden frames with wire grids the width and height of a freight car. The SS planned to use them to cage prisoners on the Gross-Rosen transports at each end of the train's cars, leaving a space in the middle of each that was the width of the sliding doors. Four SS men would be posted in that space armed with automatic weapons and grenades. There was a rumor that scores of prisoners had escaped from the Natzweiler transport, which might explain why the SS was taking these measures.[16]

The caging of the prisoners would make it much more difficult for them to break out during the attack, Janina realized. On the other hand, the armed units would now know where the SS men were and could shoot into the middle of the freight cars, which would be safer for the prisoners. Although she was happy for the prisoners who escaped the Natzweiler transport, the timing was unfortunate. She wondered whether the escapees used any of the razors and liquor that she smuggled into Field III the day before the transport departed. The tension gripping her was squeezing ever tighter. "Please, let the transport go tomorrow," she thought, "before something else goes wrong."

The next morning, however, Maria notified her that the second Gross-Rosen transport would not leave that day. Perhaps the SS were still outfitting the freight cars, Janina speculated. She received a message from Colonel Łodzia as well, confirming receipt of her latest information and that the plan would go forward. At Majdanek, Janina learned that the transport was scheduled for the next day and that forty-five more SS men had been assigned to guard it. She reported to Colonel Łodzia that fifteen SS men armed with two machine guns would be stationed in each of the forward, middle, and rear freight cars.[17]

Another sleepless night, and then Thursday, April 6, finally dawned in a cold, gray drizzle. The railway timetable indicated that the transport train would leave that afternoon. When Janina and Hanka arrived at Majdanek, the prisoners in Field III were already formed up for the march to the station. Seeing the two women, the members of the committees that had been assigned to distribute the RGO deliveries called out to them. Janina and Hanka went up to the gate and shook hands with the men through the wire. Suddenly, a car horn blasted, a sleek automobile came to a screeching halt behind them, and Thumann and Weiss jumped out.

"What are you doing here?" Thumann shouted in a rage at Janina. "I'm going to shoot you for this!" And he reached for his sidearm.

Weiss put his hand on Thumann's arm. "Do you have a permit?" he demanded of Janina.

"Yes," she replied, and pulled the paper from her pocket. "I am taking official leave of the Polish committees that you approved to distribute the provisions from my organization," she explained, as if the situation were perfectly normal.

"Now you are done and must leave," Weiss informed her. "Even with a permit, you are not allowed at this compound."[18]

Janina and Hanka moved to Field I, from which they would depart for the train station as soon as they saw the prisoners leaving Field III. SS men came marching up to Field III in their shiny black boots, all armed and helmeted, with a skull and crossbones on their collars. Janina's marrow froze at their sight, for with them were packs of dogs, howling like the hounds of hell.[19] Why had she not thought of dogs and provided drugs for them? Hanka began to sob, but Janina urged her to regain self-control.

The prisoners began to march out of Field III, four abreast, filing between the SS. In the front row, Janina saw Dr. Nowak and next to him, holding Nowak's hand, was the renowned pediatrician Dr. Mieczysław Michałowicz. As Janina watched, the frail doctor, nearly seventy, lost one of his wooden clogs in the mud. The SS shouted at him to keep moving, so he went on without it.

The time had come to race to the railway station. But when they got to the road, it was full of prisoners' relatives who had gathered in hope of seeing their loved ones pass by. The horses pulling the truck could not get through. Standing and leaning out of the truck, Janina called out that she was from the RGO and needed to get to the station before the prisoners. Slowly, the crowd gave way and they pushed through to the station. The AK liaison was waiting and immediately departed with Janina's message to Colonel Łodzia.

Janina's part in the plot was done. "It is actually happening!" she thought. And, standing in the station, she broke down in tears, the tension of the past weeks erupting out of her in sobs and gasps. "They will make it," Janina told Hanka. Some would die, Janina knew, but many, perhaps most, would soon be free. "They will make it," she said over and over.

The next day was Good Friday. There were no announcements about an attack on a transport train, and Janina assumed that her comrades would deem it too dangerous to send her a report. She included no contraband in the delivery to Majdanek that day, for her AK contact in Field I had sent a warning about a suspected spy assigned to the labor squad that unloaded the RGO deliveries.

At the gate to Field I, Janina found Dr. Perzanowska standing next to a very pretty young woman with large blue eyes, straight white teeth, and cheeks that looked almost unnaturally pink in a concentration camp. The doctor quickly introduced her.

"This is our Wiśka," she said, using the diminutive form of her name. "Everybody in the compound knows her. She is such a worry-chaser, she can cheer up anybody!" Janina immediately grasped from Perzanowska's tone that Wiśka was the suspected spy. The young woman approached Janina with a charming smile on her red lips and an innocent glow in her blue eyes.

"We shall all be free soon, Countess. One hears that the Russians are already on former Polish territory. They say the Germans in the main administration building are packing. Have you had some more recent news?"

Janina regarded her evenly and replied, "I am not at all interested in these things, only in feeding prisoners, and I am happy to have permission to do that. I hope I can bring in more food for the holidays." And after a pause, she added, "I don't think anyone can complain right now. We must be thankful if it remains as it is. No prisoner need go hungry with the food the RGO brings in. Just looking at you shows it's not so bad at all right now!"

Wiśka tried again, saying wistfully, "If only Thumann weren't here."

"Thumann?" Janina repeated, "I don't deal with him, only with the commandant."

Wiśka gave up and wished Janina a happy Easter. Janina was thankful that the other prisoners had spotted her so quickly and prevented her from seeing the cans with false bottoms.

By the next day, there was still no message about the operation nor any announcement of an attack on a train. Anxiety and doubt were eating at Janina. At Majdanek, she managed to communicate with Zelent. When she heard his news, she wanted to scream: the guards on the transport had just returned, all hale and hearty. There had been no attempt to liberate the train.

After all the planning, work, risk, and sacrifice, nothing had happened. What had gone wrong? The question tortured Janina. When more days passed without any message, she decided that she had to find Elżbieta. All Janina knew about her, however, was that she was a schoolteacher. So, Janina went shopping for lace in the store where her intermediary with Elżbieta worked. Another customer was in the shop when Janina entered. "I'm looking for a doily, blue with lace trim," she told the woman behind the counter. This was the prearranged code. The saleswoman promised to show Janina what she had after she finished with the other customer. But the woman simply could not make up her mind. Finally, the saleswoman said, "I just remembered, Madame, I sold the last blue lace yesterday. But here's the address of my friend's shop. She has exactly what you want." And she handed Janina the address of the school where Elżbieta taught.

Janina found Elżbieta, and learned that her name was Wanda Szupenko. She looked every bit as dejected as Janina felt.

"It was awful," she told Janina. "We didn't find Colonel Łodzia where he was supposed to wait for our message. When we finally found him, he was completely drunk!"

They had begged the colonel to go signal the armed units that were to liberate the transport, but he waved them off and ordered more vodka. At last, he confessed that the operation had never been approved. With no response from the high command to the request for additional forces, the AK District Command had concluded that the plan was too risky to be attempted.[20]

Janina felt overcome with fury and bitterness. The transports provided a unique opportunity to free its imprisoned comrades, but the AK refused to fire a single shot in the attempt. She directed most of her anger at Colonel Łodzia. Why had he misled her into believing that the operation would go forward, causing her to continue risking her life and, even worse, to raise false hopes in the prisoners? She imagined the prisoners who had trusted her riding in the train, whispering to comrades that they would soon be liberated, maintaining readiness for the moment of the attack that never came, and the thought of their hope gradually turning to despair crushed her.

A few days later, Colonel Łodzia appeared in Janina's office after hours. "You have been nominated for the highest military award," he announced.

Janina looked at him coldly. Though she was only a lieutenant and he was her superior officer, she said, "If it comes through your hands, I do not want it. No matter what distinction it is."

Addressing Janina by her AK code name, the Colonel muttered ruefully, "I am sorry, Stefania. You are right, you have a right to tell me whatever you want. I have no excuse."

EIGHTEEN

THE END APPROACHES

April 8, 1944, was Holy Saturday, the day before Easter, when Poles tra-ditionally prepare baskets of food to be blessed by a priest. Commandant Weiss honored his commitment to permit the delivery of special holiday food that day for Majdanek's Polish prisoners, but the camp administration notified Janina that, because the camp was being evacuated, this would be the last time the RGO would be permitted to deliver food to the prisoner compounds. Janina made sure the delivery that day was one that would long be remembered by those who partook of it.[1]

When Janina had put the call out for Easter food for Majdanek pris-oners, the people of Lublin responded with their by now customary generosity. Companies that had not donated at Christmas went all out to make up for their earlier negligence. Hams, sausages, honey, candies, chocolate bars, and gingerbread inundated the Lublin Polish Care Com-mittee's storehouse. Janina even persuaded the German authorities to allocate 2,300 kilograms of sugar, 1,200 kilograms of wheat flour, plus marmalade and candies for the Easter meal at Majdanek. Each of the 2,300 Polish prisoners remaining at Majdanek received a parcel contain-ing, in addition to cold cuts, cookies, and sweets, one babka and two eggs. There were flowers and Easter lambs as well. Children in the care commit-tee's shelters decorated the eggs and lambs, which a priest blessed. The hot meal that day consisted of borscht with beans, barley with bacon, and sausage.

When they delivered the Easter food to Majdanek, Janina and Hanka received permission to share an egg with a prisoner in each compound, in accordance with Polish custom. This provided the opportunity for Janina and Perzanowska to make their farewells, for it seemed unlikely that they would see each other again. The doctor had elected to remain with her patients, and they were to leave for Auschwitz in a few days. Perzanowska had come to feel an intimate friendship with Countess Suchodolska, as well as deep admiration for her courage and tireless dedication to helping the prisoners.

Janina held the doctor in the same regard, and as a last favor to her friend had brought with the delivery the mother of Alinka, a young nurse whom Perzanowska had taken under her wing. Both the mother and the daughter had received stern warnings not to speak or signal to each other. When Alinka approached to unload the truck on which her mother sat, the two locked eyes for a moment and began to cry silently. As she handed down items from the truck with hands wet from her tears, Alinka whispered constantly, "Mommy, Mommy, Mommy," while Perzanowska loudly counted each item.

During her deliveries to the compounds that day, many prisoners asked Janina to thank the RGO and the Polish Red Cross on their behalf. Because of the efforts of both organizations, prisoners expressed confidence that they had the strength and health to survive whatever was to come. Their thanks depressed Janina, however. How many of the prisoners she had been providing for really would survive, she wondered, now that none were to be liberated by the AK and all were going far out of the reach of the advancing Red Army? Not all, surely; perhaps not even most. All her effort and risk, it seemed, had been for naught.

The same feeling overcame her later that day, when she went to the train station to watch 2,700 prisoners depart for Auschwitz. After the train left, many of the friends and relatives of the transported prisoners who had come to see their loved ones off crowded around Janina, blessing her for all she had done to help the prisoners survive, until she was finally able to break free and flee back to her office. There she spent the evening thinking of how she could continue to help the former Majdanek prisoners. She had been collecting as much information as she could about who was on the transports, especially her AK colleagues. She forwarded the names of those sent to Auschwitz to Countess Laskowska in Kraków, who was in charge of the Underground's care for prisoners there.

Janina had hoped to send packages to the prisoners consigned to other camps. The SS informed her, however, that the RGO could not provide for Poles who were in camps outside the General Government. At those camps, the SS only permitted packages from family members. As usual, to Janina this refusal simply meant that she had to find another way to achieve her goal. So she recruited women to pose as the wives, mothers, and sisters of former Majdanek prisoners and to send them packages prepared by the Lublin Polish Care Committee. When the parcels reached the former Majdanek prisoners, other Polish prisoners sought to receive them as well, and Janina's volunteers received information about hundreds of other prisoners hoping to acquire relatives who would send them food.[2]

To help the women prisoners leaving Majdanek, Janina planned to hide money in the extra rations that transport prisoners picked up at the food warehouses as they marched out of the camp. The funds were provided by the government in exile delegation in Warsaw. The representative who brought the money marveled as he watched Janina and Hanka insert it into hundreds of little bags of butter.

"Bringing this money to you, I was in constant fear that I would be searched and arrested," he said, "but here you two are, packing money into little bags for the concentration camp as if you were doing nothing more than rolling bandages for a hospital. Your chance of being caught inside the camp is ten times greater than that of a courier traveling on the train from Warsaw to Lublin! Are you really unaware of the risk you are taking, or are you simply resigned to your fate?"

Janina did not know what to make of his question. Did he really have no idea of what they had been doing at Majdanek for the past year?

"Well," she finally replied, "it is neither ignorance nor resignation, but the conviction that what we are doing is right and must be done. Our confidence comes from our knowledge of what this money can do for the prisoners. We've often seen how helpful money can be, even in a camp: to bribe an SS guard or a kapo, or to exchange for food."

In the end, however, the women prisoners did not receive the funds. Janina learned that the kapo in charge of the rations at the warehouse was the prisoner she mistrusted because his offers to help were so insistent and indiscreet. All she could find out about him was that he was not a member of the Underground, and none of her comrades could vouch for him. The risk of betrayal was too great, she concluded, and so she had the bags withdrawn from the rations delivered to the warehouses.

Majdanek was not the only camp in Lublin to receive Easter fare thanks to Janina's efforts. On Easter Sunday, she hosted a holiday dinner at the Krochmalna Street transit camp. It was a major affair, lasting five hours and attended by the head of the district Labor Office, the district medical superintendent, and the commandant of the camp and his deputy. Janina gave formal remarks to all those in attendance, then a representative of the detainees responded, thanking Janina and the RGO for taking them under their protection. They all shared the eggs supplied by the Lublin Polish Care Committee and then dined on borscht and noodles with poppy seeds. Afterward, Janina, Wójcikowa, and three other RGO representatives distributed packages and clothes to the detainees. Although the mood was generally festive, there was some weeping among both the men and the women as they recalled past Easters in homes and with loved ones they would never see again. Some of the detainees asked the RGO representatives to autograph postcards for their families.[3]

The end of the RGO's massive feeding program at Majdanek threatened to put many of the employees involved in it out of work, but Skrzyński managed to obtain funds so that the Lublin Polish Care Committee could retain them. Soon, there was more than enough work to occupy them. In early May, 1,300 new refugees from Volhynia were placed in the Krochmalna camp and under RGO care. Hundreds more refugees followed from both Volhynia and the district, now fleeing the advance of Soviet forces as well as ethnic violence. Krochmalna could not possibly process them all, and so transports arriving at the Lublin station were regularly being sent on to other districts. Janina obtained permission to set up a care center in the station, where the Lublin Polish Care Committee provided hot meals, packages, and medical assistance to the refugees who were passing through. It was even possible to transfer the seriously injured and ill to local hospitals and to keep their families in Lublin while they recovered.[4]

The memory of Dr. Hanusz's tear-stained face begging her to get him his Bible haunted Janina. She could think of no way to smuggle it to him in Gross-Rosen, and it could not be sent in a package without being discovered and removed by the SS. Would it be possible to get the Bible to Hanusz through some official channel? From Zelent, Janina learned that Hanusz had been on good terms with Dr. Heinrich Rindfleisch, who had replaced Blancke as Majdanek's chief doctor. Perzanowska considered Rindfleisch to be the best of the SS doctors, actually capable of being humane. Janina decided to take her chances, and during a visit to Majdanek managed to find Rindfleisch in his office.[5]

She pleaded her case with the doctor, telling him that she was appealing to him not as an SS official but as a physician. "Would you refuse a sick man a harmless medicine he craved, even if you knew scientifically that it could be of no benefit?"

The doctor sprang to his feet before Janina finished. "I am a captain in the SS!"

"And a physician," Janina quickly added.

"How can you expect me to take this to him when you know it is against regulations?"

"What about your doctor's oath?" Janina rejoined. "Haven't you sworn to help the sick with every means in your power? And Hanusz is a sick man, sick unto death, and you are the only physician who can help him!" She wondered whether she had gone too far.

Rindfleisch paced the room, then asked to inspect the Bible. "Are there any markings in it?"

Janina handed it over and he inspected it carefully.

"All right," he finally sighed, "I'll take it to him, provided that I go where they have sent him. But," he added sternly, "if anyone ever finds out about this, be assured that an SS officer will know where to find you, Madame!"

He quickly left the room, and Janina hurried out as well, before anyone could see her and ask what she had been doing there.[6]

On April 19, the women's camp was officially closed when its last remaining prisoners departed on a transport to Ravensbrück. Only 180 male prisoners remained, 90 of them Poles, all housed in Field I. In addition, Field II held about 1,500 wounded Red Army soldiers in a special convalescent hospital that the SS had established for propaganda purposes. Fields III, IV, and V were empty.[7] Thumann and Weiss left in early May.[8]

Majdanek's post office closed as well, so it was no longer possible to bring or mail packages for the prisoners to the camp. However, Janina obtained permission to provide a weekly package for each of the remaining Polish prisoners, which Petrak agreed to pick up from the RGO at Lubartowska Street. In practice, he would arrange for the packages to be picked up whenever Janina called and told him they were ready, so the prisoners received packages almost daily.[9]

This arrangement ended suddenly in mid-May, when Arthur Liebehenschel replaced Weiss as Majdanek's commandant. Just a year earlier, Liebehenschel had been the second highest official in the Inspectorate of Concentration Camps, which oversaw the entire SS camp system. Then he abandoned his wife just before the birth of their fourth child for a secretary in the inspectorate office who was fifteen years his junior. Even worse, it was discovered that the secretary had been arrested years earlier on suspicion of having relations with a Jew. Himmler was scandalized. Liebehenschel was dismissed from his post and transferred to Auschwitz in November 1943, where he served as commandant of the main camp, with supervisory authority over the killing center at Birkenau. His mistress soon joined him and became pregnant. When Liebehenschel refused orders to separate from her and applied to marry her in April 1944, he was punished with the assignment to Majdanek.[10]

Liebehenschel was outraged when he learned that Polish charitable organizations had regularly provided food and medicines for Majdanek prisoners. There were to be no more such arrangements, he ordered, and that applied to the provision of packages as well. He even threatened to arrest anyone from the RGO or the Polish Red Cross who attempted to enter the camp.

Once again, Petrak came to Janina's aid. Disobeying Liebehenschel's order, he regularly came to Lubartowska Street in the evening to pick up packages that he personally delivered to the prisoners. Janina recognized that this was not a sustainable arrangement, however. Petrak could only carry a few packages at a time, and it seemed probable that he would be discovered, which would end all chances of getting permission for any kind of assistance to Majdanek prisoners. After repeated efforts, she finally obtained an appointment to meet with Liebehenschel.

Father Michalski accompanied Janina to the meeting. When they entered the commandant's office, all they could see of him was his back as he stood looking out a window. He neither turned nor spoke, even when Janina greeted him. Hostility seemed to radiate out of the man. Acting as if the situation were perfectly natural, Janina began explaining the purpose of her visit. Suddenly, the commandant erupted.

"What do you think you're doing here?" he screamed, still facing the window. "Do you imagine this is a sanatorium for bandits and enemies of our country? Is that why you keep coming here as if it were a drawing room or something? Feeding these criminals, as if they were the most precious people on earth! This is sheer Polish insolence. Don't you know that this is a concentration camp? Do you think it's a mess hall for gentlemen? You and your committee," he spat, "we should look into your activities. We should investigate all of you, including your precious charges! Those darlings that you are feeding with such dedication— why, they look much better off than our soldiers! They're healthy and strong, don't do a stitch of work all day long and are being fed like princes!"

Janina was all too familiar with such tantrums from German officials. After Liebehenschel's tirade ended, she moved to the other window in the office and, with her back to him, calmly continued. "We are an institution approved by the German authorities to care for the needy among the Polish population, and whatever we have done in Majdanek has been with the agreement of the camp administration."

Janina Mehlberg, ca. 1930s.

Photo ca. 1925–1926 of the students of Kazimierz Twardowski at Jan Kazimierz University in Lwów. Janina Mehlberg is in the bottom row, far right; Henry Mehlberg is in the top row, far left.

Henry (then Henryk) Mehlberg, ca. 1936. The photo was included in an album created by Kazimierz Twardowski's students in honor of their professor.

Wedding photo of Andrzej Skrzyński with his fourth wife, Zofia Mycielska Skrzyńska, in Wrocław, 1964.

A warning sign in German and Polish at Majdanek.

Aerial view of Majdanek showing workshops and warehouses in the center and, just above, Field I on the right and the bathing and disinfection facility with the gas chambers on the left. The "Black Road" runs from above the upper left corner of Field I to the Chełm Road.

Prisoners' barracks in one of Majdanek's compounds.

View of guard towers, fence, and crematorium chimney at Majdanek.

"Pacification" of a Polish village, either Biłgoraj or Zamość County (*Kreis*), Lublin District, June–July 1943.

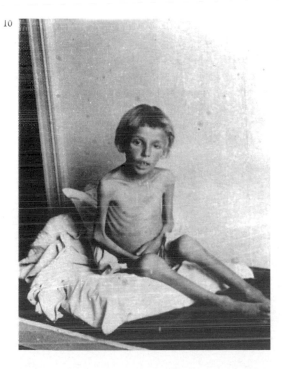

Ania Rempa, a Polish girl from Zamość, released from Majdanek in August 1943. She did not survive.

View from the village of Dziesiąta of smoke from the burning of corpses at Majdanek.

View of the Zamek prison after the German retreat from Lublin in 1944.

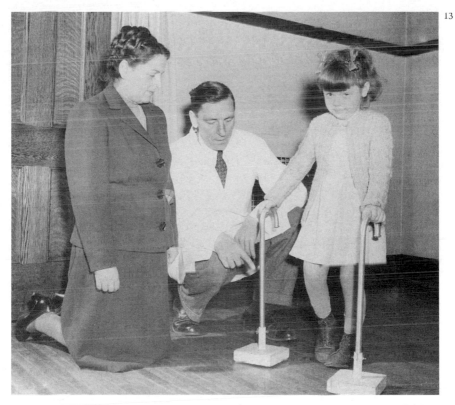

Janina Mehlberg (then known as Suchodolska) tours a Minneapolis school for children with disabilities in 1948. Janina's visit was part of her United Nations fellowship.

Photo of Janina and Henry Mehlberg, ca. 1950s.

Janina and Henry Mehlberg (middle) with their prewar friend Joseph Klinghofer and his son, Irvin, in Canada, 1961. Joseph was also a Holocaust survivor and assisted the Mehlbergs' emigration to Canada.

Photograph of Professor Josephine Mehlberg teaching a mathematics class at Illinois Institute of Technology, ca. 1960.

"Not anymore!" Liebehenschel barked.

Janina was not about to back down. "Perhaps, if there's no need for soup now, we could just send some packages," she suggested reasonably.

"You Polacks!" he shrieked, expressing all his scorn and loathing with the pejorative term. "We throw you out one door and presto, you come in by another!" Then, nonplussed by Janina's cool persistence, he shouted. "I can't hear what you're mumbling there. You're talking to the window!"

Janina turned. "And I don't hear you too well either, Herr *Kommandant*, and perhaps that is why we can't seem to come to an understanding."

At that, Liebehenschel turned to face her for the first time, and, after studying her for a moment, gestured for her to sit down. Uninvited, Father Michalski also took a seat. Janina proceeded to explain to the commandant how the RGO's help would be to his advantage as well. "You have said yourself," she pointed out, "that the people still here were kept to maintain order in the camp. You surely realize that well-fed workers are more efficient than underfed ones. If you consider soup superfluous, I won't insist on it. I could provide packages instead."

He gave up and said gruffly, "Packages, all right, but no luxuries. Only what prisoners in other camps get, nothing extra!"

Janina stood up as tall as she could and replied with dignity, "Then I shall inquire what others are getting, although I can assure you, sir, that I have quite a few years' experience in feeding prisoners." She was glad to have won this much. "May I please have a list of the prisoners to whom we may send the packages?" She already knew who they were, but the list would provide a legitimate basis for her knowledge.

The delivery of food packages for Majdanek's Polish prisoners resumed. On his own initiative, Petrak even allowed the RGO to bring the packages to the camp post office. Since one of the prisoners assigned to carry them to Field I was Janina's AK comrade Czesław Kulesza, Janina was back in occasional contact with the prisoners.

But now there were hundreds more Poles at Majdanek who were not counted in the official rolls of the concentration camp. The Wehrmacht had set up a forced labor camp in Field V to hold the workers it was drafting to build fortifications around Lublin. Most of them were peasants from nearby villages, seized at a moment's notice and interned in the camp with no way to communicate with their families. As soon as she learned of the camp, Janina went to see the German general in charge of the fortifications program to request permission to feed the prisoners. The general insisted that the prisoners' food was adequate and offered Janina the opportunity to interview some of them at a worksite, but only if she spoke to them in German. Janina refused, for the prisoners would not understand her and would view her as collaborating with the Germans. The general relented and allowed Janina to interview the forced laborers in Polish regarding their food and work. The men confirmed that they were receiving sufficient food, but some were obviously too old or weak to perform heavy labor and many had suffered injuries, especially to their feet, because their shoes had worn to tatters. All of them were desperate to get in touch with their families. Janina took down the addresses of the men she spoke to so that she could inform their families that they were in Majdanek.[11]

Janina returned to the Wehrmacht command, this time to a major with authority over the camp in Field V. She proposed that the RGO supply shoes and clothes for the prisoners, postcards that they could send to their families, and a physician to examine their fitness for labor. The last proposal was a concession that she had won for the Krochmalna Street camp, but it was too much for the major, and he refused all three of her requests. In the meantime, as a result of the letters she had written, the relatives of prisoners in the Wehrmacht camp were besieging Janina's office with pleas for help in getting their loved ones released. Local authorities applied to her as well, complaining that the Wehrmacht had left almost no one to tend the fields and so the county would face starvation in the fall.

Undeterred by the major's rejection of her proposals, Janina succeeded in getting another interview with the general. She won his permission to supply shoes and postcards for the prisoners in the Field V camp, and for the prisoners to receive packages from their families. The RGO would be responsible for delivering and distributing the packages and for retrieving and mailing the postcards. The general even ordered that a Wehrmacht physician be assigned to attend to the prisoners in the camp, stipulating that all the medicines and supplies he ordered be provided by the RGO.

The general's approval of all her requests only encouraged Janina to ask for more. She presented one additional proposal: instead of keeping the same contingent of forced laborers in the camp, the Wehrmacht could allow local authorities to assign rotating contingents of laborers who would work on the fortifications for a few days at a time and return to work their fields when the next contingent replaced them. This the general refused out of hand, probably assuming that the matter was now closed. Janina, of course, had no intention of letting it drop.

With the general's permission to distribute shoes, postcards, and packages, Janina once again had access to Majdanek, though only to Field V and via a different road than the one that ran alongside the other compounds. When the Wehrmacht doctor first arrived at Field V, Janina was already there with several assistants, handing out postcards to the prisoners and writing down their addresses and physical complaints. She encouraged prisoners who were sick or injured to go speak with the German doctor, who quickly found himself surrounded by people clamoring to him in a language he did not understand. Janina then introduced herself to the doctor and offered to supply him with an interpreter. His grateful acceptance of her offer led her to conclude that he had some decency. From that point on, the doctor was never at Majdanek without an RGO employee by his side.

By June, there were at least 1,500 forced laborers in Field V, including women and girls. Unsurprisingly, illnesses were spreading rapidly among them, requiring an infirmary to be established. The Wehrmacht could supply no extra doctors, however, or even any nurses. The overwhelmed Wehrmacht physician accepted Janina's proposal that the RGO provide nurses for the infirmary as well as a doctor to be his assistant. The RGO had no trouble finding nurses willing to work shifts at Majdanek.

These arrangements provided new opportunities for rescuing prisoners. The RGO's physician made rounds prior to the arrival of the German doctor and used the time to instruct patients about the symptoms of certain diseases. The Wehrmacht doctor treated the Polish physician as his colleague and agreed with his diagnoses. When Janina pointed out that it made little sense for the Wehrmacht to feed and house people who couldn't work, the doctor agreed and signed forms certifying that patients were unfit for labor. With these in hand, Janina succeeded in persuading the authorities to release the patients into the RGO's care.

Over two weeks, Janina arranged for four hundred prisoners to be released in this way, including all the minors. Then the major visited and found that the camp was missing over one quarter of its prisoners. "This is sabotage!" he said accusingly to Janina.

"We have nothing to do with it," Janina replied. "Your own doctor certified that all those released were unfit."

Then she broached the proposal for local authorities to supply laborers who would work on the fortifications for a few days each week in exchange for the forced laborers in the camp. The major finally agreed to the assignment of temporary workers, but would only permit the release from the camp of prisoners certified by the Wehrmacht physician as unable to work.

That evening, Janina was in Field V, distributing packages and postcards to the prisoners returning from work, when she heard a German officer make an announcement via an interpreter: "All prisoners willing to stay in the camp and work should come forward and be registered. All others will be deported." This was a bluff, Janina knew, intended to deter the prisoners from reporting sick, for they all feared being sent far away from their families. She was standing near the rear of the assembled prisoners and proceeded to squeeze her way between them from row to row, warning them in a staccato whisper not to fall for the trap. She could hear her message being passed farther on. Then she waited in suspense for the result. No one stepped forward to be registered.

"All right then," the officer announced, "tomorrow your names will be taken for the deportation transports." This sham order was withdrawn two days later.

To the prisoners remaining in Field V, Countess Suchodolska was their comforter and protector. They found out her first name and on her name day they gathered to greet her when she arrived. They had taken up a collection from the meager wages that prisoners received and pressed it on her, asking that she use it to buy packages for the neediest outside the camp. The desire of these people, enduring captivity and forced labor, to be of help to others so touched Janina that she wept. Some of the prisoners gave her

letters expressing their thanks. The wording of one, written in an awkward
scrawl, stayed with her for decades:

> May each smile that you brought to a child's face, may each tear that
> you helped wipe from a wife's or a mother's eyes, be counted in your
> favor before the throne of the Almighty. May each of your wishes, you
> who are an example for Polish womanhood, be granted. May you be
> spared and saved. Throughout the ages, Amen.
>
> Wojciech Sobol

In mid-June, Janina received a message from Kulesza, her AK comrade
in Field I. Several hundred women and children were imprisoned in the
compound, in barracks surrounded by barbed wire. They were peasants
seized in pacification operations. Some of their men were in the compound
as well, held separate from their families and subjected to regular interrogations by the Gestapo. They were not being fed by the Majdanek SS, because
they were not classified as concentration camp prisoners, and they were beginning to starve. Kulesza and the other Polish prisoners were providing
them with the contents of the packages they were receiving from the RGO,
but he begged Janina to find some way to help the pacification prisoners.[12]
    Liebehenschel refused to see Janina, claiming he had no responsibility
for the peasants. After inquiring at various offices, Janina concluded that she
would have to apply to the Gestapo. This meant she would have to go "under
the clock," to the Gestapo headquarters in Lublin.
    On the day of her appointment there, Janina took Wójcikowa with her,
but left her to wait on a bench outside. From the reception desk, Janina was
escorted under armed guard through heavy iron doors to an office where a
Gestapo officer awaited her. He asked her to state her business.
    "To feed the civilians being held in Majdanek—" she began, but he im-
mediately interrupted her.
    "Majdanek is not under our jurisdiction. You're wasting your time."
    "But the commandant of Majdanek himself directed me to you because
these inmates are under Gestapo jurisdiction," she lied.
    "You know very well," he answered, "that we keep our prisoners in

Zamek. Only after they're found guilty do they go to Majdanek." With increasing anger, he added, "And there are so many of your bandits that even your prisons can't hold them all and we've had to make camps for them. German soldiers die in battle, German civilians die from bombings, and here we keep your criminals in camps and feed them!"

As usual, Janina waited patiently for this harangue to end. Assuming an air of quiet authority, she continued, "There are prisoners in Majdanek, including women and children, who are under Gestapo jurisdiction. I represent the Polish organization authorized by the Security Police to care for prisoners in the General Government. I therefore request permission to provide food for these prisoners."

The official called around on the office intercom but could find no one who knew anything about what was happening in Majdanek. Another official arrived, and the two interrogated Janina about her identity and activities. She showed no emotion as she answered them. Finally, from the various conversations she overheard, she concluded that she would need to consult a Gestapo officer named Rohlfing, who was not in the building. So she left and retrieved Wójcikowa from the pretty little park that the Germans had created across from the building. "Just like the Germans," she thought, "to plant flowers before the gates of Hell."

On her return visit "under the clock," Janina left Father Michalski on the park bench. Her surmise that SS Second Lieutenant Rohlfing was the official she needed to speak with turned out to be correct. He was in charge of disposing of the people seized in pacification operations who were not shot for supporting the partisans. Only the able-bodied interested him, since he was charged with sending as many as possible to the Reich. Prior to this assignment, Hermann Rohlfing had charge of creating a camp in the woods outside Chełm, about forty-five miles east of Lublin, that served as both a cremation and an execution site. Jewish prisoners whom he personally selected during the Operation Harvest Festival massacre at Majdanek were forced to dig up mass graves and burn the corpses they contained, as well as the bodies of fresh victims brought to the site to be shot or murdered on the way there in gas vans. Rohlfing eradicated the evidence of tens of thousands of murders committed by the Germans of Soviet and Italian POWs as well as Jews and Poles.[13]

When Janina presented her proposal to Rohlfing, he reacted in typical German fashion. "What! You want to feed these bandits? You could be arrested yourself for asking such a thing. How dare you!"

"We have been taking care of prisoners for years," Janina explained calmly. "And besides, they're not all bandits. I saw some who were only this high," she added, holding her hand to indicate a child's height.

"How do you know that?" Rohlfing roared. "Who's your spy in there?"

"I have often visited Field V, and in the distance I noticed children and was surprised, because I didn't think they could have been convicted of any crimes."

At that moment, the air was split by a heart-stopping scream that died out in a gurgle. Janina knew that interrogations occurred on the same floor, but suspected that the sound might have been staged to frighten her. But then a nasty-looking SS man entered, juggling his gun from one hand to the other. "I put him to sleep," he reported with a smirk.

Rohlfing told the man of Janina's inquiry about some children at Majdanek. He smiled, then said he would go check. After a moment, he returned and confirmed Janina's report. Rohlfing acted surprised, claiming this was the first he had heard of the situation and promising to contact Majdanek's commandant about permitting help for the children. Janina did not believe his claim of ignorance but was satisfied. If she could get permission to feed the children, she would find a way to feed the adults as well.

In fact, after he heard from Rohlfing, Liebehenschel permitted the RGO to deliver packages for all the victims of pacification operations being held in Field I. As she had the summer before with the Zamość civilians in Majdanek, Janina persuaded the Security Police to release some of the women and children to the RGO on the grounds that they were not guilty of any crimes and were unfit for labor.[14]

Meanwhile, thanks to the arrangements Janina had set up at Krochmalna, Polish refugees were being routinely released, either because the RGO physicians found them in need of hospitalization or unfit for labor, or because they were family members of the sick or unfit, or because Lublin employers had claimed them as workers. The RGO was winning the release of as many as 95 percent of the Polish refugees. It was unable to do anything for the Ukrainian and Belarusian refugees, however, who were transported to the Reich for forced labor. It was also difficult to gain the release of young, able-bodied people who lacked labor cards and had been seized for work in the Reich. Janina sought to identify members of the AK among them and rescue them. Her contact in the Labor Office, an ethnic German woman, provided false labor cards and sent alerts about impending raids.[15]

In mid-July, Janina received notice from Rohlfing that she was to pick up a group of the pacification prisoners from Field I who were being released to the RGO. On her way to Majdanek, however, she spotted Father Michalski rushing down the street and frantically trying to flag her down. He had just been at Krochmalna and reported that Rohlfing was there and in a rage after finding that he could pack off only a tiny percentage of the Polish detainees to the Reich. He was yelling that "the goddamn bandits" were feigning sickness to be released and then rejoining their units.

"He's now screaming threats against you," Michalski warned Janina. "He blames you for everything. He kept shouting that he would have you arrested and that he was coming for you after he finished with the bandits."

The priest tearfully begged Janina not to go to Majdanek, fearing that Rohlfing would have her seized there. Janina was frightened, but saw no alternative. She could not leave those people in the camp, and only she was authorized to take custody of them.

When she arrived at Majdanek, Janina found the prisoners to be released already waiting at the guardhouse. She asked the guard whether someone would come to release them to her, but all he knew was that they no longer belonged in the camp and she was supposed to take them. So she had them board the truck and drove off.

Knowing that the Gestapo made arrests at night, Janina stopped sleeping at home, although she still went to the office during the day. No one showed up at her residence to arrest her, however. The Soviets were on the offensive again, and the Germans had other things to worry about.

NINETEEN

BLOOD ON THE STAIRS

On July 18, 1944, there was a giant traffic jam in Lublin's streets. Military convoys and tanks were heading in one direction to take up positions against the advancing Red Army. Heading in the other direction were German civilians in cars, trucks, and wagons piled high with the loot they had seized in Poland. Germans filled the city's main rail station, pushing and shoving to board the last trains departing for the Reich. The German occupation of Lublin was disintegrating.

Janina no longer lived at 22 Narutowicza Street, for the Germans had confiscated the building, giving the residents forty-eight hours to move out. Thanks to her position in the RGO, she had been allotted quarters in the German district, in a building just off Hitler-Platz. She had arranged for her "aunties," Countess Władysława and Madame Maria, to obtain housing there as well. When Janina walked out of the building that morning and saw the commotion in the streets, she decided to investigate what was happening with the German administration, using business with the BuF office as a pretext.

In the courtyard of the district administration building, Janina found the BuF secretary, Frau Stiefler, surrounded by files whose pages she was hurriedly feeding to a fire. Janina asked to see her boss.

"He isn't here today, come back tomorrow," Stiefler snapped. The woman had always treated Janina with icy disdain. But then she turned, and Janina saw that her face was etched with anxiety, her lips trembling, and her eyes filling with tears.

"Whatever is the matter, Frau Stiefler?" Janina asked in a sympathetic tone.

"Don't you know that the Bolsheviks are quite near?" Stiefler answered. "Tomorrow we'll all be leaving. The bosses have already left, but I still have some things to do before I go." Then, sobbing, she warned Janina of the horrors committed by Soviet soldiers and urged her to fill out a travel permit for herself, which the office manager could authorize.

Taking leave of Frau Stiefler, Janina went into the building, which seemed eerily quiet. The office manager was not there. Janina wandered about, knocking on various doors, and peeking inside when no one answered. Empty file drawers hung open, trash and sheets of paper were strewn about, but Janina could find no German officials. It appeared that they had all fled, leaving Frau Stiefler behind to destroy the records of their activities.

Janina hurried on to her office. Her workload had expanded in early June, when the RGO received an order to take over all of the prisoner care activities of the Polish Red Cross. The Germans decided that only an organization under their direct control should have access to their prisons, not one that answered to an international body. Skrzyński had pleaded for the transfer to be postponed. He argued that the Lublin RGO could not afford to buy all the materials and medicines that the Polish Red Cross had been supplying or to pay the extra employees needed to acquire and distribute them. The Germans refused. Nevertheless, Christians blamed Skrzyński for what he viewed as a usurpation of his authority.[1]

As a result of the change, Janina was now overseeing the provision of all packages, medicines, and medical equipment for Polish prisoners in Zamek, the nineteenth-century neo-Gothic castle built as a prison. Although it was designed to hold 700 prisoners, there were generally 2,000 to 3,000 there, held in conditions of starvation, disease, and utter squalor. Hundreds of new prisoners had been flowing into the castle in the past two months, mostly captured Polish partisans or Poles accused of resistance activities.

The overall number of prisoners did not change, however, for prisoners had been flowing out of the prison just as quickly, in buses and vans that took them to Majdanek. Not to the camp, though, but straight to the crematorium. At least one of the transports was a gas van that asphyxiated its passengers en route. The other prisoners were shot in the crematorium or in nearby trenches.[2]

Between July 19 and 21, the transports traveled constantly back and forth between Zamek and the Majdanek crematorium, whose five ovens were insufficient to dispose of all the bodies. The order had gone out to the Security Police that no prisoners should fall into the hands of the enemy. Any prisoners who could not be evacuated were to be "liquidated," and the bodies of those shot should be destroyed, whether through burning or by blowing up the prisons where they were murdered. The liquidation order particularly applied to all the Jewish tailors, cobblers, and carpenters being held in Zamek. They had been spared from Operation Harvest Festival in order to produce clothing and furniture for the Security Police.

On the morning of July 22, the people of Lublin could hear artillery fire, which steadily grew louder. Many of them took to basements and shelters, preparing for the battle that was about to engulf the city. Janina went to the office, however, for she had a vital task to complete. A courier was leaving that day for the Underground delegation in Warsaw, probably the last one to travel out of Lublin. She wanted him to take the lists she had been preparing that contained the names, addresses, and precise prisoner numbers of all the concentration camp prisoners to whom Janina and her committee of volunteers had been sending packages.

It was shortly after noon when the courier set off with the lists. Janina allowed herself to relax for a moment and savor the thought that the Germans would soon be gone, if not that day, then in the next few days. And she and Henry were still alive. They had defied the odds, after all.

Dąbrowski entered to relate to Janina what had just happened in his office. A man in Wehrmacht uniform had rushed in, claiming that he had been imprisoned in Zamek and that there had been a massacre there that morning. Dąbrowski was saying that he didn't believe the man, probably he was an *agent provocateur*.... But Janina was already out the door and flying down the stairs. She ran around the corner and started down Kowalska Street. The buildings at the top gave way to piles of debris and then fields of rubble, all that was left of the four-hundred-year-old Jewish quarter. Above this desolate landscape loomed Zamek.

Relatives of prisoners were milling about outside the outer wall. Although the entry next to the gatehouse stood open, they feared to enter. Seeing Janina running toward them, some called to her, "The Germans have left time bombs inside!"

Janina continued running up to the gate, and the cries from the crowd became louder and more urgent. "Don't go in there, don't go in, Countess! You'll die in there! They're all dead inside. That's what they want, to finish you off in there." Some dropped to their knees to pray.

Janina saw them but could not stop. She ran through the gate and toward the great arch that led to the castle's interior courtyard. The doors were open, and the Polish custodian was standing inside, holding a ring of keys. He motioned her to the left, "Straight ahead here, Countess, there might be wounded in the hospital hall."

Janina charged ahead but only saw empty beds. Her youngest assistant appeared at her side, having followed Janina from the office. Janina was surprised, for she had always thought the girl rather timid. Seeing a movement in the corner of a cell, they turned over a mattress and found a woman lying under it, still alive but too injured to move on her own. With a shock, Janina recognized her: she was a teacher at a public school in the city. Janina and her assistant half dragged, half carried the woman outside the gates. Then Janina sent her assistant back to the RGO building to fetch help and went searching for a working phone. She found one and called the Polish Red Cross to send ambulances.

She did not wait but ran back into the castle, noticing a wisp of smoke rising from the right side of the building. In the interior courtyard, she ran toward the far left corner, where she knew there were cells with political prisoners. She passed a few bodies lying in pools of blood as she sprinted to the entrance to the ward. Then she stopped. A rippling pool of blood was spreading before her, fed by rivulets of blood that were flowing down the stairs. The air was thick with the stench of a slaughterhouse.

Now she knew where she had to go. Stepping into the pool, she began to climb the stairs, clutching the railing so as not to slip. At the top, she followed the blood to her right and came upon a cell whose door was standing open. Inside were piles of twisted bodies, at least a hundred it seemed, some with skulls shattered from bullet wounds. Janina heard moans and cries and realized that the quick and the dead were mixed together. Others now joined her, and they began trying to extricate the victims who still lived. Janina followed the blood, now ankle-deep, to the end of the corridor. In a large chamber, bodies were stacked in piles more than six feet high. She estimated at least 150. Strewn between the bodies were overturned sewing machines. Some of the corpses, Janina realized, wore armbands marking them as Jews. These were the Jewish tailors, who had so long evaded the fate visited upon their families, only to be murdered at the last moment.

More victims showing signs of life were being pulled out of the piles of bodies. "How many more were still alive but being crushed to death by the weight of the corpses?" Janina wondered. "And which of those being pulled out stood a chance of surviving and should be tended to first?" The castle was shaking from the impact of shells falling nearby. There was no time to waste, she decided; a doctor needed to come immediately to conduct triage. She ran back to the working telephone to call the Lublin Polish Care Committee's physician, but she could not reach him. What doctor could she find who would risk the growing danger in the city to come to this hell?

Janina went out to search the nearby streets. A couple was hurrying by, and the man bore the insignia of a medical officer. Janina stopped him and asked him to go with her. They looked at her in horror. Janina did not understand how frightening she must appear, her clothes splattered with blood and her squelching shoes leaving bloody footprints behind her.

"Don't go, darling," the woman urged, "you'll get killed there. What's the use of having survived the occupation only to perish now?"

Janina fixed the man with a steady gaze. He knew he had a duty to go, as a physician and as a Pole, and that others would know and judge him if he neglected his duty. He went with Janina.

Back in the castle, people were laying the victims out in the courtyard, and relatives were searching among them for their loved ones. Janina saw a mother embracing the wounded head of her son, softly moaning as she wiped blood from his pale face. Nearby, an old man stood over the body of a young boy, screaming "Save my grandson! Save my grandson!" But no one came to his aid, for they were all tending to their own wounded and murdered, and the grandson was obviously dead.

Looking back toward the entrance, Janina saw that the wisp of smoke she had spotted earlier had become a billowing cloud, and she could detect a burning smell. "This place must not burn and take with it the evidence of the crimes committed here!" she thought. She dashed back to the telephone to call the fire department. It took some persuading to get the fire chief to send his crews, but Janina succeeded and the fire was extinguished.

But now the battle had reached the outskirts of Lublin and it had become too dangerous to continue searching for the living. About fifteen of those who had been found were carried on stretchers to the RGO building on Lubartowska Street to await transfer to hospitals. Relatives who found the corpses of their loved ones quickly carted them away. The rest of the victims, some three hundred, had to be left in the castle while the battle of Lublin raged. Only three days later would it be possible to retrieve them.

TWENTY

THE END

When Janina arrived home on July 22, 1944, the residents of her building were already sheltering in the basement, along with a Wehrmacht detachment led by a sergeant. He ordered the tenants to leave their apartments unlocked so that his troops could use them as observation posts. The tenants were only allowed to enter them to prepare meals. As Janina and her neighbors listened to bombs and shells exploding around them, their mood was cheerful. Soon, after nearly five years of terror, their German occupiers would be gone.

By dawn the next morning, tanks were rumbling in Lublin's streets. The soldiers in Janina's building would run out, fire their antitank weapons, and return, their faces dripping with sweat, their eyes wide with fear. A truck parked outside the building, then the sergeant appeared and ordered all the tenants to move to a different part of the basement. Rumors flew. One man claimed that the Germans had thrown grenades into a nearby basement where people were sheltering, another that the Germans were going to push women, children, and the elderly into the streets to block the Soviet tanks. A third reported that the Germans were seizing men and taking them away for forced labor. Panic spread; the tenants were arguing and shouting. Except for Countess Władysława and her sister, who quietly knelt on the damp floor and began one of their special prayers, as if they were at morning Mass.

Janina discounted the first two rumors, but the report that men were being seized for labor sounded all too plausible. Her household now consisted of Henry; Count Skrzyński's eighteen-year-old son, Ryś; and a Volhynian teenager whom Janina had rescued from Krochmalna. She was not about to lose them at this last moment. For Henry, being taken would lead to his exposure as a Jew and certain death.

All four of them went up to their apartment to prepare breakfast. Henry proposed that the three men hide in a windowless dressing room off the bedroom, against which Janina would push a chest of drawers. Janina vetoed this proposal, for their absence would be noticed, and if the Germans found the men, they would be shot. What they needed was a way to convince the Germans not to enter the apartment or seek out the men. Once again, Janina's ability to think like the Germans inspired her with a plan. Leaving the others in the apartment, she went to the basement and reported to the sergeant that Ryś Skrzyński was running a high fever and showing signs of typhoid. The sergeant immediately ordered her to return to the apartment and stay there, along with the three men, so as not to spread the disease. He also gifted her half a bottle of brandy for the patient.

They placed Ryś on a mattress in the apartment's entry, while the two men stayed in the windowless dressing room with the door open so that they would not be accused of signaling out the windows to the Soviets. Meanwhile, Janina "nursed" Ryś by giving him a thermometer, teaching him how to make it register a fever, and schooling him on the symptoms of typhoid.

That night, the wife of the building janitor knocked on the apartment door. There were some escaped Majdanek prisoners in the basement, she reported, and they were begging for men's clothes. Janina mistrusted the woman. She had claimed ethnic German status during the occupation and had snubbed Janina when she first came to the building, but in recent days had transformed into a fervently patriotic Pole. So Janina turned her away, warning that the apartment was not safe because of the presence of infectious disease.

At dawn the next morning, there was more knocking at the door. Janina opened it wide, which she had found was safest. Her blood ran cold. At the door stood the orderly of Dr. Blancke from Majdanek. Seeing him in his SS uniform, armed and helmeted, Janina's first panicked thought was that he had come to seize her. Then she remembered that the SS always came in twos to make arrests. Perhaps he wouldn't even recognize her, since her hair was hanging long rather than as he had always seen it, arranged in braids around her head and under a kerchief. But if he had come to investigate the report of typhoid, how could they fool him? He was well acquainted with the disease from his service at Majdanek. Had they survived so long, only to be taken at the last moment before freedom?

"Well, Madame, so this is where you live!" he began. "I had no idea at whose door I knocked. Nor did I expect to see you again, during this time of retreat. But this is only temporary. Assistance is coming. Then we'll get rid of these wild beasts and they'll be eating potato peels again. You should see them fighting—like animals! They come at us in a tank, we attack it, and they go right on fighting, even when the tank is on fire, even when they're wounded, right until they're all dead. But that's not what I came about. Someone is sick here?"

This bluster in an almost friendly tone gave Janina time to collect her wits. Turning to Ryś, she asked, all sweet concern, "What is your temperature this morning, dear? I haven't taken the thermometer from you yet." Ryś had popped the thermometer into his mouth just before Janina opened the door and now removed it. He reported a high fever. The SS orderly avoided coming too near the mattress, but asked questions about the symptoms. Janina answered some and referred others to Ryś. As the orderly heard their answers, a look of alarm came into his face and he backed away. He expressed surprise to hear of typhoid in this part of the city, where the water was unpolluted, but accepted the diagnosis. Withdrawing into the hallway, he wrote up a sign and fixed it to the apartment door, ordering Janina to stay inside with the others. The sign read, "Entrance Forbidden. Typhoid suspected." A while later, there was another knock, but Janina only found some bottles of medicine when she opened the door. Her plan had succeeded.

Later that day, a neighbor came up from the basement to tell them that the Germans were leaving, and shortly afterward they heard their truck roar off. But German soldiers had set the building next door on fire when they left it, so Janina and her neighbors had some tense moments, wondering whether some disaster was about to befall them. Finally, during the night, Red Army soldiers arrived with fixed bayonets and announced that they were free. Except for the escaped Majdanek prisoners who had arrived the night before. The soldiers decided they seemed suspicious and took them to Zamek.

In the early morning hours of July 25, 1944, the residents of Lublin emerged from their basements and shelters to the heartbreaking sight of their city in ruins. For block after block they saw the roofless, windowless shells of buildings, some still burning. Piles of debris, bomb craters, and burnt-out trucks and tanks rendered the streets impassible. Strewn about were body parts of humans and animals blown to pieces by explosions. Now rotting in the summer heat, the remains sent up a gagging stench and posed the threat of epidemics.[1]

Majdanek had been taken by Soviet forces three days earlier. They found 480 prisoners there, consisting of Soviet POW invalids in Field II and the victims of pacification operations in Field I. The SS had abandoned the camp just hours earlier, force-marching more than 1,000 prisoners over sixty miles and then herding them onto a train to Auschwitz. Along the way, the guards shot hundreds of prisoners who failed to keep pace.[2]

The Majdanek SS managed to destroy most of the camp's records but did not succeed in removing all the physical evidence of the crimes committed at the camp. The gas chambers were not destroyed, and although the crematorium was set on fire, much of it still stood, including all its ovens and a pile of charred human remains. Corpses of victims from Zamek still lay in the nearby trenches. Hills of human ashes and heaps of hundreds of thousands of shoes indicated that murder had been committed there on a massive scale. Majdanek was the first major German concentration camp to be liberated and the first place where physical evidence was found confirming that the Germans had committed mass murder using poison gas in stationary facilities. The Soviets brought in foreign journalists to tour the camp and distributed films showing what the Red Army had found there.[3] The reports and films met with skepticism in the West, however. The *New York Herald Tribune* counseled against crediting "the horror story that comes out of Lublin. Even on top of all that we have been taught about the maniacal Nazi ruthlessness, this example seems inconceivable."[4]

The people of Lublin quickly discovered that their liberation from the German occupier did not, in fact, mean that they were free. As soon as the Germans departed, the Lublin representative of the Underground began to form an administration that answered to the Polish government in exile in London. On July 25, however, the Soviets installed the Polish Committee of National Liberation, or PKWN (*Polski Komitet Wyzwolenia Narodowego*), in power in Lublin. Polish communists had formed it in Moscow at the behest of Stalin, who intended it to administer the Polish territories that the Red Army was liberating.

The next day, the troops of the Polish First Army marched through Lublin's streets. This force, commanded by former Polish Army officer Zygmunt Berling, was created by the Soviets and subordinate to the Red Army, which provided most of its senior officers. Although the AK had fought alongside the Red Army in liberating Lublin, the Soviet military commander of the city gave the AK a choice: join the Polish First Army or give up their weapons and disband. The AK categorically refused the former, and many of its units refused the latter. The Soviet NKVD was prepared for this response. Within days of the Germans' departure, the cells of Zamek and the compounds of Majdanek were being repopulated by members of the AK and the Underground.[5]

As soon as the fighting ceased in Lublin, Janina returned to the RGO office. There, she received an unexpected visitor: the PKWN's deputy minister of labor, social work, and health, Dr. Jerzy Morzycki.

"I am here to express the gratitude and admiration of our Government to you for your deeds of heroic and sacrificial courage during the occupation. I am here to ask you to take part in the celebration of the liberation and the rites for the dead in the Zamek prison, and to talk to us about your struggle."

But Janina had no desire to lend legitimacy to Lublin's new rulers through her participation, particularly as she had just learned that some of her comrades were imprisoned and being interrogated in Zamek. She was so upset by this news that diplomacy failed her. Struggling to keep her voice

steady and to hide her distress, she looked into the middle distance and replied, "I am unable, *Monsieur le Ministre*, to accede to this request. I have
fought, prayed, and suffered for the day of liberation to come—and so did
most of the young people who are now in Zamek."

On August 1, 1944, the AK staged an uprising in Warsaw, believing that
Soviet forces were massing just across the Vistula River from the city and
would participate in the fight. It was a fatal miscalculation. The Red Army
was not across the river in force, and although the Soviets could have provided various kinds of assistance to the Polish soldiers and civilians who
were bravely fighting the Germans in the city, Stalin did not want to help
the AK score a major victory and install the government in exile in power
in Poland's capital.

The uprising took the Germans by surprise. The people of Warsaw rallied to the AK, and its forces seized significant sectors of the city. News of
the uprising so enraged Hitler that he ordered not only that it be mercilessly
crushed but also that the city be razed and all its inhabitants killed. The Germans began bombing and shelling the city incessantly and sent in reinforce-
ments. Making no distinction between the AK fighters wearing identifying
armbands and civilians, SS forces went house to house, pulling out all inside
and shooting them. On August 5 alone, the SS shot an estimated 40,000
victims. The AK were hopelessly outmanned and outgunned. By the time
the Allies tried to airlift supplies into the city in September, they proved to
be too little and too late.

After sixty-three days of heroic fighting, the AK surrendered on October 2, 1944. The Polish death toll in the city was 150,000 to 200,000, more
than 85 percent of the victims civilians. The Germans forced the remaining
280,000 Poles in the city to evacuate to a massive camp in Pruszków, from
which 100,000 were sent to the Reich for forced labor and thousands more
to concentration camps. Then the Germans methodically looted the city
and burned it to the ground. When the Red Army finally entered Warsaw in
January 1945, more than 80 percent of the city had been reduced to rubble.[6]

Nazi Germany surrendered unconditionally on May 8–9, 1945. While
the Allies were celebrating victory, many Poles, including Janina, felt more
like mourning. Throughout the long years of terror, suffering, courageous

resistance, and horrific death, they had refused to relinquish their hope of seeing their nation restored to full sovereignty. Now, they felt that they had merely exchanged one occupier for another. It appeared that the destiny of what remained of Poland was to be the servile satellite of the Soviet Union under the yoke of a brutal regime. And for Janina, destiny promised still more danger.

TWENTY-ONE

FLIGHT

Janina and Henry had a crucial decision to make in August 1944. Now that the Germans were gone, it was at least theoretically safe for them to revert to their true identities. The temptation to do so was strong. Polish Jews who had survived in hiding were flocking to Lublin, soon joined by those who had survived in the Soviet Union. Janina and Henry yearned to connect with people who shared their trauma and grief. Among them there might be some of Janina's and Henry's family members or friends, or at least someone who could provide information about their loved ones' fate.

Janina realized that she was not out of danger, however. She was liable to arrest, perhaps even execution, should the Soviet NKVD discover her service in the AK. As an RGO official, moreover, she was automatically suspect in the eyes of the new occupier. The Soviets considered the RGO a collaborationist organization, since it was largely led by Polish aristocrats who had acted in obedience to German orders. The NKVD also suspected that the RGO was closely allied to the Polish government in exile and the AK. When NKVD agents arrested two RGO officials in early August 1944 after discovering their AK activities, the scrutiny and harassment of other RGO officials intensified.[1]

Ludwik Christians encouraged Lublin's new rulers in their negative view of the RGO. He did not share Janina's concerns about appearing to legitimize the Soviet-imposed regime. Instead, he curried its favor. The Lublin communist officials, aware of their unpopularity with most Poles, welcomed the opportunity Christians offered them to be seen as working with a highly esteemed international organization. They even gave Christians a seat on the Extraordinary Commission for the Investigation of German Crimes at the Majdanek Camp, established by the Soviets to collect and publicize the evidence of German mass murder. Even though Skrzyński was more than happy to return to the Polish Red Cross the duties that the Germans had forced the RGO to take over, Christians accused the RGO generally and Skrzyński personally of requesting their German masters to invest them with control over the affairs of the Red Cross.

Outraged by Christians's accusation, Skrzyński demanded a hearing before an honor court. There was no longer any place he could go in Poland to get his reputation back, however. His position became untenable, and he was replaced as the RGO advisor. As soon as it was safe to do so, he left Lublin altogether. In 1946, Christians would publish a book about the aid program for Majdanek prisoners in which he gave all the credit to the Polish Red Cross and made no mention of the RGO or any of its officials.[7]

In the summer of 1944, however, Janina was still popular among the people of Lublin because of her work at Majdanek and Krochmalna, and this provided some protection from the suspicion and harassment of the communist authorities. If she revealed now that she was not the countess she had pretended to be but a Jew, it might tarnish her reputation, at least with some Poles. Even with the Germans gone, it was still not safe to be a Jew in Lublin, for some of those who were coming out of hiding and attempting to return to their homes were being attacked, even murdered, by Polish bandits, partisans, and former neighbors.[8] Revealing her true identity would certainly invite questions as to how she obtained her identity papers and RGO position, with the potential result that both she and Skrzyński would be exposed as AK operatives.

Despite its mistrust of the RGO, the new regime could not dispense with the Polish Care Committees' vital work, for even with the Germans gone, the desperate needs of the Poles were undiminished. Many of the committees' workers were resigning, however. Janina was asked to stay on and given the official title of deputy to the Lublin director. Retaining her false identity would ensure that Janina could go on being of service to her compatriots, and now not only to ethnic Poles but also to Polish Jews. There were practical considerations as well: she and Henry would have an income and housing. Her position also enabled her to provide jobs for Wendrucha's wife and for Skrzyński's daughter.[4]

So Janina and Henry decided to retain their false identities, at least for the time being. Together with Countess Władysława and Madame Maria, they were allowed to move back into the Countess's building on Naruto-wicza Street.[5] When the new administration replaced the RGO with the Central Committee of Social Welfare (*Centralny Komitet Opieki Społecznej* or CKOS) at the end of 1944, Janina was named to its governing board.[6]

In 1945, the Soviets transferred the Polish administration from Lublin to Warsaw. Janina had no choice but to say farewell to her "aunties" and go. As Dr. Janina Suchodolska, social worker, she became the head of the Organization and Inspection Department of CKOS. Traveling throughout her country, Janina saw firsthand the grief and desperation of its people. Some six million Polish citizens died during the war, 18 percent of prewar Poland's population. Half were Jews. The war had orphaned 1.5 million Polish children. Hunger and homelessness were everywhere, accompanied inevitably by epidemics and crime.[7]

Like the RGO, CKOS was a voluntary welfare organization and operated through care committees and branches working at the provincial, county, and local levels. It was able to take over the RGO's facilities and some of the staff in the part of postwar Poland that had been under the General Government, but had to start from scratch in other Polish regions. Janina quickly helped to organize 2,690 committees and branches throughout the country. Her work particularly focused on children and youth, including caring for 169,000 orphans under age three and providing vocational training for the hundreds of thousands of young adults who had been denied an education under the German occupation.[8]

Much of the funding for CKOS came from abroad, from international organizations like the United Nations Relief and Rehabilitation

Administration, and from numerous aid charities and Polish diaspora organizations. Thanks to her linguistic skills, Janina was given charge of CKOS's dealings with foreign funders, and she became CKOS deputy director in April 1946. This aspect of her work brought opportunities to attend international conferences in the West, including in Geneva in 1946 and Paris in September 1947.[9]

Henry was not content to live in Warsaw as Piotr Suchodolski. He longed to resume his work on the philosophy of physics and to pursue an academic career, something he could only do as Henry Mehlberg. Other members of the Lwów-Warsaw School who survived the war also hoped to continue its work in postwar Poland. Henry was able to get a teaching position under his true name at the newly created University of Łódź, whose rector was a former Twardowski student.[10] His new job required that Henry and Janina live apart and conceal their marriage.[11]

In Łódź, Henry succeeded in reconnecting with his brothers Izydor and Juliusz through the Central Committee of Jews in Poland. They informed Henry that their parents had been gassed in Bełżec and that their two married sisters had also been murdered. Izydor had survived the war by passing as Jerzy Markiewicz and was still using that name. Juliusz had survived in the Soviet Union and was planning to immigrate to Palestine.[12]

With the exception of its surviving Jewish citizens, postwar Poland was almost entirely a mono-ethnic state. The Soviet Union annexed prewar Poland's multiethnic eastern regions, while Poland's communist regime drove the ethnic Germans out of its western lands. Even more than before the war, Jewish Poles found themselves treated as undesirable outsiders by their non-Jewish compatriots. Although they supposedly enjoyed the same rights as all Polish citizens, Jews faced rampant discrimination and harassment. Violent attacks were not infrequent, especially against survivors who returned to find their homes and businesses occupied by Poles who had no intention of relinquishing them to their rightful owners. Estimates of the number of Polish Jews killed in the first year following the end of the war range from 500 to 1,500. Local officials tended to turn a blind eye to the violence, if they didn't actively participate in it. The provisional government had no interest in alienating the vast majority of Poles by cracking down on antisemitic discrimination and attacks. Like Henry's brother Izydor, many Jews who had survived on "Aryan" papers chose to retain their wartime identities to avoid falling victim to antisemitism.[13]

The fears of Jews in Poland were crystallized on July 4, 1946. In the city of Kielce, a mob of residents together with Polish soldiers and police brutally stripped and bludgeoned Holocaust survivors who had been living in the Jewish community building. The pogrom took the lives of forty-two Jews and left perhaps eighty seriously injured.[14] After the pogrom, 70,000 Polish Jews fled the country in just a few months, preferring to live in a displaced persons camp or to journey illegally to Palestine than to continue enduring the constant fear of violence in Poland.[15]

Henry was thinking of joining them. He achieved an important career goal in June 1946, when he obtained the habilitation in philosophy that qualified him to be a full professor. If he could get to the United States, he would have far greater opportunity to attract the notice and acclaim that he believed his work deserved. He also saw little prospect that he and Janina would ever be able to live together as themselves and free from fear in Poland.

Henry and Janina managed to establish contact with Henry's uncle Joseph Mehlberg and Janina's cousin Sigmund Pines, both in New York. Pines was the grandson of Janina's grandfather Berl Spinner, who immigrated to the United States before World War I with his wife and six of their children.[16] Since both relatives were willing to sponsor the Mehlbergs' immigration to the United States, Henry applied for a visa for himself and "wife" at the U.S. consulate in Warsaw in August 1946. To complete the immigration process, however, Janina would have to produce a passport showing that she was Henry's wife, and she could not apply for one without revealing to Polish authorities that she had lied to them about her identity.[17]

Henry registered with the Central Committee of Jews in Poland, listing his wife as Pepi Mehlberg née Spinner, a teacher, and stating only that they had survived the war on false papers. As a registered Jewish survivor, he then applied to the Emigration Service Office of the American Jewish Joint Distribution Committee (JDC), which assisted Jews seeking to leave Poland. He hoped that the JDC would be able to get travel papers and an exit permit for Pepi Mehlberg without her alternate identity coming to the attention of Polish authorities.[18]

In 1947, Henry received an appointment as associate professor of philosophy at the University of Wrocław, a significant advancement in his career. Soon after he began teaching there in the autumn, however, he received a warning: communist officials had placed spies in his seminar who were reporting on his teaching.[19] Henry could not afford to take the warning lightly. Poland's communist regime had commenced a Stalinist crackdown, and tens of thousands of Poles suspected of dissent or of spreading unorthodox ideas were being arrested and given lengthy prison sentences.

Once again, the possibility that Henry was in danger jolted Janina into full rescue mode. She had to get Henry out of the country, even if it required her to stay behind in Poland. An idea occurred to her: if she could manage to go on an official trip to the United States, she would make valuable contacts that would pave the way for Henry to go there. As a result of her participation in an international child welfare conference in Paris in September 1947, she had received an invitation to represent Poland on the Council of Foreign Social Institutions. Government rules prevented Janina from accepting, but her growing international reputation as a child welfare expert was something she could leverage. She had a dear friend in New York, the zoologist Maria Anna Rudzińska, who was married to the counselor to Poland's delegation at the U.N., Aleksander Witold Rudziński. With his help, Janina obtained an offer of a U.N. fellowship to study child welfare institutions and practices in the United States. CKOS approved the fellowship on condition that Janina commit to another two years of employment with it after her return. She agreed.[20]

By December 1947, Janina was in Washington, D.C., undergoing training at the Children's Bureau of the Federal Security Agency. Then she was taken on a tour of the eastern United States and the Midwest. She visited orphanages and child care centers, observed extension services, 4-H youth clubs, and school-based extracurricular and recreational activities, and studied the work of local child welfare offices. She also met with CKOS funders and reported how their donations had been put to use.[21]

Local papers took note of the visit by U.N. fellow Dr. Suchodolska. In an interview in Raleigh, North Carolina, Janina, with her usual diplomacy, heaped praise on all that she had heard and seen. Her interviewer expressed her admiration for this "intelligent and interesting representative of the Polish people," described as "small, dark, and bright eyed with massive braids of black hair wound round her head." Although disappointed by Janina's refusal to discuss political issues, the journalist concluded that Dr. Suchodolska was "someone who puts the immediate welfare of all Polish children above politics" and was working only "for the children, the orphans of Poland, with whatever government, with whatever and all and any help that comes to hand." Janina worried that the article might get her in trouble with Polish authorities because she failed to praise Poland's regime.

Throughout her six-month stay in the United States, Janina pursued her goal of getting Henry out of Poland. She contacted philosophers at American universities, hoping to interest them in Henry's work and to arrange a fellowship or appointment for him. Impressed by her presentation, two philosophers at the University of Chicago, Rudolf Carnap and Charles W. Morris, agreed to write to other scholars on Henry's behalf. Janina did not reveal to them that she was Henry's wife but claimed that she was his friend.[22]

Janina took advantage of the lack of censorship in the United States to write freely to her friend Maria Anna Rudzińska in New York about her concerns and her efforts to get Henry out of Poland. With the help of Rudzińska and her husband, Janina was able to get money to her sister Chaja, now Clara, who was living in destitution in Argentina. Janina's other sister, Bluma, was living in Uruguay as Antonina Altmann.

In her letters to Rudzińska, Janina confided her impressions of Americans. Generally, she admired their friendliness and eagerness to help, but she thought them naïve. She also witnessed disturbing evidence of antisemitism in the United States, especially in her meetings with members of the Polish immigrant community. The spewings of one Polish American were so vile that they gave Janina a flashback to the war.

Besides contacting American philosophers about Henry, Janina was consulting his uncle Joseph and her cousin Sigmund Pines about how to get Henry out of Poland as soon as possible. They proposed that Henry go to Sweden, which Janina would transit after the end of her fellowship. She would then remain with him instead of returning to Poland and they could wait there in safety until it became possible to immigrate to the United States.

While in New York City in the spring of 1948, Janina visited the National Council of Jewish Women and spoke with Evelyn Abelson of its Service for Foreign Born. It would prove to be a fateful meeting. Janina explained Henry's situation and even confided that she was Henry's wife but living under a false identity as a Polish official. She asked Abelson for help in getting Henry to Sweden. Abelson was sympathetic, but explained that it would not be possible to obtain a Swedish visa for Henry before Janina had to leave for Poland.

Janina returned to Poland at the end of May 1948 no closer to rescuing Henry than when she had left, and her fear and stress were exacting a toll. As she confided to Rudzińska in the United States, she had not had a moment's peace in the seven years since the Germans occupied Lwów. She became sick during the journey home and arrived in Warsaw in such ill health that she was ordered to go on a rest cure for several weeks, which she spent in the resort town of Cieplice in southwestern Poland. She happened to have acquaintances there: Count Skrzyński and his family.

Meanwhile, back in New York, Abelson had not forgotten the "most involved and delicate" situation of the intriguing Polish woman who had confided in her. She forwarded Henry's biographical statement and the references Janina had gathered to the American Committee for Émigré Scholars, Writers and Artists. In July 1948, the committee arranged for Henry to receive a fellowship offer to teach in Canada from the Lady Davis Foundation, named for its funder, the Canadian Jewish philanthropist Lady Davis. The fellowship awarded an annual salary as well as travel expenses for Henry and his wife.

In order to accept the fellowship, however, Henry had first to obtain an exit permit and authorization from the Polish Ministry of Education to take a sabbatical. After some tense months, he finally set sail to New York on the flagship Polish liner MS *Batory*. Sigmund Pines pulled some strings to get permission for Henry to stay a few days in New York, during which he met with Abelson. Then he traveled on to Toronto. Following his arrival there in March 1949, he was assigned a position in the Department of Applied Mathematics at the University of Toronto.

At last, Henry was safe, and he expected Janina to join him soon. She had been elected to the executive committee of the International Union for Child Welfare (the predecessor of today's Save the Children) in August 1948 and had applied for an exit permit to attend its planning meeting in Brussels in late March. If she did not receive the permit in time, she would certainly attend the annual convention there in May. Once in Brussels, she planned to defect. Abelson alerted the JDC office there to expect her and referred Henry to the Canadian Jewish Congress for assistance in getting Janina from Brussels to Canada. Through contacts at the U.S. State Department, Henry's uncle Joseph Mehlberg ensured that U.S. consulates were informed that Janina, despite being a Polish official, was a not a member of the Communist Party. This information would be passed on to the Canadian consulate in Brussels when Janina applied there for a Canadian visa. Everything was in place for Janina to join Henry in Canada once she got to Brussels.[23]

But she never arrived there. In late February 1949, the Polish government dissolved CKOS and Janina lost her job. Her requests to attend the March meeting and the May conference in Brussels were both denied. Janina was stuck in Poland.[24]

As spring turned to summer, Henry became increasingly desperate. He was supposed to return to Poland in October. Although he had assurances that Canada would accept him as a permanent resident, he did not wish to apply as long as Janina was in Poland. In addition to appealing to Abelson and the National Council of Jewish Women, Henry turned to other agencies for help. The United Service for New Americans, the United Jewish Appeal, the United Jewish Relief Agencies of Canada, the Canadian Jewish Congress, and the Jewish Immigrant Aid Society in Canada all got involved. Henry proposed that Janina apply to immigrate to Israel through the Central Committee of Jews in Poland, where she was registered as Pepi Mehlberg. Janina realized that doing so would inevitably draw the attention of the Ministry for Public Security to her double identity, especially after she was assigned to a position in the Ministry of Labor and Welfare in

August 1949.[25] All the agencies involved in the Mehlbergs' case concluded that they could do nothing as long as Janina was in Poland. She would have to figure out how to escape on her own.

Henry obtained an extension of his sabbatical until the end of March 1950 from the Polish Ministry of Education. As the end date approached, Henry applied for a further extension. The ministry grudgingly agreed but made clear that Henry was to be back at his post in Wrocław by November 1, 1950. If Janina did not get out by then, Henry would go back, despite the danger.

Janina was not about to let that happen. In the summer of 1950, she got word to Henry that she had found a way to leave Poland for East Germany and, once there, would somehow get to the British sector of Berlin. The Canadian Military Mission in Berlin was alerted and had a visa application waiting for her. On August 16, 1950, she walked into the mission's office. It took her nine days to get there after crossing the Polish border.[26] How she managed to do that remains a mystery.

Within two weeks, Janina had permission to immigrate to Canada. It took a while longer to obtain travel papers and funds, however. As a political refugee, she turned to the International Refugee Organization for help with both, only to learn that she had missed the registration deadline of September 1, 1949. In the end, the Allied High Commission in Berlin issued her travel papers, and Henry obtained assistance from the Jewish Immigrant Aid Society in Canada.

Janina finally arrived in Toronto on October 6, 1950. Henry then wrote to the University of Wrocław that he was "pleased to announce" that he would not be returning to his post.

Henry and Janina were together again, and they were free.

TWENTY-TWO

A NEW BEGINNING

Once out of Poland, Janina constructed a new identity for her life in Canada. Using an amalgamation of her previous names, she became Dr. Josephine Janina Bednarski Spinner Mehlberg, mathematician. "Josephine" is the English equivalent of Józefa, which she had long preferred to Pepi. She may have added "Janina Bednarski" to her name in part to reconcile her Polish paperwork as Janina Bednarska Suchodolska with Henry's visa application for her as his wife. But retaining "Janina" in her name was more than a matter of bureaucratic convenience. It also acknowledged that "Janina" was the name of the woman she had actually become over the previous nine years, the identity of a version of herself—perhaps the best version—that she neither could nor wanted to relinquish entirely. Although the friends she made in her new life knew her as Josephine, Henry continued to call her Jeanine, which is Janina in French, his favorite language.[1]

Janina's aspiration to pursue her original career explains the change in her birth date from 1905 to 1915: as a woman, the odds of her getting an academic appointment in mathematics were automatically slim, and they were much worse for a forty-five-year-old than for one who was thirty-five. In listing her credentials, Janina did not specify the subject of her doctorate, correctly expecting that prospective employers would assume she had earned a PhD in math rather than philosophy.

Through Henry, Janina established contacts with mathematicians at the University of Toronto, leading to a one-year appointment as a research assistant in the university's Computation Centre. She joined Canadian mathematics organizations and was invited to give occasional lectures.[2]

Henry was finding much more professional success. His position at the University of Toronto gave him access to philosophers in the United States, where his work was attracting interest. New York University's Sidney Hook invited Henry to join the American delegation to the 1952 Conference for Science and Freedom in Hamburg. Henry's keynote address was so well received that he was one of just four conference attendees invited to speak on German radio. Unlike the others, however, Henry could not bring himself to speak in German while his memories of what he had suffered during the Holocaust were still so fresh. He spoke in English instead.[3]

Janina and Henry quickly developed a supportive social circle in Toronto, thanks to good friends from their days in Lwów, Joseph and Gisela Klinghofer. Joseph was an official of the Canadian Jewish Congress and had supported Henry's efforts to get Janina to Canada. Henry and Janina joined the CJC's education committee and participated in secular activities of Toronto's Jewish community. They also belonged to a tight circle of émigré scholars. People admired Henry's intelligence and wit and found Janina's outgoing cheerfulness utterly charming. For Janina and Henry, the ability to mix openly as themselves and as a married couple after so many years of secrecy and fear filled them with astonished relief. In 1956, they became Canadian citizens.[4]

Their professional ambitions still called them to the United States, however. Henry got his foot inside a very wide door when he received a one-year appointment as a visiting professor at Princeton University in 1955. The University of Chicago came calling and offered Henry Rudolf Carnap's old position in the philosophy department starting in 1956. On September 18, Henry and Janina immigrated to the United States by driving their car across Ambassador Bridge to Detroit. In 1961, they became U.S. citizens.[5]

In Chicago, Henry started a discussion group of local scholars that met at his and Janina's apartment. It was modeled on the philosophical school known as the Vienna Circle. In 1958, he published his first major work written in English, *The Reach of Science*, in which he elaborated upon the theories he presented in Hamburg. But the trajectory of his career stalled when illness struck, possibly as a result of a serious car crash in which both he and Janina suffered injuries. He experienced frequent bouts of aphasia in which he would speak excitedly without realizing that his words sounded like gibberish. Although his mind was as brilliant as ever, most of the scholars in the discussion group lost interest in attending. Students in his logic course would gradually slip out of the classroom as Henry wrote on the blackboard and babbled excitedly.[6]

Janina, on the other hand, experienced far more success in her career than she could have expected in Poland or Canada. In 1957, the University of Chicago hired her as a senior mathematician in its Institute for System Research, a descendant of the United States' wartime Manhattan Project that produced the first atomic bomb. Recruited for her fluency in nonlinear equations, functional analysis, and Russian, she worked on a top secret U.S. Air Force weapons project. The institute's young staff of graduate students and newly minted PhDs regarded Janina as both a respected colleague and "a beloved mother hen."[7]

Her combination of exceptional expertise with a warm and spirited personality enabled Janina to make many connections in the U.S. not only in the field of mathematics but also in engineering, for which her work had important implications. In addition to joining math and engineering societies, she served as secretary of the Chicago chapter of the American Institute of Aeronautics and Astronautics. Well versed in Henry's field of philosophy of physics, she published a paper in the journal *Current Issues in the Philosophy of Science* with the title "Is a Unitary Approach to Foundations of Probability Possible?"

In 1960, Janina joined the mathematics department at Illinois Institute of Technology as an assistant professor. She was a popular professor, scholar, and colleague there, teaching probability theory and engaging in theoretical discourse through papers and lectures. She published "A Classification of Mathematical Concepts" in 1962 as a response to renowned mathematician and department colleague Karl Menger. Within a few years, she rose to full professor at IIT. Two male students obtained their doctorates with Janina as their advisor, whereas Henry had just one.[8]

As a mathematician in the United States, Janina had to become accustomed to being the only woman in the room. She was the first woman appointed to the math department at IIT and the only one for her entire time there. At a conference organized by Dr. Edward Teller, the "father of the hydrogen bomb," she discovered that she was the only woman invited to participate. Feeling out of place, she held herself aloof at the opening reception. When one of the attendees asked why, she explained that she was nervous about giving her talk, because she had not yet acquired an American accent. Her colleague laughed and answered, "Don't you know that many American scientists spend long hours trying to acquire a foreign accent?" His joke helped her relax, and her presentation at the conference was a success. Soon afterward, she was one of the few women invited to the founding conference of the Society for Engineering Science, an interdisciplinary organization with the goal of bridging the fields of engineering, mathematics, and science.[9]

At IIT, Janina made a point of encouraging the few women engineering students who attended her classes. When the math department finally accepted its first woman graduate student, Janina took her under her wing. She was not Janina's student, but Janina agreed to serve on her defense committee. When one of the other professors on the committee began to hector the student on what he perceived as her weak spot, Janina came to her rescue:

"VY you ask her zis kvestion? She *knows* it, she *knows* it!"

The professor nodded obediently and ceased his questioning. Janina had lost none of her formidability.[10]

By the 1960s, Janina and Henry were living in financial security and considerable comfort in a large apartment overlooking a park next to Lake Michigan. The suffering and strain of their past continued to shadow their lives, however. Henry especially felt deeply bitter about all that he had lost, not only most of his family and many friends and colleagues but also time. How much more might he have achieved if Germany's murderous aggression had not interrupted the work and career that were on the brink of

success in 1939? He complained that his age should not be figured chrono-
logically from his birth date, because the lost years of the war ought to be
subtracted.[11]

Henry and Janina believed that their suffering and loss entitled them
to the reparations that West Germany had agreed to provide to Holocaust
survivors. Under the reparations agreement then in force, however, they
did not qualify: they had lived in the part of Poland occupied by the Soviet
Union in 1939, and they were never held in a ghetto, forced labor camp, or
concentration camp. These limitations seemed patently unfair to them, so
they submitted claims with an alternate history: they had been in Kraków
at the start of the war and escaped from the ghetto there in 1943, then paid
a farmer to hide them in miserable conditions until the end of the war. The
Klinghofers and Rudzińskis submitted affidavits supporting these claims.
After more than a decade of bureaucratic nitpicking, West Germany finally
decided to grant Janina a pension—two years after her death.[12]

Janina and Henry's friends knew very little about the couple's past.
Henry sometimes spoke of living under a false identity as an egg farmer
during the war, claiming that he had become an expert on the composition
of soils and fertilizers to maintain his cover. He also occasionally boasted
that Janina was a hero of the Underground and had saved him, from which
some of their friends concluded that Janina was not a Jew.[13]

Janina did not speak about her past. How could she begin to explain
what she had experienced without resurfacing the feelings of horror and
terror that still visited her in her nightmares? She tried to stay focused on
her new life as an American. But still, the ache of sorrow never left her. She
longed for the city that she and Henry had loved and would never see again;
she grieved for all the loved ones she had lost and for the people whose
suffering she had tried and too often failed to relieve; she missed the courageous friends who had risked their lives for her yet never really knew her;
and she mourned for the country that had inspired her loyalty and service
and that no longer had any place for her.

Janina's health had never been robust, and the extreme stress she lived
under as Janina Suchodolska only made it worse. She suffered from hyper-
tension, frequent migraines, and chronic gastric distress. By the late 1960s,

her heart began to fail. A heart attack in the spring of 1969 convinced her that her days were numbered, and so she sent for her sister Antonina, now widowed in Uruguay. Someone, Janina reasoned, would have to take care of Henry after she was gone. Antonina arrived on May 21. Five days later, on May 26, Janina died.[14]

Per Janina's plan, Henry applied to obtain permanent residency for his sister-in-law. As he explained in his application, he needed a housekeeper for his "huge" apartment and was confident that Antonina would be "a pleasant companion." When Henry learned that he could not obtain permanent residency for an in-law, he married Antonina on August 8, 1969, less than three months after Janina died. No doubt, she would have approved.[15]

After Henry reached retirement at the University of Chicago, his former colleague there, Charles Morris, arranged a post-retirement position for him at the University of Florida in Gainesville.[16] Antonina died there in October 1973. Less than two years later, Henry, now in failing health, married his nurse, Susie Blackman Clark. It was a marriage of convenience for both, and yet a companionable one. Henry especially enjoyed the company of Susie's children and grandchild, and she even got him to attend her church a few times.[17]

Henry spent his last years in Gainesville working on a major project. At the urging of two American leaders in the field of the philosophy of physics, Robert S. Cohen and Adolf Grünbaum, he collected and synthesized for publication in English his life's work on quantum physics and the nature of time. Henry did not live to see the result, the two-volume *Time, Causality, and the Quantum Theory: Studies in the Philosophy of Science*, but he died knowing that it would see print. After Henry's death on December 10, 1979, Grünbaum and Cohen each added an introductory essay to the first volume that paid tribute to Henry's brilliance and "astonishing erudition" and lamented that persecution and illness had prevented his work from receiving the acclaim it deserved. In his summation, Cohen wrote: "Ever creative, but a troubled victim of his times, Henry Mehlberg disciplined himself with astonishing success, for he overcame political horrors and their attendant private maelstroms. These books are a memorial to a splendid philosopher of science."[18]

There was one project Henry could not see through: the publication of Janina's memoir. Shortly before he died, Henry brought his English translation of the memoir to Dr. Arthur Layton Funk, then chair of the University of Florida's history department. Henry asked the historian to help him polish and annotate the English text to make it suitable for publication.[19] Funk was a specialist in American history, however, with no expertise on the Holocaust or wartime Poland. After Henry's death, Funk might understandably have filed the memoir away in his records. As it turned out, Henry made the right choice. Thanks to Funk's considerable efforts, Janina's story did not go with Henry to his grave.

EPILOGUE

"JANINA'S STORY"

Sometime in the last eight years of her life, Janina decided to reveal, at least on paper, the secret she had kept for more than two decades: that she was the Countess Janina Suchodolska who, as a member of the Polish resistance and an RGO official, had provided lifesaving aid to Polish victims of Nazi persecution during World War II.[1] The result was the account that is the basis for this biography.

For a memoir, Janina's account is remarkably unforthcoming. All the reader can glean about the author's identity is that at the start of the war people called her Janina (which was not actually true), she was a math teacher and the daughter of a wealthy landowner, and she was married to Henry Mehlberg, who taught philosophy. She did not even provide a title for her text. In the collections catalogue of the United States Holocaust Memorial Museum, the memoir is listed simply as "Janina's Story."

The "Janina" of the story is less the author than her alter ego, Countess Janina Suchodolska. The first twenty-seven months of the war take up just fourteen of the memoir's 155 typed pages; the rest are devoted to Janina's life as the Countess. Henry added information about her life before and after World War II in a preface that he wrote after her death and included with the text he presented to Funk. It is a moving and revealing document that deserves to be quoted here in its entirety.

This is a story by Janina Spinner Mehlberg, born in the province of Galicia, Poland, on May 1, 1915. The youngest daughter of a well-to-do Jewish landowner, she grew up happily, an academically promising young woman, gifted in mathematics, living in a comfortable environment where a traditional Polish anti-Semitism was scarcely felt in her cozy setting. She played with the neighboring children of the Polish nobility, having the same nannies as they, her home physically comfortable, the atmosphere polite and well bred.

At 18, Janina married a serious young Jewish scholar, a student of Romance philology and later of philosophy, with the modest ambition "to know everything," and they lived well in Lwow, pursuing their intense intellectual interests. Until the world impinged with gradually increasing violence on their private absorptions and turned the young mathematics teacher into an imposter, a social worker of an unusual cast, and the heroine of Majdanek. She was 24 in 1939, when it began, barely more than 5 feet tall, more than ordinarily pretty, very feminine in her style, and having no test yet in her sheltered and cultivated life of the heroic courage she was to demonstrate in the coming years. Courage not rough-hewn, but operating with an analytic intelligence, as well as passion, and in a perspective that started with a prime value—the saving of as many lives as possible, and proceeding to weigh as impersonally as possible the value of her own life against the number at stake. She based her action on the higher probability—one life was worth less than many. Against this probability rate she operated for years, under Nazi rule and under Soviet, repeatedly risking death, and the worse that might prelude it, because the help she could give to others demanded the chance—indeed, she could see no meaning in her life unless she risked. Personal safety was only the agent to secure further service to those who knew no safety; if it were only for its own sake, for nothing but personal comfort and survival, how ephemeral it was, how worthless in even the short run. She would not survive, if she would survive, having watched out for herself and her own only. It would not have been worth it. She might die, and many times knew this might be the moment, but not for nothing. Not to live uselessly, nor to die pointlessly.

This petite Jewish girl passed as a Polish countess in Lublin in the

Second World War, and for her exceptional pains knew she had the love of many ordinary people. Many the breast that was crossed for her, the candle lit for her, and the lives risked to save hers. That this was so she knew, and the knowledge was good, but the main and unforgettable goal was—"how can we save them," and "how many more can we save," and "it is still not enough—we must do more!"

The heroine of Majdanek continued her struggle for help to the people after the liberation from the Nazis. And found herself again in danger from the "liberators" who, toward a presumably different end, used some of the same means. Until she escaped. In early middle age she lived in Chicago, teaching mathematics at the Illinois Institute of Technology, while her husband taught and wrote philosophy at the University of Chicago. They lived modestly and for their work, but were plagued by a couple of automobile accidents and ill health. Until finally, worn and weakened, no doubt, by years of strain and struggle, Janina died of heart failure on May 26, 1969.

She felt it necessary to give testimony, and she is a rare witness indeed. The following is her story.

This preface provides valuable information about Janina's background and motives, as well as testifying to Henry's love and respect for her. As a starting point for verifying Janina's memoir, however, it has two distinct flaws: it misidentifies her first name, and the information it provides about her birth date and her age at subsequent events is off by ten years. Consequently, Barry began the effort to confirm that Janina was Countess Suchodolska by assuming that she was born Janina Spinner on May 1, 1915. Janina's and Henry's U.S. immigration records, obtained through Freedom of Information Act requests, and various directories of prominent American women[2] confirmed this information and noted that she obtained a PhD from the Johannes Casimirus (Jan Kazimierz) University in Lwów in 1938.

Barry discovered that her assumptions were incorrect thanks to the help of three philosophers in Poland. Dr. Jan Hertrich-Woleński and Dr. Stepan Ivanyk, both experts on the Lwów-Warsaw School, each provided her a different photo of Twardowski's students dating from 1925–1926. Henry Mehlberg appears in each, as does a woman identified in one as Pepi

Spinner and in the other as Józefina Mehlberg. Barry concluded that, based on how she was identified in the photos, the woman must be Janina, but she is clearly not age ten or eleven in the photos, as Janina would have been if she were born in 1915. Ivanyk also informed Barry that Pepi Spinner obtained a doctorate in philosophy in February 1928 as one of Twardowski's students in Lwów. She would have been precocious indeed if she had obtained a PhD at age twelve.

Dr. Anna Smywińska-Pohl finally solved the mystery of Janina's identity by obtaining her dissertation records, which show that she submitted her dissertation in 1927 as Pepi Spinner, born May 1, 1905, in Żurawno. This proved that Henry and Janina lied about her background to Canadian and U.S. immigration authorities, a lie that Henry continued to perpetuate after her death. Barry wondered whether this was cause for doubting the veracity of Janina's memoir. On the other hand, she recognized that it was not uncommon for women to conceal or change their true age when they emigrated—Barry's own grandmother had done so.

In 2018, Joanna joined the quest to solve the mystery of Janina Suchodolska's identity. And in short order, she found the definitive evidence that Janina Mehlberg was Janina Suchodolska. It was in the records of the Jewish organizations that helped Henry get to Canada. Normally, such records are not open to researchers, but Joanna won access to them by impressing the archivist with the importance of Janina's story. The records include the correspondence of Evelyn Abelson, Henry's caseworker for the National Council of Jewish Women. Generally, Abelson carefully avoided naming Henry's wife in her communications, mentioning only that she was living under a pseudonym in Poland. But in one internal memo she let the information slip: Henry's wife was Janina "Sukoldosky." In a passionate letter he wrote to Abelson from Canada seeking help in extricating his wife from Poland, Henry also revealed that she was living as Mrs. Suchodolska.

Having proved that Janina Mehlberg was Countess Suchodolska, we set out to confirm the details of her memoir and to trace her life before and after World War II. This book is the product of more than four years of research into sources held by archives and libraries in Argentina, Poland, Ukraine, Germany, Canada, and the United States; in genealogical databases and oral history collections; through contacts with scholars and genealogists in numerous countries, and with Jewish organizations in Argentina, Canada, and Uruguay; and through oral and written interviews. Much of the research was performed during the worldwide Covid pandemic, when archives and libraries were closed and traveling to conduct research was impossible. Fortunately, we reaped the benefit of the redoubled effort of many research centers to digitize their resources and make them available online. We also borrowed secondary sources from colleagues and scoured used book websites to purchase works long out of print. As archives began to reopen in Poland and Ukraine, we hired researchers and enlisted the assistance of archivists. Finally, in the spring of 2022, we were able to take part of the trip we had planned two years earlier to conduct archival research as well as to visit the sites of Janina's life and to retrace her steps during the events recounted in her memoir. Unfortunately, by that time, Russia's invasion of Ukraine precluded our going to the places where Janina and Henry lived before 1941.

Our research took us down unexpected paths to surprising sources but also to numerous dead ends. At times, it seemed as though even beyond the grave Janina wanted to retain her secrets. The only surviving vital records from Żurawno date from 1877–1885, so we could find no birth records for Janina or her siblings. We also failed to find any vital records for her parents and so we are not even sure how many siblings she had. Among the RGO records in the Lublin State Archives, a folder marked "Janina Suchodolska" turned out to be empty. Although she worked for the postwar Polish government and traveled for her official duties, the Institute of National Remembrance (IPN) could not locate any passport file on Janina Suchodolska or any of Janina's other identities. Nor could we find any record of her in the files at the IPN of the communist regime's secret service, which surely investigated her suitability for a government position and monitored her foreign contacts and travel. Janina and her sisters never had children, and we searched in vain for other relatives. It was only as we were reviewing the proofs for this book that we finally located a niece of Henry who had known both the Mehlbergs in the late 1960s.

Some valuable sources turned up in unexpected places, however. The New York Public Library digitized the letters that Maria Anna Rudzińska received from Janina during her tour of the United States as Janina Suchodolska.

Photos of Janina during this U.S. tour published in the Minneapolis *Star Tribune*, the Raleigh *News & Observer*, and the *South Bend Tribune* provide visual proof that Janina Mehlberg was Janina Suchodolska. In the application that Janina filed for compensation from West Germany, we found information about her parents and childhood. After we first drafted the final chapter of this book, a contact in Canada found the information about Janina's defection to the West in Berlin. As we were reviewing the copyedited manuscript, a genealogist extraordinaire from the Jewish Historical Institute in Warsaw provided us new information about the Spinner and Mehlberg families.

Most important, wartime records together with the postwar recollections of Majdanek prisoners, Janina's colleagues, and people she aided corroborate even the most astonishing claims in the memoir and reveal other accomplishments that it does not mention. The wealth and variety of the sources we found presented us with the challenge of how to synthesize them into a chronological narrative of Janina's life as Countess Suchodolska. Her memoir enabled us to tell her story from her perspective, but it is not a strictly chronological account and therefore was much less helpful for determining the timing and sequence of the events it relates. As is common with recollections of events that are years—or in this case decades—in the past, Janina's memoir contains some errors with respect to names and dates, and it conflates some events or confuses their chronology. For example, Dr. Blancke appears as Dr. Blaschke, and the date of "Bloody Wednesday," the Operation Harvest Festival massacre at Majdanek, is given as Wednesday, November 17, rather than Wednesday, November 3, 1943. Similarly, the recollections of Majdanek prisoners and of people who interacted with Janina are either silent about the date of events or provide conflicting timing for them. By triangulating the memoir with personal accounts, wartime records, and postwar scholarship on Majdanek and Lublin, we were able to map out the sequence of events in this book on a timeline. We then composed the narrative to connect the events. In some instances, this has required educated guesswork. Following Janina's example, we reached our conclusions through logical analysis of the sources along with judicious applications of imagination and intuition.

Two questions that have confronted us since we began this project are:

Why did Janina write her memoir, and for whom did she write it? That she waited until the 1960s to write it is not surprising. This is when many of those who had experienced the traumas and tragedies of World War II first found the ability and the will to recount what they had endured. The 1960s also saw a rise in public awareness of the Holocaust, thanks to the international sensation surrounding the trial of Adolf Eichmann in Israel in 1961. Unlike the 1946 trial of German leaders at Nuremberg, the Eichmann trial focused exclusively on Nazi Germany's effort to murder all the Jews in Europe, and the prosecutors called scores of Jewish survivors to testify. The trial was internationally televised, and trial sessions were regularly summarized on the nightly news in the United States. The trial's revelations and the testimony of the witnesses electrified non-Jews in Europe and North America and inspired other Jewish survivors to break their long-held silence about the horrors they had suffered. There was a surge of publications and films about the Holocaust as a result. In fact, the 1960s is when the word "Holocaust" became a widely recognized term for Nazi Germany's genocide of the Jews.

In Poland, the increasing willingness of Holocaust survivors to write and speak about their experiences sparked a "memory war." The narrative that emerged from the accounts of Polish Jewish survivors acknowledged both that some non-Jewish Poles had rescued Jews and that others had watched in indifference, cheered, or even participated in the persecution and murder of their Jewish neighbors by Poland's German occupiers. Wartime and postwar accounts of non-Jewish Poles fully corroborate all these varieties of Polish responses to the Holocaust. Some Poles, however, believed that survivors' recollections of antisemitic collaboration besmirched the national honor. Some also complained that the narrative of Jewish suffering during the Holocaust erased the suffering of non-Jewish Poles as victims of Nazi Germany's murderous racist policies.[3]

Poland's communist government recognized the suffering of Polish Jews under the German occupation and erected memorials at important Holocaust sites in the early 1960s. The official narrative mostly ignored the topic of Polish collaboration in persecuting Jews, however, and tended to equate the suffering of Jewish and non-Jewish Poles. The narrative focused on the heroism of those Poles who fought the occupier and rescued Jews, contrasting the Poles' actions with the supposed passivity of Polish Jews in response to their victimization.

The "memory war" in Poland intensified in 1967 with the outbreak of the Six Day War. Poland followed the Soviet Union's lead in backing Israel's Arab opponents. The Polish government launched an antisemitic campaign that depicted Polish Jews as Zionists who were in league with the West and trying to undermine Poland. In 1968, the government blamed "Zionists" for the demonstrations by Polish university students protesting government censorship and repression. Discrimination and harassment became the order of the day for the 30,000 Poles who lived openly as Jews. In addition, a special government unit ferreted out Polish Jews in official positions who had survived the Holocaust by passing as Aryans and had not reverted to their original identity. They were forced out of their jobs and pressured to emigrate. In this atmosphere, the government's Holocaust narrative preached that the Polish people had *all* collectively and heroically fought to save Polish Jews, only to be repaid by the Jews they had rescued with ingratitude and slander.[4]

Janina was certainly aware of the dueling narratives of the Holocaust and World War II in Poland. For all Polish Jews who had survived the Holocaust, including Janina, the increasingly open and virulent antisemitism in Poland in the 1960s evoked a visceral fear that Jews could once again be subjected to genocide there. According to Funk, Janina wrote her memoir in Polish, and Henry translated it into English after her death. Since Janina's written English was at least as good as Henry's, this may indicate that she did not have time to translate it into English before her death. The memoir's narrative, however, suggests that she intended it for a Polish audience. This would explain why the memoir makes so few references to Jewish suffering and only two oblique references to antisemitism among the Poles. With its emphasis on Polish suffering and heroism, Janina's memoir fits well within the official Polish narrative of the 1960s. Her account counters the exclusion of Jews from the narrative of heroism, however. She was a Polish patriot who risked her life to resist the German occupier, and she was a Jew. As a Jew, she honored Polish culture and traditions, even enabled Majdanek prisoners to celebrate Christmas and Easter. She was grateful to Count Skrzyński, the non-Jewish Pole who saved her, and, as a Jew, she aided and rescued Poles.

Janina's memoir also restores the RGO to its rightful place in the narrative of Polish resilience and self-sacrifice during World War II. Ludwik Christians erased the RGO entirely from his 1946 account of the aid program at Majdanek. His version was adopted by communist officials at that time who sought to discredit the RGO as an organization that collaborated with the Nazis in the service of the "fascist" government in exile. Many Majdanek prisoners who received RGO aid did not know who provided it. In their postwar statements about the food deliveries that saved them from starvation, they either assumed that the food had all come from the Polish Red Cross or they chose not to challenge the official narrative that the Polish Red Cross was the only organization that aided them. Janina's memoir sets the record straight, showing that it was the RGO, not the Polish Red Cross, that led the aid program at Majdanek and provided the lion's share of the food it supplied.

Janina's memoir also pays homage to the deeds of the many individuals in the RGO, the AK, and the Underground who worked with her to resist the Germans and rescue their victims. Many of their names have otherwise been lost to history. She acknowledged the heroism of Count Skrzyński, whose service to his nation during World War II was unknown even to his descendants, and she memorialized the martyrdom of Józef Wendrucha. She especially wrote about her women RGO coworkers who supported both her official and her clandestine activities. It is clear that she forged strong bonds of affection with these women who were willing to give their lives for their country and for one another. The necessity of deceiving them about her true identity must have forced her to behave with a certain reserve that deepened the loneliness of her life as an imposter.

The memoir conveys Janina's wit, courage, ingenuity, and passion, but carries an undertone of sorrow throughout. If Janina did intend her account for a Polish audience, this would explain why it is almost completely silent as to the emotions she felt as a Jew witnessing the suffering and slaughter of her people from the comparative safety of the "Aryan" side. It is almost impossible to fathom how Janina, conscious of being a Jew, dared to enter Majdanek over and over and to deal with the SS officials there, especially after the Operation Harvest Festival massacre. We suspect the answer is that she so fully suppressed the consciousness of her true identity that she essentially became Countess Suchodolska.

One enduring mystery about Janina's memoir is why it omits what was arguably her greatest service to her fellow Poles: winning the release from Majdanek of 2,106 children, women, and elderly civilian expellees in August 1943. This event is amply documented in the wartime records of the RGO, including reports that Janina filed, and she testified to Polish authorities about it in 1946. Janina's omission of this episode from her memoir may indicate that she saw it not as a successful rescue but as a failure, that her memory of the event was not of the many she saved but of the many who died in Majdanek before she could win their release, and of the many who died afterward because their release came too late. Writing the memoir required Janina to call forth many memories of terror, horror, trauma, and anguish, but there may have been some memories that, even decades later, she still could not bear to revisit. In this respect, her memoir may be seen as Janina's last courageous act.

Janina was an exceptionally intelligent and brave woman, but those attributes do not explain why and how she managed to accomplish such remarkable feats. Part of the answer lies in the patriotism that drove her actions, a patriotism not based on the lowest common denominator of ethnicity, creed, or language but on what she perceived to be her nation's highest principles. Another part of the answer lies in her compassion and empathy. They are what drove her continual quest to provide ever greater quantities and types of food, medicines, and other goods for the prisoners at Majdanek. Her compassion and empathy also contributed to her success in obtaining the goodwill and even assistance of Nazi officials and Majdanek's SS personnel. Her empathy inspired her understanding that what Majdanek prisoners needed to survive that unspeakable hell was not just food, but hope; her compassion impelled her to provide hope especially to the prisoners who had been broken and turned traitor.

Janina herself was neither fearless nor flawless, which makes her story all the more inspiring. She displayed no heroic tendencies before the war, and if world events had allowed, she would have gone on living the sheltered life of a rather pampered intellectual. Instead, she found herself in the power of people who rated some human lives as worthless, including her own. In response, she decided to measure the value of her own life by the number of lives she could help save. She pursued her mission with all her intelligence, imagination, and intuition, and with truly stubborn persistence—she simply refused to accept what others told her was impossible. As long as there were lives that needed saving, she was certain that there must be a way to save them.

In his preface to the memoir, Henry explained that Janina wrote it as her testimony. It testifies not only to the events she saw but also to what she learned about human nature by observing it within the terrible crucible that was occupied Poland. She reported the variety of responses she witnessed and analyzed what they revealed about human nature. While the memoir testifies to the heroic efforts of Poles to resist the German occupier and to help one another survive, it also cites instances of infighting and self-serving behavior that detracted from those efforts. It describes how the Germans' brutal persecution elicited responses from their Polish victims not only of courage and patriotic self-sacrifice but also of greed and cruel indifference. She wrote movingly of the agonizing choices that the occupation forced its victims to make, as in the following passage.

What would a mother do in the face of the impossible choices put to her? There was one who, with her daughter, hid in the wardrobes of her apartment during a raid. They found her daughter, but not her. The child sobbed and screamed for her mother to save her. The mother kept silent, and survived. I know this from the mother herself who, sobbing out her story, wished herself dead instead of condemned to live with this memory.

Another mother hid with her son in a bunker. . . . Her son ventured out at the wrong time; he was seized and shot right there. The mother heard and remained silent. . . .

A young Jewish woman was offered the privilege of choosing whether her mother or her husband would be executed the next day. A father was offered his life on condition he stand and watch his son being hanged and smiled all the while. If the smile left his face, he would be hanged, too. He kept smiling. . . .

And who is to judge the impulse to survive? Now, years later, I try not to judge but simply to report, since we who continue as members of the

human race are obliged to know its capacities, however grim and unbear-
able the knowledge may be. But knowledge is not the same as enduring, and
I am not sure that knowledge alone gives us the right to judge. The mystery
is too great, how we respond to unbearable demands. Because while physi-
cal and psychic tortures broke many, some reacted with what one can only
call moral grandeur. I know some and heard of many others who helped
their fellow-sufferers at the cost of their own lives, who confessed to others'
"crimes," who willingly chose death over a degrading life. So the murder of
goodness was not thorough, and this fact, too, must be reported.

Janina's memoir is a call to tolerance. The "grim and unbearable" knowledge of human capacities that her wartime experiences taught her only strengthened her belief in the fundamental value and dignity of every human life. The memoir provides examples of individual Ukrainians, Poles, and Germans who demonstrated both the capacity for what Janina termed goodness—for kindness, courage, and self-sacrifice—and the capacity for evil—to be dishonest, vicious, even murderous. She recognized that both capacities are inherent elements of human nature, and her memoir shows that the probability of a person acting on one or the other of those capacities in any given situation cannot be predicted based on ideology, national-ity, ethnicity, or belief.

Janina's memoir is also a call to mercy. She realized that, in an atmo-sphere of extreme violence and suffering, people may act in ways that would have been utterly out of character had they been allowed to live in peace. She did not wish to excuse or justify the harm caused by people's choices. She thought that people should answer for their deeds, but she also believed that people are not fully defined by either the best or the worst of their ac-tions. This belief provides grounds for both cynicism and hope: while he-roes are by nature flawed, villains may have the capacity to prove heroic.

In her relief and resistance work, Janina did not ask or care whether the people who sought her aid were deserving. They were humans and they suf-fered, and so it was her human duty to help them, to show them mercy, to give them hope.

Janina's story is a call to tolerance, to mercy, and to hope.

CODA

Janina ended her memoir with a two-page chapter titled "Return to Maj-danek." It describes a tour she took with a Swedish delegation soon after the camp was liberated. We quote from the end of the chapter here, so that Janina may have the final say regarding her story.

I walked with the delegation. I talked, pointed things out, objective and quiet. And I saw how they looked at me, wondering how I had seen all that, and survived. There wasn't much to me physically. I suppose it would be easy to imagine that dealing with this sort of matter every day for years would have crushed me. I considered their wonder inside myself, asking myself the questions that were obvious in their eyes—how had I managed, and what had made me go on? It would have been natural to give up, to stop going to Majdanek, to go to pieces, even. But then there would have been no reason to live. When so many were in such terrible need, I had to live to answer that need. I was one individual only in the vast suffering human family. If I thought only of the dangers to myself or to those I loved, I was worth nothing. But if surviving meant being useful to many, I had to find the strength to survive, which made it possible for me to feel some sense of achievement, even of pride. This, at least, was left me. I had achieved less than I had hoped, but I tried, and my efforts had made a difference, so my life had made some difference, and for that reason I had to go on.

Then I thought of those who had been broken, physically and morally, who had betrayed other lives in the hope of saving their own. Of them I spoke to these men: "None of us has the right to sit in judgment on them. No one who hasn't been in their shoes—their terrible shoes, often filled with blood. However we risked our necks, it was of our own will. But they were in bondage, and all human pride was beaten out of them. They didn't ask to be martyrs. Most of them no doubt wanted nothing more than to live out their days in an average, humdrum existence, without great impact and without glory. They were forced into martyrdom, and this is perhaps harder than willingly risking your life for an ideal."

There is nothing left to do for them but to remember. And in the way of my ancestors, intone "Yisgadal, v'yiskadash," the Kaddish for the dead, and like the real Countess Suchodolska, "Kyrie Eleison, Christe Eleison."

We will remember. . . .

ACKNOWLEDGMENTS

In the course of verifying Janina's memoir and uncovering her full story, we have benefited from the assistance, advice, and encouragement of many people in a number of countries. That Janina's memoir was preserved and came to light is thanks first of all to Henry Mehlberg, who entrusted his English translation of Janina's account to Arthur Layton Funk of the University of Florida. Funk went to remarkable lengths to make Janina's story known. In addition to giving a copy of Henry Mehlberg's translation to Barry, he created a separate version of the memoir by polishing the English and adding annotations. With the permission of Bobbie Curtis and Jeri Hough, the daughters of Henry's third wife, Susie Blackman Clark, Funk donated his annotated and edited version of the memoir to the United States Holocaust Memorial Museum (USHMM), along with photos of Janina and Henry Mehlberg.

In her early research on Janina, Barry was assisted by Katarzyna Pietrzak-Kret, then at the USHMM. Henry's former student Arthur Fine (University of Washington) shared his memories of the Mehlbergs. Fine also connected Barry with Jan Hertrich-Woleński (Jagiellonian University, Kraków), who in turn put her in touch with Stepan Ivanyk (University of Warsaw) and Anna Smywińska-Pohl (Jagiellonian University). All three shared their knowledge of the Lwów-Warsaw School, provided valuable sources, and helped Barry discover Janina's actual name and date of birth.

In 2018, when Debórah Dwork was a Senior Fellow-in-Residence at the USHMM Mandel Center for Advanced Holocaust Studies, Barry (then a

Mandel Center historian) sought her advice about authenticating Janina's memoir. Dwork recommended her former doctoral student, Joanna Sliwa, as a consultant, and thus began our partnership. We are both enduringly grateful to Dwork for the connection.

Throughout this project, we have benefited from the assistance of Alina Skibińska (Polish Center for Holocaust Research and the USHMM), who located and copied records in Poland for us and provided valuable suggestions and contacts. We are also indebted to Gunnar Berg (YIVO), who helped Joanna find and access the records that definitively confirmed for us that Janina was Countess Suchodolska.

As we were planning our research trip to Poland and Ukraine for spring 2020, the Covid-19 pandemic erupted. For the next two years, we benefited immensely from the generous assistance of individuals—archivists, scholars, activists, experts, and colleagues—in North America, South America, and Europe. We are indebted to everyone who showed solidarity, interest, and dedication despite the difficult circumstances they were facing. We could not have written this book at this time without their assistance.

We owe thanks to many colleagues at the USHMM. Throughout the pandemic, when the museum as well as its library and archive were closed, the library reference staff helped Barry access indispensable books and resources. Suzy Goldstein Snyder provided us the accession records for "Janina's Story" and put us in touch with Jeri Hough, Henry's stepdaughter. Natalya Lazar clarified details of Ukrainian history. Jacek Nowakowski introduced Barry to the story of Countess Karolina Lanckorońska. Diane Saltzman and Elizabeth (Betsy) Anthony arranged for us to present our project remotely to the museum's group of Holocaust survivor volunteers and to the Mandel Center, respectively. The support and enthusiasm of both groups were wonderfully encouraging.

Also in the United States, Jeffrey Cymbler of Jewish Records Indexing (JRI)–Poland offered genealogical advice. Sarah Coates (University of Florida), Jenifer Petrescu (Congregation B'nai Israel, Gainesville), and Carl Schramm (Montefiore Jewish Cemetery) searched their archives. Adara Goldberg (Holocaust Resource Center of Kean University) made key introductions and acquainted us with Canadian archives. We appreciated the willingness of Marjorie Senechal (Smith College) and Eugene Allgower (Colorado State University) to share with us their memories of Janina from their student days at IIT. Senechal also provided us scans of Janina's letters at the New York Public Library, shared information she uncovered about Janina's work as a mathematician, and helped us obtain information about women mathematicians in prewar Poland. Joshua Pines gave us information about Janina's cousin Sigmund Pines who supported the Mehlbergs' efforts to emigrate from Poland. We are very grateful to Henry's stepdaughter Jeri Hough for endorsing our project and sharing her memories of Henry. An invitation from the organizers of the "Heroines of the Holocaust" symposium at the Wagner College Holocaust Center allowed us to share Janina's story with international academic colleagues.

In Canada, we received archival and historical assistance from: Patti Auld Johnson (University of New Brunswick); Jocelyn Bourque (Canadian Museum of Immigration at Pier 21); Valerie Casbourn (Library and Archives Canada); Paula Draper; Sarah Fogg, Andréa Shaulis, and Eszter Andor (Montreal Holocaust Museum); Tys Klumpenhouwer (University of Toronto); Carson Phillips (UJAFED Toronto); and Janice Rosen (Canadian Jewish Archives). Donna Bernardo-Ceriz (UJA Ontario Jewish Archives) provided documentation about Janina's escape from Poland. Irvin Klinghofer shared his memories and photographs of the Mehlbergs. Hernan Tesler-Mabé (University of Ottawa) connected us with individuals in South America.

In Argentina, we are indebted to Eliana Hamra (Holocaust Museum, Buenos Aires) who obtained information about Janina's sister Clara. Emmanuel Kahan (CONICET and National University of La Plata) sought records from the country's Foreign Affairs archive. Malena Chinski connected us with Diana Wang (Generations of the Shoah in Argentina), on whose suggestion we reached out to the Argentine Israelite Mutual Association (AMIA). Grupo Reunir-Amia volunteers Clara, Elda, and Tomás uncovered information about Clara for us.

In Uruguay, Rita Vinocur (Uruguay Holocaust Remembrance Center) enthusiastically agreed to help with tracing information about Janina's sister Antonina. Jana Beris Jerozolimski (Semanario Hebreo) placed an ad in the local Jewish paper seeking information about Antonina.

In Israel, Idan Bierman, the grandson of Henry's brother Izydor, connected us with his aunt Eva Tene. Speaking from England, Tene shared with us her memories of living with the Mehlbergs in Chicago from 1965 to 1968.

In Germany, we received archival help from Wolfgang Grimm and Martin Kalibe (Bezirksregierung Düsseldorf) and guidance from Jens Hoppe (Conference on Jewish Material Claims Against Germany).

In Poland, we owe thanks to many archivists, scholars, researchers, and museum professionals. Teresa Klimowicz (Grodzka Gate–NN Theater) researched collections at the Lublin State Archive for us and later gave us an enlightening tour of her institution. Joanna Fabijańczuk (Kraków JCC) reached out to Izabela Olejnik, who copied documents at the University of Łódź. Renata Grzegórska and Barbara Krzyżanowska (University of Warsaw); Anna Jaśkiewicz (Przemyśl State Archive); Piotr Józefiak (Adam Mickiewicz University in Poznań); Karolina Anna Kołodziejczyk (Metropolitan Catholic Archives in Lublin); Grzegorz Przybysz and Magdalena Wątorska (University of Wrocław); Anna Radoń (Jagiellonian University); Agnieszka Reszka (Jewish Historical Institute); and Agnieszka Ziomek (University of Łódź) conducted archival searches in their institutions. Michał Bojanowski (Chidusz Jewish Foundation in Wrocław) put us in touch with Agnieszka Michalik, who in turn showed us sources about Janina's prewar life. Danuta Ciesielska and Krzysztof Ciesielski (Jagiellonian University) offered invaluable information about the circle of mathematicians in Lwów and pointed us to important digital sources. Tomasz Dietl (Polish Academy of Sciences) shared his recollections of Andrzej Skrzyński. Sylwia Mazurek-Męcfel connected us with Elżbieta Romiszowska-Mazurek, Skrzyński's granddaughter, who, in turn, shared information about and photographs of Skrzyński. Anna Ożyńska-Zborowska and Wojciech Rostworowski (relatives of Skrzyński's fourth wife, Zofia Mycielska Skrzyńska) responded instantly with a key postwar photograph of Skrzyński. Justyna Janiszewska (Polish-U.S. Fulbright Commission); Magdalena Kozłowska and Łukasz Krzyżanowski (University of Warsaw); and Kazimierz Rędziński (Jan Długosz University of Humanities and Sciences) made connections to researchers. Adam Kopciowski (Maria Curie-Skłodowska University) explained details about postwar Jewish life in Lublin. Noam Silberberg (Genealogy Department, Jewish Historical Institute) replied immediately with records pertaining to Janina, Henry, and their families that had eluded us and the other experts we consulted.

The staff of the State Museum at Majdanek deserve special mention for their outstanding assistance. Marta Grudzińska obtained extremely valuable sources for us and provided fascinating information about Dr. Perzanowska and the women's hospital at Majdanek. In addition to advising us on our research, Łukasz Myszała spent many more hours than he had planned giving us tours of Majdanek and Lublin and sharing his encyclopedic knowledge of both places during World War II. Wojciech Lenarczyk shared his expertise in the camp's history and helped with archival research. Dariusz Libionka provided expert historical guidance.

Also in Lublin, we thank Łukasz Krzysiak (National Museum in Lublin) for arranging a tour of the Under the Clock Museum, for the gift bags with books, and for archival advice.

Unfortunately, the Russian aggression on Ukraine in February 2022 and the ongoing war made it impossible for us to travel there. We are grateful to Volodymyr Zilinskyi (Ivan Franko National University of Lviv) and Slav Tsarynnyk (Lviv Ecotour) for their readiness to conduct research in Lviv archives. We hope for peace in Ukraine and look forward to visiting the places connected to Janina's life.

We are grateful beyond words to our literary agent, Joëlle Delbourgo. Joëlle instantly recognized the remarkable story that we wanted to tell and indefatigably advocated for us and our work. We are grateful to Debbie Cenziper for making the connection and for her advice on how to tell Janina's story to a general readership.

At Simon & Schuster, we had the good fortune to work with Bob Bender, our editor, and with Johanna Li, associate editor. Both shared our excitement in bringing Janina's story to a broader audience. Bob helped us craft a narrative for a general readership, particularly by curbing our proclivity as historians to provide more contextual detail than was strictly necessary to tell the story. We benefited from the amazing attention to detail of our copy editor, Fred Chase.

We each express our gratitude to those in our circles who have supported us in this process. Joanna thanks her supervisor at the Claims Conference, Wesley Fisher, for his broad support. Joanna's friends—Dara Bramson, Rachel Rothstein, and Magda Wróbel—understood that she often had to decline rather than accept, and yet they continued to cheer her on. Lukasz Sliwa offered his gourmet meals and signature coffee to sustain his sister over long work hours. Joanna credits her parents with inspiring her interest in history and cultivating languages that enabled her to do this research. Joanna's husband, Karol Maźnicki, an enthusiastic ally, fostered an environment that allowed her to pursue this project.

Barry is grateful to her supervisor, Patricia Heberer-Rice, director of the USHMM's Division of the Senior Historian, and to Lisa Leff and Robert Ehrenreich of the Mandel Center at the USHMM for their understanding and support as Barry reduced her hours, then took a leave of absence to work on this book. She thanks her brother, Forrest "Hap" White, for suggesting the title *Counterfeit Countess*. Throughout the long and often challenging process of producing this book, she was cheered on by her children, Lydia and Frank Blackmore, their spouses Jackson Kimbrell and Julia Lisowski, and her siblings and siblings-in-law. Her friends Lesly Berger, Trudy Clark, and Kristin Stone made sure she occasionally came up for air and human contact. Mike Meyerson provided expert legal advice as well as friendship. Finally, Barry wishes to acknowledge her mother, Edith Reynolds White, artist, poet, librarian, civic leader, World War II codebreaker, and civil rights activist. She was the first to show Barry what an intelligent and determined woman can accomplish when she refuses to accept "No" for an answer.

NOTES

The principal source for this book is Henry Mehlberg's unpublished and untitled translation from Polish of Josephine Janina Mehlberg's account of her life during World War II,
which includes a preface by Henry Mehlberg. We worked from the carbon copy of the
translation manuscript that Arthur Funk gave to Elizabeth "Barry" White in 1989. The
specific information drawn from the manuscript is not cited in the notes. Funk also created an edited and annotated version of the memoir that is available at the United States
Holocaust Memorial Museum (USHMM): Accession number 2003.333, "Janina's Story."

INTRODUCTION

1. This figure is based upon the most recent and thorough analysis of Jewish victims
   at Majdanek to date: Chmielewski, "Żydzi w KL Lublin," in *Więźniowie KL Lublin
   1941–1944*, ed. Kranz and Lenarczyk, 264–65.
2. Krzyżanowski and Soroka, "The Polish Underground Resistance in the Lublin
   Area," 145–56.
3. Like Janina and Henry Mehlberg, Lemkin studied at Jan Kazimierz University in
   Lwów.

ONE: BEFORE

1. Much of the information in this chapter about Janina's life before World War II, her
   character, and her relationship with her husband, Henry Mehlberg, is drawn from
   the following sources: Henry's preface to Janina's memoir; photographs included
   in "Janina's Story," USHMM; restitution and pension applications submitted to
   the West German government by the Mehlbergs, "Henry Mehlberg," VA 278344,
   and "Janina Mehlberg," VA 278345, State Finance Office, Compensation Payments / Landesamt für Finanzen, Amt für Wiedergutmachung—Saarburg (BEG);
   interview with Dr. Arthur Fine by Elizabeth White; interviews with Dr. Marjorie
   Senechal and Eva Tene by authors.
2. "Pepi Mehlberg," CKŻP, Wydział ewidencji i statystyki 1945–1950, 303/V/425

/M 4762/174027, Archive of the Jewish Historical Institute (AŻIH). In the late nineteenth century, only 5 percent of agricultural land in Eastern Galicia was owned by Jews. Pohl, *Nationalsozialistische Judenverfolgung in Ostgalizien, 1941–1944*, 126.

3. Under Austrian rule, Galicia was divided into western and eastern parts. Eastern Galicia encompassed the borderlands, which today is Western Ukraine. The area has been known to Ukrainians as "Halychyna."

4. Snyder, *Black Earth*, 23; Veidlinger, *In the Midst of Civilized Europe*, 37–39.

5. Böhler, "Post-war Military Action and Violence (East Central Europe)," *1914–1918 Online: International Encyclopedia of the First World War*, https://encyclopedia.1914 -1918-online.net/article/post-war_military_action_and_violence_east_central _europe, accessed September 27, 2021; Budnitsky, "Jews, Pogroms, and the White Movement," 1–23; Veidlinger, *In the Midst of Civilized Europe*, 1–5, 288–303.

6. We are grateful to Dr. Danuta Ciesielska, Institute for the History of Science, Polish Academy of Sciences, for this information.

7. For the history of the Lwów-Warsaw School, see: Woleński, *Logic and Philosophy in the Lvov-Warsaw School; Tradition of the Lvov-Warsaw School: Ideas and Continuations*, ed. Brożek, Chybińska, Jadacki, and Woleński. For the role of women in the movement, see Pakszys, "Kobiety w filozofii polskiej. Dwa pokolenia Szkoły Lwowsko-Warszawskiej."

8. "Z Uniwersytetu Jana Kazimierza we Lwowie," *Chwila*, March 9, 1928, p. 13, accessed January 6, 2021, https://libraria.ua/en/numbers/6/26480/?PageNumber =12&ArticleId=983777&Search=pepi%20spinner.

9. Henry was born on October 7, 1904, in Kopyczyńce to Nuchim Mehlberg and Sara Chane née Jamenfeld. Information about his family derives from Księgi metrykalne gmin wyznania mojżeszowego z terenów tzw. zabużańskich, 1789–1943, sygn. 2268, 2419, 2858, 3460, Main Archive of Old Records (AGAD).

10. Information about Henry's academic career derives from the following records: "Mehlberg Henryk," 1956–1951, Ministerstwo Edukacji Narodowej Departament Kadr, sygn. 3586, Archive of New Records (AAN); "Mehlberg Henryk," Archives of the University of Łódź (AUŁ); "Mehlberg Henryk," Tom I: AUW.6/2.180, p. 101, Archives of the University of Wrocław (AUW); and "Henryk Mehlberg," 387b-14, Archives of the University of Adam Mickiewicz (AUAM).

11. Archiwum Kazimierza Twardowskiego, Korespondencja Naukowa, Tom 23. Ły–Meh, pp. 96–144, Digital Archive of Combined Libraries.

12. Ibid.

13. "Letter from Kazimierz Twardowski," February 26, 1934, Roman Ingarden Digital Archive; "Odczyty," *Chwila*, January 9, 1935, p. 10.

14. "Spis prac D-ra Henryka Mehlberga," 3586, p. 9, AAN; "Letter to Kazimierz Twardowski," July 29, 1935, and "Letter to Kazimierz Twardowski," July 11, 1937, Roman Ingarden Digital Archive.

15. Archiwum Kazimierza Twardowskiego, "Księga Pamiątkowa," October 20, 1936, Digital Archive of Combined Libraries.

16. "Henry Mehlberg," VA 278344, BEG. *The 1930 Poland Industry, Business, and Finance Directory*; *The 1930 Poland Industry Directory*, vol. 4: *Food*; *The 1930 Poland and Danzig Business Directory* (*Trade, Industry, Handicraft, and Agriculture*); and *The 1932/1933 Poland Telephone Directory* (excluding city of Warsaw), Genealogy Indexer, https://genealogyindexer.org/, accessed August 10, 2022.

17. Kochanski, *The Eagle Unbowed*, 7, 22–25; Gross, *Polish Society Under German Occupation*, 9–28.

18. Pohl, *Nationalsozialistische Judenverfolgung in Ostgalizien*, 27.

19. Rędziński, "Studenci żydowscy we Lwowie w latach 1918–1939."

20. Bartov, *Anatomy of a Genocide*; Heller, *On the Edge of Destruction*; Kochanski, *The Eagle Unbowed*, 26–32.

21. Evans, *The Third Reich in Power*, 678–99; Weinberg, *A World at Arms*, 31–35.

22. In September 1939, Janina, then known as Józefa Mehlberg, published a review of *Sur la Nation de Collectif* by Jan Herzberg in *The Journal of Symbolic Logic*.

23. Announcements for Henry's talks can be found in the Jewish newspaper *Chwila*. One of them announced the Mehlbergs' joint radio program: "Słuchajmy dziś Radia," *Chwila*, 3 November 1937, p. 12.

TWO: THE BEGINNING OF THE END

1. In addition to Janina's memoir, the description of Polish attitudes and experiences during the German attack are drawn from Klukowski, *Tagebuch aus den Jahren der Okkupation 1939–1944*; Shatyn, *A Private War*, 113–19; Jolanta Jaworska, interview with Janina Wiener, Centropa, https://www.centropa.org/biography/janina-wiener, accessed November 3, 2021.

2. Kochanski, *The Eagle Unbowed*, 121; Snyder, *Black Earth*, 120, 127; Burleigh, *Moral Combat*, 152–55; Mazower, *Hitler's Empire*, 98; Beorn, *The Holocaust in Eastern Europe*, 76–77.

3. Amar, *The Paradox of Ukrainian Lviv*, 44, 50.

4. Janina Wiener oral history; Joseph Klinghofer oral history, Interview 4059, USHMM, USC Shoah Foundation Visual History Archive; Lanckorońska, *Those Who Trespass Against Us*, 1–22; Gross, *Revolution from Abroad*, 126–43.

5. Kochanski, *The Eagle Unbowed*, 125–26.

6. Ibid., 123; Gross, *Revolution from Abroad*, 106.

7. Gross, *Revolution from Abroad*, 193–97; Snyder, *Black Earth*, 57; 120–32; Asher, "The Soviet Union, the Holocaust, and Auschwitz," 898.

8. Snyder, *Black Earth*, 122.

9. Ibid., 120–23; Beorn, *The Holocaust in Eastern Europe*, 87; Pohl, *Nationalsozialistische Judenverfolgung in Ostgalizien*, 55.

THREE: TERROR COMES TO LWÓW

1. Himka, "The Lviv Pogrom of 1941," 209–43; Pohl, *Nationalsozialistische Judenverfolgung in Ostgalizien*, 54–62.

2. Pohl, *Nationalsozialistische Judenverfolgung in Ostgalizien*, 53–54; Arad, Krakowski, and Spector, eds., *The Einsatzgruppen Reports*, i–ix; Krausnick and Wilhelm, *Die Truppe des Weltanschauungskrieges*, 3–37, 150–72.

3. Zygmunt Albert, translation from *Kaźń Profesorów Lwowskich*, https://www.lwow .home.pl/lwow_profs.html, accessed November 1, 2021.

4. Pohl, *Nationalsozialistische Judenverfolgung in Ostgalizien*, 68–69; Amar, *The Paradox of Ukrainian Lviv*, 120–37.

5. Pohl, *Nationalsozialistische Judenverfolgung in Ostgalizien*, 55–58; Winstone, *The Dark Heart of Hitler's Europe*, 103–4; Berkhoff and Carynnyk, "The Organization of Ukrainian Nationalists and Its Attitude toward Germans and Jews," 150.

6. Pohl, *Nationalsozialistische Judenverfolgung in Ostgalizien*, 45–52.

7. Ibid., 64–66.

8. Ibid., 64–66; 123–25.

9. Ibid., 75–77; Winstone, *The Dark Heart of Hitler's Europe*, 106, 153.

10. Winstone, *The Dark Heart of Hitler's Europe*, 114–15; Pohl, *Nationalsozialistische Judenverfolgung in Ostgalizien*, 123–35.

11. Pohl, *Nationalsozialistische Judenverfolgung in Ostgalizien*, 119–41.

FOUR: TRANSFORMATION

1. Pohl, *Nationalsozialistische Judenverfolgung in Ostgalizien, 1941–1944*, 158–60; Document #23: diary entries of Tadeusz Tomaszewski, in *Polen*, ed. Friedrich; Redner, *A Jewish Policeman in Lwów*; Golczewski, "Polen," in *Dimension des Voelkermords*, ed. Benz, 445–46.

2. Pohl, *Von der "Judenpolitik" zum Judenmord*, 87–90.

FIVE: THE DYSTOPIAN UTOPIA

1. Akta Miasta Lublina, zespół 22, 2145/22, State Archive in Lublin (APL).

2. Kershaw, *Hitler*, 146–55; Majer, *"Non-Germans" Under the Third Reich*, 63, 625n224.

3. Aly, *Final Solution*, 34; Friedländer, *The Years of Extermination*, 11–12.

4. Koehl, *RKFDV*, 56.

5. Mallmann, Böhler, and Matthäus, *Einsatzgruppen in Polen*, 62–63; Mędykowski, *Macht Arbeit Frei?*, 7–8.

6. Gross, *Polish Society Under German Occupation*, 73–75; Burleigh, *Moral Combat*, 142.

7. Winstone, *The Dark Heart of Hitler's Europe*, 96–98.

8. Memo from Heinrich Himmler re: "Some Thoughts on the Treatment of Aliens in the East," 15 May 1940, in *Europa unterm Hakenkreuz*, ed. Heckert and Röhr, 171–72.

9. Longerich, *Politik der Vernichtung*, 273–78; 289–92; Hayes, *Why?*, 73–113.

10. Winstone, *The Dark Heart of Hitler's Europe*, 38; Majer, *"Non-Germans" Under the Third Reich*, 261–64; Burleigh, *Moral Combat*, 135–36.

11. Aly, *Final Solution*, 34–35; Madajczyk, *Die Okkupationspolitik Nazideutschlands in*

Polen 1939–1945, 405 13, Table 15; *Europa unterm Hakenkreuz*, ed. Heckert and Röhr, 56–59.

12. Gross, *Polish Society Under German Occupation*, 62–63.

13. Majer, *"Non-Germans" Under the Third Reich*, 276–82, quotation on 281; Pohl, *Von der "Judenpolitik" zum Judenmord*, 90; Winstone, *The Dark Heart of Hitler's Europe*, 43–44, 49–52.

14. Gross, *Polish Society Under German Occupation*, 148–59; Winstone, *The Dark Heart of Hitler's Europe*, 67–75, quotation on 50.

15. Akta Miasta Lublina, zespół 22, 2145/22, APL.

16. Shatyn, *A Private War*, 156–57; Madajczyk, *Die Okkupationspolitik Nazideutschlands in Polen 1939–1945*, 279.

17. Majer, *"Non-Germans" Under the Third Reich*, 290, 290f; Burleigh, *Moral Combat*, 142; Madajczyk, *Die Okkupationspolitik Nazideutschlands in Polen 1939–1945*, 347–48; Mazower, *Hitler's Empire*, 127.

18. Rations varied by district in the General Government. In the fall of 1941, the caloric value of the basic daily rations for Poles in Warsaw was 418, while in Radom, special workers could receive as much as 613 calories. Madajczyk, *Die Okkupationspolitik Nazideutschlands in Polen 1939–1945*, 283–84, 285: Table 10. According to the World Health Organization, 2,100 calories per person/per day is the minimum amount needed to sustain a population: World Health Organization, "Food and Nutrition Needs in Emergencies," 1, https://www.who.int/i/item/food-and-nutrition-needs-in-emergencies.

19. Musial, *Deutsche Zivilverwaltung und Judenverfolgung im Generalgouvernement*, 160–63.

20. Majer, *"Non-Germans" Under the Third Reich*, 272.

21. Ibid., 149–53; Pohl, *Von der "Judenpolitik" zum Judenmord*, 80; Madajczyk, *Die Okkupationspolitik Nazideutschlands in Polen 1939–1945*, 220–24, 245: Table 7; Winstone, *The Dark Heart of Hitler's Europe*, 171.

22. Gross, *Polish Society Under German Occupation*, 110.

23. The information about the Lublin Ghetto is drawn from: Photos, testimonies, and articles on the website of the Grodzka Gate–NN Theatre, especially Jakub Chmielewski, "The Ghetto in Podzamcze—boundaries and area," trans. Monika Metlerska-Colerick, https://teatrnn.pl/lexicon/articles/the-ghetto-in-podzamcze-boundaries-and-area/, accessed January 30, 2022; Martin Dean, "Lublin," *The United States Holocaust Memorial Museum Encyclopedia of Camps and Ghettos*, ed. Martin Dean, 675–78; Pohl, *Von der "Judenpolitik" zum Judenmord*, 90–95; Silberklang, *Gates of Tears*, 157–219.

24. Schwindt, *Das Konzentrations- und Vernichtungslager Majdanek*, 79.

25. Madajczyk, *Die Okkupationspolitik Nazideutschlands in Polen 1939–1945*, 454–78; Gross, *Polish Society Under German Occupation*, 186–89; Musial, *Deutsche Zivilverwaltung und Judenverfolgung im Generalgouvernement*, 145–46; Winstone, *The Dark Heart of Hitler's Europe*, 69, 104.

SIX: ANNIHILATION

1. Poprzeczny, *Odilo Globocnik*, 27–34; 61–78; Bartrop and Grimm, *Perpetrating the Holocaust*, 102–4.

2. Black, "Rehearsal for 'Reinhard'?," 220; Madajczyk, *Die Okkupationspolitik Nazideutschlands in Polen 1939–1945*, 188–89.

3. White, "Majdanek," 3; Pohl, "Die Stellung des Distrikts Lublin in der 'Endlösung der Judenfrage,'" in "*Aktion Reinhardt*," ed. Musial, 91.

4. The information in this chapter on the Lublin *Selbstschutz*, Globocnik's early forced labor camps for Jews, and plans for the reservation are drawn from: Black, "Rehearsal for 'Reinhard'?," 211–22; Mędykowski, *Macht Arbeit Frei?*, 138–77; Silberklang, *Gates of Tears*, 114–28; Winstone, *The Dark Heart of Hitler's Europe*, 77–80; Pohl, *Von der "Judenpolitik" zum Judenmord*, 49–51, 79–85; Musial, *Deutsche Zivilverwaltung und Judenverfolgung im Generalgouvernement*, 110–22; and Gruner, *Jewish Forced Labor Under the Nazis*, 244–46. Musial argues that the 50,000 to 70,000 figure, supported by Pohl and Gruner, is much too high: *Deutsche Zivilverwaltung und Judenverfolgung im Generalgouvernement*, 167.

5. Dziadosz and Marszałek, "Więzienia i obozy w dystrykcie lubelskim w latach 1939–1944," 59.

6. Musial, *Deutsche Zivilverwaltung und Judenverfolgung im Generalgouvernement*, 201–3, quotation on 203; Pohl, "Die Stellung des Distrikts Lublin in der 'Endlösung der Judenfrage,'" 91.

7. Quoted in White, "Majdanek," 4.

8. Aly, *Final Solution*, 185–86; Evans, *The Third Reich at War*, 172–75; Gerlach, *The Extermination of the European Jews*, 67–68.

9. White, "Majdanek," 3–5; Musial, *Deutsche Zivilverwaltung und Judenverfolgung im Generalgouvernement*, 202.

10. Musial, *Deutsche Zivilverwaltung und Judenverfolgung im Generalgouvernement*, 201–4.

11. For the "euthanasia" program and its connection to the "final solution," see: Friedlander, *The Origins of Nazi Genocide*.

12. Pohl, "Massentötungen durch Giftgas im Rahmen der 'Aktion Reinhardt,'" in *Neue Studien zu Nationalsozilististischen Massentötungen durch Giftgas*, ed. Morsch and Perz, 191–92; White, "Majdanek," 9; Black, "Die Trawniki-Männer und die 'Aktion Reinhard,'" in "*Aktion Reinhard*," Musial, ed., 309–52.

13. Longerich, *Politik der Vernichtung*, 441–44; Czech, *Auschwitz Chronicle, 1939–1945*, 84–87; Pohl, "Massentötungen durch Giftgas im Rahmen der 'Aktion Reinhardt,'" 191.

14. Longerich, *Politik der Vernichtung*, 466–67.

15. Friedländer, *The Years of Extermination*, 272–81; Roseman, *The Wannsee Conference and the Final Solution*, passim.

16. For a brief history of *Aktion* Reinhard and a tally of its victims, see: "Operation Reinhard (Einsatz Reinhard)," *Encyclopedia of the Holocaust*, United States Holocaust

Memorial Museum, https://encyclopedia.ushmm.org/content/en/article/opera
tion-reinhard einsatz-reinhard, accessed January 21, 2022. For the tally of Jewish
deaths at Auschwitz, see "Auschwitz," *Encyclopedia of the Holocaust,* https://ency
clopedia.ushmm.org/content/en/article/auschwitz, accessed January 21, 2022.

17. For the changes in the ghetto in the run-up to its liquidation, see: Pohl, *Von der "Judenpolitik" zum Judenmord,* 110–11; Dean, "Lublin," *The United States Holocaust Memorial Museum Encyclopedia of Camps and Ghettos,* ed. Martin Dean, 676; Chmielewski,
"The Ghetto in Podzamcze—boundaries and area," https://teatrnn.pl/lexicon/ar
ticles/the-ghetto-in-podzamcze-boundaries-and-area, accessed January 22, 2022.

18. Pohl, *Von der "Judenpolitik" zum Judenmord,* 113–17; Dean, "Lublin," 676; time-
coded English notes to July 9, 2003, oral history interview of Jacek Ossowski, RG
-50.488.0177, USHMM. The website of the Grodzka Gate–NN Theatre in Lublin
provides photos of the Lublin Ghetto and detailed descriptions of its history and of
the destruction of Lublin's Jews: https://teatrnn.pl/zydzi/en/holocaust-19391944,
accessed January 22, 2022.

19. Klukowski, *Tagebuch aus den Jahren der Okkupation 1939–1944,* 337; "The camp in
Bełżec," attachment to April 1942 report of the Polish Home Army Lublin detachment, Document 66, in *Polen,* ed. Friedrich, 260–62.

20. Anna Wylegała, "Entangled Bystanders," in *Trauma, Experience and Narrative in
Europe after World War II,* ed. Kivimäki and Leese, 132; Madajczyk, *Die Okkupa-
tionspolitik Nazideutschlands in Polen 1939–1945,* 189–90; Kłapeć, *Rada Główna
Opiekuńcza w dystrykcie lubelskim w latach 1940–1944,* 34.

21. Klukowski, *Tagebuch aus den Jahren der Okkupation 1939–1944,* 332.

SEVEN: "BETTER TO DIE A SOLDIER"

1. Zimmerman, *The Polish Underground and the Jews, 1939–1945,* 149–58; Golczewski, "Die Heimatarmee und die Juden," in *Die polnische Heimatarmee,* ed. Chiari,
with Kochanowski, 643–45, 664–65.

2. Zimmerman, *The Polish Underground and the Jews, 1939–1945,* 57; Lanckorońska,
Those Who Trespass Against Us, 20.

3. Komorowski, "Facetten des polnischen militärischen Widerstandes und seine Aktualität," in *Die polnische Heimatarmee,* ed. Chiari, with Kochanowski, 683.

4. Peploński, "Die Aufklärung der Heimatarmee," in *Die polnische Heimatarmee,* ed.
Chiari, with Kochanowski, 180–81; Biskupska, *Survivors,* 150–56. For the role of
women in the AK, see Höger, "Frauen als Kombattanten," in *Die polnische Heimatarmee,* ed. Chiari, with Kochanowski, 387–410.

5. Majer, *"Non-Germans" Under the Third Reich,* 318–19.

6. Kłapeć, *Rada Główna Opiekuńcza w dystrykcie lubelskim w latach 1940–1944,* 173–
200; Winstone, *The Dark Heart of Hitler's Europe,* 134.

7. Kłapeć, *Rada Główna Opiekuńcza w dystrykcie lubelskim w latach 1940–1944,* 120–
21; Musial, *Deutsche Zivilverwaltung und Judenverfolgung im Generalgouvernement,*
96–98.

8. Kłapeć, *Rada Główna Opiekuńcza w dystrykcie lubelskim w latach 1940–1944*, 117–21, 156–61.

9. Series of memos to the Polish Care Committees in Lublin District from Janina Suchodolska, Secretary to the RGO Advisor for Lublin District, June 1942, RGO-Lublin, sygn. 8, pp. 104–12, APL; Kłapeć, *Rada Główna Opiekuńcza w dystrykcie lubelskim w latach 1940–1944*, 156.

10. Kłapeć, *Rada Główna Opiekuńcza w dystrykcie lubelskim w latach 1940–1944*, 168–69; "Należności za podróże służbowe rowerami," June 20, 1942. APL RGO-Lublin, sygn. 8, p. 109; Majer, *"Non-Germans" Under the Third Reich*, 318–19.

11. Kłapeć, *Rada Główna Opiekuńcza w dystrykcie lubelskim w latach 1940–1944*, 150, 168–69.

12. Ibid., 117; Winstone, *The Dark Heart of Hitler's Europe*, 143–45; Kochanski, *The Eagle Unbowed*, 275; Majewski, "Konzept und Organization des 'zivilen Kampfes,'" in *Die polnische Heimatarmee*, ed. Chiari, with Kochanowski, 305.

13. Wachsmann, *KL*, 286.

14. Ibid., 261, 283; Streit, "Soviet Prisoners of War in the Hands of the Wehrmacht," in *War of Extermination*, ed. Heer and Naumann, 81, 86. British radio intercepts of Majdanek daily status reports show that 112 Soviet POWs remained at the camp on January 16, 1942; by February 19, 1942, the number dropped to 58: Kuwałek, Kranz, and Ciwek-Siupa, "Odszyfrowane radiotelegramy (. . .)," 210–32.

15. Testimony of Stanisław Goljan, October 29, 1947, GK 196/153.cz.1, pp. 73–78, Institute of National Remembrance (IPN), Chronicles of Terror, https://www.za pisyterroru.pl/dlibra/publication/3683/edition/3664/content?navq=aHR0cDo vL3d3dy56YXBpc3l0ZXJyb3J1LnBsL2RsaWJyYS9sYXRlc3Q_YWN0aW9uPV NpbXBsZVNlYXJjaEFjdGlvbiZ0eXBlPS02JnA9MA&navref=NG9tOzRucCAyd WI7MnRzIDJlbDsyZTI, accessed August 25, 2023.

16. Kranz, *The Extermination of Jews at Majdanek Concentration Camp*, 20–21; Vrba and Bestic, *Escape from Auschwitz*, 53–69. Descriptions of the suffering and death of Jews on deportation trains also available in: Klukowski, *Tagebuch aus den Jahren der Okkupation 1939–1944*, 337; "31.8.1942. 'Judenumsiedlung' in Rawa-Ruska," National-Socialism Archive, Dokumente zum Nationalsozialismus, https://www .ns-archiv.de/verfolgung/polen/rawaruska/umsiedlung.php, accessed March 28, 2020.

17. Vrba and Bestic, *Escape from Auschwitz*, 77; Ambach and Köhler, eds., *Lublin-Majdanek*, 72.

18. Marszałek, *Majdanek*, 143; Kranz, *The Extermination of Jews at Majdanek Concentration Camp*, 23; Schwindt, *Das Konzentrations- und Vernichtungslager Majdanek*, 168–70; Smorczewski, *Bridging the Gap*, 126–27.

19. The information in this chapter about Countess Lanckorońska is drawn from: Lanckorońska, *Those Who Trespass Against Us*, xvi–xxii, 53–144.

20. Kłapeć, *Rada Główna Opiekuńcza w dystrykcie lubelskim w latach 1940–1944*, 241–46.

21. Orth, *Die Konzentrationslager-SS*, 189; Wachsmann, *KL*, 117–18, 198.

22. Malm, "Przed i za drutami," in *Braterska Pomoc*, ed. Machuła and Wiśniewska, 84–109; State Museum at Majdanek, "Saturnina Malm—A 'Quiet Heroine,'" August 17, 2018, https://www.majdanek.eu/en/pow/saturnina_malm_-_a__quiet_heroine/50, accessed April 9, 2022.

23. Malm, "Przed i za drutami," 84–109; Ambach and Köhler, *Lublin-Majdanek*, 171–79; Wachsmann, *KL*, 385; Kuwałek, Kranz, and Ciwek-Siupa, "Odszyfrowane radiotelegramy (. . .)," 210–32.

24. Wachsmann, *KL*, 385–87; Marszałek, *Majdanek*, 40; Pauer-Studer and Velleman, *Konrad Morgen*, 51.

EIGHT: FROZEN CARGO

1. Madajczyk, *Die Okkupationspolitik Nazideutschlands in Polen 1939–1945*, 422–25; Kozaczyńska, "When There Were No More Tears Left to Cry," in *Crime Without Punishment*, ed. Kostkiewicz, 101–7. In addition to other sources cited in this chapter, much of the information provided regarding the Zamość resettlement operation in the winter of 1942–1943 and the RGO's response is drawn from records of the RGO, sygn. 46, pp. 1–6, 10–15, 19, 21, 41–42, AAN, and accessible at RG-15.550, 2 125_0_1.2_46. pp. 10–34, USHMM.

2. Madajczyk, *Die Okkupationspolitik Nazideutschlands in Polen 1939 1945*, 422–25; Laura Crago, "Szczebrzeszyn," *Encyclopedia of Camps and Ghettos*, ed. Dean, 713–15; Adam Kopciowski and Laura Crago, "Zamość," *Encyclopedia of Camps and Ghettos*, ed. Dean, 735–38; entries from October 21 through November 26, 1942, Klukowski, *Tagebuch aus den Jahren der Okkupation 1939–1944*, 376–87.

3. Kochanski, *The Eagle Unbowed*, 269.

4. Schwindt, *Das Konzentrations- und Vernichtungslager Majdanek*, 122–29.

5. Quotation, ibid., 123; Kranz, "Das Konzentrationslager Majdanek 1941–1944," in *Bildungsarbeit und historisches Lernen in der Gedenkstätte Majdanek*, ed. Kranz, 281–83; Minutes of October 30, 1942, Polish Care Committee meeting, RG -15.550, 2_125_0_2.1468/382, USHMM; "Tätigkeitsbericht des Polnischen Hilfskomitees für Stadt und Land Lublin für November 1942," December 18, 1942, Distrikt Lublin, sygn. 238, pp. 1–5, APL.

6. Madajczyk, *Die Okkupationspolitik Nazideutschlands in Polen 1939–1945*, 422–25; Document 123, *Europa unterm Hakenkreuz*, ed. Heckert and Röhr, 238–39.

7. Document 123, *Europa unterm Hakenkreuz*, ed. Heckert and Röhr, 238–39.

8. Kozaczyńska, "When There Were No More Tears Left to Cry," 101–4; Jaczyńska, *Sonderlaboratorium SS*, 187–97.

9. Document 123, *Europa unterm Hakenkreuz*, ed. Heckert and Röhr, 238–39.

10. Kozaczyńska, "When There Were No More Tears Left to Cry," 105–7.

11. "Protokół przesluchania świadka: Janina Suchodolska," December 2, 1946, IPN 108/272, GK 281/272; SO Kd 272, Archive of the State Museum at Majdanek (APMM).

12. Kłapeć, *Rada Główna Opiekuńcza w dystrykcie lubelskim w latach 1940–1944*, 253–59.

13. Wnuk, *Dzieci polskie oskarżaja*, 189–90, quoting the testimony of Janina Suchodolska.

NINE: THE POLISH QUESTION

1. Madajczyk, *Die Okkupationspolitik Nazideutschlands in Polen 1939–1945*, 218–19.
2. Wachsmann, *KL*, 627, 409–24.
3. Ibid., 421–27; Wiśniewska, "Pomoc więźniom Majdanka," 235–36.
4. Kuwałek, Kranz, and Ciwek-Siupa, "Odszyfrowane radiotelegramy (. . .)," 210–32; Kranz, "Konzentrationslager Lublin," 37; Grudzińska, "Polacy na Majdanku," in *Więźniowie KL Lublin 1941–1944*, ed. Kranz and Lenarczyk, 272–82.
5. Wachsmann, *KL*, 419; Document 126, *Europa unterm Hakenkreuz*, ed. Heckert and Röhr, 244; entries for January 11 and January 25, 1943, in Leszczyńska, *Kronika obozu na Majdanku*, 116, 122.
6. Wachsmann, *KL*, 421–24; Grudzińska "Polacy na Majdanku," 284–87; White, "Majdanek," 7.
7. February 17, 1943, cover letter and February 11, 1943, memo from Türk, Abteilung BuF, Hauptabteilung Innere Verwaltung, Generalgouvernment, Lublin District Office, sygn. 209, pp. 138–39, APL; Wiśniewska, "Pomoc więźniom Majdanka," 235–42. In addition to Janina's memoir, the information in the rest of this chapter, except where otherwise noted, is drawn from: "Sprawozdania Pol. K.O. Lublin z akcji dożywiania więźniów, 1943–1944," RGO sygn. 1487, AAN, in Fot. 19, APMM; Kłapeć, *Rada Główna Opiekuńcza w dystrykcie lubelskim w latach 1940–1944*, 246–47.
8. Monthly activity reports of the Polish Care Committee for Lublin city and county, August and October 1942, sygn. 209, pp. 12, 38, APL; Madajczyk, *Die Okkupationspolitik Nazideutschlands in Polen 1939–1945*, 111–13.
9. Krzymowska, *Lubelska Chorągiew Harcerek w latach 1939–44. Pomoc dla więźniów Majdanka*, VII/0-72, 193–94, APMM.

TEN: MAJDANEK

1. Hermann Florstedt SS Officer personnel file, Microfilm Publication A 3343, SSO-044B, National Archives and Records Administration (NARA).
2. Wachsmann, *KL*, 99; information provided by Łukasz Myszała, State Museum at Majdanek, May 2022.
3. The descriptions and information about Majdanek in this chapter are drawn from a wide variety of sources, as well as the authors' observations at Majdanek, consultation with Łukasz Myszała of the State Museum at Majdanek in May 2022, and review of historical photos in the museum's archive. The main primary sources, secondary studies, and accounts of former prisoners and SS personnel relied upon in this chapter include: Lenarczyk, ed., *Majdanek w Dokumentach*, particularly Documents 1.12, 1.20 through 1.25, and 4.1 through 4.5; Kuwałek, Kranz, and Ciwek-Siupa, "Odszyfrowane radiotelegramy (. . .)," 210–32; Judgment in the criminal

proceedings against Lothar Hoffmann et al., Staatsanwaltschaft beim Landgericht Wiesbaden, 8 Ks 1/70; Kranz, *The Extermination of Jews at Majdanek Concentration Camp*; Kranz and Lenarczyk, eds., *Więźniowie KL Lublin 1941–1944*; Marszałek, *Majdanek*; Marszałek, "Budowa Obozu Koncentracyjnego na Majdanku w latach 1942–1944," 21–90; Murawska, "System strzeżenia i sposoby izolacji więźniów w obozie koncentracyjnym na Majdanku," 76–132; Kwiatkowski, *485 Days at Majdanek*; statement of former administration officer at Majdanek Hans Behrstein, RG-06 War Crimes Investigation and Prosecution, .025 Central Archives of the Federal Security Services (former KGB) of the Russian Federation, 19 K-99809 006.025*19, USHMM; accounts of former Majdanek prisoners, especially Julian Gregorowicz, 148–51, and Dr. Jan Nowak, 171–79, in *Lublin-Majdanek*, ed. Ambach and Köhler; Jerzy Korcz, "15 Months in Majdanek," RG 15.271M, Zbiór pamiętników, relacji i ankiet byłych więźniów (Sygn. VII), roll 1/5-167, USHMM; Dionyz Lenard letter fragment #88, *Polen*, ed. Friedrich, 309–22; Perzanowska, *Gdy myśli do Majdanka wracają*.

4. Witte and Tyas, "A New Document on the Deportation and Murder of Jews During 'Einsatz Reinhardt' 1942," 470.

5. Elizabeth White interviews in the Federal Republic of Germany of former Majdanek guards Andreas F., January 12, 1988, Munich; Michael F., January 13, 1988, Stuttgart; Anton K., January 18, 1988, Hanau.

6. Black, "Foot Soldiers of the Final Solution," 22, 34.

7. In addition to the memoir, the information about the relief efforts at Majdanek of the RGO, Polish Red Cross, and the Underground is drawn from a variety of studies and firsthand accounts, including: Wiśniewska, "Pomoc więźniom Majdanka," 239; Malm, "Przed i za drutami," in *Braterska Pomoc*, ed. Machuła and Wiśniewska, 84–109; Brzosko-Mędryk, *Niebo bez ptaków*, 440–56; Mańkowski, ed., *Hitlerowskie więzienie na Zamku w Lublinie 1939–1944*; Kwiatkowski, *485 Days in Majdanek*; account of Antonina Łopatyńska in Anna Krzymowska, "Lubelska Chorągiew Harcerek w latach 1939–44, Pomoc dla więźniów Majdanka," VII/0-72, APMM; Perzanowska, *Gdy myśli do Majdanka wracają*; account of Zofia Orska, sygn. 129, APMM; account of Adam Panasiewicz, VII/M-234, APMM; account of Romuald Sztaba, XXII-9, APMM.

8. Document 8.3, *Majdanek w Dokumentach*, ed. Lenarczyk.

9. Grudzińska, "The Fate of Children at the Majdanek Concentration Camp," in *The Young Victims of the Nazi Regime*, ed. Gigliotti and Tempian, 171–200.

10. Grudzińska, "The Women's Medical Ward in *Frauenkonzentrationslager* Lublin (Majdanek), Presentation for Conference," *Medical Review Auschwitz: Medicine Behind the Barbed Wire*, September 12–21, 2021, https://www.mp.pl/auschwitz/confer ence/edition2021/session1/show.html?id=280502, accessed May 24, 2022.

11. Skrzyński June 1, 1943, memo; Kwiatkowski, *485 Days in Majdanek*, 173.

12. Stefania Perzanowska, "The Women's Camp Hospital at Majdanek," trans. M. Kapera, *Medical Review—Auschwitz* (January 7, 2020), https://www.mp.pl/aus

chwitz/journal/english/223573,majdanek-womens-camp-hospital#1, accessed June 3, 2022. Muhsfeldt's name is sometimes spelled Mussfeld or Mussfeldt.

ELEVEN: JANINA'S LISTS

1. Kwiatkowski, *485 Days in Majdanek*, 214.
2. Document 2.19, *Majdanek w Dokumentach*, ed. Lenarczyk; Kranz, "'Generalplan Ost' und 'Endlösung' im Distrikt Lublin," 253–54; Winstone, *The Dark Heart of Hitler's Europe*, 198–202.
3. Jaczyńska, *Sonderlaboratorium SS*, 136; Skrzyński's July 1, 1943, report on his meeting that day with Müller, 2_125_0_2.1_469/78, USHMM.
4. December 2, 1946, statement of.Janina Suchodolska, VII-135-104, APMM; Markiewicz, *Nie dali ziemi skąd ich ród*, 222.
5. Documents 2.19, 15.10, *Majdanek w Dokumentach*, ed. Lenarczyk; Grudzińska, "The Fate of Children at the Majdanek Concentration Camp," in *The Young Victims of the Nazi Regime*, ed. Gigliotti and Tempian; Gajderowicz and Skrzyniarz, "Children of the Zamość Region in the Majdanek Camp (in Selected Archive Files and Personal Accounts)," in *Crime Without Punishment*, ed. Kostkiewicz, 115–30; "Transit Camp at ul. Krochmalna 6 and 31," accessed May 26, 2022.
6. Kiriszczenko, "Mother's Death," *Majdanek Concentration Camp*, ed. Rajca and Wiśniewska, 65–57; Urszula Tochman-Welc account in *Majdanek*, ed. Grudzińska, 131–36; Kwiatkowski, *485 Days in Majdanek*, 215–18; Document 4.6, *Majdanek w Dokumentach*, ed. Lenarczyk; Wnuk, *Dzieci polskie oskarżają*, 116–21.
7. Entries for July 1943, in Leszczyńska, *Kronika obozu na Majdanku*; Wiśniewska, "Pomoc więźniom Majdanka," in *Majdanek 1941–1944*, ed. Mencel, 238; Kwiatkowski, *485 Days in Majdanek*, 215–18.
8. September 18, 1943, note re: action to help in camps at 6 and 31 Krochmalna Street, RGO 50, AAN, in Fot. 5, pp. 49–50, APMM; Markiewicz, *Nie dali ziemi skąd ich ród*, 222–25; Woroniak, "Ocalić od zapomnienia," 36–39.
9. Madajczyk, *Die Okkupationspolitik Nazideutschlands in Polen 1939–1945*, 119–21, 135; Winstone, *The Dark Heart of Hitler's Europe*, 115 (quotation), 201–3.
10. Madajczyk, *Die Okkupationspolitik Nazideutschlands in Polen 1939–1945*, 111–17, 120–21; Winstone, *The Dark Heart of Hitler's Europe*, 202; Wendler letter in SS officer personnel file of Odilo Globocnik, Berlin Document Center, also available in Microfilm Publication A3343, Series SSO, NARA.
11. Madajczyk, *Die Okkupationspolitik Nazideutschlands in Polen 1939–1945*, 122; Document 15.9, *Majdanek w Dokumentach*.
12. Poprzeczny, *Odilo Globocnik*, 342–51.
13. Skrzyński August 3, 1943, report on his August 2 meetings with Wendler and Höfle, RGO-Lublin, sygn. 19, pp. 6–9, APL.
14. Pohl, *Von der "Judenpolitik" zum Judenmord*, 115, 118, 146, 183–84.
15. Skrzyński August 3, 1943, report.

16. Skrzyński activity report for August 1943, sygn. 685, pp. 64–66, AAN; Skrzyński August 20, 1943, report to RGO Kraków on releases from transit camps, RGO 29 "Korespondencja z Doradcą Okręgu Lubelskiego" cz. 3, 1943, pp. 119–20, APL.

17. Except where otherwise noted, the narrative of Janina's efforts to obtain the release from Majdanek of expellees is based on: Suchodolska September 7, 1943, memo on taking over people from the Majdanek camp, RGO-Lublin, sygn. 19, pp. 12–13, APL; Skrzyński August 20, 1943, report; December 2, 1946, testimony of Janina Suchodolska, VII-135-104, APMM; Kłapeć, *Rada Główna Opiekuńcza w dystrykcie lubelskim w latach 1940–1944*, 252–53; Wnuk, *Dzieci polskie oskarzaja*, 118; the authors' observations at Majdanek.

18. Globocnik September 10, 1943, letter of recommendation in Florstedt's SS Officer personnel file, A 3343, SSO-044B, NARA.

19. Entries for August 9, 10, 11, 12, 13, 1943, in Leszczyńska, *Kronika obozu na Majdanku*.

20. Document 15.10, *Majdanek w Dokumentach*, ed. Lenarczyk.

21. September 18, 1943, note re: action to help in camps at 6 and 31 Krochmalna Street, RGO 50, AAN, in Fot. 5, pp. 49–50, APMM; Skrzyński activity report for August 1943; Suchodolska September 8, 1943, memo.

22. Document 2.19, *Majdanek w Dokumentach*, ed. Lenarczyk; Kranz, "'Generalplan Ost' und 'Endlösung' im Distrikt Lublin," 253–54.

23. Statement of Janina Suchodolska; Wnuk, *Dzieci polskie oskarżaja*, 189, 200–201.

TWELVE: RESCUE

1. Wnuk, *Dzieci polskie oskarżają*, 116–21.

2. Mańkowski, ed. *Hitlerowskie więzienie na Zamku w Lublinie 1939–1944*, 293; Wiśniewska, "Pomoc więźniom Majdanka," in *Majdanek 1941–1944*, ed. Mencel, 242–44; recap of July 1943, in Leszczyńska, *Kronika obozu na Majdanku*, Kiełboń and Leszczyńska, *Kobiety Lubelszczyzny represjonowane w latach 1944–1956*, 33–35.

3. Adam Panasiewicz, VII/M-234, pp. 7–10, APMM.

4. Quotation in Majdanek Museum, "Saturnina Malm—A 'Quiet Heroine'"; Malm, "Przed i za drutami," in *Braterska Pomoc*, ed. Machuła and Wiśniewska, 109–11.

5. Suchodolska September 11, 1943, memo on September 8 meeting with the Chief of the Governor's Office, RGO-Lublin, sygn. 19, pp. 10–11, APL.

6. Document 2.1, *Majdanek w Dokumentach*, ed. Lenarczyk; Skrzyński activity report September through November 1943, RG 15.550, 685/72-80, USHMM; Grudzińska, *Polacy na Majdanku*, 276–78; Kranz, "Konzentrationslager Lublin," 54; recap for August 1943, in Leszczyńska, *Kronika obozu na Majdanku*; Madej, "Erste Opfer," in *Unser Schicksal*, ed. Kranz, 17–27; Marszałek, *Majdanek*, 61.

7. Skrzyński activity report September through November 1943, RG 15.550, 685/72-80, USHMM; Skrzyński August 12, 1943, letter to Wendler, RGO-Lublin, sygn. 19, pp. 4–5, APL.

8. Suchodolska September 11, 1943, memo.

9. Lublin Care Committee minutes of September 29, 1943, meeting and monthly report for September 1943, RG 15.550, 469/117-1120, USHMM.

10. Rudling, "Historical Representation of the Wartime Accounts of the Activities of the OUN-UPA (Organization of Ukrainian Nationalists–Ukrainian Insurgent Army)," 163–89; Snyder, *The Reconstruction of Nations*, 154–77.

11. Social Report No. 38 (Oct. 9, 1943), Polish Government-in-Exile, RG-15.046M, 3/372–75, USHMM; Kłapeć, *Rada Główna Opiekuńcza w dystrykcie lubelskim w latach 1940–1944*, 260–67.

12. December 2, 1946, statement of Janina Suchodolska, VII-135-104, APMM.

13. Markiewicz, *Nie dali ziemi skąd ich ród*, 223–25.

14. Woroniak, "Ocalić od zapomnienia," 36–39; Szlachetka, "Zapomniany obóz przy ul. Krochmalnej."

15. Suchodolska October 30, 1943, memo on October 29 meeting at the BuF district office, RGO-Lublin, sygn. 46, pp. 41–43, APL.

THIRTEEN: SOUP WITH A SIDE OF HOPE

1. Globocnik September 10, 1943, note, Hermann Florstedt SS Officer personnel file, NARA; Marszałek, "Budowa obozu koncentracyjnego na Majdanku w latach 1942–1944," 39–53; Wiśniewska, "Praca więźniów Majdanka," in *Majdanek*, ed. Mencel, 177–82.

2. Oswald Pohl September 7, 1943, note on conference, Nuremberg Document NO-599, Trials of War Criminals before the Nuernberg Military Tribunals under Control Council Law no. 10 (hereafter: Green Series), 5: 377–79; Florstedt SS Officer personnel file; White, "Majdanek," 13.

3. Pohl September 30, 1943, report to Himmler, Nuremberg Document 1469-PS, Green Series, 5: 379–82; Wachsmann, *KL*, 426. The mortality figures were for registered prisoners only and did not include Jews sent to Auschwitz or Majdanek to be murdered on arrival.

4. Weingartner, "Law and Justice in the Nazi SS," 289; Kranz, "Konzentrationslager Lublin," 49; Kwiatkowski, *485 Days in Majdanek*, 202–3.

5. It was long assumed that Florstedt was executed with Koch, but no document has been found to confirm this, and there are indications that he may have survived the war and lived under an assumed name. Kranz, "Konzentrationslager Lublin" 57n; Wachsmann, *KL*, 387; Pauer-Studer, Velleman, and Cohn-Sherbok, *Konrad Morgen*, 47–53.

6. Janina Siwińska, VII/M-234, APMM; Adam Panasiewicz, VII/M-234, APMM; Marszałek, *Majdanek*, 156–61; Perzanowska, "Pomoc lubelskich organizacji społecznych więźniom Majdanka," 1–13; Zakrzewski, *A my żyjemy dalej*, 105.

7. Testimonies regarding Bajerke by Mirosława Odi and Halina Wencka in Chronicles of Terror, https://www.zapisyterroru.pl/dlibra/publication/3495/edition/3476

/content?navq, accessed June 9, 2022; testimony of Wilhelm Karl Petrak, 1383/1-8, APMM; June 27, 1969, statement of Alfred Hoffmann, Kserok. 1846, APMM.

8. Perzanowska, *Gdy myśli do Majdanka wracaja*, 28, 148; Kwiatkowski, *485 Days in Majdanek*, 114–15; Józef Korcz, VII/M-1, APMM; "15 miesięcy na Majdanku—wspomnienia," 69; Marszałek, *Majdanek*, 44–45.

9. XII-12, k. 19, k. 25, APMM.

10. In addition to the memoir, the narrative about the permission for soup deliveries is based on the following: reports of Suchodolska's October 15, 1943, meeting with the Majdanek commandant, RGO sygn. 1487, in Fot. 19, pp. 178–99 and sygn. 108, in Fot. 8, k. 32, AAN, APMM; Kłapeć, *Rada Główna Opiekuńcza w dystrykcie lubelskim w latach 1940–1944*, 247–48; Wiśniewska, "Pomoc więźniom Majdanka," in *Majdanek 1941–1944*, ed. Mencel, 239–40.

11. Pohl, *Von der "Judenpolitik" zum Judenmord*, 185.

12. In addition to the memoir, the narrative of the soup deliveries is based on: Hanna Kuskowska [*sic*: Huskowska] later Młynarska, VII/M-234, APMM; Kwiatkowski, *485 Days in Majdanek*, 249–55; Wiśniewska, "Pomoc więźniom Majdanka," 239–40. The first meeting between Janina and Perzanowska and their subsequent relationship have been described by both Janina in her memoir and by Perzanowska in several sources, including: *Gdy myśli do Majdanka wracają*, 99–102; "Pomoc lubelskich organizacji społecznych więźniom Majdanka," 6–11.

13. Mailänder, *Female SS Guards and Workaday Violence*, 163–64, 241–44; Schwindt, *Das Konzentrations- und Vernichtungslager Majdanek*, 233, 238, 260; Perzanowska, *Gdy myśli do Majdanka wracają*, 29–30.

14. Kwiatkowski, *485 Days in Majdanek*, 341–42.

15. Sahara 57/C 13. XI.43, APMM; XII-10, k. 177-178, APMM.

FOURTEEN: HARVEST OF DEATH

1. Hanna Huskowska, VII/M-234, APMM; Kwiatkowski, *485 Days in Majdanek*, 341–42.

2. In addition to Janina's account of the letter from Majdanek prisoners, the information about *Aktion Erntefest* in this chapter is based on: Kranz, *Extermination of Jews at Majdanek*, 63–69; Pohl, *Von der "Judenpolitik" zum Judenmord*, 170–74; Schwindt, *Das Konzentrations- und Vernichtungslager Majdanek*, 266–80.

3. SS and Police Leader Warsaw Jürgen Stroop May 16, 1943, report on the destruction of the Warsaw Ghetto, Nuremberg Document PS-1061, Harvard Law School Library Nuremberg Trials Project, http://nuremberg.law.harvard.edu/documents/4432-report-to-ss-officials?q=stroop+report#p.8, accessed June 17, 2022; Arad, *Bełżec, Sobibor, Treblinka*, 286–98, 322–41; "Sobibor Uprising," USHMM Holocaust Encyclopedia, https://encyclopedia.ushmm.org/content/en/article/sobibor-uprising, accessed June 17, 2022.

FIFTEEN: CHRISTMAS AT MAJDANEK

1. XII-10, k. 277–78, APMM; Kwiatkowski, *485 Days in Majdanek*, 267–68, 276; Jerzy Korcz, "15 Months in Majdanek," VII/M-1, 116–17, APMM; Kranz, "Konzentrationslager Lublin," 94.

2. Martin Gottfried Weiss SS Officer personnel file, NARA; Orth, *Das Konzentrationslager-SS*, 233–40; Schwindt, *Das Konzentrations- und Vernichtungslager Majdanek*, 271, n 386.

3. RGO Lublin report for September 1 to November 30, 1943, RG 15.550\125 Rada Główna Opiekuńcza 2_125_2.4 sygn. 685, 72–80, USHMM; XII-10, k. 271–72, APMM.

4. Christians, *Piekło XX wieku*, 187–230; Romuald Sztaba, XXII-9, APMM.

5. Marszałek, *Majdanek*, 156–161; Kłapeć, *Rada Główna Opiekuńcza w dystrykcie lubelskim w latach 1940–1944*, 248–49; November 16, 1943, meeting memo, RGO-Lublin, syg. 19, p. 1, APL; Suchodolska October 26, 1943, note, RGO 30 "Korespondencja z Doradcą Okręgu Lubelskiego" cz. 4, 1943, p. 390, APL; XII-10, k. 529, APMM; Kwiatkowski, *485 Days in Majdanek*, 281–82.

6. Christians, *Piekło XX wieku*, 263–66; XII-10, k. 415–16, APMM; Saturnina Malm, VII/M-260, 18–20, APMM.

7. Maria Gancarz, XXII-1, APMM; Ossowska, *Przeżyłam*, 302; Kwiatkowski, *485 Days in Majdanek*, 281–82.

8. Skrzyński December 15, 1943, memo, "Pełnomocnik RGO, Doradca na Okręg Lubelski. Okólniki i pisma," 1940–1941-194, RGO 24, p. 45, APL; RGO report for the period December 1, 1943, to January 31, 1944, RG 15.550\125, 2_125_2.4 sygn. 685, pp. 82–87, USHMM.

9. Perzanowska, *Gdy myśli do Majdanka wracają*, 126–27; Brzosko-Mędryk, *Niebo bez ptaków*, 545; Rebecca Voisich, "Majdanek: Revisitng Resistance," Museum of Jewish Heritage, July 23, 2020, accessed August 12, 2022, https://mjhnyc.org/blog/majdanek-revisiting-resistance/.

10. The information in this chapter about Christmas at Majdanek and Krochmalna and New Year's Eve at Majdanek is based, in addition to the memoir, on: February 2, 1944, note on Christmas and New Year's action at Majdanek, RGO 31, cz. 1, p. 101, APL; Perzanowska, *Gdy myśli do Majdanka wracają*, 126–27; Brzosko-Mędryk, *Niebo bez ptaków*, 492–95; Kwiatkowski, *485 Days in Majdanek*, 290–93, 312; Ossowska, *Przeżyłam*, 304; Stanisławski, *Pole śmierci*, 220.

11. "Mensch—bei uns in Deutschland kommt das nie in Frage," quoted in Stanisławski, *Pole śmierci*, 220.

SIXTEEN: CAT AND MOUSE

1. Rogerie, "Transporty chorych," in *Majdanek*, ed. Grudzińska, 210–14; Kwiatkowski, *485 Days in Majdanek*, 297–98; Leszczyńska, "Transporty i stany liczbowe obozu," in *Majdanek*, ed. Mencel, 9–128; Kranz, "Das Konzentrationslager Majdanek 1941–1944," 290; Kranz, "Konzentrationslager Lublin," 64–65.

2. XII-10, k. 495–96, APMM.

3. Madajczyk, *Die Okkupationspolitik Nazideutschlands in Polen 1939–1945*, 190–92; Gross, *Polish Society Under German Occupation*, 163f, 207–9; Winstone, *The Dark Heart of Hitler's Europe*, 203.

4. Marszałek, *Majdanek*, 134–35; Kwiatkowski, *485 Days in Majdanek*, 299–301, 310–11.

5. Kwiatkowski, *485 Days in Majdanek*, 114–15.

6. Marszałek, "Konspiracja w obozie," *Majdanek*, ed. Mencel, 360; Voisich, "Majdanek: Revisiting Resistance."

7. Marszałek, *Majdanek*, 165–57; Wanda Szupenko, XXI-162–65, APMM.

8. XII-10, k. 529, APMM.

9. Kłapeć, *Rada Główna Opiekuńcza w dystrykcie lubelskim w latach 1940–1944*, 152.

10. Perzanowska, "Pomoc lubelskich organizacji społecznych więźniom Majdanka," 9–13; Maria Gancarz, XX-1, APMM; Brzosko-Mędryk, *Niebo bez ptaków*, 450–56. The Polish writers whose works Janina smuggled into Majdanek included Sienkiewicz, Słowacki, Mickiewicz, Prus, and Żeromski.

11. XII-10, k. 521, APMM; Kwiatkowski, *485 Days in Majdanek*, 300; Perzanowska, *Gdy myśli do Majdanka wracają*, chapters 24 and 25.

12. XII-10, k. 495–496, APMM; Kwiatkowski, *485 Days in Majdanek*, 297–98; Rogerie, "Transporty chorych," 210–14.

13. RGO report for period February 1 to March 14, 1944, RG 15.550, 685/91-97, USHMM; XII-10, k. 521, APMM, Wiśniewska, "Pomoc więźniom Majdanka," 239–40.

14. RGO report for period February 1 to March 14, 1944; report from the camp on Krochmalna, February 1 to March 17, 1944, RGO 31 cz. 1, 304, APL; Kłapeć, *Rada Główna Opiekuńcza w dystrykcie lubelskim w latach 1940–1944*, 240–45.

15. Wiśniewska, "Pomoc więźniom Majdanka," 244–45; Kłapeć, *Rada Główna Opiekuńcza w dystrykcie lubelskim w latach 1940–1944*, 141–42.

16. November 15, 1944 staff listing, RGO 142, APL.

SEVENTEEN: THE PLOT

1. RGO Lublin report for March 15 to May 1, 1944, RGO 32 "Korespondencja ogólna Doradcy" 1944, pp. 267–71, APL.

2. Marszałek, *Majdanek*, 168–69.

3. RGO Lublin report for March 15 to May 1, 1944; Skrzyński May 5, 1944 note re: help for prisoners departing Majdanek, RGO 50, AAN, in Fot. 5, APMM; April 4, 1944, message from "Stefania" (Janina Suchodolska), XII-10, k. 663-664, APMM.

4. Wanda Szupenko ("Elżbieta"), XXI-162–65, APMM; Marszałek, *Majdanek*, 165, 168–69.

5. Marszałek, *Majdanek*, 175; entries for March 28 and 29, 1944, in Leszczyńska, *Kronika obozu na Majdanku*.

6. RGO Lublin report for March 15 to May 1, 1944; entry for March 30, 1944, in Leszczyńska, *Kronika obozu na Majdanku.*

7. Entry for March 31, 1944, in Leszczyńska, *Kronika obozu na Majdanku;* Mencel, "Konzentrationslager Lublin. General Characteristics," in *Majdanek,* ed. Mencel, 515.

8. Skrzyński May 5, 1944, note re: help for prisoners departing Majdanek; Hanna Huskowska, VII/M-234, APMM.

9. December 2, 1946, testimony of Janina Suchodolska, VII-135-104, APMM; Marszałek, *Majdanek,* 181–83.

10. Entry for April 2, 1944, in Leszczyńska, *Kronika obozu na Majdanka.*

11. April 4, 1944, message from "Stefania" (Janina Suchodolska), XII-10, k. 663-664, APMM.

12. Ibid.; Kwiatkowski, *485 Days in Majdanek,* 363–68.

13. Undated message fragment, probably from "Stefania" (Janina Suchodolska), XII-10, k. 584, APMM; Kwiatkowski, *485 Days in Majdanek,* 363–68.

14. Gajowniczek, "Choroby i epidemie. Rewir," in *Majdanek 1941–1944,* ed. Mencel, 226; Kwiatkowski, *485 Days in Majdanek,* 278.

15. Skrzyński May 5, 1944, note re: help for prisoners departing Majdanek; February 26, 196? interrogation of Wilhelm Karl Petrak in the (West German) case against Benden et al., XIX 1383/1-8, APMM; Adam Panasiewicz, "Poststelle," in *Braterska Pomoc,* ed. Machuła and Wiśniewska, 112–27.

16. Document 18.6, *Majdanek w dokumentach,* ed. Lenarczyk; Marszałek, *Majdanek,* 176; Kwiatkowski, *485 Days in Majdanek,* 361.

17. April 5, 1944, message from "Stefania" (Janina Suchodolska), XII-10, k. 663–64, APMM.

18. Skrzyński May 5, 1944, note re: help for prisoners departing Majdanek; Hanna Huskowska, VII/M-234, APMM.

19. Kwiatkowski, *485 Days in Majdanek,* 363–68.

20. Marszałek, *Majdanek,* 168–69.

EIGHTEEN: THE END APPROACHES

1. In addition to the memoir, the description of Easter at Majdanek in 1944 is based on the following: Skrzyński May 5, 1944, note about Easter food for Majdanek, RGO 32, p. 320, APL; RGO Lublin report for March 15 to May 1, 1944, RGO 32, pp. 267–71, APL; Perzanowska, "Pomoc lubelskich organizacji społecznych więźniom Majdanka," 11–12; Jadwiga Lipska-Węgrzecka, XII-49, APMM; Kwiatkowski, *485 Days in Majdanek,* 369; Marszałek, *Majdanek,* 181–83.

2. Note re: help for prisoners departing Majdanek, RGO 50, AAN, in Fot. 5, APMM; Kłapeć, *Rada Główna Opiekuńcza w dystrykcie lubelskim w latach 1940–1944,* 249.

3. Skrzyński undated note, RGO 32, p. 273, APL.

4. Protocol No. 40 of Lublin Care Committee, April 27, 1944, RGO Documents, Wydział II Organizacyjno-Inspekcyjny Dział Organizacyjny II.0.4, p. 296, APMM;

Skrzyński May 13, 1944, note on refugees from Kowel at Krochmalna, RGO 32, 274; undated report on the evacuation, RGO 31, pp. 99–100, AAN.

5. Perzanowska, "O niektórych hitlerowskich lekarzach w Majdanku," 6–7; Kwiatkowski, *485 Days in Majdanek*, 278.
6. Some months later, Rindfleisch was assigned to Gross-Rosen. Dr. Hanusz survived the war.
7. Wiśniewska, "Pomoc więźniom Majdanka," 240; Marszałek, *Majdanek*, 183.
8. Thumann transferred to Neuengamme. After the war, he was tried and executed by the British for crimes he committed there. Weiss was tried and executed by the Americans for his crimes at Dachau. Marszałek, *Majdanek*, 45, 189; Kranz, "Das Konzentrationslager Majdanek 1941–1944," 29.
9. Note re: help for prisoners departing Majdanek, RGO 50, AAN, in Fot. 5, APMM; Kwiatkowski, *485 Days in Majdanek*, 399.
10. Orth, *Die Konzentrationslager-SS*, 242–46; Kranz, "Das Konzentrationslager Majdanek 1941–1944," 291. After the war, Poland's Supreme National Tribunal sentenced Liebehenschel to death for his crimes at Auschwitz and Majdanek and he was executed. Marszałek, *Majdanek*, 45, 188.
11. In addition to the memoir, the information about the Wehrmacht forced labor camp in Field V is based on the following: June 1944 report of the Lublin Care Committee, RGO Documents Wydział II Organizacyjno-Inspekcyjny Dział Organizacyjny II.0.4, p. 325, APMM; Protocol 42 of the Lublin Care Committee, June 30, 1944, RGO documents, Wydział II Organizacyjno-Inspekcyjny Dział Organizacyjny II.0.4, p. 334, APMM; Skrzyński July 13, 1944, report, RGO 108, AAN, in Fot. 8, APMM; Grudzińska "Polacy na Majdanku," 298; Marszałek, *Majdanek*, 183; Kranz, "Das Konzentrationslager Majdanek 1941–1944," 291; Kwiatkowski, *485 Days in Majdanek*, 412.
12. December 2, 1946, statement of Janina Suchodolska, VII-135-104, APMM; Wiśniewska, "Pomoc więźniom Majdanka," in *Majdanek 1941 1944*, ed. Mencel, 240; Wnuk, *Dzieci polskie oskarżają*, 116–21; Kwiatkowski, *485 Days in Majdanek*, 416–19.
13. Angrick, "Aktion 1005," 822–40.
14. Release certificates for women and children held at Majdanek, signed Suchodolska, July 14, 1944, VI, 18/1-8, APMM.
15. Undated report on the evacuation, RGO 31, pp. 99–100, AAN.

NINETEEN: BLOOD ON THE STAIRS

1. Polish translation of June 5, 1944, letter from Schreiter, BuF, to Skrzyński, RGO-Lublin 7, pp. 64–65, APL; Lublin Care Committee Report for June 1944, RGO Documents, p. 327, APMM; Skrzyński July 13, 1944, report, RGO 108, AAN, in Fot. 8, APMM; Mańkowski, *Hitlerowskie więzienie na Zamku w Lublinie, 1939–1944*, 287; Kłapeć, *Rada Główna Opiekuńcza w dystrykcie lubelskim w latach 1940–1944*, 274–89.

2. In addition to the memoir, this paragraph and the following information in this chapter are based on the following sources: Mańkowski, *Hitlerowskie więzienie na Zamku w Lublinie, 1939–1944*, 355–56; Barbara Oratowska, Łukasz Krzysiak, and Marcin Michniowski, eds., "75 rocznica likwidacji niemieckiego więzienia na Zamku lubelskim / 75th Anniversary of the Liquidation of the German Prison in the Lublin Castle" (Lublin: The Lublin State Museum, 2019); Protocol 206 Piotr Malesza, January 25, 1946, Protocols of the Municipal Commission for the Investigation of German Crimes in Lublin, APMM; Marian Wiess, XXI-162–76, APMM; Zofia Orska, sygn. 169, APMM.

TWENTY: THE END

1. Oral histories of Janusz Andrzej Winiarski, April 19, 2004, and Łukasz Kijek, "Walki o Lublin w lipcu 1944 roku," Grodzka Gate–NN Theatre, https://teatrnn .pl/leksykon/artykuly/walki-o-lublin-w-lipcu-1944-roku, accessed August 12, 2022.
2. Marszałek, *Majdanek*, 184–85.
3. See, for example, the 1944 Soviet-produced film *Das Blut der Opfer Schreit zum Himmel!* (The Blood of the Victims Cries to the Heavens!), RG Number: RG-60.0028 | Film ID: 5, USHMM.
4. Kochanski, *The Eagle Unbowed*, 396.
5. Ibid., 377–96; Reynolds, "'Lublin' Versus 'London,'" 622–24; Harald Moldenhauer, "Der Sowjetische NKVD und die Heimatarmee im 'Lubliner Polen' 1944–1945," in *Die polnische Heimatarmee*, ed. Chiari with Kochanowski, 275–99.
6. Kochanski, *The Eagle Unbowed*, 400–425.

TWENTY-ONE: FLIGHT

1. Kłapeć, *Rada Główna Opiekuńcza w dystrykcie lubelskim w latach 1940–1944*, 274–89.
2. Ibid.; Finder and Prusin, *Justice Behind the Iron Curtain*, 32; Christians, *Piekło XX wieku*.
3. Kopciowski, "Zajścia antyżydowskie na Lubelszczyźnie w pierwszych latach po drugiej wojnie światowej," 178–79.
4. Kłapeć, *Rada Główna Opiekuńcza w dystrykcie lubelskim w latach 1940–1944*, 274–89; Suchodolska correspondence, RGO 7, pp. 1–5, APL; November 15, 1944, staff listing, RGO 142, APL.
5. Akta Miasta Lublina, zespół 22, 2145/22, State Archive in Lublin (APL).
6. Note to Piotr Suchodolski, January 14, 1946, "Henryk Mehlberg," p. 5, AUŁ; Note to Janina Suchodolska, October 24, 1945, "Janina Suchodolska" personnel file, CKOS 43, AAN; Protocol from the first meeting of CKOS, 13 December 1944, sygn. 243, AAN; Memo re: the creation of CKOS, March 3, 1947, sygn. 242, AAN.
7. Gross, *Polish Society Under German Occupation*, 85; International Conference

of Social Work, "Public Health and Welfare Technical Bulletin" (August 1948); Kornbluth, *The August Trials*, 5; "Janina Suchodolska" personnel file, CKOS 43, AAN.

8. Memo re: the creation of CKOS, March 3, 1947, sygn. 242, AAN; "Note," March 3, 1947, CKOS 242, pp. 46–47, AAN; Margarette Smethurst, "Polish Social Worker Observes Home Demonstration Activities," *News & Observer* (Raleigh, NC) January 17, 1948, 5.

9. "Janina Suchodolska" personnel file, CKOS 43, AAN; Protocol 22 of CKOS Board meeting, July 8, 1946 and Protocol 39 from CKOS meeting, September 29, 1947, sygn. 243, AAN; "Tells How UNRRA Aided Polish Child Agencies," *Daily Herald* (Chicago, IL), February 13, 1948, 14.

10. Information about Henry's academic trajectory here and later in this chapter derives from: "Henryk Mehlberg," AUŁ; "Mehlberg Henryk," sygn. 3856, AAN; "Henryk Mehlberg," 387b-14, AUAM; "Mehlberg Henryk," Tom I: AUW.6/2.180, AUW.

11. In her December 2, 1946, testimony to Polish authorities, Janina indicated that she was single, the daughter of Wojciech and Franciszka Suchodolski, and born in 1909. VII-135-104, APMM.

12. Jewish Immigrant Aid Society of Canada application submitted by Henry August 21, 1950, "Pepi Mehlberg," Ontario Jewish Archives; "Personal file of Mehlberg, Isidor, born in the year 1906 and of further persons," Reference Code 1718000_038.080, Arolsen Archives. Juliusz was a dentist and Izydor was a physician. Izydor and his wife, Helena (née Szwermer), had two daughters, Ewa and Anita. Juliusz was married to Tola (Antonina) née Mandelkorn. Information about Henry's relatives derives i.a. from the postwar registration cards of Polish Jews, Collection 303/V/425 /CKŻP, Wydział ewidencji i statystyki 1945–1950, AŻIH.

13. Kornbluth, *The August Trials*, 82–88; Gross, *Fear*, 39–72.

14. Gross, *Fear*, 78–90.

15. Historian Dariusz Stola's estimate quoted in Węgrzyn, *Wyjeżdżamy! Wyjeżdżamy?!*, 58–59.

16. In addition to Pinkas (Janina's father), Berel and Czarna (née Falik) Spinner had six children: Jonas, Aron, Pessie, Lena (Lea), Malka, and Pauline. We are grateful to Noam Silberberg, Genealogy Department of the Jewish Historical Institute in Warsaw, for providing this information.

17. Information about Janina's and Henry's emigration efforts derives from: "Henryk Mehlberg," USNA RG 246 File J-5613, YIVO Institute for Jewish Research (YIVO); "Pepi Mehlberg," Ontario Jewish Archives; "Henry Mehlberg," JDC Archives.

18. "Henry Mehlberg," JDC Archives; "Pepi Mehlberg," CKŻP, Wydział ewidencji i statystyki 1945–1950, 303/V/425/M 4762/174027, AŻIH; Warsaw Office 1945–1948, JDC Archives.

19. Interview with Dr. Arthur Fine by Elizabeth White, March 1, 2018.

20. Protocol 39 from CKOS meeting, September 29, 1947, sygn. 243, AAN; Memo,

October 24, 1947, sygn. 242, AAN. A philosopher as well as a legal scholar, Rudziński did not revert to his original name of Steinberg after the war. "Aleksander Witold Rudzinski," https://www.geni.com/people/Aleksander-Rudzinski/6000000023840977953, accessed August 3, 2022; Eric Pace, "Dr. Aleksander W. Rudzinski, 89, Polish Diplomat Who Defected," *New York Times*, April 8, 1989, 1:10.

21. The information about Janina's activities in the United States during her stay as Janina Suchodolska and about Henry's immigration to Canada comes from the following: Janina's letters to Anna Rudzińska, The Aleksander and Anna Rudzinski Collection, 1919–1995, General Research Division, New York Public Library (NYPL) (we thank Dr. Marjorie Senechal for sharing with us information about this source); "Henryk Mehlberg," YIVO; Smethurst, "Polish Social Worker," *News & Observer*; "Tells How UNRRA Aided Polish Child Agencies," *Daily Herald*; "UN Guest Visits Aid Home," *South Bend Tribune* (South Bend, IN), February 28, 1948, 21; "Welfare Program Studied by Pole," *Indianapolis Star* (Indianapolis, IN), February 23, 1948, 32; "Praises New Hampshire's Welfare Department," *Newport Daily Express* (Newport, VT), March 18, 1948, 9.

22. Other scholars Janina contacted included Ernest Nagel, Carl Gustav Hempel, and Alfred Tarski. Hempel and Tarski, both educated in prewar Europe and Henry's peers, had been part of the Vienna Circle of philosophers. Tarski, a philosopher and a mathematician, was connected to the Lwów-Warsaw School.

23. "Henryk Mehlberg," YIVO.

24. "Janina Suchodolska" personnel file, CKOS 43, AAN; CKOS protocol, March 2, 1949, CKOS 287, AAN; Brenk, "Działalność Powiatowego Komitetu Opieki Społecznej w Koninie w latach 1945–1949," 120.

25. Janina's letter to Anna Rudzińska, July 24 [1949], NYPL; October 4, 1949, letter to JDC from Janina Suchodolska, Department Head [Naczelnik Wydziału], Ministerstwo Pracy i Opieki Społecznej, JDC Archives, item 2460216.

26. The information in this chapter about Janina's escape from Poland and immigration to Canada comes from: "Pepi Mehlberg," Ontario Jewish Archives.

TWENTY-TWO: A NEW BEGINNING

1. Josephine Janina Mehlberg U.S. immigration file A10 678 524, U.S. Citizenship and Immigration Services (USCIS); "Josephine Janina Bednarski Spinner Mehlberg," https://prabook.com/web/josephine_janina_bednarski_spinner.mehlberg/1103449, accessed August 2, 2022; interview of Dr. Fine.

2. Staff Cards: Mehlberg, University of Toronto Archives.

3. Robert S. Cohen, "Editorial Note," Mehlberg, *Time, Causality, and the Quantum Theory*, xv–xvii.

4. Communication between Joanna Sliwa and Dr. Irvin Klinghofer, August 13, 2021; Josephine Janina Mehlberg U.S. Immigration File A10 678 524.

5. Josephine Janina Mehlberg U.S. immigration file A10 678 524; Henry Mehlberg Immigration File, A10 678 676, USCIS.

6. Adolf Grünbaum, "Preface," Mehlberg, *Time, Causality, and the Quantum Theory,* xiii–xiv; interview with Dr. Fine; interview with Dr. Marjorie Senechal by authors, August 18, 2020.
7. Much of the information about Janina's work as a mathematician in the United States was provided by Dr. Marjorie Senechal, including the notes and slides for her February 21, 2023, HOM SIGMAA online lecture, "Josephine Mehlberg (1905–1969)."
8. Ibid.; Josephine Janina Mehlberg U.S. Immigration File A10 678 524; "Josephine Janina Bednarski Spinner Mehlberg," prabook.com; interview with Dr. Fine.
9. Janina's talk at the University of California, Davis conference was on "Laplace Transforms in Solving Differential Equations with Complex Coefficients." "Janina Mehlberg" VA 278345, BEG; "Josephine Janina Bednarski Spinner Mehlberg," https://prabook.com/web/josephine_janina_bednarski_spinner.mehlberg/1103449, accessed August 2, 2022.
10. Interview of Dr. Fine; Senechal, "Josephine Mehlberg (1905–1969)."
11. "Janina Mehlberg," VA 278345, BEG; "Henryk Mehlberg," YIVO.
12. "Janina Mehlberg," VA 278345; "Henry Mehlberg," VA 278344, BEG.
13. Cohen, "Editorial Note"; interviews with Dr. Fine and Dr. Senechal.
14. Josephine Janina Mehlberg U.S. Immigration File A10 678 524, "Janina Mehlberg," VA 278345, BEG; Antonina Mehlberg U.S. Immigration file A18371852, RG 566, Records of the U.S. Immigration and Naturalization Service, NARA (Kansas City, MO).
15. Antonina Mehlberg U.S. Immigration File A18371852.
16. Grünbaum, "Preface."
17. Social Security Death Index entry for Antonina Mehlberg; Florida Marriage Index entry for Henry's marriage to Susie Clark (listed as Edna Benefield) on August 16, 1975; Elizabeth White phone interview with Jeri Hough, Susie Clark's daughter, September 15, 2022.
18. Grünbaum, "Preface"; Cohen, "Editorial Note," quotation on xvii; Mehlberg, *Time, Causality, and the Quantum Theory.*
19. Arthur L. Funk, "Editor's Foreword," "Janina's Story."

EPILOGUE: "JANINA'S STORY"

1. We base our dating of the memoir on two of its references: 1) Janina was unaware that Anton Thumann had been tried and executed after World War II for crimes he committed at Neuengamme, and she speculated that he was living in Argentina. Awareness that some Nazi criminals fled to Argentina after the war arose following the abduction of Adolf Eichmann in Argentina by Israeli agents in 1960 and his subsequent trial in 1961. 2) Commenting on the value of bacon as currency on the black market, Janina wrote that no one was concerned then about cholesterol levels. The first general warning about the possible connection between dietary cholesterol and heart disease was put out by the American Heart

Association in 1961. David Kritchevsky, "History of Recommendations to the Public about Dietary Fat," *The Journal of Nutrition* 128, no. 2 (February 1998): 449S–452S.

2. See, for example, *Who's Who of American Women*, 5th ed. (1968–1969).

3. Plocker, *The Expulsion of Jews from Communist Poland*, passim.

4. Ibid.; Podbielska, "'The Righteous' and March '68," 363–87.

BIBLIOGRAPHY

ARCHIVAL COLLECTIONS

Argentina

Argentine Israelite Mutual Association, Buenos Aires (AMIA)

Foreign Affairs Archive, Buenos Aires

Israelite Association of Coronel Suárez, Coronel Suárez

Canada

Canadian Jewish Archives, Montreal (CJA)

Immigration, Refugees and Citizenship Canada (IRCC)

Library and Archives Canada, Ottawa (LAC)

Ontario Jewish Archives, Toronto (OJA)

Montreal Holocaust Museum, Montreal

University of New Brunswick Libraries and Archives, New Brunswick

University of Toronto Archives, Toronto

Germany

Arolsen Archives

State Finance Office, Compensation Payments, Saarburg (BEG)

Poland

Archives of Jagiellonian University, Medical Department, Kraków

Archive of Emanuel Ringelblum Jewish Historical Institute, Warsaw (AŻIH)

Archive of New Records, Warsaw (AAN)

Archive of the State Museum at Majdanek, Lublin (APMM)

Archives of the University of Adam Mickiewicz, Poznań (AUAM)

Archives of the University of Łódź, Łódź (AUŁ)

Archives of the University of Wrocław, Wrocław (AUW)

Association of Jewish Veterans and Persecutees in World War II, Warsaw
Institute of National Remembrance, Warsaw (IPN)
KARTA Center, Warsaw
Lublin Archdiocese Archive, Lublin
Main Archive of Old Records, Warsaw (AGAD)
State Archive in Lublin (APL)
State Archive in Przemyśl (APP)

Ukraine
State Archive of Lviv Oblast, Lviv, Ukraine (DALO)

United States
Archives of the American Jewish Joint Distribution Committee, New York (JDC)
Montefiore Cemetery, New York
Mount Sinai Memorial Chapels, East Brunswick, NJ
National Archives and Records Administration, College Park, MD (NARA)
The New York Public Library, New York (NYPL)
United States Holocaust Memorial Museum, Washington, D.C. (USHMM)
University Archives and Special Collections, Illinois Institute of Technology, Chicago
    (IIT)
University of Florida Archives, Gainesville
YIVO Institute for Jewish Research, New York (YIVO)

OTHER RESOURCES
Ancestry, https://www.ancestry.com/
Auschwitz Memorial and Museum, http://www.auschwitz.org/
Center for Urban History, https://www.lvivcenter.org/
Centropa, https://www.centropa.org/
Chronicles of Terror, https://www.zapisyterroru.pl/
Digital Archive of Combined Libraries, https://archiwum.polaczonebiblioteki.uw
    .edu.pl/
Digital Libraries Federation, https://fbc.pionier.net.pl/
Genealogy Indexer, www.genealogyindexer.org/
Geni, https://www.geni.com/
Gesher Galicia, https://www.geshergalicia.org/
Greater Poland Digital Library, https://www.wbc.poznan.pl/dlibra
Grodzka Gate–NN Theatre, https://teatrnn.pl/
Harvard Law School Library Nuremberg Trials Project, http://nuremberg.law.harvard.edu/
JewishGen, https://www.jewishgen.org/databases/
Jewish Records Indexing–Poland, https://jri-poland.org/
"Josephine Janina Bednarski Spinner Mehlberg," https://prabook.com/web/josephine
    _janina_bednarski_spinner.mehlberg/ 1103449

Libraria: Ukrainian Online Periodicals Archive, https://libraria.ua/en/
Museum of Jewish Heritage, https://mjhnyc.org/
Premeditated Murder of 25 Polish Professors, https://www.lwow.com.pl/Lwow_profs
    .html
National-Socialism Archive, https://www.ns-archiv.de/
Ohistorie, https://ohistorie.eu/o-nas/
Polona, https://polona.pl/
The Roman Ingarden Digital Archive, http://ingarden.archive.uj.edu.pl/en/home/
Stanford Encyclopedia of Philosophy, https://plato.stanford.edu/
State Museum at Majdanek, https://www.majdanek.eu/
United States Holocaust Memorial Museum, https://encyclopedia.ushmm.org/
Virtual Shtetl, https://sztetl.org.pl/
World Health Organization, https://www.who.int/

NEWSPAPERS
Chwila (Lwów)
Daily Herald (Chicago)
The Indianapolis Star
The Newport Daily Express (Vermont)
News & Observer (Raleigh)
The New York Times
South Bend Tribune (Indiana)

INTERVIEWS (ORAL AND WRITTEN)
Dr. Eugene Allgower, email with authors, July 18, 2022.
Dr. Arthur Fine, interview by Elizabeth White, phone, March 1, 2018.
Jeri Hough, interview by Elizabeth White, phone, September 15, 2022.
Dr. Irvin Klinghofer, email with Joanna Sliwa, August 13, 2021.
Joshua Pines, interview by authors, online, August 27, 2020.
Dr. Marjorie Senechal, interview by authors, online, August 18, 2021.
Eva Tene, interview by authors, online, June 20, 2023.
Elizabeth White interviews in the Federal Republic of Germany of former Majdanek
    guards Andreas E., January 12, 1988, Munich; Michael F., January 13, 1988, Stuttgart;
    Anton K., January 18, 1988, Hanau.

BOOKS
Aly, Götz. *Final Solution: Nazi Population Policy and the Murder of the European Jews.*
    Translated by Belinda Cooper and Allison Brown. New York: Arnold and Oxford
    University Press, 1999.
Amar, Tarik Cyril. *The Paradox of Ukrainian Lviv: A Borderland City Between Stalinists,
    Nazis, and Nationalists.* Ithaca: Cornell University Press, 2015.
Ambach, Dieter, and Thomas Köhler, eds. *Lublin-Majdanek: Das Konzentrations- und*

Vernichtungslager im Spiegel von Zeugenaussagen. Vol. 12, *Juristische Zeitgeschichte NRW.* Düsseldorf: Justizministerium des Landes NRW, 2003.

Angrick, Andrej. *"Aktion 1005"—Spurenbeseitigung von NS-Massenverbrechen 1942–1945: Eine "geheime Reichssache" im Spannungsfeld von Kriegswende und Propaganda.* Göttingen: Wallstein Verlag, 2018.

Arad, Yitzhak. *Bełżec, Sobibor, Treblinka: The Operation Reinhard Death Camps.* Bloomington: Indiana University Press, 1999 (first published in 1987).

Arad, Yitzhak, Shmuel Krakowski, and Shmuel Spector, eds. *The Einsatzgruppen Reports: Selections from the Dispatches of the Nazi Death Squads' Campaign Against the Jews, July 1941–January 1943.* New York: Holocaust Library in cooperation with Yad Vashem, 1989.

Bartov, Omer. *Anatomy of a Genocide: The Life and Death of a Town Called Buczacz.* New York: Simon & Schuster, 2018.

Bartrop, Paul R., and Eve E. Grimm. *Perpetrating the Holocaust: Leaders, Enablers, and Collaborators.* Santa Barbara, CA: ABC-CLIO, 2019.

Beorn, Waitman Wade. *The Holocaust in Eastern Europe: At the Epicenter of the Final Solution.* London: Bloomsbury, 2018.

Biskupska, Jadwiga. *Survivors: Warsaw Under Nazi Occupation.* Cambridge: Cambridge University Press, 2022.

Black, Peter. "Die Trawniki-Männer und die 'Aktion Reinhard.'" In *"Aktion Reinhard,": der Völkermord an den Juden im Generalgouvernement 1941–1944.* Edited by Bogdan Musial. Osnabrück: Fibre, 2004, 309–52.

Brożek, Anna, Alicja Chybińska, Jacek Jadacki, and Jan Woleński, eds. *Tradition of the Lvov-Warsaw School: Ideas and Continuations.* Leiden: Brill, 2016.

Brzosko-Mędryk, Danuta. *Niebo bez ptaków.* Warsaw: Prószyński i S-ka, 2021.

Burleigh, Michael. *Moral Combat: Good and Evil in World War II.* New York: HarperCollins, 2011.

Caban, Ireneusz, and Zygmunt Mańkowski. *Związek Walki Zbrojnej i Armia Krajowa w Okręgu Lubelskim 1939–1944.* Lublin: Wydawnictwo Lubelskie, 1971.

Chiari, Bernhard, ed., in collaboration with Jerzy Kochanowski. *Die polnische Heimatarmee. Geschichte und Mythos der Armia Krajowa seit dem zweiten Weltkrieg.* Munich: R. Oldenbourg Verlag, 2003.

Chmielewski, Jakub. "Żydzi w KL Lublin." In *Więźniowie KL Lublin 1941–1944.* Edited by Tomasz Kranz and Wojciech Lenarczyk. Lublin: Państwowe Muzeum na Majdanku, 2022, 264–65.

Christians, Ludwik. *Piekło XX wieku. Zbrodnia, hart ducha i miłosierdzie.* Warsaw: Katolickie Towarzystwo Wydawnicze "Rodzina Polska," 1946.

Cichopek Gajraj, Anna. *Beyond Violence: Jewish Survivors in Poland and Slovakia, 1944–1948.* Cambridge: Cambridge University Press, 2014.

Czech, Danuta. *Auschwitz Chronicle, 1939–1945.* New York: Henry Holt, 1990.

Dean, Martin, ed. *The United States Holocaust Memorial Museum Encyclopedia of Camps and Ghettos.* Vol. 2, *Ghettos in German-Occupied Eastern Europe,* s.v. "Lublin," 675–78.

Bloomington: Indiana University Press in association with the United States Holocaust Memorial Museum, 2012.

Draus, Jan. *Uniwersytet Jana Kazimierza we Lwowie 1918–1946. Portret kresowej uczelni.* Kraków: Księgarnia Akademicka, 2007.

Evans, Richard J. *The Third Reich at War.* New York: Penguin, 2010.

———. *The Third Reich in Power.* New York: Penguin, 2005.

Finder, Gabriel N., and Alexander Victor Prusin. *Justice Behind the Iron Curtain: Nazis on Trial in Communist Poland.* Toronto: University of Toronto Press, 2018.

Friedlander, Henry. *The Origins of Nazi Genocide: From Euthanasia to the Final Solution.* Chapel Hill: North Carolina University Press, 1995.

Friedländer, Saul. *The Years of Extermination: Nazi Germany and the Jews, 1939–1945.* New York: HarperCollins, 2007.

Friedrich, Klaus-Peter, ed. *Polen: Generalgouvernement August 1941–1945.* Munich: Oldenbourg Verlag, 2014.

Gajderowicz, Magdalena, and Ryszard Skrzyniarz. "Children of the Zamość Region in the Majdanek Camp (in Selected Archive Files and Personal Accounts)." In *Crime Without Punishment: The Extermination and Suffering of Polish Children During the German Occupation, 1939–1945.* Edited by Janina Kostkiewicz. Kraków: Jagiellonian University Press, 2021, 115–30.

Gajowniczek, Jolanta. "Choroby i epidemie. Rewir." In *Majdanek 1941–1944.* Edited by Tadeusz Mencel. Lublin: Wydawnictwo Lubelskie, 1991, 194–231.

Gerlach, Christian. *The Extermination of the European Jews.* Cambridge: Cambridge University Press, 2016.

Golczewski, Frank. "Die Heimatarmee und die Juden." In *Die polnische Heimatarmee. Geschichte und Mythos der Armia Krajowa seit dem zweiten Weltkrieg.* Edited by Bernhard Chiari, in collaboration with Jerzy Kochanowski. Munich: R. Oldenbourg Verlag, 2003, 635–78.

———. "Polen." In *Dimension des Völkermords: Die Zahl der jüdischen Opfer des Nationalsozialismus.* Edited by Wolfgang Benz. Munich: Oldenbourg Verlag, 1991, 411–97.

Goldberg, Adara. *Holocaust Survivors in Canada: Exclusion, Inclusion, Transformation, 1947–1955.* Winnipeg: University of Manitoba Press, 2015.

Gross, Jan Tomasz. *Fear: Anti-Semitism in Poland After Auschwitz.* New York: Random House, 2007.

———. *Polish Society Under German Occupation: The Generalgouvernement, 1939–1944.* Princeton: Princeton University Press, 1979.

———. *Revolution from Abroad: The Soviet Conquest of Poland's Western Ukraine and Western Belorussia.* Princeton: Princeton University Press, 2002.

Gross, Jan Tomasz, and Irena Grudzińska Gross, eds. *War Through Children's Eyes: The Soviet Occupation of Poland and the Deportations, 1939–1941.* Translated by Ronald Strom and Dan Rivers. Stanford: Hoover Institution Press, 1985.

Grudzińska, Marta. "The Fate of Children at the Majdanek Concentration Camp." In *The Young Victims of the Nazi Regime: Migration, the Holocaust and Postwar Displacement.*

Edited by Simone Gigliotti and Monica Tempian. London/New York: Bloomsbury, 2016, 171–200.

————."Polacy na Majdanku." In *Więźniowie KL Lublin 1941–1944*. Edited by Tomasz Kranz and Wojciech Lenarczyk. Lublin: Państwowe Muzeum na Majdanku, 2020, 267–86.

Grudzińska, Marta, ed. *Majdanek. Oboz koncentracyjny w relacjach więźniów i świadków*. Lublin: Państwowe Muzeum na Majdanku, 2011.

Gruner, Wolf. *Jewish Forced Labor Under the Nazis: Economic Needs and Racial Aims, 1938–1944*. Translated by Kathleen Dell'Orto. New York: Cambridge University Press with the United States Holocaust Memorial Museum, 2006.

Hayes, Peter. *Why? Explaining the Holocaust*. New York: W. W. Norton, 2017.

Heckert, Elke, and Werner Röhr, ed. *Europa unterm Hakenkreuz: die faschistische Okkupationspolitik in Polen (1939–1945)*. Berlin: VEB Deutscher Verlag der Wissenschaften, 1989.

Heller, Celia S. *On the Edge of Destruction: Jews of Poland Between the Two World Wars*. Detroit: Wayne State University Press, 1994.

Himka, John-Paul. *Ukrainian Nationalists and the Holocaust. OUN and UPA's Participation in the Destruction of Ukrainian Jewry, 1941–1944*. Stuttgart: ibidem, 2021.

Höger, Katja. "Frauen als Kombattanten." In *Die polnische Heimatarmee. Geschichte und Mythos der Armia Krajowa seit dem zweiten Weltkrieg*. Edited by Bernhard Chiari, in collaboration with Jerzy Kochanowski. Munich: R. Oldenbourg Verlag, 2003, 387–410.

International Military Tribunal, *Trials of War Criminals before the Nuernberg Military Tribunals under Control Council Law no. 10, October 1946–April 1949*. Nuremberg, 1949.

Jaczyńska, Agnieszka. *Sonderlaboratorium SS. Zamojszczyzna „pierwszy obszar osiedleńczy w Generalnym Gubernatorstwie."* Lublin: Instytut Pamięci Narodowej, 2012.

Kershaw, Ian. *Hitler: A Biography*. New York: W. W. Norton, 2008.

Kiełboń, Janina. *Migracje ludności w dystrykcie lubelskim w latach 1939–1944*. Lublin: Państwowe Muzeum na Majdanku, 1995.

Kiełboń, Janina, and Zofia Leszczyńska. *Kobiety Lubelszczyzny represjonowane w latach 1944–1956*. Lublin: Wydawnictwo Test, 2002.

Kiriszczenko, Piotr. "Mother's Death." In *Majdanek Concentration Camp*. Edited by Czesław Rajca and Anna Wiśniewska. Translated by Anna Zagorska. Lublin: Państwowe Muzeum na Majdanku, 1983, 65–57.

Kłapeć, Janusz. *Rada Główna Opiekuńcza w dystrykcie lubelskim w latach 1940–1944*. Lublin: Wydawnictwo UMCS, 2011.

Klukowski, Zygmunt. *Tagebuch aus den Jahren der Okkupation 1939–1944*. Edited by Christine Glauning and Ewelina Wanke. Translated by Karsten Wanke. Berlin: Metropol Verlag, 2017.

Kochanski, Halik. *The Eagle Unbowed: Poland and the Poles in the Second World War*. Cambridge: Harvard University Press, 2012.

Koehl, Robert L. *RKFDV: German Resettlement and Population Policy, 1939–1945: A*

History of the Reich Commission for the Strengthening of Germandom. Cambridge: Harvard University Press, 1957.

Komorowski, Krzysztof. "Facetten des polnischen militarischen Widerstandes und seine Aktualität." In *Die polnische Heimatarmee. Geschichte und Mythos der Armia Krajowa seit dem zweiten Weltkrieg*. Edited by Bernhard Chiari, in collaboration with Jerzy Kochanowski. Munich: R. Oldenbourg Verlag, 2003, 679–90.

Kornbluth, Andrew. *The August Trials: The Holocaust and Postwar Justice in Poland*. Cambridge: Harvard University Press, 2021.

Kozaczyńska, Beata. "When There Were No More Tears Left to Cry: The Tragic Fate of the Polish Children Displaced from the Zamość Region in 1942–1943." In *Crime Without Punishment: The Extermination and Suffering of Polish Children During the German Occupation, 1939–1945*. Edited by Janina Kostkiewicz. Kraków: Jagiellonian University Press, 2021, 99–114.

Kranz, Tomasz. "Das KL Lublin—zwischen Planung und Realisierung." In *Die Nationalsozialistichen Konzentrationslager—Entwicklung und Struktur*, vol. 1. Edited by Ulrich Herbert, Karin Orth, and Christoph Dieckmann. Göttingen: Wallstein Verlag, 1998, 363–89.

———. "Das Konzentrationslager Majdanek 1941–1944. Zeittafel." In *Bildungsarbeit und historisches Lernen in der Gedenkstätte Majdanek*. Edited by Tomasz Kranz. Lublin: Państwowe Muzeum na Majdanku, 2000.

———. *The Extermination of Jews at Majdanek Concentration Camp*. Lublin: Państwowe Muzeum na Majdanku, 2010.

———. "'Generalplan Ost' und 'Endlösung' im Distrikt Lublin." In *Bildungsarbeit und historisches Lernen in der Gedenkstätte Majdanek*. Edited by Tomasz Kranz. Lublin: Państwowe Muzeum na Majdanku, 2000.

———. "Konzentrationslager Lublin. Powstanie, organizacja, działalność." In *Więźniowie KL Lublin 1941–1944*. Edited by Tomasz Kranz and Wojciech Lenarczyk. Lublin: Państwowe Muzeum na Majdanku, 2020, 17–132.

Kranz, Tomasz, ed. *Unser Schicksal—eine Mahnung für Euch (. . .) Berichte und Erinnerungen der Häftlinge von Majdanek*. Lublin: Państwowe Muzeum na Majdanku, 1994.

Kranz, Tomasz, and Wojciech Lenarczyk, eds. *Więźniowie KL Lublin 1941–1944*. Lublin: Państwowe Muzeum na Majdanku, 2020.

Krausnick, Helmut, and Hans-Heinrich Wilhelm. *Die Truppe des Weltanschauungskrieges. Die Einsatzgruppen der Sicherheitspolizei und des SD, 1938–1942*. Stuttgart: Deutsche Verlagsanstalt, 1981.

Kroll, Bogdan. *Rada Główna Opiekuńcza, 1939–1945*. Warsaw: Książka i Wiedza, 1985.

Kwiatkowski, Jerzy. *485 Days at Majdanek*. Stanford: Hoover Institution, 2021.

Lanckorońska, Karolina. *Those Who Trespass Against Us: One Woman's War Against the Nazis*. Toronto: Pimlico, 2006.

Langnas, Saul. *Żydzi a studja akademickie w Polsce w latach 1921–1931 (studjum statystyczne)*. Lwów: Żydowskie Akademickie Stowarzyszenie Samopomocy Środowiska Lwowskiego, 1933.

Lenarczyk, Wojciech, ed. *Majdanek w Dokumentach*. Lublin: Państwowe Muzeum na Majdanku, 2016.

Lenarczyk, Wojciech, and Dariusz Libionka, eds. *Erntefest: Zapomniany epizod Zagłady, 3–4 listopada 1943*. Lublin: Państwowe Muzeum na Majdanku, 2009.

Leszczyńska, Zofia. *Kronika obozu na Majdanku*. Lublin: Wydawnictwo Lubelskie, 1980.

———. "Transporty i stany liczbowe obozu." In *Majdanek 1941–1944*. Edited by Tadeusz Mencel. Lublin: Wydawnictwo Lubelskie, 1991, 93–128.

Libionka, Dariusz, ed. *Akcja Reinhardt. Zagłada Żydów w Generalnym Gubernatorstwie*. Warsaw: Instytut Pamięci Narodowej, 2004.

Longerich, Peter. *Politik der Vernichtung. Eine Gesamtdarstellung der nationalsozialistischen Judenverfolgung*. Munich: Piper Verlag, 1998.

Machuła, Ryszard, and Anna Wiśniewska, ed. *Braterska Pomoc. Wspomnienia dotyczące pomocy społeczeństwa Lubelszczyzny ofiarom hitlerowskiego terroru*. Lublin: Państwowe Muzeum na Majdanku, 1978.

Madajczyk, Czesław. *Die Okkupationspolitik Nazideutschlands in Polen 1939–1945*. Translated by Bertold Puchert. Berlin: Akademie Verlag Berlin, 1987.

Madej, Jósef. "Erste Opfer." In *Unser Schicksal—eine Mahnung für Euch (. . .) Berichte und Erinnerungen der Häftlinge von Majdanek*. Edited by Tomasz Kranz. Lublin: Państwowe Muzeum na Majdanku, 1994, 17–27.

Mailänder, Elissa. *Female SS Guards and Workaday Violence: The Majdanek Concentration Camp, 1942–1944*. Translated by Patricia Szobar. Lansing: Michigan State University Press, 2015.

Majer, Diemut. *"Non-Germans" Under the Third Reich: The Nazi Judicial and Administrative System in Germany and Occupied Eastern Europe, With Special Regard to Occupied Poland, 1939–1945*. Translated by Peter Thomas Hill, Edward Vance Humphrey, and Brian Levin. Baltimore: Johns Hopkins University Press, 2003.

Majewski, Piotr. "Konzept und Organisation des 'zivilen Kampfes.'" In *Die polnische Heimatarmee. Geschichte und Mythos der Armia Krajowa seit dem zweiten Weltkrieg*. Edited by Bernhard Chiari, in collaboration with Jerzy Kochanowski. Munich: R. Oldenbourg Verlag, 2003, 303–24.

Mallmann, Klaus-Michael, Jochen Böhler, and Jürgen Matthäus. *Einsatzgruppen in Polen, Darstellung und Dokumentation*. Darmstadt: Wissenschaftliche Buchgesellschaft, 2008.

Malm, Saturnina. "Przed i za drutami." In *Braterska Pomoc. Wspomnienia dotyczące pomocy społeczeństwa Lubelszczyzny ofiarom hitlerowskiego terroru*. Edited by Ryszard Machuła and Anna Wiśniewska. Lublin: Państwowe Muzeum na Majdanku, 1978, 84–109.

Mańkowski, Zygmunt, ed. *Hitlerowskie więzienie na Zamku w Lublinie, 1939–1944*. Lublin: Wydawnictwo Lubelskie, 1988.

Marczak-Bukowska, Ewa. *Przyjaciele, koledzy, wrogowie? Relacje pomiędzy polskimi, żydowskimi i ukraińskimi studentami Uniwersytetu Jana Kazimierza we Lwowie w okresie międzywojennym (1918–1939)*. Warsaw: Neriton, 2019.

Markiewicz, Jerzy. *Nie dali ziemi skąd ich ród. Zamojszczyzna 27 XI 1942-31 XII 1943*. Lublin: Wydawnictwo Lubelskie, 1967.

Marszałek, Józef. *Majdanek: The Concentration Camp in Lublin*. Warsaw: Interpress, 1986.

Mazower, Mark. *Hitler's Empire: How the Nazis Ruled Europe*. New York: Penguin, 2009.

Mazur, Grzegorz. *Życie polityczne polskiego Lwowa, 1918–1939*. Kraków: Księgarnia Akademicka, 2007.

Mędykowski, Witold Wojciech. *Macht Arbeit Frei? German Economic Policy and Forced Labor of Jews in the General Government, 1939–1943*. Boston: Academic Studies Press, 2018.

Mehlberg, Henry. *Time, Causality, and the Quantum Theory: Studies in the Philosophy of Science*. Vol. 1, *Essay on the Causal Theory of Time*. Edited by Robert S. Cohen. Holland: D. Reidel Publishing Company, 1980.

Melchior, Małgorzata. *Zagłada a tożsamość. Polscy Żydzi na "aryjskich papierach." Analiza doświadczenia biograficznego*. Warsaw: IFiS PAN, 2004.

Mencel, Tadeusz. "Konzentrationslager Lublin. General Characteristics." In *Majdanek 1941–1944*. Edited by Tadeusz Mencel. Lublin: Wydawnictwo Lubelskie, 1991, 509–19.

Mencel, Tadeusz, ed. *Majdanek 1941–1944*. Lublin: Wydawnictwo Lubelskie, 1991.

Moldenhauer, Harald. "Der Sowjetische NKVD und die Heimatarmee im 'Lubliner Polen' 1944–1945." In *Die polnische Heimatarmee. Geschichte und Mythos der Armia Krajowa seit dem zweiten Weltkrieg*. Edited by Bernhard Chiari, in collaboration with Jerzy Kochanowski. Munich: R. Oldenbourg Verlag, 2003, 275–99.

Motyka, Grzegorz. *Wołyń '43*. Warsaw: Wydawnictwo Literackie, 2016.

Murawski, Roman. *The Philosophy of Mathematics and Logic in the 1920s and 1930s in Poland*. Basel: Birkhäuser, 2014.

Musial, Bogdan. *Deutsche Zivilverwaltung und Judenverfolgung im Generalgouvernement. Eine Fallstudie zum Distrikt Lublin 1939–1944*. Vol. 10, *Deutsches Historisches Institut Warschau, Quellen und Studien*. Wiesbaden: Harrassowitz Verlag, 1999.

Orth, Karin. *Die Konzentrationslager-SS: Sozialstrukturelle Analysen und biographische Studien*. Göttingen: Wallstein Verlag, 2013.

Ossowska, Wanda. *Przeżyłam. Lwów-Warszawa 1939–1946*. 2nd ed. Warsaw: Towarzystwo Opieki nad Majdankiem Oddział Warszawski, 1995.

Pakszys, Elżbieta. "Kobiety w filozofii polskiej. Dwa pokolenia Szkoły Lwowsko-Warszawskiej," Humanistyka i Płeć. Vol. 2, *Kobiety w poznaniu naukowym wczoraj i dziś*. Edited by Elżbieta Pakszys and Danuta Sobczyńska. Poznań: Wydawnictwo Naukowe UAM, 1997, 263–82.

Panasiewicz, Adam. "Poststelle." In *Braterska Pomoc. Wspomnienia dotyczące pomocy społeczeństwa Lubelszczyzny ofiarom hitlerowskiego terroru*. Edited by Ryszard Machuła and Anna Wiśniewska. Lublin: Państwowe Muzeum na Majdanku, 1978, 112–27.

Pauer-Studer, Herlinde, and J. David Velleman. *Konrad Morgen: The Conscience of a Nazi Judge*. London: Palgrave Macmillan, 2015.

Peploński, Andrzej. "Die Aufklärung der Heimatarmee." In *Die polnische Heimatarmee. Geschichte und Mythos der Armia Krajowa seit dem zweiten Weltkrieg*. Edited by Bernhard Chiari, in collaboration with Jerzy Kochanowski. Munich: R. Oldenbourg Verlag, 2003, 169–86.

Perzanowska, Stefania. *Gdy myśli do Majdanka wracają. Wspomnienia lekarki z obozu koncentracyjnego w Lublinie*. Warsaw: Prószyński i S-ka in cooperation with Państwowe Muzeum na Majdanku, 2022 (first published in 1970).

Plocker, Anat. *The Expulsion of Jews from Communist Poland: Memory Wars and Homeland Anxieties*. Bloomington: Indiana University Press, 2022.

Pohl, Dieter. "Die Stellung des Distrikts Lublin in der 'Endlösung der Judenfrage.'" In *"Aktion Reinhardt": Der Völkermord an den Juden im Generalgouvernement 1941–1944*. Edited by Bogdan Musial. Osnabrück: fibre Verlag, 2004.

———. "Massentötungen durch Giftgas im Rahmen der 'Aktion Reinhardt.'" In *Neue Studien zu Nationalsozilististischen Massentötungen durch Giftgas. Historische Bedeutung, technische Entwicklung, revisionistische Leugnung*. Edited by Gunter Morsch and Bertrand Perz. Berlin: Metropol Verlag, 2011, 185–95.

———. *Nationalsozialistische Judenverfolgung in Ostgalizien, 1941–1944. Organisation und Durchführung eines staatlichen Massenverbrechens*. Munich: R. Oldenbourg Verlag, 1996.

———. *Von der "Judenpolitik" zum Judenmord. Der Distrikt Lublin des Generalgouvernements 1939–1944*. Frankfurt: Peter Lang, 1993.

Poprzeczny, Joseph. *Odilo Globocnik: Hitler's Man in the East*. Jefferson, NC: McFarland, 2004.

Redner, Ben Z. *A Jewish Policeman in Lwów: An Early Account, 1941–1943*. Translated by Jerzy Michalowicz. Jerusalem: Yad Vashem, 2015.

Rogerie, André. "Transporty chorych." In *Majdanek: Obóz koncentracyjny w relacjach więźniów i świadków*. Edited by Marta Grudzińska. Lublin: Państwowe Muzeum na Majdanku, 2011, 210–14.

Roseman, Mark. *The Wannsee Conference and the Final Solution: A Reconsideration*. Rev. ed. London: Folio Society, 2012.

Schwindt, Barbara. *Das Konzentrations- und Vernichtungslager Majdanek. Funktionswandel im Kontext der "Endlösung."* Würzburg: Königshausen und Neumann, 2005.

Shatyn, Bruno. *A Private War: Surviving in Poland on False Papers, 1941–1945*. Translated by Oscar E. Swan. Detroit: Wayne State University Press, 1985.

Silberklang, David. *Gates of Tears: The Holocaust in the Lublin District*. Jerusalem: Yad Vashem, 2013.

Smorczewski, Ralph. *Bridging the Gap: Reminiscences*. Leicester: Matador, 2007.

Snyder, Timothy. *Black Earth: The Holocaust as History and Warning*. New York: Tim Duggan Books, 2015.

———. *The Reconstruction of Nations: Poland, Ukraine, Lithuania, Belarus, 1569–1999*. New Haven: Yale University Press, 2003.

Sommer Schneider, Anna. "Behind the Iron Curtain: The Communist Government in Poland and Its Attitude Toward the Joint's Activities, 1944–1989." In *The JDC at 100: A Century of Humanitarianism*. Edited by Avinoam Patt, Atina Grossmann, Linda G. Levi, and Maud S. Mandel. Detroit: Wayne State University Press, 2019, 315–60.

———. *Sze'erit hapleta. Ocaleni z Zagłady. Działalność American Jewish Joint Distribution Committee w Polsce w latach 1945–1989*. Kraków: Księgarnia Akademicka, 2014.

Stanisławski, Andrzej. *Pole śmierci*. Lublin: Wydawnictwo Lubelskie, 1969.

Streit, Christian. "Soviet Prisoners of War in the Hands of the Wehrmacht." In *War of Extermination: The German Military in World War II, 1941–1944*. Edited by Hannes Heer and Klaus Naumann. New York: Berghahn Books, 2000, 80–91.

Suchmiel, Jadwiga. *Działalność naukowa kobiet w Uniwersytecie we Lwowie do roku 1939*. Częstochowa: Wydawnictwo WSP, 2000.

Twardowski, Kazimierz. *Dzienniki*, 2 vols. Warsaw: Adam Marszałek, 1997.

Veidlinger, Jeffrey. *In the Midst of Civilized Europe: The Pogroms of 1918–1921 and the Onset of the Holocaust*. New York: Metropolitan Books, 2021.

Viola, Lynne. *Peasant Rebels Under Stalin: Collectivization and the Culture of Peasant Resistance*. New York: Oxford University Press, 1996.

Vrba, Rudolf, and Alan Bestic. *Escape from Auschwitz: I Cannot Forgive*. New York: Grove Press, 1964; New York: Black Cat, 1986

Wachsmann, Nikolaus. *KL: A History of the Nazi Concentration Camps*. New York: Farrar, Straus & Giroux, 2015.

Węgrzyn, Ewa. *Wyjeżdżamy! Wyjeżdżamy?! Alija gomułkowska 1956–1960*. Kraków: Austeria, 2016.

Weinberg, Gerhard. *A World at Arms: A Global History of World War II*. Cambridge: Cambridge University Press, 1994.

Winstone, Martin. *The Dark Heart of Hitler's Europe: Nazi Rule in Poland Under the General Government*. London: I. B. Taurus, 2015.

Wiśniewska, Anna. "Pomoc więźniom Majdanka." In *Majdanek 1941–1944*. Edited by Tadeusz Mencel. Lublin: Wydawnictwo Lubelskie, 1991, 233–52.

Wnuk, Józef. *Dzieci polskie oskarżaja*. Lublin: Wydawnictwo Lubelskie, 1975.

Wójcik, Wiesław. "Budowanie środowiska matematycznego w Polsce w dwudziestoleciu międzywojennym." In *Stosunki Polsko-Żydowskie. Kultura, literatura, sztuka i nauka w XX wieku*. Edited by Zofia Trębacz. Warsaw: Żydowski Instytut Historyczny im. Emanuela Ringelbluma, 2020, 341–58.

Woleński, Jan. *Logic and Philosophy in the Lvov-Warsaw School*. Dordrecht: Kluwer Academic Publishers, 1989.

Wylegała, Anna. "Entangled Bystanders: Multidimensional Trauma of Ethnic Cleansing and Mass Violence in Eastern Galicia." In *Trauma, Experience and Narrative in Europe after World War II*. Edited by Ville Kivimäki and Peter Leese. Cham, Switzerland: Palgrave Macmillan, 2021, 119–48.

Zakrzewski, Jan. *A my żyjemy dalej (. . .) Wspomnienia więźnia Majdanka*. Lublin: Wydawnictwo Lubelskie, 1977.

Zaremba, Marcin. *Wielka trwoga: Polska 1944–1947. Ludowa reakcja na kryzys*. Kraków: Znak and Instytut Studiów Politycznych Polskiej Akademii Nauk, 2012.

Zimmerman, Joshua D. *The Polish Underground and the Jews, 1939–1945*. New York: Cambridge University Press, 2015.

ARTICLES

Asher, Harvey. "The Soviet Union, the Holocaust, and Auschwitz." *Kritika: Explorations in Russian and Eurasian History* 4, no. 4 (Fall 2003): 886–912.

Berkhoff, Karel C., and Marco Carynnyk. "The Organization of Ukrainian Nationalists and Its Attitude toward Germans and Jews: Iaroslav Stets'ko's 1941 Zhyttiepys." *Harvard Ukrainian Studies* 23, no. 3–4 (December 1999): 149–83.

Black, Peter. "Foot Soldiers of the Final Solution: The Trawniki Training Camp and Operation Reinhard." *Holocaust and Genocide Studies* 25, no. 1 (Spring 2011): 1–99.

———. "Rehearsal for 'Reinhard'? Odilo Globocnik and the Lublin Selbstschutz." *Central European History* 25, no. 2 (1992): 204–26.

Böhler, Jochen. "Post-war Military Action and Violence (East Central Europe)." *1914–1918 Online: International Encyclopedia of the First World War*, https://encyclopedia.1914-1918-online.net/article/post-war_military_action_and_violence_east_central_europe.

Brenk, Mikołaj. "Działalność Powiatowego Komitetu Opieki Społecznej w Koninie w latach 1945–1949." *Polonia Maior Orientalis* 3 (2016): 113–22.

Budnitsky, Oleg. "Jews, Pogroms, and the White Movement: A Historiographical Critique." *Kritika: Explorations in Russian and Eurasian History* 2, no. 4 (Fall 2001): 1–23.

Dziadosz, Edward, and Józef Marszałek. "Więzienia i obozy w dystrykcie lubelskim w latach 1939–1944." *Zeszyty Majdanka* 3 (1969): 54–122.

Grudzińska, Marta. "The Women's Medical Ward in *Frauenkonzentrationslager* Lublin (Majdanek)," presented at the 3rd international conference Medical Review Auschwitz: Medicine Behind the Barbed Wire, September 12–21, 2021, Kraków, https://www.mp.pl/auschwitz/conference/edition2021/session1/show.html?id=280502.

Grudzińska, Marta, and Marta Kubiszyn. "'To was tutaj tak strasznie biją? (. . .) Nie, nas nie. Tylko Żydów': Żydzi w obozie na Majdanku w świetle relacji polskich więźniów." *Studia Judaica* 21: 2: 42 (2018): 333–71.

Himka, John-Paul. "The Lviv Pogrom of 1941: The Germans, Ukrainian Nationalists, and the Carnival Crowd." *Canadian Slavonic Papers* 54: 2–4 (June-September-December 2011): 209–43.

Kopciowski, Adam. "Zajścia antyżydowskie na Lubelszczyźnie w pierwszych latach po drugiej wojnie światowej." *Zagłada Żydów Studia i Materiały* 3 (2007): 178–207.

Kritchevsky, David. "History of Recommendations to the Public about Dietary Fat." *The Journal of Nutrition* 128, no. 2 (February 1998): 449S–452S.

Krzyżanowski, Jerzy R., and Wacław W. Soroka. "The Polish Underground Resistance in the Lublin Area: A Duologue." *The Polish Review* 20, no. 4 (1975): 145–56.

Kuwałek, Robert, Tomasz Kranz, and Beata Ciwek-Siupa. "Odszyfrowane radiotelegramy ze stanami dziennymi z obozu koncentracyjnego na Majdanku (styczeń 1942–styczeń 1943 r.)." *Zeszyty Majdanka* 24 (2008): 210–32.

Łapot, Mirosław. "Incydenty antysemickie w szkołach lwowskich (1867–1939)." *Przegląd Nauk Stosowanych* 6 (2015): 107–19.

———. "Uczniowie żydowscy w szkołach średnich we Lwowie w dobie autonomii galicyjskiej." *Prace Naukowe Akademii im. Jana Długosza w Częstochowie* 26, no. 1 (2017): 309–21.

Marszałek, Józef. "Budowa obozu koncentracyjnego na Majdanku w latach 1942–1944." *Zeszyty Majdanka* 4 (1969): 21–90.

Mehlberg, Josephine J. "A Classification of Mathematical Concepts." *Synthese* 14, no. 1 (March 1962): 78–86.

Mehlberg, Józefa. Review of "Sur la Nation de Collectif" by Jan Herzberg. *The Journal of Symbolic Logic* 4, no. 3 (September 1939): 121.

Murawska, Zofia. "System strzeżenia i sposoby izolacji więźniów w obozie koncentracyjnym na Majdanku." *Zeszyty Majdanka* 1 (1965): 76–132.

Perzanowska, Stefania. "O niektórych hitlerowskich lekarzach w Majdanku." *Przegląd Lekarski—Oświęcim* (1966): 209–11.

———. "Pomoc lubelskich organizacji społecznych więźniom Majdanka." *Przegląd Lekarski—Oświęcim* (1965): 140–44.

———. "Szpital obozu kobiecego w Majdanku" ("The Women's Camp Hospital at Majdanek.") Translated by M. Kapera. *Przegląd Lekarski—Oświęcim* (1968): 169–80, https://www.mp.pl/auschwitz/journal/english/223573,majdanek-womens-camp-hospital#1.

Podbielska, Alicja. "'The Righteous' and March '68." *Kwartalnik Historii Żydów* 2, no. 270 (June 2019): 363–87

Rędziński, Kazimierz. "Studenci żydowscy we Lwowie w latach 1918–1939." *Prace Naukowe Akademii im. Jana Długosza w Częstochowie* 25 (2016): 581–601.

———. "Towarzystwo Żydowskich Studentów Filozofii Uniwersytetu Jana Kazimierza we Lwowie (1922–1939)." *Rocznik Polsko-Ukraiński* 20 (2018): 11–35.

Reynolds, Jaime. "'Lublin' versus 'London'—The Party and the Underground Movement in Poland, 1944–1945." *Journal of Contemporary History* 16, no. 4 (October 1981): 617–48.

Rudling, Anders. "Historical Representation of the Wartime Accounts of the Activities of the OUN-UPA (Organization of Ukrainian Nationalists–Ukrainian Insurgent Army)." *East European Jewish Affairs* 36, no. 2 (2006): 163–89.

Szlachetka, Małgorzata. "Zapomniany obóz przy ul. Krochmalnej." *Gazeta Wyborcza*, November 16, 2007.

Weingartner, James J. "Law and Justice in the Nazi SS: The Case of Konrad Morgen." *Central European History* 16, no. 3 (September 1983): 276–94.

White, Elizabeth B. "Majdanek: Cornerstone of Himmler's SS Empire in the East." *Simon Wiesenthal Center Annual* (1990): 3–21.

Wiśniewska, Anna. "Organizacyjny i materialny wkład lubelskiej Rady Głównej Opiekuńczej w dzieło pomocy dla Polaków osadzonych na Majdanku." *Zeszyty Majdanka* 8 (1975): 5–33.

Witte, Peter, and Stephen Tyas. "A New Document on the Deportation and Murder of Jews During 'Einsatz Reinhardt' 1942." *Holocaust and Genocide Studies* 15, no. 3 (Winter 2001): 468–86.

Wójcik, Wiesław. "Fenomen polskiej szkoły matematycznej a emigracja matematyków polskich w okresie II wojny światowej." *Zagadnienia Filozoficzne w Nauce* 53 (2013): 11–52.

Woroniak, Anna. "Ocalić od zapomnienia. Nieznane hitlerowskie obozy przejściowe w Lublinie w latach 1940–1944." *Odkrywca*, December 2008: 36–39.

Wylegała, Anna. "About 'Jewish Things': Jewish Property in Eastern Galicia during World War II." *Yad Vashem Studies* 44 (2016): 83–119.

PHOTO CREDITS

1. "Janina's Story," Accession Number: 2003.333 Courtesy of the U.S. Holocaust Memorial Museum.
2. Photo courtesy of Jan Woleński (a gift from his teacher Izydora Dąmbska) and reproduced with permission.
3. P-OM-15_AKT-KP_058_karta-034. Commemorative Book in Honor of Kazimierz Twardowski. Courtesy of Digital Archive of Combined Libraries.
4. Courtesy of Anna Ożyńska-Zborowska and Wojciech Rostworowski.
5. CAF/PAP L-314-12.jpg. Archive of the Central Photographic Agency/Polish Press Agency.
6. Courtesy of the State Museum at Majdanek.
7. Photograph 73996. Courtesy of the U.S. Holocaust Memorial Museum.
8. Photograph 65975. U.S. Holocaust Memorial Museum, courtesy of Michel Reynders.
9. Photograph 06043. U.S. Holocaust Memorial Museum, courtesy of Jerzy Tomaszewski.
10. Courtesy of the State Museum at Majdanek.
11. Photograph 83854. Courtesy of the U.S. Holocaust Memorial Museum.
12. Photograph MHMLA_007aa. Courtesy of the National Museum in Lublin.
13. *Minneapolis Tribune* photo by Roy Swan.
14. "Janina's Story," USHMM Accession Number: 2003.333. Courtesy of the U.S. Holocaust Memorial Museum.
15. Courtesy of Irvin Klinghofer.
16. 036.04.07, Dan Ryan collection, 1954–1980, Section 27, University Archives and Special Collection. Courtesy of the Paul V. Gavin Library, Illinois Institute of Technology.

INDEX

INDEX

ALSO BY PETER W. RODMAN

More Precious than Peace:
The Cold War and the Struggle for the Third World

Presidential Command

PRESIDENTIAL COMMAND

POWER, LEADERSHIP, AND THE
MAKING OF FOREIGN POLICY FROM
RICHARD NIXON TO GEORGE W. BUSH

Peter W. Rodman

Alfred A. Knopf · NEW YORK
2009

THIS IS A BORZOI BOOK
PUBLISHED BY ALFRED A. KNOPF

Knopf, Borzoi Books, and the colophon are
registered trademarks of Random House, Inc.

Library of Congress Cataloging-in-Publication Data
Rodman, Peter W.
Presidential command : politics, power, and the making
of national security policy / by Peter Rodman. — 1st ed.
p.   cm.
"This is a Borzoi Book."
Includes bibliographical references and index.
ISBN 978-0-307-26979-9
1. Presidents—United States.
2. United States—Foreign relations.
3. Political leadership.   I. Title.
JK516.R493 2009
355'.033573—dc22   2008039973

Manufactured in the United States of America
First Edition

CONTENTS

INTRODUCTION
Henry A. Kissinger

A kind Providence caused Peter Rodman's life and mine to intersect more than four decades ago. Peter was assigned to me as a tutee in 1965 at Harvard. He was part of my life ever since. It will be an emptier and less joyful world without him.

Peter wrote a brilliant undergraduate thesis. I was so impressed with him that, even as he decided to go to law school, I offered him a position as research assistant should he decide against practicing law. As it turned out, I had become President Nixon's national security adviser by the time Peter took up the offer.

Peter started work as my personal assistant. In a short time, his duties developed to supervising the assembly of documents and information relevant to the many negotiations taking place simultaneously, to see to it that an accurate record of these meetings existed, and to distill them together with his colleagues—mostly in their twenties—into recommendations for the next phase. He also helped me write speeches.

No one worked more closely with me than Peter. He sat at my side during every negotiation and was part of the team designing their tactics and strategy.

Public service was Peter's vocation. From the moment he joined my staff and for nearly four decades afterward, five presidents, from Richard Nixon through George W. Bush, benefited from his understated wisdom, his unselfish dedication, and his wry wit, as director of the Policy Planning Staff at the State Department, as presidential assistant, and as assistant secretary of defense for international security affairs. His principal weakness was a passionate attachment to the Boston Red Sox—incomprehensible for a Yankee fan.

Peter grew up during a time when America's exceptionalism had

turned on itself. It was inevitable that America would learn that there were limits even to the "shining city on the hill." But the process was painful. Throughout our history, every problem recognized as a problem had proved soluble. Vietnam proved obdurate.

The so-called greatest generation that saw us through the confrontation with Fascism and Japan had been sustained by a moral consensus and unambiguous objectives. Hence, Peter had to work on policies that were challenged not so much for their prudence as for their motive. In the 1960s and 1970s, the intellectual community, mourning the assassination of a president with whom it had identified, and perplexed by an impasse to which its own theories had contributed, interpreted its frustrations as a moral failure of the American system and experience. Dialogue evaporated and eventually turned into a kind of intellectual civil war.

Peter transcended the passions of a turbulent time. He did so by his integrity, his special kind of innocence, which caused even his intellectual adversaries to feel that they learned from him, even when they could not bring themselves to share his conclusions.

In an increasingly narcissistic age, while many of his contemporaries analyzed themselves and their motives with rapt fascination, Peter helped sustain the nation by unobtrusive commitment to the cause of freedom fought in the trenches of the bureaucracy and the battlefields of diplomacy. Peter sought fulfillment, not glory. He served to do, not to be.

Not for Peter was the debate between idealism and realism. He had seen that the key governmental decisions were close, 49.5 to 50.5 percent, and that serious people were seeking to solve them. A grasp of circumstances was essential. Yet, by themselves, experts of circumstance inspire paralysis, not direction. Events cannot be shaped, or challenges overcome, without faith in fundamental values. The highest task of a public servant is to take his or her society from where it is to where it has never been. This implies the courage to face complexity, the character to act when the outcome is still ambiguous. For Peter, the issue of courage did not arise because he perceived no alternative to pursuing his duty. And character was inherent, requiring no affirmation.

Peter was much too modest to have put his role into words as these. The fact remains that the nation has lost one of its sentinels, all the more indispensable for never having made that claim for himself.

IT WOULD NOT SERVE Peter's memory to leave him as an abstract figure on a pedestal. It was the good fortune of Peter's associates that he was

as warm a human being as he was selfless. Excessive deference was not his defining trait. At diplomatic lunches, Peter did not let note-taking interfere with his voracious appetite, eating with his left hand while scribbling with his right. On one occasion, an ambassador noticed that Peter stopped taking notes, though not eating, while I attempted a humorous point. "Don't you record the secretary's jokes?" the diplomat wanted to know. "Yes," Peter replied. "The first time."

Peter had a wicked sense of humor. One of his specialties was to produce spoofs of option papers. One such effort concerned John T. Downey, who had been imprisoned in China since the early 1950s. After Nixon's opening to Beijing, I asked Chou En-lai to release Downey on compassionate grounds so that he could see his mother one last time. When Ford became president, Peter concocted a spoof option paper with the following theme: Chou En-lai had released Downey based on our representation that his mother was dying. The mother did not die, generating a credibility problem for the United States. The president, according to Peter, therefore had the following options, in ascending order of severity: (a) he could apologize for Mrs. Downey's survival and offer unspecified compensation, (b) he could send Downey back to China, (c) he could turn the whole matter over to the CIA to terminate Mrs. Downey.

Shortly after Ford had succeeded Nixon, I slipped Peter's memorandum into a number of genuine option papers Ford was considering in my presence. When Ford came to Peter's paper, I noticed he grew red in the face, saying "no" with increasing vehemence until it was nearly a shout at the last option.

Another masterpiece of Peter's, concocted in collaboration with Bill Hyland and Winston Lord, was an apocryphal memorandum, based on a standard form developed by Bob Haldeman, preparing Nixon for an encounter with the Almighty.

BEYOND ALL THE NATIONAL PROJECTS on which we worked together and the books and articles on which he helped me as researcher and editor, I feel the loss of a surrogate son. I loved Peter, above all, for his values, his loyalty, and his utter decency. Peter treasured his parents; he adored his wife, Véronique, whom he met while he helped with my memoirs; he was proud of his two children; and he was devoted to his husky, who, though a female, was called "George." It is always unnatural

when what we expect to be the succession of generations is reversed in this manner. And Peter still had so much left to do.

As we part from Peter, he takes with him a piece of our lives. He leaves us the pride of having shared part of the way with a genuinely moving personality, who, in the process, gives us a deeper perspective on what it all meant. All whose lives he touched—whatever our previous or continuing differences—are united by our affection for Peter and our gratitude for what he contributed to the intellectual and moral content, and, above all, the nobility of our life.

—As delivered at Peter W. Rodman's memorial service,
October 10, 2008

AUTHOR'S NOTE

This book has a modest objective, and makes a few simple points. It is not an institutional history of the national security policy-making process. Others have written excellent accounts of the origins and history of the National Security Council (NSC) system and the role of the White House national security adviser. I have learned from their efforts (and list some of them in the end notes). Even less is this intended as a complete account of the tumultuous history of American foreign policy in the period covered.

But I lived through some of that history, and this book conveys my personal perspective on how presidents have responded to one of their toughest tests—how they establish their control and policy direction of the sprawling bureaucracy that is the U.S. government. I have been able to watch, at close range, the interaction of policy, politics, and personalities that determined whether they succeeded or failed. Though it is not a complete history, it is a collection of observations, impressions, examples, and conclusions by someone who was inside the process. The comparative perspective also sheds useful light on the present. In five of these administrations—those of Richard Nixon, Gerald Ford, Ronald Reagan, George H. W. Bush, and George W. Bush—I served in various positions in the White House, State Department, or Defense Department. In two Democratic administrations—those of Jimmy Carter and Bill Clinton—I did not serve, but I have included my assessments of their experience for the continuity of the story. The problems that arise are not confined to administrations of one party or the other, and the issues are not partisan.

The reader will notice that I appear in the narrative myself on occasion, Zelig-like, in different places, either describing a personal observa-

tion of people I saw in action or describing an episode or issue I was involved in. At the end of this Author's Note I have listed the positions I held throughout this period, in case there is confusion about what my vantage point was at various times. But I can summarize my story here. Henry Kissinger was my teacher at Harvard College when I was an innocent nineteen-year-old senior. Little did I know then how far my tutoring at his hands would take me. He invited me to join him in the White House in 1969; I did so in the summer after graduating law school and remained his special assistant through the Nixon-Ford period. Then I left the government with him to assist him with his memoirs. I rejoined the government in the third year of the Reagan administration. After three years at the State Department Policy Planning Staff under Secretary of State George Shultz, I returned in 1986 to the NSC staff where I remained through the end of Reagan's term and for most of the first two years of George H. W. Bush. Republicans being fortunate, a third tour came for me under George W. Bush, this time in the Pentagon as assistant secretary of defense for international security affairs. I cannot claim to have been an eyewitness to every presidential action I describe. What I can claim is to have seen much and to have formed an educated judgment about many other things.

THE BOOK CONVEYS a few simple points—lessons, if you will—about how presidents can best maintain their personal control and policy direction. They are summed up in the last chapter, but the themes are threads that run throughout the book. They have to do with the inescapable necessity for presidents to be personally and systematically engaged, lest feuds between cabinet agencies fester or bureaucracies remain unresponsive to presidential preferences. These may seem obvious points, yet the account of seven presidencies that follows includes a perhaps surprising number of negative examples that demonstrate the price that is paid when their importance is not understood.

No organization chart will tell you how an administration works in practice. In our system, intangibles reign—most importantly the personality of the president. Presidents in turn come to rely most on individuals whose judgment (and loyalty) they have most confidence in. In some instances power gravitates to personalities who seize it; in other cases, personal ambitions only provoke reactions. Sometimes tensions develop between a president and his closest White House advisers. Not every policy failure is the result of a faulty process; conversely some

great successes (Nixon's China initiative, for example) have come from highly irregular procedures.

Each of the recent presidents, we will see, exemplifies a different approach—and a different set of problems. This cumulative experience is rich in lessons for future presidents seeking to give effect to their electoral mandate. How should they manage cabinet dissent and cabinet rivalries? Which qualities should they look for—and watch out for—when they choose their key cabinet secretaries and White House advisers? What is the proper role of the White House national security adviser and NSC staff? Is there a trade-off between collegiality and policy discipline? When is it possible to delegate, and when does a president have an inescapable responsibility to take charge?

I hope to put the current debates in the perspective of longer experience, and guide future presidents to get the lessons right.

Peter W. Rodman—Positions Held

• August 1969–January 1977: Special assistant to the assistant to the president for national security affairs (White House/NSC staff)

• March 1983–March 1986: Member, then director, of the Policy Planning Staff (Department of State)

• March 1986–January 1987: Deputy assistant to the president for national security affairs (foreign policy)(White House/NSC staff)

• January 1987–September 1990: Special assistant to the president for national security affairs and NSC counselor (White House/NSC staff)

• July 2001–March 2007: Assistant secretary of defense for international security affairs (Department of Defense)

Presidential Command

CHAPTER ONE

Bureaucracy, Democracy, and Legitimacy

T HERE IS A FAMOUS STORY of President Abraham Lincoln, taking a vote in a cabinet meeting on whether to sign the Emancipation Proclamation. All his cabinet secretaries vote nay, whereupon Lincoln raises his right hand and declares: "The ayes have it!"

The story is apocryphal, but it well captures the truth of Lincoln's relations with his cabinet. That cabinet included supremely ambitious men, substantial political figures in their own right, several of whom had sought the presidency in 1860 and remained convinced that they, not the country lawyer from Illinois, should be sitting in his chair. Yet Lincoln came to dominate this "team of rivals" and seized the responsibility that was inescapably his.

Such a story brings a smile when the president under discussion is the most revered political leader in the history of the republic. But our modern political culture and sensibility are more ambivalent. When less revered presidents make controversial decisions, what do we really believe about presidential authority? How do we feel, for example, about Richard Nixon overruling the dissent of both his secretary of state and his secretary of defense to order military escalations that he thought essential to prosecute the Vietnam War? What do we think of Ronald Reagan pursuing what he thought was a strategic opening with Iran, over the objection of his chief cabinet officers? With respect to the very public anguish of Secretary of State Colin Powell and his State Department over George W. Bush's decisions on Iraq, do we identify with Bush or with Powell? How often do we read in the press about White House "interference" in the work of experts in the departments and agencies, and complaints that their work is being "politicized"? One part of our brain seems to side with the permanent government. In the age of the

3

whistle-blower, what do we really think about a president's authority to decide and carry out policies with which subordinates disagree?

The answer should not depend simply on one's own policy or partisan preferences. There ought to be neutral principles, not only to guide the public discourse but also to guide presidents. The modern trend, especially since the United States emerged from World War II as a global power, has been to expand the White House staff and institutions like the National Security Council (NSC) precisely to enable more centralized control, or at least better central coordination, over an expanding policy community. That policy community includes traditional cabinet departments with an international role (State, Defense, Treasury), other institutions (the Central Intelligence Agency, the uniformed military, and agencies in charge of trade and foreign aid policy), and departments and agencies only recently playing an important role in foreign policy (the departments of Justice and Homeland Security, the Federal Bureau of Investigation, and the Drug Enforcement Administration). But like a law of physics, presidential efforts to strengthen control over this expanding community only stimulate the countertrends that are at work—powerful centrifugal forces in Congress, in the media, and in the Executive Branch itself.

The subject of this book is not the question of presidential prerogative vis-à-vis Congress. Library shelves are already filled with books on the two "co-equal" branches, and especially the ancient debate over war powers. The issue here is presidential control over the Executive Branch.

Congress's role, however, is an enormously important factor. As scholar Richard Neustadt has expressed it, the Constitutional Convention of 1787 did not, as commonly thought, create a system of separated powers. "Rather, it created a government of separated institutions *sharing* powers." Presidents undoubtedly have more freedom of action in the national security realm than in making domestic policy. Nonetheless, cabinet secretaries and their departments have obligations to Congress by statute; they are beholden to Congress for the final disposition of their budgets and their testimony is a duty. Cabinet secretaries are thus inevitably responsive, at least in part, to Congress as well as to the president. But that only restates the problem.

Neustadt recounts that President Harry Truman in 1952, contemplating the possibility that Dwight Eisenhower would be elected to succeed him, predicted that the eminent general would have problems

adjusting: "'He'll sit here,' Truman would remark (tapping his desk for emphasis), 'and he'll say, "Do this! Do that!" *And nothing will happen.* Poor Ike—it won't be a bit like the Army. He'll find it very frustrating.'" Truman's own experience was: "I sit here all day trying to persuade people to do the things they ought to have sense enough to do without my persuading them. . . . That's all the powers of the President amount to."

That was Neustadt's analysis as well. His answer was to counsel presidents and would-be presidents on how to maximize their power to persuade. His classic book *Presidential Power*, first published in 1960, explained that a president's success depended on expanding and husbanding his personal political leverage and prestige, his mastery of tools of influence that convince his subordinates that what the president wants them to do comports with their own personal and bureaucratic interests. Neustadt graded presidents according to their "power sense"—their instinct for maintaining their personal political power; he thought Franklin Roosevelt and Harry Truman had this "power sense," but Eisenhower did not. His book was seized upon by the new administration of John F. Kennedy as a primer on how to strengthen presidential control. However, the centrifugal forces have only strengthened since then—to the point where Neustadt, in an edition of his book twenty years later, felt compelled to go out of his way to debunk the notion of the "imperial presidency" that had become fashionable in some circles in the interim. As late as 1990, even after the Reagan presidency, Neustadt was still preoccupied with what he saw as the weakness of the office: "Weakness is still what I see: weakness in the sense of a great gap between what is expected of a man (or someday a woman) and assured capacity to carry through." Part of this weakness resides in the expansion of the modern bureaucracy and the increasing difficulty of a single individual's asserting systematic control over it.

Concepts of Legitimacy

Our Constitution, on the face of it, seems unambiguous about who is in charge of the Executive Branch: "The executive power shall be vested in a President of the United States of America" (Article II, section 1). But, as usual, a closer reading of our founding document reveals a more complex picture. Passages in section 2 of the same Article II refer specifically to the "executive departments" and to Congress's power to

authorize the heads of those departments to appoint subordinates. The president's authority over the civilian establishment is less explicit than his authority as commander in chief of the armed forces. The renowned constitutional scholar Edward S. Corwin concluded that the phrase "executive power" is a "term of uncertain content."

While the United States may have a cabinet, we do not have a cabinet system, which is what the British have. The cabinet at Westminster is "the government"—the body of ministers (what we would call cabinet secretaries) headed by the prime minister, who is in theory only the "first among equals." This institution evolved in the seventeenth and eighteenth centuries as the leadership of the Parliament, which extracted from the monarch the right to form his government. In parallel it became the leadership body of the political party that held the parliamentary majority. As such it embodied the distinctive characteristic of parliamentary government—what British scholar Walter Bagehot called the "nearly complete fusion" of the executive and legislative powers.

An important element of this system is the theory of the cabinet's collective responsibility. Certainly the personal role and power of the prime minister have grown considerably over the last century and a half, and many would argue that prime ministerial government has eclipsed the cabinet. But there are occasional reminders that the system has nowhere near evolved into presidential-style government. When Winston Churchill assumed office during the great crisis of May 1940, in the first three weeks he was nearly outvoted in the war cabinet by a faction that wanted to pursue a negotiation with Hitler. Even more recent prime ministers who have achieved extraordinary political dominance have discovered that, when political fortunes ebb, the party asserts its collective will. Just ask Margaret Thatcher and Tony Blair.

There have been a few attempts in the United States over the years to limit presidential authority in a manner suggestive of British cabinet-style arrangements, but they were short-lived exceptions that prove the rule:

> • John Quincy Adams took a vote at a cabinet meeting on at least one occasion and bowed to the majority when he was outvoted. But Adams, chosen as president in 1824 by the House of Representatives after not receiving even a plurality of either the electoral or popular vote, was one of our weakest presidents. Among other things,

he adamantly refused to consider party affiliation when making government appointments. For "power sense," Professor Neustadt would have graded him an F.

• When the National Security Council was created in 1947, there were those who saw it as a way of pressing presidents to make decisions in a more collegial framework. The British system was viewed as a model. This was a reaction to FDR's freewheeling management style and to doubts whether Harry Truman was up to the job. As we shall see, Truman, acutely sensitive to any challenge to his constitutional prerogative, eluded the trap.

• When Richard Nixon was engulfed by the Watergate scandal, one of the arguments he used in his defense was that removal from office before the end of his term would alter our political system in the direction of a parliamentary system, eroding a crucial pillar of the president's constitutional independence. The argument did not convince. When his political support finally collapsed in early August 1974, it was a delegation of senior Republican Party leaders who came to see him; they could not force him to resign, but only seek to persuade him that resignation was best for the country and for the party. This he agreed to.

• An implication that the top man might not be fully up to the job may have played a role in the 1980 discussions about Ronald Reagan's taking on ex-President Gerald Ford as his running mate, with Henry Kissinger slated once again to be secretary of state. Reagan and Ford permitted their close advisers to hold a series of secret meetings at the Republican National Convention on this idea—which some dubbed a "co-presidency"—before the two principals agreed to drop it.

Our constitutional structure thus seems strong enough to withstand attempts to turn it into something it isn't.

IF ONE SOURCE of presidential authority is constitutional legitimacy, a second is democratic legitimacy. Our political system puts itself through great convulsions every four years to elect a president (though it seems more and more a never-ending process). Presumably we do this on the premise that something important is at stake in the election, namely the authority to determine the direction of national policy for the next four years. It is generally assumed that we are choosing the individual we want to set the policies that the Executive Branch will

carry out. That is what the phrase "popular mandate" refers to. Democratic legitimacy is also democratic accountability.

This calls to mind another major difference from the British system, and indeed from European and most other systems. An American president today has around three thousand so-called political appointments to make to key positions in the government, several layers down into the bureaucratic machinery. These include not only cabinet secretaries, but deputy secretaries, under secretaries, and assistant secretaries. These several layers give the president a considerable ability to put his or her political stamp on the policies that will emerge from this machinery. When a new president enters office, especially if a change of political party is involved, the turnover is huge and the transition tumultuous.

Both political parties in this country have cadres of people to bring into government with the advent of a new administration. They come from private business, the academic and policy think tank community, and congressional staffs, and thus have a claim to professionalism as well as to responsiveness to the elected president's philosophy. Many who enter at senior positions have served at lower levels in prior administrations of the same party, and thus come with experience as well.

Britain, and most other countries, have nothing resembling this. The permanent civil service populates ministries up to much higher levels of the government. Even when a general election sweeps a new party into office, the incoming political leadership consists of cabinet ministers, a few other members of Parliament who serve as junior ministers in each department, and a handful of other assistants—perhaps 100 to 120, all together, in Britain. The rest are civil servants whom they meet when they arrive. Even in the prime minister's office, the cabinet tradition severely constrains a new prime minister's freedom to bring in more than a few personal advisers in any field.

One advantage of this system is continuity. When an election brings a change of leadership, the new political team, small as it is, is easily in place in a matter of days. The principle is that the civil servants shift their loyalties immediately to the new leaders and in the most professional manner help them implement whatever changes of policy are directed. The disadvantage is that the permanent government may not be as amenable to effective political control as the theory holds.

Political control over the bureaucracy may be one of the most significant challenges to modern democratic government in the twentieth and twenty-first centuries. The American system addresses this from

two directions—by the presidential power over personnel and by congressional oversight. Especially when the two branches are controlled by opposite parties, no one can doubt the vigor of congressional oversight over the bureaucracy—certainly no one who has testified to a congressional committee in such circumstances. In parliamentary systems, in contrast, the very "fusion" of the executive and legislative branches gives the whip hand to the government; parliamentary inquiries into alleged executive malfeasance are notoriously weak.

The British in their inimitable way have immortalized these truths in a cultural masterpiece, namely two television series produced by the BBC entitled *Yes Minister* and *Yes Prime Minister*. The first series recounts the career of a bumbling politician, James Hacker, who becomes a cabinet minister. He immediately encounters his would-be helpmeet, Sir Humphrey Appleby, the permanent secretary, or career head of the department. Sir Humphrey's real preoccupation is to insure that bright ideas from the minister do not disrupt the routine of existing policies or of civil service control. "He'll be house-trained in no time," Sir Humphrey assures two civil service colleagues. He deftly manages to steer his minister away from various shoals of policy innovation, all the while convincing Hacker that he, the minister, is totally in charge and that the outcomes comport exactly with his wishes (hence the title of the show).

In the sequel, Hacker has by some freak accident of history stumbled into 10 Downing Street as prime minister; Sir Humphrey accompanies him. Issues of foreign policy and defense now broaden the agenda, and Sir Humphrey is able to collude with civil service colleagues in the Foreign and Commonwealth Office and Ministry of Defence where necessary. At one point, a difference of view with the prime minister over how to vote on a United Nations resolution elicits the Foreign Office observation: "The PM must realize that as far as Foreign Affairs are concerned his job is to confine himself to the hospitality and ceremonial role."

If this rings all too true to an American who has served in the U.S. government, it is because the American system—despite the vaunted three thousand appointees—has not solved the problem of presidential political control over our own bureaucracy. As we shall see, our cabinet departments, too, have a life and culture of their own. This can produce a number of different phenomena. Professionals in a department, whether career or "political," often develop more of a loyalty to their

cabinet secretary, with whom they work day to day, than to a president who is a more remote figure across town. To a remarkable degree, a president comes to be viewed by the professionals as an interloper in policies that their departments are immersed in on a daily basis. Career officials also know that political appointees come and go while they will remain and their own career advancement is determined mainly by their permanent institutions. In the British system, departmental parochialism has been mitigated somewhat by the "generalist" tradition of rotating civil servants among departments; in the U.S. system, in contrast, most civil servants tend to spend their careers in a single department. Even political appointees come to absorb much of the institutional culture. "Where you stand depends on where you sit," is an old Washington adage. Nixon aide John Ehrlichman once said of political appointees: "We only see them at the annual White House Christmas party; they go off and marry the natives."

This has a significant influence over how policies are originated and implemented. As many scholars have noted, the nature of society and politics in America, much more so than in Europe, fosters an egalitarian culture even in hierarchical organizations; the culture fosters two-way flows of information and ideas, not just top-down. One result is that policy recommendations often "bubble up" from lower levels, and political leaders often find themselves (as Dean Acheson once put it) in a "judicial" mode weighing what advice comes from below.

Henry Kissinger in his memoirs refers to one result of the strength of the bureaucracy. Whether or not specific ideas flow in both directions, ultimately these institutions are not likely to be sources of bold innovation:

[A] large bureaucracy, however organized, tends to stifle creativity. It confuses wise policy with smooth administration. A complex bureaucracy has an incentive to exaggerate technical complexity and minimize the scope or importance of political judgment; it favors the status quo, however arrived at, because short of an unambiguous catastrophe the status quo has the advantage of familiarity and it is never possible to prove that another course would yield superior results. It seemed to me no accident that most great statesmen had been locked in permanent struggle with the experts in their foreign offices, for the scope of the statesman's conception challenges the inclination of the

expert toward minimum risk. . . . Ultimately there is no purely organizational answer; it is above all a problem of leadership.

"A camel is a horse designed by a committee" is another old Washington adage.

The pivotal figures in the system are the cabinet secretaries. As Kissinger has observed, a cabinet secretary has a strategic choice to make:

> [H]e can see himself as the surrogate of the head of the organization [i.e., the president], taking on his shoulders some of the onus of bureaucratically unpopular decisions. Or he can become the spokesman of his subordinates and thus face the chief executive with the necessity of assuming the sole responsibility for painful choices.

Earlier administrations were conscious of the same problem. John Kennedy's special counsel Theodore Sorensen, in a public lecture in 1963, candidly pointed out that a typical cabinet secretary "was not necessarily selected for the President's confidence in his judgment alone—considerations of politics, geography, public esteem, and interest-group pressures may also have played a part, as well as his skill in administration."

Kennedy's national security adviser, McGeorge Bundy, in his post–White House reflections, was more scathing:

> The unending contest between the Presidency and much of the bureaucracy is as real today as ever, and there has been no significant weakening in the network of triangular alliances which unite all sorts of interest groups with their agents in the Congress and their agents in the Executive Branch. . . . [T]he Executive Branch remains woefully short of first-class executive agents of the President. . . . The Cabinet role which I am trying to describe . . . in its relation to the White House . . . must be at once highly autonomous and deeply responsive. It is political, but only in the President's interest. It is managerial, but only on the President's terms. . . . At a test—unless he means to resign—the Secretary should always be the President's agent in dealing with the bureaucracy, not the other way around.

The basic argument for this kind of Secretary is simply that no other instrument can give the Presidency control over its own branch of government.

Charles G. Dawes, an early-twentieth-century statesman who served as vice president, budget director, and ambassador, has been quoted as observing: "The members of the Cabinet are a President's natural enemies."

Richard Nixon's first term was one possible paradigm for dealing with this problem. This was the era in which Nixon and his assistant Henry Kissinger pulled the reins of policy into the White House (as we shall describe in Chapter 3). This was a system of maximum centralization of personal control in the president's hands, and maximum coherence of policy, but they came at the price of maximum demoralization of the rest of the government. This method achieved a number of major successes, but in the end it is not a model to be emulated. Kissinger, who served as secretary of state under Nixon and Ford after nearly five years in the White House, concluded, having experienced it both ways, that a strong secretary of state enjoying the confidence of the president is the better model:

> A foreign policy achievement to be truly significant must at some point be institutionalized; it must therefore be embedded in permanent machinery. No government should impose on itself the need to sustain a tour de force based on personalities. . . . If the President does not trust his Secretary of State he should replace him, not attempt to work around him by means of the security adviser.

All of these Executive Branch officials serve at the president's pleasure, and, as Kissinger suggests, replacing them is a presidential prerogative. In short, and in theory, he can fire them. But that is not so easy in practice. If Nixon's problem was an unwillingness to fire people, Gerald Ford's experience, as we shall see, illustrates the pitfalls of firing people. The excruciating dilemma of whether or when to replace cabinet officers, we shall also see, is one of the burdens that confronted George W. Bush over Iraq.

Thus, every administration must balance a trade-off between coherence and discipline in presidential policy on the one hand, and bureaucratic collegiality on the other. The hard choices that this poses will be a

recurring theme in this book. George H. W. Bush, we shall see, did a good job of reconciling coherence and collegiality, but other presidents considered here had a harder time of it.

WHILE CONSTITUTIONAL LEGITIMACY and democratic legitimacy underpin presidential prerogative, prudence levies its own requirements. There seems to be a third, informal, concept of legitimacy, which relates to the way decisions are made and can be measured by the bureaucratic acceptance that follows (or doesn't follow) when an important agency of the government is overruled. Professor Neustadt's recommendation of persuasion is the ideal. But what if it can't be done? If differing points of view persist, the president may have to overrule *somebody*; consensus may not be attainable (or even desirable, if it only masks hard choices that must be made). And presidents have the right—like Abraham Lincoln—to overrule a consensus of all their subordinates.

What is it that enables presidents to do this without mutiny, without rancorous charges of "cabals" and insufficient consultation? If there is such a notion of procedural legitimacy, how is it defined? How is it reconciled with the president's constitutional supremacy in his branch of government, and with the system's need for consistent personal leadership? The formal, collegial structures of modern policy-making, centered in the National Security Council process, are part of the answer, but different presidents use this mechanism in different ways.

Alexander Hamilton is well known as the champion of a strong presidency; it was his essay No. 70 in *The Federalist* that argued for "energy in the Executive." Yet in 1800, Hamilton put forward the prudential case for a president's close consultation with his cabinet. This was, to be sure, in the context of a bitter feud with the incumbent president, his political rival John Adams, but the eloquence is familiar and the advice stands on its own:

> A President is not bound to conform to the advice of his ministers. He is even under no positive injunction to ask or require it. But the Constitution presumes that he will consult them; and the genius of our government and the public good commend the practice.
>
> As the President nominates his ministers, and may displace them when he pleases, it must be his own fault if he be not surrounded by men who, for ability and integrity, deserve his confidence. And if his

ministers are of this character, the consulting of them will always be likely to be useful to himself and to the state.

Hamilton contrasted Adams with his illustrious predecessor: "Very different from the practice of Mr. Adams was that of the modest and sage Washington. He consulted much, pondered much, resolved slowly, resolved surely."

The Modern Setting

Harry Truman's Council

The growth of the White House staff and Executive Office of the President, including mechanisms like the National Security Council, is the product not only of the growth of the Executive Branch but also of the tension between the president and the cabinet. The NSC, consisting of the president, vice president, and senior cabinet-level advisers, was created by the National Security Act of 1947 "to advise the President with respect to the integration of domestic, foreign, and military policies relating to the national security so as to enable the military services and the other departments and agencies of the Government to cooperate more effectively." In other words, it was meant as a coordinating mechanism, and it has served this purpose well for several presidents since then.

For our purposes, however, both the creation of the NSC and its later history are instructive for the bureaucratic tug-of-war they involved. Some of those participating in establishing the NSC had in mind a restraint on the president's ability to act unilaterally; strong presidents changed it into something very different. An "NSC system" has developed, consisting of the council together with a supporting staff and subcommittees. But how it works and how important it is in any administration are a function of how the president chooses to exercise power. It is the modern setting for the continuing struggle of presidents to control their bureaucracy.

There is a conventional narrative that a Republican Congress foisted the National Security Council on a reluctant President Harry Truman as a kind of posthumous revenge against Franklin Roosevelt's solo policy-making during the war. This narrative is, for the most part, off the mark. In fact, the need for a better mechanism for coordinating national

security policy was a bipartisan insight shared by the Truman administration and Congress; creation of the NSC was not a matter of serious
political controversy. The most important debates about the NSC's role
and structure took place within the Executive Branch.

Despite the great reverence for Franklin Roosevelt in the Truman
administration, there was indeed a reaction to what one historian has
called the "administrative chaos" of the Roosevelt era. Many of
those who helped shape the 1947 act were envious of the British, whose
Committee of Imperial Defence (CID), established in 1904, had
the mission of "obtaining and collating for the use of the Cabinet all
the information and expert advice required for shaping national
policy in war, and for determining the necessary preparations in peace."
Chaired by the prime minister and including the relevant ministers,
the CID was technically a subcommittee that reported to the full cabinet. But in wartime it effectively turned itself into a war cabinet. It also
was aided by a permanent secretariat and various subcommittees of its
own.

The United States, in contrast, had entered World War II with only
the most rudimentary means of interagency coordination. As war
approached, FDR's secretary of state, Cordell Hull, took the initiative to
organize a Standing Liaison Committee composed of the under secretary of state, the chief of naval operations, and the army chief of staff.
But this group was more a forum for exchanging information than a
body for coordinating and directing policy; nor did it grapple with big
policy issues. It disbanded in 1943.

FDR's improvisational management style compounded the problem—
for example, famously giving the same assignments to different staffers
without their knowing, playing off their competition in order to stimulate creativity and, not incidentally, keep the reins of power firmly in his
own hands. "You know I am a juggler," he told Henry Morgenthau in
May 1942, "and I never let my right hand know what my left hand does."
In running the war, FDR dealt directly with his commanders and
service chiefs, or left it to key White House aides such as Harry Hopkins and Admiral William Leahy to handle day-to-day coordination. He
reserved major strategic decisions to himself. Secretary of State Hull
was virtually excluded.

The 1942 landing in North Africa, for example, was ordered by Roosevelt over the strong objection of Army Chief of Staff General George C.
Marshall and of Marshall's chief planner, Brigadier General Dwight D.

Eisenhower. For strategic reasons, Roosevelt wanted an early Allied counterstroke against Hitler; his commanders thought it a dissipation of effort. (Eisenhower, but not Marshall, later conceded that the president was right.) A key document in which the president conveyed his views to Marshall is signed, "Roosevelt, C-in-C [Commander-in-Chief]"—the only occasion he is known to have done this—to hammer home who was in charge.

Only in late 1944 was a senior committee set up to do important coordinated planning. The State-War-Navy Coordinating Committee (SWNCC), at the assistant secretary level, worked on postwar plans for the occupation of Germany, Austria, and Japan as well as other topics like aid to China. By 1945, also, the secretaries of state, war, and navy had begun holding weekly meetings. Truman, in office only three months when he met at Potsdam with Josef Stalin and Winston Churchill in July, praised the work of the SWNCC in preparing him for the meeting, and before leaving Potsdam he let the three departments know that he liked this system and wanted it to continue.

Another reason the NSC idea was not hugely controversial is that it was caught up in a much bigger battle over unification of the armed services—arguably the most important component of the reforms enshrined in the National Security Act of 1947. Until that act, the secretary of the navy and his Department of the Navy had full cabinet status, equal to that of the secretary of war (that is, the Army). Champions of the Navy worried that unification—including creation of a new secretary of defense above all the services—spelled subordination of the Navy. Some of them became advocates of the new council because they hoped that the gods of unification could perhaps be appeased by a forum that insured better coordination at a more exalted level of national policy-making, obviating the need for consolidation at lower levels.

Truman, in the end, turned the tables on the Navy. By the end of the process he had pocketed the National Security Council *and* gotten unification of the services, as he had long personally favored. The main issue of contention was: What kind of council? This was the subject of intense negotiations between 1945 and 1947. Some of its early advocates consciously modeled their proposed National Security Council after the British CID, hoping to incorporate some of the collective quality of the British cabinet system. Their theory was that presidential deliberations and decisions made in that framework would be more collective in

nature, restraining Rooseveltian impetuosity. Some of Truman's staff are on record as strongly suspecting that an additional motivation was an assumption that the former haberdasher from Missouri, thrust so abruptly into the presidency, was not capable of carrying the burdens of the office without that kind of support.

It was the Bureau of the Budget that weighed in to protect presidential prerogative. This organization, part of the Executive Office of the President since 1939, not only has the job of coordinating departmental budget submissions for the president and assisting him in presenting his national budget to Congress; by that very task it is also a key management arm of the presidency with respect to departmental programs. (President Nixon renamed it the Office of Management and Budget—today's OMB—in 1970, broadening its role as an instrument of presidential control over the government.) During the lengthy negotiation over the National Security Act, the various cabinet departments and military services all knew, or thought they knew, where their interests lay; the only body that zeroed in on the presidential interest was the Budget Bureau.

Key bureau officials alerted Truman to the traps. They squelched a proposal to name the secretary of defense as the stand-in for the president at NSC meetings in the latter's absence, and to house the NSC staff and secretariat in the Pentagon. Budget Bureau officials insured, in addition, that the purely advisory role of the NSC was emphasized throughout the bill and that the president would be clearly free to attend or not as he chose—so as not to be a prisoner in any way of the forum. By 1949, after amendments to the law and a further executive reorganization, it was the vice president who presided in the president's absence, and the staff and structure were formally absorbed and housed in the Executive Office of the President, not the Pentagon.

Truman understood fully what was at issue. In his memoirs, he recounts, with a tinge of sarcasm:

> There were times during the early days of the National Security Council when one or two of its members tried to change it into an operating super-cabinet on the British model. . . . There is much to this idea—in some ways a Cabinet government is more efficient—but under the British system there is a group responsibility of the Cabinet. Under our system the responsibility rests on one man—the President. To

change it, we would have to change the Constitution, and I think we have been doing very well under our Constitution. We will do well to stay with it.

At least one historian has wondered why the State Department did not play a more prominent role in all these interagency negotiations over the role and structure of the NSC system. Especially given the later experience of the 1970s, when White House national security advisers Henry Kissinger and Zbigniew Brzezinski overshadowed the secretary of state in foreign policy, it might have been foreseen that the new NSC system had large ramifications for the department. In fact, George C. Marshall, now Truman's secretary of state, did see many of these implications. When he was shown a draft in early 1947, he responded with a passionate memorandum to the president on February 7 that warned against several sections of the bill, including the new council. Marshall predicted it would introduce "fundamental changes in the entire question of foreign relations"; it would give the military establishment a role of "predominance" in foreign policy and would "dissipate the constitutional responsibility of the President," who would become an "automaton" of the council.

Marshall's reaction helped persuade the White House to take over from the Pentagon the negotiations with Congress regarding the draft bill. But there was no sustained involvement by State in the deliberations. Perhaps this was in part because Marshall could count on the Budget Bureau to fix the most obnoxious features of the original plan— namely, the Defense Department's attempts to control the council. For State, presidential control was one thing; Pentagon control would have been truly anathema. In addition, once the new NSC was up and running, the State Department's Policy Planning Staff under George Kennan managed to gain the primary role in drafting the papers and setting the agenda for NSC meetings. Neither the NSC staff nor any staff in the Office of the Secretary of Defense had yet developed the institutional capacity to compete with the substantive quality of State's work. Military representatives on the NSC staff tried their hand at broad, muscular global strategy papers on such topics as "Position of the United States with Respect to Soviet-Directed World Communism." (This was before the era of generals and admirals with Ph.D.s in international relations from major American universities.) In contrast, Kennan and his staff proposed more concrete agenda items such as (to take

an example from May 1948): "Dhahran, Tsingtao, Austrian Treaty, Japan, Philippines, and Italian Colonies." Papers on these were more useful, and most NSC meetings were devoted to such specific subjects.

The State Department's problem was more long-term in nature— gradually losing its leadership position as other departments (Defense, Treasury) strengthened their own international roles. The State Department was (and remains) organized in a way that, on its face, suits it for the leadership role in the national security community. It has a bureau of political-military affairs, and it has traditionally had the lead role on policy and budgets with respect to security assistance, police training, and other international political-military issues. It has an under secretary for economic affairs and a bureau devoted to economic and business issues. Nonetheless, other cabinet departments have been less and less willing to submit to State's direction.

Don K. Price, respected dean of the Harvard Graduate School of Public Administration, testified to Senator Henry Jackson's national security subcommittee in 1961 that the State Department simply was not well equipped for leadership over other departments when the United States became a world power and needed to integrate all these different strands of national policy:

> The situation we got into at the end of World War II was that a nation that in the 1920's and 1930's had managed to stay pretty isolationist and maintain a Foreign Service that was interested only in very restricted political functions had to take on a tremendous range of military and economic responsibilities and propaganda responsibilities all over the world. The Department of State was consequently not equipped in the slightest degree to take on the direction of those responsibilities.
>
> I think this is what forced the creation by statute of interdepartmental machinery at the Cabinet level to deal with strategy and international security affairs.

The State Department had "abdicated its primacy," Price continued, and could win it back only by years of building up the "necessary personnel and institutional habits." Over the postwar decades, as we shall see, there have been strong secretaries of state who have indeed reasserted some dominance over broad international policies—Acheson, John Foster Dulles, Kissinger, for example. But this seems mainly to have been a function of personalities at the top—of the intellectual and

physical energy of the cabinet secretary and the support of the president for this arrangement. At other times, State has been outperformed by the NSC staff, or the civilians in the Pentagon, or other cabinet departments.

IRONICALLY, while President Truman had asked Congress to create a National Security Council, he never fully overcame his sensitivity with respect to how it might affect his constitutional prerogatives. At the NSC's very first meeting, on September 26, 1947, Truman used the occasion to emphasize in characteristic fashion that it was *"his* council and that he expected everyone to work harmoniously without any manifestations of prima-donna qualities." It was decided not to establish any set schedule for NSC meetings, but to arrange them as required. Of the fifty-seven NSC meetings held from this first meeting until the Korean War (June 1950), Truman himself attended only twelve. He was determined to preserve his freedom of action, as he took pains to stress in his memoirs:

> I used the National Security Council only as a place for recommendations to be worked out. Like the Cabinet, the Council does not make decisions. The policy itself has to come down from the President, as all final decisions have to be made by him.
>
> A "vote" in the National Security Council is merely a procedural step. It never decides policy. That can be done only with the President's approval and expression of approval to make it an official policy of the United States.

Truman had two outstanding secretaries of state in George Marshall and Dean Acheson, and he tended to deal with them directly rather than through the formal NSC mechanism. He also dealt directly, outside of NSC channels, with his secretary of defense, and continued to rely as well on the Bureau of the Budget. The man he chose as executive secretary of the council, retired Rear Admiral Sidney Souers, was a trusted poker-playing friend. Truman also relied on close White House political assistants, first Clark Clifford and later Averell Harriman, to keep watch over national security affairs.

When the Korean War began in June 1950, however, Truman quickly saw value in the orderly processes of the NSC; he began to attend its meetings more frequently and he took steps to streamline its structure.

In wartime, more systematic preparation and deliberation are imperative, and the formality and staff structure enabled this. Of the seventy-
one council meetings from June 28, 1950, through January 9, 1953,
Truman attended and presided at sixty-two of them (or 87 percent).

Truman's jealous guarding of his prerogative was not directed solely
at the new council. Whatever his regard for George Marshall and Dean
Acheson, Truman often found himself railing at the indiscipline of the
State Department. State's opposition to his decision to recognize the
new state of Israel in 1948 triggered this tirade in his memoirs:

> Every President in our history has been faced with this problem: how
> to prevent career men from circumventing presidential policy. . . .
> And it has happened in the Department of State. . . . I wanted to
> make it plain that the President of the United States, and not the sec-
> ond or third echelon in the State Department, is responsible for mak-
> ing foreign policy, and, furthermore, that no one in any department
> can sabotage the President's policy. The civil servant, the general or
> admiral, the foreign service officer has no authority to make policy.
> They act only as servants of the government, and therefore they must
> remain in line with the government policy that is established by those
> who have been chosen by the people to set that policy.

One of Truman's most famous legacies is the image of the thirteen-
inch-long painted glass sign stating THE BUCK STOPS HERE, the gift of a
friend, which sits to this day on his desk at the Truman Library in Independence, Missouri. Truman wins a fairly good grade from Professor
Neustadt with respect to husbanding his presidential authority. Where
FDR did this out of an instinct for personal power, Truman did it out of
an acute consciousness of the duties of the office. Moreover, says
Neustadt, Truman "loved to make decisions"—unlike Eisenhower, who
he says tried to keep away from them, and FDR, who inclined to defer
them. Using a term that George W. Bush would later employ, Neustadt
says that Truman's image of the office "made him sensitive to anything
that challenged his position as decider and proposer."

This image of Truman should not be taken, as it sometimes is, to
mythological heights. Contrary to Neustadt, there is evidence that like
many other presidents he actually did prefer to have his senior subordinates present him a consensus recommendation if possible. "He likes
things to run smoothly," said one intimate. "He doesn't like his advisers

to disagree." Indeed, the fateful decision in the Korean War in October–November 1950 to permit General Douglas MacArthur to charge northward toward the Chinese border—which provoked Chinese military intervention—may have been the product of too much collegiality around the National Security Council table. Acheson's memoirs refer to the deep uneasiness then about where MacArthur's strategy was leading, but which no one was willing or able to express in categorical terms to the president. "I have an unhappy conviction," Acheson wrote, "that none of us, myself prominently included, served him as he was entitled to be served." The result was not only a military disaster but a step toward Truman's confrontation with and dismissal of MacArthur, which was one of the biggest domestic political crises of his presidency.

That decision to authorize MacArthur's northward offensive deserves particular attention; it was a major blunder by an administration that has been justly praised for its wisdom and creativity in shaping America's global policy after World War II. The point worth noting is not the irony that Truman, so often hailed as a great "decider," was the prisoner of a seeming bureaucratic consensus, a sin usually attributed (unfairly) to Eisenhower. Rather, the event raises a question that will recur in this book: To what extent was this a failure of *process*, as opposed to simply a failure of policy judgment? One analyst calls it an example of "groupthink," or an object lesson in Peter Drucker's maxim that "the first rule in decision making is that one does not make a decision unless there is disagreement." Acheson had the same view. "[T]o decide," he wrote, "one must know the real issues. These have to be found and flushed like birds from a field. The adversary process is the best bird dog."

On the other hand, there are examples suggesting that while that kind of adversarial process may be necessary, it may not be sufficient. In the Vietnam case fifteen years later, there was a prominent and articulate dissenter, George W. Ball. President Lyndon Johnson heard Ball's views often, but the prevailing judgment of the president and his other advisers was that the risks that Ball called attention to were manageable or were outweighed by risks on the other side of the argument. And in the case of the Iraq War, President George W. Bush heard dissents from Secretary of State Colin Powell and was aware of analyses that called attention to risks involved in overthrowing Saddam Hussein. Not only the CIA, but also Secretary of Defense Donald Rumsfeld sent his own memorandum listing things that could go wrong. Yet Bush, like LBJ, had to make his own assessment of competing risks that are always much

clearer in hindsight than before the fact. The process of weighing competing risks is not a science; nor is it made easier by counting votes among advisers. Smoking out divergent and dissenting opinions is an excellent starting point, but as we explore this question through later administrations, we need to allow for the possibility that to search for a *procedure* that assures the right decision is to pursue a mirage.

Eisenhower's "Hidden Hand"

President Dwight Eisenhower was a believer in orderly procedure, and he faulted both Roosevelt and Truman for neglecting it. Truman, he jibed, "didn't know any more about government than a dog knows about religion." In his memoirs Eisenhower wrote: "Organization cannot make a genius out of an incompetent. . . . On the other hand, disorganization can scarcely fail to result in inefficiency and can easily lead to disaster." This was a lesson he absorbed from his military career. Richard Nixon, who watched him closely for eight years as his vice president, described the "team" concept and "staff system" as they worked:

> Having chosen his Cabinet and staff on the basis of each man's ability to handle his job, he had confidence in the men working for him, trusted them, and delegated authority to them. Finally, though, in the staff system, he received the essence of the problem, the thinking that went into it, and the recommended solution. And then he either approved the decision, rejected it and substituted his own, or sent the problem back for further study.

Eisenhower institutionalized the NSC process, setting up a schedule of weekly meetings. Over his two terms, the council met 366 times; he presided at 329 of them, or about 90 percent.

During his time in the White House, this desire for orderly process led to a conventional caricature of Eisenhower as a weak leader, a prisoner of rigid staff procedures, dependent on the consensus of his advisers, inarticulate, even a bumbler. This was the widely held view among liberal journalists and intellectuals. It was propagated most vigorously by his predecessor, Harry Truman. One pungent example:

> In 1959, when Castro came to power down in Cuba, Ike just sat on his ass and acted like if he didn't notice what was going on down there,

why, maybe Castro would go away or something. Of course what happened, the Russians didn't sit on their ass, and they got him lined up on their side, which is what you have to expect if you've got a goddam fool in the White House. He was probably waiting there for his Chief of Staff to give him a report, and he'd initial it and put it in his out basket. Because that's the way he operated.

Truman was contemptuous of Eisenhower for having a chief of staff at all: "I said to him, 'The President of the United States is his own chief of staff. . . . [T]he people of the United States . . . don't elect you to sit around waiting for other people to tell you what to do.'" A more elegant version of the same theme was put forward by Richard Neustadt, whose book *Presidential Power* was published during Eisenhower's last year in office. As we touched upon earlier, Neustadt believed that Eisenhower's desire to be "above politics" weakened his hand in what is an inherently political game, and that he failed to develop the "power sense" necessary to preserve his personal leverage.

By the late 1960s, however, a revisionist view of Eisenhower began to appear in some circles of those who had disparaged him. It began with an article by liberal writer Murray Kempton in *Esquire* magazine in September 1967 entitled, "The Underestimation of Dwight D. Eisenhower"; three years later, Garry Wills included a fresh assessment of Eisenhower in a biography of Richard Nixon (*Nixon Agonistes*). This change of attitude may have come in part because, amidst the turmoil of the late 1960s, the relative tranquillity of the 1950s began to look in retrospect like a not inconsiderable achievement. But both Kempton and Wills were also influenced by a unique inside account that Nixon published in 1962. Nixon recounted among his "six crises" the chilling experience of Eisenhower's hinting in both 1952 and 1956 at Nixon's removal from the ticket. In 1952 it was because of the supposed scandal over an alleged slush fund, and in 1956 it was a more opaque suggestion by Eisenhower that, nevertheless, caused Nixon great anguish. Nixon's overall assessment of his patron is the portrait of a shrewd, cold, even calculating leader who treated his vice president at arm's length and is without doubt the dominating figure of the era. In a classic Nixonian turn of phrase, Nixon calls Eisenhower "a far more complex and devious man than most people realized, and in the best sense of those words." From Richard Nixon, this is, if not high praise, then at the very least an authoritative assessment by one battle-hardened practitioner of politics

of the handiwork of another. Eisenhower does not come across as one who was unconscious of his personal political power or of how to use it. Nixon goes on:

> Not shackled to a one-track mind, he always applied two, three, or four lines of reasoning to a single problem and he usually preferred the indirect approach where it would serve him better than the direct attack on a problem. His mind was quick and facile. His thoughts far outraced his speech and this gave rise to his frequent "scrambled syntax" which more perceptive critics should have recognized as the mark of a far-ranging and versatile mind rather than an indication of poor training in grammar.

Kempton and Wills also both cite an episode in Eisenhower's own memoirs in which, just before a presidential news conference during the Quemoy-Matsu crisis in the Taiwan Strait in 1955, his press secretary, James Hagerty, advised him that the State Department preferred that he not comment on the delicate issue. "'Don't worry, Jim,' I told him as we went out the door of my office, 'if that question comes up, I'll just confuse them.'" This anecdote, minor as it is, seemed to both Kempton and Wills first of all to bespeak a healthy self awareness and, second, to confirm Nixon's observation that Eisenhower's much derided syntax at news conferences might not indicate such a deficient intelligence after all.

A full-blown revisionist assessment came in 1982 when Princeton professor Fred I. Greenstein published *The Hidden-Hand Presidency*, a book that fleshed out, on the basis of memoirs and newly opened archives, that indeed Eisenhower was a much more dominant figure in his administration than the caricature had it. Greenstein portrays a leader who exploited his "above-politics" image as a deliberate political strategy to maximize his influence; thus by choice, not lack of ability, he eschewed the image of the "skilled, tough politician" that is Neustadt's model. "Artlessness and art" is Greenstein's description of Eisenhower's style. Where Truman had a desk ornament proclaiming THE BUCK STOPS HERE, Eisenhower had one displaying the Latin motto *Suaviter in modo, fortiter in re* (pleasantly in manner, powerfully in deed).

The most important point is that NSC meetings were hardly the only means by which Eisenhower operated. Whatever the regularity of NSC

procedures, a State Department official history of the National Security Council dismisses the idea that the president was a prisoner of them:

> In fact, Eisenhower was actively in command of his administration, and the NSC system met his instincts and requirements. There is substance in the criticism that the Eisenhower NSC became to some extent the prisoner of a rigidly bureaucratic process, but the criticism misses the point that Eisenhower and [Secretary of State John Foster] Dulles did not attempt to manage fast-breaking crises or day-to-day foreign policy through the NSC apparatus. An examination of several of the major foreign policy problems that confronted the Eisenhower administration reveals that the NSC system was used to manage some and was virtually bypassed in others. . . . Crisis situations . . . such as the Suez crisis of 1956, the off-shore island [Taiwan Strait] crises of 1955 and 1958, and the Lebanon crisis of 1958, were typically managed through telephone conversations between Eisenhower, Dulles, and other principal advisers, and through small meetings with the President in the White House.

The Suez crisis may have been the clearest example of Eisenhower's personal dominance. Eisenhower felt strongly that the British-French-Israeli attempt to seize the Suez Canal by force was objectionable on moral, legal, and political grounds; he wanted the United States to be respected in the Middle East as a mediator and friend of the Arab world, not to be tarred with the colonialist brush. He insisted on significant U.S. political and economic pressure on the three allies to force them to halt their military action. One analyst records that, after Foster Dulles was hospitalized for colon cancer in late October:

> Eisenhower took personal charge of the Middle East crisis by supervising his State Department and United Nations delegations directly from the Oval Office, holding consultations with his military and intelligence brass, and conducting intensive diplomatic maneuvering with cables and transatlantic phone calls to pressure [British Prime Minister Anthony] Eden and the French to disengage.

The recently published transcript of one such telephone conversation with Eden during the peak of the fighting reveals an insistent president ("Anthony, this is the way I feel about it . . .") succeeding in imposing

his will on an exhausted prime minister ("We are going to cease firing tonight").

There is evidence to suggest that both Foster Dulles and his brother, CIA director Allen Dulles, were rooting for the three allies to succeed in seizing the canal before the U.S. pressure kicked in. While the crisis was under way, Allen Dulles sent a message via his station chief in London that the British should either accept a cease-fire or go ahead with the invasion: "Either way, we'll back 'em up if they do it fast." After the crisis was over, a bedridden Foster Dulles, at Walter Reed Army Hospital, stunned visiting British and French leaders by asking: "Why did you stop? Why didn't you go through with it and get [Egyptian president Gamal Abdel] Nasser down?" "If ever there was an occasion when one could have been knocked down by the proverbial feather, this was it," one of the visitors (Selwyn Lloyd) later wrote. It might have been some consolation to the Dulles brothers to know that, a decade later, Eisenhower told at least two interlocutors that he had changed his mind about Suez. It had been his biggest foreign policy mistake, he concluded; U.S. policy in 1956 had only strengthened Nasser as a radical force in the Middle East and weakened the will of our best allies. But at the time, he was without doubt the driver of a very different policy.

Eisenhower's institutionalization of the NSC system included one change that was to grow in significance in future years. It was he who created the post of special assistant to the president for national security affairs. The man he chose was Robert Cutler, who had been a Boston banker, wartime aide to George Marshall, and adviser to the Truman NSC; Cutler's background and conduct of the office established the "honest broker" paradigm later exemplified by Brent Scowcroft in the administrations of Gerald Ford and George H. W. Bush. However, for all the formality of the Eisenhower machinery, the very creation of the position was another step in the strengthening of the president's hand over it.

Kennedy and Johnson

The inauguration of John F. Kennedy in 1961 brought with it two further milestones in the evolution of these institutions—one admirable, the other less so. The less admirable one is the continuation of the pattern of incoming presidents repudiating the practices of their predecessors, sometimes on the basis of politicized misimpressions of what exactly

those practices were. We have seen that creation of the NSC under Truman was in part a rebuke to FDR. Then Eisenhower revamped the NSC system as a rebuke to both Truman and FDR. Kennedy carried this to a new level in reaction to the perceived deficiencies of Eisenhower. And we shall see in later chapters that Kennedy was not the last in this chain.

Learning lessons from the experiences of one's predecessors, positive and negative, is a healthy thing—indeed it is the very purpose of this book. But the rejection of one's predecessor's arrangements should derive from some dispassionate analysis of what works the best; it should not be a political reflex. Astute observers such as I. M. Destler, Leslie Gelb, and Anthony Lake have pointed out the disservice that politicization of these matters can do to the national interest, especially when it is based on misperception and overreaction. The day may come when our political leaders will outgrow this habit. But that day may not come soon: The misadventures of George W. Bush's administration will undoubtedly lead his successors to emphasize changes in management methods and practices. Let us hope they will be the right ones.

Kennedy and his team accepted completely the then conventional view of Eisenhower as a poor leader. They agreed with Neustadt's portrayal of Ike as imprisoned in procedures and weak with respect to husbanding his political leverage over his government. Kennedy told a British television audience in April 1961 that the staff system "[o]ccasionally, in the past, I think . . . has been used to getting a pre-arranged agreement which is only confirmed at the President's desk, and that I don't agree with." As we saw in the quotations from Sorensen and Bundy in Chapter 1, the Kennedy team also came into office with considerable doubts about the competence, intellectual caliber, and loyalty of the cabinet departments.

The result was an emphasis on personal presidential authority, flexibility, and control. Journalist Charles Bartlett, a close friend of the new president, wrote in early 1961:

> The Eisenhower concept was that the bulging Federal Government could only be held in shape with a tight and precise organization at the top. Mr. Kennedy's emerging philosophy is that the gangling structure responds less to organization than to highly personalized leadership.

Sorensen explained in 1963 that:

> The parochialism of experts and department heads is offset in part by a President's White House and executive staff. These few assistants are the only other men in Washington whose responsibilities both enable and require them to look, as he does, at the government as a whole.

The Kennedy administration therefore reverted to a loose, Rooseveltian model of White House staffing, dismantled key pillars of Eisenhower's formal NSC structure, and beefed up the White House national security staff—all with the goal of strengthening the president's personal freedom of action and power of decision. The NSC met as a body less often—only sixteen meetings in the first six months of the Kennedy administration. Another important change was the streamlining and recasting of the role of the special assistant to the president for national security affairs and the NSC staff. Eisenhower had two senior men dealing with these matters: Robert Cutler (succeeded by Gordon Gray), dealing with NSC policy issues, and also Colonel Andrew Goodpaster, who as staff secretary served Eisenhower in a more personal capacity handling day-to-day national security matters including intelligence. These two functions were now combined in Bundy; he was also formally designated as director of the NSC staff. The staff was reduced to twelve substantive officers. No longer was it a large group of sixty-odd civil servants representing their departments and managing a bureaucratic process; though smaller, it was now a staff of bright young academics dedicated to the president's vision. In Bundy's telling phrase in a 1961 letter to Senator Henry Jackson, the NSC staff was now "essentially a Presidential instrument."

Many of the deliberate efforts to dismantle the Eisenhower structure were later reversed by Nixon and not revived by later presidents. But the more lasting legacy of the Kennedy model was the milestone it represented in the further strengthening of presidential control. We have seen these ideas gestating in previous administrations, but the concept of the NSC staff as a *presidential* staff was truly born then, as was the idea of a White House national security adviser and staff with the mission of giving the president independent advice, helping him direct the bureaucracy, and devoted to protecting his interests. Bundy was praised as scrupulously fair in insuring that the president heard the full range of views. But the institution that he and his aggressive staff embodied had been significantly changed.

The small size of the NSC staff in the Kennedy period reflected, paradoxically, a hope that the State Department could be prodded to take charge of implementation and coordination of policy now that Eisenhower's elaborate machinery was dismantled. But State seemed incapable of stepping up to the task. The failed invasion of Cuba at the Bay of Pigs in April 1961 only reinforced the trend of centralization in the White House. Kennedy and his inner circle concluded that the fiasco came, in large part, from excessive deference to departments and agencies that gave poor advice. "The first lesson was never to rely on the experts," wrote Arthur Schlesinger, Jr. Not only were the military and the CIA found wanting, but also State. In a memorandum to the president in June 1961, his staff delicately described its efforts to encourage more energy at State without trampling on departmental prerogatives:

> [T]he White House–NSC group has gradually encouraged the growth of responsible self-reliance in the Departments, and especially in the Department of State. . . . Quietly, but persistently, White House men have pressed for activity and energy. . . . Criticism of the sort lately leveled at White House men for work in Latin America is wildly beside the point; the President's men have sometimes filled vacuums as best they could, but they have never tried to take over the work of men who showed energy and ability of their own.

Toward the end of 1962, after both the Bay of Pigs and the Cuban missile crisis, McGeorge Bundy would sadly conclude in a private note to the president that "[t]he State Department has not proved to be as effective an agency of executive management as we hoped, and above all, it has not shown the capacity for interdepartmental coordination which we hoped to force upon it." A "bowl of jelly" was the president's own assessment, according to Sorensen.

One response was what Schlesinger euphemistically calls a "blood transfusion [at State] from the White House" at the end of 1961. This effectively purged Chester Bowles as Dean Rusk's deputy and implanted men considered Kennedy loyalists—George Ball, George McGhee, Averell Harriman, Walt Rostow, Fred Dutton. Experience had provided "convincing evidence," says Schlesinger, "that the President required people in the State Department whose basic loyalty would be to him, not to the Foreign Service or the Council on Foreign Relations."

Dean Rusk himself was an enigma to the Kennedy White House.

They saw him as personally intelligent, hardworking, and loyal to the president. But they also saw him as passive, unimaginative, and unable to give strong leadership to his department. Arthur Schlesinger recorded that at White House meetings Rusk would "sit quietly by, with his Buddha-like face and half-smile," not forcefully asserting his views. Rusk answered back many years later, saying in a book of reminiscences that he kept his thoughts to himself whenever Arthur Schlesinger was in the room since he knew Schlesinger was a notorious gossip at Georgetown cocktail parties.

White House control was strengthened in other ways. One important step after the Bay of Pigs was to shift the physical location of McGeorge Bundy's office. From the elegant Executive Office Building across West Executive Avenue, where his predecessors had resided since the 1940s, Bundy moved into the basement of the West Wing, a short run up the stairs to the Oval Office. It was a sacrifice of elegance for proximity—a sacrifice that presidential aides are usually willing to make, if not kill for. Another major step was to create the Situation Room, also in the West Basement, so that the White House could receive and send classified communications on its own and not be dependent on the departments to do so. During the Bay of Pigs crisis, decisions on naval and aircraft movements had been relayed from the Cabinet Room to the Pentagon over unclassified telephone lines. State Department historians have concluded ruefully: "More than anything else, the Sit[uation] Room allowed Bundy and his NSC staff to expand their involvement in the international activities of [the] foreign affairs community and become, in essence, 'a little State Department.'"

The Cuban missile crisis of October 1962 saw the Kennedy team revert to some degree to a more structured approach, just as the Korean War had led Truman to a greater appreciation of the National Security Council. Kennedy formally created an "Executive Committee" of the NSC (which journalists later nicknamed "ExComm"), intended as a streamlined and personalized NSC, to conduct the most important deliberations during the crisis. (ExComm's core membership consisted of fifteen top officials from State, Defense, CIA, and the White House, plus Attorney General Robert Kennedy, United Nations ambassador Adlai Stevenson, and outsiders such as Dean Acheson, John McCloy, and Robert Lovett.) ExComm proved so useful for coordinating policy during the Cuban crisis that, until it was formally disbanded in March

1963, it was given other topics to work on, such as policies toward Brazil, the Congo, Europe and NATO, and South Asia. But Bundy successfully argued against its continuation or reactivation, believing that it was not so well suited to lesser issues or for forward planning.

For our present purposes, the Cuban missile crisis is also notable for another reason. A crucial dimension of the crisis's resolution was kept well compartmented from the collegial deliberations of ExComm— namely Robert Kennedy's closely held secret communications with Soviet ambassador Anatoly Dobrynin. This is our introduction to the presidential "backchannel," which became famous—and controversial— in the context of Nixon and Kissinger's secret communications with other governments that bypassed the State Department. Private presidential channels have ample precedent, going back at least to Woodrow Wilson and his confidant Colonel Edward House, or FDR and Harry Hopkins. But in the modern period, in any discussion of good governance, the pros and cons of such irregular procedures inevitably come to be debated. Special channels sometimes offer presidents greater "secrecy and despatch," two qualities that the framers of our Constitution saw as indispensable to diplomacy and to presidential management of it. But there are always complications of one kind or another when regular procedures are bypassed.

Robert Kennedy's channel to Dobrynin did not exclude the cabinet secretaries; Rusk and Defense Secretary Robert McNamara were both part of the small Oval Office team that approved the messages passed. A more serious issue with respect to backchannels has to do with substance—that is, whether the messages passed in the special channel are consistent with what is going on in regular channels. In the case of Reagan's irregular overtures to Iran in the mid-1980s, the message conveyed was in sharp contradiction to U.S. policy at the time, which was to tilt against Iran in the Iran-Iraq War because of the ideological and geopolitical threat posed by Iran after its revolution. Of the many objections posed to this enterprise by Secretary of State George Shultz and Defense Secretary Caspar Weinberger, this to me was the weightiest— namely the policy incoherence that it embodied (see Chapter 6). As for Nixon and Kissinger, the products of their backchannels were surfaced soon enough: The China breakthrough was announced when it happened in July 1971; Kissinger's secret Paris negotiations on Vietnam were disclosed in a speech by Nixon in January 1972. On other issues such as Berlin or strategic arms limitation, understandings reached in

Kissinger's private channel to Dobrynin were quickly introduced by both parties into the official negotiations then going on.

The full extent of the compromise arrangement that settled the Cuban missile crisis—namely the explicitness of President Kennedy's promise to remove U.S. missiles from Turkey within four to five months after Moscow's removal of its missiles from Cuba—was denied in public and kept secret for more than two and a half decades until it leaked from the Soviet side. The secrecy could be justified as important to alliance management—so as not to show that the United States would sacrifice the interests of NATO or its ally Turkey in a bilateral bargain with the Soviet Union. (The U.S. missiles in Turkey were in fact obsolete, and Kennedy had ordered the State Department months before to begin consultations on their removal.) But the public refusal of such a "deal" was also an important part of the Kennedy administration's claim to have remained faithful to its alliances. Administration officials publicly rebuked Adlai Stevenson shortly after the crisis ("Adlai wanted a Munich") for having advocated what the president privately approved. In 1989, Sorensen publicly admitted that, in what historian John Lewis Gaddis wryly calls an example of "custodial historiography," he had taken it upon himself to censor Robert Kennedy's famous posthumously published memoir of the crisis, *Thirteen Days*, to edit out any suggestion that the president had approved such an explicit trade.

FOR HIS PART, Lyndon Johnson inherited and retained John Kennedy's team but the procedures worked somewhat differently. As Walt Rostow has described it:

> Johnson's advisory system for national security policy was built initially around Rusk, McNamara, and Bundy. As a colleague, he had seen these men at work for almost three years. He admired each of them. As a matter of principle, he sought continuity with Kennedy's administration.

Johnson's system proved to be less White House–centered, however, and gave more of a role to his cabinet officers. Like Kennedy he preferred small informal meetings, considering them a more congenial forum for candid discussion and decision, and—very importantly—for minimizing the risk of leaks. By early 1964 he had settled on a new format—the Tuesday lunch. In attendance were the president, Rusk,

McNamara, and Bundy (later succeeded by Rostow). Lunches were scheduled irregularly at first, but, especially as the Vietnam War heated up, almost every Tuesday. Johnson convened some 160 Tuesday lunches over the course of his presidency.

Eventually this, too, came to be caricatured by Johnson's successors. Richard Nixon and Henry Kissinger, as we shall see, had a low opinion of the Tuesday lunches, and Nixon in his 1968 campaign went so far as to attribute serious foreign policy failures to this departure from the discipline and regularity of Eisenhower's NSC. Walt Rostow makes a good case, however, that the Tuesday lunches were in fact a "rather conventional and orderly bureaucratic procedure . . . conducted in a deceptively informal setting." An agenda was prepared; presidential decisions were recorded and transmitted to concerned departments "with full formality." Yet the informal setting encouraged "extraordinary candor," Rostow argued: "Clashing, exploratory, or even frivolous views could be expressed with little bureaucratic caution and with confidence no scars would remain. It was a deadly serious but somehow intensely human occasion."

While the Tuesday lunches may have served the president well as a collegial forum for deliberation, the system still lacked a mechanism for monitoring implementation. Johnson, like Kennedy, looked to the State Department to take the primary role in this. In March 1966, a presidential directive officially—yet again—assigned to the secretary of state the responsibility for overall direction, coordination, and supervision of U.S. government activities overseas. The directive created the Senior Interdepartmental Group (SIG), chaired by the under secretary of state (a title later changed to deputy secretary), with Interdepartmental Regional Groups (IRGs) supporting it, each chaired by the assistant secretary of state responsible for the relevant region.

This was the system that Richard Nixon inherited.

CHAPTER THREE

Richard Nixon

I T WAS AN IRONIC SETTING for plotting a revolution. The Pierre Hotel is an elegant New York landmark overlooking Fifth Avenue and Central Park, its upper stories offering a spectacular panorama of the city. Built in 1930, the Pierre had begun by the late 1960s to let some of its elegance fade, though not its reputation for exclusiveness and luxury. Its guests included some of the Hollywood elite—Cary Grant, Audrey Hepburn, Elizabeth Taylor. From November 1968 to January 1969, it was the scene of a real-life historical drama, as the transition headquarters of President-elect Richard Nixon.

It was here, on the Pierre's thirty-ninth floor, that Nixon had his first conversations with Henry Kissinger, the forty-five-year-old Harvard professor he had chosen as his White House assistant for national security affairs. The two men hardly knew each other; they had met once before at a New York cocktail party a year earlier. But Nixon had read Kissinger's writings and had judged, correctly, that they shared a strategic- and geopolitical-minded view of the world. In these first discussions, Nixon talked of the changes he planned to make in American foreign policy—and in how that policy was made. Kissinger recorded on his yellow pad a blunt edict he received from his new boss: "Influence of State Department establishment must be reduced."

In the previous chapter we saw presidents Harry Truman and John Kennedy lament the State Department's unresponsiveness to presidential authority. Richard Nixon took this assessment a large step further. He had the same view of State Department stodginess, having watched the department as vice president during the eight years of the Eisenhower era. He also believed he had suffered personal slights at the

hands of the East Coast Foreign Service establishment when he was vice president, and even more when he traveled abroad as a private citizen after his political career seemed in ruins. If the Kennedy crowd thought the department was too conservative, Nixon had the opposite perspective. In 1968 he was inheriting not only the Vietnam War but the social transformations that were following in its train. If Nixon was predicting that the antiwar mood spreading in our culture would soon make its way into our foreign policy elite, he was correct.

In short, by his own account, he came into the White House fundamentally convinced that "Washington is a city run primarily by Democrats and liberals." Thus he "urged, exhorted, and finally pleaded" with all his new cabinet appointees, repeatedly, "to move quickly to replace holdover bureaucrats with people who believed in what we were trying to do. [He] warned that if they did not act quickly, they would become captives of the bureaucracy they were trying to change." This was his attitude to the entire federal bureaucracy, not only the State Department, and it would be reflected in some extraordinary measures such as his asking for the resignations of his entire administration following his reelection victory in 1972. We will trace the ramifications of that episode later in this chapter.

Nixon also shared Kissinger's critique of the national security decision-making process they were inheriting from Kennedy and Johnson. Nixon deplored its seeming lack of rigor, its informality, and what he considered its negative results. In a campaign radio address in late October 1968, he pointedly recalled his own attendance (and sometimes chairmanship) of the National Security Council during Eisenhower's eight years of peace. Citing the wars in Vietnam and the Middle East, he went so far as to blame "most of our serious reverses abroad since 1960" on Kennedy's and Johnson's dismantling of the NSC system that they had inherited from Eisenhower and Nixon.

Nixon was taking on Eisenhower's mantle, and identifying it with the National Security Council, but in fact he had something different from Eisenhower's model in mind:

> When Eisenhower selected Foster Dulles as his Secretary of State, he wanted him to be his chief foreign policy adviser, a role Dulles was uniquely qualified to fill. From the outset of my administration, however, I planned to direct foreign policy from the White House.

The New NSC System

In 1961, in its famous examination of the presidential decision making process, Senator Henry Jackson's national security subcommittee had emphasized an important truth:

> Each President will have his own style of doing business—the product of his nature and experience. Each President therefore needs great freedom to adapt his office and procedures to suit the peculiarities of his style. . . . He can use the [National Security] Council as little, or as much, as he wishes. . . . [The Council is] the President's instrument [and] exists only to serve the President.

In designing a new system to meet Nixon's requirements, Kissinger turned to now General Andrew Goodpaster, who had served as President Eisenhower's staff secretary but in 1968 was deputy U.S. commander in Vietnam. Initially agnostic himself on the question of State's proper role in the structure, Kissinger was stunned by the vehemence of not only Goodpaster but Eisenhower himself on the subject. Goodpaster took Kissinger along to visit Eisenhower at Walter Reed Army Hospital. The old man—bedridden, emaciated by his cumulative heart ailments, immobilized by a pacemaker, and having only a few months to live—expressed himself with surprising forcefulness: The system had to be pulled into the White House, he emphasized; the Pentagon would never accept interagency coordination under State Department control. For all his admiration for Dulles, Eisenhower said he had always kept control of the NSC machinery in the White House. Goodpaster later recalled:

> I recommended strongly and Henry agreed that the [senior] interdepartmental groups should be chaired by someone from the White House. The State Department tried to fight this. . . . Nixon stood fast and said, no, the chairing would be done—in other words the agenda would be set—by somebody from the White House. So, the die was cast.

To flesh this out, Kissinger turned to two men—Morton Halperin, a young former Harvard colleague who had recently served as one of Robert McNamara's civilian "whiz kids" in the Pentagon, and

Lawrence Eagleburger, a junior foreign service officer assigned by the State Department. Halperin and Eagleburger drafted a nine-page, single-spaced "Proposal for a New National Security Council System," which Kissinger presented to Nixon at the end of December in Key Biscayne, Florida. Nixon was scheduled to meet there on December 28 with his new cabinet designees William P. Rogers (State) and Melvin Laird (Defense) to discuss the new arrangements. Unbeknown to them, however, the president-elect had reviewed the paper the day before—and already approved it.

The Kissinger memorandum cited the strengths and weaknesses of the Eisenhower system, and set about to offer up a new system that improved upon it. It recommended that the National Security Council meet regularly, as the "principal forum for issues requiring interagency coordination." Below the level of the council, the assistant to the president for national security affairs would chair an NSC Review Group, which would insure that papers presented to the full council properly framed the issues for the president. An Under Secretaries Committee (chaired by State) would handle implementation and follow-up of certain issues, and the Johnson administration's assistant secretary–level Interdepartmental Regional Groups (IRGs, also chaired by State) would continue, but both these committees would become "sub-organs" of the NSC. An expanded NSC staff would monitor the day-to-day business of the cabinet departments, prepare NSC agenda papers, and do longer-range studies.

An innocuous-sounding but very pregnant "note" in the middle of the December 27 memorandum declared: "The elaborated NSC machinery [in this paper] makes the continued functioning of the existing Senior Inter-Departmental Group unnecessary." The SIG, created in 1966, had been the last effort of the Kennedy-Johnson team to give the State Department the leadership role in coordinating and integrating national policy. The memorandum proposed to abolish it, putting the Kissinger-chaired Review Group in its place.

The State Department professionals fought a tenacious rearguard action to change Nixon's mind before inauguration day. The distinguished senior diplomat U. Alexis Johnson, tapped by Nixon to be under secretary of state for political affairs, did his best to argue the matter with Kissinger—and simultaneously to explain to his new boss, William Rogers, a foreign policy novice, why all this was important from the department's point of view. Johnson in his memoirs tells of hurried

conversations in elevators with Rogers and Rogers's deputy-to-be Elliot Richardson to explain the "bureaucratic theology" that was involved, "with which, of course, they were entirely unfamiliar." Johnson's effort was in vain. Over the course of the first year, Nixon ordered other NSC subcommittees to be set up—focusing, for example, on crisis management, strategic arms control, and defense programs—and all were chaired by Kissinger. Every administration since Nixon has retained some version of the White House–centered system he put in place.

Another feature of Nixon's system was his insistence on being presented with policy options. The Key Biscayne memorandum stressed this, and Nixon highlighted it in public statements. A lengthy report sent to Congress on U.S. foreign policy after a year in office devoted a full chapter to his new NSC system. In it, Nixon declared:

> I do not believe that Presidential leadership consists merely in ratifying a consensus reached among departments and agencies. The President bears the Constitutional responsibility of making the judgments and decisions that form our policy. . . . I refuse to be confronted with a bureaucratic consensus that leaves me no options but acceptance or rejection, and that gives me no way of knowing what alternatives exist.

This emphasis on being presented with options was one of the most important features of the Nixon system. It was not really a matter of organization, but it was a central demand he made of the process. Perhaps there was some residual sensitivity that his mentor Eisenhower was still, in those days, often accused of being a prisoner of bureaucratic consensus. In any case, Nixon saw it—correctly—as a vital element of presidential control. Not every president works this way; many chief executives, before and since, have found it more comfortable to encourage their cabinet colleagues to agree on a recommendation. Nixon—his determination to dominate the process only reinforced by his suspicions of the bureaucracy's loyalty—was insistent on making the choices himself. His NSC staff had the task of forcing the bureaucracy to present policy issues in this way; if this effort was unavailing, as it often was, the staff spent much of its time writing its own memoranda to the president laying out, as fairly as it could manage, what the choices were, and the pros and cons. Not only was Nixon not afraid of choosing among sharply conflicting recom-

mendations; he was, as we shall see, fully capable of overruling his cabinet secretaries when they agreed among themselves.

Thus, under Richard Nixon the history of the National Security Council and the NSC system reached its climactic point. The institution that Harry Truman had been wary of as a possible infringement on his presidential prerogative had become, through the changes wrought by first John Kennedy and then Richard Nixon, an instrument of presidential control.

But this is only part of the story. There is much that the institutional history does not explain. The replacement of the SIG by the Review Group has become part of the folklore, perceived as a great victory for Kissinger that established his power; it has even been referred to as the *"coup d'état* at the Hotel Pierre." But Kissinger himself is skeptical of this assessment. The SIG episode, he has written, was "important less in terms of real power than in appearance and in what it foretold about the President's relations with his principal advisers"—as "the first of seemingly unending skirmishes" between Nixon and Rogers, which Rogers invariably lost. Kissinger concluded:

> [I]n the final analysis the influence of a Presidential Assistant derives almost exclusively from the confidence of the President, not from administrative arrangements. My role would almost surely have been roughly the same if the Johnson system had been continued.

Even the Nixon system was designed, on the face of it, as a collaborative bureaucratic process, albeit with the White House in the lead. Morton Halperin stresses that it worked that way at the beginning:

> The [interagency] system was not a fraud, and was not intended to be mainly a camouflage for the secret work being done for the President by Henry Kissinger. It was taken seriously by Richard Nixon and Henry Kissinger and was meant to be taken seriously by the bureaucracy.

Halperin points to some useful early interagency papers done on Vietnam, the Middle East, and strategic forces. Indeed, Nixon and Kissinger continued for the first few years to rely on the NSC process to elicit the best thinking that was available in the government.

The question then becomes: What is it that so undermined the president's confidence in the State Department that it led him to build up

Kissinger's role even further? The answer lies in a series of missteps committed by the department in the first two years of the administration, over both the procedure and the substance of policy, which compounded Nixon's suspicions and led him to strengthen White House dominance even beyond the White House–centered bureaucratic process he had started with.

Stumbles by State

For many people at State, the new NSC procedures apparently took some getting used to—particularly Nixon's insistence on policy choices. There is a classic Kissinger joke about how the bureaucracy responds to requests for options. If the president wants options, they offer him three: Option 1 is nuclear war; option 2 is surrender; and option 3 looks strangely like existing policy. Sir Humphrey in *Yes Prime Minister* would understand completely. But, alas, there is a basis for the joke. The historians who compile the invaluable archival series *Foreign Relations of the United States* have included the record of an early meeting of the new NSC Review Group, on February 13, 1969, chaired by Kissinger, on the subject of East-West relations. The account is not based on notes taken by the NSC staff or the State Department representative, as might be expected. Instead it is a summary by a neutral participant (the CIA representative), who could barely conceal his amusement at what he was witnessing. The policy paper presented to the Review Group by the State Department's European affairs bureau did not set forth alternative approaches; it was, rather, an advocacy paper on behalf of existing policy. The CIA observer continued:

> The paper contained some half-hearted gestures toward meeting the options format which Kissinger had requested, but these alternate options were patently straw men, lacking both internal logic and conviction. . . . The State Department view was that . . . in reality . . . there is only one view which "responsible people" can hold regarding policy toward East-West relations, and that view is set forth as Option 3, "Strong Deterrent with Flexible Approach." Gradually during the course of this discussion agreement was reached that Option 3 as stated was so broad that it needed to be articulated in a series of suboptions. As Kissinger put it, "Surely there is divergence between the attitudes expressed by the Arms Control and Disarmament Agency on

the one hand, and those of the Joint Chiefs of Staff on the other. Somewhere between these two outer wings are other defensible positions. The President and the NSC should be given the opportunity to discuss this range."

The State Department's difficulties carried over into substance, not only procedure. Nixon came into office with some clear views on the kind of policy he wanted to carry out, especially with respect to the two dominant issues of the period, U.S.-Soviet relations and the Vietnam War. Contrary to some accounts, Nixon never claimed in his campaign that he had a "secret plan" to end the war; that was media mischief. But he did believe that the United States had not exerted its full leverage to press the Soviet Union to exert leverage over North Vietnam. It followed from this that our diplomacy toward Moscow should feature Vietnam more prominently, and that our policy on issues that seemed to be of interest to the Soviets—especially arms control, expansion of trade, and the Middle East—should not be considered in isolation but treated as linked to other matters we cared about, especially Vietnam.

This was the famous notion of "linkage." Nixon declared in his very first news conference, for example, on January 27, 1969, that arms talks should be conducted in a way that promoted progress on "political" issues. Kissinger used the term "linkage" in a background briefing for reporters on February 6. Nixon sent a letter to secretaries Rogers and Laird and CIA director Richard Helms on February 4 laying out his reasoning in more detail.

Prevailing opinion in Congress, the media, and the State Department, however, favored strategic arms control and East-West trade as the key solvents of international tensions and thus as necessities in their own right. President Johnson had been on the verge of commencing arms talks with the Soviets in August 1968, which were canceled because of the Soviet invasion of Czechoslovakia; Nixon was pressed by his critics—and by his own diplomats—to relaunch them (what later became the Strategic Arms Limitation Talks, or SALT) as soon as possible. Crucial opportunities would be lost, he was told, if he continued to dawdle. Likewise, Congress began pressing for liberalization of U.S.-Soviet trade, and the Soviets were pressing to play a diplomatic role in the Middle East.

But Nixon did not want to be stampeded. He wanted to probe what was possible with the Soviets on Vietnam; he and Kissinger were also

concerned that more analytical work needed to be done in the U.S. government (on issues such as verification, weapons capabilities, and U.S. strategic requirements) before we would be ready to begin negotiating on SALT. Nixon also understood that in demonstrating that he could successfully withstand domestic pressures, he was gaining bargaining leverage with the Soviets. For all these reasons, he did not wish to agree immediately to a date for the relaunch of SALT.

In the State Department, the president's letter of February 4 on linkage was assumed—correctly—to have been drafted by Kissinger and his staff; this may have been thought a sufficient reason not to take it too seriously. The fact that Nixon had personally and publicly proclaimed the same doctrine in his news conference (not to mention signing and sending the letter) did not seem to register. For whatever reason, State proceeded to pursue its preferred approach. On March 19, U.S. chief negotiator Gerard Smith reassured his Soviet counterpart that the start of SALT "need not be tied, in some sort of package formula, to the settlement of specific international problems." At an April 7 news conference, Rogers predicted that SALT would begin "in the late spring or early summer." On Rogers's instructions, U.S. diplomats in Moscow suggested dates in June or July. Press leaks to diplomatic correspondents kept the world informed of this movement. Nixon, worn down and preempted by all these pressures, reluctantly agreed in early June to inform the Soviets that we were ready.

Our diplomats displayed a similar impatience over Vietnam. Peace talks had begun in Paris at the end of the Johnson administration; an understanding had been reached, through Soviet mediation, by which the United States halted the bombing of North Vietnam in return for a halt to Communist attacks on major population centers. Early in Nixon's term the Communists resumed their shelling of Saigon and other cities. This did not lessen the eagerness of American diplomats to resume the talks, which also seemed to overtake considerations of what strategy we might pursue. In January 1969, an article written by Kissinger when he was still a Harvard professor appeared in *Foreign Affairs;* it suggested a new approach to the negotiations, namely to concentrate with the North Vietnamese on resolving the military issues (cease-fire, U.S. withdrawal, and return of prisoners of war), while leaving the political future of South Vietnam to a longer-term negotiation between the Communist and non-Communist South Vietnamese. Nixon supported this approach of separating the military and political

issues (and it later became the basis of the 1973 Paris Agreement). On March 8, 1969, with the shelling continuing, and without consulting the White House, Rogers called in Soviet ambassador Anatoly Dobrynin, proposed immediate private talks with North Vietnam, and assured him we were willing to talk about political and military issues simultaneously. Kissinger complained bitterly to Nixon's chief of staff, H. R. (Bob) Haldeman, that Rogers's reversal of policy was "disastrous." This episode, as we shall see, played its part in establishing the role of a special White House backchannel to Dobrynin.

Yet another area of East-West relations proved controversial. Nixon had the idea of visiting Romania in the fall of 1969, as part of his around-the-world trip after meeting the Pacific Ocean splashdown of Apollo 11 following its return from the moon. Romania, while remaining a member of the Soviet-led Warsaw Pact, had broken with Moscow earlier in the decade, somewhat as Charles de Gaulle had struck an independent course in the North Atlantic Alliance. Nixon was the first American president to show the flag in Communist Eastern Europe; his Romanian visit in 1969 was followed by trips to Tito's Yugoslavia in 1970 and to Poland in 1972. The point of all these unprecedented visits was to demonstrate that the United States did not concede Soviet dominance in Central or Eastern Europe. This was an especially significant message for the United States to convey in the year after the Soviet invasion of Czechoslovakia and proclamation of the "Brezhnev Doctrine"—the doctrine of Soviet leader Leonid Brezhnev that demanded obeisance to Moscow as sole leader of the "socialist camp."

The State Department quickly leaked its negative view of the Romania enterprise, however. The trip arrangements having been made through White House channels, journalists sympathetic to State were quick to proclaim that the visit was a "disturbing" development and a "blunder." Nixon was accused of recklessness—of being needlessly provocative to the Soviet Union and foolishly endangering SALT and other vital negotiations with Moscow.

Events like these soon altered Kissinger's assumptions about his job. Despite the beefing-up of the NSC system, Kissinger had started out with a rather naïve idea of what his role would be. I remember his saying during the transition that he wanted to focus on basic strategy and long-range planning, and not get dragged into the "cable-clearing" business—that is, the flood of telegrams around the clock back and forth between the State Department and overseas posts, issuing instructions in the

name of the secretary of state and reporting back on overseas developments. Yet, Kissinger soon learned that this operational activity *was* our foreign policy. "Tactics turn into strategy," as he later told Haldeman. If Kissinger and his staff did not exert themselves to insure that outgoing instructions reflected the president's policies, all the brilliant strategizing in the West Wing would be overtaken by the reality of the policy being made by the State Department in its cables. In this lay the origin of one of the great melodramas of the Nixon administration—the tug-of-war between Rogers and Kissinger over operational policy.

Throughout 1969, the White House struggled to gain control over important policy cables that State sent out. In June, for example, the State Department issued instructions to U.S. diplomats at the Vietnam peace talks in Paris, including for meetings with Soviet representatives, without clearance by the White House. Kissinger called Attorney General John Mitchell to complain that the Soviets "must think we have lost our minds" on the basis of State instructions contrary to presidential guidance. (Mitchell, like Haldeman, was known to be a close political confidant of Nixon and was thus in a position to reinforce Kissinger's authority.) Mitchell agreed strongly with Kissinger's assessment— "could not be stronger about anything he has run into down there." Nixon thereupon sent a memorandum to Rogers on June 20 reaffirming his instruction that "departmental telegrams be cleared with the White House to insure that I am kept fully abreast of communications on important policy and operational matters of Presidential interest." Rogers replied that "policy" matters, of course, should be cleared with the White House but that he reserved the discretion to decide what "operational" details need not be called to the president's attention. Nixon sent another message to Rogers on June 26 reaffirming his interest in both "policy" and "operational" matters. Problems continued, to the point that Kissinger met on a Saturday morning with Mitchell on July 12, 1969, to go over a long list, compiled by his staff, of State deviations from presidential guidance on U.S.-Soviet relations and Vietnam.

Nixon then tried again. On September 1, while attending a National Governors Conference in Colorado Springs, he issued a more formal directive, this time addressed to Rogers, Laird, and Helms, reaffirming that all public statements and press releases "on matters of known or potential Presidential interest," as well as official communications "with policy implications," must be cleared by the White House. NSC staffers later discovered that the president's Colorado Springs directive was

never distributed within the Department of State—indeed, that most directives emanating from the White House were assumed at State to be merely Kissinger products and some were thought even to have been sent out without the president's knowledge. These assumptions were incorrect.

Kissinger's complaints about State continued, leading Nixon to muse in a philosophical vein to Haldeman in October 1969 about Kissinger's "overreactions" and "obsession with *total* compliance and perfection." Haldeman recorded in his diary: "K[issinger] argues that you have to maintain tight discipline on the little things or you can't control the big ones, P[resident] feels you should lose the ones that don't matter and save your strength and equity for the big battles that really count." When, later in the month, another conflict arose having to do with State's contacts with the Soviets on the Middle East, Nixon groused that Kissinger was "obsessed beyond reason with this problem." Haldeman called it a "tough one, because there *is* some real merit to K's concerns about Rogers' loyalty."

Over the next few years the conflicts between the White House and State only multiplied. The controversial U.S. and South Vietnamese military operation against North Vietnamese bases in Cambodia at the end of April 1970, which unleashed passionate protests across the United States, had their reverberations in Foggy Bottom: Fifty foreign service officers and two hundred other officials from State sent a letter to Rogers on May 8 denouncing the president's policy. Periodically, Kissinger's staff would pull together yet another compilation of instances of State's overeagerness in contacts with the Soviets, press leaks disparaging presidential policy, refusals to clear important cables at the White House, and/or efforts to curry favor with Congress at White House expense. This author helped to compile some of them. At various times, Nixon vented to Haldeman his frustration with the behavior of both Kissinger and Rogers, his tentative conclusion that one or the other would have to go, and, ultimately, his desire that someone else (Haldeman or Mitchell) handle it. But the issue for Nixon, in the end, was not personalities but policy. The most damning material in the NSC staff's burgeoning dossiers had to do with examples of real deviations from presidential policy, and Nixon knew he had to back Kissinger. Losing Kissinger would be a "major loss," Nixon commented to Haldeman in September 1970, "and then State and Rogers would run rampant which would be very bad."

At the end of November 1970, Kissinger's deputy, Brigadier General Alexander Haig, sent Haldeman a short memo listing five new items that he considered "indicative of the problems we are having with the Department of State." They included press leaks plausibly attributable to State either disparaging or distancing itself from Nixon's policies. This triggered a series of private conversations between Nixon and Haldeman over the next few days. On December 3, Nixon concluded he "may have to bite the bullet" and fire his old friend Rogers, but he wanted to "put a fully documented case together." Thus, this time it was Nixon who asked for a full dossier on press leaks attributable to State that undercut presidential policy—it was not Kissinger who volunteered it. The next day Nixon repeated his instruction to Haldeman to talk to Rogers:

> making the point that there are two different fights here. One is [between] K[issinger] and Rogers, and that the P[resident], of course, has to side with Rogers on. But the second one is much more important: that's the foreign service vs. the P. There it's unforgivable, and the P is going to have heads rolling. Since Cambodia, they've been taking on the P, leaking, etc. These things don't just happen, and from now on, it's us or them. State can't be told anything, and that's the way it is.

Haig responded to the president's request on December 7, 1970, with what the archivists call "a twenty-three-page detailed description of more than 70 press leaks concerning, among other topics, Southeast Asia, Latin America, the Middle East, Europe, and SALT." Haig's signature, but probably my work.

Nixon later became fond of quoting British statesman William Gladstone to the effect that the first requisite for a prime minister is to be a good butcher—lamenting that he lacked that quality himself. In 1970, abhorring personal confrontations, he postponed any action to discipline or replace his secretary of state. Rogers remained in office three more years.

Exclusively Eyes Only

Nixon resorted to another strategy—conducting operational policy more and more from the White House, relying on Kissinger and the

NSC staff to implement it. This was Nixon's personal rebellion against Richard Neustadt's dictum that presidential power is "the power to persuade." Given Nixon's introversion, he was never likely to attempt to follow that method. Bypassing the rest of the government was procedurally and psychologically much simpler—and also insured a centralization, consistency, and coherence in policy that has rarely been seen before or since.

A symbolic step occurred in the summer of 1970 when Kissinger's office moved upstairs. A renovation and reorganization of the West Wing shifted the White House press corps from its traditional loitering area in the front lobby to what is today the press briefing room, and turned the lobby into a dignified reception area for those visiting the president or other senior officials. This also opened up what became an elegant office on the northwest corner facing onto Pennsylvania Avenue. No longer in the basement, Kissinger—and most of his successors—now resided on the same floor as the Oval Office, and only a few steps away.

Elder statesman Dean Acheson commented on the Kissinger phenomenon in the July 1971 issue of *Foreign Affairs*, in an article written even before the dramatic announcement that month of Kissinger's trip to China. Its title was, significantly: "The Eclipse of the State Department." In it Acheson did not lament, deplore, or complain of what was happening to his beloved department; he acknowledged it and sought to explain it. To Acheson, both the Constitution and much of American history demonstrated the fundamental "fragility" of the secretary of state's position. When President William McKinley ordered the U.S. Navy to take the Philippines and destroy the Spanish fleet, thereby launching the United States into the world as a great power, he did not bother to consult or inform his secretary of state. Woodrow Wilson, once he burst on the stage as a world statesman, saw no reason to share that stage with secretaries of state he did not particularly respect; he was content, in Acheson's words, "to rely upon his own typewriter and the reports of his unofficial ambassador-at-large and collaborator, Colonel Edward M. House of Texas." Franklin Roosevelt distrusted the State Department and ignored Secretary of State Cordell Hull as we have seen. Acheson did not omit to mention John Kennedy's distrust of the department and quest for more personal control over policy. Perhaps his own close relationship with Truman had been the exception:

What has been occurring [Acheson concluded] has not been that the
White House advisers have edged the foreign office out of functions
being competently performed but that they have been needed to do
what is not being done anywhere to the satisfaction of the man
responsible, the President.

RELATIONS WITH THE SOVIET UNION, as we have noted, were a priority
for Nixon. All U.S.-Soviet negotiations had come to a virtual halt after
the Soviet invasion of Czechoslovakia in August 1968, and the Kremlin
was wary of Nixon and his reputation as a Cold War hard-liner. Soviet
ambassador Dobrynin paid his first courtesy call on President Nixon on
February 17, 1969, a month after inauguration. Kissinger had already
suggested to Nixon that he invite Dobrynin to set up a confidential
channel to the White House. Toward the end of the meeting, Nixon dismissed both Kissinger and the State Department representative from
the Oval Office and told Dobrynin he wanted this special channel
established through Kissinger. When Secretary Rogers misspoke to
Dobrynin on March 8, with respect to the president's Vietnam policy, as
noted earlier, Nixon sent Kissinger to see Dobrynin on March 11 to tell
him that the Soviets' impression of a change in U.S. policy was "premature." Nixon soon began using the Kissinger-Dobrynin channel to step
up diplomatic pressure on the Soviets to press North Vietnam into serious negotiations. In mid-April, Kissinger warned Dobrynin that Vietnam could become a major obstacle to U.S.-Soviet relations and handed
him a note, initialed by Nixon, proposing a special negotiating channel
between the United States and North Vietnam outside the existing
Paris framework. While at that time Nixon was thinking of some distinguished private American as the emissary, this later became Kissinger's
own secret talks with the North Vietnamese.

Dobrynin recounts in his memoirs that he was initially taken aback
by this "two-tier" method of diplomacy, but soon adapted to it. But while
Dobrynin mastered the complexities and delicacies of actually working
in two separate channels in Washington, he reports that his boss,
Foreign Minister Andrei Gromyko, had a more difficult time on a visit to
the United States in the fall of 1969.

The main subject of Gromyko's visit happened to be the Middle
East, on which the convolutions in the U.S. government were particularly complex. Secretary Rogers was developing a Middle East peace

plan, with Nixon's approval, but Nixon was at the same time somewhat skeptical of the effort and reserving his own judgment. Gromyko, visiting for the United Nations General Assembly, had two conversations over lunch with Rogers and was pleasantly surprised; he concluded that the United States and Soviet Union were close to an agreement on the Middle East. He was so excited he wanted to report this to Moscow. With difficulty, Dobrynin persuaded him to wait:

> Gromyko became very angry: "I came here to negotiate with the secretary of state. I don't want to listen to you."
>
> After the lunch broke up and Gromyko asked me: "What do we do now? What do we send to Moscow?"
>
> "Nothing for the time being," I replied. "Let's wait for a meeting with the president."
>
> Gromyko then became really angry. "What kind of secretary of state is this?" he said.
>
> The next day Gromyko met with Nixon and of course discovered that what Rogers had confusingly told him reflected neither the president's nor Kissinger's policy.

The Kremlin eventually got the hang of it, and Kissinger's back-channel with Dobrynin was to be the vehicle for a number of diplomatic advances. The first came when they broke a procedural impasse on SALT. The Soviets had been pressing hard to stop the anti-ballistic missile (ABM) system that Nixon had proposed to deploy; the American side wanted limits on the rapid Soviet buildup of offensive missiles. Kissinger and Dobrynin hammered out an agreement to discuss limits on both offensive and defensive systems in parallel. This was announced on May 20, 1971—and caught both sides' diplomats by surprise. A few months later came a breakthrough on Berlin. A formal negotiation had begun in early 1970 among the four powers occupying postwar Berlin (the United States, Soviet Union, United Kingdom, and France); it produced an agreement in 1971 that assured Western access to the city and essentially ended the Cold War crises over Berlin that had bedeviled the Truman, Eisenhower, and Kennedy administrations. Progress came fitfully in this complex multilateral negotiation, but was spurred by understandings reached on key points through secret communications among Kissinger, Dobrynin, and West German chancellor Willy Brandt's confidant Egon Bahr. Dobrynin was also aware of Kissinger's secret talks with

the North Vietnamese in Paris, and the channel was used occasionally, as we have seen, to try to engage Moscow to press Hanoi. In most negotiations, deadlocks are eventually raised to a higher political level for top leaders to resolve. But it is usually a cumbersome formal process involving interagency negotiations. In the Nixon administration, the backchannel kept the top political levels involved on both sides and facilitated rapid decisions.

The private channels that Nixon authorized Kissinger to set up with Dobrynin were only part of an elaborate diplomatic network that emanated from the White House. Kissinger's secret talks at safe houses in the Paris suburbs with North Vietnamese Politburo member Le Duc Tho—not the official talks at Avenue Kléber downtown—turned out to be the forum in which a Vietnam settlement was reached in January 1973. Nixon in his meetings with foreign leaders in the Oval Office or on trips abroad would tell his interlocutors that any special messages to him should be conveyed through Kissinger. Similar special channels were set up with 10 Downing Street and with the Elysée Palace, to match that with the West German Chancellery, either through their ambassadors in Washington or through the leaders' trusted advisers in their capitals; the common feature was that foreign ministries were generally excluded. White House and NSC staff documents dealing with the sensitive diplomacy received the exuberant classification marking: TOP SECRET/SENSITIVE/EXCLUSIVELY EYES ONLY.

The opening to China, probably the most celebrated product of this process, was also an illustration of how various elements of Nixon's system worked. Nixon had published an article in *Foreign Affairs* in 1967 expressing interest in easing the hostility between the United States and China that was the legacy of the 1949 Communist takeover and the Korean War. On February 5, 1969, just over two weeks into the administration, one of the first of the new National Security Study Memorandums from the White House formally instructed the departments and agencies to study various issues with respect to "Communist China" including "alternative U.S. approaches on China and their costs and risks." This produced an interagency paper by May, which contained useful analyses of China's militant ideology, the Taiwan problem, U.S. trade and travel restrictions, U.N. membership, U.S. interests in Asia, and other issues. But from Nixon's and Kissinger's perspective these analyses, while useful as a catalogue, treated the various concerns "as if they existed in a vacuum." The Soviets and Chinese had just had a

series of unprecedented military clashes along their border, and opportunities presented themselves for a more triangular American diplomacy. Nixon had already decided he wanted to signal to the Chinese that we were interested in a rapprochement and that we opposed Soviet aggression against them. The interagency process was proving decidedly unhelpful when it came to these basic questions of strategy. When Nixon's intentions in this direction became widely known—indeed, little of this was secret—delegations of senior State Department diplomats even came to the White House to counsel him against it, since it risked provoking the Soviet Union. They were not thinking the same way he was.

Thus the pattern emerged that Nixon and Kissinger looked to the bureaucracy for technical expertise, but not for strategy. On June 26, the NSC Under Secretaries Committee, chaired by Rogers's deputy Elliot Richardson, was directed to provide detailed recommendations on how the United States might modify the various legal restrictions then in effect on trade, travel, and other intercourse with China. The resulting paper was a useful, indeed indispensable, menu of all the steps one could take. But Nixon reserved for himself the decision on which ones to implement, at what pace, and in what context. Nixon was doing his own signaling to China—not only through some of these unilateral steps to liberalize exchanges, but also through public comments distancing ourselves from Soviet bullying of China, and private comments to heads of state known to have good ties with China's leadership.

Initial contacts with Beijing were made in regular diplomatic channels in 1969 and 1970 through American and Chinese ambassadors in Warsaw. But the State Department weighed the talks down with a detailed agenda of technical issues, and shared the results with at least ten foreign governments. "We'll kill this child before it is born," Nixon sighed. When the breakthrough came, it was through the sensitive Pakistani backchannel. From then on, the contacts were kept secret from the Department of State, and indeed from NSC staff members who had no need to know. Winston Lord, Kissinger's senior special assistant and colleague on the China initiative, tells of the contortions that he went through to maintain different sets of books. When Kissinger set out on an around-the-world trip in July 1971, only some members of his traveling party knew of the secret two-day detour from Pakistan into China. In fact there were three sets of briefing books:

One set for those who were going into China. . . . Another set were for those knowing that people were going into China, but were part of the cover team staying back in Pakistan. . . . And then the third briefing book was for those who didn't even know there was going to be a China leg. And I swear to God, we'd get them all updated and I'd put my head on a pillow, and Kissinger would then wake up and look at it and want it redone again, and I've got to do all three all over again.

There is a common perception that secrecy in the conduct of foreign policy is a conspiracy to conceal blunders and/or criminal behavior. On occasion, perhaps, but that is not the reason the framers of the Constitution were so forthright in recommending "secrecy and despatch" as qualities needed in the Executive Branch for the conduct of diplomacy. Most often, secrecy in negotiations is what enables compromises to be made. If one party's deliberations about possible concessions are leaked, that could doom its domestic support and undermine the whole enterprise; when negotiations are kept confidential until final results can be disclosed (and they certainly should be disclosed), the trade-off of mutual concessions is evident and domestic support more likely to be sustained.

In the China case more broadly, the reason for secrecy had to do with the desire to shield a delicate initiative from the many forces that had an interest in torpedoing it. When Nixon announced to the world on July 15, 1971, that Kissinger had just returned from China, a state that we had treated as hostile for over two decades, the effect was stunning. They had been deathly afraid of premature leaks, which could have been shaped, manipulated, or exploited by various parties that had maximum incentive to sabotage the policy—the Soviet Union, Taiwan, some of Taiwan's American supporters, et al. Controlling the China disclosure meant that Nixon's July 15 announcement could explicitly reassure friends and allies—especially Taiwan, Japan, and South Vietnam—that the United States would consult intensively before Nixon's own trip to China, which did not come until February of the following year. Premature disclosure by another party with a negative spin ("betrayal!") could have turned the July 1971 event into something wholly different from the positive event that the world now remembers. Instead of a dramatically successful initiative, the same Kissinger trip could have been turned into an even more dramatic fiasco. Control over disclosure can be a synonym for control of one's own policy.

Secrecy is not popular, especially among journalists whom it deprives of interesting stories to write. Even among historians, it is common to deplore the Nixon administration's allegedly "compulsive" devotion to secrecy, when it would be difficult to identify a president in this book who did not strive to keep important things secret and rail at leaks. Most of the substantive products of the Nixon administration's backchannel diplomacy, though, have been kindly treated. The American ambassador to Japan, Armin Meyer, who learned of the Kissinger trip only when he heard Nixon's announcement over Armed Forces Radio while sitting in a barber chair in Tokyo, conceded in his memoirs that his initial bitter embarrassment gradually gave way to acknowledgment that the Japanese government, leaky as a sieve, could not have been counted on to keep the initiative secret if it had been informed in advance. John Lewis Gaddis has acknowledged, "To have consulted the Departments of State and Defense, the C.I.A., the appropriate Congressional committees, and all allies whose interests would have been affected *prior* to Kissinger's 1971 Beijing trip would only have ensured that it not take place." Gaddis is similarly charitable toward the contribution of the backchannels during the SALT and Vietnam negotiations.

Perhaps the most massive and famous of all leaks of classified documents came on June 13, 1971, a Sunday morning that saw the opening installment of the *New York Times*'s publication of the Pentagon Papers—a documentary record of American involvement in Vietnam compiled in the Pentagon toward the end of the Johnson administration. Kissinger's deputy, Alexander Haig, briefed Nixon by telephone on what the published documents included, reassuring him that documents of the Nixon administration were better protected:

H[AIG]: It's the most incredible thing. All of the White House papers; Rostow papers; communications with the ambassadors; JCS [Joint Chiefs of Staff] studies.
P[RESIDENT]: We have been more careful, haven't we? We have kept a lot from State, I know, and enough from Defense.
H: Your White House papers are in very good shape.
P: That's why we don't tell them anything.

Nixon and Kissinger also had a conversation that afternoon, Kissinger calling in from California. Less than two weeks earlier, through the Pakistan channel, the Chinese had formally invited

Kissinger to visit Beijing in July to prepare the way for a trip by Nixon. Savoring this success made up at least in part for the shock of the Pentagon Papers, but it, too, emphasized for these men the necessity as they saw it to keep the rest of the government at arm's length. "Dulles always used to say that he had to operate alone because he couldn't trust his own bureaucracy," Kissinger said. "I just wish that we operated without the bureaucracy," Nixon responded. Kissinger laughed, and Nixon then realized the irony of what he had just said, adding: "We do." "All the good things that are being done," Kissinger said. "Yeah, we do, we do, we do," Nixon repeated.

Nixon's Trade-off

A treatment of the Nixon-Kissinger relationship published by historian Robert Dallek in 2007 makes much of the personalities—the backbiting, sniping, jealousies, insecurities, and tensions among Nixon, Kissinger, and Rogers. Personality disorder is, indeed, its explicit theme. Dallek makes use of the flood of now disclosed transcripts of meetings and telephone conversations that constitute the most intimate chronicle of an administration's inner thoughts that we will ever have. These are conversations (or at least parts of them) that could never have been meant for the historical record or public consumption. Previous administrations managed to keep such exchanges to themselves. It is unlikely that the Kennedy brothers, when they discussed their political opponents in the Oval Office, were reading responsively from the Sermon on the Mount, nor Lyndon Johnson when he conferred with his staff while doing his business on the toilet. But they were wise enough to leave no records of this. By the same token, administrations after Nixon's have undoubtedly learned their lesson and severely cut back the kind of records they keep in the first place. Thus, a few historians' gain is many historians' loss.

The more important point, however, is that preoccupation with personal idiosyncrasies is misleading. Nixon and Kissinger (and Rogers and Laird) were grappling with more profound problems of policy than most administrations are faced with—not only to extricate the country from Vietnam in honorable fashion, but to put in place the main elements of a post-Vietnam foreign policy (U.S.-Soviet relations, China, Middle East peace process) while doing so. Dallek's book has relatively little analysis to offer on the substance of these foreign policy challenges, and

much of what it does say is a rather conventional critique from the liberal point of view. The reader is left to conclude that departures from conventional liberal ideas are to be associated with personality disorder.

A richer and more illuminating account is to be found, perhaps surprisingly, in the State Department archivists' product, *Foreign Relations of the United States*. Like an epistolary novel, the documents tell a story that unfolds over the first two years of the administration. The Kissinger memoranda on the creation of the new NSC system are all there. Internal papers of the State and Defense departments record their efforts to push back. The NSC staff periodically compiles memos and press clippings to document State's deviations from presidential policies. State Department officials complain that Kissinger and his staff are having their own meetings with foreign diplomats of which the department was not officially informed. Kissinger's appeals to Nixon, Haldeman, and Mitchell for support are recorded, including vivid excerpts from Haldeman's diaries. Nixon frequently expresses his affection for both Rogers and Kissinger, his frustration at the continual conflicts, and his conclusion that he has to back Kissinger on the substance.

What comes through in this dispassionate record is the tragic aspect. As the story unfolds, all the elements of the train wreck fall into place. The leaders at State are unable to grasp at first that they inhabit not just a new administration, but a new kind of administration. They are used to a world in which presidents set broad lines of policy and leave it to the State Department to implement—indeed, presidents usually ratify broad policies that the professionals originate as well as carry out. Lyndon Johnson's decisions on the Vietnam War were usually the product of a regular bureaucratic deliberation. Even John Kennedy's high-powered NSC staff consisted of only a dozen people, who saw their job as prodding the bureaucracy, not substituting for it. But Richard Nixon was a president who came into the Oval Office after an unprecedented personal immersion in foreign affairs and who wanted not only to initiate broad policy but to control its execution in order to insure it was consistent with what he wanted.

The May 20, 1971, breakthrough on SALT was a watershed bureaucratically as well as in arms control. Until then, the NSC system for interagency deliberation had been working more or less as Nixon intended. It elicited the best information and ideas available in the U.S. government, and empowered Nixon and Kissinger to set the strategy. The secret backchannels gave the White House the option of involving

itself directly at key moments in key negotiations. They had the best of both worlds.

But in mid 1971, as the extent of Kissinger's backchannel diplomacy began to be revealed—SALT, Berlin, China, and Vietnam—the documents show the bureaucratic game beginning to change. Instead of constant White House complaints about, or efforts to prevent, State Department actions at variance with the president's wishes, it was increasingly clear that the White House was taking the policy initiative into its own hands. Foreign governments figured out that if there was any inconsistency between what they heard from the White House and from State, the White House view counted. Internal documents show the State Department struggling more and more to keep up with what the president, Kissinger, or the NSC staff were doing. When a Kissinger background briefing to the press made news, Rogers would sometimes complain bitterly to Kissinger and/or to Haldeman if he thought it inconsistent with the policy he was pursuing. When Nixon met with foreign leaders, Kissinger was usually the only other person present (perhaps besides an interpreter). Records of the president's meetings were often not sent to State, or only after a delay. Thanks to creative photocopying, the transcripts we sent to State often omitted sensitive passages for example, early exchanges with the Soviets about a possible summit meeting.

As the years went by, State's initial incomprehension eventually gave way to a twofold reaction. For Rogers personally, the reaction was one of wounded acquiescence. When the president informed Rogers of the May 20, 1971, accord on SALT, Haldeman had to go over to the State Department afterward to soothe Rogers's hurt feelings. Rogers was clearly upset—not at all by the substance of the accord but by the personal embarrassment: Haldeman recorded that Rogers was afraid of being embarrassed that it would be known that he was not involved. "[I]t was clear," Haldeman concluded, that Rogers "was very worried about the short-term impact on his own image and hadn't yet figured out the long-term implications." Much later, in January 1973, Winston Lord and I were invited by Rogers to accompany him to Paris for the official public signing—by foreign ministers—of the Vietnam agreement that Kissinger had secretly negotiated (and in which Winston and I had participated). Rogers played his ceremonial role with dignity, with consummate courtesy to the two of us, and with no outward sign of the humiliation that this Paris trip embodied.

But for the rest of the bureaucracy, some significant battles continued, especially over SALT, where the complex negotiations still depended on interagency collaboration. Kissinger and his staff continued to try to use the NSC system to elicit information, analysis, and options from the bureaucracy, as the system was designed for; they would then frame the choices for Nixon. But as the departments came to realize the pivotal role of the Kissinger backchannel, the result was not resignation but an ingenious form of revenge. Especially as Nixon's second term began, and the political climate shifted to the right, the departments discovered that they could take hard-line positions without bearing responsibility for achieving them in a negotiation with the Soviets—since that was on Kissinger's shoulders. The bureaucracy suddenly shifted to Nixon's right, when it had been on Nixon's left in his whole first term, and this fed into the national debate on foreign policy, which was itself drifting to the right once U.S. troops were out of Vietnam.

As for Rogers, his personal saga played out into the summer of 1973. Nixon finally sent Haig to tell Rogers in August that the president wished his resignation. Rogers calmly replied to Haig that if the president wanted this, he would have to ask for it himself—which, of course, Nixon was loath to do. Eventually Nixon screwed up the courage to invite Rogers in for the painful conversation. Kissinger recounts: "To everyone's surprise and Nixon's immediate intense relief, Rogers made it easy for his old friend. Without letting Nixon speak he submitted a letter of resignation free of recrimination or argument. It was a classy performance."

Nixon recounts in his memoirs that he had chosen Rogers to be secretary of state because Rogers was "a strong administrator," who "would have the formidable job of managing the recalcitrant bureaucracy of the State Department." If that is what Nixon expected, he miscalculated. The record shows many expressions of Nixon's regard for Rogers; Rogers as attorney general in the Eisenhower administration had stood by Nixon loyally and advised him astutely during the various attempts to drive him from the ticket over allegations of wrongdoing. (And Rogers, a pillar of the legal profession, seems to have been a strong attorney general.) But Nixon, as we have seen, did not want a secretary of state who actually made foreign policy. That was the trade-off: Rogers's mission was to keep the Foreign Service in line and loyally carry out the president's policy—to be "a staff man to the President on foreign policy, not the competitor," as Haldeman once put it in a conversation with Nixon.

The root of the problem is that it was difficult for Rogers to be a "strong" secretary of state when he had no background in foreign policy. This handicap made it harder to impose the president's will on a formidable career service. There is an American tradition of appointing a prominent lawyer as secretary of state. In the early years of the twentieth century, when much of America's international involvement had to do with international law, this was a natural thing. Dean Acheson and John Foster Dulles, two of the strongest secretaries in the post–World War II period, came out of that tradition, but they also had had extensive foreign policy experience before they took command of the State Department. Since 1945, given the scale and scope of our strategic challenges, policy inexperience is a weakness in any cabinet officer whose job is to impose political direction on the bureaucracy. A weak secretary of state is not a competitor of the president, certainly, but by the same token his command over the department is likely to be weak—compounding, not solving, the president's problem of managing the bureaucracy. Nixon's trade-off backfired.

Two of the presidents treated in this book who most effectively performed as "their own secretaries of state"—Nixon and George H. W. Bush—had both been, perhaps not by coincidence, immersed in foreign policy for eight years as vice president and in Bush's case had had other high-level diplomatic and policy experience. Bush picked a strong and loyal individual, James A. Baker III, who while not a foreign policy expert had been a strong treasury secretary (which involves a significant international role) and who, most important, consciously and effectively ran the State Department as an instrument of presidential policy. (See Chapter 7.) Nixon made a poorer choice, soon concluded that the State Department was not responding to his policy direction, and developed an alternative machinery to bypass it.

Naming a strong individual as secretary of state requires a considerable self-confidence on the part of a president. This self-confidence can take two forms. One is a willingness to defer and delegate to the secretary, comfortable in the belief that his or her actions will reflect loyalty to the president and the president's broad wishes. This is the model of Truman and Acheson, Ford and Kissinger. The risk involved in the future is that a president who is not a master in foreign affairs may have a difficult time keeping an energetic secretary under control. The second model is that of presidents who are confident of their own mastery of foreign policy and also confident of their ability to give direction to a

strong secretary whom they trust to know what kind of foreign policy they want. This is the model of Eisenhower and Dulles, Bush 41 and James Baker. Nixon's relationship with Kissinger as his secretary of state is another example of this, though it was heavily affected by the complexes of Nixon's first term and by the unprecedented upheaval of Watergate. Nevertheless, the converse—avoiding a strong personality out of fear of being overshadowed, or of having a competitor—is usually a bad choice for a president, compounding the president's problem of bureaucratic control.

Melvin Laird's Pentagon

Melvin Laird of Wisconsin, a distinguished conservative and Republican leader in Congress, was not only an experienced defense expert but a master politician. Back in 1967, planning his run for the White House, Nixon mentioned to former President Eisenhower that he was considering Laird for a role in his campaign. Eisenhower was hesitant; Laird was "the smartest of the lot, but he is too devious." When Nixon, as president-elect, told Eisenhower he had picked Laird as his secretary of defense, the old man repeated his doubts. Nixon reports that Laird then paid a call on Eisenhower, after which Eisenhower "told me he thought I had made a good choice. Flashing his famous grin, he said, 'Of course Laird is devious, but for anyone who has to run the Pentagon and get along with Congress, that is a valuable asset.'" This talent of Laird's would also enable him frequently to outmaneuver Kissinger, the NSC staff, and Nixon's desire to gain some control over defense policy.

Defense policy is a different animal from foreign policy. There is no way for a president to bypass the Department of Defense on military operations, or to set up an alternative mechanism for determining defense budgets and programs. Thus Laird, unlike Rogers, held a lot of the cards. He also remained influential in Congress through his friendship with key committee chairmen. Kissinger says of Laird:

> There was about him a buoyancy and a rascally good humor that made working with him as satisfying as it could on occasion be maddening. . . . Laird accepted bureaucratic setbacks without rancor. But . . . I eventually learned that it was safest to begin a battle with Laird by closing off insofar as possible all his bureaucratic or Congressional

escape routes, provided I could figure them out, which was not always easy. . . . But even with such tactics I lost as often as I won.

Laird, like Rogers, had his initial concerns about the new NSC system that the president-elect and Kissinger were designing during the transition at the Pierre Hotel. But when Kissinger met with Laird over dinner at a hotel in Washington, Laird withdrew his formal objections on the basis of some understandings that he and Kissinger reached relatively easily. One sensitive issue, however, only lightly touched upon in this initial exchange, had to do with the president's direct contacts with the Joint Chiefs of Staff, bypassing the secretary of defense. This was the subject of a written exchange between Kissinger and Laird shortly after inauguration. Kissinger did his best to assure Laird that the secretary of defense would be the addressee of "all official National Security Council communications," but that this routing was "not intended to affect the direct access between the President (and the NSC) and the Joint Chiefs of Staff, nor their statutory role as the principal military advisers to the President and the NSC." This issue remains a delicate one. No commander in chief can relinquish his right of direct communication with his military subordinates, yet if it is done in a way that weakens the standing of the secretary of defense it can do harm to another important principle, that of civilian control of the defense establishment. Empowering rather than weakening the secretary of defense is a key to that principle. Nixon, as we shall see, was to exercise this prerogative in ways that complicated his relations not only with Laird but, ironically, with the military.

The new NSC system included a subcommittee meant to provide interagency (and especially White House) supervision of defense programs and budgets. But Laird successfully fended off the intrusion. In the fall of 1969, the president approved creation of a Defense Program Review Committee (DPRC), intended to review, as he reported to Congress, "the major defense policy and program issues which have strategic, political, diplomatic, and economic implications in relation to overall national priorities." Nixon wanted to be able to review these issues while the defense budget was still in its formative stages, and to have interagency advice on the strategic context (actual and potential threats; criteria for determining requirements; etc.) and on the trade-offs with domestic priorities. He signed a directive in this vein in April 1970 after Laird had dragged his feet for several months in submitting

the Pentagon's budget and program plans to interagency scrutiny. Compliance with this directive remained grudging, fitful, and partial.

Withdrawing U.S. troops from Vietnam was the subject of another continuing tug-of-war between the president and his secretary of defense. Nixon's announced strategy in Vietnam had two components: first, Vietnamization, that is, training and equipping the South Vietnamese army so that it could take over combat responsibility from U.S. troops, and second, the negotiating track, that is, the effort to induce North Vietnam to accept a compromise settlement. Nixon all along hoped to be able to remove all U.S. troops by the end of his term—not coincidentally, around the time he would be up for reelection. But his strategy for withdrawing was, as we would say now, conditions-based. He was determined to control the timing and pace of the withdrawals, and the size of withdrawal increments, in accordance with his overall strategy, which included persuading the North Vietnamese of our staying power and maintaining flexibility to use the remaining U.S. troops for significant military operations as long as possible. He also wanted to keep his cards close to his vest, so that the impact of his announcements would not be frittered away by leaks. For example, after a number of short-term, small-increment withdrawals in 1969, to reassure the public that we were on a gradual but clear path to leave, in early 1970 he faced the problem of withdrawals potentially cutting into real fighting strength in Vietnam.(The North Vietnamese, meanwhile, were stepping up their military actions in neighboring Laos and Cambodia.) Kissinger came up with the idea, announced by Nixon on April 20, 1970, of a much larger withdrawal of 150,000 troops, to be spread out over a year. But this was to be back-loaded—keeping the bulk of the designated troops in place for most of 1970. The announcement bought more time with the American public but also preserved strategic flexibility.

Laird was responding to other imperatives, however. As a politician he was sensitive to public and congressional pressures to keep pulling troops out. The uniformed military, as an institution, was happy to be on its way out of Vietnam as well. Nixon's concerns about Hanoi's perceptions or about the blow to U.S. credibility from too fast a withdrawal were matters of broad strategy with which Laird was personally less concerned.* Laird's office was not above leaking its own, more rapid,

---

*A similar phenomenon was to be seen a generation later under George W. Bush with respect to troop withdrawals from Iraq. See Chapter 9.

withdrawal plans to the press, to force Nixon's hand or make clear that delays in getting out were Nixon's fault, not Laird's. This was the classic syndrome of a cabinet secretary insuring that the president, not he, would bear the onus of controversial decisions.

A week before the April 20, 1970, announcement, therefore, Nixon convened a meeting of his NSC principals on the subject but withheld from them that he had already decided on the 150,000/one-year plan. Instead, he solicited recommendations while pretending to be thinking of another small increment as before. While our men on the ground in Saigon, Ambassador Ellsworth Bunker and General Creighton Abrams, were aware of Nixon's thinking and supported it, Rogers and Laird were informed only a few hours before Nixon's speech. Kissinger recounts:

> The maneuvers of Nixon and Laird to steal the credit for each announced troop withdrawal from Vietnam were conducted with all the artistry of a Kabuki play, with an admixture of Florentine court politics of the fifteenth century. . . . But it was a game that Nixon, being less playful, more deadly, and holding the trump cards of the Presidency, rarely lost.

More dramatic clashes with his cabinet secretaries came when Nixon ordered controversial military operations in Indochina, overruling their dissents. The first was the U.S. and South Vietnamese attack on North Vietnamese sanctuaries in Cambodia in the spring of 1970, opposed by both Rogers and Laird; the second was the U.S.-supported South Vietnamese strike against a key node of the Ho Chi Minh Trail in Laos in early 1971, opposed particularly by Rogers. Nixon considered both these operations strategically necessary if the gradual, controlled U.S. disengagement from Vietnam was not to turn into a rout. As we saw, he was husbanding the remaining U.S. troops in order to be able actually to inflict blows on the enemy. In the heated environment of the time, this was a controversial idea.

In March–April 1970, action was forced on Nixon by a North Vietnamese offensive that threatened to overthrow the Cambodian government, which would have expanded the North Vietnamese sanctuary in Cambodia from small base camps along the border to the entire extent of the country. Nixon did not see how the U.S. strategy in Vietnam could survive this. Rogers argued that events in Cambodia were not a serious threat and that little would be gained by a military operation;

Laird supported shallow cross-border operations by the South Vietnamese but his political antennae told him that a major involvement of U.S. troops would provoke a domestic reaction. Even Kissinger had had initial doubts about a U.S. ground operation. Laird also claimed that General Abrams did not support the bigger plan—which Nixon and Kissinger, having contacted Abrams directly, knew not to be the case. In the end, Rogers and Laird were not wrong about the domestic controversy, but Nixon—like FDR and the North African campaign—had a more strategic view and made his lonely (and courageous) decision. The combination of the Tet Offensive, and the enemy's loss of Cambodia as a logistics base, virtually ended the war in the southern (and most populous) part of South Vietnam.

The bitterness of the dissension surrounding the Cambodian operation took its toll on Nixon, however. Press leaks from both departments distanced their secretaries from the decision amidst the firestorm of domestic protest, ignited not only by the military escalation but by the killing of four students by National Guardsmen at a demonstration at Kent State University a few days later. This painful experience shaped Nixon's deliberation the following year when General Abrams sent in a recommendation for a strike against the Ho Chi Minh Trail. Kissinger recounts:

> Nixon was determined not to stand naked in front of his critics as he had the year before over Cambodia. This time he would involve his key Cabinet officers in every facet of the decision-making, to force them to take some of the heat of the inevitable public criticism.

The decision-making process for the Laos operation proved somewhat less convoluted (though Rogers dissented forcefully). Unfortunately, the South Vietnamese, who in this case did all the ground fighting, were pushed back by the North Vietnamese and this operation proved controversial because it failed.

ONE LAST, but not least, dimension of Nixon's relationship with his Defense Department deserves mention here. One possible reason for the "buoyancy" that Kissinger observed in Mel Laird is that, it turns out, the Defense Department was much better informed than the State Department as to what Nixon and Kissinger were up to. The Pentagon had a three-tiered spying operation going on, targeted on Kissinger's office.

The first tier was Laird's use of the National Security Agency (NSA) and the Defense Intelligence Agency (DIA) to monitor White House backchannel activities. Laird later regaled journalist Seymour Hersh with how one of his first moves as secretary of defense was to call in the two men he had chosen to head these two DoD-run agencies: "I brought them into my office and told them they'd better be loyal to me," Laird says. "If they were, they'd get four stars after four years. . . . And goddamn it," Laird add[ed] with a laugh, "they were loyal." (And sure enough, they both received their fourth stars in September 1972, a few months before Laird left office.) Hersh asserts that Laird thus received "a steady stream of information" on Kissinger's contacts with the Soviets, Chinese, and North Vietnamese. The NSA intercepted backchannel messages; the U.S. Army Signal Corps tracked White House telephone conversations; the Special Air Missions branch of the U.S. Air Force ran the fleet of aircraft that Kissinger used. (Laird reportedly had advance knowledge of Kissinger's secret trip to Beijing by these means.)

The second tier was the famous Yeoman Charles Radford, the young Navy man assigned to the small military office in the NSC staff whose job was to serve as liaison to Chairman of the Joint Chiefs of Staff Admiral Thomas Moorer. It seems the office was not simply a transmission belt for authorized communication but had a more entrepreneurial assignment—that of stealing whatever information it could about Nixon's and Kissinger's activities. During his fifteen months on the job before being caught, Radford told Hersh, he managed to purloin some five thousand documents, through making photocopies or stealing discarded carbons or from notes he took. The liaison office was located across the street in the Executive Office Building, not in the West Wing of the White House. But Radford, an expert stenographer, ingratiated himself with Haig and accompanied Haig on three sensitive missions on which Nixon sent him to talk to leaders in Southeast Asia, such as South Vietnamese president Nguyen Van Thieu. Radford stole documents from burn bags of discarded classified material or on occasion directly from Haig's briefcase, including EYES ONLY reports that Haig sent to the president and Kissinger.

Radford hit the jackpot when he was assigned to accompany the Kissinger party on the round-the-world trip in July 1971 that included the secret detour to China. Not meant to be witting of the China stop— he was in Category 3 of Winston Lord's three categories of briefing

books—he found out nonetheless, rummaging through papers in Kissinger's room in Pakistan before the China visit. On the flight home, he delved into Kissinger's document briefcases and took notes on Kissinger's private message to Nixon on his talks with Chinese premier Zhou Enlai.

When the White House uncovered this caper in December 1971, Kissinger and Haig wanted Moorer fired. Nixon demurred, considering Moorer loyal and useful in other respects, and not wanting another scandal damaging to the U.S. military. Radford was quietly reassigned to Salem, Oregon. Nothing leaked until early 1974. According to White House assistant John Ehrlichman, who first investigated the matter, Nixon was happy to leave Moorer in place, with the admiral knowing "we had the goods," and even to reappoint him to another term as chairman. "After this, the admiral was preshrunk," as Ehrlichman put it.

A third, and perhaps even more productive, part of the Pentagon's intelligence-gathering was Chief of Naval Operations Admiral Elmo Zumwalt's private window into Kissinger's front office. Zumwalt and Kissinger got along well, at first, after the brash and innovative admiral became CNO in June 1970. Kissinger trusted Zumwalt to the extent of using Navy communications for some of the early backchannels involving Pakistan and the Berlin negotiations. While Zumwalt maintained his outward cordiality, at some point he concluded that the secretive style of the Nixon-Kissinger White House was not to his liking and Kissinger's worldview was too Spenglerian for his taste. Meanwhile, Zumwalt persuaded Kissinger that he needed more Navy personnel on the NSC staff, and for the next few years Zumwalt sent over a succession of bright young officers for one-year stints as special assistants to Kissinger. Crammed though they were into a tiny closet-sized room between Kissinger's office and Haig's in the West Wing front office, they had an unequaled vantage point on everything going on—discussions of all the most sensitive diplomacy, helping prepare the most secret plans, listening in on Kissinger's telephone conversations with Nixon, Rogers, Dobrynin, and others.

Zumwalt disclosed with some satisfaction to JCS historians in 1990 that "assigning carefully chosen lieutenants to serve as Kissinger's aides" was one of the means by which he obtained information the White House was attempting to deny. "I had my own spies," he told another interviewer. In some cases their reporting was oral and informal. In other cases it may have been more systematic. Seymour Hersh's book

on Kissinger quotes several passages from what he calls an "informal journal" kept by an unnamed close Kissinger aide and "carefully shared with at least one senior member of the government outside the White House." Its intimate revelations of goings-on in the front office are the kind of reporting that a young man sent over from the Zumwalt Employment Service would have been in a position to do.

The White House consciously shared much sensitive information with the chairman and the chiefs, to keep them informed of the president's thinking—often on condition that it not be shared with Laird. This caused frequent awkwardness inside the Pentagon when, for example, Laird's deputy David Packard peeked at Moorer's briefing book during an NSC meeting and saw a document with a White House letterhead that he and Laird had not received; the liaison office tried to solve this problem by henceforth snipping off the White House or NSC letterhead from sensitive documents before photocopying them. Zumwalt also met frequently himself with the admirals in charge of the JCS liaison office, as a way of keeping informed.

Zumwalt told the JCS historians he had concluded that the Nixon-Kissinger strategy was "to 'divide and conquer' the bureaucracy by selectively withholding information," and he saw it as his mission to overcome this. Thus was the Defense Department, too, in rebellion against Nixon's effort to centralize control over policy. Students of civil-military relations in a democracy may want to examine this further as an interesting case study. It is not clear whence derives the constitutional or statutory obligation of a president of the United States to share his most sensitive diplomatic strategies with his chief of naval operations—or even, truth be told, his secretary of defense. But it was an ironic result. The liaison office that employed Yeoman Radford had been envisioned by Nixon as a way to cultivate a special relationship with the Joint Chiefs. In Haig's recollection, Nixon wanted them to have direct knowledge of his views so that they would know "what he wanted them to do in a crisis and why he wanted them to do it." We saw above, with respect to Vietnam troop withdrawals and military operations, that direct communication with the commanders insured more accurate White House understanding of their thinking.

Whatever the root causes of this unhealthy situation, it illustrates for a president, among other things, the perils of weakening one's secretary of defense. The military is a career bureaucracy, unique in many ways, to be sure, but also meant to be subordinate to political authority; for

this, the president requires a secretary who can be the instrument of this presidential authority. Laird's reluctance to step up to this role made its own contribution to all this—his inclination to be a spokesman for the military's cautious instincts over Vietnam rather than for the president's strategy. But the principle remains, and we can see the price that Nixon paid. There is an analogy with William Rogers: If a president lacks confidence in his cabinet officer, he should replace him, not bypass him. It is hard to imagine Donald Rumsfeld agreeing to serve under an "arrangement" such as that of Nixon and Laird. A president, in his own interest, should be looking for ways to strengthen his secretary of defense, not undercut him.

Nixon and Kissinger

There are many different accounts of the Nixon-Kissinger relationship, some even accurate. They include conflicting accounts of who deserves credit for the administration's achievements with China, the Soviet Union, and the Middle East. Especially while they were in office, there were both admirers and detractors of Kissinger who were convinced that he was exerting a Svengali-like influence over the California politician. Nixon loyalists like William Safire responded with a counterimage of Nixon as the "puppetmaster" manipulating his petulant and insecure "marionette" of a national security adviser. Given the hemorrhage of intimate records, as we have seen, others content themselves with simply portraying the relationship as a dysfunctional one.

What I saw close-up, as a member of Kissinger's staff, was something different. Nixon was not only thoroughly knowledgeable in world affairs; he had the deepest intuition and shrewdest strategic judgment of any modern president. This was coupled with raw personal and political courage. A quintessential loner, withdrawn and awkward—that is, not having by any means the gregarious personality that usually characterizes American politicians, and, on top of that, having seen his career ostensibly destroyed on multiple occasions—he persevered in spite of all in a lifetime career of politics whose indignities he must have hated every waking minute. Thrusting his way back after repeated humiliations, he reached the pinnacle. The life of Richard Nixon was an astonishing display of the sheer force of will.

By the same token, he was no natural executive. For all his strategic insight and conviction, he needed subordinates to shield him from dis-

traction, sustain his morale, and implement his policy preferences (including filtering out the orders he really didn't intend to be carried out). "Nixon distrusted his own impulsiveness," Safire has noted, "and placed Haldeman between himself and the rest of the world as a safety catch on a trigger." Likewise he needed trusted subordinates to impose his policies on a recalcitrant government. He was impatient with detail and allergic to face-to-face disagreements of any kind. His loyalists, who often heard him expound brilliantly on world events, may not have been conscious of how great the distance is between exposition and execution. Therefore he needed not only a Haldeman but a Kissinger. Kissinger provided the specifics of both strategy and tactics. The scores of analytical memoranda that Kissinger provided for Nixon, especially before any important diplomatic mission by either of them, are a much better record of this than informal (and idiosyncratic) telephone conversations. Kissinger was also possessed of a remarkable (and probably unexpected) degree of bureaucratic tenacity. Without a partner with these qualities, Nixon, given his own qualities, would not have had the means to implement his visions.

But Kissinger was no natural executive either. While he had honed his competitive skills in the faculty wars of academia, he had never run or managed anything larger than a Harvard summer seminar for promising mid-career leaders from foreign countries. He had brilliance, intellectual self-confidence, and physical stamina—but in the early days he was socially shy. That is where the NSC staff and structure came in, including a capable deputy in Alexander Haig who smoothed over his rough edges in dealing with the bureaucracy. The new organizational structure did bring more of the reins of power into Kissinger's hands; the enlarged and capable staff gave him a sustained ability to monitor the rest of the government and ride herd on it—or to implement an alternative policy bypassing that government. And his celebrity—the product of a series of diplomatic achievements—as it came gradually, further strengthened his bureaucratic clout.

Thus I saw the Nixon-Kissinger relationship evolve, though not so much in their work method as in the personal intangibles. No simple description captures the relationship amid all the changes. In 1971–1972, after the revelations of Kissinger's role in significant secret diplomacy, the relationship became something very different from what it had been in 1969. Similarly, in 1973, when Nixon was weakened by Watergate and Kissinger's celebrity seemed more and more

to come at his expense, it was far different from what it had been in 1971.

At the very beginning, Kissinger was no superstar. He had real reasons to feel insecure as an outsider among Nixon's close-knit political team—a longtime associate of Nixon's rival Nelson Rockefeller; a Republican who socialized with liberals; an intellectual in a crowd of loyalist political operatives. Safire observed that "[t]o the President, he was more deferential than any of us [were]; we excused this on the grounds that he was the newcomer to the group, had never called Nixon by his first name or been made to feel needed by a man struggling to come back." While much was made of the "coup d'état" of the abolition of the SIG, the Kissinger-chaired NSC Review Group that replaced it was composed of deputy and under secretaries and hardly gave him dominance over their superiors, the cabinet officers. His continual complaints to Nixon, Haldeman, and Mitchell about State Department deviations from policy are further evidence of his lack of decisive leverage without their consistent backup. While Kissinger appeared on the cover of *Time* magazine a few weeks after taking office, he remained known mainly to foreign policy specialists and Washington insiders: He spoke to the media exclusively on an anonymous "background" basis— Nixon had given strict orders to that effect—and he did not appear on television until a CBS 60 *Minutes* segment on him in late 1970. He gave no televised news conferences until mid-1972 (his fourth year in office), and delivered no on-the-record policy speeches until his fifth year (a speech on Europe in April 1973).

Before Kissinger went off on any sensitive diplomatic mission, as mentioned, he and his staff prepared a strategy paper and the two men spent hours deliberating on strategy and tactics. Nixon made his preferences clear, but he invariably sent Kissinger off with a broad mandate to use his judgment. There were two important episodes in which Kissinger did exercise his judgment, leading to some short-term, long-distance tensions between the two. In April 1972, before a pre-summit trip by Kissinger to Moscow, Nixon wanted him to stress Vietnam with Brezhnev and not give the Soviets "a goddamn thing—unless we get something on Vietnam." Kissinger, once in Moscow, made a strong pitch on Vietnam but then decided to tempt Brezhnev with a discussion of other issues that magnified the Soviet leader's stake in the forthcoming summit. SALT and the expansion of trade were two of the issues; a third was the fact that Willy Brandt's "Eastern Treaties" (renouncing

West German territorial claims on East Germany, Poland, and the USSR) were hanging by a thread in the Bundestag and Brezhnev wanted American help. Kissinger's approach paid off. A few weeks later, the North Vietnamese launched a major military offensive against the South and Nixon retaliated on May 8 with the biggest U.S. escalation of the war—resuming the bombing of North Vietnam—but Brezhnev's huge stake in the summit (scheduled for May 22) kept him from canceling it.* The successful summit—the first-ever visit by an American president to Moscow—neutralized the antiwar protest in the United States and essentially guaranteed both Nixon's Vietnam strategy for the rest of 1972 and his reelection.

In the fall of 1972, Kissinger's North Vietnamese interlocutor Le Duc Tho began making concessions in the secret Paris talks. Kissinger was convinced that Hanoi saw the impending U.S. election as a deadline, fearing that Nixon could prosecute the war without restraint after reelection. Kissinger in fact thought Hanoi was miscalculating—that pressures on Nixon to end the war would only grow in a second term—but he saw value in squeezing the North Vietnamese up against their self-imposed deadline. Nixon, for his part, was torn. He was by that stage certain to win and did not need a peace agreement for electoral reasons; indeed, he and his political advisers were nervous that a compromise settlement before the election would only alarm his conservative base.

On October 8, bearing out Kissinger's thesis, Le Duc Tho presented to Kissinger in Paris a compromise proposal that for the first time accepted Nixon's preferred framework for a settlement—a solution to the military issues (cease-fire, U.S. troop withdrawal, and return of prisoners), leaving the political conflict to be resolved by the South Vietnamese parties. Hanoi dropped its long-standing demand that the United States turn over the South Vietnamese government to the Communists. "[I]t is the same proposal made by President Nixon himself," Le Duc Tho declared. Kissinger spent four days working out a text that pinned the North Vietnamese down on the key details. Nixon, campaigning, was sent only brief reports of what was transpiring—"more tantalizing than enlightening," as he later put it.

Yet he always backed Kissinger up. In the Vietnam case, Nixon

---

*Brezhnev's canceling the summit would also have left the Americans in bed with the Chinese, whose summit with Nixon had occurred three months earlier. It was a vindication of "linkage," though not exactly as had been anticipated in 1969.

understood that he would have no support for keeping the war going once it was known the North Vietnamese had accepted his proposal for ending it. Whether with foreign leaders or with the bureaucracy, Kissinger's decisive asset was the president's authority—his credible claim to be speaking for the president and his ability to sustain that claim. On the strategies and philosophy of foreign policy the two were intellectual allies. Compare the case of Zbigniew Brzezinski, President Jimmy Carter's national security adviser, who had the same intellectual advantage over a weak State Department but under a schizophrenic president who had no consistent foreign policy philosophy and often split the difference between Cyrus Vance's liberalism and Brzezinski's harder-line views. (See Chapter 5.) Moreover, Kissinger was fortunate enough to move to the State Department in 1973, which enabled him to rest on his own institutional base of power when that presidential authority was crumbling over Watergate.

Kissinger at the Department of State

When Kissinger became secretary of state in September 1973, he retained his post as national security adviser; he was not about to permit anyone else even to attempt to get between him and the president as he had done with Rogers. His new deputy in the White House, the trusted Air Force Lieutenant General Brent Scowcroft, managed the interagency process. When Haldeman and Ehrlichman were jettisoned in April as casualties of Watergate, Nixon pulled Kissinger's former deputy Alexander Haig out of the Army and made him White House chief of staff. Kissinger's home base was secure. Haig writes with some relief that Kissinger as secretary of state now outranked him again, "which restored not merely the appearance but also the reality of cordial relations between us."

Some observers have been tempted to speak of the Watergate period as a "Kissinger Presidency" or "Nixon-Kissinger Presidency," but this exaggerates a complicated situation. Kissinger himself acknowledges the unprecedented nature of his stewardship of foreign policy during a collapsing presidency; by accident of history he had achieved a degree of personal stature that enabled him to assert American authority internationally that could compensate in part for the loss of the president's. But the record will show that Nixon had not entirely lost his touch. During the October 1973 Arab-Israeli War, when difficulties mounted in resupplying Israel by indirect means (such as charter aircraft), it was

Nixon who straightforwardly ordered a U.S. military airlift; It was a characteristically bold Nixon decision. And, as we saw, two key moments when Nixon accepted Kissinger's exercise of diplomatic freedom of action occurred during 1972, when Nixon was at the height of his powers.

An event often cited as evidence of Kissinger's abnormal dominance is a meeting he chaired in the White House Situation Room in the late evening of October 24, 1973, toward the end of the Middle East war. Leonid Brezhnev had sent Nixon a message threatening Soviet military intervention to defend Egypt if Israel continued its military advances. The attendees at the meeting—Kissinger, Haig, Scowcroft, Defense Secretary James Schlesinger, Chairman Admiral Moorer, CIA director William Colby—agreed on an increase in the alert levels of U.S. forces worldwide as a deterrent signal to the Soviets, coupled with a stern reply to Brezhnev warning against intervention. It is commonly believed that they implemented these steps without waking the president, who had retired for the evening. This has been treated by many analysts as a virtual collapse of the presidency.

There is no doubt of Nixon's distress and distraction over Watergate during this period; his political career was entering its terminal phase. But the truth about the Situation Room meeting is less dramatic than it has been portrayed. For one thing, Nixon had emphasized to Haig, before he retired, that he wanted a strong response to the Soviets, including alert measures. (The Soviets had been telegraphing their intervention threat during the course of the day, including at the U.N.) In addition, the record suggests that Haig left the Situation Room gathering at various stages of the evening to get Nixon's blessing of what was being discussed.

HENRY KISSINGER was secretary of state for the last ten and a half months of the Nixon presidency, and then for another two and a half years under Gerald Ford. During the remainder of the Nixon period the relationship of the two men can be said to have normalized, in the sense that the bureaucratic contradictions and contortions of the previous period disappeared overnight and foreign policy was henceforth directed by a president via his secretary of state. Much of the personal awkwardness remained, however, compounded by the great transformation that was taking place: Kissinger now had an independent base and international stature; as he continued to achieve successes, it was

Nixon who began to cling to Kissinger's political authority as his own authority waned. Kissinger was awarded a Nobel Peace Prize in October 1973 for his Vietnam negotiation. Following the October Arab-Israeli War, his "shuttle diplomacy" produced landmark agreements between Israel and Egypt (in January 1974) and between Israel and Syria (May 1974), which began the modern Middle East peace process. Nixon could not wait to make his own triumphal tour of the Middle East, which he did in June as soon as the Syrian accord was finished. But the upshot was to convince his domestic opponents of Kissinger's indispensability, not his own.

Kissinger arrived at State with skepticism about the department's capacity to run foreign policy. When he wrote his memoirs after departing the office, his views had not entirely changed. The Department of State, he continued to believe, was not well suited to manage interagency affairs; that was best left to the White House national security adviser. The department's organization still inclined it to inertia, day-to-day responses to cables, and preoccupation with management of its cumbersome internal system of autonomous fiefdoms. Conceptual thinking, especially of a strategic or geopolitical variety, did not come easily to it.

The United States Foreign Service is a true elite—a tiny cadre of only around 6,500 men and women (as of 2008), selected through a process of rigorous examinations and trained to a high level of professional expertise. Overseas posts often involve working in difficult conditions— many more ambassadors have been killed in the line of duty in recent generations than generals and admirals. Yet they are perpetually underfunded by Congress and enjoy none of the popular adulation bestowed on the men and women of our armed forces. Like any other close-knit fraternity enduring hardships together, the Foreign Service has developed a strong esprit de corps only intensified by its shared sense of beleaguerment and underappreciation. This has contributed to the development of a strong institutional culture, which includes a set of institutional predispositions with respect to both the process of policymaking and its substance.

One of the hallmarks of the Department of State is its legendary internal "clearance" procedures. When Kissinger as secretary of state visited Brazil in 1976, the briefing memorandum produced for him had been "cleared" in twenty-five different offices. This is perhaps not surprising given the richness of our relations with Brazil and the necessary

contribution of offices dealing with political, economic, security, technology, and nonproliferation affairs, et cetera. But such a process of
"policy by committee" necessarily dulls sharp edges and sharp thoughts
in its intellectual product. The instinct of many into whose hands the
memo passes is to strike or soften any sentence that seems a bit
provocative or strong. Multiply that by twenty-five (and undoubtedly
that record has been broken since 1976).

But there are also institutional predispositions concerning the substance of foreign policy. The legendary Arabist bias of the Foreign Service
had in fact begun to fade in Kissinger's time, as had the traditional WASP
dominance of the department's ethnic composition. Kissinger was soon
to take charge of Middle East policy in any case. But other regional
bureaus still had their cultures and outlooks. The Europeanists, as we
have seen, had a protective interest in arms control with the Soviet Union
and a jaded view (if one may call it that) of China. Another example was
Nathaniel Davis, head of the African affairs bureau, who resigned under
Kissinger because of his objection to a covert action program against the
Cuban-Soviet military intervention in Angola.

The department as a whole has an institutional bias in favor of negotiation, dialogue, and diplomatic "engagement"; that's what they do for a
living. If a problem cannot be solved by these means, then the lead
responsibility in the U.S. government is liable to migrate to some other
agency (the Pentagon, or CIA) that disposes of cruder instruments of
policy. Thus not only policy substance but bureaucratic turf is at stake.
State, therefore, can rarely ever bring itself to admit that diplomacy is
not working; in its mind, diplomacy is perpetually deserving of "one
more chance." Sometimes this seems to degenerate into dialogue for its
own sake, without regard to results or strategy or even the leverage that
might make dialogue more fruitful.

State is also blessed with being the beat of an unusually knowledgeable corps of journalists. The title of "diplomatic correspondent" still
carries the trench-coat aura of sophistication and marks one as part of
an elite in the profession. State generally enjoys sympathetic treatment
in the media for its endeavors, especially if it is seen to be struggling
against more pugnacious elements in the government (in the White
House or Pentagon). Leaks from State are thus a familiar and sometimes effective weapon in the bureaucratic wars.

What redeemed the institution in Kissinger's eyes when he arrived

there, however, was not only the wealth of expertise within the Foreign Service but its responsiveness to strong and consistent political leadership. The Foreign Service's natural instinct is loyalty to the secretary. While under William Rogers this turned into hostility to the White House (and no little personal animosity toward Kissinger), once he arrived at State this turned in his favor. "In the hands of a determined Secretary," Kissinger wrote, "the Foreign Service can be a splendid instrument, staffed by knowledgeable, discreet, and energetic individuals." The department relished being at the center of the action for a change. While he brought a few of his NSC staff colleagues with him, by far most of his appointments to policy-making positions in the department, especially assistant secretaries, were of career people. In his frenetic diplomacy over the years of his tenure, most of the pivotal players on his team were foreign service officers. Having spent his whole life in foreign affairs, Kissinger was confident enough in his ability to provide firm intellectual direction.

A conservative critic, Ambassador Laurence Silberman, has written that while Kissinger was "astonishingly successful" at controlling the department, this did not constitute "presidential" control over foreign policy precisely because it depended so much on career officers instead of political appointees at policy-making levels. Silberman is probably right as a general matter that bringing in political appointees is a way to insure political direction. But Kissinger was an unusual case; he had the intellectual and physical energy—and closeness to the president—to accomplish the same result. When the transcripts of Kissinger's State Department senior staff meetings are published, they will vividly convey the flavor of his firm direction being given—often in his inimitably acerbic fashion—and reflecting what he knew to be his president's convictions.

In Chapter 7, we will see the contrast with another strong secretary of state, James A. Baker, who took over the department in January 1989 with an equal determination to insure its responsiveness to political direction. Baker's memoirs on this subject echo Kissinger's critique of its institutional biases and weaknesses, and with a strong emphasis on the need to insure loyalty to the president's agenda. Baker came in with a strong team of colleagues who formed an "inner circle" that members of the career service could not easily gain admission to, and resented. Kissinger, for all the coldness with which the Foreign Service greeted

him when he arrived, seems to have been more confident in his own ability to use it, guide it, and lead it.

Nemesis

The foreign policy of Richard Nixon's administration comes closest of any modern presidency to what scholar Graham Allison calls the "rational actor" model of decision making. That is, much diplomatic history, and most laymen, are inclined to view governments as unitary actors and attribute to their decisions the kinds of motivations and logical reasoning that are conventionally attributed to individuals. Allison's contribution was to present other models, based on organizational behavior or bureaucratic politics, which portray governmental decisions as the result of many contending forces. The policy-making of the Nixon administration, however, could not have been more opposite to the "government by committee" that characterizes almost every other administration since Franklin Roosevelt. The main elements of the foreign policy of the Nixon administration were largely conceived, and sometimes executed, by a committee of two; hence the endless fascination with the intellectual and personal relationship of those two. Certainly there were bureaucratic forces at work, as we have seen in this chapter. But the White House product was a remarkably coherent and disciplined policy reflecting the consistent strategic purposes of the president and his top aide.*

The extraordinary centralization that Nixon achieved in foreign policy was paralleled by a strenuous effort to centralize domestic policy-making. The significance of this for our purposes lies in the equally strenuous reaction that it caused. There is an intriguing theory of the Watergate scandal, advanced by writer Nicholas von Hoffman, that the demise of Nixon was due to no less than the revolt of the bureaucracy whose power he had striven so assiduously to break in every sphere. We know that Nixon resigned because of accumulating public evidence that he was guilty of a felony, namely obstruction of justice. But von

---

*Nixon's status as an archetype of the "rational actor" should not be deemed contradicted by his advocacy of the "madman theory." Walking along a foggy beach once with Haldeman, Nixon explained that he wanted the North Vietnamese to think he was so obsessed about Communism that he couldn't be restrained and "might do *anything*" to stop the war—"and he has his hand on the nuclear button." Nixon indeed conveyed a formidable image—magnified, it must be said, by his opponents' passionate demonizing of him—and this added to his leverage with the North Vietnamese and others.

Hoffman asks a mischievous question: Since, in his view, *most* of our recent presidents have been rogues and miscreants, why was only Nixon brought down? His answer: Nixon's attempts at centralization had so alienated so many vested interests in the American system—the very "iron triangle" of bureaucracy, Congress, and interest groups that predecessors of his had railed against—that he brought about a coalescence of opponents that not only resisted his plans but seized on his Watergate misdeeds to do him in.

On the domestic policy front, von Hoffman borrows the thesis of Richard P. Nathan that Nixon planned a comprehensive, indeed revolutionary, restructuring of national institutions. Nixon proposed a "New Federalism," including revenue-sharing with the states, to weaken the grip of the federal bureaucracy. He expanded the Bureau of the Budget into the Office of Management and Budget to strengthen its management role. After his reelection in 1972, he accelerated the transfer of trusted White House aides into key sub-cabinet positions in the departments, and he proposed a system of "super-secretaries"—a tight group of four cabinet secretaries who would be given the additional titles of "counsellor to the president" and an oversight role over other cabinet departments. Nixon saw all this as a long-overdue reform to streamline the bloated national government and give expression to a conservative philosophy that now had a mandate from the people after a generation of Eastern establishment liberalism. Nathan, in contrast, calls it a plan for an "Administrative Presidency," a concentration of power that ran counter to the theory and practice of checks and balances that applied, in his view, not only to executive-legislative relations but to the structure of the Executive Branch itself.

Perhaps the most dramatic step was Nixon's demand, announced cold-bloodedly the day after his landslide reelection, for the resignations of every noncareer official in his administration, including all cabinet secretaries and the entire White House staff. He did this to emphasize his desire to start afresh and reassert control in a comprehensive manner now that he had such an overwhelming mandate. But what this accomplished, in von Hoffman's account, was that "many of these 2,000 plus people who should have been Nixon loyalists by all rights were driven to make common cause with the already alienated bureaucracy."

Von Hoffman does not claim that Nixon was really on the verge of such a coup against the Constitution as Nathan seems to believe; rather, the attempt was enough to alienate if not frighten large vested

interests but without actually weakening their power. They resisted, then fought back. The "super-secretaries" (aka White House counselors) proved unworkable and were abandoned after five months, partly because of squabbling over turf. The CIA rejected White House efforts to suborn its cooperation in blocking the Watergate investigation on "national security" grounds. Most important, in von Hoffman's words, "[t]he bureaucracy was fighting back in the way it always does against insubordinate superiors. It was leaking." A flood of leaks poured from the government sensitive details of the FBI's investigation of White House involvement in the Watergate burglary, humiliating leaks about Nixon family tax returns, investigations of close Nixon friends, inquiries into who paid for construction of Nixon's residences at San Clemente and Key Biscayne and into a tax deduction claimed by Nixon for donation of his pre-presidential papers to the National Archives, et cetera, et cetera. The drip-drip-drip of leaks ate away at Nixon's public standing whether real impropriety was discovered or not. And of course, when von Hoffman wrote, it was not even known that Bob Woodward and Carl Bernstein's "Deep Throat" was the associate director of the FBI—a career FBI official disgruntled that a politically malleable outsider had been named J. Edgar Hoover's successor rather than a more qualified career person (such as perhaps himself).

Readers today are in a better position to separate the reality of Watergate from the melodrama. Von Hoffman, as noted, does not believe Nixon was anywhere near a "coup" against the Constitution; on the contrary, he thinks Nixon was vastly overestimating his power when he undertook such a centralization of it. He never had a chance. Professor Neustadt agreed. By the same token, the uproar over Watergate (and Vietnam) spawned a generation of institutional changes that weakened the presidency and strengthened the checks on it. Since then we have lived in an age of legally protected whistle-blowers, a vast expansion of what some would call congressional micromanagement of policy in every field, a web of legislative restrictions on presidential discretion, a strengthened Freedom of Information Act, war powers legislation, and the virtual institutionalization of leaking, including of classified documents. This is Richard Nixon's ironic legacy.

We can be thankful that such violations of legality as were committed in the Nixon era (many of which had precedents in prior administrations) are no longer with us. But what about his efforts to assert presidential control over the execution of *policy*? "The executive power shall

be vested in a President of the United States of America," says Article II of the Constitution. There is no reference in the document to disgruntled assistant secretaries and their constitutional right to undermine presidential decisions they disagree with. There are scholars who argue that the bureaucracy *should* be independent of presidential control—that in its own way it is a representative institution, given its links with Congress and interest groups, and therefore it ought to be treated as a fourth branch of government. This theory of the "representative bureaucracy" raises serious problems of its own, however. The rest of us may prefer to let regular elections continue to determine what is representative of public preferences at any given period. The vast expansion of bureaucracy in the twentieth century continues to pose a challenge to the constitutional and democratic mandates of both Congress and the president as they try to impose direction on the bureaucracy in accordance with *their* representative duties.

Nixon's determined attempt to centralize direction over policy seems to have broken a host of unwritten rules, even if the fears of constitutional transgression were overwrought. In our democratic culture some principle of collegiality and participation—some notion of procedural regularity—seems to be a source of legitimacy, in the sense of acceptance by those who are overruled. Nixon, even in exercising authority that no one disputes he had, committed an offense against this concept of legitimacy. The institutions of our government have their weapons, both offensive and defensive, to wield against a president if they choose to go to war; if it comes to that, the media and the public will watch it and enjoy it as sport, and the outcome will usually be decided by the court of public opinion as politicians fight it out. But the rest of us—and future presidents—will want to know what lessons should be drawn.

Legitimacy, we will inevitably find, cuts both ways. A president who asserts authority in ways that seem high-handed or arbitrary—and ends up alone, without allies—will usually pay the political price. Nixon is the object lesson, and it is a lesson of prudence at the very least. At the same time, any president elected by the people with a mandate for change will have no choice but to persist in the struggle that Nixon—and other presidents of both parties—have waged to give effect in our government to the popular will. Nixon's political fate, definitive as it may seem, did not by any means answer all the questions that his tumultuous presidency raised.

CHAPTER FOUR

Gerald Ford

THERE WAS AN UNUSUAL BUSTLE around the Oval Office early on a Sunday morning, November 2, 1975. President Gerald Ford was to fly that morning to Jacksonville, Florida, to meet with visiting Egyptian president Anwar Sadat, an important meeting with an important new partner of the United States. But first, Ford had to squeeze in the unpleasant task of firing his director of central intelligence and his secretary of defense.

CIA director William Colby had run afoul of the White House by delivering voluminous CIA documents, without White House clearance, to congressional committees investigating CIA misdeeds. With Defense Secretary James Schlesinger, the president felt there were clashes of personality as well as policy. Their replacement was meant to be part of a broader reshuffle of top administration personnel, but the newsmagazines had gotten wind of parts of the story and were planning to release the news Sunday night. Ford considered it the honorable course to inform the two men in person before it broke in the press. Hence the meetings early Sunday morning. Colby was scheduled first, at eight, Schlesinger at eight-thirty.

Ford's conversation with Colby was calm, brief, and "not unpleasant," Ford later recorded. He was even sympathetic to Colby, since he blamed the aggressiveness of the congressional investigations on ambitious members of Congress and their proliferating staffs. The meeting ended early, about 8:15. As Colby departed the West Wing through the basement lobby he ran into the arriving Schlesinger, who asked, "What the devil are you doing here at this hour?" Colby, having an inkling of what was in store for Schlesinger, said little and mumbled his goodbyes. In the Oval Office, young deputy chief of staff Dick Cheney was urging

Ford to go easy on Schlesinger. "[G]et that son-of-a-bitch in here so I can fire him," Ford snapped, in a display of anger uncharacteristic of him. The second conversation was much more difficult, as Schlesinger spent nearly an hour trying to talk Ford out of it.

Ford then flew off to Florida to meet with Sadat—the Arab-Israeli conflict presumably a welcome relief. He probably had no idea of the uproar that would follow when the story broke. Without knowing it, Ford had just been through one of the defining moments of his administration.

OFFICIALS WHO WORKED for both Richard Nixon and Gerald Ford are effusive about the differences between them—in personality and in the psychological environment they created at the highest levels of government. Ford was outgoing where Nixon was withdrawn, collegial where Nixon was solitary, trusting where Nixon was suspicious, at ease with himself where Nixon battled a lifetime of resentments and insecurities. "There is no guile, no convolution, no complexity in Gerald Ford," said Brent Scowcroft. "He was comfortable in who he was." Unlike Nixon, Ford had the natural gregariousness of a politician but—not having pursued the presidency as an obsession like so many of those who attain it—he was "immune to the modern politician's chameleon-like search for ever-new identities and to the emotional roller coaster this search exacts," Henry Kissinger observed. Kissinger recalls the revelation and relief of his first conversation with Ford after Ford assumed the office: For the first time in his five-year White House experience, he "left the presidential presence without afterthoughts, confident there was no more to the conversation than what I had heard." There was no hidden agenda, no complex presidential motivation to be divined. Ford had been clear, unafraid to say no, unconcerned about who should receive credit for an initiative. "With Ford, what one saw was what one got."

Historically, Ford casts a modest shadow by contrast with most of his larger-than-life predecessors—the Shakespearean flaws of Nixon, the volcanic presence of Johnson, the charisma and martyrdom of Kennedy, the world-historical figure that was Eisenhower even before he became president, and Franklin Roosevelt. Only Harry Truman was of human scale, and the resemblance is a true one: Like Truman, Ford was thrust by history into an unexpected role in the face of huge challenges (including the final stages of a war), stepped up to his responsibilities, and came to be better regarded by posterity than by contemporaries. In

his brief term in office, Ford had important achievements in domestic policy (the beginning of regulatory reform) and in foreign policy (a major step toward Egyptian-Israeli peace; the Helsinki Final Act, which enshrined human rights as a component of relations with the Communist world; creation of what is now the G-7 or G-8 grouping of major powers; and first steps toward majority rule in Southern Africa).

Ford also presided over a cabinet of heavyweights. He was comfortable with the model of cabinet government in which the president trusts that his cabinet officers are loyal to his agenda, and delegates to them:

> What I wanted in my Cabinet were strong managers who would control the career bureaucrats and not become their captives; people who knew how to build support in the Congress and the media. I would leave the details of administration to them and concentrate on determining national priorities and directions myself.

He intended to "restore authority to my Cabinet" and give them "a lot more control," to "reverse the trend" of centralization in the White House staff and Executive Office of the President. Ford's cabinet included Kissinger at State, James Schlesinger at Defense, and William E. Simon at Treasury, whom he inherited from Nixon. At Justice—an institution much bloodied by Watergate—he appointed Edward H. Levi, University of Chicago president, renowned legal scholar, and pillar of integrity. Alan Greenspan was chairman of the Council of Economic Advisers, William T. Coleman became secretary of transportation, John T. Dunlop of Harvard secretary of labor, Carla Hills secretary of housing and urban development.

Ford's legislative experience served him well with respect to many issues of substance, particularly defense and the federal budget. He had served twelve years on the House appropriations subcommittee on the defense budget, and had also dealt with intelligence appropriations. "A President controls his Administration through the budget," he knew. Officials who were used to Nixon's cursory attention were surprised by Ford's mastery of detail. In 1976 he briefed the press himself on the budget. "God, but he is good at this," one bureaucrat marveled. Kissinger found that Ford was more interested than Nixon had been in the tactics and details of his negotiations, not only general objectives.

But the job of a legislator is not the same as the job of a president. Donald Rumsfeld, who had been a colleague and ally of Ford in Congress, commented:

> President Ford came into office with wonderful training and success that didn't suit him for an executive function. He started out functioning basically like a legislator. Every day he was president he got better at being an executive. Within a year he became an exceedingly good executive. He began to delegate effectively, to become more strategic, instead of being consumed with what was in his in-box.

A management style that has been labeled one of "extreme collegiality" was eventually to give way under the pressure of events. At first, Ford wanted no chief of staff, visualizing an office (like his own as House minority leader) in which several senior aides had direct access to the boss, like spokes of a wheel. There would be no gatekeeper, no Haldeman. The exigencies of office broke down this idyllic system within six months; the open door policy meant that up to eight or nine senior aides could walk into the Oval Office, "guarantee[ing] endless discussion and infrequent resolution," in James Cannon's words, and consuming precious presidential time. Ford came around to ask Rumsfeld, who had started out with the humble title of "staff coordinator," to pull the reins into his hands and take on the traditional role of chief of staff. Yet both Rumsfeld and his successor, Dick Cheney, have complained that Ford never gave them the full authority they needed to impose discipline in the White House. A former Nixon staffer commented enviously to Ford's press secretary, Ron Nessen: "With Nixon, you had to try to save him from his worst instincts. With Ford, you have to try to save him from his best instincts."

Ford and Kissinger

When Nixon chose Ford as his vice president in October 1973 to replace the disgraced Spiro Agnew, activating for the first time the procedures of the Twenty-fifth Amendment, he exulted to Kissinger that he had purchased a kind of impeachment insurance: The Congress would easily confirm Ford because they liked him but would never think of him as capable of being president. Kissinger was not so sure, and he may have been right: Ford's selection might only have increased the Democrats'

incentive to remove Nixon because they were confident they could defeat Ford in 1976. In any event, Kissinger made it a personal priority to attend to the new vice president and ensure his familiarity with all the foreign policy issues confronting the country. At least once a week, Kissinger or his deputy Brent Scowcroft would walk across the street from the White House to the Executive Office Building and spend an hour or so briefing him thoroughly. Ford appreciated it and was confident he was being kept up to date.

"It would be hard for me to overstate the admiration and affection I had for Henry," Ford has written, and by all accounts he meant it. They had known each other for a decade or so, dating from the time that Professor Kissinger had invited the congressman to Harvard to speak to his graduate seminar on national security policy; the topic was congressional control of the defense budget. He made a good impression on the students and on the professor. They had also encountered each other frequently during Nixon's first term. Ford as vice president gave what has been called a "late-night, highball-lubricated *Air Force Two* interview" to journalist John Osborne at the end of March 1974. He confided to Osborne rather indiscreetly that if he were to become president, he would want Kissinger, a "superb Secretary of State," to stay on.

The frequent Oval Office meetings between the new president and his secretary of state were remarkable, as Kissinger has said, for their lack of psychological undercurrents, complexes, or hidden motivations. Brent Scowcroft took rough notes of these meetings, and when they are declassified they will show a relationship of complete openness and mutual confidence. Kissinger kept nothing back, briefing Ford fully on events and personalities and strategies he was proposing. Ford grasped it easily and expressed his own preferences forthrightly. Where foreign policy issues had domestic political repercussions—for example, in the debate over détente with the Soviet Union, or majority rule in Southern Africa—Ford conveyed his judgment of his political circumstances and their implications. Where there was a congressional dimension, Ford himself was the master and educated his subordinates in the ins and outs and personalities that he knew better than anyone. Rough as Scowcroft's notes were, these records will show a relationship of trust and a fullness of deliberation going to the heart of the most sensitive issues of the period.

This charmed relationship, however, came under pressure from two sources. First was the intensifying domestic debate over policy toward

the Soviet Union, especially strategic arms control, a debate that divided Ford's cabinet and generated political pressures targeting Kissinger. The second source was Ford's White House staff, some of whom were convinced that Ford, to achieve full presidential stature, had to achieve a certain independence from his overpowering secretary of state.

This is not the place for a full discussion of the debate over détente with the Soviet Union or strategic arms control. The notable point is that where Nixon and Kissinger had been vilified by the left in Nixon's first term for being too anti-Communist and too hard-line toward the Soviet Union, in the second term the public mood shifted to a greater suspicion of the Soviet Union and both Nixon's and Ford's administrations—to their monumental surprise—came under fire from the opposite direction as too soft. And where Kissinger had often been the beneficiary of public attitudes that treated Nixon as the villain and him, by comparison, as the good guy, now, with Ford the unsullied new president and Kissinger having accumulated enemies and liabilities of his own, Kissinger became more often the principal target of the attacks from both left and right.

The record is clear that as Kissinger pursued the SALT negotiations with the Soviets, he was carrying out Ford's wishes. In the end, an agreement was prevented by deep divisions in the cabinet that reflected the deep divisions in the Republican Party that almost cost Ford the presidential nomination in 1976. When Kissinger visited Moscow in January 1976, Ford at the last minute denied him the instructions that might have made an agreement possible, out of fear that his administration would not survive the rupture that an agreement would cause. At the Republican National Convention in Kansas City in August, Kissinger was such a red flag to the conservatives that Ford's aides tried to keep him away from the convention and accepted a platform plank that came close to repudiating the Ford-Kissinger foreign policy. Meanwhile, I have been told by a Democratic friend that Jimmy Carter's campaign team feared more than almost anything that Ford would sign a SALT II accord with the Soviets in 1976 and therefore be perceived by the public as a much more substantial figure in his own right; it might have made the difference in what turned out to be an extremely close election.

The strategic nuclear problem faced by the United States in the 1970s can be summed up as follows, at the risk of great oversimplifica-

tion: After the Cuban missile crisis of 1962, the United States halted its production of new intercontinental ballistic missiles (ICBMs), on the assumption that the strategic competition was essentially over. The Soviets, for their part, embarked on a major missile buildup that did not stop when they reached parity with the United States (about 1970); rather, they kept on building. Nixon's SALT I accord of 1972 was a five-year freeze on both sides' numbers, which admittedly locked in a Soviet advantage for five years but also halted the Soviet buildup while our next-generation ICBM, the MX, was to come into production at the end of the five-year period. Yet the American domestic debate in the mid-1970s was preoccupied by the seeming inequality of SALT I—blaming it on the arms control process instead of on the unilateral American decisions that had determined the American strategic program. This critique came not only from conservative Republicans but also from Democratic senator Henry Jackson of Washington state, who was himself running for president and making the critique of détente his main platform.

This campaign against SALT was fueled in large part by leaks to the media from inside the administration that depicted a president and secretary of state too eager to make concessions to the Soviets and too unwilling to demand more concessions from them. The public campaign in turn exerted its pressure on Defense Secretary Schlesinger, who became its champion inside the administration. The media perceived a titanic battle between Kissinger and Schlesinger, two brilliant policy intellectuals from Harvard (both *summas* from the Class of 1950). But Ford had a shrewder perception. When Kissinger at one point in 1975 tried to apologize to Ford for the amount of the president's time consumed by this feuding, Ford shot back: "Jim's fight is not with you but with me. He thinks I am stupid, and he believes you are running me, which he resents. This conflict will not end until I either fire Jim or make him believe *he* is running me." Within a few months, as Kissinger notes, Ford chose the first option.

Ford's reaction teaches an important lesson about bureaucratic infighting. Intramural sparring between cabinet departments is hardly new. In this case, the battle was waged by Defense Department leaks against the State Department; in other administrations, it can be the State Department sniping at Defense. The issue is not the direction, or even the substance, of the attack but how it is bound to be perceived by a president. The motive of such sniping is presumably to reduce polit-

ical support for the opposing position and thereby influence the president's decisions. The problem is, first of all, that public sniping by one department against another is, on the face of it, a sign of disarray. This is a disservice to a president because it suggests he cannot settle an issue definitively or enforce discipline in his administration. Every White House I have known perceives this. Even more serious is the problem that Ford saw: If the president has already decided on a course, or is eager to continue moving in a certain direction, the attack on the adviser whose advice is prevailing can only be seen by the president as an attack on the decision he has made, as an attempt to undermine his chosen policy. A president is likely to resent this. Bureaucratic snipers should beware—not only that they may not hit their intended target, but that their shots may ricochet badly against themselves.

The second source of pressure against the Ford-Kissinger partnership came from members of Ford's White House staff. Most of this had little to do with the substance of policy; it reflected a desire that Ford demonstrate a certain independence from Kissinger to elevate his own stature. To be sure, there was a policy dimension as Ronald Reagan's attacks on the policy mounted during 1976, which only added to the political incentive to distance Ford from Kissinger. On March 1, 1976, for example, someone persuaded Ford to announce that he was not going to use the term "détente" anymore. The difficulty with this, as we have seen, is that the controversial policies that Kissinger was identified with were also Ford's policies. How to distance oneself from one's own policies is a complex task that Ford's eager staffers never figured out how to do.

The more generic quest for "independence" took the form of wanting Ford to be seen getting advice on foreign policy matters from a wider circle than just Kissinger and his deputy Scowcroft. Various memoirs attribute this idea to Donald Rumsfeld. Ron Nessen reports that some White House aides began telling journalists that Kissinger had too much influence and Ford needed to "assert himself as the manager of foreign policy in both image and reality." Rumsfeld also convened White House meetings at which Ford would be seen giving instructions to Kissinger for speeches he was to give at international conferences. Word was also put out that the frequency of Kissinger's meetings with the president was being reduced.

One episode concerned a speech that Ford delivered at Tulane University on April 23, 1975, a week before Saigon fell to the North Viet-

namese army. A few days before flying to New Orleans, Ford had told
his staff he wanted to send the students an upbeat message that the war
that had so dominated their lives was now essentially over. "Why don't
you just say that?" aide Robert Hartmann suggested. A line was put into
the speech draft to that effect—but not included in drafts circulated to
Kissinger or Scowcroft. Ford announced to the six thousand students in
the Tulane field house that "Today, America can regain the sense of
pride that existed before Vietnam. But it cannot be achieved by refight-
ing a war that is finished as far as America is concerned." The field
house exploded in cheers, and reporters on the aircraft home asked
Ford whether Kissinger had been consulted about this language. Ford
said, simply, no. White House staffers eagerly heralded this as another
Ford "declaration of independence" from Kissinger policies. As a policy
matter, it was not ideal for the president to make a dramatic pronouncement that could have the effect of speeding up the unraveling in South
Vietnam (especially with a difficult evacuation under way). Kissinger
treats it sarcastically in his memoirs as a "typical inside-the-Beltway
bureaucratic victory," but does not claim it made a significant difference
in Vietnam. Ford does not mention the episode in his memoirs.

As Robert Hartmann writes, "Most of the tales that were told about
Kissinger losing favor with the President were more wishful than real."
Ford in fact was regularly upset at these leaks. "Goddamn it, I don't
want any more of this," he once insisted to his aides, pounding his desk
for emphasis and threatening "dire consequences" for anyone leaking
anti-Kissinger stories. Ford in his memoirs denounces as "misguided"
and "nonsense" the leaks from White House staffers trying to build up
his foreign policy credentials at Kissinger's expense, and as "totally inac-
curate" the stories that he had overruled his secretary of state on several
decisions. The fact was, as Ford says, "there never was a conflict of any
significance between us." This was arguably even more true than had
been the case under Nixon.

The Tulane speech, though, gives a clue to why the sniping from the
White House staff was so persistent. There is a tantalizing episode in
the memoir of press secretary Ron Nessen in which Ford declares once
again how mad he is at the fighting on the staff. "But he didn't seem
mad," Nessen says. "I sense that he was not unhappy at all about the
stories describing Ford's control of foreign policy as getting stronger and
Kissinger's role as getting weaker." We have already noted the president's abrupt "no" when asked by reporters on *Air Force One* whether

Kissinger had played a role in the Tulane speech. Ford clearly acquiesced in some of these staff-driven displays of "independence," but without intending them to have any substantive significance. That is a difficult line to walk. The problem was not that Kissinger was thin-skinned (which he was), but that the seeming derogation of his authority domestically was bound to erode his international authority to some degree, as well as whet appetites in Washington among those who did want to weaken his clout on substance. This was a problem for the president, not just for Kissinger, assuming (as I do) that their substantive views were close to identical.

The White House staffers failed to see that these gestures were more a reflection of weakness on Ford's part than of strength: Why should a president have to try so hard to assert his superiority over a subordinate? A strong president has no need to. And how can a president separate himself in this way from a subordinate whose views he shares? Recall the remarks of Alexander Hamilton that were quoted in Chapter 1, in his critique of John Adams's neglect of his cabinet secretaries. To paraphrase Hamilton: Since the president appointed these men, presumably he wants them around. And if not, why are they there?

A president who wishes to insure control over a strong cabinet officer should dispense with the feeble gestures of "independence" and insist, instead, on two things: a commonality of views and the subordinate's loyalty. The commonality of views can be had by the kind of intimate conversations that Ford, Kissinger, and Scowcroft had regularly in the Oval Office. The loyalty should be defined, in McGeorge Bundy's terms, as being "the president's man" in the bureaucracy, not the bureaucracy's representative in the cabinet—carrying out the policy the president wants and imposing the president's agenda on the department even if it does not comport with the institution's preferences. That is what insures presidential control over foreign policy.

Ford and Schlesinger

James R. Schlesinger is a brilliant intellectual and administrator, a pioneer in the field of defense economics, who had an extraordinary career serving in the Bureau of the Budget and as head of the Atomic Energy Commission (AEC), the CIA, and the departments of Defense and Energy. He came to President Nixon's attention for his effectiveness at the Budget Bureau and for his deft handling of a nuclear-testing contro-

versy while head of the AEC. Another matter he handled with sensitivity and acumen at the AEC was a secret project, ordered by Nixon, of cooperation with France over its nuclear weapons program.

These skills notwithstanding, his tenure as Gerald Ford's secretary of defense, inherited from Nixon, was doomed. Ford let it be known even while he was vice president that if he should succeed to the highest office, Schlesinger would not remain. In the indiscreet airborne interview with John Osborne in March 1974, Ford complained especially of what he saw as Schlesinger's mishandling of relations with Congress. In his memoirs Ford cites an example that same month (which undoubtedly prompted his comment to Osborne) in which Schlesinger intervened clumsily in a jurisdictional dispute between two powerful House committee chairmen, magnifying a mini-crisis for the administration that Ford himself had to repair with his former colleagues. Later, the problem repeated itself in October 1975 when Schlesinger publicly denounced House appropriations committee chairman George Mahon for cutting the defense budget; Ford had enormous respect for Mahon and, again, considered this a clumsy and counterproductive tactic. Ford cites other examples, including pressing too hard against budget decisions after the president had made them. In a field—the defense budget—in which Ford was a master, he found Schlesinger an undisciplined student.

In Ford's very first week in office, several major news organizations carried dramatic stories to the effect that in Nixon's final days, Schlesinger had instructed the Joint Chiefs of Staff to double-check with him any orders from the White House to insure against any untoward use of the military by Nixon. The defense secretary was quoted as concerned that a desperate Nixon or his aides might try something (unspecified), and that some Air Force and Navy officers might have formed an emotional attachment to Nixon because of his devotion to U.S. POWs in Indochina. Some stories even said Schlesinger had slept on a cot in his Pentagon office through the period. Ford was "furious" at these reports, he recalls; they were an "inexcusable" affront not only to Nixon but to the U.S. military. He complained to Schlesinger about the stories but Schlesinger gave no inkling of where they might have come from. Months later, Ford learned that Schlesinger himself had been the source, at a lunch he had had with Pentagon reporters. (No such instruction to the chiefs had in fact been issued, but the Schlesinger luncheon with reporters was real enough.)

The policy feud with Kissinger has been discussed above—in particular, Ford's increasing irritation with it which focused on Schlesinger. In addition, Ford did not even think Schlesinger was sincere in his hawkish views in the SALT debates: "In reality, the reverse was true. His views often were much more dovish than mine."

Beyond the problems of substance, the president and his secretary of defense had a severe clash of personalities. Ford, the most easygoing of men, admits that Schlesinger's "aloof, frequently arrogant manner put me off. I could never be sure he was leveling with me." Robert Hartmann writes:

> [T]he main thing that Ford didn't like about Schlesinger was Schlesinger. Whenever they talked, even alone, Schlesinger gave him the impression of a bored intellectual saying, "I know you're pretty dumb, but I'll do my best to explain it simply." Ford didn't like the fact that a Cabinet officer couldn't remember to button his shirt collar and cinch up his tie when he came to see the President of the United States.

The problems accumulated. In October 1975, at an informal meeting of Ford's "kitchen cabinet" of friends and advisers, Bryce Harlow, the wise counselor to many Republican presidents, warned Ford that the reports of feuding in the administration had created an impression of "internal anarchy" at the highest levels. He urged: "Now, Mr. President, if you have to fire 'em all, you have got to put a stop to it." As we have seen, Ford had determined at a very early stage that he would replace Schlesinger; the only question was when. Perhaps the surprise is not that it happened but that it took fourteen months to happen. While he gradually made other changes in the Nixon cabinet he inherited, Ford was waiting for an opportunity to revamp his entire national security team.

The "Halloween Massacre"

For several days in the second half of October 1975, Ford was confined to his residence upstairs in the White House nursing a cold and sinus infection. During that period of what Hartmann calls "communing with himself," Ford decided the time was ripe to make a set of changes. On a Saturday morning, October 25, he called Kissinger and Rumsfeld into

the Oval Office, sat them down in the sofas in front of the fireplace, and informed them of what he had decided to do: Not only was Schlesinger to be fired, but Colby was to be replaced as CIA director:

> The only way I could feel comfortable with my own team, I said, was to fire Schlesinger, ask Colby to submit his resignation, bring [George H. W.] Bush back to be director of the CIA, send Rumsfeld over to Defense, take away one of Kissinger's two hats and upgrade both Cheney and Scowcroft.

Kissinger and Rumsfeld were both caught by surprise. While Kissinger suspected that Rumsfeld had inspired the reshuffle in order to further his own ambitions, Ford has insisted convincingly that he came up with the idea himself, keeping both men in the dark. Rumsfeld indeed tried to talk him out of it (as did Kissinger). Kissinger was concerned that conservative critics would blame him for the loss of their hero Schlesinger, and that the reduction in his own status would impair his effectiveness.

In parallel with Kissinger and Rumsfeld, there were other acts to this drama. Ford and his vice president, Nelson Rockefeller, had their own conversation a few days later in which Ford suggested to Rockefeller that he (Ford) would be in a stronger position to head off a struggle with Reagan for the GOP nomination if Rockefeller were not on the ticket. Rockefeller, a former governor of New York (and longtime mentor of Kissinger), was a moderate Republican who was anathema to the conservatives. In a moment painful for both men, because Rockefeller had been a model of loyalty, Rockefeller withdrew his candidacy. Meanwhile, George H. W. Bush, then our envoy in Beijing, reluctantly accepted the CIA job as a matter of duty, believing it would end his political career—including giving up his chance to be Ford's running mate in 1976. (Some suspected Rumsfeld had engineered that, too.)

Whether in the best of circumstances Ford could have pulled off this complicated reshuffle, with the many interlocking controversies it contained, is a difficult question. In the event, it was blown sky-high by the press leak of the Kissinger-Schlesinger portions of the change a week after Ford's Oval Office conversation with Kissinger and Rumsfeld but before Schlesinger, Colby, et al. had been told. This forced Ford, gentleman that he was, to call Colby and Schlesinger into the Oval Office

early on a Sunday morning to give them the hard news personally, as we have seen.

The leak led to a major uproar. As we discussed in the last chapter with respect to Richard Nixon's ferocious desire to control the disclosure of the opening to China, controlling the disclosure can be synonymous with determining the nature of the event. Never has the point been better proved than by the example of Ford's loss of that control in this case. Instead of a familiar kind of reshuffle to bring in fresh faces and complete the process of replacing Nixon holdovers, explained publicly in terms that the White House would have had time to think through and prepare, it came through as a hasty improvisation, abrupt and heavy-handed, to be explained by dark personal ambitions. The media dubbed it the "Halloween Massacre." The president, asked by reporters why he had done it, responded in vague terms about "wanting my own team"—undoubtedly trying to avoid saying demeaning things about Schlesinger or Colby in public. But pundits were thereby left free to speculate on the motives of the individuals involved, often inaccurately as well as contradictorily, agreeing mainly on the proposition that the whole affair showed Ford's incompetence. Even the sympathetic John Osborne wrote scathingly (and very wrongly) that the president's explanations "and the events they concern show Gerald Ford to be intensely egoistic behind that humble façade of his, capable of an inhuman cruelty stupidly evinced, and desperately anxious to establish and prove himself as a national leader in his own right."

The firing of James Schlesinger, in particular, had significant political consequences. Conservatives were in an uproar, believing, as Kissinger predicted, that he had engineered it; the controversy over SALT only intensified. Kissinger told Schlesinger in an awkward telephone conversation after the event: "I think you and I could have held this thing together . . . perhaps only you and I." Schlesinger agreed. Indeed, a year earlier, Kissinger and Schlesinger had agreed on a SALT proposal that led to a framework agreement between Ford and Leonid Brezhnev at a summit meeting in Vladivostok.

When Rumsfeld replaced Schlesinger at the Pentagon, the State-Defense deadlocks simply reappeared, with Rumsfeld apparently unable or unwilling to make similar compromises as Kissinger and Schlesinger might have done. Schlesinger, a technocrat, had been thrust into playing a political role he may never have intended; Rums-

fold, a political figure with a political future, was inevitably caught up in the battle within the GOP and sought to protect Ford (and himself) from the growing challenge from the right. But the firing of Schlesinger only inflamed the right and singed not only Kissinger, but Ford. The departure of Rockefeller from the ticket, meant to head off the challenge from Ronald Reagan, failed utterly to do so.

Nixon, as we saw, did not have the stomach to fire people, and in part for this reason allowed dysfunction to persist in his administration. Ford, ironically, seeking to be decisive and to put in a cabinet team that he thought would work smoothly—and having the grace to dismiss people in person—saw what he did with the best of intentions blow up in his face. A noble attempt at cabinet government went badly awry. The premature leak had a lot to do with it; the scheme, in the end, may just have been too ambitious, with too many moving parts and too many political pitfalls that were not foreseen.

Later events suggest, however, that the problem bedeviling the Ford administration was not just a matter of congenial personalities or lack thereof, but institutional problems reflecting presidential weakness. The SALT stalemate in the administration persisted because the widening gulf in the Republican Party was more than an unelected president, facing a formidable challenge for the nomination, could bridge. A different dimension of institutional weakness, that vis-à-vis Congress, was reflected in the parallel events that had led to the departure of CIA director Colby.

Congress and the Intelligence Investigations

William Colby, like James Schlesinger, had had a distinguished career that propelled him to the top of his profession. Colby's quiet dignity and gray demeanor belied his extraordinary courage as a young Office of Strategic Services officer parachuting into Nazi-occupied France and Norway, and his leadership of a tough counterintelligence campaign against the Viet Cong in South Vietnam. Nixon had named Colby, a CIA professional, to be the agency's next director in May 1973 when Schlesinger was shifted from CIA to Defense. The promotion was deserved; the timing proved disastrous for both Colby and his agency. Vietnam and Watergate having generated a climate of endless scandal and political warfare fueled by tendentious leaks, the intelligence community was to be the next target.

In May 1973—the same month that Nixon nominated Colby to be Schlesinger's successor—press stories about the involvement in Watergate of ex-CIA figure Howard Hunt led Schlesinger to ask agency employees to report to him fully "on any activities now going on, or that have gone on in the past, which might be construed to be outside the legislative charter of this Agency." One week later, a memorandum landed on his desk with the whimsical title, "Family Jewels," attached to a 693-page compendium of CIA activities dating back to 1959 that could arguably have conflicted with the agency's charter, the National Security Act of 1947. Schlesinger and Colby conferred and agreed that the agency's congressional oversight committees should be notified of the compiled record—along with a firm pledge never to repeat such violations—so that it would not derail Colby's confirmation hearing.

In the climate of the time, merely to compile such a record was to do the leakers' homework for them. By December 1974, a few months into Ford's presidency, journalist Seymour Hersh telephoned Colby excitedly and said he had "a story bigger than My Lai" (the Vietnam atrocity story for which Hersh had won a Pulitzer Prize); it had to do with illegal CIA activities in the United States. Colby immediately recognized what he calls "disjointed and distorted accounts of several items" in the "Family Jewels" collection, and did his best to counter the exaggerations and distortions in what Hersh was telling him. On December 22, *The New York Times* splashed Hersh's three-column story on its front page, the lead paragraph of which accused the CIA of a "massive illegal domestic spying intelligence operation during the Nixon Administration against the antiwar movement and other dissident groups in the United States." When the predictable uproar ensued, Colby called the president to promise him a truthful account and assure him that nothing illegal was occurring on his watch.

Shortly afterward, Colby received a phone call from his predecessor, Schlesinger, during whose tenure the "Family Jewels" had been compiled. The two agreed that the article as published was a "distorted concoction of partial truths"; they also sheepishly realized that while Colby had briefed the key committee chairmen about the "Family Jewels" when they had been compiled, neither President Nixon, nor Ford, nor Kissinger "had ever been apprised" of the project. In a phone conversation with Kissinger on December 23, Colby informed Kissinger blandly that "I bundled them together and briefed my two chairmen on it, and I let the skeletons sit quietly in the closet, hoping they would stay there."

The hyped story of "domestic spying" was in fact the climax of an autumn of intelligence leaks, including allegations about the Nixon administration's efforts to block leftist Salvador Allende from becoming president of Chile in 1970 and charges that it played a role in the military coup that brought Allende down in September 1973. Other charges in the press had to do with assassination plots by the U.S. government against foreign leaders. (Extraordinarily enough, Ford himself had inadvertently generated the latter excitement by hinting, at a supposedly off-the-record luncheon with *New York Times* editors, that the intelligence investigations triggered by Hersh could do harm by opening up even more sensitive historical subjects, such as assassinations.) As a result, both houses of the Democratic Congress set up special select committees to examine the charges—in the Senate, chaired by Frank Church of Idaho, in the House under Otis Pike of New York.

Ford, in the vain hope of heading off a demagogic stampede, had already set up his own bipartisan commission under Vice President Rockefeller to look into the charges and make recommendations. But Congress ignored it, and as the congressional investigations accelerated, Ford became more and more alarmed that "some members of Congress wanted to dismantle the CIA" or "eliminate covert operations altogether." He insisted, for his part, that any investigations "had to be conducted with both discretion and dispatch to avoid crippling a vital national institution." Therefore he wanted to determine the strategy by which his administration responded to the inquiries—in Kissinger's words, "to develop some criteria by which to define transgressions and confine investigations to those subjects" and to devise "some procedure to prevent future abuses while preserving essential intelligence activities." It is in fact the norm in such situations for the White House to take charge of how the Executive Branch responds to controversial congressional investigations, if only to determine whether and when to invoke executive privilege. That is a matter of presidential prerogative. While usually the White House lawyers and congressional relations experts convene meetings with their counterparts from the concerned departments and agencies, such controversies are political at their core, and presidents invariably wish to decide for themselves how much political capital to expend and how to manage the broad strategy for the Executive Branch.

Colby had a different approach. Having prepared, at Ford's instruction, a summary report on the "Family Jewels," Colby wanted to hand it over right away to the Senate committee when he testified there in mid-

January 1975. Ford instructed him to keep it classified. Colby then delivered an opening statement virtually identical to the memorandum he had done for Ford, and agreed with the committee to release it as a public statement. Colby writes that he was "privately delighted" that the statement was published, believing it an effective rebuttal to the "misconceptions fostered by Hersh's article," but realized on his drive back from the Hill that he had not forewarned the White House of any of this: "[S]o I stopped there to give Brent Scowcroft a copy of the statement the Committee had released; the substance was well known to them, but the fact of its public release was a new bombshell."

More broadly, Colby considered that the CIA was no longer a creature of the Executive Branch exclusively; he subscribed to the view that "in 1975 the center of political power had moved to Congress and . . . the CIA's survival depended on working out satisfactory rather than hostile relations there." Therefore he unilaterally pledged to the committees his full cooperation with respect to documents and testimony, and issued a directive to CIA employees formally absolving them of their secrecy oaths with respect to testimony before Congress. In September 1975, after the House committee began publishing secret documents over administration objections, Ford prohibited the release of any additional classified material to the committee until it gave assurances about respecting their secrecy. Colby circumvented the order by "loaning" the material to the committee.

The congressional investigations were a two-ring circus. The Church Committee in the Senate respected the ground rules with regard to handling sensitive documents, but it was overeager when it came to issues of substance. One focus was on the exciting topic of U.S. government assassination plots against foreign leaders. Perhaps disappointed when it discovered that Nixon, Ford, and Kissinger were not involved in assassinating anybody, and that the most recent such plots had occurred under John and Robert Kennedy, the committee nevertheless stretched its definitions to include in its report an episode that had occurred in Chile when the Nixon administration (like the Johnson administration before it) sought by covert action to prevent Allende's coming into power. In October 1970, a group of anti-Allende military officers had hatched a plot to abduct the army commander, General René Schneider. Nixon (on Kissinger's advice) specifically disapproved this kidnapping plot; the officers went ahead anyway, bungled it, and killed Schneider by accident. While the Church Committee had to admit that no one in the

U.S. government authorized the assassination of Schneider, it managed to stretch the incident into a detailed thirty-page section of a report devoted precisely to the subject of U.S. government assassination plots.

The contortion act in the Senate was outmatched by the flaming-hoop and knife throwing act on the House side. Even Colby deplored it as a "pretty awful mess." The Pike Committee looked into a variety of alleged "intelligence failures" including historical case studies, and—even juicier—events in the Nixon and Ford administrations such as the Middle East war of October 1973 and the Cyprus crisis of 1974. Particularly egregious in Colby's eyes was its insistence on declassifying, over his objections, a reference to the Egyptian army's improved communications security before the 1973 war. The U.S. ability (or inability) to intercept foreign military communications is usually treated as an especially sensitive secret. The entire Pike Committee report, containing this and much other sensitive intelligence information, was leaked to CBS newsman Daniel Schorr, who promptly delivered it to *The Village Voice*.

Kissinger was furious at Colby throughout this ordeal, needling him at one point (referring to his Catholicism): "Bill, you know what you do when you go up to the Hill? You go to confession." In his memoirs Kissinger speculates whether at some stage in his career Colby had begun having moral qualms about his chosen profession. He was also bitter at Colby's triggering of the process that led to an unwarranted perjury indictment of his predecessor, Richard Helms, whom Kissinger regarded highly; Helms had sought to protect information about a covert operation in an open Senate hearing (having provided the same information to an appropriate committee in a closed hearing). Kissinger writes that Ford shared his disappointment with Colby's conduct but wanted to wait until the congressional ordeal was over before replacing him. Ford, in turn, treats Colby more gently in his own memoirs (especially in comparison to Schlesinger). Even in the process of dismissing him, as we have seen, Ford thanked him for the job he had done in "the most difficult of circumstances."

In truth, predictable as were the consequences of Colby's capitulations to Congress, Colby himself was not the problem. The core of the problem can be found in the passage in Colby's memoirs quoted above, in which he observed that the balance of power in Washington had shifted to Congress and he had to adapt. "I did not share the view that intelligence was solely a function of the Executive Branch and must be protected from Congressional prying," he also noted. This is an extraor-

dinary statement. The CIA is not an independent regulatory agency, like the Securities and Exchange Commission, conventionally regarded as a creature of Congress; it was created by law in 1947 as an adviser to the National Security Council, which is an arm of the president. Congressional oversight has been strengthened considerably under new procedures that developed in this period, but strengthening congressional oversight is not the same as removing the CIA from its place in the Executive Branch. Yet the reality in the mid-1970s was as Colby described it—a major weakening of the executive power: Colby was simply more afraid of the wrath of Congress than of the wrath of the president.

Losing His Hat

Ford's transition team in 1974 had included among its recommendations that Kissinger relinquish his post as assistant to the president for national security affairs while remaining secretary of state. Ford agreed, believing that the conjoining of the two jobs was "totally contrary to the purpose and intent of the NSC." But he put off any action on that front, knowing that Kissinger wanted to keep both hats and not wanting to "make any changes that might be misunderstood overseas." But over time, Ford came to the conclusion that Kissinger's deputy Brent Scowcroft would win everyone's trust as his successor, and that this move would have its logical place as part of the elaborate reshuffle in October 1975.

Ford was right about Kissinger's preference to hold on to both positions, and reasonable in the concern about international reaction. It could only be seen as a diminution of Kissinger's authority, especially by foreigners who would not be so familiar with the logic of the claim that the ouster of Schlesinger was a great victory for him. In addition he was preoccupied by the gloomy expectation that he would become more and more the principal target of Ford's conservative opposition. After brooding on all this for some weeks he began composing a long letter of resignation; like many other Kissinger products (such as speeches) he circulated it to immediate staff and friends for editorial comments. This one, I recall, was a dozen pages or so and went through several drafts until it was a fairly polished and eloquent product. All of us familiar with the project were in a state of mourning for weeks. Then Kissinger went into the Oval Office to see Ford in early January carrying the letter

still in "draft" (typed up double-spaced, without letterhead or signature), explaining to Ford that he would sign such a letter if he was becoming a political liability. Ford rejected the whole idea out of hand. If by handing over the letter in draft Kissinger was hedging against the (slim) possibility that Ford might accept it, he needn't have worried; if Ford was amused by the tentativeness of this resignation, he never let on.

On reflection, Kissinger came to see Ford's decision to separate the two positions as the right one. Not only are they separate functions; there is an obvious conflict of interest between them. With Scowcroft reverting to the classical role of the honest broker—even to become the paradigm of that role—the system worked well and Kissinger's stature cannot be said to have seriously diminished. Ford in a news conference on November 3 still spoke of Kissinger's "dominant role in the formulation of and the carrying out of foreign policy." Ford later told David Rothkopf:

> I had good relationships with both Henry and Brent, and I used them as they should have been used under the law that was passed in 1947. I depended upon a good relationship with Henry as secretary of state, and he was a first class one. But I, at the same time, used Brent and his new responsibilities as head of the NSC according to the law there as well.

Scowcroft describes his role modestly as supplementing or complementing Kissinger's role. He told Rothkopf that Ford wanted to be able to "step back and ask, 'What is this world about? What are my options?' And then Kissinger would present some options—A, B, C, D. Ford would then turn to me and ask, Are there any other options?"

In addition to this service to Ford—giving him the assurance that all bases had been covered—Scowcroft in his new role provided an important service to Kissinger, who relied on his counsel with respect to conflicts with other departments or with the White House staff. Whether on the growing controversies over SALT and détente, or over international economic issues on which Kissinger sought to launch a number of new initiatives (see below), Scowcroft was now in a stronger position to affect the outcomes or mediate the disputes. This was especially important when Kissinger was traveling (which was often) and waging the interagency battles at long distance. Knowing Ford's strate-

gic backing of Kissinger's views, Scowcroft wielded his new clout most often in Kissinger's support. Rather than attempting to be competitive with Kissinger, which Ford did not desire, Scowcroft more often than not served as Kissinger's ally in interagency squabbles. Where Ford considered that his political straits constrained him to depart from Kissinger's recommendations, Scowcroft helped manage a soft landing.

International Economic Policy

When Kissinger was White House national security adviser in Nixon's first term, one criticism of his performance was that he played no significant role in international economic policy. A widely read analysis of Kissinger's NSC staff operation, by journalist John Leacacos, included this critical observation:

> During [the] first year about 70 percent of the bureaucracy's contributions to NSC economic studies came from the Treasury Department, and only 30 percent from State. No senior interdepartmental group for economics was organized. Receiving little attention from Kissinger, the NSC's own economic specialists carried no bureaucratic clout.

This was certainly the conventional wisdom of the time, though Kissinger's reputation for lack of interest in economics may have been exaggerated. George P. Shultz gives Kissinger credit, for example, for steering Nixon toward bilateral summit meetings with key European leaders in 1971 to repair relations after Nixon's abrupt devaluation of the dollar and other unilateral measures on August 15—a necessary and inevitable "accommodation," Shultz says, "between our economic and our political interests." Leaving aside the irony that Kissinger, who was criticized in 1971 for dominating foreign policy, was simultaneously being criticized for *not* dominating international economic policy, for our present purposes there is also the irony that as secretary of state he was criticized for, indeed, trying to dominate that, too.

Kissinger's role in international economic policy under Ford is worth dwelling upon for a variety of reasons. It was an important element of the Ford administration's foreign policy; it was an example of Kissinger in action as secretary of state and his relations with cabinet colleagues other than the usual NSC players, and of how Ford managed all this. The results, too, were rather more successful than those involving the

Pentagon and CIA. It also goes to the question of the State Department's capacity for taking the lead on policy matters that cut across departmental lines.

The NSC system, as we saw in both preceding chapters, has struggled over many decades to insure smooth coordination among State, Defense, CIA, and other departments and agencies involved in the traditional national security realm. While lip service has often been paid to the need to include economic issues, the fit has never been an easy one. The National Security Act of 1947 did not list the secretary of the treasury among the statutory members of the NSC. The economic concerns that seemed most relevant in those days had to do with wartime economic mobilization—this had been the economic preoccupation in World War II and it was the Cold War expectation of those who had come out of that experience. Thus, the office in charge of resource mobilization and civil defense, in its various incarnations over the decades, was a statutory member, until Nixon removed it by executive order. Every president beginning with Truman, however, has routinely included Treasury in the NSC process, by invitation, and recommendations to include the secretary in the NSC by statute are a staple of national security reform proposals.

The more serious question and this is only half-facetious is whether the secretary of the treasury really wants to be a member, or rather, whether he wants his department roped into the national security decision-making process. All the economic departments of the government—including Treasury, Commerce, Agriculture, Energy, Labor, and the Trade Representative have powerful domestic constituencies and equally powerful congressional committees that take a proprietary interest in these agencies' activities; this is where the "iron triangle" of Congress, the bureaucracy, and interest groups is particularly strong. They are not the same committees that have oversight over foreign affairs or national defense, and the international dimension is not likely to be their main interest in life (except to promote exports).

Power has continued to gravitate to these economic agencies. There once was a time when the State Department had the predominant voice in international economic issues (with the NSC staff as its ally), with Treasury reigning supreme over the domestic economy. In recent decades, however, globalization has broken down whatever separation may once have existed between the two dimensions. As economist Fred Bergsten has put it:

Therefore, the external factors intrude across a whole range of interest groups, issues, etc., that never even heard of the world economy. Therefore, many more agencies, many more issues, many more domestic interests are involved, and it would be totally unrealistic to think State or the NSC could dominate the way it did before.

These domestic agencies strongly resist letting the "foreign policy boys and girls" play diplomatic games with their chips. That is how it often seems to them, especially in Republican administrations: The foreign policy crowd wants for political reasons to reach international arrangements that interfere with market forces, or else to impede for political reasons economic activities that the market would warrant. Therefore the economic agencies have traditionally resisted allowing major issues of concern to them to be presented to the president through the NSC process. If it goes through that process, the White House national security adviser gets to write the memorandum and the system may be skewed in the foreign policy crowd's favor. Since Nixon's time, therefore, presidents have created alternative interagency mechanisms, with varying success, to integrate all the various interests and points of view, separate from the NSC and from the exclusive control of the national security adviser. In 1971, Nixon created an interdepartmental Council on International Economic Policy (CIEP) in the White House, under first Peter G. Peterson and then Peter Flanigan as executive director; it established itself as a useful body even as a strong secretary of the treasury, John Connally, tried to stifle it.

Gerald Ford bowed to reality and established an Economic Policy Board chaired by his secretary of the treasury (William Simon)—again, separate from the NSC. This has proved a more durable model. Like George Shultz under Nixon, James Baker under Ronald Reagan, and Robert Rubin under Bill Clinton, Simon was a strong treasury secretary who took the lead in international financial policy. Ford kept a White House hand in by naming his assistant for economic affairs William Seidman as the EPB's executive director. And Seidman gave the NSC staff a behind-the-scenes role in the EPB's operations.

But what happens if a strong treasury secretary (e.g., Simon) runs up against a strong secretary of state (e.g., Kissinger)? Kissinger's initial reaction to Ford's Economic Policy Board was to ignore it. One of the preoccupations of his tenure as secretary of state—especially because of the global economic and political crisis triggered by the 1973 explo-

sion in energy prices—was a series of international initiatives in the economic field. He was aided in these initiatives by an energetic career diplomat, Thomas Enders, whose bureaucratic sharp elbows seemed to assure freedom of action for the State Department until, alas, Kissinger was pulled into the EPB by the White House (in exchange for a seat on its executive committee).

The Kissinger initiatives were based on the idea that the United States should wield its economic power in accordance with a strategy, or in furtherance of strategic objectives. One example was grain sales to the Soviet Union. The Nixon administration had been embarrassed in 1972 when the Kremlin outsmarted the Agriculture Department and bought nearly a billion dollars' worth of U.S. grain at subsidized prices; the Soviets cleverly concealed their desperate need (after a bad harvest) and played our grain companies against each other. Having been burned once, Kissinger in the Ford administration did not want to repeat the experience; he wanted to use grain sales as leverage. As one inside observer recounts:

> On the issue of leverage, Secretary Kissinger argued that the U.S. grain crop was a tremendous asset, mainly because there was no substitute for it in the world. Merely pouring out the grain for "gold" was "very painful" when appropriately managed sales could buy a year or so of good Soviet behavior. He cited the skill with which the OPEC nations used their oil resources, urged that the administration maintain an "element of uncertainty," and cautioned against excessive eagerness in dealing with the Soviets.

It was linkage again. Kissinger—a convert to the EPB now that it gave him a say in these decisions—insisted that the Agriculture Department not authorize any new sales to the Soviet Union, formally or informally, without EPB review. The upshot was a five-year agreement with the Soviets that capped the amounts sold in each year. This was a compromise that all agencies accepted (though it led to vociferous protests from the farm lobby because of its constraints on sales).

The larger challenge of the period, as noted, was the energy shock of 1973, when the Organization of the Petroleum Exporting Countries (OPEC) quadrupled the price of oil and tipped much of the world into recession. Coming at the same time as the U.S. retreat in Indochina and the Watergate crisis at home, the economic crisis led to what

Kissinger feared was a creeping demoralization in the West; the Soviets crowed that the global "correlation of forces" was shifting in favor of "socialism" and Communist parties threatened to gain electoral ground even in Western Europe.

Kissinger's idea was to counter this trend on a number of fronts. He briefed Ford on August 17, 1974, barely a week into Ford's presidency: "We have to find a way to break the cartel. We can't do it without cooperation with the other consumers. It is intolerable that countries of 40 million can blackmail 800 million people in the industrial world." Where European countries were tempted to appease OPEC, Kissinger sought to mobilize solidarity among the consumer nations as a counterweight to OPEC. The French for a time resisted this cooperation (on the Gaullist thesis that any American-led enterprise has to be resisted on principle), but eventually the French (under their new president Valéry Giscard d'Estaing) agreed to the U.S.-proposed International Energy Agency—to be headquartered in Paris, of course—and to other measures of energy cooperation among the industrial democracies.

In August 1975, Giscard proposed a meeting on economic policy among the leaders of the major economic powers; such a summit was held at Rambouillet in November. It was Ford's proposal (on Alan Greenspan's advice) to make this an annual affair. This was the origin of what soon became the Group of Seven, or G-7—the grouping of the leading industrial democracies (the United States, United Kingdom, Japan, Germany, France, Canada, Italy, plus the European Union). While the ostensible subject matter was economic—and there were significant matters of global economic policy to discuss—political topics were also discussed. Ford and Kissinger saw the forum as invaluable as a political directorate of the Western democracies, sorely needed to reinforce political solidarity and head off the demoralization threatening to engulf the West.

The second element of U.S. strategy was to split the Third World. The vast majority of developing nations—poor, and without oil—were suffering the most severe economic blow themselves from the higher oil prices. Yet they were pulled toward appeasement of their OPEC brothers by a sense of helplessness, by OPEC promises of aid (rarely kept), and by radical notions of a "New International Economic Order" in which their commodities too might someday be cartelized. Kissinger wanted the United States, by a series of multilateral economic initiatives, to demonstrate to the non-oil-producing developing countries that

their interest lay with the existing global economic system and not with Marxist ideological fantasies. In a series of major speeches to international bodies in 1974, 1975, and 1976, he let loose a steady stream of policy initiatives, including a United Nations World Food Program, a special lending facility at the International Monetary Fund to finance oil purchases for the poorest, mechanisms to improve developing countries' access to capital markets and new technology, structural improvements to the world trading system, and a special development initiative for Africa.

Pushing these economic proposals through the United States government was not easy. As noted, every single one of the proposals trod on the expertise and turf of some other department or agency with important domestic and congressional constituencies for whom Kissinger's grand strategy must have seemed a bizarre abstraction. Kissinger and his staff were also tempted occasionally by the idea of commodity agreements or other mechanisms that represented interference with market forces, on the ground that the poorer countries needed special help if they were not to be harmed by the volatility of the international economy as it was then working. These ideas ran into significant opposition among economic conservatives in the Ford administration.

Usually Kissinger simply took the bureaucratic initiative, charging his State Department experts (and NSC staff allies like Robert Hormats and me) to draft a speech for him to deliver to some important upcoming international meeting; the draft speech, laden with new proposals, would then be sent around to the other agencies for clearance—usually with not a lot of time to spare before the delivery date. His key aide Thomas Enders was sometimes accused of playing other agencies off against each other, approaching them bilaterally and sometimes misleading them about other agencies' positions. The aggressive approach was an early test of the EPB mechanism. Ford would often break the deadlocks himself if compromises could not be worked out, and as discussed earlier, the State Department was eventually domesticated into the EPB process.

Some other kinds of interagency conflicts were harder to resolve. At one point, Treasury Secretary Simon called the shah of Iran a "nut" because of the shah's aggressive promotion of OPEC price increases. The shah wanted to develop Iran rapidly and thought oil had been underpriced for too long. Despite the serious American disagreement

with him over the price hikes and the global crisis they produced, Kissinger and Ford saw the shah also as a key strategic ally in a region threatened by Soviet-backed Arab radicalism that was entrenching itself in Syria, Yemen, the Palestine Liberation Organization (PLO), and Saddam Hussein's Iraq. At Kissinger's urging, Simon retreated and announced he had been quoted out of context. Kissinger accepted the concession, though he remained puzzled as to what context might make our ally find it palatable to be called a "nut."

Kissinger's tenure as secretary of state was thus a time not only of strong political leadership of the State Department but of leadership by the department in an important area of policy involving other powerful cabinet agencies. State's role was insured by Kissinger's bureaucratic tenacity but most of all by conceptual leadership—by his articulation of a broad strategy toward the intersection of political and economic interests that Ford enthusiastically embraced. While events conspired to deny them this coherence in broad policy toward the Soviet Union, this set of issues remains an instructive example for future secretaries of state who aspire to restore at least some of their department's historical preeminence.

Straddling an Earthquake

Ford was caught by surprise by the Reagan challenge, and thrown off-balance by it. He considered himself a conservative Republican and a conservative president: He pushed for a defense buildup after a long period of decline in defense spending; he pleaded with Congress in 1974–1975 to support our allies in Indochina; he struggled to defend U.S. intelligence agencies against congressional assault. At the end of 1975, he fought to continue a U.S. covert action program against Cuban-Soviet military intervention in Angola, which Congress blocked. He considered his policy toward the Soviet Union a firm one. The arms agreement he had reached with Brezhnev at Vladivostok in November 1974 would establish equal ceilings for the strategic missiles of the two sides, correcting the (misleading) impression of inequality left by Nixon's 1972 accord. The Helsinki Final Act, which he signed at a thirty-five-nation summit meeting in the summer of 1975, enshrined human rights for the first time as a core issue of East-West relations in Europe, and also enshrined principles that delegitimated military interventions like the Soviet invasions of Hungary and Czechoslovakia. Ford and

Kissinger attempted to rebuild Western morale and unity in the wake of the energy and economic crises of the period.

Yet the Ford administration was overwhelmed by events. Its policy toward the Soviet Union was essentially taken out of its hands: Conservatives took away the carrots in its policy—such as arms control and trade—while liberals took away the sticks—the defense programs and strong geopolitical actions (as in Angola) to counter Soviet expansionism. One bellwether was the decision of George H. W. Bush, Colby's successor at CIA, to respond to conservative pressures in 1976 by appointing an outside group (dubbed "Team B") to critique U.S. intelligence on Soviet military and other activities. Team B's conclusion was that the CIA had tended consistently to underestimate the Soviet threat—which, when it leaked, became another weapon against Ford's and Kissinger's policies.

Ford's political weakness had deeper causes. In large part it was the result of the deadly economic combination of inflation and recession, as well as the Watergate debacle whose legacy still burdened Ford (especially the unpopular pardon of Nixon). A Gallup Poll in early January 1976 showed 46 percent of respondents disapproving of Ford's performance in office, with only 39 percent approving. In the foreign policy dimension the American demoralization was magnified, I am convinced, by the humiliation of the outcome in Indochina, even if that was rarely mentioned by name. There were no bitter recriminations when the war ended, no "stab in the back" theory. With the bloodbath in Indochina in April 1975 came a kind of bipartisan amnesia: Liberals were embarrassed at the grisly outcome of an abandonment they had passionately argued for; conservatives were embarrassed at the failure of an intervention they had strongly supported. Other issues, therefore, became surrogates for a nationalistic reaction. That is what propelled Ronald Reagan's powerful challenge to Ford in 1976; it is what propelled Reagan into the presidency in 1980 after the Soviet invasion of Afghanistan and President Carter's Iran hostage crisis compounded the sense of national humiliation.

The foreign policy part of Reagan's campaign against Ford in 1976 was based on the theme that the United States was falling behind the Soviets in the military field and that U.S. policy, especially arms control, was only weakening us further. Reagan called for a military buildup; he denounced Kissinger and the firing of Schlesinger. He urged Ford not to go to the Helsinki summit, as that would only concede Soviet domina-

tion of Eastern Europe. He argued that the' Panama Canal should remain U.S. property because we had built it (rather than be the subject of a negotiation with Panama to head off an explosion of Panamanian nationalism in the U.S. Canal Zone). The charismatic Reagan touched a chord in a party and a nation tired of humiliation and demoralization. Thus he launched a formidable challenge to a sitting president of his own party:

> Under Kissinger and Ford [Reagan declared], this nation has become Number Two in a world where it is dangerous—if not fatal—to be second best. All I can see is what other nations the world over see: collapse of the American will and the retreat of American power. There is little doubt in my mind that the Soviet Union will not stop taking advantage of détente until it sees that the American people have elected a new President and appointed a new Secretary of State.

The struggle lasted through a long season of hotly contested Republican primaries beginning in February with the outcome in doubt until the national convention in Kansas City in August. Ford won the early string of primaries, beginning with an ominously narrow win in New Hampshire on February 24, but moving on successfully through Florida, Massachusetts, Vermont, and Illinois, until a major upset by Reagan in North Carolina in March. Scholar Michael Barone describes what followed:

> The remainder of [the] war for the Republican nomination followed a course reminiscent of the prolonged trench warfare of World War I. Both sides fought hard and neither gained much ground. In May and June, Ford won primaries in West Virginia, Maryland, Michigan, Kentucky, Oregon, Tennessee, Rhode Island, New Jersey, and Ohio— states in which Republicans had established a presence by the time of the Civil War. Reagan won primaries in Georgia, Indiana, Nebraska, Arkansas, Idaho, Nevada, Montana, South Dakota, and California— states in which (with the exception of Indiana) Republican strength dated from some later time.

Ford made a courageous decision in April, shortly before the May 1 Texas primary, to authorize Kissinger to proceed with a major diplomatic initiative in Southern Africa, including a push to persuade Rhodesia's

white minority to accept majority rule. Ford's political advisers warned him it would hurt in Texas—indeed, Ford lost badly in Texas and this undoubtedly contributed—but he supported Kissinger's strategy to strengthen moderate forces in Africa under pressure from Marxist radicals. Ford told his political advisers: "I cannot judge whether the political impact will be good or bad. But we must do this because it's the right thing to do."

This was not just the traditional battle between two strong candidates for their party's nomination. The fact that a sitting president was under challenge was unusual. But, more than that, Barone's roster of which states were old territory for the Republicans and which were new tells the story of the political earthquake that was under way in the GOP. As political analyst Jonathan Martin elaborates:

> Where "Regular Republicans" reigned or still held considerable sway . . . the more moderate Ford did better. But in states with little in the way of a Republican tradition, Reagan won the day. . . . Ford embodied the good-government northeastern and Midwestern party of Rockefeller, [Henry Cabot] Lodge, and [Arthur] Vandenberg. He was, in many ways, representative of the end of an era. . . . Those states that, as Barone explains, Reagan won in part due to their minimal Republican tradition have something else in common—all except California are what we now call red states and form the core of the modern GOP.

IF THE SAGA of Schlesinger versus Kissinger in the cabinet was part of the narrative of the revolution engulfing the Republican Party, the drama of William Colby was emblematic of the constitutional revolution that was occurring simultaneously. Colby saw the balance of power tilting so strongly toward Congress as to render the CIA less an institution of the Executive Branch than a virtual servant of Congress. While the focus of this book is not on executive-legislative relations, the Colby phenomenon requires some explanatory context. Vietnam and Watergate left a legacy of new restrictions on presidential power that are now embedded in legislation. A paradox of the period was that while the Republican Party and the country seemed to be shifting gradually to the right, the Congress elected in November 1974 (in the wake of Watergate and the Nixon pardon) had shifted sharply to the left.

Michael Barone calls the Democrats' victory in 1974 one "of stunning proportions": They gained forty-six House seats over their 1972 numbers and controlled the House by a margin of 290 to 145, while increasing their control of the Senate by three. The previous Congress had begun the process of imposing some important restrictions on a weakened Nixon, including in Indochina and over war powers. The new Congress took up with a vengeance where its predecessor left off.

The catalogue of new legislative restraints on executive power from that period is a long one. Reagan, when he was president, used to speak of "over 100 separate prohibitions and restrictions on Executive Branch authority to formulate and implement foreign policy" enacted since the 1970s. Some of these restrictions came from conservatives (such as the Jackson-Vanik linkage of U.S.-Soviet trade to freer emigration from the Soviet Union), but the overwhelming majority came from the left:

- The War Powers Resolution, passed over Nixon's veto in November 1973.
- Prohibitions on U.S. military action in support of allies in Indochina, and reductions in security assistance to them, from 1970 to 1975.
- An embargo on U.S. military aid to Turkey after the Cyprus crisis in 1974.
- Prohibition of a U.S. covert program of military assistance to forces opposing the Cuban-Soviet military intervention in Angola.
- Expanded oversight and control over intelligence activities, resulting from the investigations into alleged intelligence abuses.
- Freedom of Information Act amendments, enacted over Ford's veto in 1974, removing the Executive Branch's exclusive power to determine what information can be kept classified on national security grounds.
- Limitations on numbers of U.S. military personnel deployed abroad, such as the ceilings on the number of U.S. Marines in Lebanon in 1983–1984 and on U.S. military trainers in El Salvador in the 1980s.
- A variety of legislated restrictions based on human rights considerations, which limit or attach conditions on economic and security assistance to friendly countries (e.g., El Salvador and Indonesia).
- A regime of nonproliferation controls and sanctions restricting various forms of bilateral cooperation with countries that have failed to comply with international safeguards or have violated unilaterally set U.S.

criteria (e.g., at various times, India, Pakistan, Brazil, Argentina, China, and Egypt).

• Limits on the president's power to impose economic sanctions or controls for foreign policy purposes (or, in some cases, conversely, mandating such sanctions without allowing presidential discretion).

• Elaborate new procedures of congressional oversight over U.S. arms transfers to friendly countries.

• Much tightened requirements for reprogramming of funds, by which congressional committees can deny presidents the flexibility they used to have in the use of authorized or appropriated funds to respond to rapidly changing conditions.

• Growing use of earmarking of aid funds to compel the expenditure of designated amounts for countries favored by Congress, which usually has the effect of squeezing out funds for other friendly countries under the fixed ceiling of the assistance budget.

Officials in recent administrations have become accustomed to struggling with these legislative restrictions, which they treat as part of the landscape. Government lawyers and accountants consume weeks and months struggling to find legal ways to perform certain tasks or to provide aid to certain allies in the national interest, sometimes in emergency conditions. Denial of presidential flexibility was a deliberate goal of these legislative constraints, and they have achieved their purpose. A few restrictions have been repealed or relaxed (like the Turkish embargo in 1978, the Angola restrictions in 1985, and the Indonesia restrictions in 2005), but that kind of effort usually takes years. The broad categories listed above embrace hundreds of statutory provisions (many of which duplicate each other, or overlap), as well as reporting requirements and restrictions that presidents can waive in certain conditions; some restrictions are presidential commitments exacted by Congress as the price of support for other presidential initiatives. But the scope of this legislative micromanagement is now enormous. In 1964, the House and Senate foreign affairs committees began publishing a handy joint compilation called *Legislation on Foreign Relations*. The 1964 edition was a volume of about 650 pages. By 1985, it had grown into three volumes totaling more than 4,000 pages. The most recent complete set comprises five volumes, published over a number of years, totaling over 9,500 pages. This represented a revolution in the balance between the two branches of government.

A Lasting Legacy

An unelected president, Ford was on the defensive from the early days of his tenure, under pressure from the conservative challenge in his party and the Democratic congressional resurgence. In the end, his race against Democratic nominee Jimmy Carter was remarkably close—a 51–48 percent loss. So the question arises whether an elected Ford, with a popular mandate and removal of the cloud over his authority, would have been able to recover lost ground, either in the party or at the other end of Pennsylvania Avenue. This is impossible to answer. Perhaps his victory would have enabled the moderate wing of the Republican Party to regain its footing and its dominance for an additional period of years, while restoring the defense budget and rebuilding popular and congressional support for his concept of a strong foreign and defense policy. We will never know. In 1976 at least, the forces arrayed against him were powerful ones, in a period of unusual turmoil. The revolution in the party might have continued regardless, with the charismatic Reagan continuing his pursuit (as he did) for 1980. Meanwhile, the Democrats' domination of Congress was to last two more decades, pulling national policy to the left. The straddle may have been more than Ford—or any president—could manage.

Those times have left their mark. A later CIA director, Robert Gates, observed in a speech in 1987 that the CIA found itself "equidistant" between president and Congress. It was an echo of Colby. (When Gates published the speech as an article in *Foreign Affairs*, he inserted the word "involuntarily" with reference to the "equidistance," in a welcome bow to the National Security Act.) Thus, even if Reagan's strong performance in the Oval Office was to remind us that the institution of the presidency was far from dead, the centrifugal pull of Congress on our bureaucracy never reverted to the earlier status quo.

Most of the officials now struggling to formulate and implement policy in this environment do not remember a time when these legislative restrictions did not exist. The burdens have been absorbed in bureaucratic routine. But one who did remember was Dick Cheney. It was a thirty-five-year-old Dick Cheney who as White House chief of staff watched President Ford and his administration being overwhelmed by this tidal wave. "It wasn't personal and it wasn't directed at Ford in that sense," Cheney said a few years later. "It was institutional in the sense that it was directed at the presidency." Decades later, he called the Ford

period "the nadir of the modern presidency in terms of authority and legitimacy."

There cannot be any doubt that this was one of the formative experiences of Dick Cheney's life. As a young member of Congress he became an outspoken champion of restoring executive authority, in both foreign and domestic policy, when other of his new colleagues (Newt Gingrich, for example) were calling for a further strengthening of Congress's role. During the congressional investigations of the Iran-Contra affair in the Reagan administration, as we shall see in Chapter 6, Cheney led the Republican minority side in an articulate defense of presidential actions and presidential prerogatives that was more impressive than anything emanating from a demoralized White House. The same conviction clearly infused his later actions as vice president—the conviction that it was not always this way, that it has done harm, and that (especially in a time of war) it was time to push back.

Jimmy Carter

J IMMY CARTER, like virtually every other president discussed in this book, came into office determined to avoid what he saw as the errors of his predecessors. When he hired Zbigniew Brzezinski as his assistant for national security affairs—another high-energy foreign-born foreign policy intellectual—he made clear to Brzezinski that he did not want him to be another Kissinger. Carter in his memoirs says he welcomed the "natural competition" between the State Department and the White House national security adviser and did not want the latter to dominate as Kissinger had done. He agreed with Brzezinski "most of the time" on substance, Carter says, but he nonetheless "appreciated" the continuing differences between the two organizations because he believed these differences maximized his own ability to make the final decisions and thereby control the process.

By the same token, Carter did not want Cyrus Vance, the distinguished lawyer he chose as his secretary of state, to be another Kissinger and to dominate the process as Kissinger had done as secretary of state. In an appearance as president-elect before the Senate Foreign Relations Committee, Carter said:

> I intend to appoint a strong and competent Secretary of State, but I intend to remember . . . that the responsibility [for the conduct of foreign policy] lies in the White House with the President. I will be the President and I will represent the country in foreign affairs.

Toward the end of his term, Carter still had Kissinger on his mind: "There have been Presidents in the past, maybe not too distant past, that let their Secretaries of State make foreign policy. I don't." As time

passed, Carter realized he had the opposite problem: Like so many other occupants of the Oval Office he came to lament the "inertia" and lack of strategic innovativeness at Foggy Bottom. While Vance, unlike William Rogers, had had prior experience in the national security field (including in the Defense Department), he proved a disappointment to Carter as Rogers did to Nixon.

Carter, in short, wanted Vance and Brzezinski to be counterweights to each other. He later told interviewers from the *Harvard Business Review*:

> I deliberately chose advisers with disparate points of view. I wanted the very conservative, stable, and cautionary reaction of the State Department on the one hand and the more dynamic, innovative advice from the National Security staff on the other hand. . . . I wanted a broad assortment of opinions before I made a judgment.

Brzezinski and Vance indeed had sharply opposing philosophies. Brzezinski, like Kissinger, came out of a European tradition that drew sober lessons from history; he was a thinker with a geopolitical world-view, realistic about the role of power in world affairs even as he shared the president's and the Democratic Party's commitment to human rights. He saw the challenge of Soviet power as a global one, and viewed other issues—especially the role of China—in the context of that competition. Like Kissinger, he was a hardened veteran of faculty politics.

Vance, like William Rogers, was a gentleman lawyer, moderate by instinct in philosophy and personality. He was comfortable reflecting the institutional views of his department. He thought it was wrong to make the competition with the Soviet Union the preoccupation of U.S. foreign policy:

> A flaw in our foreign policy during this period [Vance later wrote] was that it was too narrowly rooted in the concept of an overarching U.S.-Soviet "geopolitical" struggle. Obviously, such a conflict did exist and it was of major dimensions. But our national interests encompassed more than U.S.-Soviet relations. . . . Many developments did not fit neatly into an East-West context. . . . Global interdependence, once a fashionable buzzword, had become a reality.

Carter's memoirs bear out Brzezinski's contention that the president wanted a White House–centered rather than cabinet-centered system.

Thus, Carter leaned toward strengthening Brzezinski's hand in some respects as a way to strengthen his own. Brzezinski was given cabinet rank—which Kissinger as White House assistant never had; Brzezinski chaired a key interdepartmental group (the Special Coordination Committee), as Kissinger had done, but the other members around the table were cabinet secretaries, not deputy or under secretaries (unlike Kissinger's Review Group). Brzezinski early on, at Carter's urging, became a public spokesman for the administration, giving on-the-record interviews and appearing on television talk shows, which, again, Nixon never allowed Kissinger to do until almost the end of his first term. Brzezinski even hired his own press secretary on the NSC staff, which raised eyebrows in Washington. But there is no doubt that Carter wanted him to play this role, disappointed as he was in Vance's inability or unwillingness to be a forceful or articulate public educator concerning the administration's policies. Vance recognized in retrospect that he should have devoted more time and effort to being a spokesman, but he remained bitter at Carter for allowing Brzezinski such a prominent role.

Eventually Brzezinski was also given some important substantive assignments as Carter's special envoy in the Kissinger mode. He led the secret negotiations with China that led to normalization of relations. He negotiated a swap of Soviet spies for Soviet dissidents. He helped organize Middle East and Arab responses to the Soviet invasion of Afghanistan, and played a role in organizing West European allies' responses to Soviet missile deployments in Europe. Carter sent him to have a private conversation with Anwar Sadat about Carter's domestic political prospects and how they would affect U.S. Middle East diplomacy. He also came to take the lead, with Defense Secretary Harold Brown's support, in setting policy toward the SALT negotiations with the Soviet Union, which was managed through the Special Coordination Committee that Brzezinski chaired.

State Department officials were extremely bitter about Brzezinski's aggressiveness in excluding them from the sensitive negotiations with China. Brzezinski and Vance had different substantive approaches to the issue, with Brzezinski eager to normalize with China as leverage against the Soviet Union, and with State more cautious out of concern at disrupting the SALT talks with the Soviets. Brzezinski sent a key decision memorandum to Carter without consulting with Vance. State officials were convinced that press leaks from Brzezinski undermined

Vance's standing with the Chinese during a visit Vance paid to China; Brzezinski seems to have coaxed the Chinese into inviting *him* to visit China, where he supplanted Vance as the principal U.S. negotiator. When Brzezinski headed his own delegation to Beijing, he excluded assistant secretary of state Richard Holbrooke from a key meeting with Chinese leader Deng Xiaoping. He continued meeting secretly in Washington with Chinese envoys while taking elaborate precautions to insure that this took place without State's knowledge.

I leave it to historians to decide how this compares with how Nixon and Kissinger treated William Rogers on China policy, but there is a resemblance. In this case, too, the president sided with his national security adviser on both the substance and the procedure. In an extraordinary letter to *Foreign Affairs* in 1999, Carter put it bluntly:

> I was leery of channeling my proposals through the State Department because I did not feel I had full support there and it was and is an enormous bureaucracy that is unable and sometimes unwilling to keep a secret. . . . Secretary Vance was conversant with every dispatch we sent and had constant access to me, so I did not give much weight to his disgruntled subordinates in the State Department, some of whom had been a constant source of complaints to the news media regarding the national security advisor's having too much influence over foreign policy. If these assistants at the State Department felt excluded . . . it was because of my orders to hold information closely so that our efforts would not be subverted.

In a phenomenon we have seen before, Carter perceived the many leaks attacking Brzezinski as a "surrogate for attacks on himself," since he had made the decisions that were being attacked. In December 1978 Carter convened a meeting with Vance and Brzezinski to try to smooth out the deteriorating relations between them, and made that point explicitly. Recall that Gerald Ford made the same observation to Henry Kissinger with respect to attacks on Kissinger emanating from James Schlesinger's Pentagon. Presidents notice such things.

Despite these victories, however, Brzezinski remained continually frustrated. He encouraged Carter to do what President Kennedy had done after a year in office—clean house at the State Department to put more loyalists in key subordinate positions. But Carter did not do so. And Brzezinski chafed at his formal equality with Vance when he felt

Carter's interest lay in strengthening him further. He later told an interviewer:

> Carter, quite rightly in my judgment, wanted it to be understood as *his* system, and therefore he wasn't prepared to make the assistant's role as explicit as perhaps it should have been; moreover, he wasn't prepared to make the personnel decisions that I said earlier were necessary, namely to purge those who really were not fully loyal to his views. And as a consequence, there was always practical bifurcation, ambiguity intensified by the emphasis placed publicly on the primacy of the secretary of state.

In short, Carter was true to his word in not giving Brzezinski free rein. Reading between the lines of Carter's memoirs one can sense a certain distancing, even amid the personal compliments that seem genuine enough. Carter says he encouraged the NSC staff to be "unrestrained" in making innovative proposals—"and consequently [I] had to reject a lot of them." He and Brzezinski "had many arguments about history, politics, international events, and foreign policy—often disagreeing strongly and fundamentally." Brzezinski, in turn, lamented in his diary at the end of 1978 that "unlike Kissinger, who had in Nixon a clear ally in shaping a grand strategy for the country, I have to do it through indirection." While the president tended to be tough on specific issues of Soviet policy and sided with Brzezinski when there was a bureaucratic showdown, Brzezinski feared that Carter was "very much tempted by the vision of a grand accommodation with Brezhnev."

President Carter's "balanced" system thus made perfect sense on an organization chart, but it masked a fundamental flaw that Brzezinski's diary entry points to—the philosophical schizophrenia of the president, of his worldview, and of his resulting policies. Nixon and Kissinger were united in what might be called a conservative philosophy—a tragic view of history in which conflicts are not always reconcilable and enemies must often be resisted. It is a consistent view of how the world works and how human nature is designed; it reflects in international affairs some of the realism of the framers of our Constitution in opposing power to power and assuming the fallibility, not the perfectibility, of man. It sees the world whole, relating disparate events to each other, which is one of the meanings of taking a strategic view. Whether one agrees with this philosophy or not, having a philosophy insured

consistency—both between the two men running the policy and in the kind of policy they conducted.

Jimmy Carter was an engineer by training, not a geopolitician. As such he can be said to be part of the American pragmatic tradition, which considers issues case by case, leaning sometimes toward one view and sometimes toward the other, "on their merits." Lawyers come out of a similar tradition. Brzezinski does not conceal his disappointment at the "absence of historical perspective" in Carter, nor his gentle reproach of the "occasionally surprising naïveté" of his president, despite his own earnest and intensive tutoring over four years. Thus, the system that Carter set up only enshrined the philosophical schizophrenia of its chief. Carter indeed dominated the process as he sought, but he gave no clear direction. The "balance" of two opposing philosophies was not the system's strength but its weakness—the root of its incoherence. A senior Carter aide has commented to me that Carter had no consistent philosophy in foreign policy except that what had gone on in his predecessors' administrations was bad.

The Carter System

Carter's determination to keep the reins of control in his hands was reflected in other aspects of his management style. He, too, started out with a more open and collegial "spokes of the wheel" arrangement in the White House, as did Gerald Ford, but eventually gravitated toward appointing a chief of staff. Carter also became known for his personal micromanagement of White House affairs, appointing a Georgia cousin (Hugh Carter, Jr., known as "Cousin Cheap") to oversee White House expenses and administration. Legend had it that the president was personally managing the scheduling of reservations on the White House tennis court; this was not true, but the story reflected the intense interest he took in details of administration—to insure frugality, assert his authority, and demonstrate his engineer's technical competence. On policy matters, he read voraciously—three hundred to four hundred pages daily, Richard Neustadt was told; on foreign policy, he was given 100 to 150 pages every night, Brzezinski told Brent Scowcroft. Scowcroft was astounded and thought it too much of a burden on any president, who should be focusing on the forest rather than the trees.

If micromanagement was one problem, his aversion to politics was another. Carter's "anti-political attitude used to drive me nuts," his vice

president, Walter Mondale, later complained, "because you couldn't get him to grapple with a political problem. . . . Carter thought politics was sinful." To Professor Neustadt, this was "suggestive of a President more unpolitical in some respects than Eisenhower," which for Neustadt was not at all a compliment but a grim warning of the lack of the "power sense" that presidents need to dominate their administrations.

Carter's national security process was—in the Democratic tradition—more loosely structured than that of his Republican predecessors. The National Security Council met formally only ten times in Carter's term, compared with the 125 meetings during the eight years of Nixon and Ford. Carter much preferred a more intimate forum, his breakfast at 7:30 a.m. every Friday in the Cabinet Room with his national security team (principally his vice president, secretaries of state and defense, the national security adviser, and a few White House aides). This was, he has said, his "favorite meeting of the week." Carter resisted Brzezinski's suggestion that there be a formal agenda; instead, Brzezinski often simply suggested topics to the president shortly before they walked from the Oval Office into the breakfast. No formal records were kept, which often led to conflicting interpretations of what had been decided. Only very late in the administration, after an embarrassing foul-up that led to the public retraction of a U.S. vote on a U.N. Security Council resolution on Jerusalem in March 1980, did Carter authorize Brzezinski to circulate an authoritative summary of his decisions. Thus, the failings often laid at the door of Lyndon Johnson's Tuesday lunches—which Walt Rostow rebutted—seem to have been more true of Carter's Friday breakfasts.

This presidential event was supplemented by a weekly Vance-Brown-Brzezinski luncheon, its venue rotating among the three, without aides or notetakers. All sides seem to have found this a useful forum for ironing out some differences, and successor administrations have benefited from following the precedent. But Vance remained forever jealous of Brzezinski's direct access to the president and the leverage this gave him. Vance regrets that he did not fight harder to insist on a right to clearance on drafts of presidential directives; State Department historians also note glumly that the president often wrote marginal comments on Brzezinski's weekly foreign policy summaries and that the security adviser and his staff "used these Presidential notes (159 of them) as the basis for NSC actions."

Another important and positive innovation of the Carter administra-

tion was its elevation of the substantive role of the vice president. This had been a declared aspiration of many administrations since the April day in 1945 when Harry Truman was thrust into the Oval Office uninformed of major policies including the existence of the atomic bomb. But with Walter Mondale an experienced and substantial figure in his own right, Carter wisely brought him into the inner circle. Mondale was the first vice president to be given a West Wing office close to the president's (rescued from exile across the street in the Executive Office Building). Mondale had his own one-on-one weekly lunch with the president, and played an important role as adviser on matters of both politics (frustrated as we have seen he sometimes was) and policy. He undoubtedly added some maturity as well as Washington political savvy to a White House that needed both.

Contradictions

The contradictions in the Carter presidency were foreshadowed in the 1976 campaign, when candidate Carter strove to position himself both to Gerald Ford's right and to his left simultaneously. Carter borrowed extensively from the then current critique of U.S.-Soviet détente: He argued that détente as then practiced was one-sided, that the Soviets were exploiting it, that the United States was acquiescing in Soviet domination of Eastern Europe. A close observer has noted the parallels between some of Carter's campaign rhetoric in 1976 and some of Ronald Reagan's. Carter also put human rights front and center in U.S.-Soviet relations in a forceful way. At the same time, many other of Carter's themes were familiar liberal themes—cutting the defense budget, pursuing strategic arms control, emphasizing humanitarian rather than military assistance to friends, paying more attention to the Third World, and rejection of what he considered the amoral balance-of-power approach of his predecessors.

Some of the tensions among these different impulses quickly revealed themselves in the new administration when it formulated its approach to SALT. The framework that Ford had agreed upon with Leonid Brezhnev at Vladivostok in 1974 would put both sides at an equal level ("equal aggregates"), though at high numbers (a total of 2,400 ICBMs, with a sub-ceiling of 1,320 on ICBMs with multiple warheads). Carter had the option of completing a treaty on the basis of the Vladivostok deal, which he might have accomplished fairly quickly.

Vance favored this course, but he was overruled. Others on the new team, including Carter, rejected it for various reasons. William Hyland, an astute Sovietologist and former Kissinger aide whom Brzezinski retained on his staff, reports that many on the new team thought it beneath their dignity simply to continue and complete the approach of their predecessors. Vladivostok was dismissively branded the "If Ford Had Won the Election" option.

Carter and his team instead were attracted to the idea of a bold and more comprehensive initiative pressing the Soviets for deep reductions in ICBMs on both sides. This concept appealed to liberals because it seemed a more ambitious quest for nuclear disarmament (as opposed to mere strategic arms "limitation"). But the idea had also been advanced by many conservative critics of the Nixon-Ford policy including elder statesman Paul Nitze and Senator Henry Jackson. Conservatives liked it because it sought deep reductions particularly in the category of large, silo-based ICBMs, which posed the greatest risk to the U.S. retaliatory force and in which the Soviets had a significant advantage. The desirability of such an outcome from the U.S. point of view could not be doubted; what was less clear was whether the United States had the bargaining leverage to compel Soviet acceptance of such a result. Gerald Ford had barely begun the process of securing congressional approval of increases in the defense budget, reversing many years of decline; Carter would eventually pursue the same goal. But neither president was yet achieving anywhere near the leverage with the Soviets that Ronald Reagan would achieve by his rapid military buildup a few years later.

Carter decided to put forward a comprehensive new proposal emphasizing deep reductions (down to 1,800 to 2,000 total ICBMs, and to 1,100 to 1,200 ICBMs with multiple warheads). As a fallback, however, he decided also to present to the Soviets a more modest concept proposing some reductions in the Vladivostok numbers (to 2,000 ICBMs, to include 1,200 ICBMs with multiple warheads). These two options were hammered out at two NSC meetings on March 19 and 22.

Meanwhile, other events were taking place in the U.S.-Soviet relationship. Carter's commitment to human rights, including as a core element in U.S. policy toward the Soviet Union, was a fundamental principle of both his campaign and his presidency. But in the multifaceted relationship we had with the Soviet Union, it proved difficult to calibrate this new element. Soon after Carter's inauguration, the State

Department—on its own initiative—began issuing a flood of statements championing human rights. One such initiative was a declaration of sympathy for Charter 77, the monitoring group set up by Czechoslovak activists; another was in support of Soviet scientist and human rights champion Andrei Sakharov. Carter decided to endorse these State Department initiatives, while letting it be known that he would have appreciated their being cleared in the White House. Then the president decided that he should reply personally to a public letter addressed to him by Sakharov appealing for U.S. support for a number of Soviet dissidents. Not wanting to leave himself open to charges of moral laxity like those leveled at Gerald Ford for not receiving Aleksandr Solzhenitsyn in the White House in 1975, Carter sent Sakharov a strong letter, including a sentence of sympathy for "prisoners of conscience." In a widely circulated news photo, Sakharov proudly displayed the letter he received with Carter's signature. In addition, a White House meeting was arranged for recently released Soviet dissident Vladimir Bukovsky, who met with Mondale in the Roosevelt Room. The Soviet response to all these activities was a scathing letter from Brezhnev to Carter stressing that the Soviet leadership would not "allow interference in our internal affairs, whatever pseudo-humanitarian slogans are used to present it."

All this took place in the first few weeks of the new administration, as it was preparing its new SALT proposals to be delivered by Secretary of State Vance on a trip to Moscow at the end of March. A new administration has every right to make changes in policies; that is its mandate from the American people, and the Soviets should not have been surprised that Carter's critique of SALT and advocacy of human rights during his campaign presaged a significant change. But the Soviets were not prepared for what they were faced with. The entire history of strategic arms negotiations up to then had occurred in the Nixon-Ford-Kissinger period. The Soviets were not only unaccustomed to abrupt changes; they were also accustomed to a procedure in which Kissinger would give Ambassador Dobrynin a heads-up with respect to any new U.S. proposals so that Brezhnev would not be caught by surprise when Kissinger showed up in Moscow. This was not simple courtesy; it was a way to allow the Soviet bureaucracy time to chew on new proposals so that the Kissinger-Brezhnev discussions would be more productive. In this case, with more abrupt changes in store—and against the background of the more assertive U.S. posture on human rights—there was no such preparing of the ground.

William Hyland, the holdover on the NSC staff, was particularly amused by one aspect of the procedure. "To guard against leaks, both Carter and Brzezinski insisted that the SALT decisions be drafted without interagency clearances; thus the delegation's instructions [drafted in the White House] were a virtual secret from the other departments." Hyland was badgered during the trip by other delegation members wanting to see the president's instructions. With Vance's concurrence, Hyland had to refuse. "When I told Vance of my embarrassment, he laughed and said that while he had ordered me to protect the instructions, he had not expected me to get caught. So a Ford holdover was entrusted with the mission of keeping Carter's secrets safe from his own delegation." Hyland recognized it as a Nixonian moment.

The bigger problem, however, was that Brezhnev, presented with the deep cuts option and the modified Vladivostok option, rejected them both. This was a shock; the Carter team had assumed that the modified Vladivostok option would be a mutually acceptable fallback. The Soviets' motivation is not clear. Whether out of pique at the human rights campaign, or a rigid commitment by their military bureaucracy to the original Vladivostok numbers, the Soviets just said no. Vance, on returning home, had to admit an American miscalculation and the administration was roundly criticized in the media for incompetence. *The Washington Post* called it the most disorderly retreat from Moscow since Napoleon's.

HYLAND DOES NOT SPARE his new colleagues his own critique of their complacency, but he also believes the Soviets erred in such a peremptory response:

> Had the Soviets moved quickly to consolidate an agreement, even in vague terms, they probably could have created a better foundation for a relationship with Carter; they could have gained a tactical advantage over the Chinese and perhaps they could have avoided the problem of the new American ICBM, the MX, to say nothing of the emergence of [Reagan's] Strategic Defense Initiative. Some Soviets have since admitted to me that they missed a chance.

In any case, the abortive March 1977 trip to Moscow set the negotiations back a period of months. The experiment in getting to the right of their Republican predecessors was a failure; no Democratic administra-

tion could sustain such a hard-line posture. Soon enough, eager to achieve an agreement, the Carter administration drifted back closer to the Vladivostok framework. Its procedures, and the coherence of its positions, improved. Negotiations continued, and produced by mid-1979 a SALT II Treaty that, inter alia, capped both sides' strategic delivery systems at 2,250 (slightly below the Vladivostok ceiling of 2,400).

The problem by that point, however, was that the passage of time was very unkind to the Carter administration. By 1979, U.S.-Soviet relations were burdened with significant developments in another sphere—namely, a Soviet campaign of geopolitical opportunism in the Third World. In early 1977, there was a minor Soviet-Cuban military intervention in the Shaba region of Zaire (now Congo), from across the border in Angola. Later in 1977, Cuban troops commanded by a Soviet officer led Ethiopian forces against Somali troops that had tried to occupy the disputed Ogaden desert. The government in Afghanistan was overthrown by a Communist coup d'état in April 1978. In May 1978 came a second Shaba invasion. A coup in South Yemen pushed the Aden government further in a pro-Soviet direction. In the winter of 1978, Moscow signed a "friendship treaty" with Hanoi that encouraged Vietnam to invade Cambodia at the end of the year.

The Soviets and their allies seemed to be on a roll. Following the collapse of the American enterprise in Indochina in April 1975, and Congress's refusal to allow the Ford administration to respond to a Cuban-Soviet military intervention in Angola at the end of 1975, Leonid Brezhnev was to proclaim at the Twenty-fifth Soviet Party Congress in February 1976 that the global "correlation of forces" was tilting against "imperialism." He hailed the victories in Indochina and Angola. "No impartial person can deny that the socialist countries' influence on world affairs is becoming ever stronger and deeper," he boasted. A year and a half later, Soviet support for "national liberation movements" was even enshrined in the new constitution of the USSR. The West, as noted in the last chapter, was reeling from the energy shocks and was also worried about the growing political strength of Communist parties even in Western Europe.

All this raised an issue that became sorely divisive in the Carter administration, namely whether the United States should draw some conclusions from this and make some connection between arms control and Soviet behavior in the world. This was "linkage" again. Arms control

advocates like Vance wanted to insulate SALT from these other events; they shrank from any kind of significant response or reaction to the Soviet moves out of fear of jeopardizing SALT. On this, Harold Brown at Defense and Cyrus Vance at State were united. At White House meetings in early 1978, for example, Brzezinski urged that the United States dispatch an aircraft carrier task force to the vicinity of Ethiopia to indicate the depth of U.S. concern. Vance and Brown argued against it, and Carter sided with them.

Brzezinski was convinced that the weak U.S. response to this Soviet offensive would jeopardize not only international stability, but ultimately SALT as well. In this he was borne out, as the Soviets' aggressive behavior undermined American congressional and public support for SALT when the treaty went before the Senate in June 1979. The treaty died there—the final nail in its coffin delivered by the Soviet invasion of Afghanistan in December 1979. But Brzezinski remained convinced that the turning point had come in Ethiopia, in early 1978 when the United States had failed to react to the Soviets' Ethiopian adventure. That emboldened them to go further, and the global environment deteriorated from there. SALT was "buried," Brzezinski often said, "in the sands of the Ogaden." His "greatest regret," he admitted a few years later, was:

> that I was unable to convince the president and others to deal with the Soviet relationship in a somewhat different fashion. I always felt that we shouldn't be engaging only in the legalistic, specific, technical, and complicated negotiations, but that we should engage them also in protracted, sustained discussions in depth and at length, in which we would try to make the Russians understand what was meant by reciprocity and restraint in a genuine détente relationship. And I felt that these discussions could only succeed if they were paralleled by actions that would give credibility to what we were saying.

The administration's conceptual problem with respect to Soviet policy was further revealed in mid-1978 when the president delivered a speech on the subject at the U.S. Naval Academy in Annapolis. Vance had submitted a speech draft emphasizing the complexity of the U.S.-Soviet relationship and the need for lowering political tensions on a reciprocal basis. Carter produced his own draft, however, borrowing some of Vance's language but adding some tougher passages, especially

about the nature of the Soviet regime. Vance was frustrated by what he saw as a "stitched-together" product that only reflected the divisions in the administration. But Carter was pleased with the outcome, believing that the speech "spell[ed] out more clearly" how he saw the overall relationship with the Soviet Union.

Brzezinski continued to deplore what he saw as his State Department colleagues' tendency to "shy away from the unavoidable ingredient of force in dealing with contemporary realities, and to have an excessive faith that all issues can be resolved by compromise," and their inclination to "equate foreign policy with endless litigation and to confuse détente with acquiescence." But as we saw earlier, Brzezinski lamented that unlike Henry Kissinger he did not have consistent backing from his president. Carter was torn: "[B]ecause he was so intelligent," Brzezinski wrote delicately, "he did tend to see more sides to an issue than perhaps occasionally was necessary, and . . . he was pulled in opposite directions by conflicting advice from his immediate associates."

This was especially true on two issues. The debate over linkage in U.S.-Soviet relations was one. The other was the Iranian crisis—the revolution that toppled the shah in 1978–1979.

The Fall of the Shah

When the shah stood with Jimmy Carter on the South Lawn of the White House for the welcoming ceremony for his state visit on November 15, 1977, mounted police in the distance were trying to contain a group of anti-shah demonstrators outside the White House grounds. Wafts of tear gas reached the South Lawn and the shah, the president, their wives, and other dignitaries found themselves mopping or rubbing their eyes to contain the tears. Carter saw it as an augury of the hostage crisis to come: "The tear gas had created the semblance of grief. Almost two years later, and for fourteen months afterward, there would be real grief in our country because of Iran." But the visit was an augury for a deeper reason—because what the president said to the shah during the visit reflected the contradictions in U.S. policy that would help bring that crisis about. In the public greeting on the South Lawn, Carter repeated the strong statements of U.S. solidarity with the shah and his country that every U.S. president since Franklin Roosevelt had expressed. Once they repaired safely inside, after a larger meeting in the Cabinet Room, Carter took the shah aside to a small private room near

the Oval Office and expressed his concerns about human rights in Iran; he urged the shah to consider reaching out to dissident groups and "easing off" on police actions against them. This kind of pressure from an American president on his internal policies was new to the shah; he responded politely but firmly that he would enforce his country's laws.

As the domestic unrest within Iran grew to engulf the shah, this was to be the pattern of U.S. policy over the next fourteen months— expressions of support, coupled with recommendations for political concessions to his opponents—a pattern that confused the shah and contributed to his hesitations; it had the same effect on the Iranian military, who we were expecting to be a stabilizing factor. In the context of the upheaval that was taking place, this U.S. posture was full of contradictions, reflecting divisions within the Carter administration and, in the end, a conflict within the president's own mind.

The upheaval in Iran was the product of many causes and disparate forces. The shah failed to accompany the country's rapid economic modernization with a political modernization that could have co-opted the middle classes into the system. He dealt harshly with his opposition. In 1953, when a leftist government that tried to topple him was itself toppled by the CIA, the shah enjoyed support from many key groups in the society, including the merchant class and the clergy. By 1978, his political rigidity had alienated them. Thus the revolution against him at first appeared to be a broad-based coalition embracing the merchants, students, and many moderate elements, in addition to the reactionary clerics; only gradually did it become clear that, as in Petrograd in 1917, vacuums are often filled by the most ruthless, the most disciplined, the most fanatical. And U.S. policy was helping create that vacuum.

There were two points of view in the U.S. government. One view, strongly held in the State Department, was, in essence, that the shah was a retrograde figure, that we should seize the opportunity to help effect a transition, and that moderate elements in the revolution represented a new order that we could get along with. The opposing view, represented especially by Brzezinski (and also James Schlesinger, whom Carter had appointed energy secretary), was that the shah was a strategic ally in a vital region and that if we undermined him, or the army, we were risking strategic disaster. Carter sided with Brzezinski for much of the period, determined to bolster the shah's morale and his resistance to the revolutionary tide.

These reassurances were all the more necessary because the shah was highly susceptible to conspiracy theories. His foreign policy through his whole career had been grounded in the solid support of the United States; now he was in unfamiliar territory. From the beginning of the Carter administration he found U.S. policy to be "confusing and contradictory" and he assumed the worst. Henry Kissinger, visiting Iran as a private citizen in June 1978, found the shah convinced that Washington and Moscow were colluding to divide up Iran. Kissinger told him it was impossible. In September, the shah expounded the same theory to visiting *Time* correspondents, confiding to them his conviction that the CIA was backing the revolution. Unfortunately the head of French intelligence was telling the shah around the same time that the rumors that Carter wanted to replace him were true. And to his dying day he believed it was the American intention all along.

Despite the general view of the shah as a brutal dictator, his problem during this period was a weakness of will, exacerbated not only by these fears of American abandonment but perhaps also by the cancer that he knew (but we did not know) was killing him. During the summer and fall of 1978 he made concessions to his opposition and did not crack down ruthlessly; his police handled some protests brutally but only enough to inflame passions, not suppress them. The shah flirted with different political alternatives—either a coalition government that would seek to co-opt moderate elements from the opposition, or a military government that would restore his authority and allow him to reach out politically from a position of strength. Carter sent him a message in early November assuring him of U.S. support "without any reservation whatsoever, completely and fully," whatever course of action he chose. Brzezinski conveyed the message to him personally by phone, because he and the president were concerned that the U.S. ambassador in Tehran, William Sullivan, and the State Department, were not conveying such clear-cut support in their own communications with the shah.

Other presidents, as we have seen, have had their frustrations with the State Department. What confronted and frustrated Jimmy Carter was a group of midlevel State officials intellectually and morally opposed to the shah on human rights grounds, optimistic about America's natural affinity with a revolution they continued to see as broad-based and reformist, and tenaciously bending the implementation of U.S. policy in their preferred direction whatever instructions they received from the president. Carter and Brzezinski were unable to

impose their will on a determined Foreign Service, especially when the secretary of state acted as the spokesman and champion of the department's view.

The shah in fact established a military government in early November, but it strengthened his position only briefly. A general strike began later in the month, and the Ayatollah Ruhollah Khomeini, in exile, called for the shah's violent overthrow. Carter and Brzezinski were still seeking to buck up the shah's morale. Carter told Vance on November 10 "to be sure that the State Department officials below him supported my position—that the Shah should know that we are with him." Brzezinski later wrote:

> Sometimes the Shah expressed confidence that the military would get hold of the situation; on other occasions he would firmly state that he would not spill blood. Sullivan's cables did not give one the impression that the American Ambassador was exerting himself to reinforce the Shah's willpower.

At the turn of the year, the shah agreed to appoint the Western-educated moderate opposition figure Shapour Bakhtiar as prime minister of a coalition government. By this time the mounting pressures were so powerful that Bakhtiar felt compelled to ask, as a condition of taking office, that the shah leave Iran. This was a measure of how far and how rapidly the ground had shifted. The shah hesitated, looking to the U.S. government for advice. Whereas the president's view had been—and remained—that the purpose of any political concessions was to enable the shah to remain in power, the State Department was explicitly of the view that the possibility of a moderate pro-Western government, with army support, now depended on the shah's removal. Carter continued to reject this and was infuriated by continued leaks to the media suggesting U.S. doubts about the desirability of the shah's remaining in power.

The shah vacillated between departing, as Bakhtiar and the opposition were clamoring for him to do, and ordering the military to suppress the opposition by force. His will was clearly flagging. In early November, when *Newsweek* correspondent Arnaud de Borchgrave had told him that some of his foreign supporters would back his use of military force, the shah wept. "There had already been too much violence, he said; he would not be the cause of more bloodshed." In a meeting with Ambas-

sador Sullivan on December 26, the shah asked Sullivan point-blank what the United States wanted him to do. Sullivan's reply embodied all the ambiguity that Brzezinski was struggling to avoid:

> Sullivan reported [that he had told the shah] that the United States supported his efforts to reestablish law and order. The Shah asked then whether he was being advised to use the iron fist even if it meant widespread bloodshed and even if it might fail to restore law and order. Sullivan reported that he responded by saying that if the Shah was trying to get the United States to take the responsibility for his actions, he doubted that he would ever get such instructions from Washington. He was the Shah and he had to take the decision as well as the responsibility.

Brzezinski, disturbed by this ambiguity, arranged a meeting of principals in the White House to agree on a tougher follow-up message. The upshot was a complicated cable that Brzezinski, in his memoirs, cites as a considerable toughening of support, while Vance, in his memoirs, hails it as a clear message to the shah that we would not support his use of the "iron fist" to maintain his throne. Within days, bowing to what he saw as inevitable, the shah agreed to leave the country, in effect embracing the theory that without him, the moderate Bakhtiar government and the Iranian military could better maintain a cohesive resistance to the revolution than they could with him.

Focus then shifted to the role of the military. Carter dispatched a senior U.S. military officer, General Robert Huyser, then deputy U.S. commander in Europe, to talk to the Iranian military. Huyser's declared mission was to help the military retain their cohesion to support the moderate government and the possibility of long-term collaboration with the United States. But this assignment masked its own ambiguity: Did we want the military to take over by force if that was the only way to stop the revolution, or not? Brzezinski's hope was that it would do so. But just as Sullivan never answered that question when the shah asked him point-blank, so Jimmy Carter never answered it when Brzezinski strove to move U.S. policy to this ultimate step.

ONCE THE SHAH departed his country on January 16, 1979, the U.S. government was left with only the illusion of a policy. The momentum of revolution was irreversible (and perhaps had been for some months).

Khomeini's triumphal return to Iran swept away the Bakhtiar government, and eventually also the moderate elements in the revolution. The military—like the shah, waiting for some signal from Washington that never came—were paralyzed by the Huyser mission, not galvanized. They had no experience of politics and, without the shah, the lifelong object of their loyalty, they were directionless; and so the army, too, disintegrated under the pressure of events.

For the purposes of this book, the lesson to draw is the price paid for the contradictions in U.S. policy, the ambivalences that were never resolved. Through most of the period, Carter supported Brzezinski's view of the strategic stakes involved and repeatedly complained of leaks from State that undermined decisions he had made. But in the Carter system, State controlled the implementation of policy. The White House never trusted the U.S. Embassy to deliver categorical messages of support as the president intended, but the president's efforts to enforce his wishes were sporadic—at one point in February 1979 he met with a group of midlevel State officials and castigated them for disloyalty and leaking—and Brzezinski did not have the bureaucratic clout to enforce them on the president's behalf. Nixon's option of simply excluding and bypassing State was not available.

A second problem was that Carter's agreement with Brzezinski's tough line went only so far. As we saw, the desire to nudge the shah toward political liberalization was built into the policy from the beginning. Toward the end, the painful question was whether to advise the shah, or the military, explicitly to use force. Brzezinski favored doing so but the president did not; it reached the point that Brzezinski thought he was annoying Carter by continuing to raise it or hint at it. In the end, Carter, who prided himself on his morality and had campaigned on the contrast he drew with his predecessors, could not stomach such a course. Certainly Ambassador Sullivan was right that the shah ought not to be shifting such a burden onto our shoulders, but he did. Normally it would be a truism that the shah's survival ought to be more important to him than to us; in this case, however—especially after the nightmare the world has lived through for a generation since then—the truth of that proposition is not so obvious. Carter, in any event, took refuge in repeated public statements that we had no desire to interfere in the internal affairs of Iran. This was an evasion.

To condone or endorse a military crackdown has to be one of the most agonizing questions any president could face, given the oppro-

brium that would be heaped on the United States for whatever role it played. For a Democratic president it was probably an impossibility. Of the chief executives we are considering in this book it is easiest to imagine Nixon making such a decision. Nixon was no stranger to opprobrium; indeed he tended fatalistically to consider it part of his lot whatever he did. He and Kissinger could understand clearly what the strategic stakes were. Brzezinski and Schlesinger did as well. But in advance of events, as opposed to hindsight, one is relying on intuition, and they found it impossible to convince their president of consequences that might be avoided if their advice were taken. Nor, in fairness, could anyone have imagined the strategic enormity of what did ensue.

Lessons

The Carter administration had a number of achievements to its credit, amidst a turbulent period in international and American politics. The Camp David accords between Egypt and Israel, building upon the Kissinger shuttles, were a historic milestone in the diplomacy of Arab-Israeli peace. The "Carter Doctrine" proclaimed the vital U.S. interest in the security of the Gulf. Relations with China reached a new stage, with full normalization, and provided new leverage against the Soviet Union. In the defense field, there were advances in strategic doctrine and defense modernization, including progress in stealth aircraft technology and deployment of the MX ICBM and Trident submarine. This improving defense posture helped shore up a U.S.-Soviet strategic balance at reasonably stable levels that Carter's successor, Ronald Reagan, continued as a matter of policy even though the SALT II treaty failed of ratification. The administration began a substantial program of aid to anti-Soviet insurgents in Afghanistan that ultimately inflicted a significant strategic defeat on the Soviet Union. The Panama Canal treaties enabled the United States to maintain the defense of the canal while shedding the intrusive presence on Panamanian soil that would have assured a generation of nationalistic upheaval.

But Carter's foreign policy difficulties, which contributed to his defeat for reelection in 1980, also teach some lessons about the factors that lead to success or failure in presidential leadership.

Brzezinski argued for a time, after leaving office, that the role of the assistant to the president for national security affairs should be strengthened. He made a strong case that amid all the turbulence of the

modern era there is a premium on central direction and integration of the various elements of policy, which can come only from the White House, not the State Department. He cited the many examples of Carter's inability to impose his will on the career service. He proposed that the national security adviser's pivotal role be acknowledged, strengthened, and institutionalized by being given a statutory basis, including confirmation by the Senate.

The Senate Foreign Relations Committee held a hearing on this idea in April 1980. The committee had before it at that moment the example of two recent national security advisers, Kissinger and Brzezinski, who had to one degree or another eclipsed the secretary of state. This the committee (and many others) regretted, and from the committee's point of view the idea of making this elusive and increasingly powerful White House figure answerable to the Senate might be part of the solution. But the overwhelming majority of eminent figures whose opinion the committee canvassed—including Richard Neustadt, Andrew Good-paster, McGeorge Bundy, Walt Rostow, and Brent Scowcroft—were adamantly opposed to the idea. Making the position subject to confirmation, they believed, would only enshrine the elevated role of the national security adviser as a rival to the secretary of state, compounding the problem more than solving it. Many of them also stressed that the president in any case has need of a confidential adviser accountable to no one but the president—which is "an inside, not an outside, job," as Bundy put it.

We have Jimmy Carter's own testimony as to the problem of the State Department in his administration, but Brzezinski, in his proposed solution, may have been looking through the telescope from the wrong end. It is striking, of course, that a liberal Democratic president like Carter perceived the problem of State in terms not dissimilar from Nixon—the poor intellectual quality of its work, its institutional biases and unresponsiveness to political authority. Indeed, Carter's problem with Vance was a variant of Nixon's problem with Rogers: It was the weakness of a secretary of state unable or unwilling to impose political direction on the career bureaucracy in the president's name. One hypothetical solution is Nixon's—simply to exclude State, as if it were possible to carve out its plot of land in Foggy Bottom and float it down the Potomac. We have seen the price paid for that—and in any case, State does have its hands on the levers of implementation of policy. If Nixon's extreme exclusionary approach is itself excluded, then the solution is

not a stronger national security adviser but a stronger secretary of state. As I have suggested, "stronger" in this context has a particular meaning— a secretary of state who is loyal, both personally and philosophically, to the president and able and willing to impose the president's agenda on a recalcitrant bureaucracy. The job of the security adviser is then to arm the president so that a strong secretary of state receives firm guidance (and monitoring) from the White House.

An additional problem for Carter was the institutional weakness of the office when he inherited it after what were seen as a series of failed presidencies. In the last chapter we saw the extent of the congressional revolt against the so-called imperial presidency. Richard Neustadt asked himself in 1979, watching Jimmy Carter (after Carter then too seemed a failure): "Is the presidency possible?" Was the job simply too big and too hard for any human being in this modern era? He cited a number of causes of this institutional weakness, including the new power of Congress and complexity of dealing with it, the expansion and fragmentation of the Executive Branch, the growing power of interest groups, and the expansion of staffs all over Washington. Carter had entered office seeking to restore presidential authority by relegitimating it, which he aimed to do by displays of personal humility—walking up Pennsylvania Avenue during his inaugural parade, carrying his own luggage on and off *Air Force One*, wearing cardigans on television, insuring frugality in the White House, and so forth—all to rid the office of its "imperial" pretensions. The perverse irony of Carter's quest, however, is that his shedding of the trappings of presidential authority came at a time when that authority needed strengthening, not weakening. What Walter Bagehot called the "dignified" elements of a constitutional system have their place in inspiring people's loyalty, confidence, and deference.

A final lesson of the Carter experience is that the key is not the role of the national security adviser or the secretary of state but the role of the president. Carter built a system, as we saw, that did insure his pivotal role as the "decider." That turns out to be necessary, but not sufficient. Carter's intelligence and tenacity were often in evidence—most conspicuously, for example, in the extraordinary negotiation he mediated personally between Egypt's Anwar Sadat and Israel's Menachem Begin at Camp David. But in other, less successful, endeavors his philosophical schizophrenia tore away at the consistency that effective policy requires. Cyrus Vance wrote: "A question troubling Congress, the allies and the American public in the spring of 1980 was whether the Carter

administration had a coherent view of the international situation, a sense of global strategy, and consistent policies and objectives."

The challenge of managing conflict within one's administration is a recurring one, and often difficult to avoid. In later chapters we will see Ronald Reagan and George W. Bush wrestling with similar problems. But the difficulty is exacerbated if the president doesn't know his own mind. While Reagan and Bush 43 struggled with divisions between cabinet officers, one has the sense that they both came into office expecting a more united government and thus ended up in that position involuntarily. Carter seems to have chosen a system that enshrined his own—divided—view of the world. In such circumstances, the task of running national security policy, difficult enough to start with, becomes even harder.

CHAPTER SIX

Ronald Reagan

THE PARADOX OF RONALD REAGAN is that he was one of the most important presidents of the modern era, who left his bold imprint on his administration and on history, yet on issues on which he was less engaged, his management of his government has to be rated among the weakest. On the positive side of the ledger was, especially, the transformation of the generations-long conflict with the Soviet Union, as well as a major program of reform in domestic economic policy. In both these areas, he came with a clear sense of purpose. After leaving office Reagan told an aide: "I had an agenda I wanted to get done. I came with a script." On the negative side were lapses like the Iran-Contra affair as well as protracted conflicts among his senior subordinates that led to frustrations and failures (Lebanon being the most conspicuous). "He was better suited to leading the nation than commanding its government," his principal biographer, Lou Cannon, concluded.

But both sides of this paradox deserve their proper respect. There are studies of his administrative process (usually focusing on Iran-Contra) that tend toward the dismissive, but they thereby miss an important forest through the trees on the broad question of presidential leadership. "[T]he whole of Reagan's performance," says Cannon shrewdly, "was often greater than the sum of its parts." And those who admire Reagan (as I do) need to be clear about his weaknesses, if only to draw usable lessons for our inquiry in this book.

Reagan as president was a more enigmatic figure than most of his detractors or supporters realized. Whatever the management weaknesses, he had considerable strengths that lay elsewhere, and I do not mean just his Hollywood-nurtured ability to deliver a speech with feeling or to walk into a room with a tall, commanding stride. He did have a

remarkable physical presence in a room, which reflected an inner composure as well as whatever Hollywood had taught him. But Reagan also had an innate political shrewdness and knew his country's mood. He could not have left such an imprint on his times without embodying something of substance. Published compilations of his pre-presidential speeches and broadcasts—written by him, not ghostwriters—testify to his intellectual curiosity and grasp of issues. His presidential diaries, published in 2007, also indicate a man attentive and thoughtful, as well as "principled [and] confident," in the words of their editor. His critics alternated between denouncing him for his ideological convictions, on the one hand, and insisting (usually after one of his electoral victories) that the American people had voted only for a genial man with a smile. They could not have it both ways.

He was an unabashed believer in American exceptionalism: America was great and good and had a moral mission to be the "shining city on a hill." Where Jimmy Carter had often contrasted American ideals with American performance, Reagan cast never a doubt on his country's sincerity. Where Carter had sought, in the post-Vietnam era, to teach America its limits (especially to dampen the frustrations of the Iran hostage crisis), Reagan rejected the defeatism that this seemed to imply and sought to restore the country's faith in its limitless possibilities. It was America's Soviet adversaries, he forthrightly declared as early as 1982 and 1983, who were facing a systemic crisis. Jimmy Carter, in a sense, was an interruption of the country's recovery from the Vietnam trauma, and the foreign policy embarrassments of Carter's presidency only insured that, after him, that recovery would burst forth with a vengeance.

Similarly in domestic policy, Reagan's passion to reduce the burden of government on the economy came at a time when, fifty years after the New Deal, Western societies were discovering that an excess of bureaucracy, regulation, and taxation was burdening the entrepreneurship and innovation that are the ultimate sources of growth. At the Bonn economic summit of May 1985, all the leading industrial democracies endorsed this perception.

The intellectuals' mockery of Reagan was thus misplaced. His convictions coincided with the historical moment to powerful effect. A famous essay on intellectual history by Isaiah Berlin is based on a line from a fragment of Greek poetry: "The fox knows many things, but the hedgehog knows one big thing." Jimmy Carter was perhaps a fox but

Ronald Reagan was surely a hedgehog. He was also totally impervious to what the editorial boards of *The New York Times* and *The Washington Post* thought—a truly liberating quality for a conservative president. Nixon had been constantly tortured by the liberal criticism, struggling either to defy it or win it over.

Management Problems

Like all his predecessors, Reagan came into office with his own philosophy of the job. In contrast with Jimmy Carter, he was not shy about embracing the symbolic grandeur of the office, partly as a matter of deliberately restoring its public authority but also out of personal reverence for it: He made a point of never taking his coat off when in the Oval Office. His management style was closer to that of a chairman of the board than chief executive officer. In another conscious contrast with Jimmy Carter, he was determined to focus on the "big picture," avoiding the micromanagement that was widely held to be one of Carter's weaknesses.

Indeed he was accused of the opposite deficiency. Reagan's work habits were much derided, and he joked about it himself: "It's true hard work never killed anybody, but I figure, why take a chance?" Two weeks short of his seventieth birthday when he took office, he followed a schedule that writer William Doyle calls "ruthlessly geared to preserving his energy." He needed his eight hours' sleep, and regular rest breaks (labeled "staff time") were written into his calendar. He came into the Oval Office around 9:00 a.m. and typically returned to the Residence by 5:30 p.m.; usually he took Wednesday afternoons off and often left mid-afternoon on Friday for a weekend at Camp David.

Critiques of Reagan's management style, even from loyalists, are replete with adjectives that suggest a contradictory mixture of strengths and weaknesses: bold, stubborn, passive, lazy, incurious, inattentive, detached from the policy-making process, remote, guileless, relentlessly optimistic, innocent, et cetera. Both sides in the administration's internal quarrels, "moderates" and "ideologues," each feared that the president was being manipulated by the other. His eyes sometimes glazed over in complex discussions. When he finished reading from his five-by-eight-inch cue cards in an official conversation, the conversation often drifted off. The jokes he cracked in important meetings in the Situation Room or with foreign visitors were sometimes apt, sometimes a device

to hide his uncertainties. There are stories of his being sent a policy options memorandum with boxes for him to mark his choice and of the memo coming out of his office with all the boxes checked (though Richard Nixon did the same thing once in a distracted moment).

But the picture of a passive Reagan should not be exaggerated either. His reticence in large meetings was often simply due to a fear of leaks. He did not usually nap during his "staff time," but read mail or simply relaxed. Donald Regan, who served as chief of staff, reported:

> Every afternoon he went home complete with material—homework: briefing books, intelligence briefings, reports from State, DoD, materials submitted by Cabinet officers, legislative analysis on whether or not he should sign a particular bill. When he brought that stuff back at 8:50 or 8:55 in the morning, he not only had parts underlined, but pages annotated. You knew he had done his homework.

According to William Doyle:

> A random inspection of dozens of Reagan's diary files at the Reagan Library reveals not a somnambulant shirker but a seventy-something man who took a round of live ammunition in the chest in his second month on the job and went on to endure a tough daily schedule of frequent high-pressure private meetings and public events, plus a regular schedule of presidential functions at night, plus weekly radio addresses on Saturdays and sometimes more functions on the weekends, topped off with regular bursts of national and international travel. . . . [I]t seems the height of responsibility that he paced himself as he did.

By all accounts he was comfortable making decisions. Alexander Haig, who served both Nixon and Reagan, compared them: "[Nixon] would sit in anguish for hours over a decision before it was made. I never sensed that with Reagan. He was the most graceful and easy decision-maker I've ever seen." He demonstrated his mettle early in his first year by breaking an illegal strike by the air traffic controllers' union—a bold decision that did much to establish his political authority.

Reagan had an unusual degree of influence over events by virtue of his ideas and his communication of them. His speeches were powerful

not only in their rhetoric and masterly delivery but in the message they conveyed. Over and over again, he propagated his belief in the illegitimacy and vulnerability of the Soviet system and his confidence in the fundamental goodness and resilience of the free nations. His strength as a "conviction politician" was an important element in his leadership. He almost single-handedly transformed the terms of the domestic and international debate.

REAGAN'S DECLARED MANAGEMENT model was cabinet government. As he had governed in California, he wanted his cabinet officers, not his staffers, to be both his principal advisers in their fields and the individuals responsible for executing his policies. But while espousing cabinet government, Reagan as president did not leave himself naked. He and his White House aides made the fullest use of the presidential appointment process to place loyalists in policy jobs around the cabinet departments, and his palace guard was alert to defend his prerogatives.

Reagan himself spent two hours a week on personnel matters, at least during the first two years. To Reagan, the selection of the three thousand political appointees was vital to insure that the cabinet departments were linked to his policy priorities. "We wanted our appointees to be the President's ambassadors to the agencies, not the other way around," as longtime aide Edwin Meese put it. Before inauguration, transition teams of loyalists studied each department and agency and came up with ideas for structural reforms as well as key personnel. A staff of one hundred in the White House screened candidates for philosophy as well as competence and integrity. The Reagan team is widely regarded as having had more success than most preceding administrations in shaping the leadership of the bureaucracy by these means.

This success naturally stirred opposition. Much of the literature on the Reagan administration is filled with criticism of the "ideologues" and "crazies" who came in with Reagan and who interfered with the more "experienced" and "moderate" folks as the latter sought to conduct policy as it should be conducted. The careful reader will take this with a grain of salt. The Reagan administration was challenged in its own way by the divisions in the Republican Party that had engulfed Gerald Ford. The party had united behind Reagan, but the large talent pool that he brought with him now included many veterans of the Nixon-Ford era as well as new people of generally more conservative bent. To deny the legitimacy of the new people, however, was to deny the results of the

election as well as to deny the president the support in his own government of individuals who actually shared his beliefs. He *was* different from Richard Nixon and Gerald Ford, and this was bound to be reflected in his policies. Nor was Reagan the first to see the importance of personnel. Jimmy Carter in his time was accused of appointing scores of liberal activists to sub-cabinet positions to replace departing Republicans. Very few of our presidents have followed the self-denying (and self-destructive) approach of John Quincy Adams. "Personnel *is* policy," is another Washington maxim of very long standing that every incoming president will learn the truth of soon enough if he or she is serious about giving political direction to the policies of the government.

The palace guard was the famous "troika," sometimes dubbed the "three-headed monster." It turned out to be a formidable animal. Edwin Meese, Reagan's chief political adviser in Sacramento, had expected to be White House chief of staff, but this was blocked by Michael Deaver, who thought Reagan would be better served by someone with Washington experience. Thus, James A. Baker III—a longtime associate not of Reagan but of Vice President George H. W. Bush—became chief of staff, with Deaver as his deputy and Meese as "counselor" to the president. Reagan welcomed their presence as a buffer, and the three seem to have worked together smoothly to guard his interests. Alexander Haig, Reagan's first secretary of state, was surprised to see all three seated at the cabinet table during early cabinet meetings.

In the name of cabinet government, the position of the assistant for national security affairs was downgraded. It was to be, once again, a staff position with a coordinating function. This was a conscious decision to reempower cabinet secretaries, as well as to avoid the kind of embarrassing battles that had marked the Kissinger versus Rogers and Brzezinski versus Vance eras. Richard Allen, the first occupant of the job under Reagan, was stripped not only of the cabinet rank that Brzezinski had enjoyed but also of his direct line of access to the president; Allen was to report to the president through Meese. Allen was comfortable with all this, and indeed had proposed to Reagan during the 1980 campaign that he promise in a speech that he would restore the national security adviser to the role of staffer and honest broker. This Reagan did. And Allen is proud that he took his office physically back downstairs to the West Basement where Bundy and Rostow had labored (and Kissinger for his first year and a half). Meese took the upstairs corner office.

The flaws in this system soon appeared, as we shall see. There was considerable turmoil over eight years, including a succession of national security advisers (Richard Allen was the first of six). The Reagan presidency can usefully be divided into three periods. The first was the era of the troika, through the first term. The troika turned out to be as serious a problem for the secretary of state, at least during Haig's tenure, as any high-powered national security adviser would have been. Allen was replaced in early 1982 by William Clark, a close California friend and confidant of Reagan who by his stature upgraded the position—he reported directly to Reagan and was, effectively, on a par with the troika (which they resented). Clark's relationship with his president was one of the closest of the modern period. But Clark's relationship with two secretaries of state, Alexander Haig and George Shultz, was difficult, and for the nearly two years of Clark's tenure (until October 1983) there was indeed a replay of the State-NSC tensions that the new team had hoped to avoid.

At the beginning of the second term, the troika broke up—chief of staff James Baker switched places with Treasury Secretary Donald Regan, and Meese became attorney general. Regan dominated the White House staff, and the next two national security advisers, Robert (Bud) McFarlane and Vice Admiral John Poindexter, lacked Clark's clout. Though the office physically moved back upstairs when Meese left, functionally it reverted to a more modest honest broker role. This was the period of the Iran-Contra affair. The house-cleaning that followed led to Donald Regan's departure and to a calmer period under Frank Carlucci and then Lieutenant General Colin Powell as the national security adviser. I had returned to the NSC staff during this time, beginning under John Poindexter and remaining through the Carlucci-Powell period.

The Iran-Contra episode is usually described as the NSC staff run amok. In fact I would argue it was an aberration in a system whose dominant problem was something else—a protracted struggle between the secretaries of state and defense, which persisted through all three phases and which the White House was unable to resolve. "Nothing ever gets settled in this town," George Shultz once famously lamented. The national security adviser—deliberately weakened institutionally— was (except under Clark) unable to exert strong influence in the president's name.

Even in a system of cabinet government, the national security

adviser has an essential role in managing the process, but his (or her) effectiveness depends on presidential engagement. Where Reagan's strong convictions were engaged, he made decisions, but often the system did not produce consistent policy or effective execution. Like Nixon, Reagan detested personal confrontations with his subordinates. The result, in James Baker's words, was often "a witches' brew of intrigue, elbows, egos, and separate agendas." The looseness of the structure, and the detachment of the president's management style, left the system vulnerable to end runs into the Oval Office or to prolonged stalemates, both of which left all sides continually frustrated. We will see this problem recur through the remainder of this chapter.

The Rise and Fall of Alexander Haig

The first management crisis was the tumultuous, and brief, tenure of Reagan's first secretary of state. Alexander Haig's aborted career at State is a mystery in many ways, most of all because of the contrast between his successful performance in the Nixon administration and his frustration in Reagan's.

Haig was a bright young colonel assigned by the Pentagon to be Henry Kissinger's military assistant beginning in the 1968–1969 presidential transition at the Pierre Hotel in New York. He had come highly recommended to Kissinger by many officials in the Johnson administration. Kissinger had been advised by his predecessor and old Harvard colleague McGeorge Bundy not to appoint a deputy: Bundy had hired Carl Kaysen, a high-powered Princeton professor whom Bundy had found hard to control. So Kissinger repelled the entreaties of those civilians on his staff who yearned to be his deputy, and instead relied for administrative support on his military assistant, who so capably performed the function over the first year and a half that he became de facto deputy and was rewarded with the title in mid-1970.

It was Al Haig who smoothed out Kissinger's rough edges, who managed the NSC staff's operations and looked after its morale. Kissinger had no experience as a manager, nor the temperament for the role. Unsure of his relationship with Nixon, and preoccupied with State's continuing efforts to undermine the president's policy and himself, Kissinger was no mother hen to his staff nor a smooth bureaucratic operator. Haig, a much more gregarious personality than either Nixon or Kissinger, deployed the necessary bureaucratic finesse. After some

explosion or other in Kissinger's office, Haig would emerge and make a calm phone call to Secretary Rogers's executive assistant or Secretary Laird's military assistant and the problem would be resolved or eased or at least the message passed in some constructive fashion. Haig kept his cool. But I remember poking my head into Haig's tiny office at quiet moments and finding him seated at his desk, chain-smoking and grinning at me with a red-faced intensity that suggested his heroic self-discipline was not as effortless as it seemed.

Haig's role grew over time as Nixon got to know him, especially while Kissinger was traveling on some secret mission. As an active duty military officer, Haig owed loyalty to his commander in chief and also to his immediate boss; as differences developed between Nixon and Kissinger on some issues—for example, the tactics of the Vietnam endgame—this was a test of skill. Kissinger eased the problem by bringing Haig along with him to the Paris negotiations. Despite grumbling I heard from Kissinger at the time, I think Haig pulled off the balancing act with honor.

Haig's own starring role then came as Nixon's White House chief of staff in May 1973 after Haldeman's resignation over Watergate. Nixon, distraught, pulled Haig back from his brief stint as army vice chief of staff. Now the task was to manage Nixon, another larger-than-life personality, through a monumental political and personal trauma. Haig kept the whole U.S. government on an even keel. In the end, it meant greasing the skids for an unprecedented presidential resignation. Haig received praise from many quarters, including Watergate special prosecutor Leon Jaworski, for the integrity with which he performed this second historic mission.

All this makes the failure of Haig's third act—as Reagan's secretary of state—difficult to explain. A man of great talent, who under Nixon proved himself bureaucratically astute, under Reagan seems to have misjudged his bureaucratic situation and his president.

Perhaps there were other signs. The day after President Ford took the oath of office in August 1974, Haig came in to see him with a ten-page memorandum on White House operations that stressed the importance of his continuing role as chief of staff. Haig said that this included the power of hiring and firing, and inter alia he recommended the dismissal of Robert Hartmann, one of Ford's close aides. Ford was outwardly noncommittal, and privately shocked. It convinced him that,

superb as Haig's performance had been during Nixon's final days, he was not the right man for the Ford White House.

Consciously or unconsciously, Haig in the Reagan era may have been trying to emulate what he had seen his mentor Kissinger do successfully, in two areas. During the 1968–1969 transition, he had worked with Kissinger and other colleagues on the famous Key Biscayne memorandum to the president-elect proposing significant changes in the NSC system including taking the chairmanship of a key committee away from State. On inauguration day 1981, still in his formal clothes, Haig appeared at the White House with a draft directive on the national security policy-making process, which would among other things bring the chairmanship of a similar group back into the State Department.

Contrary to some accounts, Haig did not just spring this on his colleagues. Reagan had assured him of his support for State's lead role, and Haig had promised the president such a memorandum. Haig had also negotiated the text of the directive with the new secretary of defense, Caspar Weinberger, the new CIA chief, William Casey, and national security adviser Richard Allen, who all supported it. But Haig had not included the troika in these deliberations and they reacted badly. Meese received the document from Haig on inauguration day, asked a number of pointed lawyerlike questions, stuffed it in his briefcase, and effectively left it there for a year.

Nixon had actively sought—indeed, insisted upon—the terms of Kissinger's memo in 1968, and chief of staff Haldeman had backed Kissinger up. The troika, unfamiliar with the issue and sensitive to Reagan's prerogative, saw Haig's assertiveness as a challenge. Their antennae had been up for weeks, perhaps since Senator Paul Tsongas (Democrat of Massachusetts) had told Haig at his confirmation hearing that, given his "raw talent," he was bound to "dominate" the new administration. The comment was widely repeated in the media and became part of the conventional wisdom. The troika suspected that Haig nursed presidential ambitions of his own. Haig had also dismissed the State Department transition team—the Reaganites who had been looking into State personnel and structure—as soon as he took office, in a manner that offended loyalists. The palace guard, on alert ever after, convinced themselves that Haig's draft directive was an effort not to carry out the president's will but to impose his own.

Haig's problem was not, at bottom, ideological; it was not that he was

a moderate "Nixon-Ford retread" in an administration of Reaganites. To be sure, many of Haig's run-ins were with administration conservatives such as Weinberger, Casey, and U.N. ambassador Jeane Kirkpatrick. But in Reagan's first year it was Haig who pushed, for example, for a tougher U.S. policy against the Communists in Central America, even against Fidel Castro ("go to the source," Haig argued). But at that point the White House troika wanted Reagan's first-year priority to be his domestic economic reforms, and Mrs. Reagan weighed in with her concern that the president not do controversial things that reinforced his "belligerent cowboy" image. Haig was pushing too hard.

The second feature of Haig's approach was his frequent threats to resign. This, too, he had seen Kissinger do, indeed develop into an art form. But we know that both Nixon and Ford considered Kissinger indispensable and that his battles with others were on behalf of presidential wishes. Reagan and his minions tended to see Haig's restiveness as a bid for dominance or for presidential support on issues where the president's desires were not so clear-cut. Reagan's diaries show frequent irritation at Haig's squabbles with the White House staff as well as with Weinberger. Haig never had Reagan's consistent backing.

The fact that George Shultz, Haig's successor, endured similar struggles with conservatives in the administration shows that there was a structural problem, not only a personal one. Shultz, too, was bureaucratically tenacious and he, too, consumed a lot of his and the president's time threatening to resign over these struggles, just like his distinguished predecessors. But Shultz was better at finding allies in the White House (like Michael Deaver, and especially Nancy Reagan), and by his calm demeanor somehow managed to insure that Reagan never viewed these frequent threats of resignation as an assault on himself. If Haig had not pushed so hard he could well have ended up the "vicar" of foreign policy as he sought—and as Shultz achieved.

By January 1982, William Clark had replaced Richard Allen as national security adviser. Haig had shrewdly chosen this confidant of Reagan as his deputy secretary of state; Clark's shift to the White House seemed to bode well for Haig because it upgraded the status and clout of the security adviser and meant a potential ally among Reagan's senior team. But within months, his relationship with Clark deteriorated. In May and June 1982, for example, there were some interagency disagreements over the crisis in Lebanon. Haig was insisting that the president endorse his recommendations (such as a draft cable of instructions to

the field); Clark insisted on airing the differences before the president at an NSC meeting. Haig thought events would not brook a delay and dispatched the instructions on his own initiative. On June 25, he came in to see Reagan one more time, threatening again to resign. Reagan's diary entry for that day reads: "Today was the day—I told Al H[aig] I had decided to accept his resignation. He didn't seem surprised but he said his differences were on policy. . . . Actually the only disagreement was over whether I made policy or the Sec[retary] of State did."

The Evil Empire

Policy toward the Soviet Union in what turned out to be the terminal phase of the Cold War is the area in which Ronald Reagan has left his strongest mark on history, and he did so even amidst a good deal of bureaucratic disarray. At one level, his administration was as divided as Jimmy Carter's, with more ideologically anti-Soviet senior officials like Caspar Weinberger, Jeane Kirkpatrick, and William Casey on the one side, and more moderate individuals like George Shultz (with the backing of Nancy Reagan) on the other. The battles among these strong personalities were continual; the key question for our purposes is whether these battles reflected a schizophrenic president, like Carter, or some different management disorder.

The Reagan administration put an unusual amount of effort into articulating its basic strategy toward the Soviet Union, not only in presidential speeches but more importantly in classified policy directives. In the Reagan era, these were called National Security Decision Directives (NSDDs). In the Nixon administration, directives of this kind usually transmitted tactical decisions or, on occasion, Nixon's decisions in response to the interagency studies conducted in the NSC system; they were usually not elaborate philosophical expositions. (Nixon's broad policies were more fully articulated in his four public reports to Congress on foreign policy, drafted by Kissinger and his staff.) For Reagan, however, these internal directives were a primary vehicle for articulating broad strategies. Usually their contents were laboriously negotiated among the departments and agencies. Nevertheless, the content—especially of these early documents on Soviet policy—reflected the strong influence of a group of ideological soul-mates of the president on the NSC staff.

On U.S.-Soviet relations, three such directives, signed by the president, stand out. In response to the Communist martial-law crackdown

In Poland in December 1981, NSDD 32 (March 1982) called for tightened sanctions against the Soviet Union and a variety of means, overt and covert, of expanded aid to the Solidarity movement in Poland as part of a broader policy to "neutralize" Soviet control over Eastern Europe. Second was NSDD 66 (November 1982), on East-West economic relations, which sought to rally U.S. allies to a strategy of restricting technology transfer to the Soviet Union or energy dependence on it. Third and broadest was NSDD 75 (January 1983), which declared the following to be the "tasks" of U.S. policy toward the Soviet Union:

> 1. To contain and over time reverse Soviet expansionism by competing effectively on a sustained basis with the Soviet Union in all international arenas—particularly in the overall military balance and in geographical regions of priority concern to the United States. This will remain the primary focus of U.S. policy toward the USSR.
>
> 2. To promote, within the narrow limits available to us, the process of change in the Soviet Union toward a more pluralistic political and economic system in which the power of the privileged ruling elite is gradually reduced. The U.S. recognizes that Soviet aggressiveness has deep roots in the internal system, and that relations with the USSR should therefore take into account whether or not they help to strengthen this system and its capacity to engage in aggression.
>
> 3. To engage the Soviet Union in negotiations to attempt to reach agreements which protect and enhance U.S. interests and which are consistent with the principle of strict reciprocity and mutual interest.

NSDD 75, in its aspiration, was a significant break with decades of U.S. policy that had focused on containment of the Soviet Union's external aggression and generally eschewed "roll-back" of Soviet gains or attempts to exert direct pressure on the internal evolution of the Soviet system. Now the United States was pressing the Kremlin on several fronts. The boldness with which this new strategy was articulated owed much to the pen of Richard Pipes, a distinguished Harvard scholar of Russian and Soviet affairs and longtime critic of détente, now on the NSC staff. The "roll-back" activities would, in practice, owe much to the energy of CIA director William Casey. He would be in charge of the measures aimed at weakening the Soviet grip on Poland and Eastern Europe and expanding the covert program (inherited from the Carter administration) of aid to Afghans fighting to drive the Soviet army from

their country. The directive also stated the U.S. goal "[t]o avoid subsi-
dizing the Soviet economy or unduly easing the burden of Soviet
resource allocation decisions, so as not to dilute pressures for structural
change in the Soviet system." To advance this goal, Casey would collude
with Crown Prince Fahd of Saudi Arabia to reduce oil prices in the early
1980s to depress Soviet revenues.

Over the next few years, the United States would also step up military or financial aid to anti-Communist insurgent movements opposing
Soviet client states in Nicaragua, Angola, and Cambodia, in addition to
Afghanistan. (Legislation that had barred Ford and Kissinger from aiding the Angolans fighting the Cuban-Soviet intervention in 1975 was
repealed under Reagan in 1985.) The Soviets were overextended; the
Reagan administration perceived a Soviet vulnerability and adopted a
deliberate strategy of raising the costs to them of this Third World
adventurism.

NSDD 75 showed the signs of interagency negotiation; it had something for everyone. For the Pentagon, it contained a ringing endorsement of U.S. military modernization and the effort to restrict Western
military and dual-use technology transfers to the Soviets. The State
Department opposed the more exuberant "roll-back" language, but was
overruled. State was mollified by sections that stressed the importance
of collaboration with allies, of diplomatic engagement with the Kremlin
on arms control and other issues, and of educational and cultural
exchanges. Some of the goals in the NSDD were to prove incompatible
with each other (as when the European allies resisted the U.S. attempt
to constrain energy and technological trade with the Soviets), and many
of them were to become the subject of contention within the administration (such as when the State Department actually attempted to negotiate with Moscow on arms control and other issues).

The hard-line strategies outlined in the NSDDs were not the only
guides to Reagan's thinking, however. When it came to practice, as we
shall see, George Shultz more often than not had Reagan's backing for
his diplomacy. As early as April 1981, while still recovering from his gun-
shot wound after an attempted assassination, Reagan sent two letters to
Leonid Brezhnev—a formal letter shaped mainly by the State Department, but also a long, personal, handwritten appeal for a better world:
"Is it possible," he wrote, "that we have permitted ideology, political and
economic philosophies, and governmental policies to keep us from considering the very real everyday problems of peoples?" In April 1983, a

few weeks after his "evil empire" and SDI speeches, he noted in his diary that, despite opposition from the NSC staff, he was supporting George Shultz in his "quiet diplomacy" with the Soviets. Reagan added:

> Some of the N.S.C. staff are too hard line & don't think any approach should be made to the Soviets. I think I'm hard-line & will never appease but I do want to try & let them see there is a better world if they'll show by deed they want to get along with the free world.

In a televised address from the White House on January 16, 1984, devoted to U.S.-Soviet relations, Reagan appealed to the common interests of the two superpowers in reducing nuclear weapons, defusing regional conflicts, and improving bilateral ties.

Some liberal critics saw Reagan's policy, especially in his first term, as a mass of contradictions. Moscow, they said, could not take such U.S. overtures seriously when they were accompanied by the relentless ideological campaign to delegitimate the Soviet system; arms control proposals from Washington were hard to accept when they were blatantly one-sided and also punctuated by a series of Pentagon reports documenting allegations of Soviet cheating on prior agreements. But beneath the apparent contradictions and the bureaucratic competition in Washington, there was a logic to what Reagan was doing. As the United States and the West recovered their economic and military strength and political self-confidence, Reagan began to see himself as in a position to do business.

ONE MAJOR OBSTACLE to a breakthrough was that through the whole of his first term there was no Soviet interlocutor. "They kept dying on me," he used to joke. Brezhnev died in November 1982, his successor, Yuri Andropov, in February 1984, and Konstantin Chernenko in March 1985. Reagan tried to strike up a correspondence with Brezhnev's successors as well. But the foreign policy of the Kremlin gerontocracy seemed to be on autopilot during this period—frightened by Reagan, deepening its involvement in the Afghan morass, and preoccupied with its internal paralysis. Only when Chernenko was succeeded by Mikhail Gorbachev did serious dialogue become possible.

Between 1975 and 1985 there occurred a great reversal of historical fortune—by 1985, a palpable political recovery and economic dynamism

in the West and a Soviet system that began to see itself in crisis. That is what Reagan and Gorbachev, respectively, embodied, and Reagan sensed the opportunity. In his first term, he was laying the predicate. On September 24, 1984, at the United Nations General Assembly, he declared: "America has repaired its strength. We have invigorated our alliances and friendships. We are ready for constructive negotiations with the Soviet Union."

No one can doubt Gorbachev's pivotal role in the easing of tensions that followed. It is worth taking note, however, of Gorbachev's own analysis at the time. The essence of the "new thinking" that he and his reformist colleagues were celebrating when they came into power in March 1985 was a repudiation of the foreign policy of their predecessors—an arms race the Soviet Union now knew it could not win, quagmires in Afghanistan and other Third World conflicts from which they were struggling to extricate themselves. In a series of candid articles in authoritative journals, these Brezhnev policies were now criticized as "incompetence" and "miscalculations" that had produced "unprecedented new pressure from imperialism" and caused "enormous losses" to the Soviet Union. On October 15, 1985, seven months after he took power, Gorbachev explained to his party colleagues: "It has been necessary to work out a new understanding of the changes in the correlation of forces that are occurring." There was a "very dangerous shift" in the policies of the imperialists, he said, in seeking military superiority and suppressing liberation movements. It was "imperative to take a realistic view." The Kremlin would have to "take into account the changing situation in due time, face the reality without any bias, objectively appraise current events, and flexibly react to the demands of the moment."

"Realistic" was a compliment that Moscow had often bestowed on Western leaders who were conciliatory; they were praised for accommodating themselves to the objective trend of history that Soviet policy embodied. Reagan would be entitled to return the compliment. The new Soviet leaders repudiated the policies of their predecessors as costly miscalculations—but they were miscalculations in part because the West had reacted, and they were more costly because the United States had raised the costs. This is the evidence for those who think Gorbachev was as much the result as he was the cause of what transpired in the 1980s.

The Battle of Washington

This historical trend was partly obscured by the bureaucratic battle that raged in Washington, however. The now famous policy directives, eloquent as they were, reflected mainly aspiration and did not determine how the aspiration was to be pursued. George Shultz in his memoirs makes just one passing reference to one of them, when he cited to Reagan one of the elements of NSDD 75 that the State Department had a particular liking for (cultural exchanges). Shultz is dismissive of the ideologues on the NSC staff, and attaches more importance to memoranda of his own that he sent the president outlining a four-part agenda for a U.S-Soviet dialogue (arms control, human rights, regional conflicts, and bilateral relations).

Similarly with Reagan's speeches: The president's blunt assertion in March 1983 that the Soviet Union was an "evil empire" was generally viewed as an embarrassment at State. Usually the advance draft of a presidential speech on foreign policy was circulated to the key departments on a close-hold basis for comment, but during my years at the State Department I do not recall that most of these speeches, after the president delivered them, were widely invoked in the building as fundamental guidance. (The "evil empire" speech, made to the National Association of Evangelicals, was not thought of as a foreign policy pronouncement and State saw no advance draft.) The surprise unveiling of Reagan's Strategic Defense Initiative (SDI), tacked onto the end of a routine defense policy speech in the same month, was withheld from State until the last minute because of the likelihood of State's opposition. Speeches by the secretary of state (drafted principally by the Policy Planning Staff, which I headed for a time) received much more attention in Foggy Bottom, in part because they tended to be more detailed expositions of operational policy.

GEORGE SHULTZ HAD HIS OPENING—a mandate from Reagan to pursue negotiations. In June 1983, with Reagan's blessing, he outlined to the Senate Foreign Relations Committee a strategy to engage the Soviet leaders in a diplomatic process on concrete issues. But others in the administration had their own ideas of whether Shultz's efforts were faithful to the president's true wishes.

Strategic arms control was one such arena of bureaucratic infighting. Reagan (like Jimmy Carter before him) began his administration with

proposals that were radical departures from previous U.S. policies. While Reagan turned out to be more successful than Carter, the road to success was a rocky one. In the field of strategic (intercontinental-range) offensive missiles, Reagan like Carter proposed deep reductions; as for intermediate-range missiles (INF), he proposed their abolition. To stress the reductions, the Strategic Arms Limitation Talks (SALT) of his three predecessors were given a new name—the Strategic Arms Reduction Talks (START). Reagan had a profound personal aversion to nuclear weapons; his desire to abolish all of them was genuine. (His commitment to SDI, indeed, sprang from his faith that defensive systems could ultimately render nuclear offensive weapons obsolete.) But he presided over a bureaucratic stalemate. At times, his insistence on SDI and on deep reductions of missiles strengthened the hand of conservatives in the administration who wanted to stand fast on his original proposals, resisting compromise with the Soviets. At other times, Reagan's nuclear abolitionism strengthened the hand of Shultz, who could argue that achieving a negotiable result was the best way to achieve at least a step toward the president's vision.

No serious arms control business was likely to be accomplished with the Soviets, in any case, until they saw the failure of the massive propaganda campaign they waged in Western Europe in 1983 to block NATO's deployment of "Euromissiles," which were a response to new, multi-warhead missiles deployed by the Soviets in the 1970s. The Soviets in fact walked out of the strategic arms negotiations when the allies deployed the missiles. By that time, in addition, Reagan's SDI had injected a new element into the picture; the Soviets (who had themselves pioneered the field of anti-ballistic missile defenses) were desperately eager to stop American progress in the same field. The thrust of Soviet diplomacy after 1983 was a proposed negotiation to block or slow down SDI. This the United States was bound to reject, but Reagan at the U.N. General Assembly in September 1984 answered it by proposing a comprehensive resumption of talks on "issues of concern to both sides," including not only offensive reductions but also "the relationship between offensive and defensive forces."

The U.S. strategy, in other words, was to try to leverage Soviet concern about SDI into a comprehensive negotiation that would reduce the offensive weapons which were the main American strategic concern. (It was an echo of Nixon's strategy leading to the 1972 accords—essentially trading limits on a U.S. ABM system for limits on Soviet offensive mis-

siles.) Shultz and McFarlane saw SDI as an effective bargaining chip that would eventually bring the Soviets back to the table—as indeed it did in early 1985. However, Shultz and McFarlane had not entirely reckoned with their president, who saw SDI as a goal in itself and was not at all interested in trading it away. At the Reykjavik summit in October 1986, Gorbachev would make sweeping concessions on offensive missiles—conditioned on concessions from Reagan on SDI. Reagan refused. That summit broke up in disarray, but Reagan eventually won Gorbachev's agreement to the offensive reductions anyway.

IN WASHINGTON, the bureaucratic battles were many. The SDI proposal had not originated in the Pentagon (it had come, rather, from Reagan and his own consultations with a variety of scientists and strategists), and indeed the Pentagon had opposed it for fear of upsetting allies. But defense secretary Weinberger quickly became SDI's most ardent bureaucratic champion—"more Catholic than the Pope" on the subject, according to his military aide, Colin Powell. The Pentagon rallied to the president's concept whenever it saw the State Department as too tempted to trade some limits on SDI in exchange for a comprehensive agreement. At one point in 1985, for example, the Pentagon began to argue that (contrary to the conventional wisdom) the 1972 ABM Treaty could be interpreted to permit development and testing of space-based ABM systems; Shultz strongly objected. The Pentagon was a fervent advocate of any interpretation that freed up U.S. programs or that made compromise with the Soviets more complicated.

On the eve of Reagan's Geneva summit with Gorbachev in November 1985, Weinberger sent the president a letter cautioning him against agreeing to limits on either offensive or defensive U.S. programs. The letter somehow found its way to *The Washington Post* and *The New York Times*. Just as we saw Presidents Ford and Carter in earlier chapters react sharply to such intramural leaks, Reagan was angered. McFarlane writes that Reagan "thought the leak unnecessary, a signal that someone didn't think he could handle the account and that he needed a public goading to keep him in line. It represented lack of confidence in him and a breach of teamplay."

The story of strategic arms control in the Reagan administration is a long and complicated one, but, from today's perspective, what is notable is the difference that Reagan's personal engagement made—when it occurred. He had given Shultz a mandate, but did not actively engage in

maintaining discipline in the administration when Shultz found himself embattled. The efforts of successive national security advisers to keep peace in the cabinet did not avail. "He really disliked personal confrontation," McFarlane later told an interviewer. "It wasn't a matter of his not seeing value in the competition between Cabinet officers. But he was always quite upset about the shrillness between Cap [Weinberger] and George [Shultz]." In another interview McFarlane recounted that he had complained once to the president about the backbiting, only to be told:

> Bud, I know what you're describing, and I don't disagree with the description. These are my friends. I'm not going to fire either one. And I know that if Cap were secretary of state, I would get very bad policy advice. But he's my friend, and I'm not going to change that. I'm going to look to you to manage the relationship, and to bring the disagreements to me, with your own advice on how it ought to be resolved in each case.

Richard Nixon and Henry Kissinger had striven to insure that U.S. arms control negotiating positions with the Soviet Union reflected a coherent strategy, integrating defense and foreign policy interests, and not merely the resultant of contending bureaucratic forces. The Reagan administration set its sights lower—it considered itself successful when it managed to agree on a bureaucratic compromise at all. Reagan's personal involvement made a difference, especially his adamant refusal to sacrifice SDI. But the weaknesses of the process were exposed at the Reykjavik summit, when Gorbachev caught the U.S. side by surprise with his sweeping new proposals and the Americans hastily improvised their responses.

Another dimension of Reagan's relationship with Gorbachev—and the paradoxes of Reagan's management of his own government—are illustrated by the president's famous speech at the Berlin Wall on June 12, 1987, in which he appealed to Gorbachev to tear it down. When the White House speechwriters began to circulate the advance draft for comment, State's institutional reaction was fierce. The NSC staff had also taken on a different coloration by that time; attrition and the wake of Iran-Contra had swept away the original ideological Reaganites, many of whom had been replaced by career experts. Colin Powell, then deputy national security adviser, decided that the NSC staff would sup-

port the State Department position, which was forcefully advocated by Secretary Shultz. By that time, I had moved back to the NSC staff, where—to my eternal shame—I was one of those seeking extensive changes to the draft, including deletion of the famous line: "Mr. Gorbachev, tear down this wall!"

The changes that we bureaucrats proposed, at least the significant ones, were of two kinds. One had to do with policy content—to be specific, we wanted more of it. The speech as finally delivered included some proposals for improving exchanges between West and East Berlin, but they were thin gruel; we hoped the president would use the bully pulpit to advance U.S. positions on a host of larger issues of interest to Europeans, particularly arms control. We thought it a missed opportunity when the White House speechwriters shrank these ideas down to brief references. It is not the worst impulse of the bureaucracy to want to engage the president as the chief spokesman for his administration's policies; on the contrary, this should be encouraged. But, it is up to the president to decide these things.

The more infamous battle was over the appeal to Gorbachev to tear down the wall. The State Department argument was essentially that such rabble-rousing would embarrass the West Germans present, especially Chancellor Helmut Kohl. Kohl was a staunch NATO ally, having proved his courage in the German deployment of Euromissiles. But West Germans of all political parties had made their peace with the ugly status quo including full diplomatic recognition of the East German regime. German-Soviet relations were also poor at the time. No doubt this was not the sort of speech a West German leader would have given. It is not an accident that almost all the experts who weighed in, at State and on the NSC staff, were experts on Germany, and their preoccupation was how it would resonate in the German context.

Reagan, we can see now, had something totally different in mind. His audience was Mikhail Gorbachev. He had spent time with Gorbachev at two summits by then, at Geneva and Reykjavik, and had sensed something about the young Soviet leader who presented himself so proudly as an agent of change. Some at State, in desperation, even tried to use this against the offending sentence: After meeting Gorbachev, the president had let it be known that he did not want to "personalize" the U.S-Soviet conflict—so that was another reason to cut the line. George Shultz argued vehemently up to the last minute that the line would offend the Soviet leader. Reagan dismissed the argument.

After repeated drafts came out of the Oval Office with the sentence intact, we should have gotten the message. In his limousine on the way to the Brandenburg Gate to deliver the speech, Reagan smiled to his deputy chief of staff Kenneth Duberstein: "The boys at State are going to kill me," he said, "but it's the right thing to do."

There is no way to demonstrate that the speech changed the direction of history. In light of what later happened, certainly, watching a replay today of Reagan declaiming that line with his full rhetorical power sends chills down one's spine—though perhaps more so now than it did at the time. Nevertheless, the whole affair is a vivid example of a president's possessing a strategic and moral insight that escaped his experts. Reagan's intuition about Gorbachev was undoubtedly right. A few days before Reagan delivered the speech, thousands of young East Germans clashed with police on the other side of the wall shouting "The wall must go!" Then, in front of the Soviet Embassy in East Berlin, they chanted "Gorbachev! Gorbachev!"—appealing over the heads of their own leaders to the great reformer of the Soviet system. A year and a half later, on a visit to Germany in early 1989, one of Gorbachev's closest aides distanced the Kremlin from the wall that its puppets had built: "We didn't build this wall—this isn't our wall," declared Aleksandr Yakovlev. Later that year, when East Germany's final crisis came, Gorbachev interposed no resistance to the wall's collapse.

Central America

U.S. policy-making on Central America was a "swamp," George Shultz once wrote. Shultz blamed it on the weaknesses of an NSC process that could not resolve the bureaucratic battles and produce consistent policy. There is no doubt that Reagan saw the Central American Communists (the Sandinista regime in Nicaragua, the guerrillas in El Salvador) as a geopolitical and ideological threat, and he was wary of making political concessions to them. He fought hard for military and economic assistance to those resisting the Communists—including the anti-Sandinista insurgents dubbed the "counterrevolutionaries," or "Contras." At the same time Reagan was strongly averse to any idea of embroiling the United States militarily in Central American wars; his memoirs reveal a genuine sensitivity to Latin fears of the "Great Colossus of the North," and also a clear perception that the U.S. public would not support such involvement. It would be "lunacy" to invade Nicaragua,

the president told Shultz in January 1986. A few years later, Reagan complained to aide Duberstein about the conservatives: "Those sonsofbitches won't be happy until we have 25,000 troops in Managua, and I'm not going to do it." At times he sided with Shultz's diplomacy; at other times he sided with the hard-liners (Clark, Casey, Kirkpatrick, Weinberger) who opposed it as too accommodating to the Sandinistas.

This duality in Reagan's mind was not by itself unreasonable. With more consistent leadership, it might have been turned into a coherent, balanced policy that combined power and diplomacy, strength and flexibility. Instead, as with the strategic arms negotiations, operational policy on Central America was made by a tug-of-war between the two forces, a continuing and erratic struggle for Reagan's soul. More often than not, U.S. policy actions derived not from presidential direction but from alternating assertions of bureaucratic self-will by the various sides.

Indeed the program of U.S. covert support for the Contras itself began as a bureaucratic compromise. At the beginning of the administration, when Alexander Haig was arguing for a blockade of Cuba in order to choke off supplies to the Central American Communists, he found no takers. Weinberger wanted no part of it, believing Central America a diversion from his main task of rearming the United States against the Soviet Union; as noted earlier, the White House troika and Mrs. Reagan wanted no part of it either. Thus, when CIA director William Casey came up with a covert program of pressures on Nicaragua, it became everyone's fallback option. Reagan had no trouble approving this. It was this CIA program of pressures that later grew into a significant insurgent army.

Initially the domestic controversy focused on El Salvador, where the administration sought congressional support for military and economic assistance for a Salvadoran government resisting a Communist insurgency. This was broadly supported in the administration, but in Congress and in the country it triggered fears of "another Vietnam." In opposing Central American Communism the United States was standing against "the tide of history," Senator Chris Dodd (Democrat of Connecticut) proclaimed portentously (and very wrongly) in 1983. The administration was also accused of propping up rightist dictators and condoning death squads. The policy in El Salvador was rescued from much of its torment in May 1984 when, under U.S. pressure, a free election was held that brought to power José Napoleón Duarte, a respected Christian Democrat whose hatred of the extreme right dated

back to the early 1970s when an earlier election victory was stolen from him by the military and he was imprisoned and tortured. With this success, controversy over El Salvador ebbed, and the focus shifted to Nicaragua. Congressional pressures mounted against the increasingly visible Contra program.

Throughout this evolution, the State Department was eagerly pursuing diplomatic solutions. This began in late 1981 under Haig, when Thomas Enders—the same energetic foreign service officer who had helped Henry Kissinger make international economic policy (see Chapter 4)—pursued with the same energy a dialogue with the Sandinistas. Enders visited Managua in August 1981 and proposed a deal: Essentially the United States would accept the legitimacy and finality of the Nicaraguan revolution and normalize relations with it, provided it ended its military supply of Communist insurgencies in neighboring countries. This overture got nowhere. In fact, it was based on a serious misunderstanding of the nature of the Sandinistas, for whom support for regional revolution was the heart of their "internationalist" duty. "This revolution goes beyond our borders," Tomás Borge, one of the most militant of the *comandantes*, proclaimed in July 1981.

Enders's activities became the subject of bitter disputes between Shultz and national security adviser William Clark. Shultz in his memoirs repeatedly accuses Clark of a "grab for power" or "usurpation of power" as Clark tried to block diplomatic moves that Shultz believed he had Reagan's mandate to pursue; by the same token, Clark and his conservative staffer Constantine Menges (usually backed by William Casey) kept coming up with schemes that Shultz thought absurd. Clark and his staff, in turn, accused Shultz of bypassing an orderly interagency process by end runs into the Oval Office, denying the president the benefit of dissenting views. Menges even kept count, later claiming that over a five-year period Shultz was guilty of at least seven attempts to short-circuit interagency scrutiny, in the pursuit of diplomatic accommodations that Clark and others thought unwise. Casey once wisecracked to Shultz: "George, don't be a pilgrim." "What's that?" Shultz asked. "An early settler," Casey replied.

In early 1983, Enders came up with a new proposal—to engage Mexico and other outside countries in promoting a regional settlement. Conservatives in the administration were skeptical, believing Mexico an unlikely ally given its tilt toward the Sandinistas. Clark tried to kill it. He persuaded Reagan instead to dispatch U.N. ambassador Jeane Kirk-

patrick (a Latin America scholar) on a trip to several Central and South American countries in February to deliver a personal letter from Reagan to heads of state expressing U.S. solidarity. On her trip, one sympathetic U.S. ambassador showed her an EYES ONLY FOR THE AMBASSADOR cable that Enders had sent around to all the capitals she was to visit, saying, in effect: There is a new Central America strategy coming, which will be decided once Secretary Shultz returns from a trip to China. In other words, just ignore Kirkpatrick and the letter she is carrying. When Kirkpatrick showed the cable to Reagan upon her return, he was furious, and the episode led to Enders's transfer a few months later.

Shultz in turn was caught by surprise in July 1983 when the media reported on Big Pine II, a six-month-long U.S. military exercise off both the Atlantic and the Pacific coasts of Nicaragua in which three thousand U.S. combat troops along with Honduran troops would conduct war games on Honduran territory. Clark had persuaded the president to approve the exercise, and Shultz had not been consulted. The leak of the exercise produced an uproar in Congress and contributed to the defeat in the House a few weeks later of the administration's request for aid to the Contras.

Shultz then obtained Reagan's approval to pay a quick visit to Managua on June 1, 1984, for a dramatic airport meeting with Nicaragua's president Daniel Ortega. Weinberger, Casey, and Kirkpatrick were informed only after the president had given his approval; they were not pleased. Kirkpatrick later remarked: "[S]ince he didn't keep anybody informed, Casey or Cap or anybody, everybody felt free to develop their own fantasies, as in a Rorschach test" of what the secretary of state was up to. Enders's successor, Langhorne (Tony) Motley, a political appointee and ex-ambassador to Brazil, was a more genial fellow than Enders, but the problems continued. Though the Ortega meeting had led nowhere, State was eager to follow it up with a new diplomatic plan. When others got word of a new State plan, they managed this time to force an NSC meeting at which the pros and cons could be argued out in front of the president. At the end of the lengthy and stormy meeting, held on June 25, the president made a Delphic pronouncement that no reliable deal with the Sandinistas was likely, but continuing the diplomatic effort might help shore up congressional support for the Contras.

McFarlane and the NSC staff interpreted the discussion and the president's remarks as a rejection of State's specific plan but a general mandate to continue diplomacy; a directive was issued in this vein,

signed by the president. Shultz disagreed vehemently. Having already dispatched his negotiators to Mexico the day before to meet with the Sandinista representatives, he telephoned McFarlane to say he thought the president had given him a green light. With McFarlane's grudging acquiescence, Shultz instructed his negotiators to present the plan as it had been prepared. But this initiative, too, led nowhere.

In sum, while Shultz often complained of Pentagon obtuseness and NSC obstruction, we can see that he was no slouch himself at making his way into the White House and winning permission to pursue his diplomacy. From his point of view he was seeking (and obtaining) reauthorization from Reagan to overcome bureaucratic obstruction of what the president had already authorized. Not every State Department scheme was well thought out, however. In the absence of leverage, many of the U.S. diplomatic initiatives seemed to risk an outcome that could be a disguised formula for the consolidation of Sandinista power, with no corresponding diminution of Sandinista subversion in the region. As head of the State Department's Policy Planning Staff at the time, I told Shultz I thought we had a weak hand.

GRADUALLY U.S. POLICY acquired leverage, and coalesced around a more coherent strategy, but it took a while. The electoral success of Duarte in El Salvador, and the growth of the Nicaraguan Contras into a significant peasant army, shifted the spotlight of U.S. and regional attention onto Nicaragua's internal dictatorship. In earlier years, the State Department had been dismissive of the idea of democratization. Thomas Enders had barked to NSC staffer Constantine Menges in 1981: "Constantine, this is the real world. Get serious. There is no chance for democracy in Nicaragua." But by 1985, Nicaragua was the only dictatorship left in a region of democracies. The regime's heavy-handedness in suppressing its opposition in a 1984 election had disillusioned many of its U.S. defenders—and Reagan's own overwhelming reelection in 1984 led a group of moderate Democrats to seek to collaborate with the administration on a bipartisan policy, one of whose main consensus elements was insistence on democracy in Nicaragua.

A key figure in this evolution was Elliott Abrams, a young neoconservative intellectual who became Shultz's assistant secretary for Western Hemisphere affairs in the summer of 1985. In an earlier incarnation as assistant secretary of state for human rights, Abrams had championed a human rights policy that evenhandedly challenged dictatorships of both

left and right. (He was to have a major hand, for example, in the U.S. pressures on Augusto Pinochet in Chile that led to his stepping down from office.) When Abrams succeeded Motley in the Western Hemisphere post, he steered Shultz toward an approach that intensified diplomatic pressure on the Sandinistas' internal repression, and Shultz also became an increasingly vocal champion of U.S. aid to the Contras.

The bureaucratic tensions in the administration over Central America eased considerably, as the different factions coalesced around this approach. Conservatives championed the Contras and welcomed the ideological combat with the Sandinista regime; moderates appreciated that the leverage was being put in the service of diplomacy. Abrams thus helped put Shultz in a much better bureaucratic position vis-à-vis the administration's conservatives; the new policy put Reagan and his administration in a much better position vis-à-vis Congress; and the resulting national policy even more importantly positioned the United States in the right place strategically in Central America. Eventually the leverage of the Contras, and the focus on democracy that had been so disparaged originally by the career diplomats, produced an international agreement in 1987 that required the Sandinistas to hold a free election in 1990. Relying too much, apparently, on Chris Dodd's assessment of the tide of history, the Sandinistas were quite shocked when they lost.

The Iran-Contra Scandal

In late November 1986, the Reagan administration was shaken by the revelation that its White House/NSC personnel had been secretly selling arms to Iran and diverting some of the funds to support the Nicaraguan Contras. To many observers, this affair is emblematic of the administration's bureaucratic indiscipline in the national security field. The scandal led to joint Senate-House hearings and also to the president's appointment of a Special Review Board headed by Senator John Tower (Republican of Texas). The Tower Board, which also included former Secretary of State Edmund Muskie and former national security adviser Brent Scowcroft, published a thoughtful report in February 1987, drawing a number of lessons about the proper role of the NSC staff and national security adviser. Sound as these lessons are, however, my own view of the affair puts the emphasis somewhat differently.

It is important to separate the two dimensions of the affair—the overtures to Iran, and the diversion of funds for the Contras—since

they illustrate two different dimensions of the administration's bureau-cratic problems. The overtures to Iran were most emphatically a presi-dential decision, reflecting a policy to which the president was strongly committed. It was not a case of presidential inattention or of subordi-nates acting without his authorization. On the contrary, Reagan agreed with aides who were convinced there was potential for a strategic open-ing to Iran. Shultz and Weinberger knew of it, and strongly opposed it. I heard them joke to each other that, with all the many issues on which they were at loggerheads, here was a case where they agreed and pre-sented a common opinion to the president—and were overruled.

I moved from State back to the NSC in March 1986 and knew about the Iran policy. I also told my new NSC colleagues, including national security adviser John Poindexter and Lieutenant Colonel Oliver North, that I thought it was strategically crazy. With the Iran-Iraq War still rag-ing, a victory by Iran's new revolutionary regime would have been a strategic disaster; all America's Arab friends were backing Iraq, and U.S. policy tilted in that direction as well. The United States was waging a major diplomatic campaign, in fact, to stanch other nations' transfer of arms to Iran. Nonetheless, Bud McFarlane was called out of retirement to travel secretly to Tehran in May 1986 for what was hoped to be a political discussion. He brought with him, as tokens of goodwill, an (Israeli-baked) chocolate cake with a skeleton key design in the frosting, and a pallet of Hawk antiaircraft missile spare parts.

Reagan sincerely believed in the potential for a breakthrough with Iran, and this explains his stubborn public insistence that his policy was not a trade of arms for hostages. While he cared deeply about the hostages in Lebanon, the overarching purpose of his actions was not limited to retrieving them; it was the broader strategic opening with Iran. The various weapons that the U.S. side provided to Iran (not only Hawk parts but TOW antitank missiles) were meant as a token of the U.S. commitment to this larger goal, just as Iran's help with release of hostages was to be their token of the same. In the end, since the strate-gic relationship never materialized, operationally all that was taking place was the movement of a few arms and a few hostages; that was all that was left of the policy.

Most of the postmortems on the Iran-Contra affair focus on process—on the inappropriateness of the role of the NSC staff. In my view, however, the blunder in this case was substantive more than it was procedural. The strategy was doomed for substantive reasons no matter

how or by whom it was carried out; it seriously undercut the core U.S. policy at the time, which was to oppose Iran. That was, and remains, the basis of my own disagreement with what was done. Despite that objection, however, it is also my view that presidents deserve the benefit of the doubt on the procedural point. It was Reagan's prerogative to overrule his cabinet secretaries, and it was also his prerogative to turn to his staff for execution rather than delegate it to a bureaucracy that had made its rebellion against his decision quite clear.

The diversion of some of the proceeds to the Contras was a different matter. Poindexter and North kept this secret from the president as from everyone else. It was the revelation of the Contra dimension that turned the affair from a policy embarrassment into a political crisis, given the emotionalism that Central America was already engendering. With the Democrats' recapture of the Senate in November 1986, a maximum congressional assault was guaranteed. Democrats also charged that the diversion violated legislative restrictions on direct or indirect U.S. aid to the Contras. The fact that Poindexter went out of his way to protect the president's "plausible deniability" indicates how close to the edge he knew he was skating; thus he took on a huge political risk on his own initiative, without a safety net of any kind.

A very demoralized White House, which saw the departure of chief of staff Donald Regan as well as of Poindexter and North in the wake of the revelations, was content to blame everything on the departed employees. It was left to congressional Republicans to defend the president's prerogative and make the argument that the NSC staff's actions, however unwise, were not illegal. This they did. The most vigorous and articulate defense of the administration was made by the Republican minority report resulting from the congressional investigation—a brief shaped by Representative Dick Cheney of Wyoming. Cheney's vigorous defense of Reagan helped propel him to national recognition and toward a leadership role in the Republican Party. But it also reflected a conviction formed in the Ford years when he had witnessed firsthand the congressional assault on executive authority. Cheney's instructions to Michael Malbin, his staffer and principal draftsman on the Republican Iran-Contra report, were: "Wherever the facts of this investigation lead, let them lead. Your job is to preserve the institution of the presidency."

The Tower Board enumerated the many "mistakes of omission, commission, judgment, and perspective" committed by Reagan's NSC staff, and marked them as a warning to future officials of "potential pitfalls

they face even when they are operating with what they consider the best of motives." The board then made a number of recommendations relating to transparency, collegial deliberations, and responsible behavior on the part of the NSC staff. It recommended, for example, that the NSC staff stay out of the covert action business, and hire a senior legal adviser. It also urged that the national security adviser report directly to the president, not through the chief of staff—a correct acknowledgment that the *weakness* of the position had been its problem for much of the Reagan administration. All these recommendations were adopted. But these procedural fixes seem, in retrospect, rather small in light of the magnitude of the political crisis that had erupted.

The Tower Board is often cited for its conclusion that "[a]s a general matter, the NSC Staff should not engage in the implementation of policy or the conduct of operations." George Shultz took advantage of the opening provided by the scandal to approach the new national security adviser, Frank Carlucci, and tell him, in effect: "You shouldn't meet with foreign ambassadors; you shouldn't travel; you can't chair meetings. And State has to know everything you are doing." Carlucci politely declined. (He did promise that Shultz personally, if not State as an institution, would know everything he did.) Cyrus Vance, a decade earlier, had made similar demands on Zbigniew Brzezinski, who also politely refused. The bottom line is that there is no way to tell a president how he may or may not use his own staff.

Carlucci had it right: Transparency is a better principle to emphasize. Especially in the post-Kissinger era, no national security adviser can be expected to remain a hermit in the basement, avoiding contact with foreigners or Congress or the media. (Ironically, the one who tried hardest to do that was John Poindexter.) In professional and social Washington, the security adviser will come in contact with foreigners, legislators, and media; likewise most security advisers have been sent on missions abroad. Good governance requires not that this be stopped, but that it be in the service of policies that are transparent to other senior officials and openly deliberated upon. Which person is the best one to carry a message is a tactical question, and there will be times when a president may legitimately give the assignment to an immediate adviser who can travel less conspicuously and speak with the special authority of the White House—often to counterparts in the immediate offices of other heads of government.

These matters are for a president to decide. In the end, the Tower

Board had no choice but to recognize—as Senator Henry Jackson had recognized a quarter-century earlier—that every president needs the flexibility to choose the most congenial system of policy-making. Thus the board, after all its investigation and deliberation, recommended no legislative changes in the role, structure, or authority of the NSC or its staff.

Lebanon and the Use of Force

In relations with the Soviet Union and policy in Central America, the Reagan administration, for all its stumbles and disarray, worked its way toward successful outcomes. Ultimately it could be said that the president's policy instincts served him well even if his manner of policy-making did not. In Lebanon, however, the results were more deadly. Reagan sent U.S. military forces to Lebanon in 1982 and withdrew them in bloody and humiliating circumstances in 1984. The debacle occurred because of a policy failure in two dimensions: a miscalculation of the changing political circumstances on the ground in Lebanon, and a bureaucratic stalemate in Washington that Reagan was unwilling to break.

U.S. troops arrived in Lebanon in benign circumstances as neutral peacekeepers. Israel had invaded Lebanon in June 1982 to crush the Palestine Liberation Organization (PLO). In August a multinational force (MNF) was created, with U.S. participation, to shield the orderly withdrawal of PLO leaders and guerrillas from Lebanon. The United States contributed about eight hundred Marines, who accompanied British, French, and Italian forces. Israel, Syria, and all factions in Lebanon endorsed the exercise, and Reagan could emphasize, with justification, that there was "no intention or expectation that U.S. Armed Forces will become involved in hostilities." As the MNF was completing its mission in mid-September, seven hundred to eight hundred Palestinian civilians were killed in refugee camps at Sabra and Shatila near Beirut by Lebanese Christian militias aligned with Israel. A second MNF deployment was thereupon organized, this time with the goal of bolstering Lebanese government authority in the Beirut area. The United States contributed 1,200 Marines to this effort, with the same—legitimate—expectation that this was a neutral humanitarian mission with broad support and low risk of involvement in hostilities.

Subsequently the political ground in Lebanon shifted dramatically

under the Americans' feet, yet the U.S. government did not draw new conclusions about the mission and the vulnerability of its forces. The major new development was a peace agreement between Lebanon and Israel, mediated by Secretary of State George Shultz and signed on May 17, 1983: All Israeli forces were to withdraw from Lebanon in exchange for peace. The agreement was immediately denounced by Syria as a betrayal of the Arab cause, and Syria egged on its radical allies in Lebanon to overthrow the Lebanese government by force. Syria, though bloodied by the Israelis in their original invasion of 1982, had been rearmed by the Soviet Union and was recovering its self-confidence. Meanwhile the Israeli public was tiring of the Lebanese adventure, demoralized in part by political hand-wringing in the wake of the Sabra-Shatila disaster; Israeli forces started pulling back unilaterally.

The balance of forces in Lebanon was thus tilting badly, and the peace agreement did not reflect the new geopolitical reality. The U.S. Marines and their MNF allies found themselves in the middle of an escalating war around Beirut. Terrorists had blown up the American embassy in April; they struck the U.S. and French barracks in October, killing 241 Marines and 59 French troops.

The United States faced a choice. If the peace agreement was strategically important to us, then there was a case for using U.S. military leverage to insure the survival of the Lebanese government that had signed it. Shultz made this case, arguing that to allow Syria and its radical allies to topple a U.S.-brokered peace agreement would set an ominous precedent for Arab-Israeli diplomacy and embolden radical forces throughout the Middle East. He urged greater use of the Marines or of U.S. naval firepower offshore to assist the Lebanese government in its ongoing battle with the Syrian-backed radicals. Secretary of Defense Weinberger and the Joint Chiefs of Staff, in contrast, wanted U.S. forces in no such role; they wanted the Marines out of Lebanon, or at the very most confined to peacekeeping duties rather than taking sides in the battle.

Either Shultz's policy or Weinberger's policy would have been a coherent choice. What Reagan did, however, was evade the choice and split the difference. In August 1983 he authorized the MNF to stay, but only in a purely peacekeeping role. In December, he agreed to step up artillery fire against Syria's Druze allies lobbing shells at the Marines, but only if precise Druze targets could be identified and not against Syrian forces in the area. Every time a specific decision was presented to

him to respond to the deteriorating situation, the president would agree to an incremental increase in military pressure but never a decisive one. The mighty battleship *New Jersey*, for example, joined the naval task force off the coast but used its 16-inch guns only sporadically—never in a sustained, systematic way to affect the battle. The Pentagon interpreted Reagan's orders in minimalist fashion, concerned that greater involvement would only magnify risks. In December, it unilaterally ended reconnaissance flights over Lebanon without consultation with State.

"We're a divided group," Reagan lamented to his diary. But the upshot of his incrementalism was that the United States was engaged enough to be taking sides and staking its prestige, but not enough to win. As the Marines on the ground took casualties, congressional support eroded. An agreement with the Democratic congressional leadership in September 1983 to continue the Marine deployment another eighteen months simply collapsed after the barracks bombing. In the final phase, Donald Rumsfeld was named presidential envoy for Lebanon and the Middle East. (I accompanied him on some of his missions.) He figured out immediately that the bigger problem was not in Beirut but in Washington. He and his team came up with an alternative approach—to pull all the Marines out (since they were a political liability and performed no military mission) while stepping up training of the Lebanese armed forces and more aggressively applying U.S. naval and air power to help them win. Reagan adopted this approach in January 1984—but the situation had deteriorated so far that, while the Marines came home, the second half of the new policy was never implemented. The Lebanese government collapsed.

Just as President Bill Clinton discovered in Somalia in 1993, what started out as a relatively risk-free humanitarian involvement turned into something else as the political context changed on the ground. The policy requirement then is to draw the proper conclusions: Do we still want to be there? If not, we should get out. If yes, we need to insure that our military exertion is adequate to the goal we have decided is important. Reagan was usually reluctant to order the U.S. military to fight a war that its leaders did not want to fight. Yet he was also persuaded by Shultz's argument that the United States had a strategic stake in the outcome; thus he was always reluctant to "cut and run" until the very end when defeat was imposed. Reagan had to choose between two con-

flicting strategies, but he never did. Splitting the difference meant only incoherence.

CONTRAST LEBANON with Reagan's decisiveness over Grenada. By the fall of 1983 a radical Marxist regime was coming apart and plunging the tiny Caribbean island into anarchy, putting into apparent jeopardy not only neighboring island states but a group of American students at a local medical school. In this case, too, Cap Weinberger's Pentagon was reluctant to get involved, but Reagan overruled them. Reagan went ahead with his decision even when the Marine barracks bombing happened in Beirut a few days before execution, which took some political courage. The Normandy landing it was not, but the liberation of Grenada had its deeper importance: Its success—and popular support— marked the breaking of the post-Vietnam taboo in America against the use of military force.

An important bureaucratic factor, especially in the Lebanon case, was the Defense Department's view of its own foreign policy interests. The United States has extensive military partnerships in the Arab world; many go back to the Carter administration when moderate Arabs drew closer to us in the wake of the Iranian revolution. These relationships are a significant achievement of U.S. policy. But for Secretary Weinberger, and to some extent to the Defense Department as an institution, they meant a reluctance to fight a war against Arabs. Weinberger had no problem with the initial small Marine deployment to Lebanon which was to protect Palestinians (though he was more nervous about the second MNF mission). But when the Lebanese engagement turned into a struggle against Syria to defend an Israeli peace agreement, this Weinberger wanted no part of. By the same token, when Libyan-backed terrorists attacked the Rome and Vienna airports in December 1985, Reagan wanted to retaliate against Libya but Weinberger and the chiefs dug in their heels. A frustrated Reagan ordered Poindexter to start preparing for the next time: "I don't want any excuses." After a Libyan terrorist attack killed U.S. servicemen at a disco club in West Berlin in April 1986, Reagan, this time, ordered it.

After the Lebanon debacle, Weinberger ordered a Pentagon study of what had gone wrong, headed by a retired admiral. One of the study's conclusions was that the United States had not worked hard enough to develop "diplomatic alternatives" to resolve the political conflict, as

opposed to "military options." Shultz was outraged. He believed the diplomacy to preserve Lebanon had faltered precisely because U.S. military leverage was undercut by the Pentagon. Hearing him rail privately on this theme several times, I suggested to him that he say it publicly. He invited me to draft a speech on the subject. "It was precisely our military role in Lebanon that was problematical, not our diplomatic exertion," he declared in a speech to the Trilateral Commission in April 1984. Shultz went on in this speech to explain that power and diplomacy are not distinct alternatives but mutually dependent; in an age of complex challenges like terrorism, the United States needs to confront its enemies with an array of discriminate tools including military force.

It was this Shultz speech that prompted Caspar Weinberger to respond with his own famous pronouncement, sometimes known as the "Weinberger Doctrine," on the principles that should guide the use of force. Addressing the National Press Club in November 1984, the secretary of defense laid out six criteria that should be met whenever a president decides on the use of American military power:

- The issue should be "vital to our national interest or that of our allies."
- Once committed, we should have the "clear intention of winning."
- We should have "clearly defined" objectives and "send the forces needed" to accomplish those objectives.
- The relationship between the objectives and the size of the forces should be "continually reassessed and adjusted if necessary."
- Before we commit, "there must be some reasonable assurance" of congressional and public support.
- Committing U.S. forces to combat "should be a last resort."

The "Weinberger Doctrine" is sometimes known as the "Powell Doctrine," since a version of it was also espoused by Colin Powell, who after serving as Weinberger's military assistant went on to a brilliant career as chairman of the Joint Chiefs under Bush 41 and then secretary of state under Bush 43. In shorthand, it became known as a doctrine of avoiding incrementalism in the use of force. This is not the place for an extended discussion of the Shultz-Weinberger debate on the use of force, except to note the irony that the next significant military activity by the Reagan administration violated a number of Weinberger's criteria but had his enthusiastic support nonetheless.

This was the decision in March 1987 to provide U.S. naval convoys to protect Kuwaiti oil tankers in the Gulf against Iranian attack during the Iran-Iraq War. Despite the Weinberger emphasis on applying over-whelming force to minimize risks, this was a very limited application of military power, open-ended in its commitment, with risks that were hard to calculate, and it became the target of increasing congressional agitation. Yet the Pentagon was even more enthusiastic about this mission than State, and a colleague of mine on the NSC staff had to remind the Pentagon of the need for a plan for protecting the convoys should they come under Iranian attack. The convoying continued, without incident, until the Iran-Iraq War ended, and represented a policy success. That there was consensus in the U.S. government despite the risks was a bureaucratic success as well. Secretary Weinberger saw it—correctly—as a positive policy for the United States in the Arab world, and somehow this convinced him that it was perfectly consistent with the six criteria of his 1984 speech.

Panama and the Rogue Elephant Justice Department

A war that did *not* occur in the Reagan administration was the war to topple dictator Manuel Noriega in Panama. This, too, is a story of bureaucratic confusion—this time involving not only a recalcitrant Pentagon but a Justice Department that did not consider itself obligated to coordinate with others. Throughout this book we have seen how, over the many decades since 1947, procedures have fitfully evolved in the NSC system for coordinating or integrating the activities of the State Department, Defense Department, CIA, and the White House. In Chapter 4 we noted that successive administrations have wrestled with how to integrate international economic policy into overall national security policy-making; this is still a work in progress. By the end of the twentieth century, however, yet another problem had appeared—how to include in a coherent national security framework the growing international activities of U.S. law enforcement agencies: the FBI (which now has offices overseas), the Drug Enforcement Administration, and other Department of Justice activities.

In February 1988, federal grand juries in Tampa and Miami handed down indictments of Manuel Noriega on drug-trafficking and racketeering. These indictments launched the United States into a political crisis

with Panama for which there was no coordinated U.S. government strategy to follow up because the Justice Department had made no effort to coordinate its actions with other agencies, and the U.S. government was deadlocked for the remainder of the Reagan administration over what to do next. The crisis festered until Reagan's successor, President George H. W. Bush, ended it by war: U.S. forces invaded Panama in December 1989 and captured Noriega.

The Department of Justice, insisting on its legal responsibilities and on the sanctity of grand jury proceedings, jealously guards its prosecutorial decisions against interference from outsiders. Although indictments of foreign leaders can raise obvious issues of foreign policy, Justice's willingness to share information with other concerned agencies has been ad hoc and sporadic. Even though the president is constitutionally the chief law enforcement officer of the land, Justice has been known to resist sharing too much information even with the president or White House staff lest it tempt their assertion of a contrary opinion. Before the indictments of February 1988, Justice officials had reported occasionally to an interagency group dealing with Panama on the status of its investigations of Noriega, but not with a view to being dissuaded. The State Department's Elliott Abrams, in charge of Latin American affairs, was especially reticent for personal reasons, having run into legal trouble over his (minor) role in the Iran-Contra affair. The line between "obstructing Justice" and "obstructing justice" is a fuzzy one, and the referee who will decide whether you have crossed the line will be a very annoyed Justice Department official.

Thus there was no U.S. strategy to apprehend Noriega or to follow up in any other way. Noriega was a well-entrenched dictator. Conceivably, if there had been a concerted U.S. strategy aimed at bringing him down, indictments might have been a part of such a strategy. But that is not how events unfolded. Two U.S. attorneys launched the United States into a political crisis with Panama for which the U.S. government was unprepared.

The Reagan administration immediately deadlocked over what to do. The State Department (Shultz and Abrams) urged an aggressive policy to bring the dictator down. At Situation Room meetings, they argued, for example, for the creative use of the U.S. military presence in the Canal Zone to shake the Noriega regime (shows of force including sonic booms over the capital, exploiting dissension within the Panamanian armed forces, helping the political opposition, even a commando raid to

snatch him). Aside from sending some additional troops, however, Defense was opposed to military action. Frank Carlucci had replaced Weinberger as secretary of defense, but the Pentagon remained cautious about intervention. Thus, the pattern of Lebanon reasserted itself: Reagan wanted Noriega out but was unwilling to order his military to do something they were unwilling to do. He remained sensitive about the United States' appearing the gringo bully in Latin America.

A second bureaucratic dispute broke out over whether to offer a plea bargain to Noriega—quashing the indictments in exchange for his stepping down. State wanted to pursue this avenue, too (backed up by the shows of force). Justice was extremely reluctant, but this time Reagan stepped up to the decision and overruled it. The discussion leaked, however, and led to a storm of bipartisan protest against letting Noriega off the hook. Vice President Bush, running for president, argued passionately against the deal. The negotiation fell through, in large part because of reluctance on Noriega's side.

The bureaucratic lessons here are many. The Justice Department's coordination with other agencies has improved somewhat since then. On June 30, 1988, Attorney General Meese sent a memorandum to White House chief of staff Howard Baker promising timely notification to the White House in the future if prosecution of a foreign leader was contemplated. Today, Justice participates more regularly in interagency deliberations in the NSC system, permitting greater transparency and coordination. After the al-Qaida attack on the USS *Cole* in the port of Aden in October 2000, however, the American ambassador to Yemen and the FBI forensic team dispatched to investigate the attack clashed repeatedly over who was in charge. These relationships, too, are still a work in progress.

The most important overall lesson, of course, is the central role of the president. Sometimes there are issues on which it makes sense to split the difference between opposing views, or to navigate a jagged course among the conflicting positions of one's advisers. In arms control and on Central America, that is how Reagan proceeded. Bureaucratically it was the line of least resistance; he did not want to make a stark choice among his closest associates. Given that lengthy and complex negotiations were involved, it is arguable that no lasting price was paid; the world adjusted. Clumsy as the process was, it inched U.S. policy forward toward practical results.

Managing a crisis, however, brings other imperatives into play.

Events move rapidly, putting a premium on coherence and speed in both decision and execution. The goal must be to seize the initiative and sustain it—to make the opponent react to *our* moves and to dominate events. In such a situation, splitting the difference between conflicting strategies can only produce incoherence. Jimmy Carter in the crisis over the shah of Iran, or Ronald Reagan in the crisis in Lebanon, discovered the hard way the price that can be paid for a policy that embodies such contradictions within it. With Carter, it was a contradiction in his ultimate purposes; with Reagan, it was an impulse to evade a stark choice. In both cases the result was indiscipline in the government, with grievous consequences. Richard Nixon wanted to know what his real choices were, even if his advisers all agreed; he was prepared to step up to a stark decision. Presidents who avoid hard choices in the name of bureaucratic harmony may think they are minimizing political risks; on the contrary, they may be magnifying risks if the result is a conflicted policy that sacrifices effectiveness. They will be judged, in the end, not by the smoothness of their bureaucratic procedure but by whether they shaped events according to their purposes.

Lebanon and Panama were two important failures in what was in other respects a highly successful presidency. Some found it easy to belittle Reagan's intellectual capacities. But our analysis points to the key conclusion that the more engaged he was personally, the more successful his administration's policies were. Where he held back, or was uncertain, the system did not work. Where he did impose his will—whatever his weaknesses as a manager—he provided the decisive leadership.

George H. W. Bush

G EORGE HERBERT WALKER BUSH inherited from Ronald Reagan, among other things, the festering crisis in Panama, and the way he handled it was an early indicator that the new administration operated in a very different manner from its predecessor. Under Bush, the bureaucratic stalemate between State and Defense over this issue quickly ended. Dictator Manuel Noriega helped matters along, to be sure, with a stream of provocations, including hundreds of incidents of harassment of U.S. servicemen and their families by Panamanian troops and then, in May 1989, with the blatant rigging of an election to install a puppet of his as president of the country.

One of Bush's first acts in the Oval Office was to approve a covert action program aimed at bolstering Noriega's opposition. After the stolen election, U.S. Southern Command (SOUTHCOM), based in those days in the Canal Zone, expanded its patrols, training flights, and other military exercises in and around Panama. The U.S. ambassador, and military dependents, were called home. Two thousand additional U.S. troops were sent to Panama. These were measures of political and psychological pressure of the sort that George Shultz had advocated during the Reagan administration but that had been resisted by Frank Carlucci's Pentagon. The new secretary of defense, Dick Cheney, supported all these measures without hesitation. When the commander of SOUTHCOM was identified as part of the bureaucratic resistance to strong action, Cheney secured his replacement by an officer regarded as more aggressive.

The final provocations came in December 1989, when Panamanian troops opened fire on four U.S. officers in a car and killed a Marine lieutenant; the same night, a Navy lieutenant and his wife were stopped at

the same roadblock and detained, the wife threatened with rape before they were released after four hours. After a last briefing on the military plan on a Sunday afternoon in the residential quarters of the White House, Bush decided: "Okay, let's do it. The hell with it." An invasion force of ten thousand U.S. airborne troops, joining the forces already in Panama, overwhelmed the Panamanian military, seized the country, and captured Noriega. The U.S. attorneys in Tampa and Miami finally had their man.

The New Cast of Characters

There is a risk that a chapter on George H. W. Bush in a book such as this will be boring. Tolstoy famously observed in *Anna Karenina* that all happy families are alike, while every unhappy family is unhappy in its own way. He then wrote about an unhappy one. From the management point of view, the administration of our forty-first president was the most collegial and smoothest-run of the presidencies we are considering. It had its share of policy quarrels and bursts of ego, but nothing resembling the high drama or low melodrama of its predecessors. This is because it was led by a president who was consistently the master of his brief, and whose personal engagement preempted bureaucratic warfare. He was blessed with cabinet secretaries at State and Defense who saw themselves and acted as the president's men, imposing his agenda on their sometimes recalcitrant bureaucracies instead of becoming the spokesmen for that recalcitrance. The assistant to the president for national security affairs served effectively as honest broker and coordinator, his effectiveness insured not only by his own skill but by the palpable reality that the president, personally, was in charge.

Bush lacked the charismatic qualities of Ronald Reagan, as well as Reagan's political dominance in the Republican Party and in the country. What Bush had was an unusual accumulation of experience in foreign affairs, having been vice president for eight years, and before that the U.S. permanent representative to the United Nations, chief of the U.S. diplomatic mission in China, and director of central intelligence. Except for the brief stint at CIA, what he was accumulating was knowledge, more than executive experience. Of the presidents we are examining in this book, only Nixon had comparable background in the subject matter and comparable confidence in his own understanding of policy. Bush, like Nixon, came into office knowing most world issues and many

leaders better than his cabinet secretaries did. On an issue like China, for example, Bush himself sometimes acted as if he were the "China desk officer," to the amusement or irritation of his staff.

Bush carried with him a personal self-assurance, moreover, that Nixon's introversion denied him. Awkward as he was in some circumstances, Bush had the natural gregariousness of the politician—even more so than the aloof Reagan. Coupled with his substantive knowledge, this gregariousness guaranteed that he would engage enthusiastically in personal diplomacy, picking up the telephone and taking charge of policy implementation himself to an unusual degree. By the end of 1989, for example, Bush had found time to chat by telephone with every head of government in Latin America. This served him in good stead when he ordered the invasion of Panama that December; the goodwill he had accumulated contributed to the muted reaction from Latin leaders usually hypersensitive to the very thought of Yankee military intervention. The "mad dialer" was the name he acquired among State Department officials who had to scramble to find out what he was up to. He wanted to be a hands-on president, and he was.

His management style was open and informal. His key subordinates' access to him was easy. Regular meetings of the National Security Council gave way to smaller Oval Office meetings of the "Core Group" or "Gang of Eight"—usually including Secretary of State James A. Baker III, Secretary of Defense Cheney, national security adviser Brent Scowcroft, JCS chairman Colin Powell, White House chief of staff John Sununu, Baker's deputy Lawrence Eagleburger, Scowcroft's deputy Robert Gates, and Vice President Dan Quayle. Transparency was the cardinal rule, and most flare-ups of temper over four years had to do with cases of one principal or another being blindsided (most often inadvertently) by something that another was doing. The informality worked, first of all, because the transparency principle was generally observed; there were no end runs or attempts to bypass or exclude. Second, the president was always engaged, and deferred to. Scowcroft was the impresario and enforcer of this process, and a basic condition of trust prevailed. There were differences of view on many issues, but they were argued out and the president decided. It was a tight group, and its deliberations were remarkably free of leaks. "[W]e made the national security apparatus work the way it is supposed to," Baker wrote later.

Robert Gates, who revered Bush, has a somewhat sharper assessment:

His weaknesses in foreign policy were reflections of his strengths: he was at times too patient and too forgiving of the ambitions and game-playing of both foreign leaders and some of his own people. He was at times loyal to some who did not deserve it or return it.

And we will see below some hints of whom Gates was referring to. Jealousies and suspicions of motives and other human frailties are the norm in Washington; what is striking is that under Bush 41 they were never as debilitating as they were in some previous (or later) administrations.

BRENT SCOWCROFT was described by a journalist in 1990 as "the short, balding figure at Bush's side—at the golf course, on the speedboat, in the Oval Office, the ever-present adviser, the confidant." Trained as a fighter pilot, then earning a doctorate in international relations at Columbia, he went through his Washington trial by fire in the Nixon White House, first as Nixon's military aide, then as Kissinger's deputy through the ordeal of Watergate and the bureaucratic wars of that era. He was one of the few to survive unscathed. In 1975, Gerald Ford elevated Scowcroft to be Kissinger's successor.

Taking on the same job under George Bush, Scowcroft became the only person thus far to serve in the position twice. But it was a different job the second time around. Ford, he knew, reposed total confidence in Kissinger, and therefore his role then was to facilitate that relationship—protecting Ford's options but also Kissinger's flanks. By the time of Bush 41, Scowcroft had emerged as a significant and respected Washington figure in his own right. He had been asked by Reagan to chair a presidential commission looking into U.S. strategic forces; he had been a member of the Tower Board examining the Iran-Contra affair. By then his exemplary conduct of his office under Ford had already become the paradigm of the honest broker model of the security adviser's position—it was the "Scowcroft model." For Bush, Scowcroft would provide two key things—first, an intellectual contribution to the shaping of strategy, particularly on arms control, given his preeminent expertise in the field, and second, a strong hand for a crucial management task. Bush, the hands-on president, had appointed heavyweights James Baker and Dick Cheney to the cabinet, and would want Scowcroft's active help in maintaining presidential control. "It is probably accurate to say that the NSC staff and Brent were . . . concerned about what State might be up to," Bush observed in a dry understatement in his memoir.

Scowcroft was also responsible for a bureaucratic innovation in the NSC system that has been retained by successor administrations. It was his idea to create what is known as the Principals Committee—an interagency committee of the key cabinet secretaries, chaired by himself, in effect a National Security Council meeting without the president. This would be the forum of last resort for ironing out interagency disagreements or framing those disagreements for presidential decision. The cabinet secretaries obviously speak more authoritatively for their departments' views than their deputies can, and at such a meeting they can modify their own views as they choose (which subordinates usually may not). Thus, the forum can move issues closer to resolution in a way that can be very useful for a president. Bush appreciated Scowcroft's ability to "knock heads" and resolve some disagreements "before he let them in my door."

Zbigniew Brzezinski had chaired such a cabinet-level committee for some issues, but the idea of the national security adviser chairing a meeting of cabinet secretaries—who outrank him in protocol terms—is, on the face of it, an anomaly. In the 1940s, in the first years of the NSC, it was thought that the secretary of state or vice president would preside in the president's absence. Henry Kissinger, as noted, never chaired cabinet-level meetings when he held only the White House position; the fact that several of his successors have done so is in part a tribute to the transformation in the nature of the position that he bequeathed to them. It was also, under Bush 41, a tribute to Scowcroft's stature and reputation.

DICK CHENEY was not Bush's original choice to be secretary of defense. Senator John Tower of Texas was the first nominee, but failed of confirmation because of allegations of alcoholism and womanizing. The choice of Cheney was inspired. In light of the unusual camaraderie that the Bush team enjoyed, David Rothkopf is right to speculate that, had Tower been confirmed, "he might not have fit in as well, nor been as easy for the president to manage" given his years as an independent power in the Senate. Cheney was a team player. In Robert Gates's estimation, while Cheney "presented his views forcefully and consistently, when he lost he didn't leak or try to play games behind people's backs." By all accounts, Cheney was more hard-line in his convictions on some issues than the rest of the Bush team, especially with respect to the Soviet Union, but the disagreements never reached a level of personal

animosity, certainly not anything approaching the bitterness of the Shultz-Weinberger rivalry. They seemed, rather, to be intellectual disagreements over the substance of policy more than they were contests over the protection of bureaucratic turf. In Washington, it is the latter that give the rivalries most of their force.

Cheney's attitude to the use of American military power was not inhibited by a "Vietnam syndrome." Indeed, it was a desire to overcome the "Vietnam syndrome." When the Pentagon gave the Panama operation the name Operation Just Cause, Cheney, joking with reporters, called it "Operation Just Because"—as if to say, we did it just because we could, and we want the world to see that we can.

Cheney was also the unreconstructed Cold Warrior on the Bush team. Early in the administration, Scowcroft came up with a proposal that the United States and the Soviet Union both withdraw substantial ground troops from Central Europe, down to lower equal levels; it was meant as a test of Gorbachev and (if implemented) a significant reduction of the "smothering presence" of Soviet forces in the region. Cheney opposed it, skeptical of Gorbachev and uncomfortable with such a radical move. (Bush, contrary to his public image of caution, was eager for new initiatives and adopted the proposal.) Similarly in the Strategic Arms Reduction Talks (START), Cheney was doubtful of Gorbachev's good faith and wary of risky moves. In late 1991, as the Soviet Union headed toward breakup, it was Cheney who most openly welcomed the disintegration of our geopolitical rival, while Baker and others clung longer to Gorbachev as the benign moderate leader holding the USSR together against less benign centrifugal forces.

Cheney established his firm control at the Pentagon early on. In his first news conference as secretary of defense, he publicly rebuked the Air Force chief of staff for negotiating with members of Congress, without his authorization, on a controversial plan for missile defense. A few months later, as noted, he relieved the SOUTHCOM commander for foot-dragging over military action in Panama. Later, in the run-up to the Gulf War, he dismissed another Air Force chief of staff for loose talk to the press about plans for a bombing campaign. But he treated the chairman of the Joint Chiefs, General Colin Powell, with respect and generally gave him free rein to speak his mind to the president wherever Powell and he disagreed. There were several occasions, whether over Panama or the Gulf War, when the president and Scowcroft were suspicious that senior military planners were reluctant to provide timely or

adequate plans for war. Scowcroft reports his unhappiness with a military briefing on Iraq and Kuwait at one point in October 1990: "It sounded unenthusiastic, delivered by people who didn't want to do the job." When military planners came to the president with high estimates of the numbers of men and arms that would be needed—perhaps thinking these would discourage the president from acting—it was Cheney's strategy to advise the president that he should simply accede to the requests. "Dick led the way for the military," Bush recalled, "which I think is the model our Constitution envisioned: armed forces headed by civilians who were leading, not pushing, the military to understanding and fulfilling the missions set for them by the President."

Cheney's performance, in short, especially with respect to the use of force, was a contrast with the performance of the secretaries of defense who had preceded him in the Reagan administration. He was a classic example of a cabinet secretary acting as the president's man at the head of his department, imposing the president's agenda, not as the spokesman to the president of his department's institutional perspective. For Cheney, civilian control of the military meant responsiveness to presidential direction.

Both of these, moreover, were of a piece with his long interest in restoring presidential authority vis-à-vis Congress. Early in his term, Cheney took on the perhaps quixotic mission of challenging the accumulated congressional micromanagement of DoD's affairs. In July 1989, he appeared before the House Armed Services Committee with an array of charts demonstrating the high cost, in dollars and work-hours, of legislatively mandated reporting requirements:

> *Every working day*, for example, entails on average almost 3 new General Accounting Office (GAO) audits of DoD; an estimated 450 written inquiries and over 2,500 telephone inquiries from Capitol Hill; and nearly 3 separate reports to Congress *each* averaging over 1,000 man-hours in preparation and approximately $50,000 in cost. In addition, senior DoD officials spend upwards of 40 hours preparing for the 6 appearances as witnesses and the 14 hours of testimony that they provide on average for *each* day Congress is in session.

In January 1990, his office published a more comprehensive White Paper elaborating on the burden that congressional micromanagement

imposed on national defense policy. It catalogued a great expansion of congressional involvement in defense budget line items (including the growth of earmarks), Congress's expanded intervention in management of defense programs, a growing duplication of effort as a result of multiple and overlapping committee jurisdictions in Congress, and other problems.

The common thread in all these endeavors—whether civilian control of the military, presidential direction of defense policy, or resistance to congressional encroachments—was, for Cheney, the defense of presidential prerogative. This is the same Dick Cheney who had served in Gerald Ford's White House in a time of congressional ascendancy, and who in Congress defended Ronald Reagan over Iran-Contra. From this perspective, Cheney's later preoccupations as vice president under George W. Bush (Bush 43) do not suggest such a discontinuity as often alleged.

JAMES A. BAKER III was perhaps the most colorful character in the administration, the only larger-than-life personality in the cabinet. A close personal friend of the president from their younger days together in Houston, Baker characterized it as a "big brother–little brother" relationship. Baker had already gained substantial policy experience as White House chief of staff and secretary of the treasury under Reagan, but he considered that his strong suit was his mastery of the intersection of policy and politics. The title of his memoir of his time at State— *The Politics of Diplomacy*—tells much. "[M]ore comfortable with action than with reflection," he admits, he considered his understanding of American domestic politics a great asset since so much of recent history had underscored the importance of American public support if any policy were to be sustained. A lawyer by training, he exemplified the practical, lawyerlike, case-by-case approach to problems that we have seen in other secretaries of state from the same profession. Pragmatism was his watchword; he considered international politics as a complex negotiation—actually "a series of discrete problems that required solutions." Thus, not surprisingly, even his successes gained him a reputation as more a tactician than a strategist.

He had many successes to his credit. Formation of the broad international coalition in support of the Gulf War, the passage of key U.N. Security Council resolutions that helped mobilize the coalition, the Madrid Arab-Israeli peace conference that followed the war, the diplo-

macy that united Germany within the Atlantic Alliance, the agreement by which the former Soviet republics that had nuclear weapons on their soil yielded them up to Russia—these achievements would stand out in any administration. His personal closeness to George Bush guaranteed that he would be seen in the world as embodying the will and authority of the president; this was a considerable asset, even if internally the relationship was more complex.

Baker came to the State Department with a determination to be the president's man. There could be no doubt of his personal or political loyalty. He continually reminded his staff that the wishes of "the guy who got elected" were his and their marching orders. "I headed to State assuming that the President made foreign policy, not the Foreign Service," he wrote. This is exactly the conviction that I have been praising in cabinet officers who act on it and criticizing in those who lack it. But there was an edge to Baker's attitude that deserves comment. He was convinced, for example, that his immediate predecessor, George Shultz, had been too reliant on the Foreign Service and too much a prisoner of the institution; this he was determined not to be. This may account for his snubbing of Shultz during the 1988–1989 transition. Only toward the end of the transition period did Baker pay a call on the incumbent and outgoing secretary of state. Shultz found this rankling as well as puzzling since the Reagan administration considered that it had had a rather successful foreign policy.

Baker's memoirs contain the all-too-familiar criticism of the Foreign Service for its institutional rigidity and lack of imagination and initiative. Alas, little had changed since the days of John Kennedy. Baker's response, as he explains, was "to centralize policy authority in a small team of talented, loyal aides, and build outward from them." Unlike, say, Henry Kissinger, who brought only a few aides with him from his NSC staff and who ran the department through able career officers whom he selected, Baker brought his own team of half a dozen close aides to the seventh floor—the top floor of the building and the exalted level of the secretary and his immediate staff. It was this team that was to provide the bold ideas, discretion, and political and personal loyalty that he required to impose his (and the president's) agenda. The department's assistant secretaries, traditionally the workhorses of an administration, found themselves subordinated to this elite on the seventh floor. Baker's inner circle was an unusually talented group of individuals, and the administration's successes owe a great deal to their ideas—such as

the "Two Plus Four" diplomatic formula by which the two Germanys and the four World War II Allies (United States, United Kingdom, USSR, and France) resolved the thorny issue of German unification. This team provided much of the intellectual content of the administration's foreign policy. A strong case can be made that, as in the case of Nixon and Kissinger's groundbreaking diplomacy, a more ponderous procedure might not have produced as good results.

Yet there was a defensiveness in all this that remains puzzling in a man as self-assured as Baker surely was. Some of Baker's team made vigorous efforts to reach out to the career diplomats as time went on, and Deputy Secretary of State Lawrence Eagleburger, a Foreign Service veteran, became an important member of the team. Yet many foreign service officers never overcame their initial impression that they were distrusted and excluded from the inner workings of policy-making. On April 1, 1989, what purported to be a special edition of the State Department *Newsletter* was circulated in the building. One article, entitled, "FSO's Capture Baker Staff Member," read as follows:

> Mr. Robert B. Zoellick, the Counselor of the Department, inadvertently disembarked from a malfunctioning elevator on the Fourth Floor of the Main State building yesterday afternoon. He was promptly captured by a gang of about a half dozen toughs from the EUR [European affairs] bureau and held briefly. Zoellick managed to escape after about an hour in captivity and flee to the safety of the Seventh Floor.
>
> It is not known whether Mr. Baker will retain Zoellick in his present position since the Secretary is known to be very suspicious of any of his five trusted staff members who might have been captured by the FSOs.

A companion article reported that the secretary himself had expanded his security guard detail after the incident, lest even the boss be captured by the Foreign Service.

Earlier, I quoted a dry comment by Bush as to the need for Scowcroft and his staff to keep an eye on "what State may be up to." Even the politely worded memoirs can barely conceal the concern in the White House about the State Department's enthusiasm for diplomatic initiatives that seemed not well thought out. State's eagerness for diplomatic

activism in this case was probably due less to Baker's being captured by the Foreign Service than to his own instinct to minimize the president's domestic political risks. The Bush-Scowcroft memoir notes, more than once, Baker's reluctance to contemplate the use of force to liberate Kuwait and his eagerness to hold a high-level meeting with the Iraqi leadership before the war, despite Scowcroft's nervousness about the wisdom of such a move. Just before the ground war began (and on the same evening as the president's State of the Union address), Baker and Soviet foreign minister Aleksandr Bessmertnykh issued a joint statement that implied a relaxation of U.S. terms for a cease-fire. Not only was the content of the statement a misstep, but the president was blindsided (and his speech upstaged) and was—by Bush's own account—"furious" at Baker.

In early November 1990, during the U.S. troop buildup in the Gulf that preceded the Gulf War, Thomas L. Friedman of *The New York Times* wrote a column quoting "senior Administration officials" saying with approval that Baker had been acting as a "brake on any immediate impulse to use military force." Baker was said to look at events "less emotionally" than Bush and to be "motivated by an acute awareness of the risks, international and domestic," of going to war; therefore Baker was said to be somewhat more willing to give diplomacy and economic sanctions a chance to work. Friedman observed, moreover, that Baker had seemed to be "avoid[ing] a high profile" during the first two months of the Kuwait crisis. There is no way to determine what sources Friedman relied upon for this analysis of Baker's thinking (though it might just be worth noting that Baker devotes a long passage in his memoirs to how much he valued his off-the-record contacts with Friedman). How the president must have reacted to the Friedman column can be guessed: Other journalists reported the complaints of some of the president's closest advisers about Baker's tendency to distance himself when these controversial decisions were being made. Robert Gates, then Scowcroft's deputy, is on record with a similar observation. Gates summed up his assessment:

> Baker was a real piece of work. . . . Watching him work his counterparts abroad, members of Congress and the press, and even Scowcroft and Cheney, was to see a master craftsman of the persuasive and backroom arts at the peak of his powers. I respected Baker and came to like him. I also was always glad he was on our side.

The Transformation of Europe

It was on George H. W. Bush's watch that Mikhail Gorbachev finally lost control over events and presided over the dissolution of Moscow's Central European empire and then of the Soviet Union itself. This is not the place for a detailed discussion of this extraordinary turn of history. Suffice it to say that the peaceful evolution that took place was not foreordained. Such tumultuous events could have led in a different direction, and at times threatened to. That the outcome was one fully consistent with U.S. interests and with the long-term peace and freedom of Europe owed much to an intelligent American diplomacy in which George Bush led his government.

The pivotal issue that had to be resolved was procuring Soviet acceptance of, first, the unification of Germany and, second, of unified Germany's remaining in the Atlantic Alliance and in NATO's integrated military structures. These Soviet concessions were essential to Europe's future stability. Eventually the Soviet leaders would be brought around to understand this. Yet, four and a half decades of Soviet foreign policy since Stalin had been devoted, above all else, to suppressing such a possibility. It seemed not only a self-evident geopolitical imperative for Soviet policy but one animated by a still powerful emotion owing to the 27 million Soviet dead of World War II. In 1991, there were twenty-four Soviet divisions stationed in East Germany, totaling 338,000 troops, plus 208,000 related civilians. No satisfactory outcome was imaginable without the Kremlin's consent to remove them.

There is some irony in the fact that the Bush administration came into office with a policy toward the Soviet Union that was more hardline than Ronald Reagan's. Scowcroft, for example, believed that Reagan, having started out with his "evil empire" rhetoric, had then shifted too far to the other extreme—of believing that the Cold War's underlying confrontation had already gone away because of the new style and rhetoric of Mikhail Gorbachev. Scowcroft saw in Gorbachev a man determined to preserve and revitalize the Soviet system, not to end it, and likewise saw no willingness yet by the Soviet leadership to relinquish its military and political dominance in Central Europe. Dick Cheney and Robert Gates shared this skepticism, though in Scowcroft's case, as we have noted, it led him to come up with proposals for conventional arms reductions in Europe that might weaken that Soviet grip.

But Gorbachev had already taken a fateful step in the same direction

before George Bush had even taken the oath of office. In a major speech to the United Nations General Assembly in December 1988—the first U.N. appearance by a Soviet leader since Nikita Khrushchev's boorish performance in 1960—Gorbachev had announced an overall reduction of the Soviet military establishment by 500,000 men, including a withdrawal of 50,000 men and 5,000 tanks from Central Europe. Hard-line colleagues in the Kremlin reportedly opposed such a move as radical and risky—and they were proved right. In retrospect this troop reduction announcement is what first took the lid off—suggesting to the people of Central Europe a weakening of the Soviet commitment to maintain satellite regimes by force. As opposition to Communist rule began to bubble up during 1989 in Central Europe and in the Baltic republics of the USSR, aside from a few incidents of bloodshed the predominant signal emanating from the Kremlin was to confirm that impression. On November 9, 1989, climactically, East German border guards offered no resistance when East and West Berliners overwhelmed the wall.

Even after the wall fell, however, the prevailing assumption in Europe was that East and West Germany would respond to this new development by expanding the political and economic interchange between them, and the two German states would continue to coexist happily ever after. Anything more than that was assumed to be out of the question due to adamant Soviet opposition. West German chancellor Helmut Kohl started out with that assumption, too, but as he watched the populations of both Germanys sweep away the barriers and saw the illusion of the East German authorities' legitimacy evaporating before his eyes, he seized the initiative and, in a speech to the Bundestag on November 28, committed himself to a process leading to unification. Not only in Moscow but in Margaret Thatcher's London and François Mitterrand's Paris was this greeted by consternation. Fearing the power of a united Germany, they all wanted to slow events down.

Inside accounts of the Bush administration make clear that Bush himself was the first to see the inevitability of German unity and the first Western leader to declare unequivocal support for Kohl's initiative. The State Department was skeptical at first, comfortable in the status quo, and even Scowcroft's view was close to State's. Baker visited the East German capital in December and reported optimistically to Bush about the East German leaders' commitment to "reform and peaceful change" in their regime—missing the point that the regime was by then

a discredited shell. The president's view prevailed. As events accelerated, the administration set for itself the task of persuading its recalcitrant allies and, most important, the Soviet Union, to accede gracefully
to the absorption into West Germany of the East German regime.

When Bush met with Gorbachev on shipboard off the coast of Malta
in early December 1989, the Soviet leader was conflicted. He said he
was prepared to "let history decide the outcome" but he was angry that
"Mr. Kohl is in too much of a hurry." He called for "prudence." As if on
cue from Dana Carvey on *Saturday Night Live*, Bush readily agreed,
reassuring Gorbachev that he would continue to avoid grandstanding.
Gorbachev said he appreciated that. Bush, often criticized for his
understated management of these events, made it a cardinal point of his
strategy not to rub Gorbachev's nose in a Soviet defeat that Bush saw as
inevitable. "We're going to win the game," Bush told Helmut Kohl the
following February, "but we must be clever while we are doing it."

One could see Gorbachev's thought process gradually moving
toward where he would end up. He told Bush at Malta, for example,
that he accepted the U.S. role in Europe. This was not an empty grace
note or a favor to the United States; rather, it was a recognition that if
one had any reason to fear a united Germany in the heart of Europe,
part of the cure was a continued U.S. military presence on the Continent. But it was not until the following May that Gorbachev would follow this logic to its proper conclusion—that is, allowing united
Germany to stay in NATO's integrated military structure (and thus its
forces under U.S. command). In the meantime the Soviets were still
tempted to try to block unification or else to insist on some form of German neutrality as the price for it.

It was Baker's team at the State Department that came up with the
Two plus Four formula for a diplomatic process by which this all would
be negotiated. This allowed the two German states to work out the
terms of their merger, backstopped by the four victors of World War II,
which had up to that moment been exercising certain occupation rights
in Berlin deriving from the 1945 Potsdam agreement. The Two Plus Four
procedure gave the reluctant Europeans and Soviets a formal role but
left the ball in German hands where it belonged. It gave the United
States a role, too, and provided a framework for the Soviets to save face.
Intense legwork by the indefatigable Baker helped produce the result.
While unification was probably unstoppable, the Soviets' acceptance of
the terms that we deemed essential was not inevitable. This acceptance

undoubtedly resulted in part from the Bush administration's avoidance of triumphalism over the fall of the Berlin Wall; as its officials have insisted, this reticence was not a lack of "vision" but an intelligent strategy.

The future of the Soviet Union itself was the source of more significant intellectual hesitations within the Bush administration. As early as April 1989, while Baker was preparing for his first visit to Moscow as secretary of state, Dick Cheney blurted out in a CNN interview his pessimistic assessment that Gorbachev would "ultimately fail" in his efforts to reform the Soviet system. Baker phoned the president to complain, and Cheney himself called Baker to apologize for speaking out of turn. Baker said he did not necessarily disagree with the analysis, but the administration should not be saying this out loud (and in any case, it shouldn't be the secretary of defense saying it). Six months later, the State Department was shown for clearance the draft of a speech that Scowcroft's deputy Robert Gates planned to deliver at Georgetown University. Gates, an expert Sovietologist from his CIA days, planned to give a sober assessment of the prospects for Gorbachev's reform program. I was on the NSC staff at the time and was helping Gates with his speech. This time Baker called Scowcroft to complain; Gates's gloomy tone was too much in contrast with the positive thrust of what Baker had been saying about U.S.-Soviet relations in the wake of his own meetings with Soviet leaders. Gates revised the draft to include several upbeat quotes from Baker, but to no avail; Baker insisted the text be killed.

Baker was certainly right that the administration had to speak with one voice, and that voice should be that of the president and secretary of state. These incidents, however, small as they were, were emblematic of an important tension within the administration—between a Reaganite truth-telling and a desire to smooth Gorbachev's way forward. Generally the latter instinct won out. The prevailing view was that the United States had a strategic stake in Gorbachev and wanted him to succeed against his hard-line adversaries in the Politburo and in the country. But this approach left the administration looking flat-footed and caught by surprise when events unfolded as they did.

The test came later, in 1991, after a failed coup attempt by Soviet party and military hard-liners who held Gorbachev under house arrest for three days in August. Gorbachev was "saved" by the bold response of Boris Yeltsin—popularly elected as leader of the Russian republic—who

stood atop a tank in Moscow and faced down the coup plotters. (Strong public condemnation of the coup by the Bush administration also helped to undermine it.) But I put the word "saved" in quotation marks above because the collapse of the coup paradoxically undermined Gorbachev as well. He was surviving by a balancing act between a hard line opposition and a democratic reformist opposition; the collapse of the hard-liners tilted the balance irreversibly toward Yeltsin. The structure of the Soviet system suddenly began to look very rickety.

Soon enough, unrest in Ukraine and the Baltic republics raised the prospect of the dissolution of the USSR. Should the United States welcome this and recognize the independence of these entities? Or side with Gorbachev in trying to hold the Soviet structure together? At two crucial Oval Office meetings of the Gang of Eight on September 5 and October 11, the senior players argued it out in front of the president. Cheney argued for an "aggressive" approach: "The break-up of the Soviet Union is in our interest." He endorsed an idea of Gates's, namely to move quickly to establish American consulates in all the republics of the USSR so as to nudge events in that direction. Baker argued, on the contrary, for "strengthening the center"; our hopes for a peaceful transition to a reformed Soviet system continued to rest on Gorbachev, who was struggling against centrifugal forces that were hard-line and more troublesome for us. Baker proposed that we announce a number of principles we cared about—self-determination for the republics by democratic means; respect for existing borders; human rights; adherence to the Soviet Union's treaty obligations; central control over nuclear weapons, et cetera—and declare our principles rather than any preference as to the continuation or breakup of the USSR.

As Scowcroft later admitted, these unexceptionable principles notwithstanding, the Bush team never came around to a "tight" administration policy toward the breakup of the Soviet Union. This was partly because of the disagreements among the key people, partly because of the rush of events, and partly because of a concern about the diffusion of control over nuclear weapons. But the Baker view, in essence, became the prevailing view. The president earned criticism for a speech to the Ukrainian parliament on August 1, 1991, that cautioned: "Americans will not support those who seek independence in order to replace a far-off tyranny with a local despotism." This warning was aimed not at Ukraine but at other places where a more rabid nationalism threatened an upsurge of violence—Yugoslavia, Georgia, and Moldavia, for

example. But it nevertheless confirmed the public impression of an administration clinging to the status quo of the USSR amidst rapid— and fundamentally positive—change. In the same vein, Bush, having invested so much in the personality of Soviet leader Gorbachev, was accused—including by none other than Richard Nixon—of giving inadequate support to the Russian democratic revolution represented by Boris Yeltsin.

The Gulf War

The Gulf crisis unfolded over a period of several months—from Saddam Hussein's invasion of Kuwait on August 1, 1990, to the launching of coalition air operations on January 16, 1991, to the initiation of the ground war on February 23, to its end four days later. Through this period, American public opinion was brought around to support a war to liberate a faraway country that few Americans had ever heard of and to which we had no pre-existing defense commitment. By early December, opinion polls showed 50–60 percent support of the president's policy; by early January public support had grown to 65–80 percent. This represented a notable feat of presidential leadership; it was also an exercise in effective bureaucratic management.

At the president's first meeting of the NSC after Saddam's invasion, on the morning of August 2 in the Cabinet Room, a consensus emerged that the United States had to defend Saudi Arabia, but the conversation was inconclusive beyond that. Scowcroft reports that he was "appalled" by the undertone of resignation at that first meeting, which suggested acquiescence in the Iraqi occupation of Kuwait. The president, too, wanted better than that; after the meeting was over he and Scowcroft agreed to convene a second NSC meeting twenty-four hours later, at which they hoped to elicit more concrete proposals for action.

In the meantime, Bush flew off for a day trip to Aspen, Colorado, to deliver a speech and for a conversation with British prime minister Margaret Thatcher. Scowcroft, on the flight with Bush to Colorado, sensed the president was leaning toward the use of force to evict Saddam from Kuwait. Mrs. Thatcher, too, found Bush resolute, and she reinforced this. (Her famous admonition to Bush—that it was "no time to go wobbly"—came a few weeks later, urging that the United States and Britain vigorously enforce the economic sanctions that the U.N. Security Council had just imposed on Iraq.) On the aircraft, as well,

Bush worked the phones. He called Egyptian president Hosni Mubarak and Jordanian King Hussein, who were still hoping for some kind of peaceful path to Iraqi withdrawal; Bush warned that the continued occupation of Kuwait was "unacceptable" and urged them to convey that message to Saddam.

Meanwhile, at the Pentagon, Secretary of Defense Cheney was leaning in the same direction as the president. But his new chairman of the Joint Chiefs of Staff, General Colin Powell, was a major figure in his own right. Powell, who had become chairman on October 1, 1989, was the first man to exercise throughout his term the full powers of the chairmanship as they had been transformed by a significant Defense Reorganization Act (called the Goldwater-Nichols Act) in 1986. That legislation elevated the status of the chairman as the principal military adviser to the president and the secretary of defense. While the service chiefs remained important advisers, the chairman was no longer merely the first among equals, obligated to present the consensus recommendations of a corporate body. Likewise the 1,600-person Joint Staff now reported directly to the chairman, instead of to the Joint Chiefs as a whole. The legislation also elevated the importance of the regional commanders—in this case, General Norman Schwarzkopf, head of U.S. Central Command. In fact, the chain of command now ran from the president through the secretary of defense directly to the regional commander, bypassing the chairman of the Joint Chiefs. But there was no doubt that Powell, given his charisma and unique experience (including as President Reagan's assistant for national security affairs), was bound to use the new powers of the chairman to the full. Throughout the Gulf crisis it was Powell, not Schwarzkopf, who had most of the interaction with the president and the secretary of defense. This was partly because Schwarzkopf had moved his headquarters to Saudi Arabia, but also partly because of concern about his voluble temperament. "Norm Schwarzkopf, under pressure, was an active volcano," Powell has said. As the planning progressed, Powell was briefing the president almost daily.

But Bush, Scowcroft, and Cheney could also see early on that Powell was personally reluctant to contemplate offensive military operations. A defensive deployment of U.S. troops to deter an Iraqi attack on Saudi Arabia was one thing; offensive action to drive Iraqi forces out of Kuwait, as Powell pointed out correctly, was a much bigger task. The president, who was heading in that direction, relied on Cheney to bring the military along. "Dick was probably ahead of his military on this," Bush noted.

On August 2, in the afternoon following Saddam's invasion of Kuwait, Cheney and Powell and their top aides convened in the secretary's conference room at the Pentagon to consider what to advise the president when he returned from Aspen. Powell candidly expressed his concerns, which were political. Having been a military aide to Weinberger, Powell adhered to Weinberger's 1984 six criteria for the use of American military power—the most important of which was an assurance of public support before doing so. Powell stressed to Cheney his conviction that American public opinion would support a defense of Saudi Arabia but not a war to liberate Kuwait: "I don't see the senior leadership taking us into armed conflict for the events of the last twenty-four hours," Powell argued. Cheney's response was that the Department of Defense owed the president a recommendation: "He will look to us. The others can't do it. So what do we do?" Powell recommended the United States start with diplomatic efforts. "I am opposed to dramatic action without the President having popular support."

The next morning, August 3, with the president's approval, Scowcroft led off the second NSC meeting forcefully expressing his own view that Iraq's occupation of Kuwait should not be allowed to stand. Accommodation to the Iraqi aggression, he said, "should not be a policy option." Cheney spoke up firmly in agreement—and so did the State Department representative. Secretary Baker had not yet returned from a trip to the Soviet Union, and was represented by Deputy Secretary Lawrence Eagleburger. Scowcroft and Eagleburger were old friends, sharing the battle scars of having served as assistants to Henry Kissinger. Ironists and foreign service officers will enjoy the picture of Eagleburger the FSO being so stalwart a supporter of the military options that the president wanted aired, while his boss the secretary of state, who expressed such mistrust of the Foreign Service's loyalty to the president, was later to be chided for distancing himself from the president at various moments during the crisis.

At this NSC meeting, Powell ventured a question in front of the president along the lines of what he had said to Cheney: Was it worth going to war to liberate Kuwait? Cheney later upbraided him for overstepping his authority: "Colin, you're Chairman of the Joint Chiefs. You're not Secretary of State. You're not the National Security Advisor anymore. And you're not Secretary of Defense. So stick to military matters." Powell understood that he had been out of bounds. Cheney thenceforth insisted on absorbing the fullest information on the military

planning, and from multiple sources inside the Pentagon, not just funneled through the chairman. He spent hours peppering Powell and his staff with questions about the plans, to refine them and screen them before they were briefed to the president.

Bush soon ordered 250,000 U.S. troops to the region to bolster Saudi Arabia and bided his time. As the initial buildup neared completion, at a meeting on October 30, this time in the Situation Room, the president asked for a discussion of what his choices were—standing pat, or driving Iraqi forces out of Kuwait? Powell outlined a military plan for accomplishing the latter. As Powell recounts:

> When I finished, Scowcroft asked, "What size force are we talking about?"
>
> "We're approaching two hundred and fifty thousand for the defensive phase," I said. "But if the President opts for this offensive, we'll need a hell of a lot more."
>
> "How much more?" Scowcroft asked.
>
> "Nearly double," I said. "About another two hundred thousand troops."
>
> "Whew," Scowcroft said, his gasp echoed by others around the room. I glanced at the President. He had not blinked.

After some additional conversation, the president said simply, "Okay, do it."

Baker had returned from the Soviet Union in early August with an important trophy—Moscow's agreement to a joint declaration condemning the Iraqi invasion of Kuwait. Soviet cooperation in the Gulf crisis was arguably a significant payoff from the administration's continuing relationship with Gorbachev. Meanwhile, James Baker's State Department applied itself to mobilizing a thirty-four-nation political and military coalition, securing a series of U.N. Security Council resolutions in support of the effort, and eventually collecting on allied pledges of $53 billion to finance U.S. war costs.

Thus, the ingredients for a coherent U.S. policy were in place—a president who gave direction to his government, a secretary of defense who gave direction to his department, and an energetic diplomacy led by the president and his secretary of state in tandem. There were debates, of course. Margaret Thatcher, for one, argued strenuously, especially with Baker, against putting too much stock in U.N. Security

Council resolutions. She believed (correctly) that Kuwait and the coalition were entitled to exercise the inherent right of collective self-defense as acknowledged in Article 51 of the U.N. Charter; she did not want to set a precedent for the view that Security Council resolutions were required to authorize every use of force. The American side argued, in reply, that such Security Council resolutions would be diplomatically useful in helping to mobilize broad international support, and that—especially important to Baker—they were necessary to bring along the U.S. Congress. The Democratic-controlled Congress, voting its authorization on January 12, 1991, was indeed persuaded in part by the international legitimacy that the U.N. resolutions were seen to convey. (Twelve years later saw an interesting reversal of the process. In the run-up to the 2003 Iraq War, it was a British prime minister who insisted on the pursuit of a U.N. Security Council resolution to authorize the use of force. The administration of Bush 43, moreover, obtained congressional resolutions of support first, in the hope of using them as leverage to generate support in the Security Council.)

Baker, as we have noted, was eager for a high-level meeting with the Iraqis to demonstrate that the United States had gone the extra mile. The proposal was to invite Iraqi foreign minister Tariq Aziz to Washington for a meeting with Bush, and to send Baker to Baghdad to meet with Saddam. Scowcroft was nervous about this proposal, fearing that a clever Iraqi diplomacy could turn this into the illusion of a negotiation, confuse the issue, and weaken the coalition's resolve. But Bush approved the idea. In the end, the Iraqis accepted only a meeting between Baker and Aziz in Geneva, which took place on January 9, 1991. The Iraqi minister's performance was so stubborn and defiant that it vindicated Baker, helping strengthen the administration's case—in Congress and internationally—that it had exhausted all the options short of war. Bush later defended Baker—perhaps with another sly dig—expressing admiration for his overall performance: "I don't like the criticism of him, because his diplomacy has been absolutely superb."

The most controversial decision of the Gulf War was Bush's decision to end the ground combat after one hundred hours, leaving important units of Saddam's Republican Guard to escape and forswearing any military action to overthrow Saddam Hussein's regime in Baghdad. This is not the place to reopen the debate. The important point for our purposes is that this decision reflected unanimity in the Bush administration. Different elements in the U.S. government had different reasons for coming

to the same conclusion, and there was no internal controversy. Having achieved the liberation of Kuwait, Powell and his military colleagues strenuously opposed prolonging the killing of helpless Iraqi troops along what the media were calling the "highway of death"; they saw this as a matter of military honor. Baker and his State colleagues worried that the coalition would shatter at the unilateral American pursuit of a goal—regime change—that other countries had not signed up to, and warned that improvising an assault on Baghdad was an invitation to trouble. Dick Cheney agreed with this analysis. Bush and Scowcroft in their joint memoir concede that they acted on some mistaken assumptions: When the ground war was ended, the administration was convinced that Saddam's Republican Guard had been utterly destroyed. As it turned out, because of the swiftness of the Marines' sweep into Kuwait, many Guard reserve divisions were not drawn south into the coalition trap, and therefore survived. There was also a comfortable assumption that Saddam's regime would fall on its own, discredited by defeat, like a rotten fruit. And there was a concern about Iran, looming over the horizon—that is, a desire to calibrate the degree of defeat of Iraq so as not to leave too much of a vacuum there and unbalance the regional balance of power.

Such a fine calibration is difficult to achieve in war, in the best of circumstances, and the incomplete results of the 1991 Gulf War can legitimately be said to have left behind a strategic problem. Saddam Hussein survived, restored his tyranny, and steadily eroded the system of external restraints and sanctions that a series of postwar U.N. Security Council resolutions sought to impose on him. The difficulties that Bush 43 ran into when he imposed regime change in 2003 might be seen as proof of the unwisdom of regime change and a ringing vindication of Bush 41's restraint in 1991: Leaving a political vacuum in a major Arab country is no small problem, since diverse and powerful forces will inevitably attempt to fill it. Alternatively, it could be argued that the task might have been easier in 1991, before the ascendancy of radical Islamism that later in the decade threatened to envelop the whole Middle East. This debate will not be settled here.

Assessment

Bush's foreign policy accomplishments were substantial. Not only the liberation of Panama and Kuwait are to his credit, but his calm management of the collapse of the Soviet empire in Europe avoided a variety of

dangers that were much more real at the time than they are bound to seem in retrospect. At home, politically, he fell victim to the Churchill effect: With the world's major dangers having gone away, the American people in 1992 denied him reelection because his skills seemed no longer needed in an era when domestic policy issues seemed to dominate.

Contrary to the cliché that he lacked vision—"the vision thing," as he called it himself—Bush did articulate, repeatedly, the concept of a "new world order" that would follow the Cold War. It was the optimistic picture of a world in which relations among the major powers would remain as harmonious and cooperative as they had been during the 1990–1991 Gulf crisis, reflected in the unanimous resolutions of the U.N. Security Council that framed it. Bill Clinton would borrow the same concept and elaborate upon it. Unfortunately the great-power harmony would not survive the decade, and a violent challenge would come at us from a very different and unexpected direction early in the new century.

But Bush was always more comfortable as a pragmatist than as a conceptualizer. And this had its costs. When he announced in October 1987 his campaign to succeed Reagan as president, he declared, obliquely but deliberately, his differences from Reagan: "I am a practical man. I like what's real. I'm not much for the airy and abstract; I like what works. I am not a mystic and I do not yearn to lead a crusade." This was a true statement of fact and self-description, but it was also a position. He came into office determined to be his own man, not an appendage to Reagan. He made sweeping personnel changes among the three thousand political appointees in his administration, which came as a bit of a shock to many Republican loyalists who were expecting to stay on in a third Republican term.

But this posture of independence left Bush politically vulnerable. James Baker, his chief political strategist, was of the same mold as Bush—proudly pragmatic, problem-solving, unideological. Yet Bush owed his election in large part to Reagan's success. In drifting away from Reagan, Bush and Baker also drifted away from the base of the Republican Party as Reagan had transformed it. Bush thus left himself open to a conservative challenge to his reelection in 1992 (in the form of both Patrick Buchanan and Ross Perot). This is every incumbent's nightmare; in a reelection year one wants to tack to the center, not be pulled toward one's base. But when such a challenge occurs within

one's own party, it is a sure sign that a political miscalculation has already been made somewhere along the line.

There were also other costs. Bush's readiness to distance himself from Reagan in style and philosophy is also part of the reason why, when most Americans think of the end of the Cold War, they tend to associate it not with Bush, on whose watch it occurred, but rather with his predecessor. What Bush skillfully managed, Reagan's vision had shaped.

Bill Clinton

B ILL CLINTON WAS ELECTED at a golden moment when national
security challenges seemed no longer to rank high on our national
agenda. The Cold War had ended; it was a time of American ascendancy globally, even in crisis spots like the Middle East where moderates seemed stronger than ever in the aftermath of the Gulf War. The
main issues facing the country in 1992 seemed to be economic, whose
handling would come naturally to a Democratic administration. Clinton
promised if elected to "focus like a laser beam" on these problems, and
one of the mantras of his campaign was: "It's the economy, stupid." This
meant a focus first on the domestic economy, and on international economic issues as an adjunct to that. During the transition after his election, in a meeting with House Democratic leaders, he interrupted
veteran Foreign Affairs Committee chairman Lee Hamilton of Indiana
who was giving a brief survey of the international scene: "Lee, I just
went through the whole campaign and no one talked about foreign policy at all, except for a few members of the press."

Conventional wisdom has it that Clinton as president had no sustained interest in foreign affairs. The truth is more complicated than
that. For the first two years or so, it was probably correct that his priority
interests lay elsewhere. David Gergen, who served as an adviser to Clinton during that initial period, as well as to Republican presidents,
assessed Clinton thusly:

> In the Cold War, presidents typically spent at least 60 percent of their
> time on foreign affairs; with Bush [41], the figure could rise to 75 percent. Clinton early on reversed the tables: domestic affairs probably
> consumed 75 percent of his time, foreign affairs less than a quarter.

This was a source of a number of serious problems, including stumbles involving the use of military force and other problems that festered due to neglect. But Clinton learned lessons from this experience, and his policy-making process regained its balance in later years. More generally, the problem was not that Clinton was intellectually uninterested in foreign policy but that he was unfocused. Highly intelligent, he was subject to what his onetime political aide Dick Morris called "a tendency toward intellectual clutter," which caused him to lose focus on priorities. Nor did he want to spend a lot of political capital on foreign policy issues.

He came into office with a broad vision of a post–Cold War international order. Essentially he took George Bush's concept of a harmonious relationship among the major powers and carried it further—to a full-blooded Wilsonian vision of a world of human rights and democracy, the flourishing of the United Nations and other multilateral institutions, and cooperative responses to transnational challenges such as nonproliferation, economic globalization, and environmental protection. In his 1992 campaign he repeatedly criticized President Bush for "coddling tyrants from Baghdad to Beijing." Events would confront Bill Clinton in office with uncomfortable contradictions among these different impulses.

In Bill Clinton's eight years there were successes—economic initiatives like congressional assent to the North American Free Trade Agreement and World Trade Organization; the weathering of financial crises in Mexico and Southeast Asia; admission of three new Central European democracies to NATO; support for Russian reformers; a peace accord in Northern Ireland; agreements that brought a respite to violence in Bosnia and Kosovo; and near-success in Israeli-Palestinian diplomacy. Where he did focus himself, or delegated to capable people, there was coherence. In other cases, the loose informality of his style of decision-making often permitted bureaucratic stalemate and indiscipline.

People and Institutions

Many, if not most, administrations contain philosophical divisions— bureaucratic rivalries sharpened by ideological or policy differences. Such divisions tore at Gerald Ford's and Jimmy Carter's administrations, as well as Ronald Reagan's; as we shall see in the next chapter, they plagued George W. Bush as well. Democratic and Republican adminis-

trations alike are often tested in this way, reflecting the big-tent nature of our political parties and the broad party coalitions that presidents usually attempt to reflect in staffing their governments. But managing such a government then puts a premium on a president's leadership skills. Presidents need to be prepared for it—to have this in mind when they select their key subordinates, and ideally to have some clarity about their own convictions and to understand that they will need to resolve the differences.

In Clinton's case, part of the problem was a set of contradictions within the liberal camp—an allergy to military intervention deriving from Vietnam, challenged by a more activist humanitarian intervention-ism driven by a commitment to human rights; a tension between human rights and the much vaunted economic interests; battles over free trade and protectionism; and a tension between economic goals and tradi-tional security concerns. His decision making was made more compli-cated by public and congressional attitudes that were, for much of his term, averse to his military interventions and other dimensions of his liberal internationalism.

FOR SECRETARY OF STATE, Clinton chose Warren Christopher, a Cali-fornia lawyer who had been deputy secretary in the Carter administra-tion. Hardworking, self-effacing, and supremely cautious, Christopher, like so many other lawyers who have held the job, proudly considered himself a pragmatist, not a strategist. On issues of military intervention he was a dove, but otherwise critics saw him as having no consistent beliefs or guiding philosophy. By the criteria of this book, he was not one to impose his will forcefully on the bureaucracy. Indeed, his mem-oirs record his pride in his reliance on the Foreign Service. Clinton him-self acknowledged the doubts about Christopher's effectiveness. But there are those who believe that the last thing Clinton wanted was a forceful, independent personality with strong ideas of his own in charge of the State Department. In this case the motive was not (as with Kennedy or Nixon) to avoid having a competitor so that the president could run foreign policy himself; it was, as David Halberstam suggests, to avoid a strong figure who would only raise the prominence of issues that Clinton wanted on the back burner. As several presidents we have discussed in this book discovered, however, weakness in a secretary of state—whatever the reason—has a tendency to compound rather than to solve a president's problems.

The new national security adviser was Anthony Lake, a thoughtful ex–foreign service officer who had served in the American embassy in South Vietnam, then briefly on Henry Kissinger's NSC staff, then as director of the Policy Planning Staff at State in the Carter administration. Vietnam was the formative experience of Lake's career; he had resigned from Kissinger's staff because of discomfort with Nixon and his policy. Lake took a prominent role in articulating the new administration's philosophy, which he called a strategy of "engagement" (diplomatic and humanitarian engagement in the world) and "enlargement" (of the zone of democracy). Military intervention was something Lake cannot have been viscerally comfortable with, but as the Balkan crises unfolded he found himself in the interventionist camp because of outrage at the atrocities being committed. He admitted to being "emotional" about Bosnia, and agonized at times over his inability to formulate a stronger policy that could command support from his president.

Two committed hawks were Vice President Al Gore and Madeleine Albright, U.N. ambassador in Clinton's first term and then Warren Christopher's successor. Gore had won a claim to national security expertise by voting in the Senate in favor of Bush 41's Gulf War resolution (after agonizing over the decision until the night before). With his tenure, according to the experienced David Gergen, the vice presidency reached another new level of power and influence at the center of policy-making. Gore was a key adviser, and was given important substantive portfolios including managing cooperation with Russia. Albright came from a family that had fled Hitler; her worldview was accordingly more colored by the Munich experience than by Vietnam, and she became an advocate of muscular intervention in an administration populated by a number of more cautious souls.

A pivotal figure throughout was Samuel (Sandy) Berger, Lake's deputy national security adviser in the first term and successor in the second. A trade lawyer by background, he seemed at first glance to embody the new administration's emphasis on economics. But Berger's true talent and focus were political. He was strongly liberal by conviction—he had met Clinton when they both worked for George McGovern's 1972 campaign—but Vietnam was not for him the same traumatic experience as for Lake and others. He had been active in Democratic foreign policy salons during the long years out of office. As Lake's deputy, he served as NSC liaison to the political side of the

White House and sat in on reelection strategy meetings. As security adviser he was known most of all for his acute sense of Clinton's political needs and for policy advice that was attuned to them. Clinton's memoirs speak about Berger with a particular warmth.

Bill Clinton's relations with his military were never good. His avoidance of military service as a young man, and his announced intentions to permit gays in the military and cut the defense budget preceded him into office. The anti-military attitudes of some of his left-leaning staff also became known—including an incident reported by Elizabeth Drew in which a young woman on the White House staff, greeted by a senior military officer, responded contemptuously, "I don't talk to the military." Word of this quickly spread in the Pentagon.

These problems aside, the Defense Department under Bill Clinton was permitted to revert to the cautious, anti-interventionist mode seen in the Reagan administration. General Colin Powell, chairman of the Joint Chiefs, his prestige enhanced by the Gulf War success, was a powerful presence in the room in any deliberation; he remained a voice of caution with respect to the use of force. In his memoir he tells the story of a 1993 debate over Bosnia in which he had urged military restraint, only to be rebuked by Albright: "What's the point of having this superb military that you're always talking about if we can't use it?" Powell says he thought he would "have an aneurysm"; he was shocked by what he saw as the cavalier way this new team of civilian colleagues was ready to move U.S. troops around like toy soldiers on a board game. When Powell retired in the fall of 1993, part of his legacy was an apparent determination by Clinton not to appoint so charismatic a figure as Powell's successor. Clinton's two subsequent chairmen, Army Generals John Shalikashvili and Henry (Hugh) Shelton, were less likely to carry the political weight that Powell did either within or outside the administration. But they shared Powell's resistance to the use of force in the Balkan or other crises.

Clinton's three secretaries of defense were not activists either. Les Aspin, who had been a brilliant defense expert when a committee chairman in Congress, proved ineffectual as an executive; Powell, indeed, had warned Clinton that Aspin was not a good choice for the job. Aspin presided over a series of failed interventions in the first year, and paid the political price. His successor, William Perry, a brilliant scientist and respected defense and arms control expert, did not play a pivotal role in foreign policy discussions; he sided with the cautious military during

the Bosnia crisis until the Serb massacre of Muslims at Srebrenica in 1995 forced the administration's hand. Perry was succeeded in January 1997 by William Cohen, a former Republican senator, who in the Senate had voted with many fellow Republicans against Clinton's Bosnia intervention. Thus, unlike the tenure of Dick Cheney under Bush 41, the civilian leadership of Clinton's Pentagon was not inclined to override the caution of the military. On the contrary, in the Kosovo crisis Cohen would only reinforce it.

THE CLINTON ADMINISTRATION sought to emulate its predecessor in an important respect, by adopting its formal policy-making structure without change. Just below the level of the National Security Council, Bush and Scowcroft had come up with the innovation of the Principals Committee—the NSC without the president, chaired by the national security adviser. A level below that was the Deputies Committee, chaired by the deputy national security adviser. The Clinton team seems to have adopted this system for a variety of reasons. It made sense to be seen emulating the practices of a predecessor who had been widely regarded as a model of competence in this field. Lake, in addition, had co-authored a book that made the cogent argument that incoming administrations should shake the habit of politicizing these matters to the point of reflexively changing the arrangements they inherit just to demonstrate some kind of superiority.

The Principals and Deputies committees met frequently, under Clinton as under Bush, but the unstructured quality of the new president's engagement marked a subtle difference. Bush 41 had been more in command. Under Clinton the system seemed to rely more on the interaction of his subordinates, with presidential involvement more sporadic. "[U]nlike Bush's team, Clinton's lacked a captain," in the words of scholars Ivo Daalder and I. M. Destler. Sandy Berger has commented that formal or structured NSC meetings were reserved for times of crisis:

> Clinton did not attend NSC meetings per se. The president came to NSC meetings during crises, the Haiti meeting or Kosovo or Iraq, and he and the vice president would come down for an hour to the Situation Room and meet together. But he preferred either to let Tony [Lake] or me run the meetings and then bring him either a memo,

which laid it out so that he could decide, or we would call a meeting in the Cabinet Room or in the Oval Office.

The Clinton administration, like Reagan's, sought bureaucratic consensus among the principals. "There is a comfort you get in hearing that all your advisers agree," Lake told an interviewer. The Principals Committee was the natural place to pursue this—presumably in the hope of sparing the president the need to engage. But often there was no consensus, and there are many reports of Clinton's irritation when foreign policy disagreements were presented to him to resolve.

Even when the president was deeply engaged, discipline was not his strong suit. Meetings lasted hours; for the first several years he was notoriously behind schedule through much of the day. Colin Powell, having seen firsthand how things worked in both the Reagan and Bush administrations, was offended by the lack of discipline:

> [T]he discussions continued to meander like graduate-student bull sessions or the think-tank seminars in which many of my new colleagues had spent the last twelve years while their party was out of power. Backbenchers sounded off with the authority of cabinet officers. I was shocked one day to hear one of Tony Lake's subordinates, who was there to take notes, argue with him in front of the rest of us.

Clinton hated to be confined by formal structures: "A strict, formal structure just won't cut it," he told *Time* magazine shortly after his election. "There's too much you miss if you don't forage around yourself." As William Doyle has commented:

> This sounded much like the romantic management disorder of his hero John Kennedy, but the bitter experiences of Ford and Carter should have taught Clinton that the presidency had now grown far too enormous to be run through a "spokes of the wheel" structure without a strong chief of staff.

While the president met with Lake almost daily, regularly scheduled contact with his senior national security team was not a feature of the early years of the administration. James Woolsey, Clinton's first CIA director, had his own stories to tell. In the summer of 1993 he got

together for breakfast with Secretary of Defense Aspin, his old friend, and compared notes on their access to the president. As Woolsey later recounted:

> Aspin asked [me], "Did you think when we got these jobs that we'd get together with the president sometimes and talk to him about what we were going to do?" And I said, yeah, I thought that. He said, Well, I'm not doing that, are you? And I said, No, I'm not. I thought you were. He said, No, I'm not. And I don't think Chris [Warren Christopher] is. And he looked up at the ceiling and he said, I wonder who is.

The Economists, Stupid

The answer to Aspin's question was: the economists. On December 10, 1992, about five weeks after his election, Clinton announced his new economic team—including Texas senator Lloyd Bentsen as treasury secretary and investment banker Robert Rubin as assistant to the president for economic policy. On December 14–15, Clinton convened an "economic summit" in Little Rock of three hundred business and labor leaders and economic thinkers to brainstorm publicly about economic policy. Only on December 22, a week later, did he announce his new national security team. Soon after inauguration he issued an executive order creating a new institution called the National Economic Council (or NEC)—an "NSC for economics"—parallel to the National Security Council.

As we have seen, many recent presidents have wrestled with the question of how to integrate domestic and international economic policy with the classical issues of national security policy. Presidents beginning with Nixon have experimented with parallel structures, one of the more successful being Gerald Ford's Economic Policy Board. Clinton's NEC—its own structure consciously modeled after the NSC—was in formal terms a cabinet-level body chaired by the president, with the mandate to coordinate the process of advising the president and monitoring implementation of his decisions. The assistant to the president for economic policy (Rubin), comparable to the national security adviser, was to manage the NEC's operation and lead a staff; an interagency NEC Principals Committee would meet at cabinet level, chaired by Rubin, and an NEC Deputies Committee would be chaired by Rubin's deputy. A clever innovation to foster collaboration between

the NEC and NSC was the designation of common staffers—dual-hatted individuals serving as both the international economics experts on the NSC staff and as the national security experts on the NEC staff. By all accounts the two staffs worked smoothly together at all levels. The utility of the new institution was confirmed when Clinton's Republican successor, George W. Bush, continued the NEC system as he inherited it—returning the compliment paid to his father's NSC arrangements.

CONTENTIOUS POLICY PROBLEMS soon arose, however, which were not all amenable to smooth staff relations. They posed serious philosophical dilemmas to this Democratic administration, and many of them arose out of contradictions among the president's 1992 campaign promises. One difficult issue was relations with China.

Clinton had been particularly harsh in his campaign criticism of George H. W. Bush's policy toward China. The Tiananmen massacre of June 1989 was still a fresh memory, as was Bush's effort to maintain political relations with China on an even keel after those events. "The administration continues to coddle China," Clinton proclaimed in a December 1991 speech, "despite its continuing crackdown on democratic reforms, its brutal subjugation of Tibet, its irresponsible exports of nuclear and missiles technology, its support of the homicidal Khmer Rouge in Cambodia and its abusive trade practices." Sandy Berger later announced Clinton's view that "[t]his is going to be an arm's-length relationship at best between Washington and Beijing." But China's phenomenal economic boom was already a palpable reality, and the prospects for expansion of U.S.-China trade were powerfully attractive to many in this country—in both parties, and in Congress and the administration—interested in "the economy, stupid."

The immediate issue facing President Clinton was the annual renewal of nondiscriminatory trade status for Chinese goods (then called Most Favored Nation status, or MFN; now called Normal Trade Relations). A bitter battle immediately broke out between the champions of human rights (in the State Department, Congress, and the activist community) and the champions of economics (Commerce, the U.S. Trade Representative, and the business community). The State Department itself was divided between the human rights and East Asia bureaus, on the one hand, and bureaus dealing with economics and nonproliferation, which were interested in doing business with the Chinese.

At first, Clinton sided with the foreign policy side of the house,

which in this case meant those who wanted to link the continuation of MFN to human rights. His executive order of May 1993 renewed MFN for China for one year but conditioned it on Chinese improvements in the status of human rights. The Chinese reacted badly to this overt pressure. When Secretary of State Christopher set off on a visit to China in March 1994, the Chinese defiantly launched another crackdown against dissidents; in Beijing, Christopher was sternly lectured by Premier Li Peng that China's internal practices were none of our business, and a meeting with President Jiang Zemin was abruptly canceled. "Rough, somber, sometimes bordering on the insolent" was how Christopher described Chinese behavior in his trip report to Clinton. After these humiliations, U.S.-Chinese relations only deteriorated further. As China policy became the subject of an intense domestic political debate, the White House stepped in to take charge of the policy. The NEC staff (which had not been significantly involved in the original decision) now teamed up with the NSC staff to steer the president toward a change of direction. While Clinton was able to point to a few improvements in Chinese human rights practices over the course of the year, he essentially abandoned the linkage in his May 1994 executive order renewing MFN.

Another kind of tension within the administration came over relations with Japan. During the Cold War, Japan's importance as a treaty ally and linchpin of U.S. security policy in Asia provided an incentive to both sides to mute the tensions over the large trade imbalance and Japanese barriers to imports from the United States. Those days were over. Clinton chose as U.S. trade negotiator Mickey Kantor, a Los Angeles lawyer who had been chairman of the 1992 campaign. Kantor told the Senate in March 1993:

> Past Administrations have often neglected U.S. economic and trading interests because of foreign policy and defense concerns. The days when we could afford to do so are long past. In the post–Cold War world, our national security depends on our economic strength. . . . When all is said and done, opening foreign markets is our main objective.

As Jeffrey Garten, under secretary of commerce, put it a few years later: "Commercial diplomacy must become more central to overall foreign policy, more expansive, and more aggressive."

"Aggressive" was the appropriate word for the way the new administration approached its first trade negotiations with Japan, aiming at setting strict numerical targets for a boost in U.S. exports to Japan. Clinton visited Japan in July 1993 and claimed victory when the Japanese accepted, not numerical targets, but the principle of "objective criteria" for improvements in the trade balance. Under these pressures—and partly because of the early signs of the great Japanese economic slowdown that was coming—the Japanese government of Kiichi Miyazawa fell. His successor, Morihiro Hosokawa, refused to make significant concessions when he met with Clinton in February 1994. Administration economists began planning retaliatory sanctions, and then Hosokawa's government fell in April. The State Department—through leaks to the press—began a counteroffensive within the U.S. government, emphasizing the damage being done to the U.S.-Japan alliance and to the U.S. security position in Asia. Again, the NEC staff joined with the NSC staff to play a moderating role. A trade deal was struck with Japan by July 1995, heading off U.S. sanctions, and it was Washington that had backed away from confrontation. Said one senior official to *The New York Times*: "We all looked over the precipice and discovered we couldn't see the bottom. The sanctions were a big risk. So we took what we had in hand." By the time of a Clinton visit to Tokyo in early 1996, he was expressing a newly acquired appreciation of the importance of the security alliance.

On both China and Japan, domestic political pressures pulled Clinton in different directions until ultimately the international reality imposed itself. MFN was not going to be the weapon that would transform China's Communist system; with Japan, security trumped economics in the end as it usually does. On other issues, the NEC/NSC team managed to produce more effective results with less public embarrassment. The administration won congressional assent to the North American Free Trade Agreement in the fall of 1993, and the NEC Principals devised much of the strategy. The joint NEC/NSC staff ably performed the role of "sherpas" for the annual G-7 Economic Summits, a role that had been traditionally fought over between State and NSC.

A year later, at the end of 1994, Mexico was on the verge of financial crisis and Robert Rubin took the lead in U.S. policy, putting together a $40 billion U.S. and international financial package to restore confidence in the Mexican market and stave off a collapse. But it was Rubin—not the NEC as such—that played the lead role in the U.S.

government. Rubin had become treasury secretary, and just as when Henry Kissinger became secretary of state in 1973 the center of gravity of policy-making moved with him. Rubin's tenure at the NEC had gained him wide respect, and his performance at Treasury only added to it. The NEC remained a valuable coordinating mechanism, but power always gravitates to those in whom others (especially the president) repose the most confidence. The model of a strong and loyal cabinet officer proved itself once again. A testimony to Rubin's personal stature in the administration is that he asked to be able to continue to attend White House senior staff meetings, and was invited to do so—a faint echo, perhaps, of Kissinger's two-year retention of his NSC hat after moving to State. But it was also not an accident that the biggest international star to emerge from the Clinton administration was from the economic team, not the national security team.

Russia Policy

One of the most significant events taking place in the world in that decade was the evolution of post-Soviet Russia. It was also a subject that needed, and received, presidential attention. Clinton had eighteen meetings with Boris Yeltsin and three meetings with his successor, Vladimir Putin, and made five trips to Russia, during his term of office, in the crucial formative period of the new Russian state and its policies. The formulation and execution of U.S. policy also benefited from a clear chain of command: The man in charge was Strobe Talbott, one of Bill Clinton's oldest friends and closest foreign policy confidants. For the first year, Talbott had a complicated title as "ambassador at large and special adviser to the secretary of state on the new independent states of the former Soviet Union"; thereafter he was deputy secretary of state. As Clinton has commented: "I don't think five people could repeat Strobe's [original] title, but everybody knew what he did: he was our 'go to' man on Russia." He was in effect the U.S. secretary of state for Russia policy.

The trajectory of Russia's evolution, and of U.S.-Russia relations, was not a success story in this period. The early hopes for Russian democracy and economic reform were not fulfilled. Yeltsin's clumsy rule by decree, violent clashes with the parliament, and later alliance with the oligarchs, gave way in 2000 to the unmistakably authoritarian Putin. The early years of Russia's foreign policy were years of an extraordinary

collaboration with the United States under Yeltsin's reformist and pro-Western foreign minister Andrei Kozyrev. But by the beginning of 1996, the firing of Kozyrev and his replacement by Yevgeni Primakov symbolized the nationalist turn in Russian policy. Primakov, a shrewd and elusive veteran of the Soviet era, embodied what could be called a "Gaullist" foreign policy—a reassertion of Russia's pride and independence, especially independence from the United States, and its alignment with others (China, France) whose priority was to promote "multipolarity" in the world as an obstacle to American dominance. By the end of Clinton's term, the hopes for natural consensus in the Security Council had faded away, demonstrated particularly in the Balkan crises.

It would be unfair to lay the blame for this at Clinton's door. In the early 1990s there were debates about the alleged mistake of "personalizing" U.S. policy—that is, of investing too much in a Kremlin leader who was thought congenial to U.S. interests. International relations over the long term depend on more durable factors than personalities. Bush 41 and his team, as we have seen, came into office accusing Reagan of investing too much in Gorbachev; Bush, in turn, was accused of sticking too long with Gorbachev; and Republicans were to accuse Clinton of investing too much in Yeltsin. In a tumultuous period of Russia's evolution, however, it was hard to avoid perceiving a significant American stake in the outcome of Russia's internal struggles; Yeltsin was battling against an unappealing coalition of Communists and ultranationalists. And the formative period of the new Russian state's posture in the world was bound to be affected to some degree by what kind of international environment it was that the Russians, in turn, perceived. Even Richard Nixon, the hardheaded geopolitician, was giving private advice to Clinton that the United States had to throw its weight behind Yeltsin. "He may be a drunk," Nixon told Talbott, "but he's also the best we're likely to get in that screwed up country over there." Nixon had given the same advice to Bush.

The Clinton administration declared that its policy was a "strategic alliance with Russian reform." It devoted considerable effort with Congress and the allies to come up with significant economic assistance—on the order of $2.5 billion in U.S. aid as part of a total of $28.4 billion in international assistance. It set up a bilateral commission led by Vice President Gore and Russian prime minister Viktor Chernomyrdin to foster other cooperation. In 1994, Russia was admitted formally to the

G-7 group of industrial democracies, the annual economic summits begun in the Ford administration—no longer as a guest but as a full member of what thereafter became known as the G-8. Russia was also given formal status as a partner of NATO, through a NATO-Russia Council. The United States and its allies sought in other ways to acknowledge Russia as an equal, and to make clear their political backing of Yeltsin and the reformists.

The efforts made were considerable, but the problem was something else: The conciliatory steps were consciously intended to make it easier for Russia to acquiesce in what seemed to be the unavoidable continuing consequences of the breakup of the Communist empire. These consequences included Central and Eastern Europe's eager alignment with the West (through both the European Union and NATO); crises in the former Yugoslavia in which the West intervened to halt the Serb brutalization of Muslim populations; Western protest at Russia's military suppression of rebellion in Chechnya; and the strict conditions imposed by the International Monetary Fund in return for international aid. Other issues accumulated on which Russia and the West had different perspectives—especially our frustration with Russian nuclear cooperation with Iran, and the growing U.S. interest in deploying defenses against rogue state ballistic missiles.

To the Russians, this looked like a combination of mounting pressure, condescension, and taking advantage of Russian weakness. An impartial analyst, looking over this long list of contentious issues, might well conclude that not all were truly vital to the West and on some of them we might have cut the Russians some slack. (Unfortunately, different analysts would have different opinions about which ones to drop.) Overall, however, we were dealing with two probably inevitable historical phenomena—first, the cleanup of the unfinished business of the collapse of empire, and then, Russia's recovery (political, economic, and psychological) and quest to regain as much as possible of its lost position. As William Hyland and others have noted, the initial high hopes for both Russian democracy and "strategic partnership" were unrealistic.

In terms of process, nonetheless, Talbott's memoir is a chronicle of active engagement in Russia policy by a president conventionally perceived as disengaged from foreign policy. Talbott had bureaucratic clout, derived from his position as Clinton's intimate friend and adviser. Whatever his formal title and rank, he was credible as the agent of an

engaged president. With a small staff, he chaired the relevant inter-agency committee and ran Russia policy in State. He kept in regular and close contact with Sandy Berger, when he was not communing directly with the president. All this gave Talbott a strong hand in relations with other departments. At Treasury, he had an ally in Lawrence Summers, who as under secretary and then deputy secretary collaborated with him in putting together the U.S. and international packages of economic assistance.

The Pentagon was at first opposed to bringing the Central and East Europeans into NATO. The U.S. military was wary of expanding the formal defense commitments of the United States; it was unenthusiastic about taking on new allies whose military capabilities were thought to require vast U.S. effort and resources to bring up to NATO standards. But consultation with the Pentagon produced a creative compromise—the so-called Partnership for Peace (PfP)—put forward by General John Shalikashvili, a NATO program of defense cooperation with the new democracies. PfP was an intermediate status, a way station on the path to full NATO membership though without any definite commitment to go further. It served a number of the administration's purposes: It was the beginning of necessary defense cooperation with the Central and East Europeans. But it also enabled Clinton to fend off Republican pressure for immediate NATO enlargement—to stretch out the process in the hope of easing Russian pain.

Military Interventions

The shadow of Russian opposition lay over the Clinton administration's most significant military undertakings, in the crises in Bosnia and Kosovo. But the Russia factor only added to the inhibitions that came from other sources—especially from the series of stumbles in Clinton's first year. Clinton and his team were clearly not comfortable with military intervention. They had philosophical qualms, and the style of decision making did not easily lend itself to the sustained rigor required for such endeavors.

Bosnia came up fast on the agenda. Clinton had harshly criticized George H. W. Bush in the 1992 campaign for insufficient activism in opposing Serb predations against Muslim and Croat minorities in Bosnia. One of the new administration's first acts was to reject a compromise proposed by the international mediating team of Cyrus Vance

and David Owen, which was thought to be not tough enough on the Serbs. When it came to formulating its own policy, however, the Clinton team was divided. A stronger option, pushed by the more activist members of the administration, was called "lift and strike"—it proposed lifting the U.N. arms embargo against Bosnia so that the Bosnians could arm themselves against the Serbs (who were getting arms from neighboring Serbia), and it posed the threat of U.S. or NATO air strikes if Serb aggression did not stop. Secretary of State Christopher was dispatched at the beginning of May 1993 to visit Europe and sound out the allies. The fact that Christopher was personally opposed to the "lift and strike" idea, and was not a very forceful personality to start with, doomed the exercise. The American ambassador in London watched as Christopher made the pitch to British leaders with "all the verve of a solicitor going over a conveyance deed."

A coalition of the unwilling quickly formed—a secretary of state who had no stomach for it; a secretary of defense (Aspin) who was also against it; the U.S. military (led by Colin Powell), who invoked the Weinberger principle that limited military steps were unlikely to be decisive; Europeans who had sent peacekeepers to Bosnia but didn't want actually to fight anyone; and the more cynical French, who were pro-Serb. Most important of all was the president's own hesitation, which was visible to all. After a disconcerting conversation with Clinton at the White House, Aspin sent word to Christopher while Christopher was in Europe: "[The president] is going south on this policy. His heart isn't in it." Two more years would go by before the administration would summon the will, and the leverage, to force a satisfactory outcome.

In the summer of 1993 came a brief clash with Saddam Hussein. Kuwaiti intelligence broke up an Iraqi plot to kill former President Bush on a visit to Kuwait in April. In retaliation, Clinton in June ordered a strike by twenty Tomahawk cruise missiles against Iraqi intelligence headquarters in Baghdad, carefully staged in the middle of the night to minimize Iraqi casualties. The action was widely criticized as ineffectual. In his memoirs, Clinton attributes the modest targeting plan to Colin Powell and suggests he would have been willing to do more. Yet at the time, Clinton's discomfort at the use of military force was such that he was reported to be "tense and wobbly" after ordering it and kept asking his aides if they were sure it was the right thing to do.

In October came the debacle in Mogadishu, Somalia, immortalized in the book and film *Black Hawk Down*. As Ronald Reagan experienced

in Lebanon, U.S. forces entered Somalia on a benign peacekeeping mission, only to feel the political ground shift under their feet. Somalia was in the midst of a civil war. President Bush 41, at the very end of his term, under political pressure, had sent 25,000 U.S. troops to Somalia with the narrowly defined mission of providing security for humanitarian relief supplies. The Clinton team reduced the U.S. contingent to about 4,000 troops and expanded the mission. U.N. ambassador Albright was the most fervent advocate of a new objective—tipping the balance in the Somali civil war by defeating the warlord Mohammed Aidid. As the peacekeeping forces found themselves deeply embroiled, Aspin and Powell wanted out. They repeatedly sought guidance from the White House but received none.

When the disaster happened—two helicopters downed, eighteen American troops killed, seventy-four wounded, and the corpse of one American dragged through the street by Aidid's cheering mobs broadcast over international television—Clinton was shocked. At his hotel on a visit to San Francisco, he railed at his aides in conference calls to Washington: "How could this happen?" He had never been given a "realistic assessment" of "what we were up against." "No one told me about the downside." "We've been jerked around for months" by the United Nations, which had taken over command of the peacekeeping operation. Later he ruminated to others about firing his advisers.

Then came Haiti. This problem, too, he had inherited from Bush. Elected President Jean-Bertrand Aristide, an ex-priest who had been defrocked by the Catholic Church for his leftist "liberation theology," was overthrown by a military coup in 1991 by Lieutenant General Raoul Cédras. The Bush administration committed the United States to restore Aristide to power, but its failure to do so was another of Clinton's campaign accusations in 1992; political pressures then grew on Clinton to deliver on the promise. In July 1993, U.S. mediation produced an agreement for a peaceful turnover.

In October, a small contingent of more than two hundred lightly armed military trainers and engineers, American and Canadian, was scheduled to go to Haiti for six months for a training mission. A debate took place in the administration about whether they should go in, with Les Aspin arguing strongly that—given Cédras's unreliability—they should not. After an interagency discussion (in which the president did not participate) Aspin was overruled; Lake and Berger thought it was important to look strong. The trainers were aboard the USS *Harlan*

County off Port au-Prince when an unruly crowd of Haitians, some of them armed with handguns, appeared on the dock shouting anti-American slogans including the menacing taunt: "Somalia! Somalia!" Another debate broke out in the administration, but no one had the stomach for a fight. The *Harlan County* pulled away, as the Haitian mob cheered. Again, Clinton's reaction was anger at his staff.

The administration would recoup in Haiti a year later. Despite the Defense Department's opposition to intervention, Clinton ordered a military plan drawn up and—having learned a lesson from Somalia—he personally reviewed the plan at the Pentagon. In September 1994, the imminence of a U.S. invasion provided the leverage for a diplomacy that restored Aristide to power without bloodshed.

The stumbles of the first year left their residue, however, in the form of both increased inhibitions and diminished credibility. When Rwanda was torn apart by genocidal warfare in 1994, the administration was gun-shy. After the al-Qaida attacks on American embassies in Kenya and Tanzania in August 1998, the White House asked the Defense Department to propose options for special operations to kill or capture Osama bin Laden in Afghanistan. A similar request was made in 2000 after the al-Qaida attack on the USS *Cole* in Yemen. In neither case did the Pentagon come up with a serious plan. Military planners argued that the intelligence was insufficient and large numbers of U.S. personnel would be needed. At the White House it was suspected that the military was not inclined to undertake risky operations on behalf of a president it did not trust.

Bosnia and Kosovo

American involvement in Bosnia and Kosovo in Bill Clinton's second term is the story of a recovery of lost ground—of a president gradually leading his government to overcome its inhibitions and internal divisions and marshal the leverage to give effect to its diplomatic aspirations. While Clinton had campaigned in 1992 against Bush's alleged passivity in Bosnia, he came into office with no interest in military intervention there—a conviction only reinforced by the stumbles of 1993. "They keep trying to force me to get America into a war," he complained about the incessant television coverage of Bosnia atrocities. As the Bosnia crisis festered for the next two years, different parts of the government leaked their versions of events to the media to deflect blame or

influence the president; memos by Madeleine Albright leaked from New York, for example, with the apparent purpose of building support for her advocacy of air strikes against the Serbs. The Europeans rejected stronger options unless the United States sent troops alongside theirs— which Clinton knew that Congress would oppose. Meanwhile at Defense, the military remained strongly allergic to U.S. intervention; Secretary of Defense Perry was willing to support use of NATO air power for clearly defined purposes, but drew the line at ground troops. Perry reportedly did not consider Bosnia important enough to do battle over within the Pentagon or with the allies. In these circumstances, Clinton was content to leave Bosnia to the Europeans, and to the Principals or Deputies committees, and concentrate on other issues.

When a Bosnian Serb military offensive became the focus of international attention and protest, however, Bosnia grew into a major political problem. By 1995, Clinton was politically on the defensive. Jacques Chirac, newly elected president of France, reversed France's pro-Serb policy and began calling for allied action. In June, Clinton responded to allied pleas with the major step of promising that U.S. ground troops would indeed be available in certain conditions—if U.N. forces needed help in withdrawing, if a U.N. unit required emergency extrication, or to help police a peace agreement. But in July, Serb militiamen retook the town of Srebrenica, humiliating a Dutch peacekeeping battalion; they gathered some eight thousand Muslim men and boys in a soccer stadium and summarily executed them. Adding to the anguish in Washington was Chirac's public comment around this time that France was alone in wanting real action and that "the position of leader of the free world is vacant."

Clinton exploded. One July evening around 7:00 p.m., while he poked away at golf balls in an area near the Oval Office known as the Eisenhower Putting Green, members of his press staff and NSC staff came to talk to him about Bosnia. "This can't continue," he fumed. "I'm getting creamed!" The session went on for more than three-quarters of an hour: "This has got to stop. We've got to find some kind of policy and move ahead. Why aren't my people doing more for me?"

This presidential reengagement was an opening for Anthony Lake, who had been quietly working with his NSC staff to prepare a new, more activist strategy. The president now supported Lake. At an Oval Office meeting a few days later, Vice President Gore spoke passionately about halting the genocide. The president agreed: "The United States

can't be a punching bag in the world anymore." At the Pentagon, as well, Perry and Shalikashvili both understood that Srebrenica had changed things, and they could see the president's new commitment. Perry, Shalikashvili, and Warren Christopher made an important visit to London to a NATO conference later in July and after more vigorous presentations than Christopher's two years earlier—won a NATO consensus on a more forceful use of air power. The allies recognized that NATO's credibility was now on the line, just as Clinton had reached a similar conclusion about his own.

Richard Holbrooke was put in charge of a new diplomatic effort. Holbrooke, a dynamic if volatile star in the Democratic foreign policy firmament, had been ambassador to Germany in the first term but was eager to play in the Washington game; he was named assistant secretary of state for European affairs. He understood better than some of his colleagues that diplomacy had no chance without leverage. In August, the army of neighboring Croatia retook control of the Krajina, a region of Croatia that local Serbs had proclaimed their own territory. The prospect of a Croatian offensive had prompted nail-biting in Washington: Warren Christopher and the Pentagon feared anything that could widen the war, while Albright, Holbrooke, and others in State saw advantage in the opening of a second front against the Serbs and inflicting a defeat on them. The Croatians repeatedly asked the U.S. government whether Washington would approve, but Washington was deadlocked. American diplomats sympathetic to Croatia managed, with a wink and a nod, to convey that while there was no green light from Washington, there was no red light either. One official called it an "amber light tinted green." Clinton later said that he, too, was "rooting for the Croatians," but this does not seem to have been communicated as a presidential decision.

The Defense Department continued to betray its nervousness, however, in ways occasionally disconcerting to the diplomats. Holbrooke recounts a Principals meeting on September 11 at which Perry unexpectedly proposed a "bombing pause." Christopher, Lake, Albright, and Holbrooke all correctly opposed this, recalling the fecklessness of such moves during the Vietnam War and knowing that it would weaken U.S. diplomatic leverage. Then Admiral William Owens, vice chairman of the Joint Chiefs, spoke up and suggested that NATO was running out of bombing targets to attack and the United States would therefore either have to return to the NATO Council and the U.N. Security Council for

a broader set of targets (a nonstarter in both cases) or else wind down the bombing campaign in two or three days. Holbrooke (dubious as he was about what Owens claimed) reacted by speeding up the negotiations; he managed in three days to win Bosnian Serb agreement to halt the siege of Sarajevo, which allowed us to halt the bombing as a matter of policy.

The reversal of French policy under Chirac, the Croatian offensive in the Krajina, and the more forceful posture in Washington provided for Holbrooke the leverage for a successful diplomacy. The United States convened a peace conference in November at Wright-Patterson Air Force Base in Dayton, Ohio. Holbrooke conducted the negotiation without micromanagement from Washington. Warren Christopher attended many of the sessions, and reported to the president, but Holbrooke had no direct contact with Clinton after Dayton started. By the end of November 1995, the presidents of Bosnia, Serbia, and Croatia agreed on a complex arrangement for a federal Bosnia, enforced by a NATO-led peacekeeping force including U.S. troops. While Defense had relented on the U.S. troop contribution, it successfully blocked a significant U.S. role in training and equipping the Bosnian Muslims, which Holbrooke (and the president) had seen as an important contribution to the long-term balance of forces.

THREE YEARS LATER, however, Serbian dictator Slobodan Milosevic's belligerence had found another outlet—this time, a brutal crackdown in Kosovo, an autonomous province of Serbia populated by ethnic Albanian Muslims. Muslim refugees poured into neighboring Albania and Macedonia, threatening to destabilize the region. By the summer of 1998, NATO was planning military options to block the Serbian government's continuing military offensive. After diplomatic efforts failed, Clinton in the spring of 1999 agreed to U.S. and allied air strikes. While his national security team told him optimistically that Milosevic would fold in seventy-two hours, the NATO bombing campaign in fact went on for seventy-eight days before Milosevic desisted.

The success in Kosovo had to survive its own share of bureaucratic problems. As the crisis built in 1998, Madeleine Albright—now secretary of state—was again the hawk. Convinced that negotiations with Milosevic would fail, she repeatedly urged stronger action, including the threat of NATO air strikes. But Berger blocked her phone calls to the president and the Principals deadlocked. "We're just gerbils running on a wheel," she complained to colleagues. The new team at Defense, Sec-

retary William Cohen and General Hugh Shelton, were reluctant warriors, dubious that air strikes would work.

The pivotal figure this time was General Wesley Clark. Dual-hatted as the U.S. commander in Europe and as supreme allied commander in NATO, he was the field commander in charge of the war. A former Rhodes Scholar from Arkansas like Bill Clinton, Clark had been the Joint Staff representative on Holbrooke's negotiating team at Dayton and had strong convictions about the menace of Milosevic. In this activism he was the right man to run the war; unfortunately he found himself seriously out of step with his civilian and military superiors in the Department of Defense. Shalikashvili had been effective at bridging the bureaucratic gaps, working well with State and more supple in his relations with the White House. Shelton, a grayer figure, simply reinforced Cohen's resistance to intervention. Clark was in constant friction with Cohen; once the president ordered the bombing Clark developed his own regular contact with Sandy Berger in the White House. This only increased Cohen's resentment.

As the air campaign dragged on without result, Clark had three frustrations. One was the need for political consensus within NATO with respect to selecting targets. To hasten Serbian capitulation, Clark wanted to attack "strategic" targets, including infrastructure and command-and-control facilities in Serbia whose destruction would gain leverage over Milosevic to break his will; our European allies' sensibility would accept only "tactical" targets more directly related to the Serbian army's actions in Kosovo. Clark's second frustration was what he saw as the need to prepare for a possible ground war; this would be a fallback option if the bombing proved insufficient, and public knowledge of its preparation would add significantly to the credibility and persuasive force of the whole enterprise. He received U.S. and NATO authorization to begin planning. But Clinton feared a ground war involving U.S. troops, knowing there was no support for it in the Republican Congress. Secretary Cohen consistently opposed any serious consideration of it, determined that the air campaign succeed. Public hints of planning for a ground war probably, in the end, contributed significantly to Milosevic's cave-in, but Clinton in his memoir is adamant that he was opposed to a ground war all along.

Clark's third frustration was the way he was being treated by Washington throughout the military campaign he was leading in Washing-

ton's behalf. As we have seen, the Goldwater-Nichols defense reform of 1986 had elevated the status of the chairman of the Joint Chiefs as military adviser to the president, established an operational chain of command from the president to the secretary of defense directly to the field commander, and reduced the status of the chiefs as a collective body. This should have made Clark a key figure in the policy deliberations in Washington—not only because he was U.S. commander in the theater of war but because he was also managing the complex political task of holding a NATO coalition together. Bush 41 included General Norman Schwarzkopf in his Gulf War deliberations; though Powell overshadowed him and Schwarzkopf spent much of his time in Riyadh, he had many opportunities to communicate with the president. Bush 43, as we shall see in the next chapter, kept in continuous contact with his field commanders in Afghanistan and Iraq during both planning and operations.

But in Kosovo, the chain of command almost became unlinked. Cohen and Shelton, disliking Clark's activism, seemed determined to reduce his public visibility and his influence over presidential decisions. Clark considered that he was leading a mission that the president had ordered. When he sought guidance from Cohen as to the secretary's wishes on Balkan policy, Cohen was often uncommunicative. Yet Cohen reprimanded Clark when his news conferences seemed too exuberant for Cohen's taste. Cohen tried to exclude Clark from attending a NATO summit meeting in Washington in April (Clark attended anyway, in his capacity as allied commander); he succeeded in blocking Clark's attendance at a meeting the president held with the Joint Chiefs at the White House in early June. Clark did not believe his Pentagon superiors were conveying his views accurately to the president in his absence. Cohen seemed to use the Joint Chiefs as a buffer against Clark, frequently invoking objections that individual service chiefs put forward against requests that Clark submitted for equipment or other support. Clark wondered if this was consistent with the intent of the Goldwater-Nichols reform.

The conflicting pressures on Clark reflected the conflicting pressures on the administration. Albright and Berger, the activists, had suffered through the vacillations and humiliations of the early years, including in the Balkans, and did not want to go through the same again. In fairness to Cohen, his reluctance stemmed not only from the

reluctance of his military but from his knowledge of his former colleagues in Congress; that knowledge was, after all, one reason why he had been chosen secretary of defense. "I voted against your Bosnia policy," he once coldly reminded the president. Cohen vividly remembered the pummeling that Les Aspin had received over Somalia, and believed that that episode had done lasting damage to Clinton's credibility as commander in chief. He knew from his own conversations the aversion on the Hill to anything smacking of U.S. ground intervention in Kosovo. And the adamancy with which Clinton in his memoirs emphasizes his own opposition to the same is testimony to the objective constraints that Clark was operating under, even if he chafed at those constraints.

It was fortunate in the Kosovo case that—contrary to many experts' predictions—American air power alone proved sufficient to produce a successful result. Clinton showed political courage in persevering in the face of growing criticism as the weeks passed. But there were political casualties. One was Wesley Clark's military career. The Pentagon forced his early retirement from his command and from his career, on complicated legal grounds relating to the alleged need to put his successor on the job earlier than usual. The president, who appreciated the job that Clark had done, approved what he was told was a normal rotation; he seems not to have known, until after the fact, that he had forced Clark's early retirement.

There was also a paradoxical effect on alliance relations. Given the collective success that the Kosovo outcome represented, it should have heralded a positive era in U.S.-European relations. But in the 1990s the European allies were building their own institutions in the European Union, and the huge imbalance between American and European military capability—displayed dramatically in the Balkan crises—was painful for them to watch. Thus, Kosovo only spurred the construction of new EU political and military structures, to create a counterweight to what the French were calling the American "hyperpower." Europeans were thus pleased that the key negotiator in the Kosovo settlement was Finnish president Martti Ahtisaari—acting on behalf of the EU and not Richard Holbrooke.

As discussed earlier, U.S.-Russian relations also suffered. While Russia was given a role in partnership with NATO in the Kosovo peacekeeping force, Russia looked on with great pain as NATO demonstrated its military superiority against Slavic cousin Serbs—and as NATO did

so without any kind of endorsement by the U.N. Security Council (since Russia had blocked any such endorsement). Russia was at the beginning of a phase that was soon to become familiar—lining up, reflexively, against assertions of American power.

The Jimmy Carter Problem

A peculiar feature of Bill Clinton's foreign policy was its susceptibility on two occasions to the unsolicited diplomatic intervention of former President Jimmy Carter. One of Carter's principal activities after leaving office in 1977 was his continuing effort to engage in international diplomacy as a freelance elder statesman and peacemaker. In 1994 he offered his services to the Clinton administration to break impasses with respect to both North Korea and Haiti. That the administration assented to this intervention was another symptom of a lack of rigor, a lack of conviction with respect to its own policies, its own capability, and its own personnel. In 1995, the administration more success-fully fended off an attempt by Carter to inject himself into the Bosnia negotiation.

The personal relationship between Carter and Clinton was never warm. On the face of it, they had much in common. Two Southern governors, the only Democrats to break the Republicans' near monopoly on the White House during the entire forty-year span of this book, they both won election by positioning themselves successfully on the moderate wing of their party, closer to the center of the national debate. Most of Clinton's senior national security team had served in midlevel positions under Carter. Nonetheless, the Clinton team saw Carter's legacy as a reputation for incompetence with which they did not wish to be associated. During the 1992–1993 transition, Carter flooded the president-elect with phone calls offering his services and advice. Clinton refused to take the calls, passing them instead to Warren Christopher; Christopher, in turn, tried to pass them on to one of *his* aides. Carter was reportedly deeply wounded by how the Clinton people were treating him.

In mid-1994 the Clinton administration was engaged in a diplomatic effort to mobilize international pressure on North Korea to head off its pursuit of nuclear weapons. Pyongyang was blocking inspections by the International Atomic Energy Agency (a U.N. body), and the administra-

tion was attempting to forge a consensus in the U.N. Security Council for economic sanctions. North Korea was protesting that U.N. sanctions would be a hostile act. A sense of crisis was building; the administration was even sounding the familiar refrain that military options were not ruled out. Jimmy Carter panicked at all this. On June 1, he phoned Clinton and said he wanted to go to Pyongyang to resolve the crisis.

Clinton was extremely annoyed at Carter's intervention (and vented his anger to, among others, former President Gerald Ford). After consulting with his advisers, he authorized Carter to go—but stressed that the United States would not agree to suspend the sanctions effort unless North Korea froze its nuclear program, let the inspectors complete their work, and committed to new talks with the United States. Off Carter went to Pyongyang, where he publicly declared his opposition to sanctions and praised the regime of Kim Il-sung. He then appeared live on CNN and announced that Kim had agreed to allow the inspectors to continue, and in return for this "very positive step" the administration should back off from sanctions and agree to talks. This was not what Clinton had insisted on, but he was stuck. The effort to organize sanctions in the U.N. Security Council collapsed. By October, the talks had produced the so-called U.S.-North Korea Agreed Framework, which the Clinton administration believed halted North Korea's nuclear weapons development. Republican critics considered it an unreliable agreement, whose weaknesses were produced in part by Jimmy Carter's aborting of the international pressures that were mobilizing. In any case, Clinton came around to forgive Carter his interference.

In September 1994, Carter propelled himself into the Haiti crisis. As noted earlier, the administration was putting severe pressure, including the threat of military action, to force General Cédras's departure and President Aristide's restoration. On September 15, Carter telephoned Colin Powell (retired a year from his position of JCS chairman) and asked if Powell would join Carter and former Senator Sam Nunn (Georgia Democrat) on a peace mission to stave off an invasion. Powell said he would join if President Clinton wanted this mission to take place. That afternoon, Powell received a phone call from Clinton, who complained of Carter as a "wild card" and worried that "the next thing you know, I'm expected to call off the invasion because he's negotiating a deal." But Clinton told Powell he thought the North Korea adventure "didn't turn out too badly," and concluded that the Haiti mission could

be helpful if it confronted Cédras with the unambiguous necessity to back down.

Clinton was determined that U.S. forces would go ashore; the only question was whether it would be a forced entry or a peacekeeping mission in the context of a peaceful handover of power. While in Haiti, Carter repeatedly phoned Clinton to ask for delays in the scheduled invasion, which he "desperately wanted to avoid." Cédras finally relented, less than an hour before U.S. paratroopers were scheduled to begin arriving. The 15,000-member multinational force went into Haiti without violence.

The Haiti mission accomplished what the administration sought; in the North Korea case it is arguable either way. But in both cases it does not speak well of the administration's diplomatic team that an unwanted outsider could so easily insert himself. When a White House press release was being drafted to announce the Carter-Nunn-Powell mission, the president approved a draft that read: "With President Clinton's approval, Jimmy Carter . . ." Press secretary George Stephanopoulos intercepted it, pointing out to Clinton that "presidents don't *approve* missions like this, they *order* them." The draft was changed and the dignity of the Clinton presidency preserved.

As in other areas, Clinton learned from his mistakes. In September 1995, at a tense moment during the Bosnia crisis, Carter contacted the administration on behalf of the Bosnian Serb leadership to try to head off a resumption of the NATO bombing. Carter had a CNN camera crew standing by outside his office ready to announce a cease-fire agreement. The administration (in the person of Strobe Talbott) politely but firmly told him: No, thanks.

Assessment

William Hyland sums up Bill Clinton as "a transitional figure wedged between the end of the Cold War and the beginning of a new century." After his reelection in 1996, a poll was taken of a group of American historians supervised by Arthur Schlesinger, Jr. Schlesinger saw in Bill Clinton "a rare combination of talents and infirmities." On the one hand, he was a man of "penetrating intelligence," a skilled political leader with intellectual curiosity. On the other side of the ledger were his lack of self-discipline, his "erratic" judgment of people, and a resilience that some saw as opportunism. There is no doubt that Clin-

ton gradually became more comfortable in foreign policy—witness his personal leadership of the Camp David Israeli-Palestinian negotiation in the fall of 2000.

It was a transitional period, moreover, that postponed a number of problems. With respect to Saddam Hussein's Iraq, the goals of American policy escalated during the Clinton presidency without a corresponding commitment to means. In October 1998 Clinton signed the Iraq Liberation Act, which made it U.S. policy to remove Saddam's regime, and on several occasions he forcefully articulated the danger that was thought to be posed by Iraq's weapons of mass destruction. Saddam's constant defiance of U.N. Security Council resolutions was met by occasional U.S. air strikes without decisive effect. By 1997, however, when the administration sought new sanctions from the U.N. Security Council, France had joined Russia in opposition. By the end of Clinton's term, the cumulative effect of Saddam's repeated challenges to the United Nations was the erosion of the Gulf War coalition against him; the lineup in the Security Council became: the United States and United Kingdom on one side, Russia, France, and China on the other. A new coalition—of those interested in restraining American power as an end in itself—was forming.

The principal lesson of Bill Clinton's presidency, for our purposes, is the importance of focus, sustained engagement, and willingness to spend political capital. Success in domestic policy has an episodic quality; usually one can select an issue on which to focus and make legislative proposals. Foreign policy crises usually impose themselves, and a successful policy in response to them requires sustained, coherent, and consistent policy-making that resolves internal differences and integrates the various elements of national power. Clinton clearly gained self-confidence in his second term, and the process also worked well when he delegated to a strong individual. This was true, for example, with respect to Robert Rubin in international economic policy, Strobe Talbott in Russia policy, Richard Holbrooke in Bosnia, and former Senator George Mitchell in Northern Ireland. These individuals had credible leverage as representing the president's will and they used it. Needless to say, the same principle applies to Clinton's own engagement at Camp David II. In other administrations, we have seen this bureaucratic focus residing in a strong secretary of state.

As in previous chapters, the conclusion is that when there is a sus-

tained commitment by the president, either in person or by delegation to a strong and trusted subordinate, coherence is possible. Where there are policy or philosophical disagreements among the principals, they will not be reconciled without presidential engagement. Similarly, when a cabinet department is unresponsive to presidential wishes, only the president can impose discipline. No system—whether collegial or hierarchical, formal or informal—will work otherwise.

CHAPTER NINE

George W. Bush

O N AUGUST 23, 2001, after seven months in office, President George W. Bush paid a visit to an elementary school in his hometown of Crawford, Texas. A student asked him if it was "hard to make the decisions" as president. He replied:

> Not really. If you know what you believe, decisions come pretty easy. If you're one of those types of people that are always trying to figure out which way the wind is blowing, decision making can be difficult. But . . . I know who I am. I know what I believe in, and I know where I want to lead the country.

The controversies that engulfed him are still fresh at this writing, but it is not too soon to attempt a dispassionate analysis of his manner of leading his government. As he suggested to the students in Crawford, Bush liked to see himself as "the decider," in the Trumanesque image of a gutsy chief executive taking on tough decisions and not looking back. Indeed, the boldness of many of his policies and doctrinal pronouncements made him a consequential president, whether one liked him or hated him. Concepts such as preemption in the war against terrorism, or the promotion of democracy, are big ideas with a respectable pedigree and lasting importance whether one agrees with Bush's approach to them or not. Many of the controversies over his decisions, however, were also controversies over how these decisions were made.

The Washington Post once mischievously published a list of fourteen quotations from different sources, inside and outside the administration, calling his policy-making process "dysfunctional." The accusers included champions of both the State and the Defense departments,

the two main antagonists in the interagency struggles (who seemed to agree on at least this one thing). Like Ronald Reagan, George W. Bush presents the paradox of a leader capable of great decisiveness but who set up or tolerated a system that impeded his exercise of it. On the most momentous issues of his presidency, his own judgment was often better than that of some of his senior advisers. Yet the system floundered when it did not have his decisive intervention, and it sometimes fostered bitter bureaucratic resentments even when it did.

For a serious student of policy-making, however, the definition of "dysfunctional" has to be more than just having one's own policy preference overruled in a presidential decision. The careful reader will need to discount for that factor in many accounts that have appeared up to now. That one loses out in an interagency debate does not automatically mean the process is not working right. Those who compiled the multiple occurrences of the term "dysfunctional" usually failed to note that many of the critics quoted were making contradictory accusations: Some were criticizing a reputed "cabal" of Vice President Dick Cheney and Defense Secretary Donald Rumsfeld who were said to tip the scales of policy-making unfairly in their direction and whom national security adviser Condoleezza Rice failed to control. Others were referring to what they saw as insubordination and rebellion by the Department of State and Central Intelligence Agency against decisions the president made, which, likewise, the national security adviser was said to be unable to control. Others, more neutrally, were referring to bureaucratic stalemates that were allowed to fester.

In truth, the facts varied from issue to issue; the bureaucratic balance of forces fluctuated over time. The most important question to ask is: Where was the president during these various debates? Did he decide the matter, siding with one group of advisers over the other, as was his right? Or did he fail to decide, allowing deadlocks to persist? What was the nature of the problem or problems he faced in his cabinet subordinates and how did he cope with them?

Team Bush

White House speechwriter David Frum, who spent many hours observing Bush, painted a complex portrait of contradictory qualities. He described Bush as "relentlessly disciplined," a man able to inspire great loyalty, and bold in his ideas—yet also a man "sometimes glib, even dog-

matic; often incurious and as a result ill informed; more conventional in his thinking than a leader probably should be." But Frum also listed Bush's virtues—decency, honesty, rectitude, courage, and tenacity.

Bush, like Reagan, was probably surprised by the intensity of divisions in his administration. He won his party's nomination in 2000 by positioning himself successfully in the party's center; he was seen as more conservative and "tougher" than his father, yet he benefited from the reflected glow of his father's moderate image, not to mention the political organization he inherited, and he espoused what he called a "compassionate conservatism." When he formed his government after the 2000 election, he seems to have intended a collegial policy-making process like his father's. He put together what was regarded as an impressive national security team of seasoned veterans.

Bush had absorbed some principles of management from his Harvard Business School education and from his experience as owner of the Texas Rangers baseball team. Published accounts of this business experience, and of what it taught him, present a rounded impression of an executive who aimed at decisiveness and collegiality, boldness and patience, loyalty and accountability. As with Reagan, again, there was a heavy emphasis on trust in subordinates and delegation to them, and a desire for consensus among them. When that consensus was not to be had, as we shall see, the system often broke down.

First, like most of his Republican predecessors, Bush 43 saw his job as focusing on the big picture and delegating the details. Just as Reagan and his colleagues saw this approach as a positive contrast with Jimmy Carter, so George W. Bush saw it as a needed change from Bill Clinton, who like Carter was criticized for immersion in details at the expense of vision. The president's job was to make the big decisions confidently, as Bush told the Crawford students.

Second, one of the lessons taught at Harvard Business School is that executives must often make decisions under conditions of uncertainty. There is never perfect information, yet managers must act before all the desired information is available. How to cope with this? Students are taught to analyze facts, make reasonable inferences, weigh probabilities, and assess as best they can the costs and benefits of acting or not acting. This is not only a business school principle; it is a stark necessity of presidential leadership. Henry Kissinger wrote many years ago of the dilemma of the statesman—that to shape events he must act before all the facts are clear; if he waits for perfect certainty the moment when

events could be shaped will have passed. This puts a premium on a leader's vision, intuition, and courage. It is a dilemma inherent in the responsibility of any leader who wants to impose purpose on events and not become their prisoner.

Bush told Bob Woodward that he trusted his intuition: "I'm not a textbook player. I'm a gut player." Intuition, we all know, has its limits. Bush famously said after he met Vladimir Putin in June 2001 that he had gotten a "sense of his soul," discovering spiritual qualities that had not hitherto been widely observed in the ex-KGB operative. Conservative writer Richard Brookhiser, in another perceptive portrait of Bush, pointed out that the tendency of the president and his aides to exalt the virtues of instinct could "seem like a rationalization, a cover for his lack of more obvious qualifications, such as intellect conventionally measured." But Brookhiser also quoted White House aide Karl Rove's comparison of Bush to Eisenhower, on the ground that both men had a "wiliness about being underestimated."

Third, Bush startled Bob Woodward with a comment contrasting himself with his father: "[T]he vision thing matters. That's another lesson I learned." According to many accounts, Bush's model of leadership was not his father, but Ronald Reagan. No one can claim that Bush 43 shied away from ambitious actions and large ideas, whether in foreign policy or in domestic policy. Despite the controversy surrounding his election victory in 2000, Bush considered that he had a mandate to be a purposeful leader and to spend whatever political capital he had for his agenda.

Bush as baseball executive revealed another feature of his concept of leadership. As managing general partner of the Texas Rangers he was not the master of baseball strategy or financial details but by all accounts he acted skillfully and energetically as the leader of an executive team. "He very much believes that the chief executive's responsibility is to manage the other executives," a former associate said. He made strategic decisions, and did so easily; he hired good people and held them accountable; he had "an uncanny ability," according to another account, "to create consensus and contentment among prickly peers and subordinates." He organized the effort to fund and build a new ballpark. He had a gift for public relations that disarmed the skeptics with a "beguiling charm" and "vastly improved the brand." He sat in the stands with the fans, even during team slumps, absorbing their complaints and promoting the team.

This psychological dimension of leadership has its significance. During tense moments in the war to liberate Afghanistan in 2001, for example, Bush saw it as his duty to demonstrate resolve, both to the public and to his subordinates. In an important and revealing passage, he told Bob Woodward:

> [A] president has got to be the calcium in the backbone. If I weaken, the whole team weakens. If I'm doubtful, I can assure you there will be a lot of doubt. If my confidence level in our ability declines, it will send ripples throughout the whole organization.

Woodward tells the story of a moment in late October 2001 when the U.S. military effort in Afghanistan seemed to have bogged down and critics were clamoring that it was a "quagmire." National security adviser Condoleezza Rice informed Bush that there was hand-wringing among some in his government, which annoyed him much more than the criticism in the media. He summoned his senior people to an NSC meeting on October 26 and asked them stern questions: Is this the military plan we all agreed on? (Yes.) Does anyone have any new or different ideas to propose? (No.) Well, then, we need to be steady and see it through: "Resist the second-guessing. Be confident but patient. It's all going to work." His cabinet officers came away braced and encouraged. Two weeks later the war broke decisively in favor of the United States and its Afghan allies.

One man's courage can be another man's stubbornness, of course. Whether a display of presidential resolve is the one or the other may not be obvious right away, and some of these assessments may be better left to the historians. Bob Woodward entitled a later book on Bush *State of Denial*, which captures the writer's harsher judgment of Bush's refusal to shift course in Iraq. But Bush was on to something. Military experts know this resolve to be a principle of command.

Holding subordinates accountable is another basic management tenet. Bush came to the White House asserting that "a good executive is one that understands . . . how to hold people accountable for results." In Texas, he had shown he meant it. When the club president, manager, and general manager could not deliver a successful baseball team, Bush dismissed them. In the presidency of his father, when White House chief of staff John Sununu was judged to be an obstacle to the smooth running of the White House team, President Bush 41 assigned to his

son the task of approaching Sununu to seek his resignation. As we shall see, Bush 43 found this principle of accountability harder to implement in his own administration.

The upshot of all this was that, whether or not he realized it, George W. Bush by his style of leadership was raising the stakes for his administration. For one thing, to pursue a bold agenda with a weak political mandate was to magnify political risks. But his concept of leadership as purposeful and resolute also put a premium on coherence of policy-making and discipline in execution. His reliance on a "team" made their collegiality and their performance all the more important.

Colin Powell at State

Colin Powell is one of the outstanding public figures of the last generation. I served under him on the NSC staff when he was the deputy national security adviser and then the national security adviser in the last two years of the Reagan administration. As an active duty lieutenant general, dependent on the U.S. Army for his career, he could have been pulled by conflicting institutional loyalties or suspected of the same, while occupying a White House position in which being an honest broker remains the model. Yet Powell carried it off with integrity and came away with universal respect, demonstrating a fine political skill in the best sense of the word. A few years later, as chairman of the Joint Chiefs under Bush 41, despite his professional unease about the Gulf War he carried out the president's orders loyally and was one of the architects of a brilliant military victory. Charismatic as well as capable, as a private citizen a few years later he passed over a serious opportunity for the 1996 Republican presidential nomination, and perhaps even for the presidency itself. Politically, he called himself a "Rockefeller Republican," though in his 1995 memoir he admitted that "[n]either of the two major parties fits me comfortably in its present state."

When George W. Bush named him secretary of state, Powell entered the office in January 2001 with a clear concept of how he intended to lead the department. During a telephone conversation I had with him then about a possible job at State, Powell described his desire to give the main role to career professionals and to run the organization in a traditional way. By this he meant two things. One was a determination to streamline the structure of the department in order to clarify the chain of command. When he arrived, for example, he found that there were

fifty-five "special envoys" or ambassadors-at-large reporting to the secretary; he abolished as many of them as he could (some had a statutory origin), ultimately eliminating twenty-two. The point of this streamlining was to restore responsibility to the regular regional and functional offices in the building—to "empower the desks at the State Department," as White House press secretary Ari Fleischer put it at the time.

There were other indicators of the same intention. Richard Haass, an experienced policy expert who had served on Bush 41's NSC staff, took the job of director of State's Policy Planning Staff. This is a job I had held under George Shultz. The office can be of value to a secretary of state as a gadfly to the bureaucracy by providing strategic perspectives different from what the secretary receives from the bureaus and desks. But Powell did not want gadflies, and Haass never had the impact that he might have had. By the same token, the seventh-floor position of "counselor" of the department, which James Baker had filled with a key member of his inner circle, went unfilled throughout Powell's tenure. He had little use for offices that did not exercise operational responsibility. Undoubtedly, much of this reflected Powell's experience with the military principle of "not jumping the chain of command"— that is, respecting the hierarchical structure and deferring to the operational responsibility of the officials in the chain.

Even more important, Powell's desire to "empower the desks" meant reliance on the Foreign Service. Most key assistant secretary positions went to career officers, and in the principal policy-making jobs there were only a few political appointees. White House aide Karl Rove clashed with Powell over this early in the administration, but gave way. As Powell said in his confirmation hearing, "part of my plan with the State Department is to put our Foreign Service officers in charge of the work of the Department, to motivate them, to give them a sense of responsibility and let them know we trust them, we have confidence in them."

The most eminent of the political appointees who made it through was John Bolton, who became under secretary of state for arms control and international security affairs and a pivotal figure on issues such as the nuclear weapons programs of Iran and North Korea. Bolton believes that Powell saw the value of having a true-blue conservative in his entourage. "You do cover my right flank," he told Bolton once, "and it needs covering." Bolton's memoir records that Powell stood by him loyally during all the congressional political assaults that he (Bolton) came

under. But the memoir also reflects Bolton's constant frustration and isolation in a department in which most of the important officials reflected a policy mind-set he considered out of step with the president's.

Bolton tells of instances in which Powell took on the bureaucrats. One issue was the new International Criminal Court (ICC), which Bill Clinton's administration had agreed to but which the Bush administration decided to disengage from. The Bush team was convinced that this new court, unaccountable to any government, its prosecutions not subject to U.N. Security Council veto—imagine Kenneth Starr on an international scale—was likely to become a politicized weapon against American officials and military personnel. The Bush administration not only withdrew its signature from the ICC treaty but launched a campaign to reach bilateral agreements with as many countries as possible not to surrender each other's citizens to the ICC. Such agreements were eventually reached with more than one hundred countries—a remarkable achievement by the State Department, which some of the senior career diplomats virtually refused to assist in until they were bluntly ordered to do so by Powell. Another instance was Bush's condemnation of Iraq, Iran, and North Korea as the "axis of evil" in his January 2002 State of the Union address. This was followed by leaks to the media by State Department officials denying that these characterizations would have any relevance to U.S. policy toward those countries. Powell surprised a meeting of his senior staff by declaring sternly that the president believed strongly in what he said and no one in the State Department "should try to take the edge off what the president said, or try to spin it."

Powell was later criticized by liberals for excessive loyalty to the president, especially over the Iraq War. These examples cited by Bolton show him, indeed, striving to be loyal and to impose this loyalty on his department. But Powell had helped create, or magnify, his own problem. The philosophy of "empowering the desks" reflected a view of stewardship of the department at odds with much of the philosophy we have seen earlier in this book. Where Henry Kissinger and James Baker had come into the building with a determination to impose political direction on the career service, Powell chose to embrace the organization. He seems to have done this as a matter of orderly management as he saw it; his own moderate instincts on policy only reinforced it. Whatever the intention, the result was to increase the probability that when

controversial issues presented themselves, whether Iraq or Iran or North Korea, Powell's State Department would find itself out of step with the more conservative members of the administration—which very often included the president.

Thus, one of the key building blocks was in place for a divided government. It was inevitable that the moderate views of the State Department, led as it was by a moderate who generally shared its institutional philosophy, would leave the institution out of sync with a conservative secretary of defense and vice president. What was not inevitable was that the feuds would be so persistent—and that the president would have such difficulty in managing them.

EARLY IN THE ADMINISTRATION, Powell made a public misstep on the subject of North Korea. He declared at a news conference on March 6, 2001, that the Bush team would "engage with North Korea to pick up where President Clinton and his administration left off." The Clinton administration had reached an Agreed Framework with North Korea in 1994 intended to halt its nuclear weapons program, and was moving toward normalizing relations with Pyongyang. Powell, in speaking this way, was reflecting the preference of the career diplomats of his East Asian and Pacific affairs bureau, many of whom had helped shape the Clinton policy. In December 2000, during the transition, Powell had been briefed at his home in McLean, Virginia, by Clinton's State Department North Korea team, and he seemed impressed by what he heard. At the time Powell spoke in March, however, the Bush administration had made no decisions on the matter, and conservatives such as the vice president, secretary of defense, and the Republican congressional leadership viewed the Clinton diplomacy as seriously flawed. The president himself called Rice at 5:00 the next morning, furious when he read Powell's remarks in The Washington Post. Rice called Powell to tell him of the president's displeasure, and Powell later publicly confessed he "got a little too far forward on my skis." The incident was a harbinger of the bureaucratic brawl that would begin in earnest a year and a half later when North Korea was caught cheating on the 1994 agreement.

It took Powell a long time to develop a personal camaraderie with the president. "There existed a distance between these two affable men," Bob Woodward wrote, "a wariness—as if they were stalking each other from afar, never sitting down and having it out, whatever the 'it' was."

Only in the late spring of 2002—after some sixteen months in office—did Powell ask the president for periodic private meetings with him in the Oval Office, a common—and obviously crucial—opportunity for harmonizing views and building confidence (recall Kissinger's regular meetings with Ford). Apparently Powell thought to ask for this only after he got wind of the fact that Rumsfeld was requesting and having such meetings. Powell, recalling from his own experience as Reagan's national security adviser that everyone in the world wants face time with the president, had not wanted to intrude on the president's time. His deputy, Richard Armitage, an experienced bureaucratic operator, convinced him that he needed the same access as Rumsfeld. So he began having such meetings, and later declared himself satisfied that he was having the access he wanted.

But the mutual unease between Bush and Powell seems never to have gone away, and much of the problem had to do with the substance of policy, not simply personality. By all accounts, Powell was uncomfortable with what he saw as an impetuosity in the White House and inadequate attention to the benefits of international consensus-building. He and his State Department colleagues blamed Cheney and Rumsfeld for skewing U.S. policies in this direction. Those who sympathized with Powell complained that a "cabal" of the vice president and secretary of defense had undue influence over the president, putting a "thumb on the scales" of the policy-making process. But another revealing moment in Woodward's *Bush at War* is the weak response that Bush gave when asked about Powell's contributions. "Powell is a diplomat," Bush responded. "And you've got to have a diplomat." This was less than a passionate presidential embrace of what Powell was engaged in.

Associates and friends of Powell have said that often when he thought he had persuaded the president of some moderate diplomatic course to pursue, the president reversed direction after a short period, apparently due to the influence of Cheney and Rumsfeld. "Somebody got to the President after I did," he used to lament. The premise of that characterization is that the president's natural inclination lay with Powell, and the influence of others was a distortion. An alternative hypothesis would be that this president's natural instincts lay on the conservative side, and that when Powell thought he had fully persuaded the president in a private conversation without the presence of those with contrary views, he was often mistaken. George Shultz had had a similar experience with Reagan: Reagan most often sided with Shultz in

their private sessions, but there were occasions (especially on Central America) when the issue was forced into an NSC meeting in which all the players could argue it out in front of the president, with the result that the president tilted back to the conservative side. Victories won by bureaucratic end runs are often short-lived. The disorderliness of this procedure—of competitive end runs into the Oval Office—is a serious management deficiency in itself. (Colin Powell, when he was Reagan's national security adviser, had seen it as part of his job to head off this sort of thing.) In any case, the president's wishes are the ultimate and legitimate arbiter. If the "cabal" consistently includes the president, it's not a cabal but a presidential preference.

Rumsfeld at the Pentagon

Where Colin Powell took charge of the State Department with the intention of empowering the existing organization, Donald Rumsfeld took over at the Department of Defense with the opposite intention. It was widely believed in Republican circles that civilian control of the military had weakened in Bill Clinton's presidency and political authority needed to be reasserted. (Some of this impression, ironically, was due to the charismatic Colin Powell's tenure as a strong chairman of the Joint Chiefs.) Having served once before as secretary of defense (under Gerald Ford) and having run two major corporations successfully, Rumsfeld had experience as a hands-on executive not shy about imposing his will. His friend Newt Gingrich linked some of Rumsfeld's style to his experience as a college wrestler at Princeton: "The sport," Gingrich said, "tends to produce very confident people who don't mind being visible, because everybody can watch them, and ain't nothing between them and winning and losing." Rumsfeld, he said, was smart, "stunningly competitive," with a "disciplined, focused ability to think about things."

Rumsfeld quickly asserted his control. He returned for his second tour in the E-ring office of the secretary of defense with an agenda, which he called "transformation." He had the president's explicit mandate to "challenge the status quo inside the Pentagon," and he went about it with gusto. There is no doubt this is what animated Rumsfeld the most and what he most wanted to leave as his legacy. He was convinced that the U.S. military had not yet shaken off the doctrines, structures, and systems of war-fighting left over from the Cold War; in the twenty-first century the United States would face threats from unpre-

dictable directions, including from possible new rivals, rogue states, terrorists, and others with weapons of mass destruction and missiles to deliver them. Therefore he wanted the U.S. military to restructure itself rapidly to emphasize flexibility, agility, better intelligence, innovative use of information technology and outer space, defenses against missiles, and new ways of war-fighting. He expanded the scope and missions of special operations forces, and he introduced a new process for more frequently updating war plans. Overseas, he launched a realignment of U.S. bases and forces, questioning Cold War deployments and forcing commanders to rethink what the requirements were in a new era.

Much of this was met with bureaucratic resistance from a military establishment—one of the most conservative of institutions—that had not experienced so assertive a reformist civilian leadership since Robert McNamara in the 1960s. Rumsfeld's abrupt personal style also rankled. There were those who found him intimidating. (My own impression was that he respected those who stood their ground—such as General Tommy Franks, the commander who planned the Afghan and Iraq campaigns.) After a while, management procedures in the department became more regular. Relations with the Army, however—the service that had the hardest time adjusting to new missions and concepts following the demise of its Soviet land-army rival—remained difficult the longest; the struggle over its modernization was quickly followed by the stresses of the prolonged Afghanistan and Iraq deployments. The liberation of Afghanistan in 2001 seemed to vindicate Rumsfeld's emphasis on innovation and flexibility. He was delighted by photos of U.S. Army Special Forces in Afghanistan—on horseback—with laser designators calling in precision air strikes from their handheld radios. The Iraq War, however, not only put considerable stress on U.S. ground forces but required a rapid relearning of counterinsurgency skills that the Army had forgotten since Vietnam.

RUMSFELD'S ROLE in the interagency battles over policy became controversial; he and his old friend the vice president were the "cabal." As a statutory member of the NSC, the secretary of defense has a voice in foreign policy discussions just as the secretary of state has a voice on any other topic. On diplomatic issues, generally, agencies tend to defer to State, but most of the big national security issues facing the Bush administration—withdrawal from the ABM Treaty; negotiations over North Korean and Iranian nuclear programs; Afghanistan and Iraq—

involved interests of many departments. Indeed, the need to integrate the diplomatic, military, and other dimensions of policy is why the National Security Council was created.

The vehicle by which Rumsfeld prepared himself for these interagency deliberations was the office of the under secretary of defense for policy, headed by Douglas Feith. My office—assistant secretary for international security affairs—was responsible for advising Rumsfeld on policies in most regions of the world, under Feith. (A parallel assistant secretary dealt with Europe; I had the rest.) We were the foreign policy arm of the Pentagon. The Policy office, as it was known, and especially my staff of regional experts, was quite small compared with the large organizations in each of the regional bureaus at State, but we churned out papers for Rumsfeld and briefed him before his attendance at meetings of the NSC or Principals Committee. Feith or I often accompanied Rumsfeld (or his deputy, Paul Wolfowitz) to these meetings, as well as attending meetings of the Deputies Committee ourselves.

On any issue on the NSC table, the Defense Department is entitled to submit its own paper outlining a proposed policy or strategy, or to propose amendments to papers drafted by others. The frequency with which we took the initiative to do this has turned, in some quarters, into another example of the Pentagon's undue influence over U.S. policy. This is puzzling. Marc Grossman, who was State's capable under secretary for political affairs and Feith's counterpart, is on record stating his admiration for the speed and quality of the papers that the Policy office produced. The White House, for its part, found our efforts helpful as well. I recall a moment when my Latin America experts mentioned to Feith that the interagency drafting of a new presidential strategy for the Western Hemisphere (a National Security Presidential Directive, or NSPD) was expected to take six months. Feith, incredulous, asked why such a noncontroversial document would take so long. He proposed that our office do its own draft in the next few days and submit it to the White House to jump-start the process. We did, and it did. But as policy controversies developed on many other issues, Feith's office became a bureaucratic and journalistic target.

The Unprecedented Vice President

Lynne Cheney, wife of the vice president, turned up on Comedy Central's *The Daily Show* in October 2007 to promote a memoir she had

written. To the surprise of host Jon Stewart and amusement of her audience, she presented Stewart with a gift—an eighteen-inch statue of Darth Vader—the dark villain who, for some, had become the image of her husband. She called it a "family heirloom."

There is no dispute that Dick Cheney had an unusual influence in national security policy as George W. Bush's vice president, and, as with all recent president–vice president relationships, its mystery is only deepened by the fact that only the two men know the real content of their private conversations. As a former White House chief of staff, congressional leader, and secretary of defense, Cheney was bound to carry substantive weight. His close personal and philosophical bond with Donald Rumsfeld—for whom he had once worked as a young aide in his first job in Washington—was also a bureaucratic factor of undeniable importance. But, even more important, he seems to have established an intimate relationship with the president.

The modern vice presidency can be said to have begun with Walter Mondale in the administration of Jimmy Carter. As we have seen, Carter treated Mondale as a valued political ally and granted him a West Wing office, where most of his predecessors had been confined to the old Executive Office Building next door. Mondale was an important source of political advice in a White House that had few senior people of Washington experience. Carter's attorney general, Griffin Bell, complained at length in his memoir that Mondale and his strategically placed former staffers had undue influence over Carter's policy-making on a range of domestic, legal, and foreign policy issues. Al Gore was believed to have unprecedented influence, as we have seen, in Bill Clinton's administration. Gore's national security adviser, Leon Fuerth, was "a very major player" in the NSC staff's work. While comparisons are difficult—the size of the vice presidential staff and office budget have not recently been disclosed—some experts believe Cheney's staff was about the same size as Gore's in total, though Cheney's national security staff may have been somewhat beefed up. Some have said that Cheney enjoyed "considerably more time with the president" than his predecessors—not only a weekly private lunch and the formal meetings (cabinet and NSC) but also hours of additional time together—but I have not seen documentation of this comparison.

The accusation often made was that Cheney's close relationship with the president, his statutory role on the NSC, his participation in Principals Committee meetings, his affinity of views with Rumsfeld, the

beefing up of his national security team, and his staff's participation in NSC staff and interagency meetings, all added up to a decisive tilting of the policy-making process. This is the origin of the "cabal" thesis and it seems to have been the perception at the State Department. Wherever Cheney and Rumsfeld were was said to be the "center of gravity" of U.S. policy.

My perception from the Pentagon was different. There were undoubtedly issues on which the vice president's private views communicated to the president had a particular impact, but they were not as many as generally claimed. The attempt to assert broad presidential powers over detention and surveillance of alleged foreign terrorists is clearly one such category. Given Cheney's historical passion to preserve what he saw as the constitutional powers of the executive, especially in wartime, reports of his strong convictions on this score are credible. The secrecy of most of the relevant internal debates leaves it difficult for outsiders to know, but the testimony of former Justice Department and Pentagon lawyer Jack Goldsmith is also credible with respect to the influence of the vice president and his staff. In any event, I am told authoritatively that the vice president's passion to preserve presidential powers was also shared by other senior White House officials, and it is easy to believe it was the president's natural conviction as well.

On other issues, we in the Pentagon perceived a more level playing field than did those from other agencies whose accounts have generated most of the public commentary. We considered that our views were rejected by the president on many issues—including on important points over Iraq—and our frustrations with the slow deliberative process were similar to the frustrations expressed by others. I was present at Principals meetings at which Secretary Powell's recommendations on diplomatic courses of action were approved by national security adviser Condoleezza Rice despite the vice president's disagreement. Cheney strongly opposed Powell's U.N. diplomacy before the Iraq War, but the president sided with Powell. There were times when we were convinced that Powell had a special relationship with Rice, bypassing the formal interagency procedures that would allow us to interject our view. There was no evidence for any such "special relationship" between Powell and Rice; indeed, subsequent accounts suggest the relationship between them was strained. The State Department even considered at times that she was in collusion with Cheney and Rumsfeld, or an "enabler" to their

nefarious influence, or attempting too much to "position" herself to personal advantage. As I read these accounts, I am struck most of all by the mirror-image quality of the suspicions on both sides. Below, when we consider particular issues, we will see a more complex picture than what either side imagined. The pivotal factor was always the president. Sometimes he sided with one side, sometimes with the other; sometimes he deferred judgment.

ON AUGUST 26, 2002, during the run-up to the Iraq War, Cheney gave a speech to the Veterans of Foreign Wars warning of the menace of Saddam Hussein's weapons of mass destruction, and he cautioned that the return of U.N. inspectors to Iraq would bring "false comfort." This time it was Powell's turn to be furious, since the president had decided at an NSC meeting ten days earlier that he would go before the U.N. General Assembly in early September to challenge the U.N. to confront Saddam. While the president had made no decision on a role for U.N. inspectors, Cheney's remark seemed to commit the United States to oppose it. Rice took her and Powell's concerns to the president, who agreed. He told her: "Well, why don't you call Dick and tell him what you want him to do?" She did, delicately chiding him for foreclosing the president's options. Cheney steered clear of the issue in subsequent speeches.

As for the vice president's allegedly decisive influence, White House insiders scoffed at the notion. They saw Cheney as a heavyweight counselor, given his deep knowledge of both policy and process, but they recalled many occasions when the president did not follow his advice. Speechwriter David Frum concluded: "Cheney was certainly a powerful figure within the administration. But those who identified him as a shadowy shogun who secretly controlled Bush, the weak mikado, could not have been more wrong."

Rice, Hadley, and the Interagency Process

The device of the Principals Committee was invented by President Bush 41. As we have seen, it was a forum of cabinet secretaries chaired by the assistant to the president for national security affairs (then Brent Scowcroft). Bill Clinton's administration made use of it, somewhat differently. In its own way it was emblematic of some of the problems under Bush 43.

Control of the Principals Committee was the subject of an early test of strength between Rice and Cheney. In the early years of the NSC, particularly the Eisenhower administration, the vice president presided at NSC meetings in the president's absence. Since the Principals were, in effect, the NSC minus the president, Cheney took a run at asking Bush to appoint him chairman of the Principals. "She threw a fit," according to a colleague, invoking the more recent precedent and pleading with Bush: "[T]his is what national security advisers do." He agreed. Thus it came about that the supposedly all-powerful vice president sat at the table with cabinet secretaries at Principals meetings chaired by an assistant to the president.

The job of assistant to the president for national security affairs contains within it a number of functions—staffing and advising the president, managing the interagency process, monitoring implementation of presidential decisions. Condoleezza Rice saw the first role as the most important. She spent extraordinary amounts of time with him, not only as confidante and counselor but virtually as a member of the family. David Rothkopf recounts:

> On a typical day as national security advisor, she saw him seven or eight times, and many days she was by his side between four and six hours. She worked out in the gym with him. She spent so much time with him at Camp David that she had her own cabin there. She joined the Bush family for Sunday dinner on a regular basis.

Rice's closeness to the president and her chairing of the Principals Committee gave her, on the face of it, an enormous advantage. In the Pentagon we sometimes feared that she was interpreting agencies' views to the president, at the expense of our ability to present our views directly to him, as Rumsfeld could do at an NSC meeting. (Principals meetings were more frequent than NSC meetings.) This was a source of suspicions. But apparently the State Department's fears were similar to ours. More generically, Rice came to be accused of being weak and of neglecting her responsibility to manage the growing conflicts among the cabinet heavyweights. Armitage once cracked that she was an "acceleratron," meaning that she reinforced Bush's wrong impulses when she should have been putting a brake on them.

With respect to Iraq, for example, she has been criticized harshly for not challenging assumptions or pressing alternative points of view on

the president before he made his decisions. Perhaps she might have done more of this. But (as we will see below in our discussion of Iraq) I am not convinced that the main mistakes in Iraq policy were mistakes of process.

My own view of Rice is more sympathetic. First of all, it is no small task to provide psychological support to the person on whose shoulders rests the heaviest burden of decision in the world. Helping the president achieve a level of substantive and psychological comfort with this burden is indeed part of the job; Henry Kissinger considered it one of his most important tasks with Richard Nixon. As for managing the bureaucratic conflicts, it is clear she tried. Her inability to resolve serious deadlocks was not a matter of personal deficiency: No one elected *her* to decide major controversies of national security policy. Just as Zbigniew Brzezinski attempted (and often failed) to wield presidential influence as Kissinger had done, it was not credible to the bureaucracy if the president was not visibly backing it up. Just as Ronald Reagan's national security advisers were perceived as weak, the problem was not their personal qualities but the president's unwillingness to break the deadlocks himself. Bush 43, like Reagan, was often not prepared to break decisively with one side or the other in a policy dispute; he preferred his subordinates to reconcile their conflicts for him if they could. Sometimes Rice would ask him to call a cabinet officer to make his wishes clear, and he would say no, it was for her to do. He did not want to referee every dispute. (Note that in the August 2002 incident involving Cheney's speech, Bush asked Rice to make the call.) To break major deadlocks she would need more presidential backing than that.

Bush's preferred method of resolving disputes was to encourage a consensus of his advisers. At Principals or Deputies meetings, Rice and her deputy Stephen Hadley repeatedly conveyed the president's injunction to reconcile disagreements, to "merge" or "blend" or "bridge" competing proposals, to split the differences, to come up with compromises. Even where it was known where the president's substantive preference lay, we had the picture of a president reluctant to impose his own will; he wanted his preferred outcome to emerge from the process and to reflect the consensus of his government. This approach was reflected also in the work of the NSC staff. When I served in the Nixon administration, the NSC staff's most important product was memoranda to Nixon laying out options for his decision; Bush 43's NSC staff crafted

laborious statements of broad policy attempting to capture the state of the interagency consensus, which the Deputies Committee laboriously argued over. Hadley told the NSC staff that good governance required this pursuit of consensus—apparently in the hope that it would minimize controversy and gain legitimacy for the outcomes.

As for Armitage's complaint that Rice "accelerated" Bush's wrong instincts, this was a misreading if not disingenuous; it more likely reflects State's disgruntlement at being overruled in cases where the president did choose sides. From the Pentagon's vantage point, State wasn't doing so badly. Colin Powell, given his national and international stature, had considerable leverage in the interagency struggles, whatever the president's preferences. Hadley was heard saying more than once during tense moments over Iraq in 2002–2003 that "we can't let the NSC fly apart"—meaning that State had to be mollified in some way (or, perhaps, that they could not afford to have Powell resign). This insured that State—despite its frequent public complaints—won many battles for the president's ear (if not his soul) or at least held its own sufficiently to cause unhappiness in the Pentagon when our preferences were not adopted. Indeed, it is part of the explanation for the deadlocks that frustrated everyone. Many times I heard Rumsfeld echo George Shultz's famous complaint. "Nothing ever gets settled in this town."

Cases and Controversies

A variety of problems arose in the Bush administration from this management system. In some cases, the pursuit of consensus led to frustrating delays. To take an example, Bill Clinton had begun an improvement of U.S. relations with India and Bush was eager to take it further. The Cold War had distorted the relationship of the two largest democracies— because of India's assertive neutralism in the early years, then the U.S. success in bringing China (India's rival) into the game against the Soviet Union (India's ally). The Cold War's end banished these distortions, and the new strategic reality of China's rise was pushing India and the United States together. The obstacle that remained was India's nuclear weapons program. Its nuclear weapons test in 1998 had forced the Clinton administration to apply legislatively mandated economic sanctions. A logical and promising avenue of U.S.-Indian rapprochement in the new century was to expand cooperation in high technology between the two mature economies in such areas as civilian space programs, civilian

nuclear energy, missile defense, and other high-tech trade. The two countries needed to work out a plan for steps by India that would enable the United States to remove the legislative and regulatory obstacles to make such cooperation possible.

At a Deputies meeting in March 2003, Hadley announced that the president considered it was time to transform the relationship with India. But before any proposition could be put before the Indians, a divided U.S. government had to thrash out what it would be. Both State and Defense were internally split. In both departments, people who were focused on India policy favored trade liberalization for strategic reasons, while those responsible for U.S. nonproliferation policy considered India a conspicuous miscreant because it had never signed the Nuclear Non-Proliferation Treaty and they saw any significant concession to India as a weakening of the international nonproliferation regime.

In the Pentagon we worked out our differences fairly quickly. My office, responsible for regional relations, favored rapid improvement of ties with India. My colleague J. D. Crouch, responsible for nonproliferation policy, shared the concerns of his counterparts at State. Both of us worked for Douglas Feith, who supported the president's desire to move forward with India and asked Crouch and me to work out some compromises on the technical issues, which we did. In State, however, the impasse took much longer to resolve. The obstacle was John Bolton, who as State's nonproliferation "tsar" was adamantly against concessions to India that would legitimate its nuclear programs. It was ironic that the issue on which the usually frustrated Bolton seemed to have the most influence at State was an issue on which he was at odds with his conservative allies in the rest of the government. Lunching once with Bolton in the elegant eighth-floor dining room at State, I asked him half-jokingly if he planned to add democratic India to the president's "axis of evil" list. John just smiled.

As a result it took six months for the U.S. government to work out its position. The Defense and Commerce departments pushed for liberalization; State leaned in that direction but was hobbled by its internal divisions. I remember asking NSC staff friends why the president could not be presented with, say, two or three options, so he could just decide the matter. I was told that the president—despite his clear desire to change U.S. policy—wanted the departments and agencies to negotiate it.

While the India deliberation produced an agreement in the end,* on other issues the deadlocks were never resolved. One example was Iran. In the spring of 2003, the president asked his departments and agencies to develop an NSPD for him to sign setting forth a U.S. policy toward the Islamic republic. As our contribution to the deliberation, we in the Policy office in the Pentagon turned out "action plans" for increasing pressures on Iran; as drafts of the NSPD were circulated, we added our points. State disagreed with many of our points, leaning more toward diplomatic engagement. Repeated Deputies meetings chaired by Hadley failed to iron out the philosophical disagreements. The president reportedly sided with those skeptical of diplomatic engagement, but with the Iraq War heating up he also shied away from escalation of a conflict with Iran. The draft NSPD went nowhere—except to generate a few press leaks from State about the bellicosity of the Pentagon.

North Korea policy was another example of the president's attempting to split the difference between conflicting positions. Within the State Department, the Bureau of East Asian and Pacific Affairs (EAP), headed in the first Bush term by James A. Kelly and in the second by Christopher Hill, was the ardent champion of bilateral negotiations with North Korea. It was EAP that encouraged Colin Powell in his admiration for the Agreed Framework of 1994, which the Clinton administration believed had halted the North Korean nuclear weapons program. It had long been an article of faith among congressional and conservative Republicans, on the other hand, that the 1994 agreement was a mistake: While it placed international controls on North Korea's Yongbyon nuclear reactor complex, it provided no visibility into whatever else North Korea might be doing, in a country known to have the most extensive network of secret underground facilities on the planet. In return for this, the Clinton administration had eagerly pursued normalization of relations, with a high-profile visit by Secretary of State Madeleine Albright to Pyongyang and a near-agreement on a visit by President Clinton himself just before the end of his term.

In the new administration, the president let it be known through Rice that he wanted a North Korea policy "180 degrees" different from Clinton's, that he found the regime of Kim Jong-il "abhorrent," and that

*Eventually a game plan was agreed in the U.S. government in the fall of 2003 and with the Indians in January 2004. Its culmination was an accord on peaceful nuclear cooperation, reached in July 2005. As of late 2008 the fate of this accord was in the hands of the legislatures of the two countries.

we could have no more "business as usual" with North Korea. Bush told Bob Woodward of his visceral "loath[ing]" of Kim Jong-il, who starved his people and ran a massive system of prison camps. Any new agreement would have to include strict verification of all North Korean nuclear programs. Under pressure from Powell and from the liberal South Korean government of Kim Dae-jung, Bush in June 2001 authorized continued bilateral contacts with North Korea (through its U.N. mission in New York) and continued adherence to the 1994 Agreed Framework. But Bush toughened the U.S. position in other ways: He insisted on improved implementation of the Agreed Framework, on verifiable constraints on North Korean missiles, and on changes in North Korea's conventional military posture that would be less threatening to South Korea.

This would become the pattern of North Korea policy in Bush's first term—acceding to the need for diplomacy, but reassuring administration conservatives by toughening the content of the U.S. positions. This approach frustrated both sides. The firmer substantive positions were much less likely to appeal to the North Koreans, which was frustrating to State, yet the president's go-ahead for continued diplomacy gave State many opportunities to pursue its own quiet overtures toward North Korea, which continually aroused the conservatives' suspicions. One example was Powell's "accidental" meeting with the North Korean foreign minister at a Southeast Asian nations' conference in Brunei in July 2002—a meeting that Powell's aides acknowledge they had choreographed for days and on which he had not consulted beforehand with the White House. On at least two other occasions, Powell ignored opposition from elsewhere in the administration to authorize his diplomats to engage with the North Koreans, without consulting the White House.

In the summer of 2002, the administration was preparing a new diplomatic initiative toward North Korea when U.S. intelligence discovered that North Korea had a secret program to build a nuclear weapon via highly enriched uranium (HEU). This program, circumventing the restraints on the Yongbyon reactor, meant that North Korea was violating not only the 1994 Agreed Framework but also three other agreements it had signed—the Nuclear Non-Proliferation Treaty, the North-South Joint Declaration on Denuclearization of the Korean Peninsula (1992), and an International Atomic Energy Safeguards Agreement (1992). The HEU program had apparently been under way for a number of years, since the Clinton administration. A visit to

Pyongyang in October 2002 by a delegation headed by assistant secretary of state James Kelly, originally conceived as an occasion to offer a new U.S. initiative, instead became the occasion of a dramatic encounter in which Kelly confronted the North Koreans with the U.S. knowledge of their HEU program, and the North Koreans, to everyone's amazement, admitted it. State's diplomats were unhappy, however, that Kelly's instructions and talking points—vetted by an interagency process in Washington—did not permit him to engage in any give-and-take with the North Koreans. "A trained monkey who can speak English could do this job," Kelly griped. Thus, again, State was given the form but the conservatives were given the content.

The next major diplomatic step was China's agreement in early 2003 to host a six-party negotiation on the North Korean nuclear problem (United States, China, Japan, South Korea, North Korea, and Russia). While this initiative came as a surprise to most of us in the Pentagon— it was apparently worked out in White House backchannels, with State participation but not the Pentagon's—we understood that it reflected the president's desire for closer cooperation with China; thus it had a wider strategic purpose in his mind, whatever results it produced on North Korea. The six-party forum had the additional benefit that it included five countries all committed to the denuclearization of North Korea; this was expected to be a vehicle of diplomatic pressure. The North Koreans always preferred direct bilateral talks with the United States, so as to head off such a coalition, to go over the heads of the South Koreans, and to place their own agenda of demands on an equal footing to that of the United States. To avoid this and to maintain the multilateral pressure on their illicit nuclear activities, the White House instructed negotiator Kelly that he was not to have private bilateral conversations with the North Koreans in these multilateral meetings.

The State Department felt passionately, however, that direct bilateral talks with the North Koreans were the only possible avenue to success. Likewise, State was convinced that the administration would have to abandon its harsh rhetoric against the regime and be willing, in the end, to come to terms with it. In Senate testimony in February 2003, Richard Armitage suggested that the United States would have to talk to North Korea. Soon after, a Democratic senator called Armitage to tell him, "I saw the president after that, but the president said to us, 'That wasn't my policy.'" To which Armitage answered, "You watch. It will be the policy." The president was reportedly not amused when he heard of this.

Within two years, however, U.S. diplomats were congratulating themselves that they had turned the six-party talks into a façade behind which all the serious business was conducted bilaterally with the North Koreans.

In Bush's second term, shifts in personnel shifted the balance of forces within the administration. Rice replaced Powell as secretary of state; her deputy Stephen Hadley replaced her as national security adviser. John Bolton, who had fought a rearguard action within State on the North Korean issue, left to become U.S. permanent representative to the United Nations. Robert Joseph, who had done his best, as umpire on the NSC staff, to split the differences, left the NSC to replace Bolton at State, but at State he discovered that Rice most often sided with Christopher Hill of the East Asian and Pacific bureau. Rumsfeld, preoccupied with Iraq and politically weakened, fought less hard on these issues; briefing him before NSC and Principals meetings, I detected an air of resignation on this. (Robert Gates, who replaced Rumsfeld, played even less of a role.) Bolton, who became involved in the subject again in 2006 when the issues of North Korean missile and nuclear tests came before the U.N. Security Council, noticed that U.S. policy in New York toughened whenever the president got personally involved. But Rice, given her special relationship with the president, now had the upper hand in the government, and she pushed the agenda of State's East Asian and Pacific bureau. A spate of press articles appeared hailing the new dominance of Foreign Service professionals in Rice's State Department.

In February 2007, after several rounds of bilateral talks, Christopher Hill reached an agreement with the North Koreans in Berlin. To its critics, the new accord strongly resembled Bill Clinton's 1994 Agreed Framework in that, while it shut down the Yongbyon reactor again, it provided no credible verification of whatever else North Korea might be doing clandestinely elsewhere in the country—or in other countries. Possible obstacles to the conclusion of this agreement, in the form of critical views elsewhere in the administration, were bypassed. State Department officials let it be known to the media, with some apparent pride: "Rice telephoned Bush from Germany, and national security adviser Stephen J. Hadley walked the president through its terms line by line. The layers of interagency discussion that had previously thwarted policy toward North Korea were simply eliminated." Days passed after the public announcement of the Berlin accord before the

secretary of defense and chairman of the Joint Chiefs were informed of its content.

Usually, leaks about the bypassing of regular procedures come from the bureaucratic party that is aggrieved by the practice. Leaks like these, boasting of the maneuver, are more unusual. But the State Department was pleased with its success. It is reported that U.S. diplomats considered the Berlin setting for the final stage of the negotiation to be particularly symbolic because Berlin had been the venue for many Clinton-era bilateral negotiations with North Korea. Similarly, the U.S.-North Korean working group set up by the Berlin agreement to explore normalization of relations found a particular satisfaction in being able to meet, in the Waldorf Towers in New York, in what had been the official residence of John Bolton, who had left his U.N. post after failing of confirmation by the Senate.

Bush had second thoughts about the Berlin accord, according to three former colleagues of mine in his administration. "Buyer's remorse" is a phrase I heard. But the president had left himself no recourse but to accept it. In the first term, the evidence is ample that he was among the skeptics, and his skepticism was a restraint on the exuberance of a diplomacy that he seems to have tolerated more than enthused over—a diplomacy that was heading in a direction he had said he did not want to go. But essentially he was only splitting the difference. Like Reagan on START or Central America, the result was a messy process that frustrated both sides in the interagency debate—those who wanted to do more and those who wanted to do less. Bush managed the disagreements, instead of choosing a clear-cut position. In the second term, weakened politically by Iraq, Bush was not in a position to take on the foreign policy establishment in another battle; he seemed to acquiesce in the new balance of forces in his administration instead of shaping it. If he had a view contrary to what the State Department professionals were pursuing, he did not assert it.

The War in Iraq

This is not the place for a full-length treatment of the Iraq War and its controversies. Nor can I claim to be a neutral observer, having been involved in policy-making in the Department of Defense with respect to it. Nevertheless I will attempt to assess, in as balanced a way as I can manage, a few of the issues that relate to the topic of this book, that is,

how Bush ran his government. At this writing (2008), the goal Bush set out to achieve in overthrowing Saddam Hussein—a stable, moderate Iraq in the place of a tyrant with hegemonic ambitions—may be within reach. But no one can deny that it has been a more costly and painful enterprise than its supporters expected.

Not everything that goes wrong in foreign policy is the result of a failure of process, however. In the Iraq War, the most fundamental problems in my view were substantive—some important assumptions with respect to its difficulty that proved to be mistaken. It is not clear that a different procedure would have led the president to decide the big questions differently.

The most important mistaken assumption related to the extent of the political vacuum that would be left by the removal of Saddam's regime. The U.S. government expected to find Iraqi *institutions*—civilian and military—to which it could give direction and then assist the Iraqis in finding new leadership for. But these disintegrated; no department or agency predicted the depth of the institutional implosion that occurred. Many of the problems encountered flowed from this. An important prewar debate that is relevant to this had to do with whether the United States should have an occupation at all, or whether an Iraqi political structure should be put in place as soon as possible after liberation. We will discuss this below, but it is an issue deserving of serious consideration by historians because it was at the heart of how postwar events unfolded.

A second fundamental problem in Iraq was the failure to adapt quickly to the difficulties once they arose. There is a military maxim that no war plan ever survives the first contact with the enemy. The requirement then is to respond with timely decisions that address the unexpected challenges, and do not compound them. Some of the problems of this kind were indeed management failures, and we will discuss them. But other of these problems, too, were the result of policy judgments and unanticipated developments more than they were failures of process. The security vacuum that opened the door for an insurgency, for example, was the product of a number of separate factors: a war plan that emphasized speed over mass (and thus limited the numbers of U.S. troops); the decision to build a new Iraqi army from scratch instead of trying to reconstitute the remnants of the old; collapse of the Iraqi police; lower numbers of international forces than had been expected; Turkey's last-minute denial of access for the 4th Infantry Division; and so on. Then came a

delay in recognizing the seriousness of the insurgency and in designing a strategy to defeat it. For all this, Donald Rumsfeld was ultimately held accountable, though the factors had a variety of origins.

THE PRESIDENT'S DECISION to go to war, made finally in January 2003, came after more than a year of deliberation within the administration. The adequacy of planning—if it were to be measured by the volume of effort alone—would be difficult to fault. All agencies were involved. There were dozens of meetings of the NSC, the Principals, and the Deputies on all aspects of the war and on a variety of postwar contingencies. A working-level Executive Steering Group was set up in August 2002 under NSC staff chairmanship to develop interagency plans. Subgroups were devoted to political-military issues, humanitarian and reconstruction needs, energy infrastructure, coalition affairs, and public affairs. Serious potential problems such as Saddam's destruction of the oilfields were anticipated and avoided in the major combat phase.

Rumsfeld brought in General Tommy Franks of Central Command and JCS chairman General Richard Myers to brief the president on a regular basis on the war plan. There was an unprecedented degree of transparency and communication among the president, the secretary of defense, and the military leadership, marking a significant improvement over Bill Clinton in Kosovo or Richard Nixon in Indochina. Colin Powell, who had serious reservations about the drift toward war, spent more than two hours with the president over a private dinner on August 5, 2002, laying out all the risks as he saw them and the need for the maximum international support. Powell was confident afterward that he had had the chance to make his case in full, and indeed the president accepted his recommendation to seek international support via the U.N. Security Council. Powell also had private conversations, soldier to soldier, with General Franks, expressing misgivings about the small size of the invasion force but receiving Franks's assurances that he (Franks) was comfortable with it.

In October 2002, Rumsfeld sent Bush his own memo listing things that could go wrong, and the CIA sent forward its assessments of the risks of a possible conflict. The president had to weigh those risks against the risks of inaction as they were seen at the time, including Saddam's hegemonic ambitions, his links to terrorism, his (near universally assumed) possession of stocks of WMD, and the erosion of the policy of containing him through sanctions.

George Tenet, then CIA director, has complained that there was no single meeting in which the president asked his senior subordinates their view on the "central questions" of whether the United States should go to war or not. Bush admitted this to Bob Woodward, saying he did not need to canvass his cabinet in such a formal way because he knew their views. Was this a serious mistake, or not? The value of hearing multiple views at the same time was once stated concisely and persuasively by that master of organization, Dwight Eisenhower:

> I know of one way in which you can be sure you have done your best to make a wise decision. That is to get the responsible policy makers with their different viewpoints in front of you, and listen to them debate. I do not believe in bringing them in one at a time, and therefore being more impressed by the most recent one you hear than the earlier ones.

This is undoubtedly a good model, and it may go a long way to answering the question raised in Chapter 1 about procedural legitimacy—that is, what kind of process increases the likelihood that those overruled in a presidential decision will accept its fairness. Future presidents would be wise to follow this practice where they can.

Two qualifications come to mind, however. One is that there is no such thing as a guarantee that those overruled will not feel aggrieved anyway, or will not avail themselves of the opportunity to distance themselves afterward—especially if the policy runs into difficulties. Cynical as it may sound, the quietude of the overruled may depend more on how a presidential decision fares after it was made than on how it was made in the first place. The second point is that in the case of an intense deliberative process lasting over a year, Bush had a point. He knew everyone's views, he had heard every argument, and all sides had had ample opportunity to speak their minds. It is not clear that a grand debate in the Situation Room would have added significantly to the president's understanding of what wisdom there was in the U.S. government as to the risks of action or inaction. My impression is that insistence on a formal Eisenhower-like interactive process would have made more difference to the administration's North Korea policy than to the decision to go to war in Iraq.

.   .   .

SOME OF THE FAMILIAR BUREAUCRATIC PROBLEMS of the Bush administration did assert themselves, however, and the president and his policy making process did not deal with them decisively. Even Bush's decision to endorse Powell's U.N. diplomacy had about it the air of splitting the difference. Cheney argued strongly that the pursuit of a U.N. Security Council resolution might well fail and leave us worse off diplomatically: If Saddam were clever, he could tie up the U.N. inspectors in endless evasions; nor did the United States have any assurance that it could achieve U.N. blessing for the use of force in any foreseeable circumstances, given French, Russian, and Chinese opposition. Bush sided with Powell on this issue, despite reservations, presumably hoping at the very least to demonstrate a degree of deference to his increasingly restless secretary of state. As it turned out, Powell was initially vindicated by the U.N. Security Council's unanimous passage of Resolution 1441 in November 2002, which declared Iraq to be in "material breach" of its obligations to renounce WMD and warned of "serious consequences." It was the quest for a second resolution—more explicitly endorsing the use of force—that ran aground, however. British prime minister Tony Blair desperately wanted explicit U.N. authorization to satisfy his Labour Party. Meanwhile, the French government was quietly telling the Bush White House to "just do it"—to go to war on the basis of Resolution 1441 and not put Paris on the spot a second time. On this, Bush sided with his ally Blair—and was humiliated by French sabotage of the second resolution. Such are the joys of multilateralism.

Planning for postwar reconstruction was hampered by a number of bureaucratic problems. Given the importance of the principle of unity of command, Rumsfeld fought hard for this to be put under Defense Department control. This was done. State inevitably chafed as many of its personnel came under military command. The Executive Steering Group chaired by the NSC staff chafed at Rumsfeld's unwillingness to let activities that the president had assigned to the Pentagon be vetted by a working-level interagency committee. In October 2002, the White House asked Rumsfeld to delay setting up an office for postwar Iraqi reconstruction because of fear that it would undercut the president's diplomacy. At a time when Bush was trying to reassure the world of his desire for peaceful solutions, how could he explain why the Pentagon was already staffing an organization to run Iraq after the overthrow of Saddam? Eventually, an Organization of Reconstruction and Humanitarian

Assistance (ORHA) was created, under retired Army Lieutenant General Jay Garner, in January 2003, just two months before the war began.

At this point, Rumsfeld made a misstep that seriously embittered relations with the State Department. In February, Garner reported to Rumsfeld on his progress in identifying skilled people to serve as senior advisers to the various Iraqi ministries. When Garner showed him a chart listing several men and women from the State Department and the U.S. Agency for International Development, Rumsfeld bristled. For the most important ministries he instructed Garner to develop a different kind of process; he wanted to know the criteria for selection, the skills needed, and then multiple candidates for each job, including experienced private sector people and others outside the U.S. government. He then started crossing names out on the chart next to the key ministries. This created havoc for Garner, who had been trying to put a team together on an urgent basis, and at State, where these individuals presumably had volunteered for this hazardous duty and begun making personal plans. The bitterness at State was deep and lasting. There was also irony in view of Rumsfeld's later campaign to mobilize greater participation from State and other agencies in postwar duties in Iraq and Afghanistan.

A bigger problem for ORHA was that it became a political football within the Pentagon. U.S. military doctrine treated postwar reconstruction (sometimes called "stability operations") as "Phase IV" of any military plan.* The "planning order" sent by the chairman of the Joint Chiefs to General Franks in July 2002 included this requirement. For a considerable period, however, General Franks seemed to believe that others would be taking this burden off his shoulders—either Feith, the under secretary for policy (an office that is not in the military chain of command); or ORHA, which he treated as Rumsfeld's baby, not his; or the State Department. On December 19, an updated "planning order" was sent to Franks, calling attention again to Phase IV. As the Joint Staff grew nervous about Phase IV, an "execute order" was issued on January 10, 2003, which enlisted a separate command (U.S. Joint Forces Command) to assist Central Command with the work involved. These orders made clear that ORHA reported to Central Command (that is, to General Franks).

There is no doubt that the delays hindered preparation. What also

---

*Phase I, typically, is planning and preparation; Phase II is "shaping the battlespace," often by air operations; Phase III is major combat operations.

stands out in retrospect, however, is how badly the Defense Depart ment and the entire U.S. government were organized for the nature and scale of the postwar reconstruction activities that turned out to be urgently required. The Joint Staff, in a post-Iraq "lessons learned" assessment, correctly concluded that stability operations should not be viewed as sequential to but as an integral part of combat planning. In November 2005, Rumsfeld signed a directive establishing that the Department of Defense should henceforth treat stability operations as a core mission in war-planning. A month later, the president signed an NSPD establishing the coordinator for reconstruction and stabilization in the Department of State, to coordinate government-wide economic assistance efforts. To the regret of many, however, including in the Pentagon, the new office in State was given little funding.

On another crucial issue, Bush reversed an important decision he had made, in part out of deference to the man in the field. One of the central prewar debates in the administration, as I have noted, was whether there should be a U.S. occupation at all, or for how long, or whether an interim Iraqi political structure should be put in place as soon as possible after liberation. Long before the war, we in the Pentagon were strongly urging that a lengthy occupation would be a mistake, only delaying the Iraqis' ability (and necessity) to fill the vacuum with their own new institutions. A memorandum I wrote to Rumsfeld on this subject in the summer of 2002 is featured prominently in a book written by Feith. Our fear was that the U.S. political authority would end up sitting in Baghdad imagining that it was running Iraq, while all sorts of hostile forces would run loose in the country. While no agency of the government, as noted earlier, predicted the extent of the vacuum that occurred, the situation that we encountered arguably strengthened the case for helping the moderate Iraqis fill it as soon as possible.

The opposing view, held strongly in State and CIA, was that to prepare such an Iraqi political structure in advance would mean undue reliance on the half-dozen exile groups with which we had been working; their legitimacy and ability were questioned, and one of them, Ahmed Chalabi's Iraqi National Congress, was a particular object of State and CIA suspicion. The hope was that new, locally based Iraqi leaders would emerge after liberation, and that with time a more representative leadership group would develop. (Five years later, almost all the leading Iraqi politicians came from the external groups.) I

raise this issue not simply to complain that the Pentagon was overruled, but because of its importance and because of the way it was handled.

Before the war, after interagency debate, Bush decided at an NSC meeting on March 10 that we would establish an Iraqi Interim Authority "as soon as possible after liberation." This was not to be a provisional government but a vehicle for enabling Iraqis, both "internals" and "externals," to begin sharing responsibility for running the country. The president's decision was spelled out in unusual detail in the official "summary of conclusions" of the NSC meeting circulated a day later. After Baghdad fell, however, the difficulties encountered in Iraq gave Washington cold feet. When Ambassador L. Paul Bremer was chosen in May 2003 to be head of the Coalition Provisional Authority, the president suggested to him that the process of Iraqi self-government would "take a long time." On arrival in Baghdad, Bremer concluded that a multi-year U.S. occupation would be necessary before the Iraqis could run their own affairs, and he halted the efforts begun by Jay Garner to help Iraqi moderates organize. He shared State's view that the external groups could not be relied upon and that moderate forces and institutions needed to be built from scratch. Everyone in Washington (including the president, vice president, and Rumsfeld) deferred to Bremer. After a few months, Washington had second thoughts again. By October, Bremer was persuaded to agree to turn over sovereign authority to Iraqis by the end of June 2004—earlier than he had originally wanted. Nonetheless, the formal occupation lasted fourteen months. As to its effects, historians can debate whose arguments proved correct.

The chain of command with respect to the occupation was an anomaly in itself. Bremer's charter stated that he was subject to the "authority, direction and control of the Secretary of Defense." But he also had the title of "presidential envoy," and he concluded reasonably enough that his most important tie was to the White House. He developed a close personal connection with the president, and telephoned national security adviser Rice virtually every day. Meanwhile, many of his senior colleagues in Baghdad were from State. A tireless and forceful executive, with courage as large as the burden on his shoulders, Bremer skillfully made use of the bureaucratic complexity to carve out considerable freedom of action.

As problems mounted in postwar Iraq, the State Department, feeling itself the aggrieved party in these many bureaucratic battles, found ways of distancing itself. It let its views be known through friendly media, and shone special light on its rivals in the Defense Department. Beginning in 2003, there was a flood of tendentious leaks attributing all the difficulties in Iraq to alleged failings of the Defense Department—failure to do any postwar planning, suppression of State Department planning efforts, intent to install Ahmed Chalabi as leader of Iraq, and so on. Not all these leaks came from State Department sources, but many of them clearly did. It was a natural reflex of State to try to distance itself from the problems in Iraq, but it was equally natural of the White House to perceive that this was harming the president. Many of the accusations against the Pentagon essentially called into question presidential decisions. Senior White House officials made calls to Powell's office rapping knuckles over the leaks.

What the White House did not do in this case, however, was to launch a vigorous defense of the president's original decisions. Whether the issue was postwar planning or the failure to find WMD, the president and his aides shied away from defending his decisions or the rationale for going to war. They attempted to focus on the future—on Iraq's democratic hopes and the stakes in the Middle East. Thereby, they not only conceded much of the ground to the critics but underestimated how much the leaks were delegitimating and undermining the president's whole Iraq policy. Perhaps only when Democratic candidate John Kerry threw these same accusations at Bush during the 2004 presidential campaign did the White House realize the full extent of the damage these leaks had done to him.

The CIA was also heard from. The fall of 2004—just before the U.S. presidential election—saw an unusual proliferation of leaks from intelligence sources embarrassing to the administration. On September 16, *The New York Times* reported on a secret National Intelligence Estimate (NIE) with a grim prognosis for Iraq, including civil war as a "worst-case" outcome. Two weeks later, the *Times* cited prewar intelligence reports that had allegedly predicted serious internal problems in Iraq. Also in September, a senior CIA Middle East analyst was reported to assert that CIA warnings before the war had gone unheeded. A second senior intelligence officer, an expert on counterterrorism, was permitted

by the agency to publish a book highly critical of its performance against al-Qaida; he commented to *The Washington Post* that "[a]s long as the book was being used to bash the president, they [his superiors] gave me carte blanche to talk to the media." In October, the Knight Ridder/ Tribune chain reported that a secret CIA assessment contradicted what the administration was saying about Saddam's ties with al-Qaida. Patrick Lang, a retired Defense intelligence analyst with friends at the CIA, later commented: "Of course they were leaking. They told me about it at the time. They thought it was funny. They'd say things like, 'This last thing that came out, surely people will pay attention to that. They won't re-elect this man.'"

The CIA has not succeeded in overthrowing a hostile foreign government in a few generations; alas, its effort to overthrow the American government fared no better. Joking aside, what we saw was a breakdown in professionalism. The phenomenon is not unheard of; during the Indochina conflict the Johnson and Nixon administrations were targets of similar intelligence leaks. But in general we expect more discipline in these matters from the CIA than from, say, the State Department, and it is healthier for the republic if this expectation is lived up to. Many of the press reports over Iraq were misleading. The CIA's supposed prediction of a postwar insurgency, for example, was a speculation at the tail end of a long report and not even mentioned in the "key judgments" at the front of the paper. Overall, some of the CIA's prewar analysis turned out to be right, but much of it turned out to be wrong (including on the stocks of WMD and the reliability of the Iraqi police). Their judgments in this regard were not strikingly better than others'.

The main issue for us here is that politicization of our intelligence professionals is a serious matter for the longer term. Politicization can come from either of two directions—from the leadership of an administration, or from an impulse to oppose the leadership of an administration. The latter is no more desirable than the former. Future presidents of whatever party will come to regret the bureaucratic indiscipline, even if it has been indulged lately in some quarters because partisan temptations were too hard to resist. When it happens, it is not only the political leadership of an administration that suffers. It is decidedly unhealthy for the intelligence professionals to expose themselves to such political pressures; they risk losing credibility if they let themselves be drawn into positions of policy advocacy. In December 2007, for example, the unclassified summary was published of an NIE that asserted that Iran had

halted its nuclear weapons program—a conclusion that undercut the administration's policy of mobilizing international pressure on Iran. The published summary was clumsily drafted and misleading. The resulting furor engulfed not only the Bush administration's policy-makers; the CIA was bombarded by accusations that it had crossed the line between intelligence analysis and attempts to change policies it didn't like.

The "Surge"

A final example of Bush policy-making in Iraq is the process that led to the president's announcement on January 10, 2007, that he was temporarily increasing the U.S. commitment in Iraq by five brigades (more than twenty thousand troops), in what was dubbed a "surge" of forces. I was part of the interagency team that was called together in the fall of 2006 to review Iraq strategy. It was a successful process, which produced a clear-cut course of action that led in turn to a strategic improvement on the ground in Iraq. Yet the process reflected all the paradoxes of George W. Bush's leadership. His own instinct was decidedly better than that of his principal advisers. He understood that his existing strategy was not succeeding; he opted for a show of additional American strength in Iraq rather than for an elegant retreat as many in our national debate were urging upon him. In these judgments he was both correct and courageous—he was the "calcium in the backbone," as he aspired to be. Yet he did not want to impose such a decision on his subordinates; he wanted it to emerge as the recommendation of his senior advisers, especially the military. The reluctance of the U.S. military to make such a recommendation forced Bush into what was for him an unusual assertiveness that extracted, if not imposed, what he wanted. The complex process took four months.

Bush and his closest colleagues in the White House came to the conclusion in the late summer of 2006 that the Iraq strategy was not working. The political progress evidenced by the series of successful Iraqi elections in 2005 had not translated into a stable and unified government, and the terrorist bombing of the Shi'a Golden Mosque in Samarra in February 2006 had let loose a vicious spiral of sectarian killing, especially in Baghdad. Despite the growing clamor to begin withdrawals, Bush sensed, on the contrary, that security in Iraq needed bolstering. Some outside critics had long been calling for troop increases. In September, Bush asked national security adviser Stephen

Hadley to begin rethinking the strategy, and at the beginning of October Hadley asked his senior NSC defense staffer, William Luti (a former colleague of Feith and me in Rumsfeld's Pentagon), to prepare a briefing on the military direction the United States should take. A week later, Luti produced a paper outlining the concept and mission for a surge of forces. In mid-November, Hadley's deputy J. D. Crouch (another former colleague from the Pentagon) called together a Deputies-level group from key agencies, announcing that the president wanted a new approach in Iraq and that he hoped for a unified recommendation from all his advisers. Only after a few weeks of inconclusive discussion did Crouch ask agencies to offer up concrete proposals reflecting their individual preferences. State's paper suggested the beginning of a military disengagement from major cities, leaving it to the Iraqis to suppress the sectarian violence. (Even the Joint Staff considered that unrealistic.) With more wisdom, the State paper also foresaw that more political progress might be made among the feuding Iraqi communities at the local or provincial level than at the national level, where political accommodation was deadlocked.

The Department of Defense, however, was suffering its own internal deadlock. General George Casey, commander on the ground, firmly resisted any suggestion of additional troops; he argued that they would only prolong Iraqi dependency and the image of the United States as an "occupier." Chairman of the Joint Chiefs General Peter Pace and General John Abizaid (Franks's successor at Central Command) supported Casey. I told Rumsfeld that based on my conversations with NSC staffers I believed the president wanted the Defense Department to put the surge on the table as an option. Rumsfeld was torn. Given the worldwide strains on the U.S. Army and Marines, the military's preference was to limit itself to the existing strategy of training and equipping the Iraqi forces so that U.S. forces could "transition out." That approach, however, had made strategic sense only before Samarra, when the Iraqi political process had seemed to be succeeding. The Samarra bombing, and the unprecedented blow it struck to Iraqi political cohesion, had created a new strategic situation that called for a reimposition of U.S. military power to suppress the sectarian violence—which was the precondition for any hope of recovery of the political process.

The interagency negotiation gradually produced the outline of a potential bargain: State and other agencies made a maximum commitment to deploy their civilian personnel in greater numbers—a "civilian

surge" to match the military one—and all sides acknowledged that an improvement in security could not be sustained unless the Iraqis made political progress. These were the Pentagon's desiderata. But even then, the military made no commitments. An outside political figure who supported a troop surge asked Hadley in mid-November if the president would support it; Hadley's answer was: yes, but only if the military recommended it. As the Pentagon continued to drag its feet, the president encouraged Hadley to step up his quiet lobbying. Hadley called in General Pace and handed him Luti's paper; Crouch and Luti lobbied the Joint Staff representatives on the interagency group. The president stepped up his own lobbying, but still by indirection. In a December 13 meeting with his generals at the Pentagon, he told them: "What I want to hear from you is how we're going to win, not how we're going to leave."

The new secretary of defense–designate, Robert Gates, told the president he supported a surge. But the problem remained of how to bring along the military. On this, Rumsfeld did the president one last service. He continued to work with General Pace on a paper setting forth a unified Defense Department position; the memo was painstakingly massaged over seventeen drafts by Rumsfeld, Pace, the Joint Staff, and my office. Before departing the Pentagon, Rumsfeld approved it and sent it to the White House. Buried in the four-and-a-half-page paper was the suggestion that a surge of military resources might be useful if in support of clearly defined objectives and if accompanied by a surge in political, economic, and other efforts by the civilian side of the U.S. government.

PERHAPS PROFESSOR NEUSTADT would see Bush's indirect approach as a good example of a president exercising his "power to persuade." Bush told a journalist that he wanted to be "thoughtful and sensitive" in his handling of the military. Probably he had absorbed the conventional conservative wisdom about Lyndon Johnson and the Vietnam War, namely that presidents should not micromanage military operations. But on matters of strategy the commander in chief need not be so shy. As scholar Eliot Cohen has shown in his classic study, *Supreme Command*, strategic judgment and direction often come only from the political leadership, and successful war leaders have provided it—such as Lincoln, or Churchill. In this book, for example, we have taken note of Roosevelt's assertion of command over the North African campaign and of Nixon's in Cambodia.

In fairness to Bush in this instance, he had boxed himself in polit-

ically. Amidst all the deterioration in Iraq during 2006 he had taken public refuge in his reliance on what his generals were advising him; it was
bound to be difficult to shift course so explicitly and be seen suddenly
overruling them. If the generals he relied upon wanted to come home,
why was he sending more troops? But the complex process also
reflected his natural management style as we have seen in many other
areas. As Hadley told an NSC staffer after the president's decision, "It
had to come from the military."

In the summer and fall of 2006, as Bush gave the first indications of a
shift of course, he seems also to have made his decision to relieve Donald Rumsfeld. After three years, Rumsfeld was held accountable for the
failures of strategy—for the failure of the generals to respond effectively
to the growing insurgency, for their persistence in a strategy that wasn't
working. Rumsfeld—so much criticized for imperiously imposing his
will on the uniformed military in the Pentagon—ironically paid the
price for being excessively deferential to the commanders in the field.
As he did with respect to many of Bremer's decisions, Rumsfeld repeatedly told aides he was reluctant to second-guess his field commanders.
Quite possibly he shared the military's not-so-hidden desire to extricate
itself from Iraq, to leave "nation-building" behind, and yearned to get on
with "transformation" for the long term. In any case, for the president,
who was focused on the strategic necessity of succeeding in Iraq, it
must have been acutely painful to dismiss the cabinet officer in whom
he had seemed to repose the greatest trust. When Bush announced, on
November 8, 2006, that Rumsfeld was being replaced, the phrase "loyal
to his president" featured conspicuously in his words of praise.

"Decider" or "Dissident"?

In 2007, Bush made the surprising comment to an Egyptian pro-
democracy activist that he, too, often felt like a "dissident" in Washington. His bureaucracy, he said, was not responsive to his policy of
promoting democracy. "Bureaucracy in the United States does not help
change." As we have seen in this book, Bush was not the only president in
the modern era who believed his government to be unresponsive to his
wishes. Like Jimmy Carter during the Iran crisis, Bush came face-to-face
with the reality that execution of policy is in the hands of the permanent
government. A president needs not only the "power to persuade" but also
a variety of political tools to reinforce his powers of persuasion—political

appointees in the departments who are attuned to his wishes, and cabinet officers for whom the presidential agenda is the top priority.

Bush had problems with both the State Department and the Defense Department, but the problems were of different natures. In a conservative administration, State under Colin Powell often seemed the outlier. When Condoleezza Rice took over the State Department in the second term, this was thought to solve the problem; she had been more attuned than anyone else to Bush's thinking. On the strategic initiative toward India, for example, State suddenly moved decisively in the direction the president had presumably always wanted to go; the agreement with India on nuclear cooperation was reached early in her tenure in 2005. On Iran as well, State's policy under Rice seemed to some observers tougher than it had been under Powell, as she unveiled increasing support for democratic opposition groups in Iran.

Over time, however, the role of the career service reasserted itself in the department, and State's policy drifted in that direction. Especially with the departure of Rumsfeld, the balance of forces in the administration as a whole shifted in the State Department's direction. Hadley often acted as Rice's partner—perhaps analogous to Scowcroft's role in covering Kissinger's flanks in the Ford administration. Yet, unlike Gerald Ford, Bush 43 (if the North Korea case is an example) seemed ambivalent about the policy results.

The problem at the Pentagon was different. Here the issue was not a philosophical disconnect but a failure to deliver results. I will leave the specific debates on troop levels, strategy, and so on to the historians, but the president ultimately reached his own conclusions and held Rumsfeld accountable. The 2007 surge represented an assertion of Bush's personal leadership.

Bush followed it up in 2008, as another debate occurred in the administration over how fast to reduce U.S. troops in the wake of the apparent success of the surge. Rumsfeld's successor, Robert Gates, won plaudits for his more congenial style with Congress as well as the military. Initially Gates sided with those in the Pentagon who wanted U.S. troop reductions to continue in the second half of 2008—withdrawing not only the increment associated with the surge but as many as five additional brigades. This was responsive to those in the Pentagon concerned about the stress on the overall force and those in Congress eager to withdraw. The president, however, sided with General David Petraeus, Casey's successor as commander on the ground in Iraq, who

wanted to stabilize force levels in the second half of 2008 to consolidate the gains that had been made. Unlike Melvin Laird during the Vietnam War, Gates deftly shifted to support the president once the president (again) made his wishes clearly known.

FROM MY VANTAGE POINT, the iconic figure in the Bush administration was not Dick Cheney, the Darth Vader caricature, but Stephen Hadley, the pursuer of bureaucratic consensus. That consensus was Rice's goal, as well, as chair of many Principals meetings, but Hadley—the calm, careful lawyer, the judicious and always even-tempered referee—epitomized it to me in the many Deputies meetings that I saw him chair in the first term, and then as Rice's successor. The model of good governance that they both sought to follow—clearly at the president's instruction—was noble in intent. But as Ronald Reagan discovered, the pursuit of bureaucratic compromise can be a fool's errand. Bush, like Reagan, was often surprisingly diffident about imposing his will. It was puzzling above all because Bush, in meetings where I saw him, was focused, determined, and well versed in the issues—more so than my recollection of Reagan in a number of such meetings.

Bush I believe was attempting to follow a management model from the business world, delegating to senior subordinates and relying on their judgment. But there are large differences between a president's situation and a CEO's. In a typical corporation, a CEO's senior subordinates have a more acute sense of whom they answer to; certainly there are nothing like the centrifugal forces that pull on a cabinet secretary—the congressional and media pressures, the institutional cultures and biases, the career professionals' knowledge that they will be there for the long term while their political masters are only temporary. Any president, of course, has to delegate to subordinates. But yet again we see that without the sustained strategic leadership of the president, a collegial system of management is subject to breakdown. Two kinds of problems can result, and Bush suffered from both of them. One major problem arises when there are deep disagreements among strong cabinet secretaries; these only the president can resolve. And second, even when there is consensus, it can be a lowest common denominator—a papered-over compromise that conceals the president's real choices. This was Richard Nixon's insight. It was not an accident that Bush's surge of forces in Iraq—the decision that may prove to save his legacy—did not originate in any bureaucratic consensus.

CHAPTER TEN

Lessons Learned

L IMITS ON THE POWER OF THE PRESIDENT, it is worth reminding
ourselves, are built into our constitutional structure. While the
framers, I believe, intended the president to have a significant degree of
flexibility in the conduct of foreign affairs and as commander in chief, I
doubt they would be surprised to learn of the centrifugal forces at work
on the presidency in the contemporary period. Justice Louis Brandeis
famously said of the doctrine of separation of powers that it was
adopted "not to promote efficiency, but to preclude the exercise of arbitrary power." Richard Neustadt, reaffirming in 1990 his conviction that
the modern president was a weak (rather than an "imperial") office, hastened to add that "most of the time, he is supposed to be weak. And in
the normal course, getting what he wants is supposed to be hard. Those
actually are attributes of constitutional government in the United
States."

If the issue before us is limitation of the power of government,
however, there is another perspective that should concern us today.
The growth of the modern bureaucratic state has posed a particular
problem—namely, how to insure the political legitimacy and political
control of its actions. Governance is impossible without the modern
state, but who is in charge of it? How does a president insure that decisions he makes are implemented? Democratic societies are not the only
ones wrestling with this question. Indeed, it has been one of the most
fundamental challenges to the philosophy of government in the modern
era. The Communists thought they had the solution: They had a parallel institution—the party—to impose political direction on the state
institutions. What they discovered, however, was that the party became
a bureaucracy of its own, losing its revolutionary purity, weighed down

by inertia and corruption. The Communists then thought they had the answer to that problem, too—the permanent purge, cracking the dictator's whip on the party itself. Mao Zedong's murderous "Cultural Revolution" in the late 1960s and early 1970s can be understood as a desperate and horrific lashing out to prevent what he saw as the descent of the party he founded into bourgeois mediocrity, led by bureaucrats seduced by the temptations of "the capitalist road."

Free societies are in the fortunate position that they have methods available to them that are not only less repugnant but also more effective. Americans may be the most fortunate in that our constitutional structure may be better equipped than some other democracies for insuring political direction of the administrative machinery. The system of presidential appointments and congressional oversight may be better able to exert such control than parliamentary systems, with their "fusion" of the executive and legislative branches and the greater power of the civil service. But all the democracies benefit from the most important feature of all: Political legitimacy in our societies is not bestowed in perpetuity by history or anyone else on a privileged group or institution. Legitimacy is instead a renewable resource, a source of authority bestowed—or withdrawn—by the people at regular intervals.

Our professional diplomats, uniformed military, and intelligence officers are the backbone of our national security institutions. They are the executors of policy, the institutional memory, the repository of experience, and the fount of expertise. As these words are being written, many of them are putting their lives on the line in distant theaters on behalf of national policies. To say that they deserve our admiration and gratitude is an understatement. Duty and professionalism are the standards of their performance. In the back of our minds, perhaps, there is a technocratic model of government in which these professionals should be left to go about their business uncorrupted by politics or even by policy influence from elected or appointed officials who may have their own philosophy or objectives in the matter. But in truth, this is the wrong model. The political process that is the ultimate determinant of national policy is not a corruption; it is the source of legitimacy. The abolition of politics is a mirage, and a dangerous one. There are differences of view about national policies; that's the point. How the choices get made is the essence of the matter. "The truth," British scholar Bernard Crick has written, "is that there is nothing, in this world at least, above politics. Politics is freedom."

The technocratic model is the source of some of the controversies that bedeviled George W. Bush's administration. One major controversy, for example, concerned alleged White House politicization of the role of U.S. attorneys, the appointment of U.S. attorneys having always been a matter of presidential discretion. Whatever the merits of White House conduct in that affair, the awkward and sensitive position of the Justice Department has been the subject of many debates since Watergate, with a perceived tension between the president's role as chief law enforcement officer and the department's role as guardian of the integrity of the law. (We saw this tension in the Panama case.) Jimmy Carter even proposed during his 1976 campaign that the independence of the Justice Department be insured by giving the attorney general a term of office not coterminous with the president's—virtually removing him from the president's cabinet. After his inauguration, Carter's attorney general Griffin Bell (who had suggested the idea) regretfully reported to Carter that Justice Department lawyers had concluded the idea was unconstitutional: Since it is the president's duty to "take care that the laws be faithfully executed" (Article II, section 3), the attorney general has to be answerable to the president.

In an earlier chapter we saw CIA director William Colby come to the conclusion that the CIA even though its founding statute places it firmly under the president—was more than ever beholden to Congress, particularly in a political climate in which a weakened presidency was being attacked for past abuses. A later director, Robert Gates, wrote of the CIA as "involuntarily equidistant" between the two branches. It should not be surprising that the controversies surrounding George W. Bush—who was accused of politicizing intelligence analysis in connection with the 2003 Iraq War—have stimulated more of the same. Retired intelligence officer Paul Pillar, writing in 2006, took this idea to its logical conclusion, proposing that the CIA become an independent agency, separated from presidential control—modeled after the Federal Reserve, a "quasi-autonomous body overseen by a board of governors with long fixed terms."

There are many practical problems with such a proposal. Even if intelligence analysis were made independent to avoid risk of politicization, what about covert action? The trend of all intelligence reforms since the 1960s and 1970s has been to strengthen presidential accountability for intelligence operations, not to dilute it. Would we have to separate operations and analysis in order to achieve more autonomy for the

latter—when another trend of recent decades has been to try to integrate them more closely?

But the problems with such proposals are not merely practical; they go to the heart of our notion of government. Again, the concept is wrong. I know of no political system in which intelligence is not part of the executive function, with respect to collection, analysis, and covert action. Precisely because of its sensitivity, it should remain part of the accountable structure of government—reporting to an accountable, elected president, subject to reasonable procedures of congressional (and judicial) oversight. The controversies over intelligence in the Iraq War were thoroughly investigated by the Senate Intelligence Committee and by an independent bipartisan commission. But separating these functions from policy supervision would only diffuse responsibility, as well as rendering them less responsive to the policy-makers who *ought* to be the ones giving them guidance as to their priorities, weighing the risks of their activities, and taking responsibility for the results.

Accountability is what presidents provide. Their ability to give effective policy direction to their government is the other side of the coin of that accountability. This book has explored how they can most effectively provide that policy direction.

Broad Lessons

I do not hide my unapologetic support for presidential authority in the Executive Branch. One of the main reasons is the principle just stated—of democratic legitimacy and accountability. But on the practical level, where the requirement is coherence of policy, the preceding chapters of this book should have provided more than enough examples of the price that is paid for its absence. In a turbulent world, the U.S. government—and therefore the president—needs to get ahead of events and shape them; this puts a premium on bold, timely, purposeful, and consistent policy-making. This includes the faithful implementation of policies as the president has decided them. These qualities are not the natural product of bureaucracies operating without strong political direction. The policy machinery will simply not work without effective presidential control over it.

The differences among the presidents we have discussed are striking, yet there are threads running through their experiences, and broad lessons to be drawn from each.

Richard Nixon represents one paradigm. His White House–centered system produced what was probably the most centralized, consistent, and strategically coherent policy-making of any modern presidency (China, Soviet Union, Vietnam)—but it came at the price of demoralization and alienation of the rest of the government. The exclusionary style of his management is not a model to be emulated. Yet his White House–centered NSC structure has essentially been followed by most of his successors. Nixon was also a president who jealously guarded his right to decide, because he insisted on knowing what his real choices were and he abhorred being presented with bureaucratic compromises. Nixon, more than Truman or Bush 43, deserves the title of the "decider."

Gerald Ford tried hard to avoid what were seen as the flaws of Nixon—he sought to restore cabinet responsibility and a collegial style of deliberation. But his collegial system failed because he never gained political control over the forces tearing his administration apart (particularly over policy toward the Soviet Union). The authority of the presidency was under assault, and his party was undergoing a revolution. Ford's aspiration to collegiality did not avail when his personal political strength and the strength of the presidency as an institution were in question.

Jimmy Carter set up a system to insure that he heard different points of view—from his conservative national security adviser Zbigniew Brzezinski and his liberal secretary of state Cyrus Vance. Carter (like Nixon) wanted to be able to decide, and thereby to be in control. This made sense in the abstract, on an organization chart, but Carter's system also reflected a philosophical confusion at the very top: What kind of a president is it who is so unsure from one day to the next whether his foreign policy should be conservative or liberal? The lack of intellectual consistency impaired Carter's ability to impose consistent political direction on a recalcitrant bureaucracy, which (as in the crisis over the shah) remained in control of the levers of policy execution.

Ronald Reagan's has to be regarded as one of the most significant presidencies of recent history. But it is also an object lesson in the need for consistent hands-on policy management. On many crucial issues—especially Soviet policy—Reagan imposed his will. On issues on which he was less engaged (Central America, Lebanon), however, his government was often rudderless; in such cases he hoped for a consensus of his advisers. Where consensus was unattainable, conflicts persisted.

Thus Reagan's attempt at collegiality, too, turned out at times to be a formula for policy incoherence.

George Bush 41 was, from a management point of view, more successful. His cabinet was a cabinet of heavyweights; its collegial operation was a function of strong direction from a president who was deeply engaged, thoroughly knowledgeable in the substance of policy, and comfortable imposing his will. Nor was he shy about commanding his generals (as in Panama and the Gulf War). If there were limits to his historical legacy, they were not the product of faulty procedures.

Bill Clinton was elected at a moment in history when domestic and economic issues seemed to dominate and to supplant traditional security challenges. Yet he was confronted by such challenges regardless— as will all future presidents. Conflicts festered not only in his bureaucracy but in the world, until crises forced themselves upon him. Through trial and error Clinton learned the importance of presidential focus, more disciplined procedures, and a willingness to spend political capital.

The travails of George Bush 43 present a number of paradoxes. The problem was not to be found in conspiratorial "cabals" run by the vice president's office but in a systemic failure to manage conflicts among his advisers. A president capable of great decisiveness adhered paradoxically to a management model that elevated the principle of deference to top subordinates. As with Reagan, Bush and his White House team strove hard for interdepartmental consensus, and where consensus was not to be had, the result was often protracted bureaucratic deadlock. Bush's chosen system of management impeded his exertion of presidential will and his ability to control dissension in his government.

Specific Lessons

There are a number of more specific lessons that can be learned from this historical experience. The first group relates to issues of procedure. A second group involves issues of structure. A third group deals with issues of personality.

Presidential Engagement. The most obvious thread running through the accounts of several of the recent presidencies is the lesson that where presidents did not engage personally, consistently, and forcefully, they often lost control. We saw this especially in the cases of Ronald

Reagan, Bill Clinton, and George W. Bush. These three men could not have been more different from one another, and yet, for different reasons, they sought to delegate to subordinates and rely on them in circumstances that, on occasion, rendered this a disability. With Reagan, the reasons probably had to do with age and a laid-back temperament. Bill Clinton could never be accused of an allergy to detail—he was hailed (or mocked) as an arch "policy wonk"—but in foreign affairs his problem was a lack of focus. With George W. Bush it seems to have been a CEO management model. All three had their successes when they did impose their will—Reagan on broad policy toward the Soviet Union; Clinton on Russia; Bush on the surge in Iraq. But when they hung back, for whatever reason, their administrations fell prey to feuding among senior subordinates and/or the problem of departments and agencies unresponsive to presidential wishes (Reagan in Lebanon; Clinton's early policy in Japan, China, and Bosnia; Bush in North Korea and Iraq).

There is no structure or policy-making procedure that can fix these problems. The National Security Council mechanism—the council, the subcommittees, the NSC staff—remains a flexible instrument that successive presidents have used in different ways. Bush 43 used the formal NSC procedures extensively for consultation; Bill Clinton much less so. But both leaders suffered from the similar problem that no structure can substitute for a president's sustained and credible engagement. The word "credible" is important here because it is the key to empowering a subordinate to act in the president's name. If the boss is thought not to care all that much about an issue, even an energetic subordinate will find his or her ability to act in the president's name undercut. This applies to a cabinet secretary as much as it does to a White House adviser: Nobody elected *them*. Thus, a vicious circle arises—feuds will not be resolved; delegation will not be effective. Credible presidential backing of a subordinate—as Nixon and Ford provided for Henry Kissinger, or Reagan (for the most part) for George Shultz, or Bush 41 for James Baker—makes delegation possible. Bill Clinton did this ad hoc (and not usually for his secretary of state).

Much, of course, depends on the quality of a president's team (more about that later). But whether the subordinates are weak or strong, presidential authority needs to be asserted. Weak subordinates will only shift the onus of making and enforcing hard decisions back onto the

president; strong subordinates need even more to be under presidential control.

The Mirage of Bureaucratic Consensus. Chairman Mao used to write long essays on the issue of how to handle "contradictions." But it is not only Marxist-Leninists who are forced to confront the dialectics of policy conflict. Contradictions will always exist in an administration, given the big-tent diversity of American political parties, the exuberance of campaign promises, the institutional interests of different parts of the government, congressional and media pressures, interest groups, and so on. Another dimension of the imperative of presidential engagement is to face up to this. Yet many of our recent presidents seem to have yearned for their subordinates to resolve as many conflicts as possible before presenting the remaining differences to the president to resolve. To a certain degree, this is inevitable and desirable. A president cannot possibly be immersed in every issue without risking total exhaustion, and subordinates owe it to the boss to save him for the toughest and most important decisions. That is what any decision-making process should aim to do. But if there is no consensus on an important issue, pushing the departments and agencies to negotiate a compromise outcome can be an abdication.

For Richard Nixon, being presented with the real choices was the key to his authority and the raison d'être of his policy-making procedures. Shaping the national strategy was, in his view, his job. Other chief executives of the recent past, however, seem to have identified good governance with the fostering of bureaucratic consensus, as a matter of principle. This, too, is the wrong model. On key issues of policy, the president ought to be made aware of the options and the arguments, pro and con. Then it is up to him (or her) to decide; there is no compelling reason for a president to shun this duty within the limits of time and physical capacity. Bureaucratic consensus is often purchased at a high cost in terms of policy sharpness or coherence; bold ideas usually won't survive, and the results may well be anemic compromises. On the other hand, when the president has settled the basic issues—strategy, objectives, and policy direction—it makes sense to delegate to subordinates (say, the Principals Committee) to work out by consensus the program of steps to implement what the president has decided. This the president can be informed of, and bless, but that can be where the line

is drawn between what needs to be decided at the very top and what can be delegated to others.

More serious risks can come from a president's trying to split the difference between sharply opposing positions. On many issues of domestic policy, and even in formulating U.S. positions in a prolonged negotiation, seeking compromise by splitting the difference can be a convenient method of buying bureaucratic peace. This is far from ideal, but probably the foreign government we are negotiating with is formulating policy in the same clumsy way. This can work sometimes, but as Reagan found in Lebanon, there will be cases—most importantly in the management of a crisis—where the price paid in policy incoherence is too high. These are times when splitting the difference is a false option and a president may have to choose between positions that are not reconcilable.

Often a president just has to overrule somebody (or everybody), even if it is unpleasant. A president will be judged by the efficacy of his policies, not by the smoothness of his bureaucratic procedures—by whether American policies have shaped world events according to American purposes, not by whether there is perfect morale inside the government. Boldness and coherence tend not to emerge from bureaucratic compromises; they are what a president is required to supply.

End Runs. When there is no bureaucratic consensus, and the process is deadlocked, the process becomes especially susceptible to end runs. Our judicial system is allergic to what lawyers call ex parte communications—roughly translated as contacts with a judge on behalf of one party, either without the knowledge of the opposing party or without giving the opposing party the opportunity to answer. The bureaucratic equivalent is an end run by one cabinet secretary into the Oval Office to try to get the president's approval of something behind the back of a cabinet rival who disagrees. Most White House national security advisers see it as their job to head off such maneuvers. As we have seen, victories won by end runs can be notoriously short-lived—in part because their legitimacy is usually not accepted by others.

The principle against ex parte communication is a valid one. The Eisenhower precept cited in the last chapter—the value of hearing one's advisers debate together in person—has considerable merit. Problems arise, however, if one attempts to apply the edict against ex parte communication too literally. Private time with the president is, in fact, essential for a cabinet secretary as a means of getting authoritative guid-

ance and insuring harmony with the president's views. Secretaries of state and defense, even intelligence chiefs, should have such opportunities. Whether it's Henry Kissinger with Gerald Ford, or Colin Powell with George W. Bush, it's a good thing. Meanwhile the national security adviser and NSC staffers, for their part, are having conversations with individual colleagues in the bureaucracy every hour of the day. If the principle were taken to an extreme, every meeting would have to be a mass meeting and every phone call a conference call. The proper standard, rather, is to achieve a reasonable transparency in these separate dealings so that departments know the state of play in any deliberation and always have a fair chance to make their case. But this standard exists, it is worth pointing out, not merely for the edification of the cabinet departments but for the benefit of the president. As Eisenhower's precept implies, it is a way to insure that the president knows every argument, and its counterargument, before making a decision.

Leaks and How to Read Them. Unauthorized and/or tendentious disclosures to the media, as we have seen, are a favorite instrument of bureaucratic warfare. In a country with a First Amendment and no Official Secrets Act, they are here to stay. But all presidents deplore them. Walt Rostow, Lyndon Johnson's national security adviser, delicately described the sense of betrayal that a president can feel, which in LBJ's case often led to volcanic eruptions of temper:

> Presidents assume that their task is not easy and that a good deal of frustration is to be expected from the American political process and an intractable and volatile world. But leaks to the press from their own subordinates, usually inaccurate but complicating inherently difficult business, appear one more burden than their oath of office really required.

There is an art to reading leaks in the press. Even those inside the government—perhaps especially those inside the government—read these leaks avidly, not so much to learn new substantive information as to monitor the course of the bureaucratic wars being waged by extrabureaucratic means. For the outsider, it is usually more difficult to tell who is winning, or even to understand what kind of blow is being struck. Often the most interesting part of the story—the leaker's real motive—is not being told. The careful reader will need to ask: If one

part of the government is criticizing another, is there a larger bureaucratic battle of which this story is a part? What seems to be the leaker's purpose? What seems to be the other side of the story, which so frustrates the leaker, and which the journalist may not always give a voice to? There is always more than one side to the debate. The reader should also be wary of leaks complaining about improper procedures—more often than not, the story is really that the leaking side got overruled and is now trying to mobilize pressures to get a decision reversed, or slowed down in implementation. The aggrieved party would probably have had no problem with irregular procedures if the decision had gone the other way (as in the North Korea example in the previous chapter).

This brings us back to our topic, which is the Oval Office perspective. A leak in the morning papers can be a source of important intelligence for a president about his own government: Who is playing by the rules and who is not? Who is stirring up pressure against the White House? If the leak is from one department against another, what are its implications for the president? Aside from the embarrassment of having dirty interagency linen aired in public, it could also be an instance of what Gerald Ford spoke about to Kissinger—a rebellion against the president for a decision he has made, or is about to make, and an attempt to mobilize public or congressional pressures against him. Even if the president's name is not mentioned, the leak could be—or quickly become—part of a bigger controversy. The president and his White House advisers are thus likely to draw their own conclusions from leaks, which are not always those intended by those doing the leaking. Bureaucrats need to be reminded that the president is watching.

Secretary of State and National Security Adviser. On this issue of policy-making structure, I have stated my conclusions in the early chapters. Richard Nixon in his first term, and Jimmy Carter, were frustrated by the State Department's lack of responsiveness to presidential direction in important areas of policy. Both presidents therefore relied on their national security advisers not only for advice but to attempt to wrest control over policy execution. Zbigniew Brzezinski in his memoir recommended expanding the role and power of the national security adviser for this purpose. Henry Kissinger, having become secretary of state and thereby having seen it from both perspectives, put forward a different proposition: If the president has no confidence in his secretary of state, he should replace the secretary of state with someone he has

confidence in, rather than attempt to bypass the State Department by creating an alternative machinery in the White House.

The Kissinger-Brzezinski phenomenon in the 1970s began a long period of fascination with the national security adviser and the role of the NSC staff. Based on recent decades of experience, however, the best model in my view is one in which the pivotal figure in the system is a strong and loyal secretary of state. But "strong" and "loyal" have a particular meaning. They mean a secretary of state who is trusted by the president to carry out policies in harmony with the president's wishes, and who sees himself or herself as the president's agent in the department, not the spokesman of the department in the president's cabinet. It is likely to mean resisting, rather than absorbing, the views and inclinations of the career service.

John Kennedy, Richard Nixon, and Jimmy Carter paid a price for choosing a weak figure as secretary of state in the expectation that this would enhance their own dominance of the system. On the contrary, it only added to the centrifugal tendencies of the department and compounded the president's problem of a department that was unresponsive to his preferences. As presidential scholar Stephen Hess has pointed out, no president need fear being overshadowed by a cabinet officer: "Cabinet members cannot successfully compete with a President, regardless of their past standing." Bill Clinton may have chosen a weak secretary of state for another reason—to keep foreign policy on the back burner—but this, too, backfired, in that it contributed to policy weaknesses that eventually led to crises.

A crucial and difficult question arises about presidential appointments in cabinet departments below the level of secretary. McGeorge Bundy, who as we saw was fervently of the view that cabinet secretaries must be loyal agents of the president, also believed that those secretaries ought to be allowed to choose their own subordinates. Since they are accountable to the president, they should be left to choose the staffs that they feel best enable them to do their jobs. Bundy saw little value in what he ridiculed as the "oh-so-skillful insertion of a President's man into the second or third level of a department" (as Kennedy had done at State at the end of 1961).

My own view is different, for two reasons. One is that the appointments power is a major tool of presidential control that I do not believe a president can or should trade away. The dictum "personnel is policy" has too much truth in it, in my experience. Using this tool was one of

Reagan's strengths. If there are individuals whom the president values for sharing his policy philosophy, then there should be a place for some of them in the departments that are in charge of implementation of his decisions. Second, the institutional strength of the career service normally requires more than one individual at the top, no matter how forceful a personage, to provide direction to it. Kissingers are rare. A cabinet nominee ought to welcome the prospect of bringing in other outsiders to help him assert control over the operations of the department. Indeed it has been suggested that this ought to be part of the definition of presidential control. If a cabinet nominee, conversely, views presidential appointees as potential adversaries rather than allies, then a problem lurks not far beneath the surface that will erupt sooner or later between the department and the White House.

While I am arguing here for a model that rests on the foundation of a strong secretary of state, an effective national security adviser remains indispensable—to arm the president for the policy engagement that is required; to insure that the bureaucratic process provides what the president needs; to help protect presidential interests. The security adviser is the guardian of the president's independence of judgment, and is also in a position to provide a strategic overview over the whole of national security policy. The Brent Scowcroft model (especially in his second incarnation, with Bush 41) was a model not only because of Scowcroft's reputation for fairness but for his being a strong right arm for a president who had no intention of being dominated by anybody. Scowcroft had important influence under Bush—not as a substitute for a weak secretary of state but as an instrument for presidential control of a strong secretary of state.

The role of the NSC staff, similarly, is to arm the president—to monitor what is going on in the government; to generate ideas for presidential initiatives; to provide the president with the wherewithal to make decisions and conduct diplomacy. In the previous chapter I noted the peculiar practice of George W. Bush's NSC staff of crafting long papers trying to capture the state of the bureaucratic consensus; these papers were offered up at interagency meetings, presumably to be blessed as a reflection of the consensus and then forwarded to the president for his endorsement. In the Nixon administration, by contrast, the more important role of the NSC staff was to craft memoranda to the president setting forth issues, options, and pros and cons to enable the president to decide things.

Should the NSC staff never have an "operational" role? I would answer as follows. The Nixon-Kissinger model of executing all the most important policies (China, Vietnam, Soviet Union) from the White House, bypassing State, is a nonstarter in any normal conditions. Resort to it in that period was the product of exceptional circumstances; while it achieved important results, a price was paid for it. One is reminded of the television ads for high-performance automobiles, which show hair-pin turns and other death-defying maneuvers, followed by a message on the screen: "Drivers are professionals. Do not attempt yourself." In normal times the most efficient system is to treat the implementation of policy as the province of the departments and agencies that, in fact, have their hands on the instruments of execution. Policy direction then needs to be insured by other means.

But no one is in a position to dictate to a president that he or she may not use a trusted adviser for a confidential or other mission. The precedent for that is ample, stretching back over a century. Normally the principle of transparency ought to govern at the top levels of the administration, so that the use of NSC personnel becomes merely a tactical question in the framework of a well-understood policy. So long as presidents are frustrated by the performance of their departments, however—which seems to be a recurring phenomenon—the temptation will be there to rely on the trusted adviser whose office is just down the hall. Not only Nixon but Carter felt that temptation. Dean Acheson conceded this point many years ago.

A word here about the Principals Committee. This innovation has lasted through three administrations, at this writing (Bush 41, Bill Clinton, and Bush 43). We have seen that it operated differently in each case, and future presidents will want to look at it carefully and at how it would fit their needs. It should (as in Bush 41) be a way of enhancing the president's role, not substituting for it or reducing it (which is one interpretation of how it worked under Clinton). And it needs to be managed in so transparent a manner by the national security adviser that cabinet secretaries do not worry that it is a screen behind which the national security adviser is exerting influence in unpredictable ways (a problem in Bush 43). The best cure for this, again, is the confidence that the main issues will be argued out in front of the president or that the president will, in other ways, have complete knowledge of everyone's views before deciding.

Institutional Reform. The concern expressed above about the performance of cabinet departments brings us to a larger structural issue that future presidents should take hold of—the project of reforming the interagency system. Sometimes it goes by the name of "a Goldwater-Nichols Act for the interagency process." Concretely, this involves building up the capacity of, particularly, the civilian departments of the government to carry out functions—postwar stabilization and reconstruction, for example—that have in recent years been left to the Department of Defense. More broadly it would mean that departments would cede some of their turf in the name of presidential flexibility, just as our individual armed services have given up much of their parochialism in the name of joint planning and operations. The result would be that in some instances the president could give State the lead; in other instances, Defense. From a presidential perspective, the benefit is to widen the range of tools and options available, as well as improve overall performance. Reforms of this kind will require reforms in executive-legislative relations as well, since much of the inflexibility built into today's system is the result of thirty-five years of legislation rigidly controlling Executive Branch programs and limiting presidential discretion.

Reform of the State Department is a related subject. A more capable State Department would affect the equation of our discussion—strengthening the department's traditional claim to interagency leadership, clarifying the answers to many of the questions raised earlier about the proper balance of forces in the government. Various reform proposals have been put forward by bipartisan commissions and think tanks. Some would involve a radical restructuring of the department's organization; others are more modest. The hope is not only to improve State's operational performance, but also to lay claim to greater support from a Congress whose chronic underfunding of State has created a vicious circle: The deprivation of funds only weakens the department further. One of the other lessons of recent history is that strong secretaries of state who enjoy the confidence of the president have managed to restore the department to a position of leadership in the government. This does not diminish, however, the desirability of improving the department's effectiveness by internal reforms.

A broader reform agenda could also be undertaken. Most of our national security institutions in the U.S. government—as well as international organizations—are the legacy of the Cold War era and might well stand in need of revision for a new era. This applies to U.S. institu-

tions relating to public diplomacy, for example; they have not yet responded effectively to the urgent needs of the ideological struggle against violent Islamist extremism (in part because current law is weighted toward insulating them from U.S. policy objectives instead of helping advance them). Likewise international institutions like the United Nations, World Bank, and International Monetary Fund—all created in the mid-1940s—may need significant revisions to respond adequately to the very different political and economic conditions of a new century.

Civil-Military Relations. The U.S. military, we have seen, is also a career service whose bureaucratic role can be expected to reflect institutional interests like any other. But recent years have put unusual stresses on civil-military relations. First, as writers like Thomas Ricks have pointed out, there may be a worrisome and growing cultural divide between a more liberal, permissive society and a military community that still predominantly adheres to traditional values of self-discipline and patriotism; an all-volunteer military caste could drift further toward a regrettable isolation from the society as a whole. Second, the stresses of the Afghanistan and Iraq campaigns have reopened sensitive questions about the propriety (or duty, as some believe) of military personnel speaking out against national policies. A small number of retired generals, for example, called out publicly for the firing of Donald Rumsfeld in the spring of 2006—some with the implication of prompting their colleagues still on active duty to stand up more boldly against policy decisions they considered unwise. Both these problems raise profound issues that may loom larger in the years ahead, whichever party is in office.

Personalities. A final word about personalities. A president, staffing an administration, needs to look at more than paper qualifications. It is remarkable that John Kennedy picked Dean Rusk as secretary of state without knowing him. So much depends on personalities—the energy level of the cabinet officer; the compatibility of cabinet officer and president; the degree to which presidents have confidence in their subordinates' personal and policy loyalty. The tension between James Schlesinger and Gerald Ford was considerably exacerbated by personal styles. The president's dilemma is that so little can be predicted. On the face of it, from congressional experience and intellectual mastery of the subject matter, Les Aspin should have been a great secretary of defense.

A president always has the option of firing someone who turns out to be ineffective or disloyal. Richard Nixon and Ronald Reagan, however, were personally reluctant to fire people. Gerald Ford was less so, but he found out how risky it can be. Interestingly, prime ministers seem to have more flexibility to reshuffle their cabinets; it is accepted as a regular practice, and it gives prime ministers a mechanism both to weed out poor performers and to strengthen their own political dominance. (Of course, the civil service is there as a cushion when reshuffles take place at the top of departments.) But presidents, who put a whole new administration in place when they arrive, are not expected to be doing too much of this; it looks like sloppiness if they do. Ford thought he was straightening things out in his administration by a grand reshuffle; it went badly. As a result, most presidents endure silently for long periods before pulling the plug, if they do so at all. But a price is paid.

Presidents who enter office with a background in foreign policy will have the most options in selecting their cabinet. They need not be afraid of choosing strong personalities, either as White House adviser or cabinet secretary. As we have seen, they only benefit from it. Nixon (with Kissinger) and Bush 41 (with Baker and Scowcroft) are in this category; their own unusual experience and extensive exposure to the subject matter insured their self-confidence and their leadership, and their key subordinates were attuned to their desires. Ford, too, was unafraid to be surrounded by strong figures in his cabinet; he was undone by larger political forces beyond his control.

But a president who is less a master of foreign policy when coming into office, or who chooses not to engage systematically, can count on having difficulties. The system will then be inherently vulnerable to many of the problems we have traced in this book. Choosing weak cabinet secretaries, or secretaries who become spokesmen for their institutions, is in this circumstance likely to foster inertia and unresponsiveness. This was Jimmy Carter's and Bill Clinton's problem. Ronald Reagan had a stronger cabinet, and he imposed his will on matters he cared about, such as the competition with the Soviet Union. But on issues like Lebanon he remained aloof and tolerated debilitating conflicts in the government. A president who chooses—for whatever reason—not to sustain a dominant role in policy formulation would, on balance, as I have argued, be better off with strong cabinet officers. But such a president would also need to exercise special care in choosing cabinet officers who can be counted on to hew faithfully to presidential

desires. (National security advisers in that environment would have their work cut out for them.)

Thus, the decisive factor in how national security policy-making works is not what kind of procedure, or what kind of structure, but what kind of people. And the American system depends to a breathtaking degree on the qualities of the one person in charge. The growth of a national security bureaucracy, and of coordinating mechanisms like the NSC system, was meant to help the president. That they have done, but they have also created a new dimension of challenges; the large modern machinery of government may be harder than ever to control. For those who care about national security policy, therefore, the key question turns out to be: not what we should look for in a policy-making process, but what we should look for in a president.

ACKNOWLEDGMENTS

For the opportunity to write this book I owe a special debt to Strobe Talbott and the Trustees of the Brookings Institution, who invited me to join them on my departure from government service in 2007. Strobe and I disagree often on issues of public policy, but his loyal friendship over three and a half decades has reflected a graciousness and warmth of spirit that are tragically rare in Washington and therefore particularly precious. My new colleagues at Brookings have reflected a similar spirit.

For financial support at Brookings I am very much indebted, first, to the Stephen and Barbara Friedman Endowed Fellowship. The Smith Richardson Foundation stepped in with a specific grant in support of this project: My special thanks go to Dr. Marin Strmecki, Senior Vice President and Director of Programs, whose advice and support have meant so much in the past. Significant additional support for my other work at Brookings is coming from the Starr Foundation, under the able chairmanship of Maurice R. (Hank) Greenberg, for which I am deeply grateful.

A number of individuals took upon themselves the burden of reading the entire manuscript and offering advice. These include Strobe Talbott, Henry Kissinger, Stephen Hess, and Aaron Friedberg. They also include William G. Hyland, a dear friend and former colleague who tragically passed away in 2008 but left me his characteristic legacy of pungent as well as wise comments on the text, which took on a special poignancy (and persuasiveness) after his loss. A number of other colleagues read portions of the text, including James Cannon, Robert Hormats, Nicholas Rostow, John O'Sullivan, Douglas Feith, and William Luti. I benefited also from numerous conversations with a variety of individuals in sensitive positions in several administrations whose candor to me in private should not have to come at the risk of any personal embarrassment to them. Therefore I have chosen not to list them by name. And much of the content of this book comes, of course, from my own observation.

Heather Messera was an exceptionally talented senior research assistant. Intrepid in exploring, discovering, and organizing material, as well as offering good editorial judgment, Heather also—being young—was able to assure that my labors did not evaporate into the computer ether when I pushed a wrong button. A truly indispensable service.

My editor at Alfred A. Knopf, the brilliant Andrew Miller, was a constant source of astute and fair-minded advice on substantive content as well as presentation. It

was a pleasure to talk over the issues with him and to work with him. To my agent, Andrew Wylie, the best in the business, I owe a special debt for the birth of this project. Having seen many negotiators at work, I was duly awed by the opportunity to see him in action.

The special friendship of Henry and Nancy Kissinger, which stretches back over four decades, now goes far deeper than what I can adequately describe here or any where else. I touch briefly upon some of my debt to Henry in the Author's Note, but I cannot omit to repeat it here.

My wife, Véronique, to whom this book is dedicated, also read portions of the manuscript. Never shy in her thoughts, she was an incisive and unfailing source of good advice. I am grateful to her for that, and needless to say, much, much more.

The usual disclaimer must be repeated here. The opinions and conclusions in this book are not the responsibility of any of the aforementioned (or anonymous) individuals or institutions but are solely mine.

NOTES

Presidential speeches, news conferences, and other documents are readily available in several official compilations. The same is true of most statements by secretaries of state. I have done my best to identify such source documents by date and title to aid the reader.

AUTHOR'S NOTE

xi Others have written excellent accounts: See especially David J. Rothkopf, *Running the World: The Inside Story of the National Security Council and the Architects of American Power* (New York: Public Affairs, 2005); the many products of Ivo H. Daalder and I. M. Destler's National Security Council Project, sponsored by the Center for International and Security Studies at Maryland and the Brookings Institution, including a forthcoming book entitled *In the Shadow of the Oval Office* (New York: Simon & Schuster, 2009); Amy B. Zegart, *Flawed by Design: The Evolution of the CIA, JCS, and NSC* (Stanford: Stanford University Press, 1999); and Karl F. Inderfurth and Loch K. Johnson, *Fateful Decisions: Inside the National Security Council* (New York: Oxford University Press, 2004).

CHAPTER ONE: BUREAUCRACY, DEMOCRACY, AND LEGITIMACY

3 The story is apocryphal, but it well captures: See the number of episodes that approximate it in Doris Kearns Goodwin, *Team of Rivals: The Political Genius of Abraham Lincoln* (New York: Simon & Schuster, 2005), e.g., pp. 288–89, 464, 482, 669.

4 "Rather, it created": Richard E. Neustadt, *Presidential Power: The Politics of Leadership* (New York: John Wiley & Sons, 1960), p. 33.

5 "'He'll sit here'": Ibid., pp. 9–10 (emphasis in original).

5 felt compelled to go out of his way to debunk the notion of the "imperial presidency": Richard E. Neustadt, *Presidential Power: The Politics of Leadership from FDR to Carter*, rev. ed. (New York: John Wiley & Sons, 1980), pp. 279–80n.46.

5 As late as 1990 . . . Neustadt was still preoccupied: Richard E. Neustadt, *Presidential Power and the Modern Presidents: The Politics of Leadership from Roosevelt to Reagan*, rev. ed. (New York: Free Press, 1990), p. ix.

6 The president's authority over the civilian establishment: Harvey C. Mansfield, "Reorganizing the Federal Executive Branch: The Limits of Institutionalization," *Law and Contemporary Problems*, vol. 35, no. 3 (Summer 1970), p. 462.

6 The renowned constitutional scholar: Edward S. Corwin, *The President: Office and Powers, 1787–1957*, 4th rev. ed. (New York: New York University Press, 1957), p. 3ff.

6 "nearly complete fusion": Walter Bagehot, *The English Constitution* (Introduction by R. H. S. Crossman) (London: Collins/Fontana Library, 1963), p. 65.

6 the theory of the cabinet's collective responsibility: Ibid., pp. 21–22 (Crossman), 67–69 (Bagehot).

6 many would argue that prime ministerial government: Ibid., pp. 51–53 (Crossman).

6 When Winston Churchill assumed office: John Lukacs, *Five Days in London: May 1940* (New Haven: Yale University Press, 1999).

6 John Quincy Adams: Sen. William Pitt Fessenden (Republican of Maine) told Gideon Welles, Lincoln's secretary of the navy, in 1862, that he had heard Adams discuss the episode on the floor of the House. Gideon Welles, *Diary*, Vol. 1 (Boston: Houghton Mifflin, 1911), p. 197. See also Goodwin, *Team of Rivals*, p. 491.

7 he adamantly refused to consider: Robert V. Remini, *John Quincy Adams* (New York: Times Books, 2002), pp. 76–77, 101, 110.

7 Reagan and Ford permitted: Ronald Reagan, *An American Life* (New York: Pocket, 1990), pp. 215–16; Michael K. Deaver with Mickey Herskowitz, *Behind the Scenes* (New York: William Morrow, 1987), pp. 92–96; Walter Isaacson, *Kissinger: A Biography* (New York: Simon & Schuster, 1992), pp. 717–20.

8 three thousand so-called political appointments: This is the current number used by Paul C. Light of New York University, the foremost expert on the federal bureaucracy. It includes about seven hundred to nine hundred Senate-confirmed senior officials, six hundred to eight hundred members of the Senior Executive Service subject to noncompetitive appointment, and 1,600–1,800 "Schedule C" or "political" appointments exempted from the competitive service because of confidential or policy determining duties. It excludes ambassadors, U.S. marshals and U.S. attorneys, advisory boards and commissions, and a variety of less central positions that, if included, would double or triple the total number. Communications to the author from Paul C. Light, May 9 and October 5, 2007.

9 two television series produced by the BBC: See, in book form, Jonathan Lynn and Antony Jay, *The Complete Yes Minister: Diaries of a Cabinet Minister, by the Right Hon. James Hacker MP* (London: BBC Books, 1989); and Jonathan Lynn and Antony Jay, *The Complete Yes Prime Minister: The Diaries of the Right Hon. James Hacker* (London: BBC Books, 1989).

9 "He'll be house-trained": Lynn and Jay, *Yes Minister*, p. 21.

9 "The PM must realize": Lynn and Jay, *Yes Prime Minister*, p. 165.

10 the "generalist" tradition of rotating civil servants: Eugene B. McGregor, Jr., "Politics and the Career Mobility of Bureaucrats," *American Political Science Review*, vol. 68 (March 1974), pp. 18–26.

10 "We only see them": Ehrlichman quoted in Richard P. Nathan, *The Plot That Failed: Nixon and the Administrative Presidency* (New York: John Wiley & Sons, 1975), p. 40.

10 "bubble up" from lower levels: Zbigniew Brzezinski and Samuel P. Huntington, *Political Power: USA/USSR* (New York: Penguin, 1977), pp. 207–8. They quote

Dean Acheson, "Thoughts About Thought in High Places," *New York Times Magazine,* October 11, 1959, p. 20ff.

10 Henry Kissinger in his memoirs: Henry Kissinger, *White House Years* (Boston: Little, Brown, 1979), p. 39.

11 a cabinet secretary has a strategic choice to make: Ibid., pp. 24–25. Kissinger cites Michel Crozier, *The Bureaucratic Phenomenon* (Chicago: University of Chicago Press, 1964), pp. 44–55, 187–98.

11 Theodore Sorensen, in a public lecture: Theodore C. Sorensen, *Decision-Making in the White House: The Olive Branch or the Arrows* (New York: Columbia University Press, 1963), p. 68.

11 Bundy . . . was more scathing: McGeorge Bundy, *The Strength of Government* (Cambridge: Harvard University Press, 1968), pp. 37–39.

12 "The members of the Cabinet": Neustadt, *Presidential Power,* 1960 ed., p. 39.

12 "A foreign policy achievement": Henry Kissinger, *Years of Upheaval* (Boston: Little, Brown, 1982), p. 434. See also Kissinger, *White House Years,* p. 30.

13 "energy in the Executive": Alexander Hamilton, "The Federalist No. 70," in *The Federalist* (Introduction by Edward Mead Earle) (New York: Modern Library, n.d.), p. 454.

13 "A President is not bound to conform": Alexander Hamilton, "The Public Conduct and Character of John Adams, Esq., President of the United States" (1800), in Henry Cabot Lodge, ed., *The Works of Alexander Hamilton,* Federal Edition, Vol. 7 (New York: G. P. Putnam's Sons, 1904).

14 Hamilton contrasted Adams: Ibid.

CHAPTER TWO: THE MODERN SETTING

15 "to advise the President": National Security Act of 1947, Public Law 253, 80th Congress (61 Stat. 495), section 101 (a).

16 a bipartisan insight shared by the Truman administration and Congress: Amy B. Zegart, *Flawed by Design: The Evolution of the CIA, JCS, and NSC* (Stanford: Stanford University Press, 1999), pp. 54–57.

16 "administrative chaos" of the Roosevelt era: Alfred D. Sander, "Truman and the National Security Council: 1945–1947," *Journal of American History,* vol. 59 (September 1972), p. 369.

16 "obtaining and collating for the use of the Cabinet": Arthur J. Marder, *From the Dreadnought to Scapa Flow: The Royal Navy in the Fisher Era, 1904–1919,* Vol. I: *The Road to War, 1904–1914* (London: Oxford University Press, 1961), pp. 341–44. On the American view of the CID, see Sen. Henry M. Jackson, ed., *The National Security Council: Jackson Subcommittee Papers on Policy-Making at the Presidential Level* (New York: Frederick A. Praeger, 1965), pp. 102–3 (testimony of Adm. Sidney Souers, May 10, 1960) and p. 247 (testimony of Don K. Price, August 17, 1961).

16 The United States, in contrast: Ernest R. May, "The Development of Political-Military Consultation in the United States," *Political Science Quarterly,* vol. 70 (June 1955), in Karl F. Inderfurth and Loch K. Johnson, *Fateful Decisions: Inside the National Security Council* (New York: Oxford University Press, 2004), pp. 8–9, 11–12; Mark M. Lowenthal, *The National Security Council: Organizational History,* Report No. 78-104 F (Library of Congress/Congressional Research Service, June 27, 1978), pp. 4–7.

16 FDR's improvisational management style: Arthur M. Schlesinger, Jr., *The Age of Roosevelt*, vol. 2: *The Coming of the New Deal* (Boston: Houghton Mifflin, 1958), pp. 520–22.

16 "You know I am a juggler": Henry M. Morgenthau, Jr., Presidential Diary, May 15, 1942, Morgenthau Papers, Franklin D. Roosevelt Library, quoted in William Doyle, *Inside the Oval Office: The White House Tapes from FDR to Clinton* (New York: Kodansha International, 1999), p. 19.

16 Secretary of State Hull was virtually excluded: Dean Acheson, *Present at the Creation: My Years in the State Department* (New York: W. W. Norton, 1969), pp. 87–88.

16 The 1942 landing in North Africa: Brig. Gen. Charles F. Brower, "The Commander-in-Chief and TORCH," lecture at the Franklin D. Roosevelt Presidential Library on the 60th anniversary of Operation Torch, November 12, 2002, at http://www.fdrlibrary.marist.edu/cbtorch.html.

17 The State-War-Navy Coordinating Committee: May, "The Development of Political-Military Consultation," p. 13.

17 had begun holding weekly meetings: Office of the Historian, Department of State, *History of the National Security Council, 1947–1997* (August 1997), p. 2 (at http://www.whitehouse.gov/nsc/text/history.html).

17 Truman . . . praised the work of the SWNCC: Harry S. Truman, *Memoirs*, vol. 2: *Years of Trial and Hope* (Garden City, N.Y.: Doubleday, 1956), p. 58.

17 Some of them became advocates of the new council: Inderfurth and Johnson, *Fateful Decisions*, pp. 17–20; Paul Y. Hammond, *Organizing for Defense: The American Military Establishment in the Twentieth Century* (Princeton: Princeton University Press, 1961), pp. 210–13; and Zegart, *Flawed by Design*, pp. 64–66.

18 Some of Truman's staff are on record as strongly suspecting: Anna Kasten Nelson, "President Truman and the Evolution of the National Security Council," *Journal of American History*, vol. 72 (September 1985), pp. 361 (citing interview with Elmer Staats) and 366 (citing interview with James B. Webb); Sander, "Truman and the National Security Council," pp. 378–79.

18 Key bureau officials alerted: Sander, "Truman and the National Security Council," pp. 378–79.

18 Truman understood fully: Truman, *Years of Trial and Hope*, p. 60.

19 At least one historian has wondered: Sander, "Truman and the National Security Council," p. 380.

19 Marshall . . . did see many of these implications: Michael J. Hogan, *A Cross of Iron: Harry S. Truman and the Origins of the National Security State, 1945–1954* (Cambridge, UK: Cambridge University Press, 1998), pp. 56–57; Nelson, "President Truman and the Evolution of the National Security Council," p. 363; Hammond, *Organizing for Defense*, p. 222; Rothkopf, *Running the World.*, pp. 55–56.

19 the State Department's Policy Planning Staff: Nelson, "President Truman and the Evolution of the National Security Council," pp. 369–70.

20 "The situation we got into": Jackson, *The National Security Council*, pp. 250–51 (testimony of Don K. Price, August 17, 1961).

20 "abdicated its primacy": Ibid., p. 251.

21 At the NSC's very first meeting: Walter Millis, ed., *The Forrestal Diaries* (New York: Viking, 1951), p. 320; Nelson, "President Truman and the Evolution of the National Security Council," p. 366.

21 "I used the National Security Council": Truman, *Years of Trial and Hope*, p. 59.

21 he tended to deal with them directly: Office of the Historian, Department of State, *History of the National Security Council*, pp. 3–4.

21 When the Korean War began: James S. Lay, Jr. and Robert H. Johnson, *Organizational History of the National Security Council During the Truman and Eisenhower Administrations*, August 1960, Study Submitted to the Committee on Government Operations, United States Senate, by Its Subcommittee on National Policy Machinery, Committee Print, 86th Cong., 2nd Sess., 1960, pp. 17–18.

22 "Every President in our history": Truman, *Years of Trial and Hope*, p. 165.

22 THE BUCK STOPS HERE: Doyle, *Inside the Oval Office*, pp. 55, 351n.

22 Truman "loved to make decisions": Neustadt, *Presidential Power*, 1960 ed., pp. 172, 178.

22 "He likes things to run smoothly": "Mr. Truman After Five Years: Sizing Up His Faults and Merits," *U.S. News & World Report*, April 14, 1950, pp. 13, 14, 17; see sources collected in Doyle, *Inside the Oval Office*, pp. 60–62.

23 "I have an unhappy conviction": Acheson, *Present at the Creation*, pp. 466–68; other sources in Doyle, *Inside the Oval Office*, pp. 62–65.

23 "groupthink," or an object lesson in Peter Drucker's maxim: Irving L. Janis, *Victims of Groupthink: A Psychological Study of Foreign Policy Decisions and Fiascoes* (Boston: Houghton Mifflin, 1972), p. 60; Peter F. Drucker, *Management: Tasks, Responsibilities, Practices* (New York: Harper & Row, 1974), p. 472, quoted in Doyle, *Inside the Oval Office*, pp. 64–65.

23 Acheson had the same view: Acheson, *Present at the Creation*, p. 733.

23 In the Vietnam case fifteen years later: E.g., Leslie H. Gelb with Richard K. Betts, *The Irony of Vietnam: The System Worked* (Washington, D.C.: Brookings, 1979).

24 Truman, he jibed, "didn't know any more": Doyle, *Inside the Oval Office*, p. 82.

24 "Organization cannot make a genius": Dwight Eisenhower, *Mandate for Change: The White House Years 1953–1956* (Garden City, N.Y.: Doubleday, 1963), p. 114.

24 "Having chosen his Cabinet and staff": Richard M. Nixon, *Six Crises* (Garden City, N. Y.: Doubleday, 1962), p. 140.

24 Eisenhower institutionalized the NSC process: Office of the Historian, Department of State, *History of the National Security Council*, p. 5; Fred I. Greenstein, *The Hidden-Hand Presidency: Eisenhower as Leader* (New York: Basic Books, 1982), p. 124.

24 One pungent example: Merle Miller, *Plain Speaking: An Oral Biography of Harry S. Truman* (New York: Berkley, 1973, 1974), pp. 343–44.

25 "I said to him": Ibid., p. 344.

25 a revisionist view of Eisenhower began to appear: Murray Kempton, "The Underestimation of Dwight D. Eisenhower," *Esquire*, September 1967, p. 108ff.; Garry Wills, *Nixon Agonistes: The Crisis of the Self-Made Man* (Boston: Houghton Mifflin, 1970), esp. Part I, Chapter 6.

25 Nixon recounted among his "six crises": Nixon, *Six Crises*, pp. 73–129, 158–67.

25 "a far more complex and devious man": Ibid., p. 161.

26 "Not shackled to a one-track mind": Ibid.

26 " 'Don't worry, Jim' ": Eisenhower, *Mandate for Change*, p. 478. A fuller account of the episode, and of the news conference, is in Greenstein, *The Hidden-Hand Presidency*, pp. 68–70.

26 A full-blown revisionist assessment: Greenstein, *The Hidden-Hand Presidency*, pp. 5, 31, 36, 57.

27 "In fact, Eisenhower was actively in command": Office of the Historian, Department of State, *History of the National Security Council.*, p. 6.

27 "Eisenhower took personal charge": Doyle, *Inside the Oval Office*, p. 87.

27 The recently published transcript: Ibid., p. 88.

28 Allen Dulles sent a message via his station chief: Chester L. Cooper, *The Lion's Last Roar: Suez, 1956* (New York: Harper & Row, 1978), p 181.

28 After the crisis was over, a bedridden Foster Dulles: Selwyn Lloyd, *Suez 1956. A Personal Account* (New York: Mayflower, 1978), pp. 219, 257–58; Christian Pineau, *1956 Suez* (Paris: Laffont, 1976), p. 195.

28 Eisenhower told at least two interlocutors: During the 1967 Middle East crisis, Eisenhower spoke in this vein both to Richard Nixon and to Israeli ambassador Avraham Harman. See Richard Nixon, "My Debt to Macmillan," *The Times* (London), January 28, 1987, p. 16; and author's communication in 1992 with Israeli diplomat Ephraim Evron, who was Harman's deputy chief of mission and was debriefed by Harman after his visit to Eisenhower in Gettysburg before the 1967 war. See sources collected in Peter W. Rodman, *More Precious than Peace: The Cold War and the Struggle for the Third World* (New York: Scribner's, 1994), pp. 84–86, and p. 560 nn.73–78.

29 Astute observers: I. M. Destler, Leslie H. Gelb, and Anthony Lake, *Our Own Worst Enemy: The Unmaking of American Foreign Policy* (New York: Simon & Schuster, 1984), e.g., pp. 179–85.

29 "[o]ccasionally, in the past, I think": President Kennedy, Transcript of Interview for British Television, April 19, 1961.

29 "The Eisenhower concept was": Charles Bartlett, *Chattanooga Times*, early February 1961, quoted in Bromley K. Smith, *Organizational History of the National Security Council During the Kennedy and Johnson Administrations*, monograph written for the National Security Council, September 1988, p. 15.

30 "The parochialism of experts and department heads": Sorensen, *Decision-Making in the White House*, p. 70.

30 The NSC met as a body less often. McGeorge Bundy, "The National Security Council in the 1960's," letter to Sen. Henry M. Jackson, September 4, 1961, in Jackson, *The National Security Council*, pp. 276–78.

30 "essentially a Presidential instrument": Ibid., p. 278; Office of the Historian, Department of State, *History of the National Security Council*, pp. 7–8.

30 Bundy was praised as scrupulously fair: Office of the Historian, Department of State, *History of the National Security Council*, p. 8; Inderfurth and Johnson, *Fateful Decisions*, p. 66.

31 "The first lesson was never": Arthur M. Schlesinger, Jr., *A Thousand Days: John F. Kennedy in the White House* (London: Andre Deutsch, 1965), p. 268.

31 "[T]he White House–NSC group has gradually encouraged": Memorandum for President Kennedy, "Current Organization of the White House and NSC for Dealing with International Matters," June 22, 1961, in *Foreign Relations of the United States, 1961–1963*, Vol. 8: National Security Policy (Washington: Government Printing Office, 1996), Document 31, pp. 107–8.

31 "[t]he State Department has not proved to be as effective": McGeorge Bundy, memorandum to the President in response to John McCone's report of Eisenhower criticism, mid-November 1962, quoted in Bromley Smith, *Organizational History of the National Security Council*, p. 49.

31 A "bowl of jelly": Theodore C. Sorensen, "The President and the Secretary of State," *Foreign Affairs,* vol. 66, no. 2 (Winter 1987–1988).

31 "blood transfusion [at State]": Schlesinger, *A Thousand Days*, pp. 390, 395.

32 "sit quietly by, with his Buddha-like face": Ibid., pp. 384–86.

32 Rusk answered back: Dean Rusk with Richard Rusk and Daniel S. Papp, *As I Saw It* (New York: W. W. Norton, 1990), p. 520.

32 decisions on naval and aircraft movements: Bromley Smith, *Organizational History of the National Security Council*, p. 37.

32 "More than anything else, the Sit[uation] Room": Office of the Historian, Department of State, *History of the National Security Council*, p. 7.

33 But Bundy successfully argued against: Bromley Smith, *Organizational History of the National Security Council*, pp. 45–48.

33 "secrecy and despatch": Alexander Hamilton, "The Federalist No. 70," in *The Federalist* (Introduction by Edward Mead Earle) (New York: Modern Library, n.d.), p. 455.

34 The full extent of the compromise arrangement: For a full summary, see Jim Hershberg, "Anatomy of a Controversy: Anatoly F. Dobrynin's Meeting with Robert F. Kennedy, Saturday, 27 October 1962," Cold War International History Project (CWIHP), *Bulletin*, no. 5 (Spring 1995), pp. 75–80. See also Dobrynin's memoir, *In Confidence: Moscow's Ambassador to America's Six Cold War Presidents* (New York: Times Books, 1995), pp. 87–88. On Sorensen's admission, see Bruce J. Allyn, James G. Blight, and David A. Welch, eds., *Back to the Brink: Proceedings of the Moscow Conference on the Cuban Missile Crisis, January 27–28, 1989* (Lanham, Md.: University Press of America, 1992), pp. 92–93; and John Lewis Gaddis, *We Now Know: Rethinking Cold War History* (Oxford: Clarendon Press, 1997), pp. 271, 381n.65.

34 "Adlai wanted a Munich": The quote about Stevenson came from an unnamed official to two journalists known to be close to the president. See Stewart Alsop and Charles Bartlett, "In Time of Crisis," *Saturday Evening Post*, vol. 235, no. 44 (December 8, 1962).

34 As Walt Rostow has described it: W. W. Rostow, *The Diffusion of Power: An Essay in Recent History* (New York: Macmillan, 1972), p. 358.

35 Johnson convened some 160 Tuesday lunches: Bromley Smith, *Organizational History of the National Security Council*, p. 63; Office of the Historian, Department of State, *History of the National Security Council*, p. 9. See also Henry F. Graff, *The Tuesday Cabinet: Deliberation and Decision on Peace and War Under Lyndon B. Johnson* (Englewood Cliffs, N.J.: Prentice Hall, 1970).

35 "rather conventional and orderly": Rostow, *The Diffusion of Power,* pp. 359–60.

35 In March 1966, a presidential directive: On the SIG/IRG system, see Office of the Historian, Department of State, *Foreign Relations of the United States, 1964–1968 (FRUS)*, Vol. 33, Organization and Management of U.S. Foreign Policy; United Nations.

CHAPTER THREE: RICHARD NIXON

36 "Influence of State Department establishment": Henry Kissinger, *White House Years* (Boston: Little, Brown, 1979), p. 43.

37 "Washington is a city run primarily by Democrats": Richard Nixon, *RN: The Memoirs of Richard Nixon* (New York: Grosset & Dunlap, 1978), pp. 352, 355–56.

37 In a campaign radio address: Richard Nixon, address on CBS Radio Network, October 24, 1968, in *Nixon Speaks Out: Major Speeches and Statements by Richard M. Nixon in the Presidential Campaign of 1968* (New York: Nixon-Agnew Campaign Committee, October 1968), pp. 242–43.

37 "When Eisenhower selected Foster Dulles": Nixon, *RN*, p. 340. See also Stephen Hess, *Organizing the Presidency* (Washington, D.C.: Brookings, 1976), pp. 113–14.

38 In 1961 . . . Senator Henry Jackson's national security subcommittee: Sen. Henry M. Jackson, ed., *The National Security Council: Jackson Subcommittee Papers on Policy-Making at the Presidential Level* (New York: Frederick A. Praeger, 1965), pp. 5, 30, 39.

38 Goodpaster took Kissinger along: Kissinger, *White House Years*, pp. 42–46.

38 Goodpaster later recalled: Goodpaster quoted by David J. Rothkopf, *Running the World: The Inside Story of the National Security Council and the Architects of American Power* (New York: Public Affairs, 2005), p. 115.

39 The Kissinger memorandum: Memorandum from the President's Assistant for National Security Affairs-Designate (Kissinger) to President-Elect Nixon, "Proposal for a New National Security Council System" (Tab A of Document 1: "Memorandum on a New NSC System," December 27, 1968) in Office of the Historian, Department of State, *Foreign Relations of the United States (FRUS), 1969–1976*, Vol. 2: Organization and Management of U.S. Foreign Policy, 1969–1972, pp. 1–10. On the drafting of the memorandum, see Morton H. Halperin, "The 1969 NSC System," unpublished paper drafted for the Commission on the Organization of the Government for the Conduct of Foreign Policy (the Murphy Commission), 1974.

39 An innocuous-sounding but very pregnant "note": Kissinger Memorandum to President-Elect, December 27, 1968, in *FRUS, 1969–1976*, Vol. 2, pp. 4–5.

39 The distinguished senior diplomat: U. Alexis Johnson with Jef Olivarius McAllister, *The Right Hand of Power* (New York: Prentice Hall, 1984), pp. 513–14, cited in *FRUS, 1969–1976*, Vol. 2, Editorial Note, pp. 10–11.

40 other NSC subcommittees to be set up: The best account is Chester A. Crocker, "The Nixon-Kissinger National Security Council System, 1969–1972: A Study in Foreign Policy Management," published by the Murphy Commission (June 1975), Vol. 6, Appendix O, pp. 79–99.

40 "I do not believe that Presidential leadership": Richard Nixon, *U.S. Foreign Policy for the 1970's: A New Strategy for Peace*, a report to the Congress (The White House, February 18, 1970), Part I: The National Security Council System, p. 22.

41 "coup d'état at the Hotel Pierre": This is the title of Chapter 2 of Roger Morris, *Uncertain Greatness* (New York: Harper & Row, 1977).

41 "important less in terms": Kissinger, *White House Years*, pp. 44, 47.

41 Morton Halperin stresses that it worked that way: Halperin, "The 1969 NSC System," pp. 25, 29.

42 the record of an early meeting of the new NSC Review Group: R. J. Smith, Deputy Director for Intelligence, CIA, "Memorandum for the Record: NSC Review Group Meeting on 13 February," February 13, 1969, in *FRUS, 1969–1976*, Vol. 2, Document 27, pp. 64–65 (paragraph numbers omitted).

43 Nixon never claimed in his campaign: William Safire, *Before the Fall: An Inside View of the Pre-Watergate White House* (Garden City, N.Y.: Doubleday, 1975), p. 48.

43 Kissinger used the term "linkage": Excerpts from the Kissinger background briefing can be found in *FRUS, 1969–1976*, Vol. 1: Foundations of Foreign Policy, 1969–1972, Document 11: Editorial Note.

43 Nixon sent a letter: This discussion of "linkage" draws on Nixon, *RN*, p. 346, and Kissinger, *White House Years*, pp. 128–36.

44 In January 1969, an article written: Henry A. Kissinger, "The Viet Nam Negotiations," *Foreign Affairs* (January 1969), pp. 211–34.

45 Kissinger complained bitterly: Kissinger comments to Haldeman, March 9 and 10, 1969, in H. R. Haldeman, *The Haldeman Diaries: Inside the Nixon White House* (New York: Berkley, 1995), pp. 47–48.

45 The State Department quickly leaked: Kissinger, *White House Years*, pp. 157 and 1478n.18.

46 "Tactics turn into strategy": Kissinger comment to H. R. Haldeman, September 20, 1970, in Haldeman, *Diaries*, p. 234.

46 Kissinger called Attorney General John Mitchell: Editorial Note, in *FRUS, 1969–1976*, Vol. 2: Document 50, pp. 109–11, 115–16.

46 Kissinger met on a Saturday morning with Mitchell: Memorandum from the President's Military Assistant [*sic*] (Haig) to the President's Assistant for National Security Affairs (Kissinger), "Items to Discuss with the Attorney General, 2:30 p.m., Saturday, July 12, 1969," Document 63, July 12, 1969, in *FRUS, 1969–1976*, Vol. 2, pp. 135–39.

46 Nixon . . . issued a more formal directive: Telegram from President Nixon to Secretary of State Rogers, Secretary of Defense Laird, and Director of Central Intelligence Helms, Document 70, September 1, 1969, in *FRUS, 1969–1976*, Vol. 2, p. 151.

46 NSC staffers later discovered: Memorandum from W. Anthony Lake of the National Security Council Staff to the President's Assistant for National Security Affairs (Kissinger), "Relations with the State Department," November 14, 1969, Document 86, Attachment A: "The Problem and Its Consequences," in *FRUS, 1969–1976*, Vol. 2, pp. 184, 186.

47 leading Nixon to muse in a philosophical vein: Haldeman, *Diaries,* entries for October 9, 11, 13, 15, 27, 1969, pp. 116–20, 123–24.

47 Fifty foreign service officers and two hundred other officials: David E. Rosenbaum, "50 in State Dept. Chided on Letter," *New York Times*, May 21, 1970. The two hundred others included officials from the Agency for International Development and the Arms Control and Disarmament Agency, which were divisions of State.

47 Periodically, Kissinger's staff would pull together: E.g., Memorandum from the President's Military Assistant [*sic*] (Haig) to the President's Assistant for National Security Affairs (Kissinger), "Continuing Problems with State Department," Document 85, October 29, 1969, in *FRUS, 1969–1976*, Vol. 2, pp. 177–82, and a similar memo from Haig, Document 96, February 21, 1970, in ibid., pp. 213–16.

47 Losing Kissinger would be a "major loss": Haldeman, *Diaries* (Multimedia Edition), entry for September 26, 1970, quoted in Editorial Note, *FRUS, 1969–1976*, Vol. 2, p. 271. See also Haldeman, *Diaries*, entry for March 3, 1971, p. 306.

48 Nixon repeated his instruction to Haldeman: Haldeman, *Diaries,* entry for December 3, 1970, p. 256; Editorial Note, Document 129, in *FRUS, 1969–1976*,

Vol. 2, pp. 277–78, quoting the Multimedia Edition of Haldeman, *Diaries*, and other sources.

48　Nixon later became fond of quoting British statesman William Gladstone: E.g., Richard Nixon, *Leaders* (New York: Warner, 1982), pp. 334–35.

49　Elder statesman Dean Acheson commented: Dean Acheson, "The Eclipse of the State Department," *Foreign Affairs* (July 1971), p. 605.

50　Nixon . . . told Dobrynin he wanted this special channel: Kissinger, *White House Years*, p. 141; Nixon, *RN*, p. 369; Anatoly Dobrynin, *In Confidence: Moscow's Ambassador to America's Six Cold War Presidents (1962–1986)* (New York: Times Books, 1995), p. 199.

50　Nixon sent Kissinger to see Dobrynin: Kissinger, *White House Years*, p. 264.

50　Kissinger warned Dobrynin that Vietnam could become a major obstacle: Nixon, *RN*, p. 391; Kissinger, *White House Years*, pp. 267–68.

51　"Gromyko became very angry": Dobrynin, *In Confidence*, pp. 205–6.

51　A formal negotiation had begun in early 1970: Kissinger, *White House Years*, esp. pp. 805–10, 823–33.

52　Nixon had published an article: Richard Nixon, "Asia After Viet Nam," *Foreign Affairs* (October 1967).

52　one of the first of the new National Security Study Memorandums: Kissinger, *White House Years*, pp. 169–70, 178.

53　delegations of senior State Department diplomats: Ibid., pp. 189–90.

53　"We'll kill this child before it is born": Ibid.

53　In fact there were three sets of briefing books: Winston Lord comments in Ivo H. Daalder and I. M. Destler, moderators, "The Nixon Administration National Security Council," The National Security Council Project: Oral History Roundtables (Washington, D.C.: Center for International and Security Studies at Maryland/University of Maryland, and the Brookings Institution, December 8, 1998), p. 42.

55　The American ambassador to Japan: Armin Meyer, *Assignment Tokyo* (Indianapolis: Bobbs-Merrill, 1974), pp. 133–37.

55　John Lewis Gaddis has acknowledged: John Lewis Gaddis, *The Cold War* (London: Penguin, 2007), p. 172. But see his criticisms of Nixon's allegedly "compulsive" secrecy concerning military and intelligence operations of which he disapproves. Ibid., pp. 172–76.

55　Gaddis is similarly charitable: Gaddis, *The Cold War*. He quotes Nixon's defense of secrecy in *RN*, p. 390.

55　Alexander Haig, briefed Nixon by telephone: Transcript of Nixon-Haig telephone conversation, June 13, 1971, in Editorial Note, Document 154, in *FRUS, 1969–1976*, Vol. 2, p. 323.

55　Nixon and Kissinger also had a conversation that afternoon: Transcript of Nixon-Kissinger telephone conversation, June 13, 1971, 3:09 p.m. (White House Tape WHT-5, Cassette 825, Conversation 5-59), transcribed by National Security Archive.

56　A treatment of the Nixon-Kissinger relationship: Robert Dallek, *Nixon and Kissinger: Partners in Power* (New York: HarperCollins, 2007).

57　Lyndon Johnson's decisions on the Vietnam War: Leslie H. Gelb with Richard K. Betts, *The Irony of Vietnam: The System Worked* (Washington, D.C.: Brookings, 1979).

58　Internal documents show the State Department struggling: E.g., Memorandum

from the Executive Secretary of the Department of State (Theodore L. Eliot) to the Under Secretary of State (John N. Irwin),"Your Luncheon Today with Henry Kissinger," October 28, 1970, Document 127, in *FRUS, 1969–1976*, Vol. 2, p. 275.

58 Rogers would sometimes complain bitterly: E.g., Transcript of Telephone Conversation Between Secretary of State Rogers and the President's Assistant for National Security Affairs (Kissinger), September 25, 1970, and Haldeman, *Diaries,* entries for September 25, 26, and 27, 1970, Documents 123 and 124, in *FRUS, 1969–1976*, Vol. 2, pp. 267–71.

58 Haldeman had to go over to the State Department afterward: H. R. Haldeman Diary Entry, May 19, 1971, in *FRUS, 1969–1976*, Vol. 2, Document 148, pp. 310–13 (citing Multimedia Edition of Haldeman, *Diaries*).

59 the departments discovered that they could take hard-line positions: E.g., Henry Kissinger, *Years of Upheaval* (Boston: Little, Brown, 1982), p. 1017.

59 "To everyone's surprise and Nixon's immediate intense relief": Ibid., p. 422.

59 Nixon recounts in his memoirs: Nixon, *RN*, p. 339.

59 Rogers as attorney general in the Eisenhower administration: Richard M. Nixon, *Six Crises* (Garden City, N.Y.: Doubleday, 1962), passim. There is another view, held by a number of Nixon's senior aides, that Nixon felt that Rogers had condescended to him in the Eisenhower period and secretly relished subordinating Rogers now that he was president. See the views of John Ehrlichman and Elliot Richardson quoted in Walter Isaacson, *Kissinger: A Biography* (New York: Simon & Schuster, 1992), p. 196, and Kissinger, *White House Years*, p. 29.

59 "a staff man to the President on foreign policy": Editorial Note, in *FRUS, 1969–1976*, Vol. 2, Document 152, transcript of Oval Office conversation between Nixon and Haldeman, June 12, 1971, pp. 320–21.

61 Nixon mentioned to former President Eisenhower: Nixon, *RN*, p. 289.

61 "There was about him a buoyancy": Kissinger, *White House Years*, pp. 32–33.

62 Laird withdrew his formal objections: Ibid., pp. 44–45. See Memorandum from Secretary of Defense-Designate Laird to the President's Assistant for National Security Affairs-Designate (Kissinger), "Your Memorandum Dated January 3, 1969 Concerning a New NSC System," January 9, 1969, Document 6, in *FRUS, 1969–1976*, Vol. 2, pp. 22–24.

62 "all official National Security Council communications": Editorial Note, Document 16, in *FRUS, 1969–1976*, Vol. 2, p. 42.

62 intended to review, as he reported to Congress: Nixon, *U.S. Foreign Policy for the 1970's,* February 18, 1970, Part I: The National Security Council System, p. 20.

62 He signed a directive in this vein: Memorandum from President Nixon to the Chairman of the Defense Program Review Committee (Kissinger), April 2, 1970, Document 102, *FRUS, 1969–1976*, Vol. 2, p. 224.

64 Rogers and Laird were informed only a few hours before: See, e.g., Memorandum from the President's Assistant for National Security Affairs (Kissinger) to President Nixon, "Interdepartmental Meeting on Fourth Redeployment Increment from South Vietnam, 5:00 p.m., April 13," April 13, 1970, Document 228, in *FRUS, 1969–1976*, Vol. 6: Vietnam, January 1969–July 1970, p. 806; Kissinger, *White House Years*, pp. 479–81.

64 "The maneuvers of Nixon and Laird": Kissinger, *White House Years*, pp. 32–33. See also Dale Van Atta, *With Honor: Melvin Laird in War, Peace, and Politics* (Madison: University of Wisconsin Press, 2008), p. 183.

64 Nixon considered both these operations strategically necessary: Nixon, *RN*, pp. 448–50; Kissinger, *White House Years*, pp. 483–505; and the extensive documentation in *FRUS, 1969–1976*, Vol. 6, especially Documents 215–72, pp. 741–917.

65 "Nixon was determined not to stand naked": Kissinger, *White House Years*, p. 994. See also pp. 502–3.

66 Laird later regaled journalist Seymour Hersh: Seymour M. Hersh, *The Price of Power: Kissinger in the Nixon White House* (New York: Summit, 1983), pp. 207–8. See also Van Atta, *With Honor*, pp. 224, 298.

66 Laird reportedly had advance knowledge of Kissinger's secret trip: Van Atta, *With Honor*, p. 300.

66 the famous Yeoman Charles Radford: United States Congress, Senate, Committee on Armed Services, *Transmittal of Documents from the National Security Council to the Chairman of the Joint Chiefs of Staff, Hearings*, 93rd Cong., 2nd Sess., Part I (February 6, 1974), and Part 2 (February 20, 21, 1974); Hersh, *The Price of Power*, pp. 466–70.

67 Kissinger and Haig wanted Moorer fired: Nixon, *RN*, pp. 531–32; Kissinger, *Years of Upheaval*, pp. 806–9; Editorial Note, Document 164, in *FRUS, 1969–1976*, Vol. 2, pp. 334–38. Ehrlichman comments in Hersh, *The Price of Power*, Chapter 33, esp. p. 476.

67 Kissinger trusted Zumwalt: Kissinger, *White House Years*, pp. 722, 810.

67 Zumwalt . . . concluded that the secretive style: Elmo R. Zumwalt, Jr., *On Watch: A Memoir* (New York: Quadrangle, 1976), esp. Chapter 14.

67 Zumwalt disclosed with some satisfaction to JCS historians: Historical Division, Joint Secretariat, Joint Staff, *The Joint Chiefs of Staff and National Policy*, Vol. 10: 1969–1972, p. 9, quoted in Editorial Note, Document 159, in *FRUS, 1969–1976*, Vol. 2, p. 328.

67 "I had my own spies": Isaacson, *Kissinger*, p. 202.

67 In some cases their reporting was oral and informal: Conversation with an individual with direct knowledge.

67 Seymour Hersh's book on Kissinger: Hersh, *The Price of Power*, p. 569. See also pp. 583, 591, 597, 621, 630, 637.

68 David Packard peeked at Moorer's briefing book: Zumwalt, *On Watch*, p. 370.

68 Zumwalt also met frequently: Historical Division, Joint Secretariat, Joint Staff, *Joint Chiefs and National Policy*, in *FRUS, 1969–1976*, Vol. 2, p. 328.

68 he saw it as his mission: Ibid.

68 In Haig's recollection: Alexander M. Haig, Jr., with Charles McCarry, *Inner Circles: How America Changed the World: A Memoir* (New York: Warner, 1992), p. 245n.

69 Nixon as the "puppetmaster": William Safire, "Puppet as Prince," *Harper's*, March 1975.

69 The life of Richard Nixon: A good portrait of Nixon's many layers and contradictions is in Safire, *Before the Fall*, esp. pp. 97–106. See also Henry Kissinger, *Years of Renewal* (New York: Simon & Schuster, 1999), pp. 43–91.

70 "Nixon distrusted his own impulsiveness": Safire, *Before the Fall*, p. 112.

71 Safire observed: Ibid., p. 157.

71 While Kissinger appeared on the cover of *Time*: *Time*, February 14, 1969.

71 Nixon had given strict orders to that effect: Memorandum from the President's Assistant (Haldeman) to the Director of Communication for the Executive

Branch (Herbert G. Klein), March 24, 1969, Document 32, in *FRUS, 1969–1976*, Vol. 2, p. 77.

71 pre-summit trip by Kissinger to Moscow: Kissinger, *White House Years*, pp. 1135–37, 1148; Nixon, *RN*, pp. 587–88. The quote on Vietnam is from an Oval Office conversation between Nixon and Kissinger on April 19, 1972, in *FRUS, 1969–1972*, Vol. 39, *European Security*, p. 274.

72 In the fall of 1972 . . . Le Duc Tho: see Kissinger, *White House Years*, pp. 1347–52; Nixon, *RN*, pp. 691, 700–702.

73 Haig writes with some relief: Haig, *Inner Circles*, p. 345.

73 Some observers have been tempted to speak: E.g., Robert Dallek, "The Kissinger Presidency," *Vanity Fair*, May 2007, and Dallek, *Nixon and Kissinger*, Chapter 16.

74 a characteristically bold Nixon decision: Kissinger, *Years of Upheaval*, pp. 513–15; Haig, *Inner Circles*, p. 412.

74 An event often cited: Dallek, *Nixon and Kissinger*, p. 530.

74 But the truth about the Situation Room meeting is less dramatic: Haig, *Inner Circles*, pp. 415–16; Haig communications with the author, February 27 and April 16, 2008; Henry Kissinger, *Crisis: The Anatomy of Two Major Foreign Policy Crises* (New York: Simon & Schuster, 2003), p. 355.

75 When he wrote his memoirs: Kissinger, *Years of Upheaval*, pp. 432–46.

76 The legendary Arabist bias of the Foreign Service: Robert D. Kaplan, *The Arabists: The Romance of an American Elite* (New York: Free Press, 1993).

76 Another example was Nathaniel Davis: Henry Kissinger, *Years of Renewal* (New York: Simon & Schuster, 1999), pp. 800–809, 827; Nathaniel Davis, "The Angola Decision of 1975: A Personal Memoir," *Foreign Affairs* (Fall 1978).

77 "In the hands of a determined Secretary": Kissinger, *Years of Upheaval*, p. 442.

77 most of the pivotal players on his team: See the observations of Helmut Sonnenfeldt and Winston Lord in Daalder and Destler, "The Nixon Administration National Security Council," pp. 15, 55–56.

77 A conservative critic, Ambassador Laurence Silberman, has written: Laurence H. Silberman, "Toward Presidential Control of the State Department," *Foreign Affairs* (Spring 1979), pp. 888–89.

78 what scholar Graham Allison calls the "rational actor" model: Graham T. Allison, *Essence of Decision: Explaining the Cuban Missile Crisis* (Boston: Little, Brown, 1971).

78 the "madman theory": H. R. Haldeman with Joseph DiMona, *The Ends of Power* (New York: Times Books, 1978), p. 83 (emphasis in original).

78 an intriguing theory of the Watergate scandal: Nicholas von Hoffman, *Make-Believe Presidents: Illusions of Power from McKinley to Carter* (New York: Pantheon, 1978); Nicholas von Hoffman, "Unasked Questions" (review of Bob Woodward and Carl Bernstein, *The Final Days*), *New York Review of Books*, vol. 23, no. 10 (June 10, 1976).

79 Nixon saw all this as a long-overdue reform: Nixon, *RN*, pp. 761–69.

79 Nathan, in contrast, calls it a plan: Richard P. Nathan, *The Plot That Failed: Nixon and the Administrative Presidency* (New York: John Wiley & Sons, 1975). For a calmer assessment of the Nixon administration's restructuring plans, see Hess, *Organizing the Presidency*, Chapter 7.

79 But what this accomplished: Von Hoffman, "Unasked Questions." The number two thousand corresponds to what is today about three thousand.

79 Von Hoffman does not claim: Von Hoffman, *Make-Believe Presidents*, pp. 30–32.

80 The "super-secretaries" . . . proved unworkable: George P. Shultz and Kenneth W. Dam, *Economic Policy Beyond the Headlines*, 2nd ed. (Chicago: University of Chicago Press, 1998), pp. 169–70.

80 The CIA rejected White House efforts: Vernon A. Walters, *Silent Missions* (Garden City, N.Y.: Doubleday, 1978), Chapter 29.

80 "[t]he bureaucracy was fighting back in the way it always does": Von Hoffman, *Make-Believe Presidents*, p. 34.

80 Professor Neustadt agreed: Richard E. Neustadt, *Presidential Power and the Modern Presidents: The Politics of Leadership from Roosevelt to Reagan,* rev. ed. (New York: Free Press, 1990), pp. 203, 226.

81 bureaucracy *should* be independent: On the theory of the "representative bureaucracy," see the work of Norton E. Long and Peter Woll, cited sympathetically in Nathan, *The Plot That Failed*, pp. 89–90.

CHAPTER FOUR: GERALD FORD

82 the newsmagazines had gotten wind: Ron Nessen, *It Sure Looks Different from the Inside* (Chicago: Playboy Press, 1978), p. 156. Most sources refer to a *Newsweek* scoop, but my Brookings colleague Strobe Talbott, then a *Time* correspondent, assures me that *Time* was pursuing the story too.

82 Ford's conversation with Colby: Gerald R. Ford, *A Time to Heal: The Autobiography of Gerald R. Ford* (New York: Harper & Row and Reader's Digest Association, 1979), pp. 328–29. For Colby's account, see William Colby and Peter Forbath, *Honorable Men: My Life in the CIA* (New York: Simon & Schuster, 1978), pp. 8–11.

83 "[G]et that son-of-a-bitch in here": Stephen F. Hayes, *Cheney: The Untold Story of America's Most Powerful and Controversial Vice President* (New York: Harper-Collins, 2007), p. 97.

83 "There is no guile, no convolution": Scowcroft interview in William Doyle, *Inside the Oval Office: The White House Tapes from FDR to Clinton* (New York: Kodansha International, 1999), p. 201.

83 "immune to the modern politician's chameleon-like search": Henry Kissinger, *Years of Renewal* (New York: Simon & Schuster, 1999), p. 30.

83 "left the presidential presence without afterthoughts": Ibid. p. 25.

83 "With Ford, what one saw was what one got": Ibid.

84 "What I wanted in my Cabinet": Ford, *A Time to Heal*, pp. 131–32. On the quality of Ford's cabinet, see David S. Broder, "How Ford's Legacy Still Serves," *Washington Post*, December 28, 2006, p. A27.

84 "A President controls his Administration": Ford, *A Time to Heal*, p. 352.

84 "God, but he is good at this": Hugh Sidey, "Beyond the Facts and Figures," *Time*, February 2, 1976, p. 11, quoted in Doyle, *Inside the Oval Office*, p. 202.

84 Kissinger found that Ford was more interested than Nixon: Kissinger interview, ibid., p. 205.

85 "President Ford came into office with wonderful training": Rumsfeld interview, ibid., p. 220.

85 "extreme collegiality": Ibid., p. 206.

85 There would be no gatekeeper, no Haldeman: Richard B. Cheney, "Forming and Managing an Administration," in Kenneth W. Thompson, ed., *The Ford Presi-*

dency: Twenty-two Intimate Perspectives of Gerald R. Ford, Portraits of American Presidents/Vol. 7 (Lanham, Md.: University Press of America/The Miller Center, University of Virginia, 1988), p. 62.

85 The exigencies of office broke down this idyllic system: Robert T. Hartmann, *Palace Politics: An Inside Account of the Ford Years* (New York: McGraw-Hill, 1980), Chapter 12; James Cannon, *Time and Chance: Gerald Ford's Appointment with History* (New York: HarperCollins, 1994), pp. 356, 369.

85 Yet both Rumsfeld and his successor: John Osborne, *White House Watch: The Ford Years* (Washington, D.C.: New Republic Books, 1977), pp. xxxii–xxxiii.

85 "With Nixon, you had to try": Nessen, *It Sure Looks Different from the Inside*, p. 162.

85 he exulted to Kissinger that he had purchased: Henry Kissinger, *Years of Upheaval* (Boston: Little, Brown, 1982), p. 514. Nixon said something similar to Nelson Rockefeller. See James Cannon, *Time and Chance*, pp. 275–76.

86 Ford appreciated it: Ford, *A Time to Heal.*, p. 121; James Cannon, *Time and Chance*, p. 266.

86 "It would be hard for me to overstate": Ford, *A Time to Heal*, p. 129.

86 He made a good impression on the students: Kissinger, *Years of Renewal*, p. 20.

86 Ford as vice president: John Osborne, "White House Watch," *The New Republic*, April 13, 1974, quoted in James Cannon, *Time and Chance*, p. 275. For the description of it as a "late-night, highball-lubricated *Air Force Two* interview," see Thomas M. DeFrank, *Write It When I'm Gone: Remarkable Off-the-Record Conversations with Gerald R. Ford* (New York: G. P. Putnam's Sons, 2007), p. 8.

86 Brent Scowcroft took rough notes: Scowcroft's handwritten notes of these meetings were very sketchy. The typed records now in the archives should not be treated as verbatim transcripts for any purpose. His rough notes, often difficult to read, were deciphered and fleshed out somewhat by a staffer who was familiar with the subject matter but had not been present in the room (usually me) so that they would acquire some clarity and coherence, and then were typed up to be available for reference.

87 Kissinger was such a red flag to the conservatives: Nessen, *It Sure Looks Different from the Inside*, pp. 229–31, 233–34.

87 Meanwhile, I have been told by a Democratic friend: Told to me by an individual who later served in the Carter administration. See also I. M. Destler, Leslie H. Gelb, and Anthony Lake, *Our Own Worst Enemy: The Unmaking of American Foreign Policy* (New York: Simon & Schuster, 1984), p. 23.

88 Ford shot back: "Jim's fight is not with you": Kissinger, *Years of Renewal*, pp. 181–82.

89 Various memoirs attribute this idea: Hartmann, *Palace Politics*, p. 288; Nessen, *It Sure Looks Different from the Inside*, pp. 132–33.

89 Ron Nessen reports: Nessen, *It Sure Looks Different from the Inside*, p. 133.

89 One episode . . . Tulane University: Ibid., pp. 107–9; Hartmann, *Palace Politics*, pp. 321–23; Kissinger, *Years of Renewal*, pp. 534–36.

90 As Robert Hartmann writes: Hartmann, *Palace Politics*, p. 363.

90 "Goddamn it, I don't want any more of this": Nessen, *It Sure Looks Different from the Inside*, p. 162.

90 The fact was, as Ford says: Ford, *A Time to Heal*, p. 355.

90 "But he didn't seem mad": Nessen, *It Sure Looks Different from the Inside*, p. 135.

92 cooperation with France over its nuclear weapons program: See Richard H. Ullman, "The Covert French Connection," *Foreign Policy*, no. 75 (Summer 1989).

92 In the indiscreet airborne interview: Osborne, *White House Watch*, pp. 219–20 (reprinting article in *The New Republic* dated November 15, 1975).

92 that Ford himself had to repair: Ford, *A Time to Heal.*, pp. 320–21.

92 Schlesinger had instructed the Joint Chiefs: Ibid., pp. 136, 322–23; Alexander M. Haig, Jr., with Charles McCarry, *Inner Circles: How America Changed the World: A Memoir* (New York: Warner, 1992), p. 529.

93 In addition, Ford did not even think: Ford, *A Time to Heal*, pp. 323–24; Hartmann, *Palace Politics*, p. 364.

93 Ford, the most easygoing of men: Ford, *A Time to Heal*, p. 324.

93 Robert Hartmann writes: Hartmann, *Palace Politics*, pp. 364–65.

93 Bryce Harlow, the wise counselor: Ibid., p. 360.

93 Ford decided the time was ripe: Ibid., p. 364.

94 "The only way I could feel comfortable": Ford, *A Time to Heal.*, p. 326.

94 Ford has insisted convincingly: Ibid., pp. 323–28; also Rumsfeld conversation with the author, 2006. See also Ford comments to Bob Woodward in "Ford Disagreed with Bush About Invading Iraq," *Washington Post*, December 28, 2006.

94 Rockefeller withdrew his candidacy: Ford, *A Time to Heal*, pp. 327–28.

94 Meanwhile, George H. W. Bush: Kissinger, *Years of Renewal*, pp. 842–43; Hartmann, *Palace Politics*, p. 370.

95 Even the sympathetic John Osborne: Osborne, *White House Watch*, p. 217 (reprinting article in *The New Republic* dated November 15, 1975); Hartmann, *Palace Politics*, pp. 378–79; Nessen, *It Sure Looks Different from the Inside*, pp. 159–60.

95 Kissinger told Schlesinger in an awkward telephone conversation: Kissinger, *Years of Upheaval*, p. 842.

97 One week later: The "Family Jewels" compendium, with redactions, was declassified by the CIA on June 26, 2007. See www.gwu.edu/~nsarchiv/NSAEBB/NSAEBB222/family_jewels_full_ocr.pdf.

97 Schlesinger and Colby conferred and agreed: Colby, *Honorable Men*, p. 345.

97 they also sheepishly realized: Ibid., pp. 389–94.

97 In a phone conversation with Kissinger: Kissinger, *Years of Renewal*, pp. 312–13.

98 Ford himself had inadvertently generated the latter excitement: Colby, *Honorable Men*, p. 409.

98 Ford, in the vain hope: Ford, *A Time to Heal*, p. 266.

98 "to develop some criteria": Kissinger, *Years of Renewal*, p. 320.

99 Colby writes that he was "privately delighted": Colby, *Honorable Men*, p. 402.

99 More broadly, Colby considered: Ibid., p. 404.

99 Colby circumvented the order: Kissinger, *Years of Renewal*, pp. 322–23.

99 While the Church Committee had to admit: United States Senate, Select Committee to Study Governmental Operations with Respect to Intelligence Activities, *Alleged Assassination Plots Involving Foreign Leaders, Interim Report*, 94th Cong., 1st Sess. (Washington, D.C.: Government Printing Office, November 20, 1975), p. 262. The section on Schneider is pp. 225–54.

100 Even Colby deplored it: Colby, *Honorable Men*, p. 433.

100 Particularly egregious in Colby's eyes: Ibid., pp. 434–35.

100 Kissinger was furious at Colby: Ibid., p. 16.

100 In his memoirs Kissinger speculates: Kissinger, *Years of Renewal*, p. 336.

100 perjury indictment of his predecessor: Ibid., p. 343; Richard Helms with William Hood, *A Look over My Shoulder: A Life in the Central Intelligence Agency* (New York: Random House, 2003), Chapters 40, 44; Colby, *Honorable Men.*, pp. 383–87.

100 Ford shared his disappointment: Kissinger, *Years of Renewal*, p. 838.

100 Ford, in turn, treats Colby more gently: Ford, *A Time to Heal*, pp. 265–68, 329.

100 "I did not share the view that intelligence": Colby, *Honorable Men*, p. 404.

101 "totally contrary to the purpose and intent of the NSC": "A Conversation with President Ford," at a 1999 session of a John F. Kennedy Institute of Politics study group, in Aaron Lobel, ed., *Presidential Judgment: Foreign Policy Decision Making in the White House* (Hollis, N.H.: Hollis Publishing, 2000), p. 80. See also DeFrank, *Write It When I'm Gone*, pp. 90–91.

101 But over time, Ford came to the conclusion: Ford, *A Time to Heal*, pp. 325–26.

101 Kissinger . . . carrying the letter still in "draft": Ibid., p. 354; Kissinger, *Years of Renewal*, pp. 839–40, 843.

102 On reflection, Kissinger came to see: Kissinger, *Years of Renewal*, p. 839.

102 Ford later told David Rothkopf: David J. Rothkopf, *Running the World: The Inside Story of the National Security Council and the Architects of American Power* (New York: Public Affairs, 2005), p. 154.

102 Scowcroft describes his role modestly: Ibid., p. 155.

103 A widely read analysis of Kissinger's NSC staff operation: John P. Leacacos, "Kissinger's Apparat," *Foreign Policy*, no. 5 (Winter 1971–1972), p. 19.

103 George P. Shultz gives Kissinger credit: George P. Shultz and Kenneth W. Dam, *Economic Policy Beyond the Headlines*, 2nd ed. (Chicago: University of Chicago Press, 1998), pp. 12, 116.

104 As economist Fred Bergsten has put it: Bergsten quoted in Ivo H. Daalder and I. M. Destler, moderators, "International Economic Policymaking and the National Security Council," The National Security Council Project: Oral History Roundtables (Washington, D.C.: Center for International and Security Studies at Maryland/University of Maryland, and the Brookings Institution, February 11, 1999), p. 38.

105 John Connally, tried to stifle it: Shultz and Dam, *Economic Policy Beyond the Headlines*, pp. 175–76.

106 Kissinger was pulled into the EPB: Roger B. Porter, *Presidential Decision Making: The Economic Policy Board* (Cambridge, U.K.: Cambridge University Press, 1980), pp. 49–55.

106 the Kremlin outsmarted the Agriculture Department: Henry Kissinger, *White House Years* (Boston: Little, Brown, 1979), pp. 1269–73.

106 The upshot was a five-year agreement: Porter, *Presidential Decision Making*, Chapter 5; the quote about Kissinger is on p. 127.

107 "We have to find a way to break the cartel": Kissinger, *Years of Renewal*, p. 669.

107 The second element of U.S. strategy was to split the Third World: Ibid., esp. Chapter 22, as well as pp. 734–36.

108 The aggressive approach was an early test of the EPB: Porter, *Presidential Decision Making*, pp. 49–54.

108 Simon called the shah of Iran a "nut": Kissinger, *Years of Renewal*, p. 670.

110 an outside group (dubbed "Team B"): See Richard Pipes, *Vixi: Memoirs of a Non-Belonger* (New Haven: Yale University Press, 2003), pp. 132–38. See also Strobe

Talbott, *The Master of the Game: Paul Nitze and the Nuclear Peace* (New York: Alfred A. Knopf, 1988), pp. 145–47.

110 A Gallup Poll in early January 1976: Ford, *A Time to Heal*, p. 347.

111 "Under Kissinger and Ford": Quoted in ibid., pp. 373–74.

111 Michael Barone describes: Michael Barone, *Our Country: The Shaping of America from Roosevelt to Reagan* (New York: Free Press, 1990), p. 552.

112 "I cannot judge whether the political impact": Ford, *A Time to Heal*, pp. 380–81.

112 As political analyst Jonathan Martin elaborates: Jonathan Martin, "The Moderates' Last Stand: Gerald Ford and the GOP," *National Review Online* (December 28, 2006).

113 "of stunning proportions": Barone, *Our Country*, p. 533.

113 "over 100 separate prohibitions and restrictions": President Ronald Reagan, "America's Foreign Policy Challenges for the 1980's," address at the Center for Strategic and International Studies, Washington, April 6, 1984.

114 The most recent complete set comprises five volumes: U.S. House of Representatives, Committee on International Relations, and U.S. Senate, Committee on Foreign Relations, *Legislation on Foreign Relations Through 2005*, Vols. 1-A and 1-B (January 2006); *Legislation on Foreign Relations Through 2000*, Vols. 2 and 3 (May 2002); *Legislation on Foreign Relations Through 1996*, Vol. 4 (December 1997); *Legislation on Foreign Relations Through 1988*, Vol. 5 (December 1989).

115 the CIA found itself "equidistant": Robert M. Gates, "CIA and the Making of American Foreign Policy," address at the Woodrow Wilson School of Public and International Affairs, Princeton University, September 29, 1987; Robert M. Gates, "The CIA and American Foreign Policy," *Foreign Affairs* (Winter 1987–1988), p. 225.

115 Cheney said a few years later: Cheney remarks in Thompson, *The Ford Presidency*, p. 64.

115 Decades later, he called the Ford period: Cheney quoted in Kenneth T. Walsh et al., "The Cheney Factor," *U.S. News & World Report*, January 23, 2006.

116 As a young member of Congress Cheney became an outspoken champion: See the contrasting views of Congress's role expressed by Cheney and Gingrich in John Charles Daly, moderator, "Revitalizing America: What Are the Possibilities?," AEI Forum 49, December 9, 1980 (Washington, D.C.: American Enterprise Institute, 1981).

116 The same conviction clearly infused his later actions as vice president: See Hayes, *Cheney*, p. 490; Walsh et al., "The Cheney Factor."

CHAPTER FIVE: JIMMY CARTER

117 Carter in his memoirs says: Jimmy Carter, *Keeping Faith: Memoirs of a President* (New York: Bantam, 1982), pp. 51, 54.

117 In an appearance as president-elect: Carter remarks, November 1976, quoted in Karl F. Inderfurth and Loch K. Johnson, eds., *Fateful Decisions: Inside the National Security Council* (New York: Oxford University Press, 2004), p. 71.

117 Toward the end of his term: Carter, Town Hall appearance, Nashville, Tennessee, October 9, 1980.

118 he came to lament the "inertia": Carter, *Keeping Faith*, pp. 53–54.

118 He later told interviewers from the *Harvard Business Review*: Interview with Jimmy Carter, *Harvard Business Review* (March/April 1988), p. 62, quoted in

William Doyle, *Inside the Oval Office: The White House Tapes from FDR to Clinton* (New York: Kodansha International, 1999), p. 234.

118 "A flaw in our foreign policy during this period": Cyrus Vance, *Hard Choices: Critical Years in America's Foreign Policy* (New York: Simon & Schuster, 1983), p. 27.

119 But there is no doubt that Carter wanted him: Carter, *Keeping Faith,* pp. 53–54.

119 Vance recognized in retrospect: Vance, *Hard Choices*, pp. 15, 35–36.

119 Brzezinski was also given some important substantive assignments: Zbigniew Brzezinski, *Power and Principle: Memoirs of the National Security Adviser, 1977–1981* (New York: Farrar, Straus & Giroux, 1983), p. 536; Brzezinski comments in "A Forum on the Role of the National Security Adviser," co-sponsored by the Woodrow Wilson International Center for Scholars and the James A. Baker III Institute for Public Policy of Rice University, in Houston, Texas, April 12, 2001, reprinted in Inderfurth and Johnson, *Fateful Decisions*, pp. 151–52.

119 State Department officials were extremely bitter: See the account in David J. Rothkopf, *Running the World: The Inside Story of the National Security Council and the Architects of American Power* (New York: Public Affairs, 2005), pp. 187–95. Cf. Brzezinski, *Power and Principle,* Chapter 6. See also Ivo H. Daalder and I. M. Destler, moderators, "China Policy and the National Security Council," The National Security Council Project: Oral History Roundtables (Washington, D.C.: Center for International and Security Studies at Maryland/University of Maryland, and the Brookings Institution, November 4, 1999), esp. pp. 11–16.

120 In an extraordinary letter to *Foreign Affairs*: Jimmy Carter, "Being There," letter to the editor, *Foreign Affairs* (November/December 1999), pp. 164–65; see also Carter, *Keeping Faith,* p. 194, and Brzezinski, *Power and Principle,* pp. 202–6.

120 In December 1978 Carter convened a meeting: Brzezinski, *Power and Principle,* p. 41; Carter, *Keeping Faith,* pp. 59–60.

121 "Carter, quite rightly in my judgment": "The Best National Security System: A Conversation with Zbigniew Brzezinski," *The Washington Quarterly* (Winter 1982), p. 75.

121 Reading between the lines of Carter's memoirs: Carter, *Keeping Faith,* pp. 53–54.

121 Brzezinski, in turn, lamented in his diary: Brzezinski, *Power and Principle,* p. 520.

122 Brzezinski does not conceal his disappointment: Ibid., pp. 23, 525.

122 A senior Carter aide has commented to me: Conversation with former senior Carter national security aide, March 30, 2007.

122 Legend had it that the president was personally managing: Doyle, *Inside the Oval Office,* pp. 227–31.

122 Richard Neustadt was told: Richard E. Neustadt, *Presidential Power: The Politics of Leadership from FDR to Carter*, rev. ed. (New York: John Wiley & Sons, 1980), p. 208.

122 Scowcroft was astounded: Brent Scowcroft, "Ford as President and His Foreign Policy," in Kenneth W. Thompson, ed., *The Ford Presidency: Twenty-two Intimate Perspectives of Gerald R. Ford* (Lanham, Md.: University Press of America/The Miller Center, University of Virginia, 1988), p. 311.

122 "anti-political attitude used to drive me nuts": Mondale quoted in Peter G. Bourne, *Jimmy Carter: A Comprehensive Biography from Plains to Postpresidency*

(New York: Scribner, 1997), p. 419, cited in Doyle, *Inside the Oval Office*, pp. 231–32.

123 "suggestive of a President more unpolitical in some respects": Neustadt, *Presidential Power*, 1980 ed., pp. 215, 276–77n.21.

123 The National Security Council met formally only ten times: Office of the Historian, Department of State, *History of the National Security Council, 1947–1997* (August 1997), p. 12.

123 "favorite meeting of the week": Carter, *Keeping Faith*, pp. 55–56.

123 Carter resisted Brzezinski's suggestion: Brzezinski, *Power and Principle*, p. 68.

123 after an embarrassing foul-up that led to the public retraction: Ibid.; Office of the Historian, Department of State, *History of the National Security Council*, p. 12.

123 a weekly Vance-Brown-Brzezinski luncheon: Brzezinski, *Power and Principle*, p. 70; Vance, *Hard Choices*, p. 39.

123 But Vance remained forever jealous: Vance, *Hard Choices*, p. 37.

123 State Department historians also note glumly: Office of the Historian, Department of State, *History of the National Security Council*, p. 12.

124 Mondale was the first vice president to be given: See the discussion in Event Summary, "The Office of the Vice Presidency," Woodrow Wilson International Center for Scholars, April 26, 2007, at http://www.wilsoncenter.org/index.cfm?fuseaction=events.print&event_id=228842.

124 A close observer has noted the parallels between: William G. Hyland, *Mortal Rivals: Superpower Relations from Nixon to Reagan* (New York: Random House, 1987), pp. 174–75.

125 Vance favored this course: Vance, *Hard Choices*, pp. 48–49.

125 Vladivostok was dismissively branded: Hyland, *Mortal Rivals*, p. 208.

125 Carter and his team instead were attracted: Ibid., pp. 208–10; Carter, *Keeping Faith*, p. 216.

125 Soon after Carter's inauguration, the State Department: Hyland, *Mortal Rivals*, pp. 204–6; Brzezinski, *Power and Principle*, pp. 155–56.

127 William Hyland, the holdover on the NSC staff: Hyland, *Mortal Rivals*, pp. 211–12.

127 *The Washington Post* called it: Editorial, "The Retreat from Moscow," *Washington Post*, April 5, 1977, p. A18.

127 " Had the Soviets moved quickly to consolidate an agreement": Hyland, *Mortal Rivals*, p. 218. See also Vance, *Hard Choices*, p. 54.

128 The Soviets and their allies seemed to be on a roll: On the Soviet geopolitical offensive, see Peter W. Rodman, *More Precious than Peace: The Cold War and the Struggle for the Third World* (New York: Scribner's 1994), esp. pp. 147–52.

129 SALT was "buried   in the sands of the Ogaden": Brzezinski, *Power and Principle*, p. 189.

129 His "greatest regret," he admitted a few years later: "The Best National Security System: A Conversation with Zbigniew Brzezinski," p. 79.

129 a speech on the subject at the U.S. Naval Academy: Brzezinski, *Power and Principle*, pp. 320–21; Vance, *Hard Choices*, p. 102; Carter, *Keeping Faith*, p. 229.

130 Brzezinski continued to deplore: Brzezinski, *Power and Principle*, e.g., pp. 42, 520.

130 Carter was torn: Ibid., p. 522.

130 Carter saw it as an augury: Carter, *Keeping Faith.*, pp. 433–34.

130 Carter took the shah aside: Ibid., pp. 436–37.

131 As the domestic unrest within Iran grew to engulf the shah: An excellent account of the crisis is Michael Ledeen and William Lewis, *Debacle: The American Failure in Iran* (New York: Alfred A. Knopf, 1981).

132 he found U.S. policy to be "confusing and contradictory": Mohammad Reza Pahlavi, *Answer to History* (New York: Stein & Day, 1980), pp. 164, 169; Mohammad Reza Pahlavi, "How the Americans Overthrew Me," *NOW!* (London), no. 13 (December 13–17, 1979), p. 34.

132 Henry Kissinger, visiting Iran as a private citizen: This author accompanied Kissinger to Iran.

132 the shah expounded the same theory to visiting *Time* correspondents: Author's conversation with Strobe Talbott, one of the correspondents.

132 Unfortunately the head of French intelligence: Count [Alexandre] de Marenches and David A. Andelman, *The Fourth World War: Diplomacy and Espionage in the Age of Terrorism* (New York: William Morrow, 1992), p. 178.

132 And to his dying day he believed it: Pahlavi, *Answer to History,* p. 165.

132 did not crack down ruthlessly: Vance, *Hard Choices,* p. 324.

132 Brzezinski conveyed the message to him personally: Carter, *Keeping Faith,* p. 439; Brzezinski, *Power and Principle,* p. 365.

133 Carter told Vance on November 10: Carter, *Keeping Faith.,* p. 440.

133 Brzezinski later wrote: Brzezinski, *Power and Principle,* p. 368.

133 Carter continued to reject this: Carter, *Keeping Faith.,* p. 443; Ledeen and Lewis, *Debacle,* pp. 170–71.

133 "There had already been too much violence": The shah quoted in Ledeen and Lewis, *Debacle,* p. 140.

134 "Sullivan reported [that he had told the shah]": Brzezinski, *Power and Principle,* p. 375.

134 The upshot was a complicated cable: Compare ibid., p. 375, with Vance, *Hard Choices,* p. 333.

134 Brzezinski's hope was that it would do so: Brzezinski, *Power and Principle,* pp. 379–82.

135 castigated them for disloyalty and leaking: Ibid., pp. 389–90.

135 Brzezinski thought he was annoying Carter: Ibid., pp. 393, 396–97.

136 Brzezinski argued for a time, after leaving office: Ibid., pp. 533–36.

137 The Senate Foreign Relations Committee: U.S. Senate, Committee on Foreign Relations, *The National Security Adviser: Role and Accountability,* Hearing, April 17, 1980, 96th Cong., 2nd Sess. (U.S. Government Printing Office, 1980), esp. pp. 24–25 (Scowcroft), 29–31 (Neustadt), 147–48 (Goodpaster), 148–49 (Bundy), and 149–50 (Rostow). Brzezinski, too, seems to have had second thoughts about the idea. See his comments in "A Forum on the Role of the National Security Adviser," in Inderfurth and Johnson, eds., *Fateful Decisions,* p. 156.

138 Richard Neustadt asked himself: Neustadt, *Presidential Power,* 1980 ed., pp. 208, 212–14.

138 the "dignified" elements of a constitutional system: Walter Bagehot, *The English Constitution* (Introduction by R. H. S. Crossman) (London: Collins / Fontana Library, 1963), pp. 61–62.

138 "A question troubling Congress": Vance, *Hard Choices,* p. 395.

CHAPTER SIX: RONALD REAGAN

140 "I had an agenda I wanted to get done": Lou Cannon, *President Reagan: The Role of a Lifetime* (New York: Simon & Schuster, 1991), p. 845n.2.

140 He was better suited to leading the nation": Ibid., p. 147.

140 "[T]he whole of Reagan's performance": Ibid., p. 185.

141 Published compilations of his pre presidential speeches: E.g., Kiron K. Skinner, Annelise Anderson, and Martin Anderson, eds., *Reagan, in His Own Hand* (New York: Free Press, 2001).

141 "principled [and] confident": Douglas Brinkley, ed., *The Reagan Diaries* (New York: HarperCollins, 2007), p. xiii.

141 At the Bonn economic summit: See the Economic Declaration issued by the G-7 economic summit participants in Bonn, May 4, 1985.

141 A famous essay on intellectual history: Isaiah Berlin, *The Hedgehog and the Fox: An Essay on Tolstoy's View of History* (New York: Simon & Schuster/Clarion, 1970).

142 He made a point of never taking his coat off: Michael K. Deaver with Mickey Herskowitz, *Behind the Scenes* (New York: William Morrow, 1987), p. 143.

142 determined to focus on the "big picture": Edwin Meese III, *With Reagan: The Inside Story* (Washington, D.C.: Regnery Gateway, 1992), p. 22. See also Carnes Lord, *The Presidency and the Management of National Security* (New York: Free Press, 1988), p. 24.

142 "ruthlessly geared to preserving his energy": William Doyle, *Inside the Oval Office: The White House Tapes from FDR to Clinton* (New York: Kodansha International, 1999), p. 252.

142 He came into the Oval Office around 9:00 a.m.: Lou Cannon, *President Reagan*, pp. 144–45.

142 Both sides in the administration's internal quarrels: E.g., Lou Cannon, *President Reagan*, Chapter 10; Doyle, *Inside the Oval Office*, pp. 252–55, 265–69; Constantine C. Menges, *Inside the National Security Council: The True Story of the Making and Unmaking of Reagan's Foreign Policy* (New York: Simon & Schuster, 1988), pp. 382–88.

143 He did not usually nap during his "staff time": Lou Cannon, *President Reagan*, p. 146.

143 Donald Regan, who served as chief of staff: Regan interview in Doyle, *Inside the Oval Office*, p. 254.

143 According to William Doyle: Doyle, *Inside the Oval Office*, pp. 254–55.

143 Alexander Haig, who served both Nixon and Reagan: Haig interview in Lou Cannon, *President Reagan*, p. 151.

144 "We wanted our appointees to be the President's ambassadors": Meese, *With Regan*, p. 77.

144 The Reagan team is widely regarded: James Q. Wilson, *Bureaucracy: What Government Agencies Do and Why They Do It* (New York: Basic Books, 1989), pp. 261–62; Lord, *The Presidency and the Management of National Security*, p. 30.

145 Jimmy Carter in his time: Wilson, *Bureaucracy*, pp. 261–62.

145 Reagan welcomed their presence as a buffer: Deaver, *Behind the Scenes*, pp. 124, 128.

145 Alexander Haig . . . was surprised: Alexander M. Haig, Jr., *Caveat: Realism, Reagan, and Foreign Policy* (New York: Macmillan, 1984), pp. 80–81.

145 Richard Allen: In Ivo H. Daalder and I. M. Destler, moderators, "The Role of the National Security Advisers," The National Security Council Project: Oral History Roundtables (Washington, D.C.: Center for International and Security Studies at Maryland/University of Maryland, and the Brookings Institution, October 25, 1999), p. 3.

146 The Reagan presidency can usefully be divided: This useful construct is from Doyle, *Inside the Oval Office*, p. 264.

146 Clark's relationship with his president: Paul Kengor and Patricia Clark Doerner, *The Judge: William P. Clark, Ronald Reagan's Top Hand* (San Francisco: Ignatius Press, 2007).

146 "Nothing ever gets settled": Secretary of State George P. Shultz, "Iran and U.S. Policy," testimony before the U.S. House of Representatives, Committee on Foreign Affairs, December 8, 1986.

147 "a witches' brew of intrigue": James A. Baker III with Thomas M. DeFrank, *The Politics of Diplomacy: Revolution, War and Peace, 1989–1992* (New York: G. P. Putnam's Sons, 1995), p. 26.

148 Watergate special prosecutor Leon Jaworski: Jaworski letter introduced into the record of Haig's confirmation hearing, U.S. Congress, Senate, Committee on Foreign Relations, *Nomination of Alexander M. Haig, Jr.,* Hearings, 97th Cong., 1st Sess. (Washington, D.C.: Government Printing Office, January 1981), Part 1, p. 276. See also Theodore H. White, *Breach of Faith: The Fall of Richard Nixon* (New York: Atheneum, 1975).

148 Ford was outwardly noncommittal: James Cannon, *Time and Chance: Gerald Ford's Appointment with History* (New York: HarperCollins, 1994), p. 357.

149 Haig had also negotiated the text: Haig, *Caveat*, pp. 56–61, 74.

149 Senator Paul Tsongas: U.S. Senate, *Nomination of Alexander M. Haig, Jr.,* Part 2, p. 109.

150 In May and June 1982, for example: For Haig's account, see Haig, *Caveat*, pp. 310–14. For his critics' version, see Lou Cannon, *President Reagan*, pp. 199–205. See also Kengor and Doerner, *The Judge*, pp. 152, 180–85.

151 "Today was the day—I told Al H[aig]": Brinkley, ed., *The Reagan Diaries*, pp. 90–91.

151 Nixon's broad policies were more fully articulated: Nixon's four reports to Congress, all entitled *U.S. Foreign Policy for the 1970's*, were published on February 18, 1970; February 25, 1971; February 9, 1972; and May 3, 1973.

151 On U.S.-Soviet relations, three such directives: NSDDs 66 and 75 can be found, e.g., in Norman A. Bailey, *The Strategic Plan That Won the Cold War: National Security Decision Directive 75* (McLean, Va.: The Potomac Foundation, 1998). For NSDD 75, see also Appendix B to Robert C. McFarlane and Zofia Smardz, *Special Trust* (New York: Cadell & Davies, 1994), pp. 372–80.

152 owed much to the pen of Richard Pipes: Richard Pipes, *Vixi: Memoirs of a Non-Belonger* (New Haven: Yale University Press, 2003), pp. 188–202.

152 William Casey . . . would be in charge: See John O'Sullivan, *The President, the Pope, and the Prime Minister: Three Who Changed the World* (Washington, D.C.: Regnery, 2006), and Peter Schweizer, *Victory: The Reagan Administration's Secret Strategy That Hastened the Collapse of the Soviet Union* (New York: Atlantic Monthly Press, 1994).

153 Casey would collude with Crown Prince Fahd: Schweizer, *Victory,* esp. Chapter 8.

153 the Reagan administration perceived a Soviet vulnerability: Stephen Sestanovich, "Do the Soviets Feel Pinched by Third World Adventures?," *Washington Post*, May 20, 1984, p. B1. Sestanovich was the NSC staff's Soviet specialist
at the time of this article. See also Ronald Reagan, "Freedom, Regional Security,
and Global Peace," a White House document published on March 14, 1986, and
Peter W. Rodman, *More Precious than Peace: The Cold War and the Struggle for
the Third World* (New York: Scribner's, 1994), esp. Chapter 11.

153 The State Department opposed: Interview with Richard Pipes in Kengor and
Doerner, *The Judge*, p. 170.

153 "Is it possible," he wrote: Reagan, *An American Life*, pp. 271–73.

154 "Some of the N.S.C. staff are too hard line": Brinkley, ed., *The Reagan Diaries*,
p. 142.

154 Some liberal critics saw Reagan's policy: E.g., Raymond L. Garthoff, *The Great
Transition: American-Soviet Relations and the End of the Cold War* (Washington,
D.C.: Brookings, 1994).

154 Reagan tried to strike up a correspondence: E.g., the correspondence with
Andropov in Reagan, *An American Life*, pp. 576–82.

155 In a series of candid articles in authoritative journals: See sources collected in
Rodman, *More Precious than Peace*, Chapter 12, and also Peter W. Rodman,
"Reversal of Fortune," in Kiron K. Skinner, ed., *Turning Points in Ending the
Cold War* (Stanford: Hoover Institution Press, 2008), pp. 186–88. Some of the
discussion of Reagan in this chapter is also adapted from *More Precious than
Peace*.

155 Gorbachev explained to his party colleagues: Mikhail Gorbachev, Report to the
Plenary Meeting of the CPSU Central Committee, October 15, 1985, quoted
in *On the New Edition of the CPSU Programme* (Moscow: Novosti, 1986),
pp. 13–15; also in FBIS-SOV-85-200, October 16, 1985, pp. R3, 6.

156 George Shultz in his memoirs: George P. Shultz, *Turmoil and Triumph: My Years
as Secretary of State* (New York: Scribner's, 1993), pp. 265–66, 275–76.

156 The surprise unveiling of Reagan's Strategic Defense Initiative: McFarlane, *Special Trust*, pp. 232–33.

156 In June 1983, with Reagan's blessing: Secretary of State George P. Shultz, "U.S.-
Soviet Relations in the Context of U.S. Foreign Policy," statement to the Senate
Committee on Foreign Relations, June 15, 1983.

158 their president, who saw SDI as a goal in itself: See President Reagan's news
conference, September 17, 1985, and McFarlane, *Special Trust*, p. 234.

158 "more Catholic than the Pope": Colin L. Powell with Joseph E. Persico, *My
American Journey* (New York: Random House, 1995), p. 295.

158 Shultz strongly objected: Shultz, *Turmoil and Triumph*, pp. 578–81.

158 Reagan "thought the leak unnecessary": McFarlane, *Special Trust*, p. 317.

159 "He really disliked personal confrontation": McFarlane interview in Doyle,
Inside the Oval Office, p. 267.

159 "Bud, I know what you're describing": McFarlane interview in Daalder and
Destler, "The Role of the National Security Advisers," p. 42.

160 I was one of those seeking extensive changes: Peter Robinson, the chief draftsman of this speech, tells his account in Peter Robinson, *It's My Party: A Republican's Messy Love Affair with the GOP* (New York: Warner, 2000), pp. 13–18, and in
Peter Robinson, *How Ronald Reagan Changed My Life* (New York: Harper-
Collins, 2003), pp. 101–3.

161 "The boys at State are going to kill me": Robinson, *How Ronald Reagan Changed My Life*, p. 103.

161 thousands of young East Germans clashed with police: Serge Schmemann, "Rallying Cry of East Berliners: 'Gorbachev!,'" *New York Times*, June 10, 1987, p. A7.

161 "We didn't build this wall": Yakovlev quoted in *Tagesspiegel*, January 10, 1989, quoted in Garthoff, *The Great Transition*, p. 602.

161 a "swamp": Shultz, *Turmoil and Triumph*, p. 322.

161 sensitivity to Latin fears of the "Great Colossus": Reagan, *An American Life*, pp. 239–40.

161 It would be "lunacy": As recounted by Shultz at the time to his State Department senior staff (including me).

162 "Those sonsofbitches won't be happy": Lou Cannon, *President Reagan*, p. 337.

162 Thus, when CIA director William Casey came up with: See, e.g., Brinkley, ed., *Reagan Diaries*, pp. 52, 110; Lou Cannon, *President Reagan*, pp. 345–56.

162 standing against "the tide of history": Sen. Christopher J. Dodd, "Democratic Response to President Reagan's Address to Joint Session of Congress," April 27, 1983, News Release, p. 7.

163 This overture got nowhere: The best account of U.S. policy in Central America in this period is Robert Kagan, *A Twilight Struggle: American Power and Nicaragua, 1977–1990* (New York: Free Press, 1996). On the Enders mission, see Chapter 20.

163 "This revolution goes beyond our borders": Speech by Tomás Borge at ceremonies marking the second anniversary of the Nicaraguan revolution, July 19, 1981, in FBIS-LAM-81-139, July 21, 1981, p. P10.

163 Shultz in his memoirs repeatedly accuses Clark: Shultz, *Turmoil and Triumph*, pp. 306–22. Clark says he was "shock[ed]" by the treatment of him in Shultz's memoirs. See Kengor and Doerner, *The Judge*, p. 241.

163 Clark and his staff, in turn: Menges, *Inside the National Security Council*, p. 94.

163 "George, don't be a pilgrim": Shultz, *Turmoil and Triumph*, p. 305.

164 On her trip, one sympathetic U.S. ambassador: Menges, *Inside the National Security Council*, pp. 107–9; Lou Cannon, *President Reagan*, pp. 376–77.

164 Shultz in turn was caught by surprise in July 1983: Shultz, *Turmoil and Triumph*, pp. 310–11.

164 "[S]ince he didn't keep anybody informed": Lou Cannon, *President Reagan*, pp. 380–81.

164 At the end of the lengthy and stormy meeting: An account of the meeting can be found in Kagan, *A Twilight Struggle*, pp. 312–14, and in Rodman, *More Precious than Peace*, pp. 253–54. Strictly speaking it was a meeting of the National Security Planning Group (NSPG), a more restricted forum.

165 With McFarlane's grudging acquiescence: Compare Menges, *Inside the National Security Council*, pp. 126–27, and Shultz, *Turmoil and Triumph*, pp. 415–16.

165 As head of the State Department's Policy Planning Staff: Rodman, *More Precious than Peace*, p. 254.

165 Thomas Enders had barked to NSC staffer: Menges, *Inside the National Security Council*, pp. 105, 113.

165 A key figure in this evolution was Elliott Abrams: Kagan, *A Twilight Struggle*, pp. 419–20; Rodman, *More Precious than Peace*, pp. 410–13.

166 The Tower Board . . . published a thoughtful report: President's Special Review
      Board, *Report* (Washington, D.C.: Government Printing Office, February 26,
      1987).

167 Bud McFarlane was called out of retirement: McFarlane, *Special Trust*,
      pp. 53–65.

168 a brief shaped by Representative Dick Cheney: U.S. Congress, Senate Select
      Committee on Secret Military Assistance to Iran and the Nicaraguan Opposi-
      tion and House Select Committee to Investigate Covert Arms Transactions with
      Iran, *Report of the Congressional Committees Investigating the Iran-Contra Affair*,
      S. Rept. No. 100-216/H. Rept. No. 100-433, 100th Cong., 1st Sess. (Washington,
      D.C.: Government Printing Office, November 1987), Section II: The Minority
      Report, pp. 431–586.

168 Cheney's vigorous defense of Reagan helped propel him: Stephen F. Hayes,
      *Cheney: The Untold Story of America's Most Powerful and Controversial Vice Pres-
      ident* (New York: HarperCollins, 2007), pp. 197–200.

168 The Tower Board enumerated the many "mistakes": President's Special Review
      Board, *Report*, p. I-2.

169 All these recommendations were adopted: Paul Schott Stevens, "The Reagan
      NSC: Before and After," *Perspectives*, vol. 19, no. 2 (Spring 1990), pp. 118–22.
      Stevens was NSC executive secretary when the reforms were made.

169 The Tower Board is often cited for its conclusion: President's Special Review
      Board, *Report*, p. V-4.

169 George Shultz took advantage of the opening: Carlucci quoted in Daalder and
      Destler, "The Role of the National Security Advisers," p. 12.

169 Cyrus Vance, a decade earlier: Zbigniew Brzezinski, *Power and Principle: Mem-
      oirs of the National Adviser, 1977–1981* (New York: Farrar, Straus & Giroux, 1983),
      p. 36.

170 Thus the board, after all its investigation: President's Special Review Board,
      Report, Part V.

170 The debacle occurred because of a policy failure: A good account is in David C.
      Martin and John Walcott, *Best Laid Plans: The Inside Story of America's War
      Against Terrorism* (New York: Harper & Row, 1988), pp. 87–153.

170 "no intention or expectation that U.S. Armed Forces": Letters from President
      Ronald Reagan to Speaker of the House Thomas P. O'Neill on the role of U.S.
      forces in Lebanon, August 24 and September 29, 1982.

171 In August 1983 he authorized the MNF to stay: Shultz, *Turmoil and Triumph*,
      p. 222.

171 In December, he agreed to step up: Brinkley, ed., *Reagan Diaries*, pp. 201–2.

172 "We're a divided group": Ibid., p. 201.

173 Cap Weinberger's Pentagon was reluctant: Shultz, *Turmoil and Triumph*,
      pp. 329, 331, 342–43; Russell Crandall, *Gunboat Democracy: U.S. Interventions
      in the Dominican Republic, Grenada, and Panama* (Lanham, Md.: Rowman &
      Littlefield, 2006), pp. 139–40.

173 A frustrated Reagan ordered Poindexter: Conversation with John Poindexter,
      January 2007; Shultz, *Turmoil and Triumph*, pp. 677, 680–82.

174 "It was precisely our military role in Lebanon": Secretary of State George P.
      Shultz, "Power and Diplomacy in the 1980's," address to the Trilateral Commis-
      sion, Washington, April 3, 1984.

174 Caspar Weinberger to respond: Secretary of Defense Caspar Weinberger, "The

Uses of Military Power," address at the National Press Club, Washington, November 28, 1984. Weinberger wanted to deliver his response to Shultz earlier, but the White House delayed it to after the election. See also the discussion in Caspar W. Weinberger, *Fighting for Peace: Seven Critical Years in the Pentagon* (New York: Warner, 1990), pp. 401–2, 433–45.

175 Yet the Pentagon was even more enthusiastic about this mission: Weinberger, *Fighting for Peace*, Chapter 13, esp. pp. 395–97.

175 somehow this convinced him that it was perfectly consistent: Ibid. See also Secretary of Defense Caspar W. Weinberger, *A Report to the Congress on Security Arrangements in the Persian Gulf* (Department of Defense, June 15, 1987).

175 These indictments launched the United States into a political crisis: A good account is in Crandall, *Gunboat Democracy,* Chapter 4.

176 Justice has been known to resist sharing too much information: Nicholas Rostow, "Law Enforcement and Foreign Policy," unpublished draft paper, July 1994, p. 3.

176 At Situation Room meetings, they argued: Shultz, *Turmoil and Triumph,* pp. 1054, 1058; Crandall, *Gunboat Democracy,* p. 194.

177 the Pentagon remained cautious: Powell, *My American Journey,* p. 416.

177 The negotiation fell through: Shultz, *Turmoil and Triumph,* pp. 1058–79.

177 After the al-Qaida attack on the USS *Cole*: National Commission on Terrorist Attacks upon the United States ("9/11 Commission"), *Final Report* (New York: Norton, [2003]), Section 6.3, pp. 190–92.

CHAPTER SEVEN: GEORGE H. W. BUSH

179 covert action program . . . SOUTHCOM: Russell Crandall, *Gunboat Democracy: U.S. Interventions in the Dominican Republic, Grenada, and Panama* (Lanham, Md.: Rowman & Littlefield, 2006), pp. 195–97; James A. Baker III with Thomas M. DeFrank, *The Politics of Diplomacy: Revolution, War, and Peace, 1989–1992* (New York: Putnam's Sons, 1995), Chapter 11.

179 Cheney secured his replacement: Stephen F. Hayes, *Cheney: The Untold Story of America's Most Powerful and Controversial Vice President* (New York: HarperCollins, 2007), p. 221.

180 Bush decided: "Okay, let's do it": Colin L. Powell with Joseph E. Persico, *My American Journey* (New York: Random House, 1995), p. 425.

181 "China desk officer": comment of NSC staffer Robert Suettinger in David J. Rothkopf, *Running the World: The Inside Story of the National Security Council and the Architects of American Power* (New York: Public Affairs, 2005), p. 291.

181 Bush had found time to chat by telephone: George Bush and Brent Scowcroft, *A World Transformed* (New York: Alfred A. Knopf, 1998), pp. 61–62.

181 "mad dialer": John Bolton, *Surrender Is Not an Option: Defending America at the United Nations and Abroad* (New York: Threshold/Simon & Schuster, 2007), p. 36.

181 "Core Group": Bush and Scowcroft, *A World Transformed,* pp. 41–42.

181 "[W]e made the national security apparatus": Baker, *The Politics of Diplomacy,* p. 22.

181 Gates . . . has a somewhat sharper assessment: Robert M. Gates, *From the Shadows: The Ultimate Insider's Story of Five Presidents and How They Won the Cold War* (New York: Simon & Schuster, 1996), p. 454.

182 Scowcroft was described by a journalist: David Lauter, "The Man Behind the

President," *Los Angeles Times*, October 14, 1990, p. A1, in Karl F. Inderfurth and Loch K. Johnson, *Fateful Decisions: Inside the National Security Council* (New York: Oxford University Press, 2004), p. 203.

182 "It is probably accurate to say": Bush and Scowcroft, *A World Transformed*, p. 36.

183 Scowcroft's ability to "knock heads": Ibid., p. 35.

183 had Tower been confirmed: Rothkopf, *Running the World*, p. 264.

183 In Robert Gates's estimation: Gates, *From the Shadows*, p. 457.

183 By all accounts . . . the disagreements never: Baker, *The Politics of Diplomacy*, pp. 21–24; Hayes, *Cheney*, p. 209.

184 "Operation Just Because": One of the journalists present, Strobe Talbott, recounts the story in Strobe Talbott, *The Great Experiment: The Story of Ancient Empires, Modern States, and the Quest for a Global Nation* (New York: Simon & Schuster, 2008), p. 264.

184 "smothering presence" of Soviet forces: Scowcroft in Bush and Scowcroft, *A World Transformed*, p. 43.

184 Similarly in . . . START, Cheney was doubtful: Ibid., pp. 208–10.

184 as the Soviet Union headed toward breakup: Gates, *From the Shadows*, pp. 529–31.

184 In his first news conference as secretary: Hayes, *Cheney*, pp. 215–16.

184 Later, in the run-up to the Gulf War: Ibid., pp. 234–38; Powell, *My American Journey*, pp. 476–78.

184 But he treated the chairman of the Joint Chiefs: Gates, *From the Shadows*, p. 457; Hayes, *Cheney*, p. 234.

185 Scowcroft reports his unhappiness: Bush and Scowcroft, *A World Transformed*, p. 381; see also pp. 353, 354, 431.

185 it was Cheney's strategy: Baker, *The Politics of Diplomacy*, p. 409.

185 "Dick led the way": Bush and Scowcroft, *A World Transformed*, p. 354; see also Hayes, *Cheney*, pp. 227, 233–34.

185 In July 1989, he appeared before: Secretary of Defense Richard Cheney, "Cost of Congressional Reporting Requirements," Testimony to the House Armed Services Committee, July 1989. The quote is from the related report, Secretary of Defense Dick Cheney, *Defense Management: Report to the President*, July 1989, p. 27 (emphasis in original).

185 In January 1990, his office published: Office of the Secretary of Defense, *White Paper on the Department of Defense and the Congress*, January 1990.

186 "big brother–little brother": Baker, *The Politics of Diplomacy*, p. 19.

186 "[M]ore comfortable with action": Ibid., pp. 38–40.

186 "a series of discrete problems": Ibid., pp. 134–35.

187 "the guy who got elected": Bolton, *Surrender Is Not an Option*, p. 36.

187 "I headed to State assuming that the President": Baker, *The Politics of Diplomacy*, pp. 29–30.

187 Shultz found this rankling: Author's conversations with Shultz during the period.

187 Baker's memoirs contain the all-too-familiar criticism: Baker, *The Politics of Diplomacy*, pp. 31–32.

188 never overcame their initial impression: E.g., John M. Goshko, "Poor Morale, Drift Seen at Baker's State Dept.; Inner Circle Aloof, Bureaucrats Charge," *Washington Post*, March 6, 1989, p. A1.

188 On April 1, 1989, what purported to be: Copy of *"Newsletter"* in author's collection. Note the date.

189 The Bush-Scowcroft memoir notes, more than once: Bush and Scowcroft, *A World Transformed*, pp. 354, 437, 463.

189 "furious" at Baker: Ibid., p. 461. Baker's account, only partially contrite, is in *The Politics of Diplomacy*, pp. 391–95.

189 Thomas L. Friedman . . . wrote: Thomas L. Friedman, "Mideast Tensions; Baker Seen as a Balance to Bush on Crisis in Gulf," *New York Times*, November 3, 1990.

189 Baker devotes a long passage in his memoirs: Baker, *The Politics of Diplomacy*, p. 131.

189 Other journalists reported: *U.S. News & World Report, Triumph Without Victory: The Unreported History of the Persian Gulf War* (New York: Times Books, 1992), p. 104.

189 Robert Gates . . . is on record: Gates, *From the Shadows*, p. 456.

190 Scowcroft, for example, believed: Bush and Scowcroft, *A World Transformed*, pp. 12, 135, 154.

191 Hard-line colleagues in the Kremlin: Raymond L. Garthoff, *The Great Transition: American-Soviet Relations and the End of the Cold War* (Washington, D.C.: Brookings, 1994), p. 367.

191 Inside accounts of the Bush administration: Bush and Scowcroft, *A World Transformed*, pp. 187–88.

191 Baker visited the East German capital: Baker, *The Politics of Diplomacy*, pp. 174–75.

192 the Soviet leader was conflicted: Ibid., pp. 167, 172.

192 "We're going to win the game": Baker, *The Politics of Diplomacy*, p. 230.

192 accepted the U.S. role in Europe: Ibid., pp. 170–71.

192 Baker's team at the State Department: The definitive account of the Two Plus Four process is Philip Zelikow and Condoleezza Rice, *Germany Unified and Europe Transformed: A Study in Statecraft* (Cambridge: Harvard University Press, 1995).

193 Baker phoned the president to complain: Baker, *The Politics of Diplomacy*, p. 70.

193 a speech that Scowcroft's deputy Robert Gates: Ibid., pp. 156–58; Gates, *From the Shadows*, pp. 480–81.

194 At two crucial Oval Office meetings: See Bush and Scowcroft, *A World Transformed*, pp. 541–44; Baker, *The Politics of Diplomacy*, pp. 560–61; Gates, *From the Shadows*, pp. 529–31.

194 As Scowcroft later admitted: Bush and Scowcroft, *A World Transformed*, p. 544.

194 This warning was aimed: Ibid., pp. 515–16.

195 none other than Richard Nixon: See Thomas L. Friedman, "Nixon Scoffs at Level of Support for Russian Democracy by Bush," *New York Times*, March 10, 1992; Marvin Kalb, *The Nixon Memo: Political Respectability, Russia, and the Press* (Chicago: University of Chicago Press, 1994).

195 By early December, opinion polls: Bush and Scowcroft, *A World Transformed*, pp. 427n., 439n.

195 Scowcroft reports that he was "appalled": Ibid., p. 317.

195 Scowcroft . . . sensed the president: Ibid., p. 318.

195 Mrs. Thatcher, too, found Bush resolute: Margaret Thatcher, *The Downing Street Years* (London: HarperCollins, 1993), pp. 817–18, 820.

195 Her famous admonition to Bush: Ibid., pp. 823–24.
196 Bush worked the phones: Bush and Scowcroft, *A World Transformed*, pp. 318–19.
196 "Norm Schwarzkopf, under pressure": Powell, *My American Journey*, p. 492.
196 "Dick was probably ahead of his military": Bush and Scowcroft, *A World Transformed*, p. 354. See also ibid., pp. 353, 381, 431, 477, and Hayes, *Cheney*, pp. 233–34.
197 Powell candidly expressed his concerns: Michael R. Gordon and Gen. Bernard E. Trainor, *The Generals' War: The Inside Story of the Conflict in the Gulf* (Boston: Little, Brown, 1995), pp. 31–34.
197 Scowcroft led off the second NSC meeting: Bush and Scowcroft, *A World Transformed*, pp. 315–24.
197 Powell ventured a question: Powell, *My American Journey*, pp. 464–66.
197 Cheney thenceforth insisted: Ibid., pp. 425–26, 503.
198 "When I finished, Scowcroft asked": Powell, *My American Journey*, pp. 488–89.
198 Margaret Thatcher, for one: Thatcher, *The Downing Street Years*, pp. 821, 827–28; Bush and Scowcroft, *A World Transformed*, pp. 384–87.
199 Baker, as we have noted, was eager: Bush and Scowcroft, *A World Transformed*, pp. 419, 437–38.
199 Bush later defended Baker: Ibid., p. 487.
200 Powell and his military colleagues: Powell, *My American Journey*, pp. 519–22.
200 Baker and his State colleagues: Baker, *The Politics of Diplomacy*, pp. 436–38.
200 Dick Cheney agreed: Hayes, *Cheney*, pp. 249–51.
200 Bush and Scowcroft . . . concede: Bush and Scowcroft, *A World Transformed*, pp. 488–90.
201 "I am a practical man": Quoted in Jon Margolis, "Bush Opens Run as 'Own Man,'" *Chicago Tribune*, October 13, 1987.

CHAPTER EIGHT: BILL CLINTON

203 he interrupted veteran Foreign Affairs Committee chairman: Quoted in David Halberstam, *War in a Time of Peace: Bush, Clinton, and the Generals* (New York: Scribner, 2001), p. 168.
203 David Gergen . . . assessed Clinton thusly: David Gergen, *Eyewitness to Power: The Essence of Leadership: Nixon to Clinton* (New York: Simon & Schuster, 2000), p. 276.
204 "a tendency toward intellectual clutter": Dick Morris, *Behind the Oval Office: Getting Reelected Against All Odds* (Los Angeles: Renaissance, 1996), p. 51.
204 Nor did he want to spend a lot of political capital: Ivo H. Daalder and I. M. Destler, *In the Shadow of the Oval Office: The President's National Security Adviser and the Making of America's Foreign Policy* (New York: Simon & Schuster, forthcoming), Chapter 7.
204 He came into office with a broad vision of a post–Cold War: Strobe Talbott, *The Great Experiment: The Story of Ancient Empires, Modern States, and the Quest for a Global Nation* (New York: Simon & Schuster, 2008), Chapter 15.
205 otherwise critics saw him: Elizabeth Drew, *On the Edge: The Clinton Presidency* (New York: Simon & Schuster, 1994), p. 140.
205 pride in his reliance on the Foreign Service: Warren Christopher, *Chances of a Lifetime* (New York: Scribner, 2001), pp. 80–81.

205 Clinton himself acknowledged the doubts: Bill Clinton, *My Life* (New York: Alfred A. Knopf, 2004), p. 455.

205 there are those who believe: Halberstam, *War in a Time of Peace*, p. 174; Daalder and Destler, *In the Shadow of the Oval Office*, Chapter 7.

206 Lake took a prominent role in articulating: See Anthony Lake, "From Containment to Enlargement," speech at the Johns Hopkins University School of Advanced International Studies, September 21, 1993 (at http://www.mtholyoke.edu/acad/intrel/lakedoc.html).

206 He admitted to being "emotional": Drew, *On the Edge*, p. 143; Halberstam, *War in a Time of Peace*, pp. 283–92.

206 the vice presidency reached another new level of power: Gergen, *Eyewitness to Power*, pp. 295–96.

206 Berger's true talent and focus: R. W. Apple, Jr., "A Domestic Sort with Global Worries," *New York Times*, August 25, 1999, p. A1; Halberstam, *War in a Time of Peace*, pp. 404–9.

207 Clinton's memoirs speak about Berger: Clinton, *My Life,* pp. 737–38.

207 "I don't talk to the military": Drew, *On the Edge*, p. 45.

207 In his memoir he tells the story: Colin L. Powell with Joseph E. Persico, *My American Journey* (New York: Random House, 1995), p. 576.

207 apparent determination by Clinton: Halberstam, *War in a Time of Peace*, pp. 324, 389, 412–14.

207 Powell, indeed, had warned Clinton: Powell, *My American Journey*, pp. 563, 578–80.

208 Lake . . . had co-authored a book: I. M. Destler, Leslie H. Gelb, and Anthony Lake, *Our Own Worst Enemy* (New York: Simon & Schuster, 1984), p. 279.

208 "[U]nlike Bush's team, Clinton's lacked a captain": Daalder and Destler, *In the Shadow of the Oval Office*, Chapter 7.

208 Sandy Berger has commented: Berger interview in David J. Rothkopf, *Running the World: The Inside Story of the National Security Council and the Architects of American Power* (New York: Public Affairs, 2005), p. 381.

209 "There is a comfort you get": Lake interview in Daalder and Destler, *In the Shadow of the Oval Office*, Chapter 7.

209 there are many reports of Clinton's irritation: E.g., Halberstam, *War in a Time of Peace*, pp. 223, 262–65, 272, 279–80, 316–17.

209 Colin Powell . . . was offended: Powell, *My American Journey*, p. 576.

209 he told *Time* magazine: Michael Kramer, "What He Will Do," *Time*, November 16, 1992, p. 31.

209 "This sounded much like": William Doyle, *Inside the Oval Office: The White House Tapes from FDR to Clinton* (New York: Kodansha International, 1999), pp. 304–5.

209 James Woolsey . . . had his own stories to tell: Woolsey interview in Rothkopf, *Running the World*, p. 327.

210 National Economic Council: Kenneth I. Juster and Simon Lazarus, *Making Economic Policy: An Assessment of the National Economic Council* (Washington, D.C.: Brookings, 1997).

211 "The administration continues to coddle China": Gov. Bill Clinton, address at Georgetown University, December 12, 1991.

211 "[t]his is going to be an arm's-length relationship": Berger quoted by Sandra Kristoff in Ivo H. Daalder and I. M. Destler, moderators, "China Policy and the National Security Council," The National Security Council Project: Oral His-

tory Roundtables (Washington, D.C.. Center for International and Security Studies at Maryland/University of Maryland, and the Brookings Institution, November 4, 1999), p. 28.

212 "Rough, somber, sometimes bordering": Christopher, *Chances of a Lifetime*, pp. 238–39.

212 The NEC staff (which had not been significantly involved). Juster and Lazarus, *Making Economic Policy*, pp. 26–27, 44–45.

212 Kantor told the Senate: Mickey Kantor, testimony before the Senate Finance Committee, March 9, 1993, quoted in William G. Hyland, *Clinton's World: Remaking American Foreign Policy* (Westport, Conn.: Praeger, 1999), p. 128.

212 As Jeffrey Garten, under secretary of commerce: Jeffrey E. Garten, *The Big Ten: The Big Emerging Markets and How They Will Change Our Lives* (New York: Basic Books, 1997), p. 141.

213 The State Department—through leaks to the press: E.g., Daniel Williams and Clay Chandler, "U.S. Aide Sees Relations with Asia in Peril," *Washington Post*, May 5, 1994.

213 Again, the NEC staff joined with the NSC: Juster and Lazarus, *Making Economic Policy*, pp. 37, 44.

213 Said one senior official: David E. Sanger, "At the End, U.S. Blunted Its Big Stick," *New York Times*, June 30, 1995, p. A9.

213 Robert Rubin took the lead: A good account of Rubin's role in the Mexican crisis is in Rothkopf, *Running the World*, pp. 358–62.

214 A testimony to Rubin's personal stature: Ibid., p. 361.

214 "I don't think five people could repeat": Clinton, *My Life*, p. 504. Talbott's account is told in Strobe Talbott, *The Russia Hand: A Memoir of Presidential Diplomacy* (New York: Random House, 2002).

215 Nixon told Talbott: Talbott, *The Russia Hand*, p. 46; see also Clinton, *My Life*, pp. 505, 593.

216 the initial high hopes for both Russian democracy: Hyland, *Clinton's World*, pp. 85–90.

217 Clinton had harshly criticized George H. W. Bush: E.g., "Statement by Gov. Bill Clinton on the Crisis in Bosnia," July 26, 1992.

218 "all the verve of a solicitor": Raymond Seitz, *Over Here* (London: Phoenix, 1998), p. 329.

218 A coalition of the unwilling: See Halberstam, *War in a Time of Peace*, pp. 224–31; Rothkopf, *Running the World*, pp. 364–66.

218 "[The president] is going south on this": Drew, *On the Edge*, pp. 157–58.

218 In his memoirs, Clinton attributes: Clinton, *My Life*, pp. 525–26.

218 Yet at the time, Clinton's discomfort: Evan Thomas et al., *Back from the Dead: How Clinton Survived the Republican Revolution* (New York: Atlantic Monthly Press, 1997), p. 1.

218 immortalized in the book and film: Mark Bowden, *Black Hawk Down: A Story of Modern War* (Berkeley: Atlantic Monthly Press, 1999); the film *Black Hawk Down*, 2001, produced by Jerry Bruckheimer and Ridley Scott and directed by Scott.

219 They repeatedly sought guidance from the White House: Halberstam, *War in a Time of Peace*, p. 259.

219 At his hotel on a visit in San Francisco: Drew, *On the Edge*, pp. 317–18, 335. See the similar assessment of blame in Clinton, *My Life*, pp. 550–53.

219 Then came Haiti: On the *Harlan County* episode, see Drew, *On the Edge*, pp. 333–34; Halberstam, *War in a Time of Peace*, pp. 267–72. Drew estimates the number of Haitians on the dock at forty to sixty, Halberstam at "more than one hundred."

220 he personally reviewed the plan at the Pentagon: Clinton, *My Life*, pp. 616–19.

220 At the White House it was suspected: Steve Coll, *Ghost Wars: The Secret History of the CIA, Afghanistan, and bin Laden, from the Soviet Invasion to September* 11, 2001 (New York: Penguin, 2004), pp. 497–501, 533–34.

220 "They keep trying to force me": Morris, *Behind the Oval Office*, p. 245.

221 memos by Madeleine Albright: Rothkopf, *Running the World*, p. 366.

221 Meanwhile at Defense: Ivo H. Daalder, *Getting to Dayton: The Making of America's Bosnia Policy* (Washington, D.C.: Brookings, 2000), pp. 105, 169–70.

221 In June, Clinton responded to allied pleas: Ibid., pp. 66–67.

221 "the position of leader of the free world is vacant": Chirac quoted in Michael Dobbs, "Bosnia Crystallizes U.S. Post–Cold War Role; As Two Administrations Wavered, the Need for U.S. Leadership Became Clear," *Washington Post*, December 3, 1995.

221 One July evening around 7:00 p.m.: Bob Woodward, *The Choice* (New York: Simon & Schuster, 1996), pp. 260–61; Halberstam, *War in a Time of Peace*, pp. 316–17.

221 "The United States can't be a punching bag": Woodward, *The Choice*, pp. 262–63.

222 American diplomats sympathetic to Croatia: Daalder, *Getting to Dayton*, pp. 120–22; Richard Holbrooke, *To End a War* (New York: Modern Library, rev. ed., 1999), pp. 72–73.

222 "rooting for the Croatians": Clinton, *My Life*, pp. 166–67.

222 Holbrooke recounts a Principals meeting: Holbrooke, *To End a War*, pp. 144–46.

223 Holbrooke had no direct contact with Clinton: Morris, *Behind the Oval Office*, p. 261.

223 Defense . . . successfully blocked: Holbrooke, *To End a War*, p. 277.

223 While his national security team told him optimistically: Adm. Vern Clark quoted in Bob Woodward, *State of Denial* (New York, Simon & Schuster, 2006), p. 61. See also Ivo H. Daalder and Michael E. O'Hanlon, *Winning Ugly: NATO's War to Save Kosovo* (Washington, D.C.: Brookings, 2000), p. 91ff.

223 "We're just gerbils": Daalder and O'Hanlon, *Winning Ugly*, p. 71; Daalder and Destler, *In the Shadow of the Oval Office*, Chapter 7.

224 Clark developed his own regular contact with Sandy Berger: Steven Lee Myers and Eric Schmitt, "Crisis in the Balkans: The Leadership," *New York Times*, May 30, 1999.

224 Clark wanted to attack "strategic" targets: Gen. Wesley K. Clark, *Waging Modern War: Bosnia, Kosovo, and the Future of Combat* (New York: Public Affairs, 2001), esp. pp. 236–38, 265–66, 271.

224 Secretary Cohen consistently opposed: Ibid., pp. 269, 285, 332.

224 Public hints of planning for a ground war: Ibid., p. 405; Daalder and O'Hanlon, *Winning Ugly*, pp. 184, 203–4.

224 Clinton in his memoir is adamant: Clinton, *My Life*, pp. 851, 859. But see Daalder and O'Hanlon, *Winning Ugly*, pp. 156–61.

225 Cohen was often uncommunicative: Clark, *Waging Modern War*, pp. 98–99, 106.

225 Clark wondered if this was consistent with the intent: Ibid., pp. 288, 319.

225 The conflicting pressures on Clark: For this paragraph, see Halberstam, *War in a Time of Peace*, pp. 441–43.

226 The president . . . seems not to have known: Halberstam, *War in a Time of Peace*, pp. 478–79.

226 a paradoxical effect on alliance relations: This point is expanded upon in Peter W. Rodman, *Drifting Apart? Trends in U.S.-European Relations* (Washington, D.C.: Nixon Center, June 1999), pp. 64–67 (at http://nixoncenter.org/publica tions/monographs/drifting.pdf).

227 Carter's legacy as a reputation for incompetence: Halberstam, *War in a Time of Peace*, pp. 175, 280.

228 to, among others, former President Gerald Ford: Thomas M. DeFrank, *Write It When I'm Gone: Remarkable Off-the-Record Conversations with Gerald Ford* (New York: G. P. Putnam's Sons, 2007), pp. 148, 164.

228 he authorized Carter to go: Clinton, *My Life*, pp. 602–3.

228 Carter telephoned Colin Powell: Powell, *My American Journey*, pp. 597–98.

229 "desperately wanted to avoid": Clinton, *My Life*, p. 617.

229 the president approved a draft that read: George Stephanopoulos, *All Too Human* (Boston: Little, Brown, 1999), p. 313; Halberstam, *War in a Time of Peace*, p. 280.

229 Carter contacted the administration: Holbrooke, *To End a War*, pp. 121, 147–50.

229 William Hyland sums up: Hyland, *Clinton's World*, p. 202.

229 Schlesinger saw in Bill Clinton: Arthur M. Schlesinger, Jr., "The Ultimate Approval Rating," *New York Times Magazine*, December 15, 1996. See also the fuller analysis in Arthur M. Schlesinger, Jr., "Rating the Presidents: Washington to Clinton," *Political Science Quarterly*, vol. 112, no. 2 (1997), p. 188.

230 forcefully articulated the danger that was thought to be posed; See, e.g., President Clinton's address to the Joint Chiefs of Staff and Pentagon staff, at the Pentagon, February 17, 1998.

CHAPTER NINE: GEORGE W. BUSH

232 Bush liked to see himself as "the decider": He used this formulation notably in April 2006 in reply to a barrage of press questions on whether he was considering firing Secretary of Defense Donald Rumsfeld: "I'm the decider, and I decide what is best." See "President Bush Nominates Rob Portman as OMB Director and Susan Schwab for USTR," White House press release, April 18, 2006.

232 *The Washington Post* once mischievously published: Alasdair Roberts, "The Bush Years, in a Word," *Washington Post*, January 1, 2007, p. A13. See also David Rose, "Neo Culpa," *Vanity Fair* (January 2007), p. 85; David J. Rothkopf, *Running the World: The Inside Story of the National Security Council and the Architects of American Power* (New York: Public Affairs, 2005), pp. 406, 415, 436; Glenn Kessler and Peter Slevin, "Rice Fails to Repair Rifts, Officials Say," *Washington Post*, October 12, 2003, p. 1.

233 Some were criticizing a reputed "cabal": Lawrence B. Wilkerson, "The White House Cabal," *Los Angeles Times*, October 25, 2005.

233 Others were referring: See, e.g., Rose, "Neo Culpa," pp. 85, 90 (Richard Perle), 90, 144 (Frank Gaffney).

233 Team Bush: The title is borrowed from Donald F. Kettl, *Team Bush: Leadership Lessons from the Bush White House* (New York: McGraw-Hill, 2003).

233 White House speechwriter David Frum: David Frum, *The Right Man: The Sur-*

prise Presidency of George W. Bush (New York: Random House, 2003), pp. 28, 146, 272–77. In a later book, Frum expressed more disappointment in Bush's performance. David Frum, *Comeback: Conservatism That Can Win Again* (New York: Doubleday, 2008), Chapter 1.

234 a needed change from Bill Clinton: Kettl, *Team Bush*, p. 149.

234 one of the lessons taught: Thomas Lifson, "GWB: HBS MBA," *American Thinker*, February 3, 2004.

234 the dilemma of the statesman: Henry A. Kissinger, *Nuclear Weapons and Foreign Policy* (New York: Harper & Bros., 1957), p. 424.

235 "I'm not a textbook player": Bob Woodward, *Bush at War* (New York: Simon & Schuster, 2002), pp. 136–37, 145, 168, 342.

235 Conservative writer: Richard Brookhiser, "Close Up: The Mind of George W. Bush," *The Atlantic* (April 2003).

235 "[T]he vision thing matters": Woodward, *Bush at War*, p. 341.

235 According to many accounts, Bush's model of leadership: See esp. Lou Cannon and Carl M. Cannon, *Reagan's Disciple: George W. Bush's Troubled Quest for a Presidential Legacy* (New York: Public Affairs, 2008).

235 Bush considered that he had a mandate: Bob Woodward, *Plan of Attack* (New York: Simon & Schuster, 2004), pp. 28, 410; Charles O. Jones, "Governing Executively: Bush's Paradoxical Style," in John C. Fortier and Norman J. Ornstein, eds., *Second-Term Blues: How George W. Bush Has Governed* (Washington, D.C.: American Enterprise Institute and Brookings, 2007), pp. 123–24.

235 "He very much believes": Quoted in Dick Kirschten, "Bush as Boss: The Leadership Style of the Man Who Could Be Government's Next CEO," *Government Executive* (July 2000).

235 "uncanny ability": Dana Milbank, "Dispelling Doubts with the Rangers," *Washington Post*, July 25, 2000. See also Fred I. Greenstein, "George W. Bush: The Man and His Leadership," in Fortier and Ornstein, *Second-Term Blues*, p. 43.

236 "[A] president has got to be the calcium": Woodward, *Bush at War*, p. 259. See a similar observation by Bush in an interview in Robert Draper, *Dead Certain: The Presidency of George W. Bush* (New York: Free Press, 2007), pp. x–xi.

236 Woodward tells the story of a moment: Woodward, *Bush at War*, pp. 260–63.

236 Military experts know this resolve: Eliot Cohen, "What Combat Does to Man: Private Ryan and Its Critics," *The National Interest*, 1998–1999 (Winter). Cohen mentions a scene in the film *Saving Private Ryan* in which Tom Hanks's character, Capt. John Miller, seeks refuge in a solitary shell hole when he is about to crack with grief and doubt, determined that his men not see him, knowing how much they depended on confidence in his strength.

236 "a good executive": Remarks by Bush on announcing three new cabinet appointments, January 2, 2001.

237 in his 1995 memoir: Colin L. Powell with Joseph E. Persico, *My American Journey* (New York: Random House, 1995), p. 608.

238 "empower the desks": Ben Barber, "Bush Welcomes Sharon Victory, Fresh Start to Peace," *Washington Times,* February 8, 2001, p. A10. On the "special envoys," see Richard Boucher, State Department spokesman, Daily Briefing, March 12, 2001, p. 10.

238 Karl Rove clashed with Powell: Woodward, *Plan of Attack*, p. 127.

238 As Powell said in his confirmation hearing: U.S. Senate, Committee on Foreign Relations, *Nomination of Colin L. Powell to Be Secretary of State*, Hearing, Janu-

ary 17, 2001, 107th Cong., 1st Sess., p. 97 (exchange with Senator Chris Dodd, Democrat of Connecticut).

238 "You do cover": John Bolton, *Surrender Is Not an Option: Defending America at the United Nations and Abroad* (New York: Threshold/Simon & Schuster, 2007), pp. 47, 54.

239 International Criminal Court: Ibid., pp. 85–87.

239 "axis of evil": Ibid., pp. 103–4.

239 Powell was later criticized by liberals: E.g., Karen De Young, *Soldier: The Life of Colin Powell* (New York: Alfred A. Knopf, 2006).

240 during the transition, Powell had been briefed: Charles L. Pritchard, *Failed Diplomacy: The Tragic Story of How North Korea Got the Bomb* (Washington, D.C.: Brookings, 2007), p. 73.

240 The president himself called Rice: Elisabeth Bumiller, *Condoleezza Rice: An American Life: A Biography* (New York: Random House, 2007), pp. 145–47.

240 "got a little too far forward on my skis": Powell interview, May 14, 2001, with Andrea Koppel of CNN, quoted in Bolton, *Surrender Is Not an Option*, p. 102.

240 "There existed a distance": Woodward, *Bush at War*, p. 13.

241 later declared himself satisfied: Powell interview in Rothkopf, *Running the World*, p. 409.

241 a "cabal" of the vice president and secretary of defense: Wilkerson, "The White House Cabal."

241 "thumb on the scales": Rothkopf, *Running the World*, pp. 389, 407.

241 "Powell is a diplomat": Woodward, *Bush at War*, p. 342. See also the *Time* cover story, "Where Have You Gone, Colin Powell?," September 10, 2001, alleging his declining stock in the White House, discussed by Woodward, p. 14.

241 "Somebody got to the President": Interview with Lawrence Wilkerson in Yoichi Funabashi, *The Peninsula Question: A Chronicle of the Second Korean Nuclear Crisis* (Washington, D.C.: Brookings, 2007), p. 142. I heard a close friend of Powell's give the same account in a conversation in November 2007.

242 Colin Powell, when he was Reagan's: Powell, *My American Journey*, p. 338.

242 His friend Newt Gingrich: Rowan Scarborough, *Rumsfeld's War: The Untold Story of America's Anti-Terrorist Commander* (Washington, D.C.: Regnery, 2004), p. vii.

242 He had the president's explicit mandate: President-elect Bush's announcement nominating Rumsfeld, December 28, 2000. See also candidate Bush's speech, "A Period of Consequences," at The Citadel, South Carolina, September 23, 1999.

244 Marc Grossman . . . is on record: Quoted in Rothkopf, *Running the World*, p. 410. Grossman is incorrect, however, in claiming to Rothkopf that the Office of the Secretary of Defense had superior numbers of people.

244 The White House, for its part: Favorable comments on Feith's work by deputy national security adviser Stephen Hadley are reported in Bob Woodward, *State of Denial* (New York: Simon & Schuster, 2006), p. 208.

245 Carter treated Mondale: Woodrow Wilson International Center for Scholars, "The Role of the Modern Vice President," *Centerpoint* (June 2007), summarizing a Center Director's Forum on the topic held on April 26, 2007 (at http://www.wilsoncenter.org/index.cfm?fuseaction=events.print&event_id=228842).

245 Carter's attorney general: Griffin B. Bell with Ronald J. Ostrow, *Taking Care of the Law* (New York: William Morrow, 1982), pp. 22–36.

245 Leon Fuerth . . . "a very major player": Daniel Poneman, NSC staffer, quoted in Ivo H. Daalder and I. M. Destler, moderators, "The Clinton Administration National Security Council," The National Security Council Project: Oral History Roundtables (Washington, D.C.: Center for International and Security Studies at Maryland/University of Maryland, and the Brookings Institution, September 27, 2000), p. 4.

245 some experts believe Cheney's staff : Bradley H. Patterson, Jr., quoted in David Nather, "The Vice Presidency: An Office Under Scrutiny," *CQ Weekly Online*, June 11, 2007, p. 17ff.

245 "considerably more time with the president": Rothkopf, *Running the World*, p. 423.

245 The accusation often made: This is the thesis set forth, for example, in ibid., Chapter 12.

246 The attempt to assert broad presidential powers: Jack Goldsmith, *The Terror Presidency: Law and Judgment Inside the Bush Administration* (New York: W. W. Norton, 2007).

246 shared by other senior White House officials: Conversation with former senior Bush White House official.

246 subsequent accounts suggest the relationship between them: E.g., Bumiller, *Condoleezza Rice*, pp. 159–60, 177–78, 217–19; Bolton, *Surrender Is Not an Option*, pp. 69–70, 76.

247 Rice took her and Powell's concerns: Bumiller, *Condoleezza Rice*, pp. 189–90.

247 White House insiders scoffed: Conversation with several senior Bush White House officials.

247 "Cheney was certainly a powerful figure": Frum, *The Right Man*, p. 62.

248 "She threw a fit": Bumiller, *Condoleezza Rice*, pp. 136–37.

248 Rice saw the first role as the most important: Ibid., p. 134.

248 "On a typical day": Rothkopf, *Running the World*, p. 393.

248 Rice came to be accused of being weak: E.g., Karl F. Inderfurth and Loch K. Johnson, "Crucial flaw demands immediate reform," *Chicago Tribune*, June 20, 2004.

248 "acceleratron": Bumiller, *Condoleezza Rice*, p. 134.

248 she has been criticized harshly: Ivo H. Daalder and I. M. Destler, *In the Shadow of the Oval Office: The President's National Security Adviser and the Making of America's Foreign Policy* (New York: Simon & Schuster, forthcoming), Chapter 8.

249 Henry Kissinger considered it: E.g., Henry Kissinger, *White House Years* (Boston: Little, Brown, 1979), p. 31.

249 He did not want to referee every dispute: Conversations with two former senior officials, one in the White House and the other on the NSC staff.

250 Hadley was heard saying more than once: Author's conversation in August 2007 with a former White House official. See also Woodward, *State of Denial*, pp. 244–45.

252 The president reportedly sided: Connie Bruck, "Exiles: How Iran's Expatriates Are Gaming the Nuclear Threat," *The New Yorker*, March 6, 2006, pp. 53–54.

252 he wanted a North Korea policy "180 degrees" different: Bolton, *Surrender Is Not an Option*, p. 105.

253 Bush told Bob Woodward: Woodward, *Bush at War*, p. 340.

253 Powell's "accidental" meeting . . . in Brunei: Pritchard, *Failed Diplomacy*, p. 31.

253 On at least two other occasions: Ibid., pp. 31–32, 57–58.

253 to build a nuclear weapon via highly enriched uranium (HEU): The facts of the North Korean HEU program, and of the North Koreans' admission of it, are not

disputed. See the convergent accounts of two men on opposite sides of the policy debate: John Bolton, in *Surrender Is Not an Option*, Chapter 4, and Charles Pritchard, in *Failed Diplomacy*, Chapter 2. Pritchard was part of Kelly's delegation in Pyongyang, as was a member of my staff.

254 "A trained monkey": Kelly quoted in Funabashi, *The Peninsula Question*, p. 162.

254 The State Department felt passionately: This is one of the main themes of Pritchard, *Failed Diplomacy*, esp. Chapter 11.

254 would have to abandon its harsh rhetoric: Ibid., esp. pp. 9–21, 140–41.

254 a Democratic senator called Armitage: Funabashi, *The Peninsula Question*, p. 164; Nicholas D. Kristof, "Secret, Scary Plans," *New York Times*, February 28, 2003, p. 25.

255 Within two years, however, U.S. diplomats: This is the assertion of Pritchard, *Failed Diplomacy*, pp. 109–12.

255 U.S. policy in New York toughened: Bolton, *Surrender Is Not an Option*, pp. 299, 300, 304, 310.

255 A spate of press articles: E.g., Elaine Shannon, "How Rice's Posse Struck Back," *Time*, March 19, 2007, p. 28; Matthew Lee, "Diplomats Reclaim Foreign Policy Roles," Associated Press, August 22, 2007.

255 "Rice telephoned Bush": Karen DeYoung and Glenn Kessler, "Policy Successes—or U-Turns; Views Differ on Bush Moves on Iran, N. Korea, Mideast," *Washington Post*, March 11, 2007. See also David E. Sanger and Thom Shanker, "Rice Is Said to Have Speeded North Korea Deal," *New York Times*, February 16, 2007.

256 U.S. diplomats considered the Berlin setting: Pritchard, *Failed Diplomacy*, pp. 158–59.

256 meet, in the Waldorf Towers in New York: Ibid., p. 185.

256 Bush had second thoughts: Conversations in 2007 and 2008 with three senior sources in the Executive Branch who had heard the president on the subject.

258 The president's decision to go to war, made finally in January 2003: This is the assessment of Woodward, *Plan of Attack*, p. 254.

258 an unprecedented degree of transparency and communication: Powell was struck by the preeminent role of the CENTCOM commander and the reduced role of the chairman of the JCS, compared with his experience in the 1991 Gulf War. See De Young, *Soldier*, pp. 394–95. Probably this will vary in the future, depending on personalities and geography. The chairman is chief military adviser to the president, but the combatant commander is the chief planner and is in the chain of wartime command. Both have a claim on being included.

258 Powell . . . spent more than two hours with the president: Woodward, *Plan of Attack*, pp. 149–53; De Young, *Soldier*, pp. 401–2.

258 Powell also had private conversations . . . with Franks: Woodward, *Plan of Attack*, pp. 80, 125–26; De Young, *Soldier*, pp. 396, 426.

258 Rumsfeld sent Bush his own memo: Douglas J. Feith, *War and Decision: Inside the Pentagon at the Dawn of the War on Terrorism* (New York: Harper, 2008), pp. 332–35.

259 George Tenet, then CIA director: George Tenet with Bill Harlow, *At the Center of the Storm: My Years at the CIA* (New York: HarperCollins, 2007), pp. 307–8.

259 Bush admitted this: Woodward, *Plan of Attack*, pp. 251–52.

259 "I know of one way": Dwight D. Eisenhower, Columbia University Oral History

Interview, July 20, 1967, uncorrected transcript, quoted in Greenstein, "George W. Bush: The Man and His Leadership," pp. 65, 69n.36.

260 French sabotage of the second resolution: An authoritative account is Charles Cogan, *French Negotiating Behavior: Dealing with La Grande Nation* (Washington, D.C.: United States Institute of Peace Press, 2003), pp. 186–214.

260 The Executive Steering Group . . . chafed: Woodward, *State of Denial*, pp. 108–10.

260 the White House asked Rumsfeld to delay: Feith, *War and Decision*, pp. 316–17.

261 Rumsfeld made a misstep that seriously embittered: Rajiv Chandrasekaran, *Imperial Life in the Emerald City: Inside Iraq's Green Zone* (New York: Vintage, 2007), p. 37; Feith, *War and Decision*, pp. 386–89.

261 The "planning order" sent by the chairman: See the timeline in the Joint Staff briefing, "Operation Iraqi Freedom: Strategic Lessons Learned," August 29, 2003, in Scarborough, *Rumsfeld's War*, pp. 175–77.

261 For a considerable period, however, General Franks seemed to believe: Feith, *War and Decision*, pp. 291–93, 317–18, 349–50, in answer to Woodward, *State of Denial*, pp. 91, 144–45. See also Michael R. Gordon and General Bernard E. Trainor, *COBRA II: The Inside Story of the Invasion and Occupation of Iraq* (New York: Pantheon, 2006), pp. 68, 70, 138.

261 On December 19, an updated "planning order": See the timeline in Joint Staff briefing, "Operation Iraqi Freedom: Strategic Lessons Learned," in Scarborough, *Rumsfeld's War*, p. 178.

262 a post-Iraq "lessons learned" assessment: Ibid.

262 Rumsfeld signed a directive: DoD Directive 3000.05, "Military Support for Stability, Security, Transition, and Reconstruction (SSTR) Operations," November 28, 2005.

262 A memorandum I wrote to Rumsfeld on this subject: Feith, *War and Decision*, Appendix 7 ("Who Will Govern Iraq?" Rodman Memo, August 15, 2002), pp. 546–48. See also the discussion in ibid., pp. 252–57, 497–501.

263 The president's decision was spelled out in unusual detail: Ibid., pp. 406–8.

263 Bremer concluded that a multiyear U.S. occupation: His account is in Ambassador L. Paul Bremer III with Malcolm McConnell, *My Year in Iraq: The Struggle to Build a Future of Hope* (New York: Simon & Schuster, 2006), pp. 43–49, and also in L. Paul Bremer III, "Facts for Feith," *National Review Online*, March 20, 2008 (at http://article.nationalreview.com/print/?q=NDIwN2MzOTlj OTNlODdiMDIzZWQ5ZmZjZ).

263 By October, Bremer was persuaded to agree: Chandrasekeran, *Imperial Life in the Emerald City*, pp. 218–19; Feith, *War and Decision*, pp. 455–66.

263 Bremer's charter: Presidential letter of appointment, May 9, 2003.

264 there was a flood of tendentious leaks: E.g; Jonathan S. Landay and Warren P. Strobel, "Postwar U.S. Plan for Iraq Called Flawed," *Miami Herald*, July 12, 2003; Peter Slevin and Dana Priest, "Wolfowitz Concedes Iraq Errors," *Washington Post*, July 24, 2003; James Fallows, "Blind into Baghdad," *Atlantic Monthly*, January/February 2004; David Rieff, "Blueprint for a Mess," *New York Times Magazine*, November 2, 2003. Other leaks, criticizing the conduct of the war, came from military sources. On, e.g., the allegation that the State Department had a significant planning effort that was suppressed, see Gordon and Trainor, *COBRA II*, p. 159; and Bremer, *My Year in Iraq*, p. 25. On the Pentagon's alleged plan to install Chalabi, see Feith, *War and Decision*, pp. 279, 383, 487–90.

264 Senior White House officials made calls: Conversation with former senior White House official, December 2007.

264 Thereby, they not only conceded much: Feith, *War and Decision*, pp. 474–77, 491–93.

264 Democratic candidate John Kerry: E.g., Sen. John Kerry, Remarks to the American Legion Convention, September 1, 2004. Kerry also raised some of these points directly with Bush in the debates on September 30 and October 8, 2004.

264 *The New York Times* reported: Douglas Jehl, "U.S. Intelligence Shows Pessimism on Iraq's Future," *New York Times*, September 16, 2004.

264 the *Times* cited prewar intelligence: Douglas Jehl and David E. Sanger, "Prewar Assessment on Iraq Saw Chance of Strong Divisions," *New York Times*, September 28, 2004.

264 a senior CIA Middle East analyst was reported: Robert Novak, "Is CIA at War with Bush?; A National Intel Officer Tells of Secret, Unheeded Warnings of War in Iraq," *Chicago Sun-Times*, September 27, 2004.

264 A second senior intelligence officer: Dana Priest, "CIA Officer Criticizes Agency's Handling of bin Laden," *Washington Post*, November 9, 2004.

265 In October, the Knight Ridder/Tribune chain: Warren P. Strobel, Jonathan S. Landay, and John Walcott, "CIA Review Finds No Evidence Saddam Had Ties to Islamic Terrorists," Knight Ridder/Tribune News Service, October 5, 2004, cited in Hayes, *Cheney*, pp. 456–57.

265 Patrick Lang, a retired Defense intelligence analyst: Lang quoted in Robert Dreyfuss, "The Yes-Man; President Bush Sent Porter Goss to the CIA to Keep the Agency in Line. What He's Really Doing Is Wrecking It," *The American Prospect*, November 2005.

265 The CIA's supposed prediction: Gordon and Trainor, *COBRA II*, pp. 570–71. On the CIA's assessment of the Iraqi police and other lapses, see ibid., pp. 136, 161, 202–3, 212–13, and 466.

265 the unclassified summary . . . of an NIE: National Intelligence Council, "Iran: Nuclear Intentions and Capabilities," National Intelligence Estimate: Key Judgments, November 2007. For critical comments, see, e.g., Henry A. Kissinger, "Misreading the Iran Report: Why Spying and Policymaking Don't Mix," *Washington Post*, December 13, 2007, and John R. Bolton, "Our Politicized Intelligence Services," *Wall Street Journal*, February 5, 2008.

266 Bush and his closest colleagues: Bumiller, *Condoleezza Rice*, pp. 299–302; David E. Sanger, Michael R. Gordon, and John F. Burns, "Chaos Overran Iraq Plan in '06, Bush Team Says," *New York Times*, January 2, 2007; Michael Abramowitz and Peter Baker, "Embattled, Bush Held to Plan to Salvage Iraq," *Washington Post*, January 21, 2007.

267 General George Casey . . . firmly resisted: See Casey quoted in Sanger, Gordon, and Burns, "Chaos Overran Iraq Plan in '06."

268 Hadley's answer was: yes, but only if the military recommended it: Conversation with senior NSC staff member.

268 "What I want to hear from you": Sanger, Gordon, and Burns, "Chaos Overran Iraq Plan in '06."

268 "thoughtful and sensitive" in his handling of the military: Fred Barnes, "How Bush Decided on the Surge," *The Weekly Standard*, February 4, 2008, p. 23.

268 As scholar Eliot Cohen has shown: Eliot A. Cohen, *Supreme Command: Soldiers, Statesmen, and Leadership in Wartime* (New York: Free Press, 2002).

269 As Hadley told: Conversation with a senior NSC staffer with whom Hadley spoke.

269 made his decision to relieve Donald Rumsfeld: Bumiller, *Condoleezza Rice*, pp. 298–300.

269 Bush made the surprising comment: Peter Baker, "As Democracy Push Falters, Bush Feels like a 'Dissident,'" *Washington Post*, August 20, 2007, p. A1.

270 On Iran as well, State's policy under Rice: Bruck, "Exiles," pp. 62–63.

271 Gates deftly shifted to support the president: Gates's early view may be found in Michael Abramowitz and Thomas E. Ricks, "Pentagon Chief Talks of Further Iraq Troop Cuts," *Washington Post*, September 15, 2007, p. A1. Compare with the president's remarks at Camp Arifjan, Kuwait, after meeting with Gen. David Petraeus and Ambassador. Ryan Crocker, January 12, 2008, and Gates's revised position as reported in Lolita C. Baldor, "Gates Hopes to Continue Iraq Drawdown," Associated Press, February 22, 2008.

CHAPTER TEN: LESSONS LEARNED

272 Justice Louis Brandeis: Brandeis dissent in *Myers v. United States*, 272 U.S. 293 (1926).

272 Richard Neustadt, reaffirming in 1990: Richard E. Neustadt, *Presidential Power and the Modern Presidents: The Politics of Leadership from Roosevelt to Reagan*, rev. ed. (New York: Free Press, 1990), Preface, p. xvii.

272 The Communists thought they had the solution: E.g., Milovan Djilas, *The New Class: An Analysis of the Communist System* (New York: Praeger, 1957), and Zbigniew K. Brzezinski, *The Permanent Purge: Politics in Soviet Totalitarianism* (Cambridge: Harvard University Press, 1956).

273 "The truth . . . is": Bernard Crick, *In Defense of Politics* (London: Pelican, 1964), p. 199.

274 politicization of the role of U.S. attorneys: The accusations made are summarized in Karen Tumulty and Massimo Calabresi, "Inside the Scandal at Justice," *Time*, May 21, 2007, pp. 44–49.

274 Jimmy Carter even proposed during his 1976 campaign: Griffin B. Bell and Ronald J. Ostrow, *Taking Care of the Law* (New York: William Morrow, 1982), p. 28.

274 "involuntarily equidistant": Robert M. Gates, "CIA and the Making of American Foreign Policy," address at the Woodrow Wilson School of Public and International Affairs, Princeton University, September 29, 1987; Robert M. Gates, "The CIA and American Foreign Policy," *Foreign Affairs* (Winter 1987–1988), p. 255.

274 Retired intelligence officer Paul Pillar: Paul R. Pillar, "Intelligence, Policy, and the War in Iraq," *Foreign Affairs* (March/April 2006), p. 27.

275 The controversies over intelligence in the Iraq War were thoroughly investigated: U.S. Senate, Select Committee on Intelligence, *The U.S. Intelligence Community's Prewar Intelligence Assessments on Iraq, Report*, S. Report 108-301, 108th Cong., 2nd Sess., July 9, 2004; The Commission on the Intelligence Capabilities of the United States Regarding Weapons of Mass Destruction (Laurence S. Silberman and Charles S. Robb, co-chairmen), Report to the President of the United States, March 31, 2005. Both inquiries found that prewar intelligence analysis on Iraq was not skewed by policy or political pressures from elsewhere in the administration.

280 The Eisenhower precept: Dwight D. Eisenhower, Columbia University Oral History Interview, July 20, 1967, uncorrected transcript, quoted in Fred I. Greenstein, "George W. Bush: The Man and His Leadership," in John C. Fortier and Norman J. Ornstein, eds., *Second-Term Blues: How George W. Bush Has Governed* (Washington, D.C.: American Enterprise Institute and Brookings, 2007), pp. 65, 69n.36.

281 "Presidents assume that their task": W. W. Rostow, *The Diffusion of Power: An Essay in Recent History* (New York: Macmillan, 1972), p. 368.

282 Zbigniew Brzezinski in his memoir: Zbigniew Brzezinski, *Power and Principle: Memoirs of the National Security Adviser, 1977–1981* (New York: Farrar, Straus & Giroux, 1983), pp. 533–37.

282 Henry Kissinger, having become secretary of state: Henry Kissinger, *Years of Upheaval* (Boston: Little, Brown, 1982), p. 434.

283 "Cabinet members cannot successfully compete": Stephen Hess, *Organizing the Presidency* (Washington, D.C.: Brookings, 1976), p. 193.

283 McGeorge Bundy, who . . . was fervently of the view: McGeorge Bundy, *The Strength of Government* (Cambridge: Harvard University Press, 1968), pp. 39–40. See also Hess, *Organizing the Presidency*, pp. 187–88.

284 Indeed it has been suggested: Laurence H. Silberman, "Toward Presidential Control of the State Department," *Foreign Affairs* (Spring 1979), pp. 888–89.

285 Dean Acheson conceded this point: Dean Acheson, "The Eclipse of the State Department," *Foreign Affairs* (July 1971).

286 "a Goldwater-Nichols Act for the interagency process": See, e.g., the joint testimony of Secretary of State Condoleezza Rice and Secretary of Defense Robert Gates before the House Armed Services Committee, on "Building Partnership Capacity and Development of the Interagency Process," April 15, 2008; Hans Binnendijk, "At War but Not War-Ready," *Washington Post*, November 3, 2007, p. A19; and Kenneth R. Dahl, "New Security for New Threats: The Case for Reforming the Interagency Process," unpublished paper, May 30, 2007, for the Twenty-first Century Defense Initiative of the Brookings Institution.

286 Various reform proposals have been put forward: A radical proposal for reform of the State Department's structure may be found in the U.S. Commission on National Security/21st Century (Hart-Rudman Commission), "Road Map for National Security: Imperative for Change," Phase III Report, March 15, 2001, pp. 52–63; more modest reforms were proposed by Frank C. Carlucci, chair, "State Department Reform," Report of an Independent Task Force Cosponsored by the Council on Foreign Relations and the Center for Strategic and International Studies, 2001.

286 A broader reform agenda: Donald Rumsfeld, among others, has been a strong advocate of this. See Donald Rumsfeld, "The Smart Way to Beat Tyrants Like Chavez," *Washington Post*, December 2, 2007, p. B3.

287 as writers like Thomas Ricks have pointed out: Thomas E. Ricks, *Making the Corps* (New York: Scribner's, 1997).

287 Both these problems raise profound issues that may loom larger: See Richard H. Kohn, "Coming Soon: A Crisis in Civil-Military Relations," *World Affairs* (Winter 2008), pp. 68–80.

INDEX

DATE